ORGANIZATIONAL BEHAVIOR CONTINGENCY VIEWS

The West Series in Management

Consulting Editors:

Don Hellriegel
and
John W. Slocum, Jr.

ORGANIZATIONAL BEHAVIOR
CONTINGENCY VIEWS

DON HELLRIEGEL
Texas A&M University

JOHN W. SLOCUM, JR.
The Pennsylvania State University

WEST PUBLISHING CO.
St. Paul · New York · Boston · Los Angeles · San Francisco

Library of Congress Cataloging in Publication Data

Hellriegel, Don.
    Organizational behavior: contingency views

    Bibliographies
    Includes index.
    1. Organization. 2. Management—Case studies
I. Slocum, John W., joint author. II. Title.
HD31.H448   658.4   75–41404
ISBN 0–8299–0078–0
3rd Reprint—1977

PREFACE

In studying chemistry, biology, or physics, one can bring the real world into the laboratory. The student need not rely on verbal explanations or pictures to describe certain events in the real world. If students doubt Galileo's theory, they can test the theory for themselves by rolling a ball down an inclined plane. In laboratory settings, students can learn how to do scientific experiments, practice the necessary skills for carrying out the scientific approach, and acquire the needed knowledge for attaining graduate degrees in science.

A major problem in teaching organizational behavior effectively, and a major problem for the students learning it, is to provide an effective counterpart for the laboratory. Firsthand experience in many organizations is hard to come by. We cannot always find the factory, church, hospital, university, or other organization that will allow full access to the behavior of its members, or that wants to be used as a "guinea pig." Therefore, an organizational-behavior textbook needs to be imaginative in presenting knowledge about organizations and helping students develop skills that are essential to the effective management of people.

Organizational behavior is a difficult area to study and teach, in part, because many of the concepts appear as abstractions. One of the goals of this book is to present concepts and frameworks that deal with organizational behavior at the appropriate level of abstraction. This goal is implemented by presenting conceptual frameworks, along with numerous case illustrations and examples from actual organizational settings. Abstract concepts and concrete examples are further blended throughout the book. This is accomplished by providing brief critical incidents, scenarios, and discussion questions at the end of each chapter, as well as more extensive cases that are located in the last section of the book.

A second major goal in preparing this book has been to include topics and illustrations of high interest to students, professionals, and managers.

A third major goal of the book is to help you understand why certain behavioral processes and events occur in organizations. Human behavior in organizations, as elsewhere, is exceedingly complex, and there are no simple solutions. Some individuals are continually trying to find the "one best way to motivate" or the "one best leadership style." Possibly no other management topics claim as much time as those revolving around the human side of the organization. Managers are continually attempting to find answers to problems of designing organizational structures, intergroup conflicts, motivation, leadership, group processes, organizational change, and the like.

This book provides conceptual frameworks for studying and understanding organizational behavior. To do this, we attempt to integrate theory, research and applications into a contingency approach. The contingency approach requires you to diagnose each behavioral situation as partially unique, and then apply the conceptual frameworks, as needed. Therefore, the conceptual frameworks we present are designed to help you fill in the specifics of any behavioral situation, so that you can understand better what is happening and what can be done. This approach stems implicitly from an open systems orientation. More about this in Chapter 1.

Skill at diagnosing situations is achieved only through effort. Thus, as you go back and forth between concepts, exercises, and cases, we hope your skills at using the ideas will be developed so that you can better appreciate your behavior and that of others. To breathe life into concepts, we sometimes include shortened versions of research instruments to help clarify their use and, possibly, to permit application to your own experiences.

This book consists of five interrelated parts. We begin with a study of organizations. In this part, we describe the contingency approach and introduce the notion of how environmental, individual, group, and organizational properties affect the behavior of all employees in organizations. We note that these four properties are the bases for presenting the material in this text. The first part also introduces some of the basic fundamentals for learning about behavior in organizations. Careful efforts are made not to be technical or to introduce statistical problems. The remainder of this part examines the external environment and the way values of employees affect their behavior. Attention is given to ways that managers can use information to assess their relevant environment(s).

The second part includes discussions of the individual. Performance of an organization can partially be understood through knowledge of individual members' behavior. Here the important topics include learning, perception, individual problem-solving styles, communications, and methods of individual conflict resolution. Individuals bring to organizational settings personal tendencies to behave in certain ways. The central concern of this section is to understand the individual's behavior in organizations.

The third part stresses the group aspects of organizations. We discuss the desirable and undesirable functions of groups, why an individual may be attracted to a group, and several suggested ways of assessing the nature of effectiveness. The part concludes with a focus on relations between groups, the factors that affect the relations between groups, and the major mechanisms that can be utilized for managing intergroup relations.

The fourth part introduces two important dimensions—motivation and leadership—that can influence the effectiveness of employees. A critical factor in increasing the effectiveness of the employee is understanding the relationship between the motivational bases of the employee and the need to design the job to solicit these motivations. One of the possible ways is through job enrichment and another is through a supervisor's leadership style, which is dependent on several factors that are discussed in this part.

The part concludes with a discussion of the concepts of organizational climate, structure, and physical settings. There is a discussion of how elements of an organization's structure can affect the behavior of employees and also their perceptions regarding the structure. The introduction of physical settings represents an attempt to focus attention on how the design of an individual's immediate surroundings affects his or her behavior. In sum, Part IV addresses a number of the relationships between the individual, the group, and the organization.

The fifth part focuses on planned organizational change. Effective organizations are continually making changes to cope with their customers and workers, with governmental bodies, and with other external publics. A critical factor is knowing what to change, the forces working for or against a change, and the role of the manager in the change process. After addressing these issues, this part concludes with a discussion of various approaches and their relative emphasis in making changes in the organization's structure, people, task, or technology. An effort is made to clarify the ways in which the approaches can be employed and under what conditions they would have a greater chance for success.

A desire to avoid sexist connotations has created a few minor editorial problems in the writing of this book. An attempt has been made to avoid the inference, by the use of personal pronouns such as "he," that all managers are male. Thus, we usually use terms such as "leader," "change agent," "manager," or the double pronoun "he or she" where possible.

We are keenly aware of the many contributions by others to this book. We wish to thank those whom we know about and ask those inadvertently overlooked to accept our apologies as well as our thanks.

For the intellectual stimulation and guidance that their reviews have provided us, we are grateful to Al Bartlett, University of South Florida; Art Brief, University of Iowa; Dan Costley, New Mexico State; Fred Crandall, Southern Methodist University; Jack Duncan, University of Alabama; Dick Dutton, University of South Florida; David Gustafeson, University of Missouri, St. Louis; Herbert Hand, University of South Carolina; L. G. Hrebiniak, Pennsylvania State University; Jerry Hunt, Southern Illinois University—Carbondale; Ed Huse, Boston College; Ralph Kilmann, University of Pittsburgh; James Richie, Brigham Young University; Randy Schuler, Cleveland State University; Chuck

Snow, Pennsylvania State University; John Stinson, Ohio University; Dick Steers, University of Oregon; and Paul H. Thompson, Brigham Young University.

We thank H. Kirk Downey, Oklahoma State University, for significant help with the entire manuscript and John Slocum (*New York Times*, retired), who made numerous stylistic and grammatical revisions. For being with us in the vitally important testing of the materials in courses at Pennsylvania State University, we warmly thank Bill Joyce, and the students who unfortunately are too many to be named here.

For the cases they have written so that others might learn, we thank all the casewriters. For permission to use many of the cases in this book, we thank the President and Fellows of Harvard College and express gratitude to Professor Charles Gebhard for help in securing permissions. The authors of each case and other copyright information appears at the beginning of each case. The cases utilized are located after the last chapter in the book.

For excellent support and assistance, we thank the people at West Publishing Company. For prompt, accurate, and cheerful typing, we thank seven superb secretaries: Sharalyn Bowersox, Dot Dorman, Nancy Hillard, Linda Platou, Marie Straka, Ildiko Takacs, and Jo Ann Thomas. Without them, it is doubtful that this manuscript could have ever been completed.

Appreciation is also expressed to Dean Gene Kelley and Michael Hottenstein, Pennsylvania State University, as well as Dean John E. Pearson and B. Douglas Stone, Jr., Texas A&M University, who were most helpful in providing assistance and other needed resources.

D.H.
J.W.S., Jr.

College Station, Texas
University Park, Pennsylvania
November, 1975
Don Hellriegel
John W. Slocum, Jr.

CONTENTS

†

PART I

FOUNDATIONS

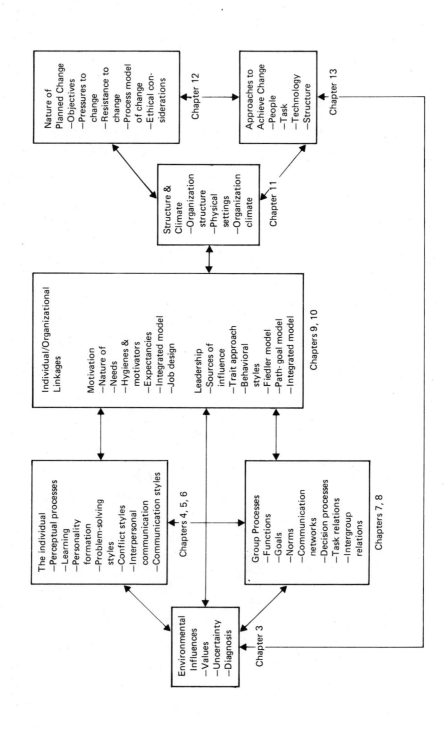

The individual
—Perceptual processes
—Learning
—Personality formation
—Problem-solving styles
—Conflict styles
—Interpersonal communication
—Communication styles

Chapters 4, 5, 6

Group Processes
—Functions
—Goals
—Norms
—Communication networks
—Decision processes
—Task relations
—Intergroup relations

Chapters 7, 8

Individual/Organizational Linkages

Motivation
—Nature of
—Needs
—Hygienes & motivators
—Expectancies
—Integrated model
—Job design

Leadership
—Sources of influence
—Trait approach
—Behavioral styles
—Fiedler model
—Path- goal model
—Integrated model

Chapters 9, 10

Structure & Climate
—Organization structure
—Physical settings
—Organization climate

Chapter 11

Environmental Influences
—Values
—Uncertainty
—Diagnosis

Chapter 3

Nature of Planned Change
—Objectives
—Pressures to change
—Resistance to change
—Process model of change
—Ethical con- siderations

Chapter 12

Approaches to Achieve Change
—People
—Task
—Technology
—Structure

Chapter 13

1
A FRAMEWORK FOR UNDERSTANDING BEHAVIOR IN ORGANIZATIONS

The aim of this book is to develop an understanding of behavior in organizations. Organizations are social systems. If we wish either to work in them or to manage them, it is necessary to understand how they operate. To do this, we must achieve a sense of an organization's entirety by studying and understanding the complexity of its parts. The character of an organization will influence the behavior of the entire organization and, to a great extent, the behavior of individuals within it as well. For example, the organization's character influences the degrees of personal freedom people have, the kinds of opportunities they have for advancement, the types of control imposed upon them, and even the way they think and feel about working in the organization. Identifying the critical parts of an organization's character and their interrelationships enables us to bring about change and to predict the consequences of employee behavior.

Employee behavior in organizations is rather unpredictable, from your present viewpoint. It is unpredictable because it arises from the needs and the nebulous value systems of many different people. However, it can be partially understood by developing frameworks from the behavioral sciences, which represent a systematic body of knowledge pertaining to why and how people behave as they do. This book has the special objective of integrating behavioral science concepts within formal organizations. There are no simple cookbook formulas for working with people. There is no "one best answer," no "ideal organization."

A key problem to understanding behavior in organizations is knowing what to look at or for. You may begin by trying to see the "whole" organization, or you can begin by looking at small parts of various sizes. Examples of these parts might include individuals, teams, groups, or departments. Of course, focusing on a particular part of an organization only partially solves our problem. It is unfortunately true that, to understand the behavior of individuals in organizations, we must know something about the interrelationships between the various parts of the structure.

One way to avoid the feeling of hopelessness in understanding behavior is to assume that explanations of behavior are simple and simply found. The tendency to think only in causal terms is an example of this simple reasoning. The automobile accident was "caused" by the carelessness of one of the drivers, or by dangerous road conditions, or by any one of a single number of factors, which can be and are cited in a particular instance of an automobile collision. We could draw up an infinite list of these single causes of automobile accidents, and if we did so, we might be struck by the fact that many, if not all, of the items on our list play some causative role in any single accident we might examine.

If the single-cause assumption is inadequate, an obvious substitute is the assumption that events are caused by many forces working in complex reaction to each other. If we are interested in establishing the conditions within which the frequency of automobile accidents is reduced, then we would be well advised to study the primary factors associated with collisions and the relationships of those factors to one another. The notion of a "system" in essence assumes multiple causation and complex interrelation of forces. In the simplest sense of the word, everything is related to everything else. Organizations can be thought of as systems, such as work-flows, reward structures, communication networks, and role structures. All of these, functioning together, constitute what we commonly refer to as an organization. The system concept is critical in our understanding of behavior. It emphasizes the interrelatedness of parts and suggests the importance of interpreting an individual part only in the context of the whole.

To be effective managers, we do not need to know *all* that can be known about every relevant system. (If this were the case, we would never get through analyzing the first problem we encountered, since everything is related to everything else in an infinitely complex chain of interdependence.) Instead, we establish who we are, our role, our competencies, and our goals. Then we choose to analyze the systems whose conditions are something we want to control or understand. Other systems whose conditions lie beyond our competence and/or control are taken into account only insofar as they affect the systems we are trying to influence. For example, the individual is a subsystem in his own right, with certain goals, needs, and expectations. Not all of these goals, needs, and expectations will coincide with those of his work group. We could study only those that are in conflict with the group's goals.

Since the purpose of this book is to deal with the behavior of individuals within organizations, we shall have to learn about individuals, groups, and structures that affect the behavior of people in organizations. We shall analyze the individual's behavior in the group, groups themselves, relationships between work groups, and groups within organizations. We shall try to describe and explain the interrelationships within and among various parts in the organization. Because our emphasis is on dealing with causes of human behavior in organizations, the structure of the organization, its technology, and job designs are all important. Individual behavior can best be understood by studying topics such as job design, motivation, leadership, group dynamics, communication, interpersonal styles, and the like.

THE CONTINGENCY APPROACH

Traditional management theory emphasized the development of principles that were appropriate to all organizations and managerial tasks.[1] These universal principles were generally prescriptive—there was only one way to manage organizations and people. Management scientists have tended to emphasize this approach and stressed the logical and rational view of managerial decision-making. The use of linear programming and other mathematical models attempts to prescribe the "best" solution. Many behavioral scientists have also emphasized a particular approach to management. For example, if one assumed that the workers were inherently lazy and irresponsible and needed to be coerced to work, an autocratic managerial style was appropriate. Similarly, if a manager assumed that employees are basically industrious and responsible, then a democratic managerial style was appropriate.

Another approach to the study of behavior is by analyzing each situation as a unique case. By considering the variables in a given situation, the manager can intelligently analyze the relationships that have developed. If the manager is a good interpreter, he or she can discover the most appropriate forms of behavior under the circumstances to increase productivity, improve morale, or cut costs.

Figure 1-1 reflects the different orientations of these approaches and indicates that the contingency approach is a blend of different approaches. The contingency approach rejects the notion that universal principles are appropriate to all situations.[2] The contingency approach suggests some themes concerning different types of behavior under different conditions. Most contingency approaches emphasize that there is no one best way for designing jobs and/or organizations, managing people who work in all types of organizations, and achieving change in an organization. There is a wide variety of managerial responses that are appropriate. It all depends upon the particular circumstances in the specific situation. It is only after the situation has been properly analyzed by a manager that certain "rules" can be followed.

A play by James Barrie, "The Admirable Crichton," illustrates a basic concept underlying the contingency approach to leadership. A butler was employed for a wealthy family in England. The butler's job was to drive the family to its destination safely, answer the door, answer the telephone, and announce the presence of various visitors of this family, among other tasks.

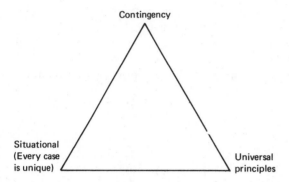

Figure 1–1   Alternative Frameworks for Understanding Behavior

The family told the butler what to do, how to do it, and when to perform his tasks. One day the family decided to take a cruise and asked the butler to accompany them on their boat. While at sea, a storm arose and capsized the boat, but all persons were able to swim ashore safely. On the shore, the family had no knowledge of basic survival practices, but the butler was knowledgeable in this area. Therefore, he assumed the leadership role and instructed the family in the performance of various tasks, telling them what to do, and when and how to do it. In normal circumstances, the butler had been performing a subordinate role, but the new situation (a contingency) changed the leadership roles in the group. The head of the family was no longer effective in directing the butler's behavior because the butler alone had the expertise needed to accomplish the task—survival.

Does the contingency approach provide a panacea for solving all an organization's problems? The answer is *no;* this approach does not provide us with the five easy steps to success in management. Cookbook approaches, while seemingly practical and easy to understand, are usually short-sighted and don't work. Fundamental contingency concepts are more difficult to grasp, but they do facilitate a more thorough understanding of complex situations and increase the probability that appropriate action will be taken.

The contingency view seeks to understand the interrelationships within and among the various parts of an organization. Each part can be analyzed separately or as a unit interacting with other parts in the organization's system. We may examine the conduct of an employee who is involved in the actual production of goods and/or analyze his behavior in relation to achieving the goals of his work group. In this instance, the individual is part of a larger system, the work group. The individual assembly-line worker at the Vega plant in Lordstown, Ohio, who wants to work overtime is dependent upon management's willingness to offer overtime work, as well as upon the agreement of other members of his work group to work overtime, since they must provide the worker with materials, equipment, and the like. A worker's desire to work overtime is "contingent" upon others' desire to work overtime. Stated more formally, a contingency approach recognizes that subsystems within the organization are dependent upon and influence each other.

A Contingency Model

In building a contingency model to understand behavior of employees in organizations, we have included four major areas. These are:

1. Environmental properties

2. Individual properties

3. Organizational properties

4. Group properties

The relationships between these areas are shown in Fig. 1–2, which sets forth the themes presented in this book and represents a conceptual model. It includes some of the dimensions in the major areas that will be discussed. The analysis of the areas and their key dimensions provides a pattern for understanding behavior in organizations. The relationships between these major areas are much too dynamic to allow us to set forth "laws" about their relationships. We recognize that the relationships indicated in Fig. 1–2 are tentative because of the variety of events that can affect the behavior of people in organizations. For example, consider the routine characteristics of an airline flight, which suddenly change when the hijacker says, "Fly this plane to Cuba." The behavior of the flight crew and the passengers is changed and their behavior is "contingent" upon the demands of the hijacker. This example highlights three important things in applying a contingency approach to understanding behavior.

First, the behavior of individuals within a system is dependent on their *environment,* which gives them a framework within which to perform their tasks. In the airliner example, the relevant environment is the plane that is being hijacked. Other environments, such as the kind of a car a person drives, the type of job he has, his home, his family life, are not relevant determiners of behavior in the present situation.

Second, the *behavior* of individuals in an environment is dependent on their alternatives. In the present example, most of us would sit quietly and try not to disturb the hijackers. Alternatives, such as jumping out the window, starting a riot, wrestling with the hijacker, may all result in consequences detrimental to the person.

Third, the *consequences* of any behavior must be understood in that particular environment. Consequences are always contingent upon the behavior within the environment. In this example, the consequence of jumping out an airliner's window will probably be death, whereas the consequences of follow-

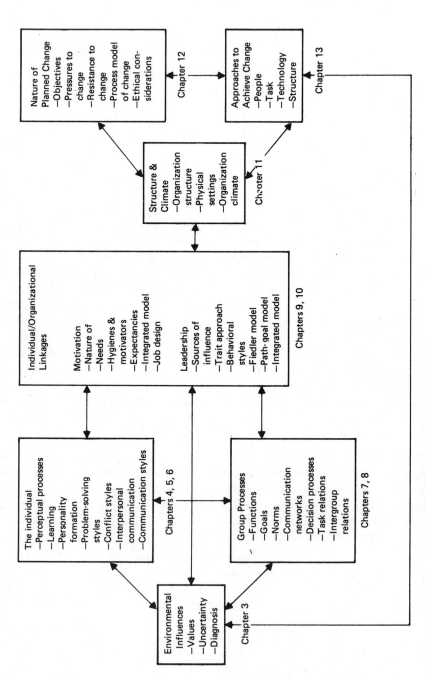

Figure 1–2 Contingency Model of Organizational Behavior

ing the hijacker's orders will involve considerable personal frustration and anxiety, but may not result in death.

It is our purpose in writing this book to identify patterns of relationships among areas as they affect the organization, environment, individual, and group.

Environmental Properties

As we proceed to examine the four major areas in more detail and assess the applicability of contigency views, it is important to recognize that each organization operates in its own relevant environment. These environments include consumers, suppliers, competitors, and regulatory agencies. The organization must identify its "relevant" environment, for its success lies in its ability to secure resources from the environment, transform these resources into goods and services, and then return them to the market place.[3] In the case of a local church, the environment might be relatively stable in terms of the number of active church members, few other "competitors" in the locale, and little interference from local, state, and federal regulatory agencies. The effect that this type of environment has on the individual, the church's organizational structure, group processes, and the like will affect the success of the church in achieving its goals. In thinking about the environment of an organization, it is very important to understand that to analyze *every* relationship in an organization's environment would be a slow and painstaking process. Thus, we include in our discussion only those dimensions that will ultimately facilitate your understanding of behavior in organizations.

Individual Properties

Each of us makes assumptions about the people with whom we work, whom we supervise, or with whom we engage in leisure activities. These assumptions, to some extent, influence our behavior towards others. The effective manager should understand the psychological influences that determine his or her own behavior before attempting to influence the behavior of others. Chapters 4 through 6 focus on a number of properties and determinants of individual behavior. As indicated in Fig. 1–2, the individual represents the "core" of the contingency model. There are several reasons for this. First, an organization's performance can best be understood when the determinants of its individual members' behavior are clear. Second, the level of analysis we are primarily concerned with is that of the individual. The individual is also a system, comprised of a number of physiological subsystems—digestive, nervous, circulatory, reproductive—each of which can be considered as a system in its own right. One can also look at the individual from a psychological perspective. Here the important variables are one's attitudes, motives, feelings, values, and the like. In this book, we follow the "psychological" perspective in studying the individual as a complete system and also as a subsystem of the organization. Third, the individuals are inevitably engaged in a number of different systems. Managers deal with personality systems (perhaps many of them), social systems, and formal systems of varying sizes and interrelationships. Any particular individual behavior is likely to affect behavior in any or all of these other systems.

A set of tools for thinking about individual behavior is outlined in Fig. 1–2. In Chapter 4, the individual's personality, and his perceptual and adaptation processes are explored. Learning theory is used as a vehicle to explain how the past history of the individual is instrumental in determining the behavioral patterns brought to the organization.

The ways in which particular personality, perceptual, and learning processes affect behavior is the focus of Chapters 5 and 6. The learned manner in which individuals relate to others in the building of interpersonal relationships will influence the quality of relationships that exist among people. It will also bear on the emotional climate that will characterize their interactions, and on whether or not there will be problems of communications. People make important decisions about what information will be processed, irrespective of organizational and group considerations. Individuals bring to organizational settings tendencies to behave in certain ways. They prefer certain interpersonal styles that significantly influence the flow of information in an organization. Central to understanding behavior in organizations, therefore, is an appreciation of the complexities of various interpersonal styles.

Group Properties

The importance of the social aspects of work roles has been extensively documented by behavioral scientists.[4] Almost every work role involves membership in one or more groups. It is safe to conclude that even where social satisfactions are not of primary importance for the individual coming to work, they generally affect performance. In Chapter 7, we lay out the major components of intragroup relations. These include a discussion of the desirable and undesirable functions of groups, the major forces that influence group members' behavior, and several ways for studying, analyzing, and assessing the nature of group effectiveness. In Chapter 8, the focus is on relations between groups—that is, how several factors can influence relations between two or more groups in organizations. We also are concerned with creating an awareness on the part of the manager of the major mechanisms and processes for managing intergroup relations. As with the individual, the parts of the group and their relations with other groups in the organization must be understood in order to determine why groups of people behave as they do. As you will discover, many of the factors that were important in shaping the behavior of the individual are also important in shaping the behavior of the work group.

Individual/Organizational Linkages

To understand the operation of values, personality, interpersonal style, and group processes, we need to know about the characteristics of work settings that are motivationally important to the individual. Recently, much attention has been focused on the "blues" experienced by rank-and-file workers. The hopelessness and boredom resulting from meaningless work and the effect of such reactions on the health and attitudes of workers have been the cause of a growing concern on the part of managers. The critical factor in the relationship between the quality of working life and employee productivity is the motivational bases of the employee; these bases are examined in Chapter 9. Once these bases have been explored, managers may see the desirability of allowing employees to become more involved in the activities of the firm. This may be accomplished through the redesigning of tasks to permit the employees a broader role in decision-making, the formation of self-governing work groups, setting up job-enrichment programs, and the like.

Managements today need leaders who have the ability to integrate the goals of the employees and those of the organization. The focus of Chapter 10 is on understanding the leadership process. At times, this may involve adapting the organization to the needs of employees, while at other times, it may involve influencing employees toward the attainment of the organization's goals. While the group is the natural home of the leader, just as the organization is the natural home of the group, not every person is going to be able to influence the group in the direction best suited for the group. In its simplest terms, effective organizational leadership depends upon the degree to which the person's ability and style, as well as the group's situation, provide him with control and influence to act effectively in the situation.[5] Despite the fact that the organization's structure is supposed to govern the way people work and that it is shaped to some extent by technological considerations, the leader still has some latitude to influence people. The formal structure is often shaped by the ideas of the man in charge. Within any given structure, as a result of supervisory behavior or group influences, patterns of relationships emerge that are different from the relationships that the formal structure says should apply. For example, a leader with a directive, controlling nature is likely to set up structures and procedures that differ from those established by a leader with a permissive predisposition, even though both leaders are concerned with essentially the same products and technology. Of course, decisions will affect, and be affected by, the social groupings and informal norms which emerge in the group's system.

Organizational Climate

The character of an organization is often referred to as the organization's climate. An organization's climate is composed of a number of descriptive dimensions (much as meteorological climate includes temperature, humidity, amount of precipitation, etc.), and these dimensions contribute to the various impressions that people form about their organization. Just as precipitation may be used to measure the amount of rain, sleet, snow, etc., climate dimensions refer to properties of the organization, such as pay, working conditions, leadership styles, degree of individual decision-making, that affect an individual's motivations and job performance. Different climates arouse different behavioral actions among employees, and these result in various consequences such as satisfaction, productivity, absenteeism, and turnover. If an organization's climate can affect employee behavior, what are the determinants of an organization's climate? How does the physical setting and design of an organization affect its climate? How do jobs make differences in the workers' perceptions of the climate that affect their attitudes and behavior? The ways in which jobs, physical settings, and tasks are designed may be several of the most important influences on the work motivation and productivity of individuals in organizations.

Change

One intent of managerial decision-making is to move the organization from one condition where outputs are unsatisfactory to another condition where we could expect to find outputs more satisfactory. In the broadest sense, this involves changing the organization to make it more effective and efficient, as well as more satisfying for its participants. These objectives have a contingency flavor because a balance must be maintained in order to ensure the long-run survival of the firm. Effective solutions to organizational problems must be tempered with considerations of costs, in order to be realistic. For example, let's assume we feel it is necessary to replace our method of posting accounts receivable from a hand operation to one using new electronic data-processing equipment. This new equipment should increase output and decrease cost per unit simultaneously. What do we do with the people who previously posted these accounts—fire, transfer, promote them, or what? Overemphasis on efficiency at the expense of employee satisfaction might result in slow-down tactics, or high turnover rates throughout the company, and could create an undesirable atmosphere of conflict and tension.

In Chapters 12 and 13, we present some of the major ideas and techniques concerning the initiation and facilitation of change in organizations. The emphasis is on changing the behavior of organization members. While we discuss approaches concerned with change in such things as the administrative structure, technology, and work flow, in the final analysis, the members of the organization are called upon to do things differently. In this sense, behavioral change is involved in all organizational change efforts.

Chapter 12 presents some critical dimensions in the nature of the change process. Why do some organizations change, while others do not? What are the various pressures to change in an organization and in its environment?

Why do people and/or organizations often resist change? While this chapter does not present cookbook solutions to questions, it does provide you with a general process model of a change. It also discusses the job of a change agent and the ethical considerations surrounding any organizational change.

Chapter 13 discusses the available techniques a manager has at his or her disposal to initiate a change in the organization. An effort is made to clarify the ways in which the technique can be employed to specify the conditions under which such devices may be successful. The change effort is likely to be successful as long as the effort is consistent with the organization's relevant environment. The importance of teams and team development is also discussed. The emphasis is upon the group and group interaction, rather than on individual behavior only.

The essence of these two chapters is that organizations must learn to adjust effectively to meet the unstable demands of their relevant environment. Managers who see themselves as "change agents" and who know how to function effectively in this capacity are clearly among the most valuable members of the organization.

SUMMARY

Individual and group behavior in an organization are determined by a host of factors. An initial step of identifying patterns of relationships can be of major importance. The contingency framework permits the manager to design his organization and/or his motivational program in such a way that it will be most effective in a given situation. To study behavior in organizations in more detail, it is important to recognize that many managers do and will continue to use a contingency approach intuitively and implicitly. The thrust of the contingency view is an attempt to understand the fundamental concepts of behavior and to develop normative or prescriptive statements that should be applicable to the specific situation.

Basic ideas from learning theory, perception, and personality processes provide the manager with insights necessary to comprehend how the organization influences its members and shapes their behavior. Group structure and processes serve to maintain and/or change the attitudes, perceptions, and motivation of individuals. Knowing the nature of the organization's relevant external environment can be a basis for understanding the formal structure of the organization. Finally, to change the system, alterations can be made by way of individual retraining, organizational development, and organizational redesign.

Discussion Questions

1. What does one gain by viewing organizations as social systems?

2. What is the contingency approach?

3. Give an example of a contingency approach to your own study habits.

4. What are the differences among the contingency, traditional management, and case approaches to the study of organizational behavior?

CRITICAL INCIDENT

Robert Millman, age about 40, worked as assistant general foreman of a large steel mill in the eastern United States. He had been an assistant manager for fifteen years, but his work was so ordinary that no manger wanted him. His present manager had tried to move him out several times by transferring him to other company mills, but he kept returning. When he was transferred to a new mill, the manager would soon learn of his record and return him to the home mill. At last, Carl Anderson, the manager of the Standard Steel mill, although tempted to transfer Millman back to his home mill, decided to try to motivate him, and asked Gene Kelley, Millman's boss in the home mill, if Millman could be transferred to his mill. Naturally, Kelley honored the request. Carl Anderson soon learned that Millman had no economic needs, because his wife had always worked and he had no children.

During Millman's first month in his new assignment, Carl Anderson made little headway with him and twice considered trying to fire him. Occasionally Millman would develop a drive, but then would lapse into his old nonproductive ways again. After a careful analysis of Millman's situation, Carl concluded that Millman's needs for tangible goods were satisfied, but he might respond to more recognition. On the mill's first anniversary, the manager held a party for all managerial personnel and their wives in the local country club. Carl had the caterer prepare a large cake and write on the top of the cake an important product line that was under Millman's jurisdiction and which was successful. Millman was greatly moved by the recognition and took a lot of kidding from other employees that night. Shortly after the party, Carl noticed that Millman's work improved and within several years, Millman became a successful general foreman in the plant.

Questions:

1. What do you think happened in this situation?

2. From a contingency perspective, what are the important features of this incident?

REFERENCES

1. Hellriegel, D., and J. Slocum, *Management: A Contingency Approach.* Reading, Mass.: Addison-Wesley Publishing Co., 1974.

2. Tosi, H., and C. Hamner, *Organizational Behavior and Management: A Contingency Approach.* Chicago: St. Clair Press, 1974. Moberg, D. and J. Koch, "A Critical Appraisal of Integrated Treatments of Contingency Findings," *Academy of Management Journal,* 1975, **18,** pp. 109–124.

3. Lawrence, P., and J. Lorsch, *Studies in Organization Design.* Homewood, Ill., Richard D. Irwin and Co., 1970. "Differentiation and Integration in Complex Organizations," *Administrative Science Quarterly,* 1967, **12,** pp. 1–47.

4. Roethlisberger, F., and Wm. Dickson, *Management and the Worker.* Cambridge, Mass.: Harvard University Press, 1941. Homans, G. *The Human Group.* New York: Harcourt & Brace, 1960.

5. Fiedler, F., and M. Chemers, *Leadership and Effective Management.* Chicago: Scott, Foresman & Co., 1974.

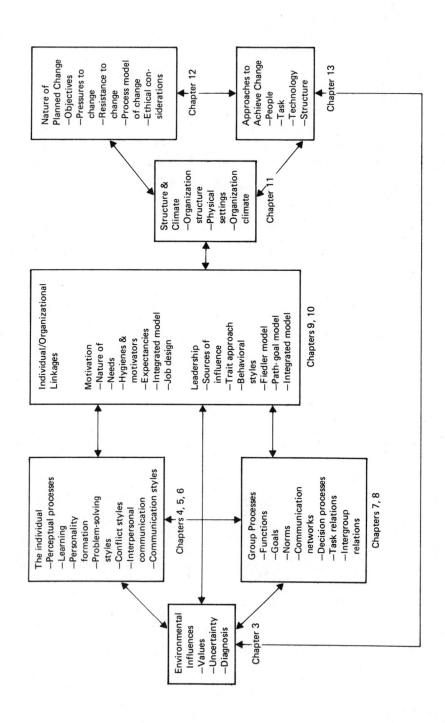

Nature of
Planned Change
—Objectives
—Pressures to
  change
—Resistance to
  change
—Process model
  of change
—Ethical con-
  siderations

Chapter 12

Approaches to
Achieve Change
—People
—Task
—Technology
—Structure

Chapter 13

Structure &
Climate
—Organization
  structure
—Physical
  settings
—Organization
  climate

Chapter 11

Individual/Organizational
Linkages

Motivation
—Nature of
—Needs
—Hygienes &
  motivators
—Expectancies
—Integrated model
—Job design

Leadership
—Sources of
  influence
—Trait approach
—Behavioral
  styles
—Fiedler model
—Path-goal model
—Integrated model

Chapters 9, 10

The individual
—Perceptual processes
—Learning
—Personality
  formation
—Problem-solving
  styles
—Conflict styles
—Interpersonal
  communication
—Communication styles

Chapters 4, 5, 6

Group Processes
—Functions
—Goals
—Norms
—Communication
  networks
—Decision processes
—Task relations
—Intergroup
  relations

Chapters 7, 8

Environmental
Influences
—Values
—Uncertainty
—Diagnosis

Chapter 3

2
LEARNING
ABOUT
ORGANIZATIONAL
BEHAVIOR

The study of organizational behavior is pursued by such diverse professionals as psychologists, sociologists, anthropologists, political scientists, economists, practicing managers, industrial engineers, and management scientists. These professionals often use different methods to focus on specific aspects of behavior. The common denominator among all these professionals is their attempt to study organizational behavior by the scientific approach.

The whole scientific procedure is based on the assumption that events do not occur merely by chance, but, rather, that events are linked together. For you, it may appear that good days and bad days are completely random, or related as much to your horoscope as to anything else. One of the major purposes of this chapter is to give you clues so that, with some skill, you may be able to discover the causes that underlie good and bad days. The manager should be in a position to do something about creating good days and avoiding bad days, and not just be a victim of circumstances.

While horoscopes or other forms of superstition are attempts to establish some regularity in the relationship between events, a manager relies on laws. As you will discover in this book, human behavior can be astonishingly lawful. For example, when we make a phone call, another person answers it; people report to work on time; when we buzz our secretary, the secretary enters the office; most people stop at red lights; paychecks arrive at the end of the month, and so on. However, there are exceptions. Occasionally, the secretary does not respond, the phone call is unanswered, a person runs the light, or the paycheck is late.

What good management is all about is being able to make good predictions. The first element in being able to make good predictions is to make an *observation* of behavior. For the manager, this is people, their behavior, and the results they attain. The second element is tied closely to the first. It is *measure-*

ment. The manager measures such variables as productivity, progress to a goal, ability, worker satisfaction, and many other variables associated with people, money, and materials. The third element in the approach is *prediction* on the basis of measurements and observations. The following are some examples of managerial questions concerned with the prediction element: Will productivity increase? Will scrap costs be reduced? How much will job satisfaction improve? What will be the impact on absenteeism? and the like.

As suggested in Fig. 2–1, the three basic elements in the scientific approach are closely interrelated.

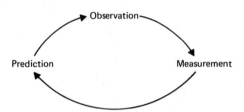

Figure 2–1   The Scientific Approach

Let's consider a brief example of the application of the scientific approach to management. A manager observes the work carried out by a new subordinate. The manager starts to make *observations* on the reports from this worker that come across her desk for approval. Each day more observations are made of the worker's performance. After a number of days, there are enough data to apply yardsticks to *measure* the worker's behavior. These measures indicate that the employee's performance is of superior quality and quantity. These measures provide a basis for *predicting* that the subordinate's work would continue to be exceptional even if not continuously checked. Accordingly, the subordinate is provided feedback on the outstanding performance and given the authority to issue certain reports without the manager's prior approval. The manager might now carry out further observations and measurements by checking through every tenth report or so. This will provide a basis for determining the accuracy of the manager's predictions. If the predictions are true over a period of time, the manager may decide to delegate more authority to this particular subordinate.

The purpose of this chapter is to help you understand the fundamental nature of research in organizational behavior. One cannot appreciate the limitations and contributions of the organizational behavior field without some understanding of how we learn about behavior within organizations. To accomplish this major purpose, the chapter has six objectives:

1. To discuss the basic elements of research designs;

2. To examine the four research designs commonly used by behavioral scientists and the manager/researcher;

3. To assess the managerial implications for each of these designs;

4. To suggest some methods for collecting data;

5. To discuss how often you need to collect the data; and

6. To examine the ethical and legal obligations of the manager/researcher.

RESEARCH DESIGNS

A research design is a plan, structure, and strategy of investigation developed to obtain answers to one or more questions.[1] The *plan* is the overall scheme or program of the research effort. It includes an outline of everything the investigator will do from the start until the final analysis of the data and submission of the report. A plan should include types of data to be collected, sample populations, research instruments, tentative target completion dates, and the like. The *structure* is also an outline, but specifies the variables to be measured. When we draw diagrams outlining the variables and their relationships we are building a structural schema for accomplishing the research. If we wish to examine students' learning in a class, the structure might indicate a direct relationship between student evaluation of faculty performance and academic achievement. The *strategy* represents the methods used for gathering and analyzing the data—that is, how the research objectives will be reached and how the problems encountered in the research will be resolved. The strategic issues in the previous example are likely to focus on how to validly measure academic achievement and faculty performance. Other strategic questions might be: What happens when students are absent and do not fill out the faculty evaluation? What statistical tests will be used to measure the degree of association between the two variables?

Purposes of Research Designs

A research design has two major purposes: to provide answers to questions and to provide control for nonrelevant effects that could affect the results of the study. These effects are those things the researcher has little control over, but which could have a great impact on the results. In our student evaluation example, some effects might include whether half the class was absent or whether an examination was returned the day measurements were taken. Research designs are invented by the investigator to obtain answers to questions as validly, objectively, accurately, and economically as possible. How does a research design help in accomplishing these aims? Research designs set up the framework for "adequate" tests of relations among the variables. The design communicates, in a general sense, what observations to make, how to make them, and how to quantitatively or qualitatively analyze the observations. It provides a guide to the investigator as to directions to pursue and avenues to avoid. For example, to research the automobile accident mentioned in Chapter 1, the investigator might include variables such as the speed of the car, road design and conditions, weather and driver conditions, and the condition of the car. The researcher might omit the place of the accident, the time, make and style of car, and a host of other variables. Any conclusions the investigator draws from the study are limited to those variables studied. In our example, this would preclude the investigator from making inferences about accidents involving different makes and models of cars, places of accidents, and other variables excluded from the research design.

Fundamentals of Research Designs

While we realize that a research design can rarely satisfy all the criteria usually associated with the scientific method, we should strive to satisfy as many as possible. If the research design is poorly conceived, the ultimate findings may be invalid or limited in applicability. If it is well conceived structurally, the ultimate product has a greater chance of being worthy of serious attention.

Before discussing the types of alternative designs, let us explain that our discussion is limited in scope and does not pretend to be encyclopedic. There are many research designs and textbooks written on the subject.[2] Our limited discussion arises from the growing recognition that a basic knowledge of certain research methods is needed by the present or prospective manager to adequately understand the contributions and limitations of the enormous and growing body of research in organizational behavior. In addition, this discussion should be useful in tempering a tendency to rush into cause-and-effect solutions to questions that frequently confront managers.

Typically, the entire design of a research project has the ultimate purpose of providing for the collection of data about a hypothesis in such a way that inferences of a causal relationship between an independent (causal) and dependent (effect) variable can be legitimately drawn. A hypothesis is a statement about the relationship between two or more variables. It asserts that a particular characteristic or occurrence in one of the factors (independent variable) determines the characteristic or occurrence of another factor (dependent variable). Examples of hypotheses might read: group study for examinations contributes to higher academic achievement than studying alone; profit-sharing plans lead to reduced turnover; and young college graduates are likely to experience more job dissatisfaction than older college graduates. In the first example, we have a statement that represents a relation between one variable, group study, and another variable, grade achievement. Group study is the independent variable and grade achievement is the dependent variable.

Let's consider another hypothesis: Business students will have more positive attitudes towards business and choose it more frequently as an occupation than psychology students. Again, we have a relation stated between one variable, students (business and psychology) and two other variables, favorable attitudes and occupational choice. In this example, the student's academic major is the independent variable and attitudes toward business and occupational choice are the dependent variables. The investigator often attempts to specify hypotheses and let the facts determine the probable truth or falsity of the hypothesis. Of course, as our comments about systems in Chapter 1 suggest, it is not easy to establish simple cause-and-effect relations. Similarly, managers informally pose hypotheses on a day-to-day basis to structure their decision-making processes. With these in mind, let us examine the basics of common research designs.

Experimental Design

The classic design involves an experimental group and a control group. These two groups are usually randomly chosen. The experimental group is the group receiving a "treatment" not given to the control group. For example, one group of executives may be exposed to a human-relations training program and another group of executives is not. The executives enrolled in the training program would be labeled as the experimental group; those not enrolled, the control group.

A control group is especially critical to increase the validity of the findings. For example, suppose the Director of Personnel is testing the hypothesis that the use of executive human-relations training will lead to greater performance on the job. The Director might arrange for the selection of executives to take training (the experimental group exposed to the "treatment") but not for others (the control group, not exposed to the treatment). At the end of the training program or some later period of time, the Director might compare the job performance data of the managers in the experimental and control groups. If the executives in the training program score higher on the average than those executives who did not take the training, there might be a basis for concluding that human-relations training programs and executive job performance are related.

The use of a control group permits the Director to rule out some other possible causes for the improvement in job performance. These other causes might be: (1) natural maturing or development of the executives, which has nothing to do with training; (2) other simultaneous events, such as new performance appraisal forms, the firm's active involvement in stopping pollution, procurement of new types of equipment that will change the process of getting work accomplished; and (3) the measurement process.

In any design involving the comparison of two groups exposed to different treatments (conditions), there is an underlying assumption that the groups being compared are equivalent before the introduction of the treatment. It is, however, virtually impossible to form groups that are equivalent in all respects.

There are two reasons for trying to establish equivalent groups: (1) to provide a basis for inferring differences in results that do not result from initial differences between the two groups; and (2) to increase the ability of the research design to measure the effects of the treatment. Equivalent groups can be obtained either through randomization or by matching.

Random assignment of subjects to experimental and control groups means that each subject must have the same chance as any subject of being assigned to either the experimental or control group. For example, one may flip a coin for each subject, assigning the individual to the experimental group if the coin comes up "heads," to the control group if it comes up "tails." Although random assignment, where it is feasible, is the most effective method of assignment, *matching* is another frequently used technique. Matching requires all subjects to be equal on the factors regarded relevant by the researcher. The equating process involves matching individuals in each group, person by person. For example, we might select subjects who are at the same managerial level, have been with the company for five years, and are making $25,000.00 dollars, for both the experimental and control groups.

The matching of individuals is often a difficult task. First, a large number of individuals are typically needed to achieve adequate matching. Second, it is also difficult to know in advance which factors are the most important to match against. Third, it is difficult to match on three or more factors. Finally, it may be difficult to obtain adequate measures for all the factors on which it is important to match. An example of the last difficulty is attempting to match a subject's past performance records when the company has not maintained a consistent performance evaluation form.

COMMON RESEARCH DESIGNS

Several of the designs used in the study of organizational behavior are well established. The four most common research designs are probably the case study, the laboratory experiment, the field experiment, and survey research. The purpose of this section is to review the advantages and disadvantages of these designs. The interrelationships of these four designs may be represented in numerous ways. One way of suggesting the relationships between the designs is by means of the diagram in Fig. 2–2. Although other feedback loops are possible (e.g., survey to case study, laboratory experiment to survey, case study to laboratory, etc.), the rationale for the relationships shown in Fig. 2–2 is appealing. At times a case study of an organization can identify one or more of the important variables that a researcher may wish to investigate by means of a survey. The major relationships uncovered in the survey will probably leave unanswered questions concerning their dynamics. The researcher may then choose to pursue the problem of relationships among the important variables in a laboratory setting. If the experiment yields a relationship of general significance to theory and/or practice, the researcher may then wish to explore the importance of the relationship in a field experiment.

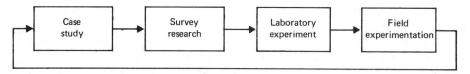

Figure 2-2 Interrelationships of Research Designs

Adapted from: William Evan, *Organizational Experiments: Laboratory and Field Research.* New York: Harper & Row, Publishers, 1971, p. 4. Reproduced by permission of publisher.

Case Study

Researchers working in relatively new areas, where there is little experience to serve as a guide, have found the case study of selected individuals and/or firms to be a particularly fruitful method for stimulating insights into what the problem(s) might be.[3] The case-study approach is incorrectly perceived in the narrow sense of studying the historical records kept by an organization. While the case method may include the examination of existing records, it may also involve interviewing, observation by the researcher, or some other approach.

There are several distinctive features of the case approach that make it an important strategy for stimulating new insights. A major one is the attitude of the investigator, which should be one of alert receptivity, of seeking rather than testing. Instead of limiting oneself to the testing of existing hypotheses, it is best to be guided by the features of the object being studied. A second feature is the intensity of the study. The researcher attempts to obtain sufficient information to characterize and explain the unique features of the case being studied and those other cases with which it has common features. A third feature is reliance in the researcher's ability to draw together the many diverse bits of information into a unified interpretation.

If careful attention is given to these three key points, the case can be a very effective research technique for the analysis of organizational behavior. It is highly adaptable to many problems found in organizations. For example, the case study might be a useful approach for obtaining the reactions of strangers and/or newcomers to an established group. A newcomer tends to be sensitive to social customs and practices that members are likely to take for granted. For example, a six-man work group loses one member because of retirement and his or her place in the group is taken over by a newcomer to the plant. The social practices of the work group (e.g., lunch breaks, bowling and golf leagues, and its production standard of 100 axles per day) must be communicated to this newcomer. The depth of analysis attained through the case study is its major advantage. However, there are no simple rules governing the incidents to be studied, experiences to be investigated, and the like.

The various limitations of the case study of a particular organization, whether it be a governmental agency, hospital, research laboratory, or university, must be considered by the researcher. This method's most prominent disadvantage is that it is not usually practical and/or logical to generalize the results of one case analysis to other cases. That is, only rarely does one find two cases that can meaningfully be compared in terms of essential characteristics (e.g., growth potential, number of employees, location, number of products made, levels of hierarchy, and the like). Therefore, case studies can rarely be repeated or their findings held true in other settings.

A further disadvantage is that a case study does not usually lend itself to a systematic investigation of cause-and-effect relationships. Although a case study extending over time can offer the opportunity to determine changes, the range of variations observed in the case study may be too limited for practical analysis. Hence, case studies may not afford definitive proof of a hypothesis, but they are frequently rich in clues and insights for further investigation.

Field Survey

A field survey involves collecting data, either by interviewing or by a questionnaire, from a sample of people selected to accurately represent the group under examination. The intent of a field survey is to gather information. It is not intended to change or influence the respondent. The aim is simply to find out how things are and how people feel and think. To carry out these aims, each person in the sample is asked the same series of questions. The answers obtained are put together in an organized way so that conclusions can be drawn. The use of the sample means that a small number of people can be selected to represent the whole, making it possible to avoid the very extensive and time-consuming procedure of taking a complete census (a "census" would involve a complete accounting of every person in the group being studied).

The content, or type of information gathered, usually concerns people's behavior, their attitudes, and other types of data. The manager might want to gather data about employees' *behavior, attitudes,* and *environment.* Many organizational surveys deal with the behavior of employees. For example, a superior's leadership behavior, the respondent's recreational habits, and the like. Some surveys concern the employees' opinions, attitudes, past experiences, or job expectations. This type of information includes many of the most interesting motivational questions available to the manager/researcher. Finally, the manager/researcher may want to know the circumstances in which employees live, in order to interpret their responses more accurately. This would include information about the local neighborhood, membership in groups and organizations, use of public transportation, and so on.

Most managers make extensive use of field surveys to measure the attitudes of employees. If a manager wishes to determine whether there is a relationship between job satisfaction and performance, a questionnaire is administered to a select sample of employees. Assuming that the questionnaire is a reliable and valid measuring instrument (see page 35) for a discussion of these terms), the manager can use the results from this sample to draw certain conclusions about the relationship between job satisfaction and performance, how to increase job satisfaction, what employees like or dislike about their jobs, and the like. Companies also use surveys to find out about employees' reactions to new rules and regulations, buildings, working hours, products, and other related issues.

Certain kinds of data cannot be validly obtained by using the survey design. Survey research typically taps data only about things of which an individual is consciously aware. For example, if the individual's preconscious and subconscious motivations are important, in-depth personal interviews might be most fruitful. Second, a large number of people usually must be sampled before we can draw any meaningful inferences from the results. Whereas the case study is restricted to a single firm or very few firms, people, or other units, the survey has very broad coverage.

The problem of getting individuals sampled to respond must be considered. Typically, only 40 to 50 percent of the people receiving a questionnaire fill it out. If the sample is limited, it is difficult to generalize the findings to a broader population.

Last, there remains the problem of inferring cause-and-effect relationships. A case in point is the analysis of the relationships among job satisfaction, leadership styles, and performance. Does job satisfaction lead to higher performance and then does the leader change his or her personal style? Or is leadership related to job satisfaction, which is then associated with high performance? Because of the large number of variables typically investigated in a survey, problems concerning the causal relationships among the variables are often still unanswered. [4]

Laboratory Experiment [5]

Compared with the case study and field survey, the laboratory experiment increases the ability to establish cause-and-effect relationships between variables. The researcher has an increased ability to create and control the exact conditions desired. The choice of the activity in which the group and/or the individual is to be engaged is somewhat dependent upon the variables being investigated. The essence of the laboratory experiment is to observe the effects of manipulating an independent variable(s) on a dependent variable(s). For example, one group of three blindfolded subjects is instructed by an autocratic leader to build a tower as high as they can with Tinker Toys. Another group of subjects is instructed by a democratic leader to perform the same task. The dependent variable is the height of the tower, and the independent variable is leadership style.

There are several disadvantages in using the laboratory design. Given the practicalities of the situation, the subjects are usually college students. It is difficult to justify the use of college students as representatives of actual managers involved in decision-making processes. That is, students are very transitory and their academic livelihood is usually not dependent on successful completion of a task under laboratory conditions. Therefore, to what populations and treatment variables can the laboratory results be generalized? Simulating many properties of organizational structure and process in the laboratory may increase the "realism" of the experiment at the cost of decreasing experimental control and precision.

Another general problem is that much of the work undertaken in the laboratory deals with phenomena that cannot be reproduced in the "real" world. For example, it would be difficult to recreate the effects of different status hierarchies in organizations. However, experiments in the laboratory should derive their direction from studies in real-life situations and results should be continually checked by studies in real-life situations. Finally, many behavioral problems in organizations cannot be meaningfully isolated to permit their examination under lab conditions; thus researchers tend to focus narrowly on problems that can be implemented in the laboratory setting.

Field Experiment [6]

In the case of the field experiment, there are fewer difficulties in introducing real-life organizational behavior problems. This design constitutes an attempt to apply the laboratory method to on-going, real-life situations. The field experiment permits the researcher to manipulate one or more independent variables in an on-going organization. The changes in the dependent variables can be studied and the direction of causality can be inferred with some degree of confidence.

The subjects ordinarily know they are under investigation. There is a need to adopt procedures that will decrease the possibility of subjects changing their behavior simply as a result of being observed. The field researcher usually lacks some degree of control over the situation, as compared to the control in the laboratory design. The researcher must make the assumption that events are affecting both groups equally and that these events will not be a major determinant of the dependent variable.

An example of a field experiment consisted of one group of executives who were randomly selected to attend an executive development program for fifteen weeks, and another group of executives from the same company who were not. The independent variable was the training program and the dependent variables were job satisfaction and performance. Prior to training, the groups were similar on these two variables.

Eighteen months after the conclusion of the training program, the researchers measured the dependent variables again and concluded that those executives who participated in the program were more satisfied with their jobs and earned higher salary adjustments than those executives not enrolled in the program. Superiors of the men in the training program were aware of their involvement, while the supervisors of the men in the control group were not. The possible effect of this awareness on performance evaluations of the executives in the program was beyond the control of the researcher.[7]

Comparison of Research Designs

The research designs previously discussed have both strong and weak points. By selecting one design, the researcher must often forego some of the advantages of alternative designs. Let's quickly compare the major designs on a few points.

Realism.   One of the major advantages of doing research in a natural setting, such as within an organization, is the ability to increase the level of realism. The researcher has some confidence that the subject (e.g., managers, workers, administrators) are behaving under conditions that are natural and on-going. While this is an advantage over the laboratory, which typically uses "artificial" conditions, the researcher in the field loses the ability to manipulate the independent variable(s) as freely as in the laboratory condition.

Scope.   One advantage of the field experiment and field survey is that they are usually broad in scope and incorporate many variables of interest to the researcher.

Precision.   Research undertaken in the laboratory setting is usually more precise than is typical in the field setting. The use of multiple measures of the same variable(s) under controlled conditions allows the researcher to obtain more accurate information about the variables than with other strategies. The use of video tape, for example, permits the researcher to tape the entire experiment and then study the tape at a later time, to examine such things as styles of behavior, motives, and gestures. The intention is to measure more accurately the variables under consideration.

Control.   The manager also wishes to control the situation in such a way that the events under observation are sure to be related to the causes he or she thinks exist and not to some unknown events. Control over the situation in which we wish to take our measurements provides several advantages. First, we can produce the situation over and over again. This means that we do not have to rely on a single observation to form our impressions. Second, by replicating the study, we can refine our predictions about cause-and-effect relationships from "sometimes" to "95 times out of a hundred." Third, many factors occur in the field (personnel changes, employees forgetting to fill out the questionnaire) over which the manager has little control.

In our discussion we have emphasized that each method has its unique strengths and weaknesses. Before choosing among the alternatives, the researcher should accurately assess each method in light of the questions to be answered. For example, most historical studies are based on information drawn from several sources, and inferences are often necessary to reconcile records originally collected for other purposes. Thus, a case study usually requires a lengthy narrative. Does the question warrant this elaboration?

DATA COLLECTION

In the previous section, we discussed some of the design strategies available to you. Let's assume you have chosen one and now are faced with the task of developing methods for collecting the data. What are the alternatives open to you?

Interviews

The interview is probably one of the oldest and most often used devices for obtaining information. This is a face-to-face situation in which one person, the interviewer, asks a person being interviewed, the respondent, questions designed to obtain answers pertinent to the research problem. An interview has three general purposes:

First, it can be used as an exploratory device to help understand the variables in question. For example, if you are attempting to predict what job a candidate will take, you might interview several candidates to find out what they are looking for in their work (e.g., salary, challenging job assignments, opportunity to continue their education). After you have discovered what job characteristics attract candidates, you might hypothesize that corporations with the desired job characteristics will be more attractive to candidates than corporations without these characteristics.

Second, the interview can be used as the major instrument of the research. For example, if you want to understand why people are absent, you could interview employees who are frequently absent and those who are rarely absent. The responses may assist you in answering your question.

Third, the interview can be used to supplement other data-collection methods. A major strength of this method lies in its ability to obtain a great deal of information in a fairly straightforward manner on selected questions. Though questions may have to be carefully worded, respondents can and usually will give much information directly. Of course, the research purposes should determine the types of questions asked, their content, sequence and wording.

There are, on the other hand, several major shortcomings in the interview method. First, there are certain types of information respondents may be unwilling to provide readily in a face-to-face situation. An employee may be unwilling to express negative attitudes about a superior when the interviewer is from the personnel department. Second, interviews take time and this large investment in time costs money. Third, to achieve reliability, interviewers must be well trained and questions must be pretested to achieve validity; interviewers' personal biases must be eliminated and questions must be tested for unknown biases.

Questionnaires

Managers sometimes feel that interviewing large numbers of employees costs too much and that it takes employees away from production while they are being interviewed. One alternative is to use a questionnaire to measure the beliefs, opinions, and attitudes of the employees. There are two general types of questionnaire: objective and descriptive.

The *objective* questionnaire presents the individual with a question and a choice of answers, in such a way that the employee merely has to mark the answer which is his or her choice. This type of questionnaire is illustrated in Fig. 2–3. In this type of questionnaire, the individual reads all the answers to each question and then marks the answer which is nearest to how he or she feels. This questionnaire is part of a larger study conducted by your authors at Mack Trucks, measuring the climate of this organization. The instructions ask the employee to mark a numerical value in the space provided, indicating his or her opinion as to the accuracy of the description contained in the statement. The chief advantage of an objective questionnaire is that it is easy to administer and to analyze statistically. This permits much of the analysis to be performed on computers, which is an important cost consideration when hundreds of employees are surveyed.

The *descriptive* questionnaire presents the questions to the employee, but lets the employee answer in his or her own words. His or her responses are encouraged in a directed manner. The directed question focuses the employee's attention on a specific part of his or her job and questions him or her about it. An example is "What do you think about the air-conditioned cafeteria?" In this way, management in general determines the questions that will be asked. The descriptive questionnaire gives the employee more leeway in answering the question than does the objective questionniare.

Projective Methods [8]

Projective methods involve the presentation of an unstructured situation. A major intent is to obtain the subject's perception of the world. The situation should be capable of arousing many different kinds of reactions. Examples are an ink blot that can be perceived in different ways or a picture that can elicit a variety of stories. There are no right or wrong answers; nor are the subjects faced with a limited set of alternatives. The emphasis is on the subjects' percep-

Figure 2-3   Organizational Climate Questionnaire

Instructions: We would like you to describe the "climate" of your plant. To do this, read each statement and ask yourself how descriptive this statement is of your plant. We are not asking whether you think the statement should or ought to be descriptive, rather whether it actually is descriptive.

To indicate how well each statement describes your plant, write a number in the blank beside each statement, based on the following scale.

1	2	3	4	5	6
Never true	Almost never true	Sometimes true	Frequently true	Nearly always true	Always true

_____ 1. In this plant, a manager's superior watches over him carefully to make sure he does things correctly.

_____ 2. As long as he keeps within broad limits, a manager can plan and schedule his work as he wants to.

_____ 3. A manager's boss tries to supervise him too closely here.

_____ 4. Managers here must submit frequent oral and written reports concerning what they are doing.

_____ 5. There are many close friendships among managers in this company.

_____ 6. This plant's management is sympathetic with the personal problems of its employees.

_____ 7. There are a lot of policies and standard procedures in this plant that a new manager must know before beginning a job.

_____ 8. This organization has excellent benefits for its managers.

_____ 9. The most deserving managers are the ones who get promoted.

_____ 10. This plant has a real drive to be number one.

_____ 11. Top management personnel are called by their first names.

_____ 12. Traditions are so strong here that it is difficult to modify established procedures or undertake new programs.

_____ 13. Decision-making in this organization is accomplished through shared authority (by which top and lower levels of management arrive at decisions jointly).

_____ 14. As long as he keeps within broad limits, a manager can plan and schedule his work as he wants to without consulting other members of the plant.

Source: Hellriegel, D., W. Joyce, and J. Slocum, Unpublished questionnaire, Pennsylvania State University, July, 1975.

tions of the material, the meaning they give to it, and the way they organize and/or manipulate it. The nature of the stimuli and the way in which the materials are presented do not clearly indicate the purpose of the researcher or the way in which the responses will be interpreted. The individuals are not asked to talk directly about themselves. However, the responses are often interpreted as indicating the individual's own view of the world, personality structure, needs and feelings, and ways of interacting with people.

Look at Fig. 2–4. What is this man thinking? What has led up to this situation? You might want to write a brief response to these questions. In presenting the picture in Fig. 2–4 to executives, some typical responses include: (1) an executive relaxing in an airplane after a board meeting; (2) a man thinking it will be nice to spend some time home after a tiring business trip; and (3) an executive thinking how to swing a big deal over on his competitors. The responses to pictures such as these have been used as a bases for assessing individual's motivational needs. We shall have more to say about this in our chapter on motivation.

Figure 2–4   Sample Picture Used for "Unstructured" Stimulus. Just look at the picture briefly (10–15 seconds).

Source: David A. Kolb, Irwin M. Rubin, and James M. McIntyre, *Organizational Psychology: An Experiential Approach,* © 1971, p. 65. Reproduced by permission of Prentice-Hall, Inc., Englewood Cliffs, New Jersey.

One of the most difficult problems with projective techniques is that many inferences may be drawn from a person's written responses. The method demands extreme reliance on the interpretive skill of the researcher.

Observation

Everyone observes the actions of others. We look at people and talk with them. We often infer what others mean when they speak and infer their motivations, feelings, and intentions on the basis of these observations. We may say, "What a rip-off artist," suggesting that the individual is shrewd and demonstrates nongenuine behavior.

A major difficulty with the observation method is inherent in the observer. The researcher must digest the information derived from the observations and then make inferences about problems. Due to human fallibility, these inferences may be incorrect. Suppose, for example, an individual who is strongly antagonistic to major university football observes the game, the recruiting of candidates, and the pressure to win. This individual's personal biases may well invalidate the observations and inferences about the sport. One method for reducing this problem is the development of an observational form, on which the observer(s) records specific acts. For example, two graduate students observed individuals approaching the ticket office of an X-rated movie in a university town. Some of the observational categories were:

1. Sex, M or F;

2. Alone, or with group;

3. Stag group or mixed;

4. How did patron pay?—fumbled around with money, quickly paid, looked to see who was around;

5. Age bracket: 18 and under, college age, 25–30, over 31;

6. Apparent occupation: student, businessman, housewife, retired.

Sitting in a car across from the theater, each observer marked a place on the form for each theatre patron. If there were discrepancies between the two observers in describing the behavioral characteristics, a third observer could be used, or the two observers could reach a mutually agreeable decision on the patron.

Secondary Sources

If we wish to know something about an individual, instead of asking the person directly we may turn to secondary sources for our information. Secondary sources represent data others have compiled. Company records have provided researchers with valuable data on absenteeism, turnover, grievances, performance ratings, and demographics. In some cases, this source of data may be more accurate than that obtained directly by questioning the subject. For example, company records on individual job performance may yield greater accuracy than would direct questions to the individual.

Figure 2–5 presents a summary of the problems and potentials for collecting data using the four major methods. This figure roughly classifies and orders the methods according to four factors:

1. The control over the investigator's question;

2. Investigator's control over the respondent's answer;

3. Degree of precision; and

4. Breadth and depth of respondent's potential responses.

In general, as more and more constraints are placed on the investigator and respondent, the unknown biases of the method decrease while the precision increases. For example, if the respondents must confine themselves to a specific topic, say, pay satisfaction, and their answers must be placed in one category (e.g., highly satisfied with my pay, satisfied with my pay, dissatisfied with my pay, very dissatisfied with my pay), their answers become more directly comparable one to another.

The questionnaire is a method that increases the investigator's control over the question posed, and the respondent's answer to the question. At the same time, the questionnaire cannot tap the breadth of potential responses that the individual wants to give to the question because of the limited number of questions asked. On the other hand, if a researcher wants to increase the respondent's breadth and depth of answers, a projective method easily affords the researcher an opportunity to gather such data. With this method, the respondent has a high degree of control over the answer given, and can vary in the degree to which he or she answers the question. For example, turn back to page 31. How many interpretations of this picture are possible? Almost an infinite number. Since the investigator cannot control the potential number of interpretations, he or she loses control over the possible number of responses but gains insight into the nature of the problem.

Criteria for a Good Measure

How is it possible to make sure a measure accurately reflects only the characteristic we are interested in studying? To answer this question, we need some understanding of the criteria for a good measure. Figure 2–6 presents the major criteria and illustrates how each applies to a physical variable, such as room temperature, and a psychological one, such as motivation.

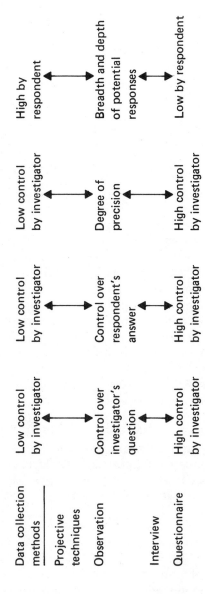

Figure 2-5 Classification of Methods to Gather Data

Criteria of a good measure	Meaning	Temperature	Application to motivation
Sensitivity	Measure reflects underlying variable sensitivity	Column of mercury rises regularly as heat is applied	Behavioral measure reflects motivational need states
Uniqueness	Measure reflects changes in that variable only	Column of mercury does not rise as pressure is applied	Behavioral measure is relatively uninfluenced by habits, values, etc.
Reliability	Measure gives same reading under same conditions	Mercury rises to same temperature if some heat is applied	Behavioral measure gives same value when used by two different raters
Validity	Measure reflects the importance of a variable	Temperature as measured by a thermometer is theoretically and practically useful in predicting what will happen to weather under various conditions	Motive measure shows theoretical properties of a motive and is useful in predicting behavior under various conditions

Figure 2–6 Criteria for a Good Measure

Source: Adapted from: David C. McClelland, *Assessing Human Motivation*. Morristown, N.J.: General Learning Press, 1971.

The *sensitivity* criterion requires the measure to fluctuate with the characteristic which it is intended to represent. If heat is applied at the base of a column of mercury in a glass tube and the mercury does not rise, the mercury is an insensitive indicator of temperature change. If a motivational questionnaire is designed to measure a need for affiliation and we know the person is about to join a social fraternity but, with our questionnaire, scores low on his or her need for affiliation, the questionnaire is probably not a sensitive indicator of affiliative needs.

The *uniqueness* criterion requires that the indicator not be influenced by unintended variables. Thus, a person's score should not vary for reasons that have nothing to do with motivation. For example, people will often say they have a need for affiliation because it is "socially desirable" to have this need and want to be around others.

The *reliability* criterion means that, if two observers look at the same phenomenon, they should arrive at the same interpretation. For example, the two graduate students observing theatre patrons should be able to rate the same patron accurately on the desired dimensions if the report has reliability.

Validity is also important because it answers the question: Does the method measure what it is supposed to measure? It is possible to devise a measure that is sensitive, unique, and reliable but that is quite unimportant in that it does not tell you anything else about the person. The utility of a motivation index is judged by the relationship between it and other things that a person does. That is, its predictiveness. For example, if a person scores high on the need for affiliation but the score is not related to anything else (e.g., needs, job performance, job satisfaction), it does not have predictive validity.

Timing of Data Collection

After you have decided on the method(s) for collecting the data and on your research design, you must still decide how often you will collect these data. Some frequently used methods are single times, *after* measure only, and before-and-after measures.

Single time.   This approach attempts to collect data about the subjects' attitudes, performance, or other characteristics at only one point in time. A control group is usually not used. It is our estimate that 80 percent of the researchers use this approach. Thus, it is important to understand its usefulness and limitations.

This approach is most often used to investigate current practices and/or events. For example, student evaluations of professors have become increasingly popular on many campuses. The students enrolled in the class are sampled and their perceptions are recorded. Single-time measurements are often limited to a description of the situation at the current time. Within organizations, management uses single-time measures primarily to determine the relevance of certain practices and trends, or to compare its practices against trends in the industry. This approach can also be employed to investigate relationships between two or more groups of data. If we measure an individual's job satisfaction and obtain a measure of job performance, we then can test the degree of relationship between job satisfaction and performance.

There are two limitations of the single-time measurement. First, the data do not demonstrate how the variables are related—no causal relationships can be claimed. Secondly, the data reported hold true only under the conditions at a specific point in time. In this respect, single-time measurements resemble photographs.

After-only.   As the name implies, the experimental and control groups are measured with respect to the dependent variable only after the experimental group has received a "treatment." The main difference between this method of data collection and the "single-time" method is the formation of control and experimental groups. It has been estimated that about 90 percent of the researchers and managers involved in human-relations training use this type of research design.[9]

Perhaps the most serious weakness of this design is the researcher's assumption that the two groups were equal prior to the exposure of the experimental group to the treatment. Thus, it might be incorrectly concluded that the differences between the groups can be attributed to introduction of the treatment. Without prior measures, it is necessary to assume that both groups hold similar attitudes toward some object, or that they have similar job-performance profiles. It is also necessary to assume that the groups were exposed to the same environmental and maturational processes between the time when the groups were selected and the time the measures were taken.

Before-after design.   The use of both experimental and control groups and before-and-after measurements is a reasonable design for most managers to use. This improves the ability of the researcher to conclude that changes in the experimental group were in fact due to the "treatment," rather than due to passage of time or to some uncontrolled change. The logic of this research design is indicated in Fig. 2–7. Two groups are selected either by random assignment or by a matching process. Measures of the dependent variables are made in the experimental and control groups. The experimental group is then given a "treatment," such as a human-relations training program, a change in leadership style, or a modification of its task structure.

The possible effect of the treatment is subsequently evaluated by again measuring the dependent variables in both groups. The differences between the two groups after the treatment, minus the differences that may have existed before, is considered to be the effect of the treatment. In Fig. 2–7, the effect of the experimental variable is $(E_A - C_A) - (E_B - C_B)$. This research design is the closest we have come in organizational behavior to demonstrating cause and effect. This type of design is particularly important in evaluating the

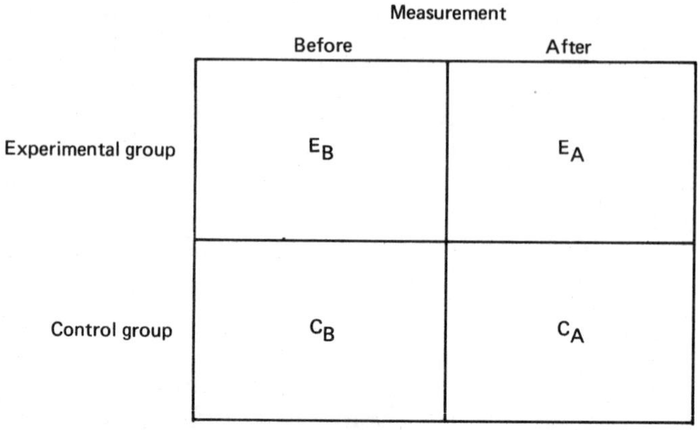

Measurement

	Before	After
Experimental group	E_B	E_A
Control group	C_B	C_A

Figure 2–7   The Basic Experimental Design

effectiveness of organizational change programs and may be used in any "real-world" setting.

Comparison of Research Strategies

To understand the complexity of learning about organizational behavior more clearly, Fig. 2–8 provides a means for comparing and contrasting all of the strategies, methods of gathering data, and the timing of the measurement processes. Each research design is described in terms of its usual procedures for gathering data and the timing of the measurement processes. The characteristics assigned represent our interpretation of the "best fit" for each strategy. Thus, there is latitude for debate and discussion on some of the characteristics assigned to certain of the designs.

ETHICS

To the extent that data are derived from the general public, students, or company employees, there arises the question of the ethical and legal obligations owed by the researcher to these subjects. Some of these obligations may be implicit in the conduct of any kind of relationship, and others have specific application to the subject matter and techniques under discussion.

One of the primary ethical requirements is the confidential nature of the relationship between the researcher and subject(s). For example, if a researcher is testing the relationship between job satisfaction and performance, the individual's performance data must be obtained. Let's assume the researcher determines that employees who are highly satisfied with the company and its policies are better performers than those employees who are not satis-

Figure 2–8   Comparison of Research Designs

Research design	Typical method(s) of data collection	Typical timing of data collection
Case study	Observation Interview Secondary source	Single-time
Field survey	Questionnaire Interview	Single-time
Laboratory	Projection Observation Interview Questionnaire	Before-after
Field experimentation	Questionnaire Observation Interview Secondary sources	Before-after

fied. Someone in the company may want to know which employees are in each group. However, the researcher should maintain the confidentiality of his data sources to protect the anonymity of the respondents.

By their very nature, certain types of research designs require naiveté on the part of the respondent, which is impaired under conditions of complete candor. In marketing research, for example, subjects are often asked to evaluate two samples of a product that are identical, but are presented in different packages. Obviously, the research would be largely worthless if the respondents were informed prior to the evaluation that the contents of the packages were identical.

Similar practices are common in psychology, wherein false statements are presented, or true statements are attributed to false sources, in order to determine various influences of credibility. The code of ethics of the American Psychological Association requires ". . . only when a problem is significant and can be investigated in no other way is the psychologist justified in giving misinformation to research subjects. . . ."[10] Many researchers feel an ethical obligation to inform the subjects of any falsehoods as soon as possible after the research has been terminated.

The U.S. Department of Health, Education, and Welfare has issued an extensive report for the protection of human subjects.[11] To protect the respondent, objective and independent reviews of research projects and activities involving the use of human subjects are conducted by a committee. At the Pennsylvania State University, the independent review committee is composed of various Directors of Research from the colleges within the University.[12]

Each member of the review board arrives at a decision based on his/her professional judgment as to whether or not the research will place the participating subjects "at risk." If a majority of the review committee members feel that the procedures to be employed will not place the subject at risk, the proposal will be approved. After the proposal has been approved, each subject must sign an agreement of consent. The basic elements of informed consent include:

1. A fair explanation of the procedures to be followed, including those that are experimental;

2. A description of the study;

3. A description of the benefits to be expected;

4. An offer to answer any inquiries concerning the procedures; and

5. An instruction that the subject is free to withdraw consent and to discontinue participation in the activity at any time.

When the research has been completed, an abstract of the report should be made available to all interested subjects who took part in the study.

We recognize that procedures such as the ones we've mentioned do not resolve all of the possible ethical issues associated with organizational behavior research. However, they do suggest some of the positive steps that we believe should be taken to minimize risks to human subjects.

SUMMARY

The purpose of research is to discover answers to questions through the application of scientific procedures. These procedures have been developed to increase the likelihood that the information gathered will be relevant to the questions asked and will be reliable. Throughout this chapter, we have tried to concern ourselves with the basic requirements of research and with some of the methods frequently used by researchers.

The four major research designs were discussed: case method, survey, laboratory, and field experiments. Each has its own unique features and limitations. The final research problem addressed in this chapter is the gathering of data to test hypotheses. The interview, questionnaire, projection, observation, and secondary sources of obtaining data were discussed. An attempt was also made to cross-classify the methods of gathering data with the four research design strategies. We concluded with discussion of several ethical considerations involved in the use of humans as research subjects.

Discussion Questions

1. What are the purposes of a research design?

2. What are the basic variables in an experimental design?

3. What are some of the major research designs used by managers today?

4. Compare the research designs in terms of (a) realism; (b) control; and (c) precision.

5. What types of data-gathering methods are used by managers? Evaluate the strengths and weaknesses of each method.

6. What is reliability? What is validity? Give examples of each.

7. Why should researchers be concerned with ethics?

8. Prepare a plan for using a survey in a bank or large department store to determine customers' attitudes toward a new billing system.

CRITICAL INCIDENT

Westminster College is a small (1500 students) private liberal arts college. For most of its history, it has operated on a conventional semester program with no classes during the summer months. In order to bring money into the college during the summer months, efforts have been made by the Director of Continuing Education to bring conferences to the campus and thereby achieve more productive use of the idle facilities during the summer. These efforts have never been very successful.

All administrative activities slowed down during the summer and it had been the custom to close the office at 3:30 P.M. rather than the normal hour of 5:00 P.M. The revised hours usually started immediately after commencement activities in the spring and extended through Labor Day. Approximately 75 clerks, typists, and other secretarial personnel were affected by the change. Each year, the Vice-President for Academic Affairs notified these personnel about the new summer hours in a memo.

In January of 1975, the Board of Trustees approved a plan to switch Westminster College to an academic quarter plan and enroll some freshman students in both summer and fall quarters. This was done in the belief that the facilities of the college would be used more fully, and that the added income would alleviate the financial strain on the college. It was also hoped that this plan would enable students to graduate more quickly because some students would attend college on a year-round basis.

Academic plans for the switch-over had been going smoothly, and Dr. Watson, Business Manager and Vice-President for Financial Planning, called a staff meeting in early May to review the overall plan. During the course of the meeting, Mr. Richards, the treasurer of the college, indicated that with 300 freshman students entering the college within a month, his staff was going to have difficulty getting its work accomplished in the shortened work hours, and that he assumed that the shortened summer hours were now a thing of the past.

Dr. Kelley, the Director of Public Administration, said that it was his understanding that the reduced summer hours would still be in effect. He further noted that many of his staff had already made plans on the basis of the traditional summer working hours. Others at the staff meeting echoed Dr. Kelley's thoughts. The Vice-President for Academic Affairs immediately replied that no memo had gone out this year indicating that the shortened summer hours schedule would be in effect in 1975. He reasoned that employees should not assume that the usual changes would take place unless they received a memo from his office to that effect.

After the meeting, the word spread among the nonacademic staff that there would be no shortened work hours in 1975. During the rest of May, most administrators noticed that the morale was low, the technical quality of the work was substandard, and the problems that should have been handled by senior clerical personnel were being neglected.

Questions:

1. What happened in this situation to trigger poor workmanship and low morale?

2. What types of data would you like to gather and how would you design a research program to analyze the problem?

REFERENCES

1. Kerlinger, F., *Foundations of Behavioral Research.* New York: Holt, Rinehart & Winston, 1965, pp. 275–290.

2. For example, see Selltiz, C., M. Jahoda, M. Deutsch, and S. Cook, *Research Methods in Social Relations.* New York: Holt, Rinehart & Winston, 1965. Borgatta, E., and G. Bohrnstedt (eds.), *Sociological Methodology.* San Francisco: Jossey-Bass, Inc., Publishers, 1970. Kirk, R., *Experimental Design: Procedures for Behavioral Sciences.* Belmont, Calif.: Brooks/Cole, 1968. Edwards, A., *Experimental Design in Psychological Research.* New York: Holt, Rinehart & Winston, 1965. Campbell, D., and J. Stanley, *Experimental and Quasi-Experimental Designs for Research,* Chicago: Rand McNally & Co., 1963.

3. Towl, A. "The Use of Cases for Research," in *The Case Method at the Harvard Business School.* McNair, M. (ed.). New York: McGraw-Hill Book

Co., Inc., 1954, pp. 223–230. Yin, R., and K. Heald, "Using the Case Survey Method to Analyze Policy Studies," *Administrative Science Quarterly*, 1975, **20,** pp. 371–381.

4. Kerlinger, F., "Survey Research," in *op. cit.,* pp. 392–411.

5. Festinger, L., "Laboratory Experiments," in *Research Methods in the Behavioral Sciences.* Festinger, L., and D. Katz (eds.). New York: Holt, Rinehart & Winston, 1953, pp. 136–172.

6. Barnes, L. "Organizational Change and Field Experiment Methods," in *Methods of Organizational Research.* Vroom, V. (ed.). Pittsburgh, Pa.: University of Pittsburgh Press, 1967, pp. 77–111.

7. Hand, H., and J. Slocum, "A Longitudinal Study of the Effects of a Human Relations Training Program in Managerial Effectiveness," *Journal of Applied Psychology,* 1972, **56,** pp. 412–417.

8. Berelson, B., and G. Steiner, *Human Behavior: An Inventory of Scientific Findings.* New York: Harcourt, Brace & World, 1964, pp. 32–33.

9. Hand, H., M. Richards, and J. Slocum, "Organizational Climate and the Effectiveness of a Human-Relations Training Program," *Academy of Management Journal,* 1973, **16,** pp. 185–195.

10. "Ethical Standards of Psychologists," *The American Psychologist,* 1963, **18,** pp. 56–60.

11. *The Institutional Guide of DHEW Policy on Protection of Human Subjects.* Washington, D.C.: Department of Health, Education, and Welfare, 1971.

12. Osborn, R. *Policy and Procedure in Research: The Pennsylvania State University,* University Park, Pa.: Pennsylvania State University, 1970.

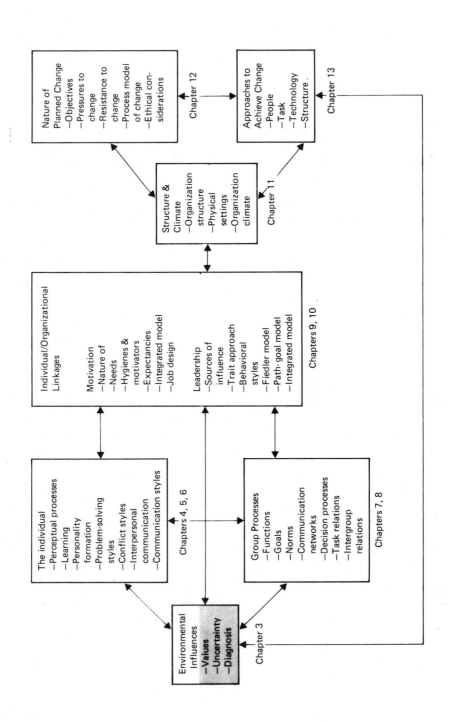

Nature of Planned Change
—Objectives
—Pressures to change
—Resistance to change
—Process model of change
—Ethical considerations

Chapter 12

Approaches to Achieve Change
—People
—Task
—Technology
—Structure.

Chapter 13

Structure & Climate
—Organization structure
—Physical settings
—Organization climate

Chapter 11

Individual/Organizational Linkages

Motivation
—Nature of
—Needs
—Hygienes & motivators
—Expectancies
—Integrated model
—Job design

Leadership
—Sources of influence
—Trait approach
—Behavioral styles
—Fiedler model
—Path-goal model
—Integrated model

Chapters 9, 10

The individual
—Perceptual processes
—Learning
—Personality formation
—Problem-solving styles
—Conflict styles
—Interpersonal communication
—Communication styles

Chapters 4, 5, 6

Group Processes
—Functions
—Goals
—Norms
—Communication networks
—Decision processes
—Task relations
—Intergroup relations

Chapters 7, 8

Environmental Influences
—Values
—Uncertainty
—Diagnosis

Chapter 3

3
ENVIRONMENTAL
INFLUENCES
AND
ASSESSMENT

Just a few years ago the CEO (Chief Executive Officer) of a big company spent 10% of his time on external matters ... Today the figure is generally 40%.[1]

Alonzo L. McDonald, Jr.
Managing Partner of McKinsey & Co.

It's an odd world we're living in. We're sitting on a volcano of conflicting interests.[2]

Frank A. Nemec, Chairman of the
Board, Youngstown Sheet and Tube Co.

All organizations are likely to experience turmoil in their environments through the 70's. This turmoil is wide ranging, encompassing such issues as employee relations and working conditions, marketing and financial power and practices, consumerism, environmentalism, equality of opportunity, individualism, productivity, governance, community and government relations, international operations, inflation and controls, health and safety, and the role of organizations in society. Jerome Jacobson, senior vice-president of Bendix Corporation, observed "In a rapidly changing economic environment, some plans are out of date in three to six months." [3; p. 46] The importance of new expectations for organizations, especially large ones, is suggested by chief executives spending more of their time on environmental influences. However, this may be analogous to the tip of an iceberg. Managers and individuals at all levels of organizations are having to confront new issues, problems, and opportunities created by the changing environment, particularly in the United States.

Within this chapter, the discussion of environmental influences is highly selective. It is impossible to deal with all the concepts and issues relevant to a comprehensive development of the interface between environments and organizations, particularly as they relate to individual and group behavior within those organizations. The potential breadth, complexity, and interdependencies in and with the environment have been expressed this way:

> The whole world is by now a richly interactive system. It is running according to various tenets (doctrines): cultural tenets, legal tenets, financial tenets, industrial tenets, political tenets. These tenets prescribe the rule governing a great many of the interactions. [3, p. 198]

Accordingly, the objectives of this chapter are:

1. To develop an understanding of the nature and importance of values and value systems for differentiating and predicting the behavior of individuals and organizations;

2. To develop a sensitivity for the past, present, and future with respect to specific types of managerial values;

3. To present a framework for diagnosing various dimensions of work-related values for individuals;

4. To describe a framework for assessing types of organizational environments and understanding how varying environments should be associated with varying practices and processes within organizations; and

5. To describe General Electric's strategy of environmental assessment as one example of a sophisticated system for helping management anticipate and react to changes in a planned manner.

This chapter will provide the reader with "mental maps" and concrete examples for recognizing and diagnosing the interrelationships between practices internal and external to the organization and its members.

Part One of this chapter focuses on values and value systems because: they often represent the foundation for the legal, financial, industrial, and political tenets mentioned in the above quote; they provide one source of explanation for some of the actions by individuals, groups, and organizations; they provide an understandable way of considering differences in the past, present, and possibly the future for both individuals and organizations; they represent a major part of the meaning and significance we assign to our personal lives and to the organizations within which we work; and they provide a background for maintaining perspective on many of the more specific concepts and issues discussed in later chapters. These assertions as to the role of values and value systems will be illustrated and made more explicit as the chapter unfolds.

Part two of the chapter concerns a discussion of two models that indicate how managers can assess their organizational environments. The first model suggests the key variables and the interrelationships among them that should be considered when attempting to decide how to organize and the types of relationships between individuals that might be encouraged. The second model presents the strategy General Electric uses in attempting to assess the significance of various environmental forces. These two models recognize the role of values and value systems, but include other elements as well, such as political and economic factors.

As emphasized in the contingency model (Fig. 1–2) in Chapter 1, the definition of environment is a relative matter. [4] It depends upon the unit of analysis that is of interest (such as an individual, a group, a division of an organization, an organization, etc . . .), as well as the issues and problems being considered. For example, if we are interested in understanding and predicting the productivity of an individual employee, it might be useful to know something about the internal and external environment of the organization. In this example, relevant variables in the internal environment of the organization might include the expectations held by fellow workers, leadership practices, the nature of reward systems, and the like. One of the relevant variables in the external environment could be the prevailing value system regarding the importance attached to hard work. A second variable could be the alternative employment opportunities provided by the economic system. Thus, internal and external environmental variables may affect the employee's receptiveness to the expectations for certain levels of productivity. Of course, the value of hard work will only assume importance if it has been personally accepted by the employee.

Individuals, groups, and organizations not only may be affected by their environments but may actively influence their environments as well. For example, General Motors, which found itself with too few economy cars during the energy crisis of 1974, speeded up its timetable for the introduction of new compacts. At the same time, some of the divisions, particularly Oldsmobile and Cadillac, launched major advertising campaigns promoting the safety and comfort features of larger cars. This campaign was accompanied by the claim that the additional gasoline costs to operate the larger cars, compared to those for compacts, might be less than $200 per year for the average driver. Our intent in this example is not to pass judgment as to whether these actions are good or bad. Rather, it is to illustrate the possibility of individuals, groups, and organizations being reactive as well as proactive with respect to their environments.

A *reactive* orientation refers to the tendency to take action as a consequence of being affected by some external influence, event, force, or the like. A *proactive* orientation refers to the tendency to take actions as a consequence of ideas, goals, perceived opportunities, and the like, which are created or formulated by the individual, group, or organization. Typically, proaction is intended to create greater self-control relative to the environment and/or to influence the actions of others in the environment. From an individual point of view, the reactive and proactive conceptions are consistent with the now common view that behavior is a function of the individual and the environment.

VALUES AND VALUE SYSTEMS

Nature and Importance

The nature and importance of values presented here is substantially based upon the five assumptions articulated by Rokeach:

> 1. The total number of values that a person possesses is relatively small. 2. All men everywhere possess the same values to different degrees. 3. Values are organized into value systems. 4. The antecedents of human values can be traced to culture, society and its institutions, and personality. 5. The consequences of human values will be manifested in virtually all phenomena that social scientists might consider worth investigating and understanding. [5, p. 3]

There are several qualifications we would make to these assumptions. First, our thrust is primarily with values related to individuals within organizations and organizations within society, especially the United States. The focus is not on abstract values of mankind in general. Secondly, our discussion of types of managerial values is primarily related to profit-making organizations in a private enterprise system. However, the discussion of alternative work values is applicable to both private and public organizations.

The definition of value and value system, as set forth by Rokeach, substantially represents the meaning we would like to assign to the concepts. Rokeach states:

> A *value* is an enduring belief that a specific mode of conduct or end-state of existence is personally or socially preferable to an opposite or converse mode of conduct or end-state of existence. A *value system* is an enduring organization of beliefs concerning preferable modes of conduct or end-states of existence along a continuum of relative importance. [6, p. 5]

Let's briefly consider the component parts in the definition of a value. A value is a belief that does not change from day to day. But, the idea of *continuity* in a value does not mean it is completely stable or rigid. One of the attributes and problems of contemporary industrialized societies is the increased rate of change and instability in values. In industrialized countries, there is a greater probability for subgroups within the societies to possess different values that may come into conflict. The *belief* element in the value definition is quite complex, consisting of three distinct, yet related components: cognitive, affective, and behavioral. *Cognition* means the individual has a conception or knowledge of what is desirable. To suggest that an individual accepts the value of "working hard" is to say that, cognitively, this person knows that the appropriate way to behave on the job is to work hard. The *affective* component of a value means that the individual can experience emotions or feelings about the value, both negative and positive. The individual who believes in the value of "hard work" may feel good about working hard, as well as experiencing resentment and even hostility toward those who don't share this belief and are low performers. Finally, the *behavioral* component of the value suggests that it influences the actions of individuals. The individual who believes in "hard work" is more likely to translate this value into action by actually working hard. The modes of conduct and end-state of existence elements in the previous definition of a value are also distinct, yet interrelated. *Modes-of-conduct* values are typically instrumental in the attainment of values specifying end-states of existence. The value frameworks presented in this chapter are primarily concerned with modes-of-conduct values. According to Rokeach, *end-states of existence* might be concerned with values such as: a comfortable life, a sense of accomplishment, a world of beauty, equality, freedom, happiness, inner harmony, mature love, pleasure, salvation, self-respect, social recognition, and wisdom. [7] It is quite possible for two individuals to share similar end-states-of-existence values but hold different and possibly conflicting modes-of-conduct values. Two individuals may believe strongly in freedom but differ substantially over issues involving freedom, such as relative rights of workers and managers, the appropriateness of government controls over an organization's activity, and the like. Finally, a value is a conception of something that is personally or socially preferable. This means an individual's values are not necessarily intended as applying equally to oneself and to others. A manager, with no thought of being inconsistent, might say: "I believe in competition in our economic system because it increases efficiency" and "There are too many firms in our industry engaged in cutthroat competition—what we need is more cooperation if we are going to survive." In the one instance, the manager is applauding the modes-of-conduct value of competition, in the other the modes-of-conduct value of cooperation. In everyday life, values are often used flexibly; they may be viewed as applicable to ourselves and not to others, or vice versa; and they may be used as a single or double standard of behavior.

From the standpoint of organizational behavior, an understanding of values is extremely important because they influence the decisions or choices made by employees and managers, and help to determine how we relate to the world around us. [8]

Models of Managerial Values

I am concerned about a society that has demonstrably lost confidence in its institutions—in the government, in the press, in the church, in the military—as well as in business. [9, p. 87]

Richard C. Gerstenberg, President
General Motors (1973)

We are witnessing the development of a responsive corporation which . . . should be increasingly capable of handling new issues whether they be "business" or "social." They will probably have different values, as has been rather widely suggested. [10, p. 61]

Raymond A. Bauer, Professor
Harvard Business School (1974)

Whether you agree or disagree with the pessimism of Gerstenberg or the optimism of Bauer, they are both claiming that the value framework by which managers of our major institutions, particularly business, have operated is rapidly going out of existence. [11] Depending upon one's personal value system, this changing reality can be either a problem or an opportunity. Based on studies of the values of high school and college age population, it would appear that changes in the value framework of organizations would be considered desirable by America's youth. In a review of studies on the values of youth, Miner concludes:

America's youth is becoming more negative to authority, less trusting of authority, less desirous of exercising authority, less accepting of the legitimacy of authority, more rebellious and defiant of authority, less tolerant of authority, less accepting of the moral values held by established authority, and more opposed to organizations viewed as authoritarian . . . [11, p. 108]

From the perspective of managers in organizations, it is difficult enough to function in an environment in which traditional values are being rejected with increasing frequency. The current situation is made even more turbulent since new values are not well defined or easily implemented in our day-to-day working lives. The unfamiliarity and diversity in new value systems naturally lead to states of personal uncertainty and possibly fear. [12]

To illustrate these concepts, we will outline three alternative managerial value systems. These have emerged in historical phases within the United States, somewhat as follows: profit-maximizing management, 1800—; trustee-ship management, 1920—; quality-of-life management, 1960—. These three types of managerial value systems and the following descriptions of them is adapted from the analysis and synthesis of Hay and Gray. [13] These three value systems are presented as somewhat "pure" types to emphasize differences and their possible implications. Thus, it should not be assumed that a single manager can be described as representing only one of the three types. [14]

Profit-Maximizing Management

The profit-maximizing managerial value system is the simplest and most limited compared to the other two. The manager's value and the value of the organization should be to maximize profits. All other managerial decisions and actions should be directed toward this sole end. While this value system promotes a selfish outlook, it was advanced as a desirable and appropriate form of behavior within a particular type of economic system. It was assumed this selfish interest would be pursued in an economic system with the following attributes:

1. Consumers would have complete knowledge about alternatives and the characteristics of the products and services. /

2. There would be so many sellers and buyers that none of them could independently control the number of items produced.

3. The suppliers would have no control over price; i.e., they would have to sell at the price established by the impersonal interaction of market forces.

4. Government would not interfere with the economic system.

While there are a number of other assumptions underlying this type of economic system, the key point is that it was assumed that the exclusive pursuit of profits would ultimately result in the lowest prices for the consumers. Profit-maximizing management was thus accompanied by values such as: individualism (survival of the fittest); individual property and private ownership of the major means of production; competition; and the less government control and intervention into the economic system the better.

Along with the development of profit-maximizing management, there were major changes in religious beliefs. These changes start with the Protestant Reformation, which was led by Martin Luther in the early 1500's. Over time, a value system emerged that is often referred to as the Protestant ethic. While the development of this ethic is beyond our scope, it does emphasize the importance and desirability of hard work, self-discipline, simplicity of life, sobriety, frugality, individualism, and like qualities. [15] These religious values served to justify and reinforce the values in profit-maximizing management.

There are several personal modes-of-conduct values in profit-maximizing management that are extremely important for the understanding of managerial behavior. The decisions and actions toward customers are likely to reflect the value of caveat emptor ("let the buyer beware"). Within the organization, employees would probably be considered little more than another resource needed to create the firm's goods and services. These human resources should be hired, fired, demoted, and promoted only on the basis of what is considered best by the managers for the owners of the organization. Employees are only *means*, not ends! It is typically assumed that the top managers of the firm would also be the owners. As a consequence, there should be no conflict between the interests of the owners and those of key managers. The leadership style might be one of a rugged and authoritarian individualist. This is consistent with the underlying "survival of the fittest" value. Thus, the welfare of employees should be considered only from the standpoint of helping the organization to maximize its profits. Ultimately, it is assumed that the employees' welfare and that of society in general would benefit from competition between firms.

The rationale for the profit-maximizing manager might be somewhat as follows: "I have to survive in an impersonal and competitive marketplace. If my employees can do better in the labor market, it is their choice to quit. But if I start considering my employees' needs beyond what my competitors do, this will drive up my costs, eliminate all profits, and result in failure. Thus, I will not have survived and my employees will be out of work. So what did I accomplish? You should also remember that the plight of most of my employees is not due to me. It is a consequence of their own weakness and inability to compete. Look at me! I brought myself up by hard work and sticking to it. If they weren't so lazy, they could be much better off. Through hard work, they could have money and wealth, too. But I guess it's God's will that only some of us will make it. These radicals, who think they can change things, don't realize that the laws of nature and God control our destiny. If they would only listen . . ." We fully recognize that this description is not necessarily an actual portrayal of how all profit-maximizing managers did or do act and feel. Rather, it describes one of our three "pure" types of managerial value systems. The profit-maximizing value system was most often and vocally expressed in the 1800's and early 1900's. Parts or all of the profit-maximizing managerial value system are probably still accepted by various groups in contemporary society.

Trusteeship Management

The trusteeship-management value system was superimposed upon profit-maximizing management in the 1920's. This occurred when the structure of the economic and social system no longer adequately mirrored the assumptions of profit-maximizing management. The economic system was increasingly characterized by large-scale, complex organizations that functioned as oligopolies, where a few suppliers provided 70 percent or more of the goods and services in a particular industry. The tire industry, which is dominated in the United States by Goodyear, Firestone, B. F. Goodrich, General Tire, Uniroyal, and Dunlap, is often considered an oligopolistic industry. Monopolies, such as telephone, electric, and natural gas companies, were also increasing in relative size and importance.

There was a growing tendency for the ownership of these complex organizations to be widely diffused among thousands of stockholders and for the managerial group to control, but have little stock ownership, in these firms. The practical effect of this change for the average stockholder, if he became dissatisfied with the management and the performance of the firm, was to impel him to simply sell his shares. While stockholders were legally the owners, their actual status became somewhat closer to that of creditors and bondholders of the firm. The concept of trustee management gained the greatest recognition among the managers of these large and complex organizations.

Another change that accompanied the development of the trusteeship-management value system was the conception of the United States as a pluralistic society. A pluralistic doctrine means ". . . counterbalancing interests and institutions in society prevent one group or interest from achieving hegemony [dominance]. Offsetting businesses are the regulatory organs of the government . . ., organized labor, competing interests within business, and the legal system that affords means of redress for the average consumer or his representatives." [16, p. 26] The extent to which society actually mirrors pluralism remains subject to debate and different interpretations. (A consideration of this debate is beyond our scope).

Pluralism suggests that the power and the right to influence an organization is diffused among a number of groups and does not reside only in the owners. Accordingly, managers were supposed to be responsible to those groups with important stakes in the firm, particularly the workers, customers, stockholders, creditors, suppliers, and the community. With these diverse demands on the organization, management's role was to balance and reconcile the claims of the various groups.

The value system of trustee management is broader and more complex than profit-maximizing management, for there are no longer the clear and well defined goals serving as guidelines in managerial decision-making. Questions illustrating these uncertainties might include: What are the tradeoffs, if any, between improved working conditions for employees and dividends for stockholders? Should we impart information about our products to customers if it enables them to make more informed choices, but has the consequence of revealing that there are virtually no differences as compared with lower-priced products of competitors? Should we pay employees at the market rate even if it barely permits subsistence? If we pay employees above the market rate, how much above should it be, and does this really result in lowering the profits that rightfully belong to the stockholders? Numerous questions are left to be answered by the managers and possibly by the group(s) that have the greatest relative power to affect the survival and growth of the organization.

While trustee management created ambiguities such as the ones mentioned, it also was followed by several critical modes-of-conduct values regarding the management of employees. Individuals are more likely to recognize that employees' needs go beyond simple economic ones, including needs such as security, belonging, and recognition. Individuals in the organization are viewed as much more complex in nature. While still adhering to the importance of individualsim and the individual, the trustee-management value system is less likely to be accompanied by the assumptions of the inevitability of intense competition and the "survival of the fittest" doctrine. There is likely to be some recognition of the value of group and individual participation in decisions. Employees are viewed as both a means and an end. They are more than a resource to be hired and discarded in the impersonal labor market.

Employees have certain rights that must be recognized. If they are not recognized, they have the ability and the right to form employee groups, such as unions, to focus attention on their interests.

Within the concept of trustee management, there is still a strong sense of self-interest and the need to earn certain targeted profit levels. Earning a satisfactory profit level, such as 20 percent return on investment, becomes a major guide to decision-making, rather than simply profit maximization. There might be a strong feeling of "what's good for the company is good for the country." While the necessity of government is recognized, it is one of those evils to be maintained at a minimum level of influence, particularly with regard to the economic system. In sum, the trustee-management value system is probably the one most frequently espoused today by managers. Henry Ford II seemed to articulate a version of the trustee-management model in these words:

> There is no longer anything to reconcile—if there ever was—between the social conscience and the profit motive.

> The first duty of a company to society as well as to its owners is still to strive for profit . . . the difference between capital investment and social is much more a difference of degree than of kind. [17, p. 278]

Quality-of-Life Management   [18]

This value system represents an extension of the trustee-management model. It is the newest of the models and probably has the fewest advocates in the management community. There is a recognition of the need for profits, but a preference for them to be rationalized in terms of social benefits, rather than just those of the owners. Profits are viewed more as a means than an end. The need for responsiveness to various groups with a stake in the organization is expanded to include the interests of society as a whole. As a corollary, there is a greater tendency to think "what is good for society is good for our company." The major changes occur in viewing people, both within and outside the organization, as more important than money, materialism, and technology. The humanistic bias in quality-of-life management means that the dignity and worth of each employee is recognized. The managers recognize that individuals bring all of themselves to the workplace. A serious concern is shown by designing jobs so that they enable the individual to utilize his or her skills and abilities. Group and individual participation in the organizing, planning, and controlling of work relevant to the job domain is viewed as necessary and desirable. Participation is considered necessary because it increases the probability of the organization being successful and it is one of the primary avenues for recognizing the dignity and humanness of individuals and groups.

At the top executive level of the organization, managers are more prone to feel that society's problems require cooperation between business and government. In certain social areas, business managers are likely to feel that government must and should play a leading and vigorous role. The necessity of a vigorous government is seen, for the first time, in a favorable light. This has also been substantially confirmed in a study of the values expressed in the speeches of top executives of American firms. This study of almost 500 executive speeches also suggests there is no unified expressed value system among the top officials in the eleven industries studied—providing some indirect verification of the pluralistic doctrine mentioned previously. [19]

The value system in quality-of-life management continues the shift from individualsim, competition, and raw self-interest to sharing, cooperation, and enlightened self-interest. Life is seen less as "I win when you lose" and more as "I win when you win." It remains an unanswered question whether the value system that makes up quality-of-life management will be widely accepted by managers and, more importantly, practiced by them. There is also the fundamental question of whether managers, given the present institutional system within the U. S., should or even can adapt to quality-of-life management in all its forms. For example, Xerox Corporation has been regarded as a ". . . leader in providing job training to disadvantaged workers and financial and other aid to ghetto businesses [and] can be considered by some to be a prime example of a socially responsible corporation, while others can consider it to represent an 'immoral investment.' " [20, p. 41] Xerox Corporation was viewed by some as an immoral investment because it does business in South Africa and thus, it is claimed, indirectly supports apartheid (strict segregation between whites and blacks) and racism.

Assessment

The three managerial value systems we have reviewed are probably all operating, to varying degrees, among different managers and managerial groups. However, we want to reemphasize several of our earlier points about the nature of human values, especially the following ideas: values are not necessarily intended to apply equally to oneself and to others; and values are not always translated into the types of behaviors and decisions which seem to be warranted by the espoused values. The three managerial value systems of profit maximizing, trustee management, and quality-of-life management have been articulated and developed by leaders in the management community or by those closely associated with management. Since our purpose was to convey the representative value systems most commonly espoused in managerial circles, this was an appropriate strategy.

There are certainly groups that might contend that the trusteeship and quality-of-life models are essentially propaganda and rhetoric designed to hide the true nature of the values actually being implemented by managers. Some groups contend that organizational and managerial values are beyond change and must be eliminated through various means. Their thoughts might be summarized as follows. We should and could eliminate the nonsensical concern with profits by having the benefits of the organization shared with all the people. This means that private ownership should cease and these huge organizations, including big business, big unions, and big government, should be broken up to permit real decentralization to the people. The idea of pluralism is a big joke. The managers of the big institutions are cooperating and feeding off the efforts of the common working man. Only a revolution and tearing apart to start anew will bring about any meaningful changes in the values that influence the way organizations are run and the way people are treated within them.

Views such as these are disturbing, if not frightening, to leading managers of American industry. The quality-of-life management value system might have obtained some impetus from those within or associated with American management who see the necessity for responding to some of the problems pointed out by radical groups. However, these spokesmen are not likely to go so far as the radicals hope to, because they believe a revolution in the institutional system is likely to bring more problems than cures. Regardless of one's personal beliefs as to the "right" managerial values, there will probably continue to be major concern with this area in the business community and various segments of society over the next ten years. Our primary purpose has been to consider the outlines of the major alternatives being considered—not to prescribe an answer.

In conclusion, values are extremely important in organizational behavior because they influence people's actions. The tangible relationship between managerial values and behavior can be illustrated by suggesting what top management might do about water pollution from one of the company's plants, given each value system. With profit-maximizing management, there might be a tendency to do the minimum required and to use the courts to delay complying with government orders to clean up the water they use before dumping it back into the river. With the trustee-management value system, there is likely to be a tendency to react positively and to work with the government agency after they have been notified of being in noncompliance. With quality-of-life management, there might be a tendency to be proactive in recognizing the need to clean up their waste water, possibly even before governmental action is implemented. The theme of alternative managerial values is extended and expanded to the level of the individual manager and the individual employee, in the next section.

Individual Values in Organizational Settings

The types of values the individual holds, either consciously or subconsciously, within organizational settings could have an impact on behavior and decision-making in all organizational roles, including peer, subordinate, and superior roles. Individual value systems, particularly of managers, are of significance because they influence such things as:

1. The way other individuals and groups are perceived, thereby influencing interpersonal relationships;

2. The decisions and problems solutions chosen by an individual;

3. The perceptions of situations and problems an individual faces;

4. The limits for determining what is and what is not ethical behavior;

5. The extent to which an individual will accept or resist organizational goals and pressures; and

6. The perception of individual and organizational success and its achievement. [21, p. 2]

Since this theme is developed more specifically throughout the book, we shall give only brief examples here of the possible implications of varying values for individual behavior and decision-making. The value framework and examples which follow draw heavily upon the work of Tannenbaum and Davis. [22]

Continua of Values

Figure 3–1 provides an abbreviated outline of a limited number of individual values within organizational settings. Each value dimension is presented as a continuum (e.g., from viewing other individuals as inherently bad, to viewing them as inherently good). The continua have a neutral point labeled as "O" in the middle. The continua also recognize that each value dimension can vary in intensity or strength. The intensity of each value dimension varies from a low intensity of one point to a high intensity of three points. When viewing all of the value dimensions together as a potential representation of a value system, it might be reasonable to find some consistency in emphasis between dimensions. Thus, an individual is not likely to vary radically from the extreme left to the extreme right of the continuum between each dimension.

While you might find it interesting and useful to indulge in a little introspection, by assessing your own values in terms of Fig. 3–1, there are several limitations in doing this. First, the characteristics on the right have strong social desirability attributes. Thus, there is a possibility of responding on the basis of what one would like his or her values to be or what others think are "good" values, rather than on the basis of ones' actual values. Secondly, there is the related issue, discussed in later chapters, of the degree of self-awareness by the individual. Thirdly, the individual may want to respond on the basis of recalled experiences and conclude that the response would depend upon which experiences are used as the frame of reference. An individual may recall being very distrusting of others in one organization and trusting in another because of the different organizational climates. The initial perception of Fig. 3–1 in terms of experiences and situational factors is quite reasonable. But our primary focus is on personal values rather than differences in past experiences.

Figure 3–1   Individual Values in Organizational Settings

	High			Neutral			High	
	3	2	1	0	1	2	3	
1. Individuals as bad								Individuals as good
2. Individuals as fixed								Individuals in process
3. Individuals as workers								Individuals as whole persons
4. Resistence and fear of differences								Acceptance and use of differences
5. Closed to feelings								Open to feelings
6. Game-playing behavior								Authentic behavior
7. Self-centered status								Developmental status
8. Distrusting								Trusting
9. Competitive								Collaborative

Adapted from: Tannenbaum, R., and S. A. Davis, "Values, Man and Organizations," *Industrial Management Review,* 1969, **10**, pp. 69–80.

With these qualifications in mind, let's briefly consider the dimensions of individual values presented in Fig. 3–1.

Dimensions of Individual Values

The question of man as essentially "bad" or "good," because of one's inherent or genetic nature, is as old as recorded history. The inherent view of man's nature might affect the ways by which we attempt to influence others. It has been noted:

> ... we assume that man himself is bad, *a priori,* we are prone to assume that misbehavior is caused by something within him which we cannot alter directly. Accordingly, our attention will focus on limiting his freedom to choose and to act through external curbs or controls. [23, p. 178]

There might be a natural tendency to influence others somewhat more through such means as punishments, direct and close checking, and minimizing areas of freedom if one views others as basically bad.

The conceptions of others as basically fixed in terms of skills, knowledge, interests, and the like, may also have an impact on how one sees the others in relation to change. There might be a bias, in the fixed view, against spending resources on individual and group development and training. The cliché "you can't teach an old dog new tricks" is likely to prevail. At the other end of the continuum, individuals are viewed as "in process." By this, we mean the individual is more likely to see and anticipate that people, within limits, are capable of continuous change and development.

In the third dimension, an individual may vary in perceiving others, seeing them first only in terms of their formal positions, ultimately coming to view them as whole persons. In the "individuals as workers" view, other individuals are likely to be seen as only means, whereas in the whole person conception they are prone to be seen more realistically as both means and ends. At one end of the continuum, an individual might be categorized, stereotyped, and evaluated primarily on the basis of the pecking order of his or her position in the formal hierarchy. A person working as a clerk is pigeonholed one way and a manager another way, by virtue of the attributes of their jobs rather than the attributes they possess as whole persons.

In the fourth continuum, the resistance to and fear of differences in others, versus the acceptance and use of differences, is increasingly a concern in organizations as women and minority workers gain positions that are equal (or higher) in formal status than those of white males. One supervisor in a production department expressed concern about the differences occurring among subordinates this way:

> People here aren't what they used to be. Several years ago most of our employees had WASP (White, Anglo-Saxon Protestant) values ... We still have some of these, but now we're getting some different types who are difficult to supervise. Some are hippies who are bright enough, but their ideas are far out, and they don't seem to care about pay, job security, or recognition from their supervisors. [24, p. 7]

The acceptance and use of differences does not imply that one has to adopt or personally subscribe to the differences seen in others. Rather, there is a greater tendency and attempt to work through differences where necessary, utilize differences for purposes of stimulating creativity, and consider differences whenever possible, as the inherent right and part of individual uniqueness.

In American organizations, it is often claimed that there is a widespread fear and avoidance of expressing feelings, particularly among males. [25] Feelings may be considered irrational, improper, and unrelated to job performance. The fifth continuum, closed versus openness to feelings, refers to the extent to which we recognize and accept the role of our own and others' feelings in influencing actions and decisions.

The sixth continuum, game-playing versus authentic behavior, focuses on various personal orientations. These orientations might include: whether or not a person is predisposed to say what he really thinks and feels; whether or not manuevering others is highly valued; whether there is a desire to create artificial impressions in the minds of others about oneself; and the like.

Status and status symbols play an important role in most of our lives. The emphasis in the seventh continuum is not whether status systems exist or whether they are important to us. The key question concerns an individual's use of status systems. Self-centered users attempt to maintain and increase personal power and prestige. In contrast, developmental uses of status are based more on relevant knowledge, experience, and expertise within the individual.

The eighth continuum zeroes in on the idea that a distrusting or trusting predisposition is likely to have considerable impact on how one relates to others and how they come to relate to oneself. A predisposition to distrust is more likely to result in the individual attempting to influence others through outside pressures, i.e., "from the outside in," whereas, with a trusting predisposition, the individual is more likely to see others as being motivated from the "inside out." Accordingly, there is likely to be more emphasis upon self-direction and control and more open and authentic communications.

The last continuum refers to a competitive versus collaborative predisposition, which was also discussed in the quality-of-life management value system. This continuum is used in the sense of whether individuals tend to see relationships with others and problems more in a win-lose (I win as you lose) or a win-win (I win as you win) frame of reference. However, there is no intent to suggest that all competition is "bad" or all "collaboration" is good.

Interrelationships Between Value Dimensions

There are several interrelationships between our discussion of individual values and the prior discussion of alternative managerial values. With several exceptions (to be noted), the profit-maximizing management value system is probably most compatible and consistent with the individual values on the lefthand side of Fig. 3–1. Managers are more likely to resist and fear differences, be closed to feelings, distrust others, be competitive, and the like. In the trustee-management value system, the individual values are more likely to be wide ranging and possibly inconsistent. On the one hand, there could be extensive attempts to increase collaboration through participation in decision-making and group meetings. On the other hand, there could be a formal performance appraisal system, which evaluates fellow employees against one another, thereby stimulating competitive relationships. In the quality-of-life management value system, individual values are more likely to be consistent with the values toward the right side of the continuua in Fig. 3–1. Managers would be more predisposed to trusting, risk-taking, collaboration, authentic behavior, openness to feelings, and the like.

Values such as those in the righthand column of Fig. 3–1 are increasingly being articulated by new members to the work forces. In a study of the occupational values expressed by business administration students, the author reached several conclusions. The students rejected ". . . narrow, closely defined jobs and prefer work situations which allow a strong sense of independence, individual responsibility, achievement, and recognition. They also prefer to work with co-workers with skill and competence equal to theirs in a cooperative team relationship or as a group of colleagues rather than in an interpersonal competitive relationship." [26, pp. 430–431]

These new values and trends seem to be emerging for both college and noncollege young adults. This conclusion is partially based on surveys of attitudes and values of individuals from 16 to 25 years old conducted during 1969 and 1973 by Daniel Yankelovich, Inc. [27] For the 1973 survey, they conducted about 3,500 personal interviews, among a representative sample of 1,000 college students and 2,500 noncollege young people. We will briefly review the findings and trends related to work values for the college and noncollege groups between the measurements taken in 1969 and 1973.

Their most striking finding was a growing similarity in the values between 1969 college and 1973 noncollege young people.

Noncollege individuals expressed about the same values in 1973 as the college respondents expressed in 1969. The belief that hard work always pays off was agreed with by 79% of the noncollege respondents in 1969 and 56% of them in 1973. In 1969, 56% of the college respondents agreed with this statement and only 44% in 1973. Both groups of young people said they were *willing* to work hard, but many have apparently lost the confidence that hard work will pay off in psychological and economic rewards.

The desire to have a position enabling one to do more than make a living is also indicated by these findings. Among young blue-collar workers, job security is 15 percentage points below interesting work as an important criterion in choosing a job. The chance to make a lot of money ranks among the bottom ten on a list of 35 possible job criteria.

Since most young people eventually find employment in business firms, particularly large ones, it is useful to note their expressed views toward big business. In 1969, 37% of the noncollege respondents agreed with the statement "big business needs reform or elimination" and 54% agreed in 1973. For college respondents, only 24% agreed in 1969, but this figure shot up to 45% in 1973. Data such as these are partially responsible for the sample of quotes of executives presented earlier in this chapter and an increasing number of articles for managers like the one which appeared in the January, 1974, issue of *Fortune* entitled "Who Will Do the Dirty Work Tomorrow?" There appears to be a shift in the values expressed by young people toward the adoption of a value system somewhat more consistent with quality-of-life management. The changing values these new employees are bringing to the work setting may increasingly represent a powerful environmental influence on organizations.

While suggestions for coping with value changes are developed later in the book, it is important to recognize two essential points. First, the types of changes desired by various groups in the environment of organizations are often turbulent and conflicting. Some employees may desire more meaningful jobs with greater responsibility, while other employees may focus on job security and are fearful of changes in jobs. Secondly, the means for bringing about changes which are agreed upon are often complex and not well defined. Chrysler Corporation has made some efforts to enrich jobs of production workers but has encountered numerous difficulties in keeping production costs from increasing, maintaining the concept of job security, making equitable adjustments in reward systems, and revising labor management agreements. While the general goal of making the workplace more meaningful and humane is widely applauded, the means for doing so without also revising other desired goals is not as clear.

This part of the chapter has emphasized the importance of value changes in society as representing a major environmental influence on organizations. The second part of this chapter shifts focus somewhat by suggesting "mental maps" or models for diagnosing and assessing the environment of an organization. Moreover, these assessment approaches will include many environmental forces in addition to values. This discussion will primarily emphasize the types of environments managers may confront and the problems they have to diagnose. We will continuously refer to the present discussion in later chapters by suggesting how different environments are often associated with different management patterns and practices in effective organizations.

ASSESSING THE ENVIRONMENT

The first key concept in discussing environmental assessment is to recognize that an organization encounters and interacts with many external environments—rather than with simply a single environment. In a practical sense, an organization breaks down its environment into subenvironments, each of which may be primarily dealt with by different individuals or groups in the organization. Relationships between one subenvironment and organizational group may have implications for relationships with another subenvironment and organizational group. For example, one of your authors was involved with a major U. S. tire manufacturer that threatened to cancel about a million dollars a year in shipping business with a trucking firm when it discovered this firm was not purchasing any of its truck tires.

A second key concept is that there are differences in these subenvironments which require differences in the ways of organizing and managing to match up with the characteristics of the particular subenvironment. For example, a research and development unit has a different environment than an assembly plant. The specific management implications will be developed in later chapters.

Thirdly, an organization is typically faced with demands from its subenvironments that exceed its available resources. For example, consumers may want lower prices, suppliers desire higher prices, the state wants more taxes, the federal government desires more pollution control, etc.

The first two concepts presented will be made more explicit in the following discussion of the Change-Complexity Model, whereas, the third concept is illustrated in the description of General Electric's environmental assessment strategy.

Change-Complexity Model

The change-complexity environmental model is adapted from the work of Duncan. [28] Environment is defined as "the totality of physical and social factors that are taken directly into consideration in the decision-making behavior of individuals in the organization." [29, p. 314] The breadth of this definition permits recognition of an internal environment, i.e., within the boundaries of the organization, and external environment, i.e., outside the organizational boundaries. In this part, we are primarily concerned with the external environment.

Specific external subenvironments are likely to vary among types of organizations. The subenvironments and the relative importance of each may well differ among industrial organizations (Ford Motor Co.), private service organizations (State Farm Insurance), government organizations (Social Security Administration), hospitals (Mayo Clinic), universities (Penn State), and the like. However, our discussion of individual values, the changes occurring within them, and the differences in values among individuals, represents one environmental component which affects all organizations.

Even here, the impact is not likely to be the same among all organizations. Societal changes in instrumental values may not be as relevant, in the short run, to managers of a firm located in a rural and stable community (in terms of religious, political and economic values) as they would be to managers of a firm located in a major metropolitan area with a labor force that is diverse in terms of value orientations. In addition to the values of the population and the work force, the following subenvironments may be particularly relevant to industrial organizations: customers, suppliers, competitors, government agencies, labor unions, consumer groups, environmental groups, and the like. Subenvironments such as these might be assessed in terms of two key dimensions: the degree of complexity and the degree of change. (Since we are somewhat oversimplifying the definition and classification of organizational environments, the interested reader may want to see Jurkovich for a more comprehensive framework of organizational environments. [30]

Degree-of-Complexity Dimension

This dimension refers to the degree to which an individual or group in an organizational unit must deal with few or many factors that are similar or dissimilar to one another. The people in an organizational planning unit are typically confronted with a complex environment, whereas the members in the custodian unit face a relatively simple environment. The degree of complexity might be determined by asking the individuals what factors they consider in making decisions and determining how many of them are located in different subenvironments. A discussion of the detailed methods for arriving at the quantitative values of this is beyond our scope.

The important point is that the degree of complexity depends upon both the number of factors and the number of subenvironments in which these factors are located. Five factors located in one subenvironment, such as the customer subenvironment, would not be given as high a point rating on complexity as five factors located in three subenvironments, such as customers, suppliers, and competitors. From a psychological perspective, we need to add the qualifying statement that the degree of complexity is somewhat influenced by whether or not decision-makers perceive their environments as complex or noncomplex. [31, p. 382] Thus, the perception of a simple or complex environment is likely to be influenced by both the nature of the environment and the nature of the individuals perceiving their environment (see especially Chapter 5).

Degree-of-Change Dimension

This dimension refers to the extent to which the environmental factors considered by an individual or group in a particular work unit of the organization are in a constant process of change, or remain basically the same over time. The individual values of organizational members, while they have always been complex, are changing rather than remaining static and stable. It is also becoming increasingly necessary to get individuals to work together who have varying and oftentimes conflicting value systems. Another example might be the frequency with which the customers change their requests for different levels of output, or different characteristics in the output for a given product. The degree-of-change dimension is assessed by asking the individuals in a work group how often the environmental factors change (that they had already identified as being important in their decision-making). Response categories could vary on a five-point scale, such as: 1 = never; 2 = almost never; 3 = sometimes; 4 = frequently; and 5 = very often.

A second aspect of the degree-of-change dimension is the frequency with which individuals in a work group have to consider new and different factors in their decision-making process. For example, a marketing group has to consider many classes of customers, such as automobile dealers, car rental firms, and auto supply stores. Again, the frequency of considering new and different factors in decision-making might also be determined along the same type of five-point scale (from 1 = never to 5 = very often). The scores obtained on each aspect of the degree-of-change dimension can be combined, to obtain an overall index.

A more general aspect of the degree-of-change dimension, is the number of major changes in goals or objectives during a given period. The greater the number of changes in goals or objectives over a given period, the higher the rate of change; the lower the number, the lower the rate of change. [32, p. 386]

Perceived Environment

The overall perceived environment for a specific work group or organizational unit is dependent upon both the degree-of-complexity and the degree-of-change dimensions, as suggested in Fig. 3–2. The vertical axis in Fig. 3–2 shows the degree-of-change dimension as varying along a continuum from static to dynamic. The degree-of-complexity dimension is represented as varying along a continuum from simple to complex. Each of the cells in Fig. 3–2 indicates the amount of uncertainty that is likely to be associated with each of the four extreme situations, such as a static/simple situation (Cell #1) versus a dynamic/complex situation (Cell #4). Without going into the mechanisms for measuring uncertainty, some of the questions that might be presented to determine the amount of uncertainty for various factors include:

a) How often do you believe that the information you have about each factor (such as customer preferences) is adequate for decision making in your work unit?

b) How often is it hard to tell how each factor (such as customer preferences) will react to, or be affected by a decision of your work unit before it is actually implemented?

c) How often do you feel the work unit can tell if the decisions made will have a positive or negative effect on its and the organization's performance?

d) How sure are you about how each factor (such as customer preference) would affect the relative success of your work unit and the organization?

Figure 3–2   Environmental Change—Complexity Model

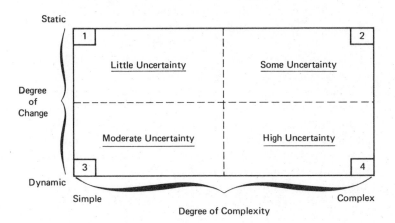

Source: Duncan, R., "Characteristics of Organizational Environments and Perceived Environmental Uncertainty," *Administrative Science Quarterly*, 1972, **17**, pp. 313–327.

A few of the implications of different levels of perceived uncertainty, which will be developed more fully in later chapters, might be briefly mentioned. As implied in our earlier discussion of individual values, some individuals may experience anxieties and tensions if their work units confront a dynamic/complex environment versus a simple/static environment. Other individuals may perceive the same environment more favorably. [33] At a group level, there is often a greater need for job related interaction and communications among peers and with their manager in a complex/dynamic environment versus a simple/static one.

At an organizational level, the level of skills and knowledge needed by individuals in work units is likely to vary partially as a function of the degree of change and complexity in the external environment. Finally, the ease or difficulty in managing work groups varies somewhat, according to their external environment. Many issues, problems, and recommendations in the field of organizational behavior are partially dependent upon the character of the external environment confronting a work unit or individual.

The second framework and approach for assessing environmental influences is issue-oriented and focuses on the organization as a whole. It describes a framework used by General Electric to evaluate the relative importance of different charges, complaints, threats, and demands from the external environment.

GE's Assessment Strategy

Although our discussion of General Electric's strategy for environmental assessment focuses on the organization as a whole, the actions taken as a consequence of these assessments will have an impact on individuals and groups throughout the organization. The commitment by top management to equal employment opportunity may well result in white male employees finding they have minorities and females as peers and superiors.

Much of the following discussion is adapted from a more extensive description of General Electric's strategy for environmental assessment by Estes. [34] There are several assumptions in this description. First, we make no assumption that General Electric is a "good" or "bad" organization in relating to its external environment. Our focus is on the systematic process G.E. has developed for environmental assessment and the types of issues it has identified. Secondly, there is no assumption that the types of issues identified as being most consistent with broader societal trends and backed up by the greatest amount of pressure are inherently more worthy of response from the organization than other issues. Thirdly, there is no assumption that General Electric is adequately or inadequately taking action on the basis of its findings.

Structural Impact.   General Electric has attempted to give greater attention to the external environment by creating a Public Issues Committee as part of its board of directors. This committee has a chairman who is a board member from outside of the company; the majority of the committee members are also from outside the corporation. A senior executive vice-president from the corporate executive staff serves as the formal link between company management and the commitee. Within General Electric, a business environment studies unit has been created to serve the committee and management. The unit's primary role is to identify and evaluate issues requiring broader consideration by top management and the board of directors.

Dilemmas. The top management of General Electric contends they are faced with the traditional demands of economics; the need for the firm to be concerned with efficiency, productivity, and profits; and the new and emerging expectations and pressures from various segments of society. Since G.E. assumes that these expectations and pressures exceed its resources and capabilities (at least in the short run), its managers are faced with several fundamental questions. What demands should they respond to? What constituencies and pressure groups should they listen to? Implicit in their approach is the desire to devote scarce resources to those issues that will yield the greatest benefit to the firm. Resources expended on an issue that is a passing fad, even if there is strong current pressure behind it, might be viewed as resources that should have been used for some other issue or some other purpose (higher salaries, bigger profits, more comfortable offices, etc.)

Assessment Approach. Since G.E. assumed it was impossible to respond to every pressure on an equal basis, the management felt a need for some approach to analyze environmental pressures, and establish priorities.

They grouped, on the basis of judgment, environmental pressures in terms of eight broad categories: marketing and finance, production operation, employee relations and working conditions, governance, communications, community and government relations, defense production, and international operations. Within each category, they identified the charges or complaints being levied against large business firms. The demands and threats that accompanied these charges and complaints were also inventoried. They identified 97 different demands and threats within the eight categories. These 97 demands were then subjected to a priority analysis. This involved assessing each demand in terms of two key dimensions.

One dimension was the variable called *degree of convergence with trends.* This required the development of expected major societal trends over the next ten years (through 1982). Thirteen societal trends were identified. The complete list of trends includes:

> ... increasing affluence; rising level of education; proliferating technology; emergence of "post-industrial society" (services economy); growing interdependence of institutions (including business–government partnerships); increasing emphasis on individualism; growing pluralism (groups, organizations) and diversity of lifestyles; the "equity revolution"; growing emphasis on "quality of life" (ecology

culture, education), Maslow's levels 4 and 5; redefinition of work/leisure patterns; continued increase in foreign competition; growing/changing role of government; continued urbanization. [35, p. 27]

Each of the 97 demands was evaluated in terms of its degree of convergence or collision with each of the thirteen trends. This was accomplished by making judgments about each demand on a scale of 1 to 10. A rating of 10 meant high convergence between a demand and a trend, and a rating of 1 meant no convergence or a collision with a trend.

The second dimension was the *degree of pressure* or power behind each demand. Each demand was evaluated in terms of its relative importance or interest to each of fourteen constituencies or pressure groups in the environment. These fourteen constituencies were identified as: customers and consumer groups, share-owners, unions, blue-collar workers, managers and professional staff, government (federal, state and local), small businesses, minority groups, women's groups, college youth, environmental groups, "populists," academic critics, and "moralists" (including church groups). Each demand was given a 4, 3, 2, or 1 score according to the estimate of whether it fell in the first, second, third, or lowest quartile of a group's demands or interests. In combining the point values for the 14 constituencies or pressure groups, there was also the recognition that not all groups necessarily have the same power or ability to enforce their demands, and they may not be equally active in working to achieve their demands.

Model.   The two dimensions for ranking the demands are brought together to form a model, such as that shown in Fig. 3–3. This environmental assessment model permits the demands to be plotted in terms of both dimensions. In Fig. 3–3, the dimension "degree of convergence with trends" is on the horizontal axis and is shown as varying from low to high. The "degree-of-pressure" dimension is shown as varying from low and diffuse pressure to high and intense pressure.

The demands that fell in the upper right quadrant of the model provided a first approximation of those that should receive highest priority. This is based on the fact that they were ranked high on both convergence with trends and on pressures. G.E.'s expressed intent is to work these priorities into their strategic planning which, in turn, provides a basis for resource allocation. This process of environmental assessment and defining priorities is claimed by G.E. to be a continuous process and thereby subject to change and modification.

Some Findings.   G.E.'s detailed findings as to high- and low-priority issues have not been disclosed to the public. However, some of the general issues (demands) that are most germane to organizational behavior and that received a high priority analysis include: job enlargement; flexible work scheduling; equality of opportunity; participation and individualization; external constraints on employee relations, particularly in equal employment opportunity, health and safety, and federalization of fringe benefits; coalition bargaining by

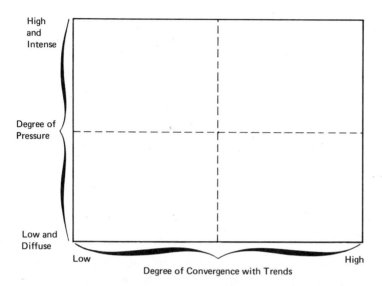

Figure 3–3   Environmental Assessment Model

unions; broader public representation on board of directors; disclosure of information; and accountability and personal liability of managers and directors in matters relating to organizational governance.

The full spectrum of pressures and demands identified for the major grouping they called "employee relations" is shown in Fig. 3–4. It might be useful and interesting to evaluate the pressures and demands in terms of your own value system, as well as in terms of your perceptions of future changes in employee relations. Do you agree with the pressures and demands identified by G.E.? Do you think some of these are much more important than others? If so, which ones? Do you feel the pressures and demands identified are complete or exhaustive? If not, what is missing?

The pressures identified in the lefthand column of Fig. 3–4 should not be read as aligned with the demands directly to their right. Many of the demands and threats are a consequence of several of the pressures (charges or complaints) mentioned in the lefthand column of Fig. 3–4.

The discussion of General Electric's environmental assessment process has served three main purposes. First, it illustrated one possible approach for systematically evaluating the relative importance that might be assigned to the numerous charges, complaints, demands, and threats from the environment of organizations, particularly large business firms. Secondly, it illustrated the types of pressure and demands from the environment regarding the human-resource component of organizations. Many of the issues identified in Fig. 3–4 will be discussed in greater detail in various parts of this book. Finally, the issues identified in Fig. 3–4 and the ones that G.E. feels should have high priority provide some concrete illustrations of possible shifts in the managerial and individual values discussed earlier in the chapter.

Figure 3–4   Pressures and Demands in Employee Relations

Pressures (Charges and complaints)	Demands (Threats)
Authoritarian, hierarchical systems suppress individual initiative and participation in decisions affecting employees' interests.	Best talent drawn away from large corporations.
Profit, not employee welfare, is determinative in decisions, e.g., regarding layoffs.	Deterioriation in productivity of employees at all levels.
Work, whether in the plant or in the office, is monotonous, deadening, dehumanizing.	Alienation of blue-collar workers and, to a lesser extent, middle management and professional personnel.
Profit emphasis corrupts individual value systems (of managers and others) and distorts decision-making.	More participative management, employee involvement in decisions affecting their interests.
"The system" retaliates against "whistle-blowers:" it demands unconditional loyalty ("organization men").	Appoint managers capable of dealing with change and "new work force."
Working conditions, especially in plants, show minimal regard for occupational health and safety.	Job enlargement/enrichment (team and individual work in plants and offices). More flexible scheduling of work.
Management thinks only of an "adversary role" vis à vis unions' legitimate demands for better wages, benefits, and conditions.	Greater employment security (guarantees of income or work; government as "employer of last resort"); massive WPA-type programs.
Business is racist, denying equal opportunity (in hiring, training, promotion) to minorities.	Increasing shortages of technicians and craftsmen.
Business is sexist, denying equal opportunity to women.	More attention to career development, retraining; growing obsolescence of skills at all levels. More leisure time; longer vacations; earlier retirement; sabbaticals.
Business is elitist, favoring "crown princes," and concentrating power in the hands of a few.	Federalization (or federal control) of many benefits, e.g., health insurance, pensions.
Business has a "brick curtain," preventing movement from shop to office.	Affirmative action on hiring, training, promotion of minorities and women (compliance reviews, termination of government contracts).
Employees are cheated out of their pension rights through unreasonable vesting provisions or none at all.	Equal pay (and benefits) for equal work. Provision (or support) of day-care centers.
Business is no longer capable of creating and maintaining a sufficient number of jobs at all levels (blue-collar, professional, management).	Tighter enforcement of occupational health and safety standards. Due process for employees (ombudsman).

Figure 3–4   (Continued)

Pressures (Charges and complaints)	Demands (Threats)
Corporations pay too little attention to the needs of middle management—both with respect to compensation benefits and job security and with respect to more subtle aspects of corporate life.	Human-assets accounting, to reveal managerial performance re human resources.
	More "whistle-blowing" by employees, with protection for their rights.
Top management people vote themselves excessive salaries for work that has little to do with the useful, productive enterprise of producing and delivering goods and services.	Special groups—e.g., minorities, women—demand separate collective bargaining rights.
	Strikes, sit-ins, class-action suits to enforce demands.
	White-collar unionization including middle management, professionals.
	Restrictions on "management rights" (to limit exercise of arbitrary authority).
	"Coordinated (coalition) bargaining" with major companies/industries.
	Escalation of labor's bargaining power.
	Union political power overshadows that of business.

Source: Estes, R. M. "The Business-Society Relationship: Emerging Major Issues," in Steiner, G. A., *Selected Major Issues In Business Role In Modern Society.* Los Angeles: UCLA: Graduate School of Management, 1973, pp. 36–38. Used with permission.

SUMMARY

This chapter has explored some trends, concepts, issues, and approaches for assessing the environment of organizations. Although our major intent was not to be prescriptive or to make simplistic judgments about "what is right," we know some of this occurred. One bias has been our tendency to consider only pressures from the environment and possible reactions by organizations. There is considerable data to suggest that organizations influence and are very proactive with their environments as well. A second obvious bias is simply the choice of concepts, trends, and issues presented. One of our guiding principles in making these choices was to present materials that might have the greatest relevance to an understanding of individual and group behavior within organizations and that could be built upon and extended in later chapters.

Discussion Questions

1. What similarities are there between the three managerial value systems and the pressures and demands in employee relations presented in Fig. 3–4?

2. What differences are there between the three managerial value systems?

3. What difficulties do you think a manager would have if he or she possessed individual values like those along the righthand column of Fig. 3–1?

4. Do you think the values of young people are really changing, as suggested by the studies reported in this chapter? Explain the basis for your conclusions.

5. What do you like and dislike about G.E.'s approach for assessing their environment? Why?

CRITICAL INCIDENT

In the May, 1975, issue of *Fortune,* there is an article entitled "What's Really Wrong at Chrysler." The author suggests that Chrysler is having difficulties because its management has never clearly answered three fundamental questions that confront all organizations: "What is our purpose? What are we trying to do? Whom are we trying to serve?" In the case of Chrysler, it is claimed that top management has never been able to decide the types of cars it wants to build or the types of customers it wants to serve. As a result, Chrysler is said to continuously shift gears—thereby missing out on its strengths and reinforcing its weaknesses. The author goes on to assert:

> Any successful business is founded on a concept of a product it can make or a market it can serve. This idea becomes the company's central heritage. Over time it comes to dominate both the strategy and the spirit of the company, so that problems and opportunities are seen in relation to the fundamental principle. Organizations can often move beyond their original concept, but they can seldom abandon it.

Questions:

1. Discuss the implications of the chapter materials in substantiating, or being at odds with, the quote and comments presented above.

2. In what ways do you agree and/or disagree with the quote and comments presented above?

REFERENCES

1. "The Top Man Becomes Mr. Outside," *Business Week,* May 4, 1974, p. 38.

2. "Corporate Planning: Piercing Future Fog In the Executive Suite," *Business Week,* April 28, 1975, pp. 46–54.

3. Beer, S., "The World We Manage," *Behavioral Science,* 1973, **18,** pp. 198–209.

4. Moos, R. H., "Conceptualizations of Human Environments," *American Psychologist,* 1973, **28,** pp. 652–665.

5. Rokeach, M., *The Nature of Human Values.* New York: Free Press, 1973.

6. *Ibid.*

7. *Ibid.*

8. Laszlo, E., "A Systems Philosophy of Human Values," *Behavioral Science,* 1973, **18,** pp. 250–259.

9. Gerstenberg, R. C., *1973 Report on Progress in Areas of Public Concern,* Feb. 8, 1973.

10. Banks, L., "The Mission of Our Business Society," *Harvard Business Review,* 1975, **53,** pp. 57–65.

11. Miner, J. B., *The Human Constraint: The Coming Shortage of Managerial Talent.* Washington, D.C.: Bureau of National Affairs, 1974.

12. Toffler, A., *Future Shock.* New York: Random House, 1970. Lodge, G. C., "Business and the Changing Society," *Harvard Business Review,* 1974, **52,** pp. 59–72.

13. Hay, R., and E. Gray, "Social Responsibilities of Business Managers," *Academy of Management Journal,* 1974, **17,** pp. 135–143.

14. Behling, O., C. Schriesheim, and J. Schriesheim, "Hay and Gray's Phases of Social Responsibility: An Empirical Assessment," 1975, unpublished manuscript.

15. Long, J. D., "The Protestant Ethic Reexamined," *Business Horizons,* 1972, **15,** pp. 75–82.

16. Perrow, C., *The Radical Attack on Business: A Critical Analysis.* New York: Harcourt Brace Jovanovich, 1972.

17. Ford, H., II, "The Reduction of Human Misery—Voluntary Contributions," *Vital Speeches,* 1966, **27,** pp. 278–280.

18. Richman, B. M., and K. Marcharzina, "The Corporation and the Quality of Life: Part I: Typologies," *Management International Review,* 1973, **13,** pp. 3–16.

19. Seider, M. S., "American Big Business Ideology: A Content Analysis of Executive Speeches," *American Sociological Review,* 1974, **39,** pp, 802–815.

20. Malkiel, B. G., and R. E. Quandt, "Moral Issues in Investment Policy," *Harvard Business Review,* 1971, **16,** pp. 37–47. *Also see:* Carson, J., and G. A. Steiner, *Measuring Business Social Performance: The Corporate Social Audit.* New York: Committee for Economic Development, 1974.

21. England, G. W., O. P. Dhingra, and N. C. Agarwal, "The Manager and the Man: A Cross-Cultural Study of Personal Values," *Organization and Administrative Sciences,* 1974, **5,** pp. 1–97.

22. Tannenbaum, R., and S. A. Davis, "Values, Man, and Organizations," *Industrial Management Review,* 1969, **10,** pp. 69–80. *Also see:* Dimarco, N., and S. Norton, "Life Style, Organization Structure, Congruity, and Job Satisfaction," *Personnel Psychology,* 1974, **27,** pp. 581–591.

23. Knowles, H. P., and B. O. Saxberg, "Human Relations and the Nature of Man," *Harvard Business Review,* 1967, **45,** pp. 22–40 ff.

24. Myers, M. S., and S. S. Myers, "Toward Understanding the Changing Work Ethic," *California Management Review,* 1974, **16,** pp. 7–14.

25. Argyris, C., *Intervention Theory and Method: A Behavioral Science View.* Reading, Mass.: Addison-Wesley Publishing Co., 1970.

26. Ondrack, D. A., "Emerging Occupational Values: A Review and Some Findings," *Academy of Management Journal,* 1973, **16,** pp. 423–432.

27. "College, Noncollege Youth: Same Values," *New York Times,* Section E, May 26, 1974, p. 7.

28. Duncan, R., "Characteristics of Organizational Environments and Perceived Environmental Uncertainty," *Administrative Science Quarterly,* 1972, **17,** pp. 313–327. Duncan, R., "Multiple Decision-Making Structures in Adapting to Environmental Uncertainty: The Impact on Organizational Effectiveness," *Human Relations,* 1973, **26,** pp. 273–291.

29. *Ibid.,* p. 314.

30. Jurkovich, R., "A Core Typology of Organizational Environments," *Administrative Science Quarterly,* 1974, **19,** pp. 380–394.

31. *Ibid. Also see:* Downey, H. K., D. Hellriegel, and J. W. Slocum, Jr., "Environmental Uncertainty: The Construct and its Operationalization," *Administrative Science Quarterly,* in press.

32. *Ibid.*

33. McCoskey, M. B., "Tolerance for Ambiguity and the Perception of Environmental Uncertainty in Organization Design," presented at the Man-

agement of Organization Design Conference, University of Pittsburgh, 1974.

34. Estes, R. M., "The Business-Society Relationship: Emerging Major Issues" in Steiner, G. A., *Selected Major Issues in Business' Role in Modern Society.* Los Angeles: UCLA Graduate School of Management, 1973, pp. 19–43. *Also see:* House, P. W., R. C. Livingston, and C. D. Swinburn, "Monitoring Mankind: The Search for Quality," *Behavioral Science,* 1975, **20,** pp. 57–67.

35. *Ibid.,* p. 27.

*

PART II

INDIVIDUAL PROCESSES

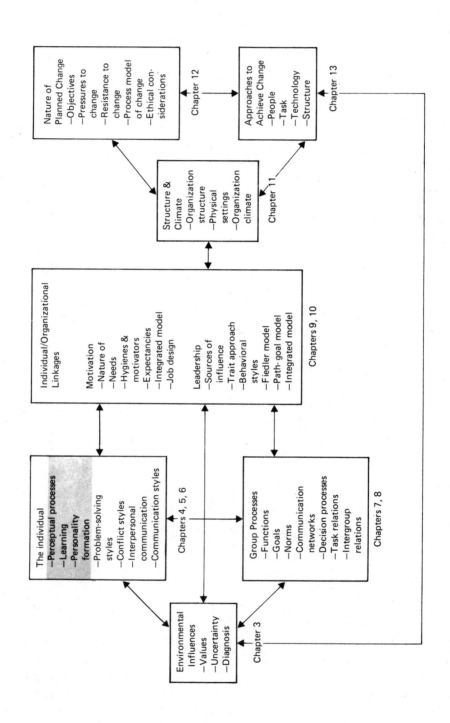

The individual
- **Perceptual processes**
- **Learning**
- **Personality formation**
- Problem-solving styles
- Conflict styles
- Interpersonal communication
- Communication styles

Chapters 4, 5, 6

Individual/Organizational Linkages

Motivation
- Nature of
- Needs
- Hygienes & motivators
- Expectancies
- Integrated model
- Job design

Leadership
- Sources of influence
- Trait approach
- Behavioral styles
- Fiedler model
- Path-goal model
- Integrated model

Chapters 9, 10

Group Processes
- Functions
- Goals
- Norms
- Communication networks
- Decision processes
- Task relations
- Intergroup relations

Chapters 7, 8

Environmental Influences
- Values
- Uncertainty
- Diagnosis

Chapter 3

Structure & Climate
- Organization structure
- Physical settings
- Organization climate

Chapter 11

Nature of Planned Change
- Objectives
- Pressures to change
- Resistance to change
- Process model of change
- Ethical con- siderations

Chapter 12

Approaches to Achieve Change
- People
- Task
- Technology
- Structure

Chapter 13

4
INDIVIDUAL: PERCEPTION, LEARNING, AND PERSONALITY

In our observations of others it is clear that responses to a given situation differ from person to person. By now you have spent some time studying and discussing some of the materials presented in this book with other students. In doing so, you may have noticed that perceptions about the materials presented varied, yet presumably all were using the same text to understand the materials. The differences among you, the differences in what you perceived and thought about the class materials are all important if you are to begin to understand the interpersonal relations in organizations. Often our explanation of the situation is that "They didn't see it that way," or "They wanted to do things differently." Or we might explain the differences by saying "She does that because she's naturally bright." People do indeed differ in their responses to the same situation, and the explanations offered by individuals depend on individual differences.

Our primary purposes in this chapter are to:

1. Discuss how perceptual processes affect your behavior;

2. Examine the basic factors in the perceptual process;

3. Discuss how individuals learn;

4. Assess different reinforcement schedules used by managers and their effects on the individual's behavior; and

5. Discuss the nature of personality and its determinants.

PERCEPTION

Individuals are constantly being bombarded by sensory stimulation. There are sight, noise, smell, touch, and taste sensations. Yet with all these sensations, you are somehow able to process this information without being hopelessly confused. This process is known as *perception* and may be defined as the process of selection and organization of sensations to provide a meaningful experience for the individual.[1] In essence, the individual receiving information assembles it and incorporates it into this experience. The process is essentially subjective; if a photograph is projected on a screen before you, your response to the photo is inherently personal. You can become aware of another person's perception of the same photograph only though observation of the behavior of that person. Very commonly, you report what you see. The inability of another person to measure your perceptions means that it is often difficult for the other person to know what you have seen.

Figure 4–1 depicts the basic perceptual process. In everyday life, impressions and judgments of other persons and events are formed in a wide variety of situations. The left block shows the various basic forms of stimuli or sensations. The middle block lists the factors that affect the perceiver's reaction to the stimulus information, such as his previous experience with the stimulus, the association of the information with certain stereotypes of persons, and the perceiver's self-concept. The righthand block lists the types of impressions formed. The perceiver attributes specific traits to the other person, he forms feelings of likes and dislikes, respect, etc., and finally forms impressions, whether these impressions were caused by a situational factor or whether they are intentionally formed.

Most of us recognize interpersonal events as we see them, but these are not necessarily the same as the "real world." To illustrate the concepts in Fig. 4–1, consider the drawing in Fig. 4–2. Here are some questions about the figure: (1) How old is the woman at the time of the picture? (2) Is she reasonably attractive or ugly? If you have seen this picture before, approximately equal numbers of you will see it either as young woman with her face turned

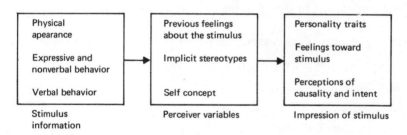

Figure 4–1   Factors in the Perceptual Process

Abridged from: Secord, P. and C. Backman, *Social Psychology*. New York: McGraw-Hill Book Co., 1964, p. 51.

up far enough so that her mouth is hidden and only the tip of her nose can be seen, or as a rather old woman with her chin buried in her fur collar and with a large Roman nose seen in profile.

There is an important point in this picture. If we are to have a fundamentally sound idea of how individuals operate, we must come to see how their functioning is determined by factors that are in their environment. If we see an old woman in Fig. 4–2, then we may be demonstrating one type of behavior; a young woman, another type of behavior.

Factors Influencing Perception

While social and environmental cues can help us to form impressions of others, there are two basic factors affecting our perceptual process: selection and/or screening, and organization.

Figure 4–2   Wife or Mother-in-Law?

From: Frederick Perls, M.D., Ph.D., Ralph F. Hefferline, Ph.D., and Paul Goodman, Ph.D., *Gestalt Therapy: Excitement and Growth in the Human Personality.* New York: Julian Press, 1951; Dell paperback, 1965, p. 27.

Selection

Perception is a selective process. We select a certain amount of information from the environment because we simply cannot assimilate all of the incoming information. Think of the times, for example, you were disturbed by the talking of other students in class when you were trying to concentrate on what the instructor was saying. The noise made by other students is not typically selected. That is, you notice it only because an examination is near. If the talking is constant, the screening process will help you avoid processing the irrelevant conversation. Suppose, though, that while you are successful in ignoring the background talk, someone starts shouting. At this point, when the unpleasantness becomes intense, you stop defending and may begin responding. In this case, you may turn to the individuals and tell them to shut up. This reversal seems to happen suddenly, at some specific threshold. The distant irritation increases to a threshold point at which it becomes so real that you no longer screen out the others' behavior and you tell them to shut up.

In some situations, nonverbal cues may contribute to the screening process. The selection of information may be based on facial features, appearance, body build, expressive movements, and gestures. In those everyday situations where stimulus information is limited, nonverbal cues may be used as a basis for screening. Such screening may well lead the perceiver to draw conclusions concerning the person. For example, heavy, fat persons typically are characterized as "loving physical comfort," "slow to react," and "relaxed." Persons with athletic builds have been described as "energetic," "assertive," and "loving physical exercise."[2] Thus, these body types convey certain impressions of one person to another and can obscure the true feelings and characteristics of the other person. To some extent, gestures and other expressive movements also act as screening mechanisms for the individual. These movements act as cues in the judgment and evaluation of others. In the absence of other cues, commonsense psychology suggests that a person with a slumped posture who moves slowly would be judged listless, dull, and depressed. A weak handshake may suggest a lack of strength and warmth, and self-confidence.

Organization

The second component of the perceptual process is organization. The information that has passed through our screening process must be organized in some fashion that allows us to ascribe meaning to the information. The stimulus provides cues as to its nature. For example, all of us have a conceptual category that includes the following properties: wood, four legs, seat, back, arm rests, etc. This is your concept of a chair. You can form this concept in your mind without seeing a chair. When you see a picture of an object and the properties of this object match your concept, you will categorize this sensory input as falling within the boundaries of the concept and will assign many of the properties of a chair to the object you see. These categories may be more or less complex but their central function is the reduction of complex information into simpler categories. How does one choose to select and categorize information in his own unique fashion?

The first factor is the individual's familiarity with the stimuli. Individuals tend to perceive familiar stimuli more quickly than unfamiliar ones. Conversion to the metric system in the United States, for example, has been a slow process. Individuals are more familiar with distances expressed in inches, feet, and yards than they are with centimeters and meters. Thus, if a highway sign states New York City is 966 kilometers away, most people will not know how far it is to New York City (answer 600 miles).

A second factor influencing the categorization of information is one's feelings towards the objects or persons in question. There is research evidence that those objects toward which we hold strong positive feelings will be recognized more readily than adverse and/or neutral stimuli.[3] In general, it appears that we select things about which we hold positive feelings and also avoid the recognition of things that lead to a negative response or feelings.

The third factor is the importance of the stimuli to the person. A frightened person is more likely to perceive fearful objects than an unfrightened person; a hungry person is more likely to perceive food objects than a person who has just eaten. Both historical variables, such as past experience, and contemporary factors, such as needs and expectations, influence the importance of the stimuli to the person.

Perception of others is not a single skill. People differ in the ways they describe others. That is, some use physical characteristics, such as tall, dark, and handsome to describe someone, while others might use a central trait, sly, tricky, and ruthless. One's ability to perceive others accurately depends on how sensitive one is to differences between people and also to the norms for judging them. The manager who wishes to perceive someone else accurately must look at the other person, not at himself. The characteristics we look for in someone, however, are influenced by our own personality traits and how we perceive ourselves.

Perceiving Oneself

So far we have talked about perceptions of things and other people. We perceive ourselves as we think we are and also as we would like other people to see us. There is a tendency for each of us to use ourselves as the norm or standard by which we judge and/or perceive others. In general, there seem to be two sets of variables that are important in understanding one's self-perceptions.

First, one's own social and personality characteristics make a difference.[4] Secure people (compared to insecure) tend to see others as warm rather than cold, more independent than dependent, and to have a higher tolerance for ambiguity. The person with Machiavellian tendencies is more likely to view others in terms of power and is less sensitive to the social needs of others than is the low-Machiavellian individual. That is, high Machiavellians tend to manipulate others, win more, and are less persuaded by others in face-to-face interactions than are low Machiavellians.[5]

Second, if the perceiver knows and accepts himself, it is easier to see others accurately because of the wider range of vision used in seeing others.[6] People who know themselves are less likely to view the world in black-and-white terms and to give extreme judgments about others.

The Situation

The final set of circumstances that are related to one's perception of others is the situation in which one finds oneself. If you are traveling in a foreign country, you may find that your interaction with a fellow North American is more important than if you interact with this person at home. The familiarity of the situation is important in terms of norms and expectations. When members of the Peace Corps, for example, volunteered for an assignment in a different country, they often experienced "cultural shock." That is, they had to adjust quickly to the norms and expectations of the local community if they were to be effective in their mission. To soften this "shock," Peace Corps members were often sent out in pairs. Even under this condition, some volunteers returned home because they couldn't adjust to the situation.

Perception of the situation is also dependent upon some historical factors. Our past experience, culture, and learning influence these judgments, as do the factors in the current situation. It has been found that when a committee is composed of congenial members who are willing to continue to work in the same group, they will develop similar perceptions and be more effective in reaching a social goal than members who are not able to work with each other.[7] The implication from this research seems clear: Do not place together those individuals with a history of personal fights. If they must be on the same committee, individuals should be helped by the managers to see that they are expected to work toward the common group goal.

One's position in the organization is also likely to affect one's perception of problems. In a study of executives from sales, production, and accounting, it was found that sales executives looked at sales and related marketing problems as most important, production managers tended to view production and organizational issues as most important, and accountants looked primarily at income and financial data. Each executive perceived those aspects of the situation that related specifically to the activities and goals of his or her work unit.[8]

Barriers to Forming Impressions of Others

The forming of accurate impressions of others is an important task. A manager is confronted many times with the task of forming impressions of other persons, a secretary interviewing for a position, a visiting member from the home office, a customer he has not personally met before. His own needs, values, and expectations will play a major part in the impressions formed. Several of the more obvious factors that typically operate to influence the individual's perception were shown in Fig. 4–1—that is, physical appearance, and verbal and nonverbal behaviors. In the casual situations in which we must form impressions of others, it is a natural tendency to jump to conclusions and form impressions without adequate evidence. Too often in forming impressions, the perceiver does not know what is relevant, important, or predictive of later behavior. It is an old cliché that, accurate or not, first impressions are lasting.

It is possible to identify some distorting influences in the process of forming impressions of others. Research has focused on four typical errors: stereotyping, halo effect, projection, and perceptual defense.

Stereotyping. The word "stereotype" often has a negative connotation, but we mean it simply as the "picture" one has in mind when regarding a hypothetical "kind" of person. That is, the words "undergraduate," "cop," and "VIP" each call to mind a mental picture that is a stereotype. Persons have many attributes differing greatly in visibility and distinctiveness. People select certain attributes as a means of identifying categories of persons, and ignore others. These attributes may be physical—such as age, or sexual or racial characteristics; they may involve membership in a group or organization—such as an occupation, church, or national organization. In other words, a stereotype is a special form of categorical response; membership in a category is sufficient to evoke the judgment that the person possesses all the attributes belonging to that category.

We often find ourselves using categorical information about a person. If you were asked to think about an individual who is a professor, student, policeman, or football player, what impressions come to your mind? Where additional information about the individual is minimal, this type of categorical information is likely to strongly affect our perceptions of that person. This process of assigning attributes to a person solely on the basis of a category to which that person belongs is known as stereotyping. The grouping of individuals into a category meaningful to us is often helpful in forming impressions of others. However, it also tends to limit our view of the differences between people whom we lump into a category.

One of the troublesome aspects of stereotyping is that it is so commonplace. In one study, labeling one photograph as a representative from management caused an impression to be formed of that person different from that formed when the identical photograph was labeled as that of a union leader. Management and labor formed different impressions, each perceiving the person as less dependable than if he had been a member of the interviewee's own group. Managers also felt that other managers were better able to appreciate labor's point of view, while unionists felt that other unionists were better able to appreciate management's point of view.[9]

Halo Effect.   This refers to a process in which an impression, either favorable or unfavorable, is used to evaluate a person on other dimensions. The "halo" serves as a screen keeping the perceiver from actually seeking the attribute that is supposedly being judged. The "halo" has received much attention in the rating of employee performance. In the rating situation, a manager may single out one trait and use this as the basis for judgment of all other performance measures. For example, an excellent attendance record may produce judgments of high productivity, quality work, and so forth. The halo effect can also have a general effect on forming impressions. In one study, knowledge that the company was in receivership caused employees to devalue the higher pay and otherwise superior working conditions of their company compared to those of a financially secure firm.[10] We also often link together certain traits. For example, we may assume that when a person is aggressive, he or she will also have high energy, dominance and achievement, or that when a person is friendly, he or she will also be generous and warm, and have a good sense of humor. While the conclusions reached may be correct about a person, the manner by which they were reached are examples of the halo effect.

Projection.   In projection, a person distorts the source of the unacceptable thought or motive. One attributes the cause of the unacceptable thought or feeling to someone else. In a sense, rejecting the unacceptable thought by giving it to another person is the process of *projection.* For example, the manager who has been passed over for promotion may project this lack of success to the ability of those promoted to get close to the boss, or to their having "connections." In this case, the manager is trying to block out the thought that he may be an ineffective manager. The tennis player who muffs a stroke and looks at the tennis racket for the offending "hole" would be another example.

Our perceptions may characteristically be distorted by emotions we are experiencing or by personality traits we may possess.[11] For example, a manager frightened by rumors of impending organizational changes may not only judge others to be more frightened than they are, but also assess various policy decisions as more frightening than they are. People high in personality traits such as stinginess, obstinacy, and disorderliness tend to rate others higher on these traits than would those who are low in these personality traits.

Perceptual Defense.   Another distorting influence is putting on blinders to defend ourselves from seeing those events that may disturb us. An example may be the front-line foreman who sees any new ideas suggested by a new young Industrial Engineering staff manager as worthless. This example of perceptual defense offers an excellent description of perceptual distortion at work. By refusing to consider the young engineer's ideas, the foreman may avoid potential inconsistencies. For example, if the foreman were to consider the engineer's ideas, he might be confronted with a fact (younger manager can have good ideas) inconsistent with a stereotype already held (people must be around long enough to earn the right to make a decision). Thus, by refusing to consider the new ideas or by perceiving all of the new man's ideas as worthless, the foreman can eliminate any potential inconsistency. The foreman has a defense against changing his stereotype of new, young engineers.

Summary

Managers frequently base their decisions and actions on their perception of other individuals. In this section, we have indicated some guidelines and precautions to use in this complex process. First, we discussed some basic factors in the nature of the perceptual process and then examined organizational and situational influences on the perceptual process. Finally, some of the barriers to forming accurate impressions of others were discussed.

LEARNING

When individuals enter organizations, they bring with them their own unique ways of perceiving and responding to their environment as a result of their past experiences. A manager's ability to deal effectively with complex decisions, the lathe operator's ability to machine parts to exact tolerances, and a secretary's mode of dress and bearing are all things that have been learned. As managers, we often fail to recognize that these common, everyday phenomena have been learned by employees. Since a large portion of the manager's time is devoted to influencing behavioral patterns of subordinates so that they will be more oriented toward the goals of the organization, it is only natural that we examine the principles and processes that govern learning.

Definition of Learning

There seems to be general agreement among behavioral scientists that learning can be defined as a "relatively permanent change in the behavior that results from reinforced practice or experience."[12] There are several important elements in this definition.

First, learning involves a change, but not necessarily an improvement in behavior. Learning usually has the connotation of improvement, but remember that stereotypes, prejudices, projections, and the like are also learned.

Second, the change in behavior must be relatively permanent. This rules out behavioral changes resulting from fatigue, temporary memorization of materials, and other temporary behavioral adaptations.

Third, some form of practice or experience is necessary for learning to occur. For example, a secretary may attend a secretarial school and know the mechanical processes of typing a paper, but must practice typing before being able to type accurately 120 words per minute.

Fourth, practice or experience must be reinforced for learning to occur. If reinforcement does not accompany the practice or experience, the behavior will eventually disappear.[13]

Applying these points to the study of organizational behavior implies that learning is the acquisition of knowledge or skill and performance is the translation of knowledge or skill into practice. The primary effect of reinforcement is to strengthen the practice.

Models of Learning

As stated in Chapter 2, the basic purpose of any model or theory is to be able to predict the phenomenon under study. Thus, a model of learning should explain all aspects of learning, be universal in scope, and predict learning in all conditions. To date, no such model exists. While behavioral scientists have agreed upon a basic definition of learning, there is disagreement on the model behind the definition. However, the lack of agreement on "the" model should not rule out the importance of learning. Even though controversy surrounds nearly every model of learning, there is widespread and basic agreement on many of the concepts of simple and complex learning. This knowledge has direct implications for managers, as will be illustrated in the forthcoming pages.

Classical Conditioning

Pavlov's classical experiment with dogs provided behavioral scientists with a quantity of knowledge about the learning process. He noticed, while studying the automatic reflexes associated with digestion, that when he presented to the dogs a piece of meat (unconditioned stimulus), the dogs salivated (unconditioned response). On the other hand, the ringing of a bell (neutral stimulus) had no effect on the dogs' salivation. Pavlov next accompanied the presentation of the meat with the ringing of the bell. After repeating this sequence several times, the dogs salivated not only when the meat was presented alone, but also when he rang the bell alone. In other words, the dogs had become conditioned to salivate (conditioned response) to the sound of the bell (conditioned stimulus) alone.

While it is important to understand that primary needs can be conditioned by this process, classical conditioning principles are of very limited use to managers. Most behavioral scientists would agree that the learning of primary needs represented only a small part of the human's total learning.[14] In organizations, these primary needs have little relevance to more complex behavior. Of greater importance to the manager are the complex behavioral actions of employees that are learned through conditioned or secondary reinforcers. Conditioned reinforcers, such as money, social approval, praise, responsibility, recognition, are important for most organizational participants.

Operant Conditioning

The contemporary psychologist most closely associated with operant conditioning is B. F. Skinner, the author of *Walden Two*[15] and *Beyond Freedom and Dignity*.[16] Operant conditioning is primarily concerned with learning that occurs as a consequence (rewards and punishments) of behavior. In classical conditioning, the sequence of events is independent of the subject's behavior. For example, in Pavlov's experiment, the dogs had no control over the unconditioned or conditioned response, but were at the mercy of the experimenter and his past conditioning history. In operant conditioning, the subject must do something in order to get a reward. Performance is important in getting the reward. For example, if you take a break from studying and go to a vending machine to purchase a Coke and put a penny (performance) in the machine (stimulus), nothing will happen (reinforcement). However, if you put a quarter (performance) in the machine (stimulus), you will probably receive a Coke (reinforcement). In this case, your behavior is important in determining the reinforcements that will accrue to yourself. Note, however, that for voluntary behavior, the presence of a reinforcer is dependent on the behavior of the individual in a given stimulus setting. Reinforcement is not given every time the stimulus is presented, but only when correct performance is made. This sequence is illustrated in Fig. 4–3. For example, following the sequence in the figure, the manager asked the employee to increase the productivity rate from 24 axles per shift to 30 axles per shift. The employee responded by performing at the higher rate. The manager rewarded the employee for higher productivity by increasing the decision-making discretion and giving the employee more money. However, if the manager did not reward the employee and if sometime in the future the manager asked the employee to increase productivity, the employee's response might not be to increase the productivity rate in accordance with the wishes from the manager.

In this example, the interrelationships among the three components of (1) stimulus, (2) performance, and (3) reinforcements are known as the contingencies of reinforcement.[17] Therefore, an adequate formulation of the interaction between an individual and performance must always specify three things: (1) the occasion upon which a performance occurs, (2) the performance itself, and (3) the reinforcing consequences. To change behavior, the reinforcers of behavior often need to be changed.

Contingencies of Reinforcement.   The term reinforcement is very closely related to the psychological process of motivation, which is discussed in Chapter 9. Although reinforcement and rewards are often used interchangeably, a more precise definition is that reinforcement can be anything that increases the strength of the performance and tends to induce the behavior that preceded the reinforcement.[18] Managers intuitively use rewards in their attempts to modify and influence the behavior of their subordinates, but these efforts often produce limited results because the methods are used improperly, inconsis-

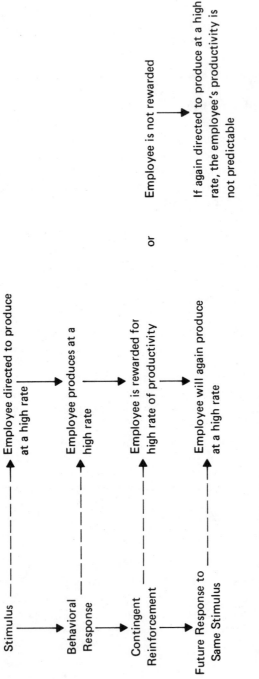

Figure 4-3 The Impact of Contingent Reinforcement on Employee Behavior

Source: Adapted from Brief, A. and Filley, A. "Contingency Management: Poor People and the Firm," MSU Business Topics, 1974, 22, No. 2, p. 47. Reprinted by permission of publisher, Division of Research, Graduate School of Business Administration, Michigan State University, 1975.

tently, and inappropriately. In many instances, rewards are given to workers, but they are not made conditional or contingent on the behavior the managers wish to encourage.

One of the reasons managers may fail to influence the behavior of their subordinates is the lack of understanding of the contingencies of reinforcement available to them. There are four basic ways the managers can arrange the contingencies available to them—positive reinforcement, avoidance learning, punishment, and extinction.[19] The first two ways represent methods to strengthen *desired* behaviors, while the latter two are methods of weakening *undesired* behavior.

Positive Reinforcement. [20]   A positive reinforcer is one that strengthens an association between a stimulus and response (performance). A positive reward is usually pleasurable and desirable. Three basic ideas should be kept in mind when using positive reinforcers. First, it is important to note that what is rewarding to one person may not be rewarding to another. A manager should determine whether the reinforcement has reward value to the worker. Second, it is necessary to design the reinforcement contingencies in such a way that reinforcing events are made contingent upon desired behavior. Rewards should result from performance, and the greater the performance, the greater the rewards. Money is not the only reward available for the manager. In most unionized shops, the manager has limited direct control over the wages that are tied to performance. However, the manager may be able to influence other forms of rewards, such as recognition, praise, and promotion that can be made contingent on proper performance. For a manager to maintain desired behavior, it is important for him to design a reward system that differentiates among employees based on their level of performance and is administered contingent on the level of performance observed. Third, the contingencies should be designed in such a way that a reliable procedure for achieving the desired performance level can be established and generalized to other situations. Through the process of generalization, the more nearly alike the new situation is to the original one, the more likely the old reinforced behavior is likely to be recalled. For example, if you hire a contractor to build a custom house, he is able to bring with him enough old behavioral patterns to this unfamiliar setting (a new custom house) to erect your house. He has learned through past reinforcement history that one way to operate in a new environment is to recall behavior that has been used successfully in the past, and use that behavior in this new situation. That is, excavate the land and pour the foundation prior to engaging a plumber. Perhaps this is one reason why employers look for persons with experience.

Avoidance Learning.   Just as with positive reinforcement, this is a method for strengthening desired behavior. Avoidance or escape learning can be used when proper behavior on the part of an employee can prevent the occurrence of an undesired stimulus. For example, punctuality of students in the classroom may be maintained by avoidance learning. The undesired stimulus is the criticism by the professor for being late. To avoid criticism, students may make an effort to reach class on time. In an organization a worker may learn to escape a boring job with no challenge by daydreaming during working hours. After work, the worker may become very serious-minded. There is a distinction between this process of strengthening desired behavior by means of positive reinforcement and avoidance learning. In the former case, the worker exerts energies to gain the reinforcements that result from good work. In the latter instance, the individual works hard to avoid the noxious aspects. In both cases, the same behavior is strengthened.

Extinction.   While positive reinforcement and avoidance techniques are often used by managers to strengthen desired behavior, extinction and punishment are methods for reducing undesired behavior. When positive reinforcement for a previously desired behavior is withheld, individuals may continue to exhibit that behavior for some period of time. However, under this condition of repeated nonreinforcement, the behavior will deteriorate and eventually disappear. This decline in behavior as a result of nonreinforcement is defined as *extinction.* For example, a student may be reinforced (praise, grades) by the teacher for raising his hand and asking brilliant questions. However, if the teacher begins ignoring this behavior (hand-raising), the behavior might eventually be extinguished because it was not reinforced.

Punishment.   A second method of reducing the frequency of undesired behavior is through the use of punishment. Punishment involves the presentation of an aversive stimulus immediately after the response. While managers and supervisors typically use some form of punishment in attempting to influence subordinates' behavior, most learning theorists would agree that while punishment has an immediate effect of stopping the undesired behavior, punishment has several undesirable side effects.[21] First, punishment may not always reduce or eliminate the undesirable behavior. Sometimes when the punishing agent is removed or the punishment is discontinued, the behavior recurs. Second, if no acceptable alternative to the punished response is provided, the punished person does not know what to do the next time the same situation occurs where the previous response was punished. Finally, the punished response may not be made under conditions deemed appropriate. For example, the staff manager may assume additional authority on a project that the company is bidding on. This behavior may be punished by a line supervisor who feels that the staff manager is overstepping his bounds. The punishment may generalize to the point where the staff man's initiative to assume additional responsibility on other projects is inhibited.

Techniques for Administering Reinforcement

With the exception of prisons, mental hospitals, and other custodial institutions, most workers enter an organization voluntarily. For this reason, important influences on individual behavior are the presence of positive reinforcers.[22] Modification of certain behaviors, such as absenteeism, lateness, shoddy workmanship, may be influenced by the positive reinforcement schedule used by the manager. Positive reinforcers are generally more effective than negative reinforcers in influencing behavior. Positive reinforcers indicate what needs to be done and are result-oriented. Thus, how the reward is administered can greatly influence the specific behavior of the individual. The contingencies of reinforcement concern primarily the pattern of the relationship between the reinforcer and the response. This pattern is referred to as the reinforcement schedule.

Basically, there are two types of reinforcement schedules: continuous and intermittent. Under continuous reinforcement, every time a specific behavior is engaged in by the individual, it is followed by a reward. That is, an employee receives a bonus for each unit he or she produces or a commission for each unit he or she sells. Door-to-door sales people selling encyclopedias or Fuller brushes, are usually paid on a continuous reinforcement schedule. When behavior is continually reinforced, learning is most rapid. However, if reinforcement is terminated, extinction of behavior learned under continuous reinforcement is more rapid than that which has been reinforced only intermittently. Since it is usually impossible for a manager to continuously reinforce the behavior of his or her subordinates, the intermittent schedules are usually more appropriate for modifying employees' behavior. There are four major intermittent techniques for administering rewards: fixed-ratio, variable-ratio, fixed-interval, and variable-interval. In the ratio schedules, the individual is reinforced after giving a certain number of specific types of behavior. Under the fixed-ratio schedule, the number of behaviors is held constant, while under a variable-ratio schedule it changes. In an interval schedule, the individual is reinforced on the first appropriate behavior after a particular time has elapsed. In fixed-interval scheduling, the time required is held constant, while under a variable-interval schedule, the time changes from period to period. Let's examine these intermittent reinforcement schedules as they apply in typical organizational settings.

Fixed-Ratio Schedule.   Under this schedule, reinforcement is given only after a certain number of responses. A common example of this schedule is the piecework incentive system. A worker is paid (reinforced) on the basis of how many pieces he produces (responses). Administering a reward under a fixed-ratio schedule tends to produce a steady response.

Variable-Ratio Schedule.   Under this schedule, the reward is given after a number of responses, but the exact number is varied. When the variable ratio is expressed as some number, say 25, this means that on the average the individual is reinforced after twenty-five responses. The first common industrial example is its application to the salesman who works for a commission. The salesman's reinforcement schedule is highly variable when it depends upon the number of customers contacted. For most industrial organizations, this plan would be impossible to use as the only plan for scheduling reinforcement because of the numerous financial commitments (e.g., mortage payments, life insurance, etc.) that demand regular payment. However, Christmas bonuses and salesmen's commissions would be examples of this schedule for reinforcement which are supplemental to other forms of reinforcement (i.e., the fixed-interval schedule).

Fixed-Interval Schedule.   The most common way to administer a monetary reward is on a fixed-interval schedule. Under this schedule, reinforcement is given after a specified period of time and not after a specific response, as under the fixed-ratio schedule. Most workers are paid on a weekly, bi-weekly, or monthly plan based on a certain number of hours worked, assuming that the worker was performing at some acceptable level. Behavior resulting from the fixed-interval schedule is difficult to reinforce. The reinforcement is not given immediately following a specific response. Therefore, it is difficult for the worker to know exactly what behavioral acts should be continued and those that would be stopped,[23] except perhaps going to work on payday.

Variable-Interval Schedule.   Under this schedule, reinforcement is administered at some variable interval of time around some average.[24] Since the reinforcers are given unpredictably (for example, in the case of promotions, or administering praise), variable schedules generate higher rates of response and more stable and consistent behavior. For example, the manufacturing vice-president of Standard Steel Corporation makes it a point to walk through the melt shop on an average of once a day but at varied times, i.e., twice on Monday, once on Tuesday, not on Wednesday, not on Thursday, and twice on Friday. As you would expect, performance will be higher and have less fluctuation than under the fixed-interval schedule because the reinforcers are dispensed unpredictably.

In general, the timing of the reinforcement should be kept reasonably close to the desired behavior. In Table 4–1, the effect of each of the types of reinforcement schedules and the various methods of arranging reinforcement contingencies on worker performance is summarized. Understanding and applying what is known about the administration of reinforcement can have a great impact on the behavior of employees. Several researchers[25] have suggested areas whereby the systematic use of positive reinforcement can be used to increase organizational effectiveness. The areas include training and development, job design, compensation systems, and organizational design. Since

Table 4-1 Operant Conditioning Summary*

Type of Reinforcement	Schedule of Reinforcement	Effect on Behavior When Applied to the Individual	Effect on Behavior When Removed from the Individual
	Continuous Reinforcement	Fastest method to establish a new behavior.	Fastest method to extinguish a new behavior.
	Intermittent Reinforcement	Slowest method to establish a new behavior.	Slowest method to extinguish a new behavior.
	Variable Reinforcement Schedules	More consistent response frequencies.	Slower extinction rate.
	Fixed Reinforcement Schedules	Less consistent response frequencies.	Faster extinction rate.
Positive Reinforcement Avoidance Reinforcement		Increased frequency over preconditioning level.	Return to pre-conditioning level.
Punishment		Decreased frequency over preconditioning level.	Return to pre-conditioning level.

*Adapted from: Behling, O., C. Schriesheim, and J. Tolliver, "Present Theories and New Directions in Theories of Work Effort," Journal Supplement and Abstract Service of the American Psychological Corporation, 1974, ms. no. 385, p. 57. Reprinted by permission.

these topical areas will be covered in different chapters of this book, they will not be elaborated on here. However, several guidelines for the use of operant conditioning techniques might be briefly mentioned.[26]

First, do not give all people the same rewards if their performances differ. The behavior of high performers may be diminished while average-performance and poor-performance workers' behavior is being strengthened by positive reinforcement.

Second, failure to respond has reinforcing consequences. The way managers use rewards at their disposal will influence the behavior of the employee. Managers must be careful that they examine the consequences of their nonaction as well as of their action. Nonaction is a means of reducing undesired behaviors.

Third, be sure to communicate to the person what he can do to be positively reinforced. By making the contingencies of reinforcement known to the worker, the employee will have a standard against which to measure perfor-mance and will have a built-in feedback system that will allow accurate judg-ments about his own work.

Fourth, be sure to tell a person what he or she is doing wrong. As a general rule, people do not like to fail. If a manager fails to explain to an employee why a reward is being withheld, the employee may associate it with past desired behavior instead of past undesirable behavior. Managers should not use extinction as the sole method of modifying behavior, but use it in combination with positive reinforcement principles.

Lastly, make the consequences equal to the behavior. Many managers find it difficult to praise employees; others find it difficult to counsel an employee about what he or she is doing wrong. If a manager fails to use the proper reinforcement techniques, the manager is actually reducing organizational effectiveness. When a worker is overrewarded, guilt feelings may be devel-oped. On the other hand, when a worker feels underrewarded, frustration will result and he will not contribute his best efforts toward the management's goals. If the situation persists, the worker may leave the organization.

Application of Positive Reinforcement: Emery Air Freight Corporation [27]

E. J. Feeney, Vice-President for Emery Air Freight Corporation, used the five guidelines just discussed when he designed a positive reinforcement program at Emery. First, he introduced a performance audit that indicated which were the biggest potential profit payoffs for the company and areas that needed substantial improvement. For example, managers at Emery were certain that containers were used for shipping about 90 percent of the time. The perfor-mance audit indicated that containers were used only 45 percent of the time. Thus, the performance audit provided a specific objective base line against which to measure future performance.

Second, Feeney established performance standards and goals for each worker. The goals were defined in measurable terms. It is important that the goal-setting activity follow the performance audit and that the goals be tied directly to the job. The involvement of employees in setting standards was encouraged.

Third, each employee was given the basic data so that he or she could keep track of the work. This is a continuous reinforcement schedule and gives the worker immediate knowledge about the results of his work and whether or not the goals are being met. Prompt direct feedback is, of course, knowledge of results, which is one of the most important principles of learning.

The fourth step involves the use of supervisor-to-feedback performance reports to the worker. The behavior should be reinforced as soon as possible and be expressed in specific rather than nonspecific phrases. For example, "Keep up the good work, Harry" is an example of what Feeney calls "gumdrops," generalized praise. Specific phrases such as "Marie, I liked the imagination you used in scheduling production," or "Ildiko, you are running fairly consistent at 98 percent of standard" are specific positive reinforcers. Emery Air Freight encourages a variable-ratio reinforcement, with supervisors giving praise and recognition to each employee. The use of negative reinforcement is discouraged.

The results at Emery have been exceptionally good. In the three divisions that are using the positive reinforcement approach, management has reported a saving of over $3 million in the past three years. What does this prove? In those instances in which Emery has used positive reinforcement, behavior modification has been dramatic, sustained, and uniformly in the desired direction. Positive reinforcement has been used selectively at Emery in areas where work could be measured and quantifiable standards set if they did not already exist, and areas where observation showed that existing level of performance was far below standard. On the basis of Emery's success, other corporations, such as United Airlines, IBM, IT&T, Procter and Gamble, and Ford Motor Company, have used positive reinforcement approaches with tentative but similar results.

PERSONALITY

In the first two sections of this chapter, we discussed two of the important bases for understanding individual behavior in organizations—perception and learning. In this section of the chapter, we bring these two concepts together. Most administrators need more facts than those provided by perception and learning in order to understand individual behavior. In essence, the individual operates as a "whole" man, and behavior is not readily understood as distinct parts or entities. The process of intergrating these parts is accomplished through the study of personality. Personality has been defined as "how a person affects others, how he understands and views himself, and his pattern of inner and outer measurable traits."[28] There are three important notions in this definition. First, how a person affects others primarily depends upon one's external appearance (height, weight, etc.) and behavior. The ramifications from our discussion of perceptual processes would influence our judgments of others. Second, each person is unique. Each individual forms a self-concept that is derived from successive interactions with the environment. Third, each individual possesses traits or dimensions and it is how these traits interact that shape the total pattern of the individual's personality.

It is assumed, in the definition of personality, that an individual's personality is constantly changing. Individuals are influenced by situational factors; they learn new ways and vary their behavior in many of their more accustomed roles. The employee who enters the organization will be significantly influenced by the demands of that organization's environment (see Chapter 3). One's personality may change as a result of this mutual interaction. Personality development may occur as a result of everyday experience within an organization. Different situations bring different responses, which may be either strengthened or weakened as a result of their reinforcement contingencies. Thus, personality is a description of psychological growth and development.

The Nature of Personality

The concept of personality as a changing and developing system can be more easily understood by an examination of several propositions. Each of these propositions will be reviewed and their relevance to administrative practice indicated.[29]

1. *Human behavior consists of acts.*   In any complex behavioral form, the whole individual acts. While processes such as learning and perception may be important aspects, they are parts of the total behavioral pattern of the individual. Thus, a view of personality must focus on the pattern of total acts rather than the specific aspects of it. For example, in responding to a managerial request to increase productivity, the individual may behave. The consequences of the managerial request may take the form of increased productivity.

2. *Personality conceived of as a whole actualizes itself in a specific environment.*   This proposition indicates that the individual cannot be understood apart from the environment in which he is operating. The employee is a part of a work unit and this affiliation may interact with the total organization atmosphere to influence his or her personality. Other people are important sources of an individual's identity and self-concept. Various facets of one's personality can be drawn out by facets of others' personalities. Thus, a person is a product of the characteristics of those around him. The interactional nature of the individual, the small group, and the formal organization will be developed more specifically in Chapters 7, 8, and 11.

3. *Personality is characterized by self-consistency.*   The normal personality is in a state of dynamic equilibrium. This means it is flexible, but tries to maintain a consistency. For example, individuals who are internally oriented (individuals who see themselves as able to control their environment) have been found to show higher motivation toward achievement than external personality types (individuals who believe that others control their fate).[30] However, this does not mean that in every instance, internals will demonstrate achievement. Over the long run, internals will tend to demonstrate this type of behavior. Attempts to maintain self-consistency may not always lead to improved organizational effectiveness. Individuals will learn to avoid discussing various topics and avoid noticing events in their environment as means of protecting their self-concept.

4. *Personality is goal-directed behavior.*   The choice among goals or motives is a distinguishing feature among individuals. The individual strives for more than self-consistency; the person tries to obtain goals and satisfy motives. For example, one of the outstanding features about individuals is that most people live in groups. The fact that employees who feel accepted, respected, and needed by others are more satisfied with their jobs has long been accepted.

5. *Personality is a time-integrating structure.*   Personality embodies the past, present, and the future. The individual is partly a product of conditioned responses and habits learned from past reinforcement contingencies. However, we are also future-oriented. The planning function in an organization would be an example of the organization's future orientation, just as the individual planning his career would be an example of a future orientation.

6. *Personality is a process of becoming.*   Each individual personality is striving to actualize itself—become what one is capable of becoming. Organizational value changes, as indicated in Chapter 3, suggest that the quality-of-working-life managerial value system attempts to create an environment that will allow the individual to determine his own goals and satisfy these goals within the organization. The concept of actualizing is important in most theories of motivation (Chapter 9) and interpersonal styles.

Determinants of Personality

What determines personality? There is no single answer to this question because there are too many variables that contribute to an individual's personality. However, several writers suggest that clear and orderly thinking about personality formation will be facilitated if four determinants, and their interactions, are examined: constitutional; group-membership; role; and situational.[31]

Constitutional Determinants.   Constitutional factors, such as body type, sex, muscular and nervous systems, and some glandular processes, are determined by heredity. People appear to have different biological rhythms, varying potentials for learning, reaction time, and tolerance for frustration. Such characteristics influence a man's needs and expectations. As mentioned earlier in this chapter, the way others react to an individual's appearance and physical capacities affects personality formation. Occasionally, a physically weak youth, such as Theodore Roosevelt, may be driven to achieve feats of physical strength as a form of overcompensation, but usually an individual will learn to avoid situations that he or she perceives as threatening to his or her self-concept.

Group-Membership Determinants.   Anthropologists working in different cultures have clearly demonstrated the important role that culture plays in the formation of the individual's personality. Individuals within any given culture are exposed to beliefs and values (see Chapter 3). For example, the North American culture often rewards people for being independent and competitive. However, there are extreme differences among individuals within a single culture. The Protestant work ethic is usually associated with Western culture, but it is wrong to assume that all individuals within this culture exhibit the same degree and/or the same intensity of this value. Thus, it is important for the manager to recognize that culture does have an impact on the development of workers' personalities, but it is wrong to assume that all workers are equally affected by their culture or that all cultures are homogeneous.

Membership in a group also carries with it exposure to a social environment. The individual adjusts in the presence of others. Our personality is molded by the particular members of the group with whom we have personal contact and by our perceptions of the group as a whole. Groups define the role played by the individual along with his or her social standing in the group.

Role Determinants.   Culture defines how the different roles necessary to group life are to be performed. In this sense, the role determinants are a special class of group-membership determinants. Each individual is capable of playing a number of different roles at various times, because everyone participates in several groups, and the roles an individual plays are influenced by the groups within which that individual acts. For example, the roles of a husband and father are partially determined by the cultural environment in the family, while the roles of a shop foreman or secretary are largely determined by their immediate work groups. Actors wear different masks in a play to represent different individuals. From one point of view, this represents a disguise. It also operates to conceal the individual's own underlying motivations from others. The medical doctor who demonstrates little emotional distress in emergency situations has been trained in medical school to adopt that role.

Situational Determinants.   Situational determinants are unique factors that influence an individual's personality. A student, say, who is undecided as to his professional career, or who is equally drawn to several different vocations, happens to sit down in an airplane next to a lawyer who is an engaging and persuasive advocate of the legal profession. This may set off a chain of events that puts the student into situations that are decisive in shaping his or her personality and/or changing his or her academic program.

Situational determinants also include things that happen in the immediate family. A divorce, a father whose occupation keeps him away from home much of the time, the fact of being the only child, or youngest or eldest in a series, may all affect the individual's personality development. One research study of twenty executives who had risen from a lower-class neighborhood to hold top ranking positions with business firms clearly indicated that parents who reinforced values conducive to achievement had a great deal of influence on the personalities of this group of business executives.[32]

Interdependence of the Determinants. The personality of an individual is the product of inherited disposition and environmental experiences. These experiences occur within the field of physical, biological and social environment, all of which are modified by the culture and immediate group ties. A balanced consideration of these determinants is needed. For example, in every society, the child is differentially socialized according to sex. Also, in every society, different behavior is expected of individuals in different age groups, although each culture makes its own unique prescriptions as to what behavioral responses are to be reinforced. The personalities of men and women, of the young and old, are differentiated, in part, by the experience of playing these various roles in conformity to cultural norms. Since age and sex are biological facts, they also operate as constitutional determinants of personality.

SUMMARY

In this chapter, we examined three concepts that have great importance and usefulness in understanding the individual's behavior: perception, learning, and personality. Perception involves the selection, organization, and interpretation of sensations from the environment. It was defined as a process whereby cues from the environment are organized. The individual selectively accepts certain cues from the environment and classifies them according to past experience with the cues. This process enables one to screen out unwanted sensations and aids in the organization of the environment into a consistent whole.

Learning theory illustrates how individuals respond to circumstances in their environment and develop different responses. The differences between classical and operant conditioning were discussed. Classical conditioning has limited usefulness for the administrator. In operant conditioning, reinforcement is critical. When behavior is reinforced, it is likely to occur again in response to a particular stimulus. If behavior is reinforced positively, the probability of recurrence of the behavior is increased, but if behavior is negatively reinforced, the likelihood that this reponse will occur again is decreased. Useful guidelines for the manager in using the concepts in practical situations were examined.

A basic assumption in this chapter and in Chapter 3 is that values and culture mold individual personality. In the third section of this chapter, we discussed the dimensions of personality. The personality of an individual is a product of inherited disposition and environmental experiences. These experiences occur within the field of one's physical, biological, and social environment, all of which are modified by the culture of one's total environment.

Discussion Questions:

1. Why is an understanding of a person's perceptual processes important for managers?

2. What are some of the factors affecting an individual's perceptual processes?

3. How does stereotyping affect a person's perception? Give an example of this process.

4. What are some barriers to forming accurate impressions of others?

5. What are some differences between classical conditioning and operant conditioning?

6. What is meant by contingencies of reinforcement? Give some examples.

7. Discuss the nature of personality. What are some major factors affecting the formation of one's personality?

8. Why should managers be concerned with employees' personalities?

9. What potential drawbacks exist when you attempt to use operant conditioning at work?

CRITICAL INCIDENT

The School Board Problem

Late on Friday afternoon Mr. Babcock, the head of the school board, received a petition of complaints bearing some 725 signatures of parents in the local school district. The petition urged the board to take some action other than the busing of children to alleviate overcrowding at a local school. Among those things cited were such matters as inadequate music rooms, inadequate storage and arts rooms, and ever-increasing enrollment for kindergarten with no apparent effort by the school board to introduce new methods for handling these problems. The petition threatened that if corrective actions were not taken immediately, the parents would be forced to go to the State Department of Education, which would result in a period of extreme distress at a critical time in the local school district's economy.

Having had no problems with the parents previously, Mr. Babcock was somewhat alarmed at the sudden appearance of these numerous problems and the opposition to busing. He immediately phoned Mr. Stevens, principal of the elementary school, in an effort to gain a better picture of the situation. He knew Mr. Stevens was an excellent principal and would probably be able to better explain what was happening. However, Mr. Stevens was attending a professional meeting in another state and would not return for several days. Then Mr. Babcock placed a phone call to Mr. Hughes, director of the elementary system, and bluntly asked what the petition was all about. Mr. Hughes said he had received no petition from parents and was sure that Mr. Babcock need not worry, since there was no problem that he (Hughes) couldn't handle. Mr. Babcock called in one of his assistants to look into the matter and get back to him in a day or so with more information.

Questions:

1. What do you think led up to the petitions signed by the parents?

2. Analyze Mr. Hughes' reaction(s) to Mr. Babcock's phone call.

CRITICAL INCIDENT

The faculty of the Organization and Management Department of a large state university decided to automate the preparation of student examinations in multiple-section classes. Mr. Pitts, an Assistant Professor, who also acted as a coordinator for these classes, was assigned the task of accomplishing this. Originally, Mrs. Smith, who had several years of secretarial experience, was selected to implement the program. She had quickly proved too technically and socially incompetent to perform the needed tasks, which demanded integration of the university's program and the faculty's examination procedure.

Somewhat in desperation, Mr. Pitts then chose Ms. Takacs, one of the younger and more capable secretaries, as her replacement. The system implementation was more than successful. Ms. Takacs, through taking several computer-science courses in the evening, had learned the intricacies of computer programming and managed to convert many of the heretofore different faculty tests into one form, such that all faculty members could readily use it.

At the end of the year, Mr. Pitts called Ms. Takacs to his office for her annual performance appraisal review. Ms. Takacs was of the opinion that her dual efforts as secretary and examination coordinator were worthy of a greater reward and told this to Mr. Pitts. His explanation was that due to her past raises as a secretary she was already approaching the pay scale of long-tenured secretaries and that a substantial increase would create dissension among these secretaries. Ms. Takacs refused the raise that Mr. Pitts awarded her, claiming that it was an insult.

While it was not stated in so many words, Mr. Pitts read this as a forewarning that she would probably resign. Knowing that this would affect the entire examination procedure, an event certain to dismay many of the faculty members, and also being aware that a substantial raise would most certainly cause disharmony in the office, he was faced with a dilemma.

Question:

What should he do to assure the continued success of the examination procedure and at the same time to maintain a reasonable level of harmony in the
office work force?

REFERENCES

1. Asch, S., "Forming Impressions of Persons," *Journal of Abnormal and Social Psychology,* 1946, **40,** pp. 258–290.

2. Sheldon, W., and S. Stevens, *The Varieties of Temperament: a Psychology of Constitutional Differences.* New York: Harper & Row Publishers, 1942.

3. Secord, P., and C. Backman, *Social Psychology.* New York: McGraw-Hill Book Co., 1964, pp. 22–24.

4. Bossoom, J., and A. Maslow, "Security of Judges as a Factor in Impressions of Warmth in Others," *Journal of Abnormal & Social Psychology,* 1965, **55,** pp. 147–148.

5. Siegel, J., "Machiavellianism, MBA's and Managers: Leadership Correlates and Socializational Effects," *Academy of Management Journal,* 1973, **16,** pp. 404–412.

6. Omwake, K., "The Relation Between Acceptance of Self and Acceptance of Others Shown by Three Personality Inventories," *Journal of Consulting Psychology,* 1954, **18,** pp. 443–446.

7. Zalkind, S., and T. Costello, "Perception: Implications for Administration," *Administrative Science Quarterly,* 1962, **7,** pp. 218–235.

8. Dearborn, D., and H. Simon, "Selective Perception," *Sociometry,* 1958, **21,** pp. 140–143.

9. Haire, M., "Role Perceptions in Labor-Management Relations: An Experimental Approach," *Industrial Labor Relations Review,* 1955, **8,** pp. 204–216.

10. Grove, B., and W. Kerr, "Specific Evidence on the Origin of Halo Effect in Measurement of Morale," *Journal of Social Psychology,* 1951, **34,** pp. 165–170.

11. Sears, R., "Experimental Studies of Perception. 1. Attribution of Traits," *Journal of Social Psychology,* 1936, **7,** pp. 151–163.

12. Luthans, F., *Organizational Behavior.* New York: McGraw-Hill Book Co., 1973, p. 362.

13. Hamner, C., "Reinforcement Theory and Contingency Management in Organizational Settings," in *Organizational Behavior & Management: A Con-*

tingency Approach. Tosi, H., and C. Hamner, (eds.). Chicago, St. Clair Press, 1974, p. 87.

14. Hill, W., *Learning: A Survey of Psychological Interpretations.* San Francisco: Chandler Publishing Co., 1963.

15. Skinner, B. F., *Walden Two.* New York: Macmillan Publishing Co., 1948.

16. Skinner, B. F., *Beyond Freedom and Dignity.* New York: Alfred A. Knopf, 1971.

17. Luthans, F., and R. Kreitner, *Organizational Behavior Modification.* Glenview, Ill.: Scott, Foresman & Co., 1975.

18. Adam, E., and Wm. Scott, "The Application of Behavioral Conditioning Procedures to the Problems of Quality Control," *Academy of Management Journal,* 1971, **14,** pp. 178–179.

19. Rachlin, H., *Modern Behaviorism.* New York: W. H. Freeman & Co., 1970.

20. Most of this discussion is taken from Bandura, A., *Principles of Behavior Modification.* New York: Holt, Rinehart & Winston, 1969. Hamner, C., "Reinforcement Theory and Contingency Management in Organizational Settings," in *Organizational Behavior and Management: A Contingency Approach.* Tosi, H., and C. Hamner, (eds.). Chicago: St. Clair Press, 1974, pp. 86–112.

21. Kendler, H., *Basic Psychology.* 2nd ed. New York: Appleton-Century Crofts, 1968, pp. 290–291.

22. Whyte, F., "Skinnerian Theory in Organizations," *Psychology Today,* 1972, **5**(11), p. 67 ff. Hinton, B., and J. Barrow, "The Supervisor's Reinforcing Behavior as a Function of Reinforcement Perceived," *Organizational Behavior & Human Performance,* 1975, **14,** pp. 123–143.

23. Behling, O., C. Schriesheim, and J. Tolliver, "Alternatives to Expectancy Theories of Work Motivation," *Decision Sciences,* 1975, **6,** pp. 449–461.

24. Bandura, A., *op. cit.*

25. Jablonsky, S., and R. DeVries, "Operant Conditioning Principles Extrapolated to the Theory of Management." *Organizational Behavior and Human Performance,* 1972, **7,** pp. 340–358. Yukl, G., and G. Latham, "Consequences of Reinforcement Schedules and Incentive Magnitudes for Employee Performance: Problems Encountered in an Industrial Setting," *Journal of Applied Psychology,* 1975, **60,** pp. 294–298. Kim, J., and C. Hamner, "Effect of Performance Feedback and Goal Setting on Productivity and Satisfaction in Organizational Settings," *Journal of Applied Psychology,* 1976, in press. For an excellent critique of behavioral modification approaches in applied settings, see Kazdin, A., "Methodological Assessment

Consideration in Evaluating Reinforcement Programs in Applied Settings," *Journal of Applied Behavioral Analysis,* 1973, **6,** pp. 517–531.

26. These are taken from Hamner, C., *op. cit.,* pp. 96–98.

27. Feeney, E. J., "At Emery Air Freight: Positive Reinforcement Boosts Performance," *Organizational Dynamics,* 1973, **1,** pp. 41–50.

28. Ruch, F., *Psychology and Life.* 6th ed. Chicago: Scott, Foresman, & Co., 1963, p. 354.

29. Bonner, H., *Psychology of Personality.* New York: Ronald Press, 1961, pp. 38–40.

30. Joe, V., "Review of the Internal–External Control Construct as a Personality Variable," *Psychological Reports,* 1971, **28,** pp. 619–640.

31. Sarason, I., R. Smith, and E. Diener, "Personality Research: Components of Variance Attributed to th Person and the Situation," *Journal of Personality and Social Psychology,* 1975, **32,** pp. 199–204.

32. Abegglen, J., "Personality Factors in Social Mobility: A Study of Occupationally Mobile Businessmen," *Genetic Psychology Monographs,* 1958, **58,** pp. 101–159.

*

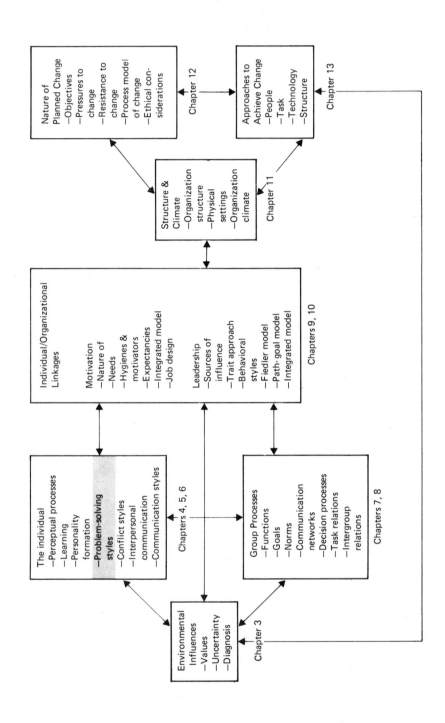

Nature of
Planned Change
—Objectives
—Pressures to
 change
—Resistance to
 change
—Process model
 of change
—Ethical con-
 siderations

Chapter 12

Approaches to
Achieve Change
—People
—Task
—Technology
—Structure

Chapter 13

Structure &
Climate
—Organization
 structure
—Physical
 settings
—Organization
 climate

Chapter 11

Individual/Organizational
Linkages

Motivation
—Nature of
—Needs
—Hygienes &
 motivators
—Expectancies
—Integrated model
—Job design

Leadership
—Sources of
 influence
—Trait approach
—Behavioral
 styles
—Fiedler model
—Path-goal model
—Integrated model

Chapters 9, 10

The individual
—Perceptual processes
—Learning
—Personality
 formation
—Problem-solving
 styles
—Conflict styles
—Interpersonal
 communication
—Communication styles

Chapters 4, 5, 6

Group Processes
—Functions
—Goals
—Norms
—Communication
 networks
—Decision processes
—Task relations
—Intergroup
 relations

Chapters 7, 8

Environmental
Influences
—Values
—Uncertainty
—Diagnosis

Chapter 3

5
INDIVIDUAL
STYLES:
PROBLEM-SOLVING

Donald C. Burnham is a shy executive who shuns the spotlight, keeps his distance from the press, and nurses a long glass of tomato juice at cocktail parties . . . Robert E. Kirby . . . not only will take a hard drink, he'll also take your picture, join a jazz band for a few riffs, and maybe even do a few magic tricks. The two men do, however, have one thing in common: both have held the chief executive-ship of Westinghouse Electric Corporation . . . Whereas Burnham [1963 through 1974] kept in touch with Westinghouse's multifarious activities through a staff of specialists, . . . Kirby [as of 1975] has formed an operations committee of seven members, all of whom are encouraged to render advice on any or all segments of the company. Then, too, Burnham used his staff as a screen between himself and his line managers. Kirby prefers face-to-face contact. [1, p. 34]

What would the *ideal* organization look like? How would you describe a day in your life three years from now? How do you go about making important decisions? What are your typical ways of responding when you disagree with others? How willing are you to communicate openly with others? Would you expect individuals you know well to answer these questions differently from the way you do yourself? These questions provide the primary thrust of this and the following chapter.

The subsequent chapters will explore individual problem-solving, conflict, and communication styles. Our analyses make no assumptions that there is only one ideal type of style within each of the domains (i.e., problem-solving, conflict, and communication), nor that a single individual can utilize only one style within each domain. Either consciously or subconsciously, individuals may be capable of exercising somewhat different styles to cope with different situational requirements and personal needs. However, individuals often have a natural tendency or predisposition to use one style more than the others within each domain.

Our use of the word "style" is captured in the following two phrases from Webster: ". . . a manner or method of acting or performing . . ."; and ". . . the peculiarly distinctive technique or methods characteristic of or identified with a particular individual, usually in the performance of a particular activity . . ."

While personality is likely to have a strong influence on the use of particular problem-solving styles, conflict styles, or communication styles, the differences in individual style should not be interpreted as synonymous with differences in personality. This chapter, which selectively draws upon a very limited body of personality theory, makes no attempt to discuss the numerous perspectives or conflicting positions exisitng within the field of personality theory. Our use of personality theory is consistent with the properties and definition of personality presented in the last chapter. Personality was defined as how a person affects others, how she or he understands and views oneself, and the person's pattern of inner and outer measurable traits. The selective application of personality theory is based on the conclusion ". . . no substantive definition of personality can be applied with any generality . . ." and the recommendations that personality should be "defined by the particular empirical concepts which are a part of the theory of personality employed by the observer." [2, p. 9] Thus, it is recognized that there are personality concepts and theories different from the ones we employ, which could also be used to examine some of the issues and questions of concern in this chapter.

With this brief outline of the nature and limitations of this and the following chapter, we can set forth the following major objectives of the chapter:

1. To present and explain a model for differentiating problem-solving styles of individuals;

2. To develop an understanding of some contingencies under which certain problem-solving styles are likely to be more effective for individual and organizational performance;

3. To further develop the ability to diagnose and recognize one's own and others' problem-solving styles; and

4. To increase empathy and understanding of individual differences.

UNDERLYING PERSONALITY THEORY

The theoretical and empirical work that serves as the primary basis for this discussion of problem-solving styles was undertaken by Carl Jung. [3] We draw primarily upon this framework for the orientation ("attitudes") of personality, including extroversion or introversion and the four basic psychological functions, which include thinking, feeling, sensing, and intuiting. Before discussing several of the specific characteristics of Jung's personality theory, it should be useful to mention the major themes in his framework. First, Jung maintained that the individual's behavior is influenced by both his history or past, as well as by his goals and aspirations for the future. The individual is not simply a "slave" to the past. Rather, the individual can be proactive in selecting goals and influencing one's own destiny. Secondly, there is the possibility for constant and creative development of the individual. Jung's personality theory assumes an optimistic versus pessimistic view of the individual and a personal potential for growth and change. Thirdly, Jung suggests an open-systems view of personality. Personality is said to consist of a number of differentiated but interacting subsystems. The open-systems view of personality leads to at least two important considerations. The subsystems within the personality can be receptive to inputs and exchanges between each other. Also, the personality as a whole, or one of its subsystems, can change as a result of inputs and interactions with the external environment, particularly influences from other individuals. The only subsystems within Jung's personality theory that we will consider include the ego, personal unconscious, basic attitudes (extroversion–introversion), and the psychological functions (thinking, feeling, sensing, and intuiting).

The *ego* refers to the conscious mind. It consists of feelings, thoughts, perceptions, and memories of which we are aware and which we can articulate to ourselves and others. The *personal unconscious* includes: experiences and wishes which have been repressed (i.e., suppressed below the level of consciousness); feelings and thoughts that lie below conscious awareness (but have never gone through the process of repression); and feelings and thoughts that have *not yet* reached consciousness but that provide the basis for certain forms of future consciousness, such as creativity. The personal unconsciousness is often first expressed in the form of dreams and fantasies, and it can change its "contents" in coordination with the conscious mind. [4] The personal unconscious and conscious are often in a compensatory relationship to one another. The principle of compensation is a key element in Jung's personality theory. Jung contends that, for the normal personality, one subsystem may compensate for the weakness of another subsystem. A period of intense extroverted behavior may be followed by a period of introverted behavior. A person who is characterized by the psychological functions of thinking and feeling in the conscious mind, may emphasize the intuitive and sensation psychological functions in the unconscious mind. The principle of compensation serves as a means of balancing contrasting types, thus preventing the personality from becoming neurotically unbalanced. [5]

PURE TYPES

Attitude Types

According to Jungian theory, the two attitude-types or orientations of the personality are extroversion and introversion. While these are opposing orientations, they are both present in one's personality. One of them is usually dominant and exists in the conscious mind, while the other is subordinate and exists in the unconscious. Jung refers to extroversion and introversion as "attitudes" because they are potentially variable within an individual; i.e., they can change over one's lifetime. The introvert attitude is "normally character-ized by a hesitant, reflective, retiring nature that keeps to itself, shrinks from objects, is always slightly on the defensive, and prefers to hide behind mistrust-ful scrutiny." On the other hand, the extrovert is "normally characterized by an outgoing, candid, and accommodating nature that adapts itself easily to a given situation, quickly forms attachments, and, setting aside any possible misgivings, will often venture forth with careless confidence into unknown situations." [6] In terms of problem-solving styles, an introverted individual often likes "quiet for concentration, uninterrupted work on one subject, [has] some problems communicating (with others), and work[s] contentedly alone." On the other hand, "extroverts like variety and action, are impatient with long, slow jobs, usually communicate well, like to have people around, and are good at greeting people." [7] Most of us can probably think of individuals that tend to characterize the extremes of introversion and extroversion. But, as sug-gested by Fig. 5–1, individuals can vary in the degree to which they are extro-verted, introverted, or relatively balanced between the extremes. You might want to take a moment to reread the descriptions of the extrovert and introvert types, and think about where you might fit on the continuum in Fig. 5–1 with respect to your conscious mind. Since there are obvious problems of distor-tion, as discussed in the previous chapter, in any assessment process which relies on perception and especially on self-perception, it might be useful to also ask individuals who know you well how they perceive you in terms of the continuum in Fig. 5–1. In sum, the extreme extrovert and introvert types are so contrasting that their differences become obvious to almost everyone, once they are pointed out. [8]

Extrovert and introvert types are widely distributed among the popula-tion within such categories as high and low education levels, women and men, and a variety of occupational classifications. As might be expected, extroverts seem to be disproportionately represented in the managerial occupation. Some research even suggests that extroversion is important to managerial success. [9] Since the manager's role often involves identifying and solving problems with and through other individuals, a certain degree of extroversion is likely to be functional. But an extremely extroverted attitude can result in the individual literally sacrificing oneself to external conditions and demands. The manager who becomes totally immersed in the job at the cost of all other concerns might be one example of this. The extreme extrovert's limitation is

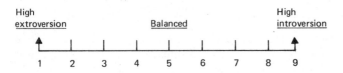

Figure 5–1 Continuum of Attitude-Types

one of getting "sucked" into external objects or demands and completely losing himself or herself in them. On the other hand, the introvert tends to interject a *subjective* view between his perception of external demands and factors, and his decisions. As a consequence, the introvert may choose courses of action that don't as readily fit the external situation. There tends to be more concern with personal factors in relation to external factors. As Jung is quick to emphasize, when external understanding is overvalued, we are actually repressing the importance of the subjective or personal factor, which simply means a denial of ourselves. Perception and cognition (i.e., knowledge and understanding) are not simply externally determined, but are also subjectively determined and conditioned. The world exists not merely in itself, but also as it appears to us. [10]

While extroversion and introversion are a direct basis for differentiating problem-solving styles, they can operate indirectly through the four psychological functions as well. Moreover, they operate differently between the conscious and unconscious mind. Because of the limited objectives of this chapter, our primary orientation in discussing the four psychological functions will be in terms of the conscious mind and the extroverted attitude.

Psychological Functions

As mentioned previously, Jung has identified four psychological functions, including thinking, feeling, sensation, and intuition. The thinking and feeling functions represent the two opposite types of basis upon which an individual may prefer to operate in making decisions and arriving at judgments. As with introversion–extroversion, the feeling–thinking functions are paired opposites, which should be thought of as extreme ends of a continuum, as shown in Fig. 5–2. Feeling and thinking represent the extremes of individual decision-making orientations for making evaluations and judgments about external "facts" and the "fact world."

The psychological functions of sensation and intuition are paired opposites as well, and may also be thought of as extreme ends of a continuum, as shown in Fig. 5–3. Sensation and intuition represent the extreme orientations to perceptions that may be preferred by individuals. As used here, perception refers to the process of "information" gathering, i.e., the ways by which we can become aware of people, things, situations, or ideas.

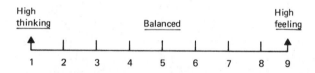

Figure 5–2 Continuum of Individual Decision-Making Orientations

Figure 5–3 Continuum of Individual Perceptual Orientations

According to Jung, only *one* of the four functions is dominant in each individual. The dominant function is normally backed up by only *one* of the functions from the other set of paired opposites. For example, the thinking function may be supported by the sensation function, or sensation may be supported by thinking. These two combinations are regarded as most characteristic of modern man in Western industrialized societies. As a consequence, feeling and intuition are the functions which are considered most likely to be disregarded, undeveloped, or repressed. We will first consider each of the four psychological functions as a dominate type, and then consider the two perceptual orientations (sensation and intuition) in combination with the two decision-making orientations (thinking and feeling).

Feeling-Thinking Orientations

Feeling types are "... aware of other people and their feelings, like harmony, need occasional praise, dislike telling people unpleasant things, tend to be sympathetic, and relate well to most people." [11] Feeling types are likely to engage in a high degree of conformity, and accommodate themselves to other individuals. This type of individual may tend to make decisions that are likely to result in approval from others (peers, subordinates, and superiors). There may also be a strong tendency to avoid problems that are likely to result in disagreements. When avoidance or smoothing of differences is not possible, the feeling type is more prone to change his or her position to one more acceptable by others. The establishment and maintenance of friendly relations may even supersede, and possibly interfere with, a concern for achievement, effectiveness, and decisions. [12] A feeling-type manager may have an extremely difficult time suspending or discharging a subordinate for inadequate performance that is widely recognized by others, including the poor performer's own peers. In sum, the feeling type is likely to emphasize affective and personal processes in decision-making.

At the other extreme, *thinking* types are "... unemotional and uninterested in peoples' feelings, like analysis and putting things into logical order, are able to reprimand people or fire them when necessary, may seem hardhearted, and tend to relate well only to other thinking types." [13] The activities and decisions of this individual are usually controlled by intellectual processes. These intellectual processes are based upon external data and/or generally acceptable ideas and values. There tends to be a desire to fit problems and their solutions into standardized formulas. The application of external data and impersonal formulas to decision situations may result in the loss of all personal considerations, even when they affect the decision-maker's own welfare. For the sake of some goal, the decision-maker may neglect health, finances, family, or other interests that others would normally regard as important. The thinking function, when dominant, is often positive and productive because it results in the discovery of new facts, new concepts, or new models, which are based upon seemingly unrelated empirical data. In terms of a problem-solving style, thinking types are likely to:

a) Make a plan and look for a method to solve the problem;

b) Be extremely conscious and concerned with the approach they take to a problem;

c) Carefully define the specific constraints in the problem;

d) Proceed by increasingly refining their analysis; and or

e) Obtain and search for additional information in a very orderly manner. [14]

There is considerable similarity between the thinking type, the major elements in the scientific method, and what our society often characterizes as rational problem-solving. Our educational institutions have also probably been most concerned with developing the thinking type of function. While the elements of this type are obviously crucial to any advanced industrialized society, Jung's concern and ours is with the too frequent one-dimensional emphasis on the assumed functional nature of thinking versus feeling.

A useful summary of the difference between the thinking and feeling types has been expressed this way:

> A thinking individual is the type who relies primarily on the cognitive process. His evaluations tend to run along the lines of abstract true/false judgments and are based on formal systems of reasoning. A preference for feeling, on the other hand, implies the type of individual who relies primarily on affective processes. His evaluations tend to run along personalistic lines of good/bad, pleasant/ unpleasant, and like/dislike. Thinking types systematize; feeling types take moral stands and are interested and concerned with moral judgments. [15, pp. 447–478]

Sensation-Intuition Orientations

In terms of our continuum of individual perceptual orientations (see Fig. 5–3), the sensation-type of individuals ". . . dislike new problems unless there are standard ways to solve them, like an established routine, must usually work all the way through to reach a conclusion, show patience with routine details, and tend to be good at precise work." [16] The sensation type usually dislikes coping with unstructured problems, which contain considerable uncertainty.

In most cases, unstructured problems require the individual to exercise some degree of judgment in deciding upon a course of action and how to implement it. In the popular vernacular, sensation types are satisfied and are good performers as "detail" persons or "bureaucrats." As used here, bureaucrat refers to an individual whose organizational life primarily revolves around the implementation and use of rules, regulations, and standard operating procedures. It is not unusual to find lower-level organizational jobs designed like this. Sensation types may adequately fill such jobs because they require a minimal need to exercise discretion. Discretion refers to the amount of uncertainty and the level of responsibility in a job (see Chapter 3 for a discussion of uncertainty). [17]

A sensation type may well experience considerable anxiety due to the uncertainties that are inherent in making decisions in "hazy" areas. The mental set of the sensation type is highly oriented to realism, external facts, and concrete experiences. Along with the love of concrete or physical reality, this type of person is not inclined toward personal reflection and introspection into his or her experiences or self.

The type of job (routine and structured) enjoyed and performed well by a sensation type is likely to be disliked and poorly performed by an intuitive type. An *intuitive* types is one who ". . . likes solving new problems, dislikes doing the same things over and over again, jumps to conclusions, is impatient with routine details, and dislikes taking time for precision." [18] Whereas the sensation type tends to perceive the external environment in terms of details and parts, the intuitive type tends to perceive the whole or totality of the external environment, as it is and as it might change. In terms of a problem-solving style, intuitives tend to:

a) Keep the "total" or overall problem continuously in mind as the problem-solving process develops;

b) As the process unfolds, show a tendency, willingness, and openness to continuously redefine the problem;

c) Rely on hunches and unverbalized cues;

d) Almost simultaneously consider a variety of alternatives and options; and/or

f) Jump around or back and forth in the elements or steps in the problem-solving process. (After presumably defining a problem, identifying alternatives to the problem, and evaluating consequences of each alternative, the intuitive may suddenly jump back to a reassessment as to whether the "true" problem has even been identified.)

e) Very quickly consider and discard alternatives. [19]

Unlike the sensation type, the intuitive is suffocated by stable conditions and seeks out and creates new possibilities. Intuitives may often be found among business tycoons, politicians, speculators, entrepreneurs, stockbrokers, and the like. This type can be extremely valuable to the economy and society by providing a service as initiators and promoters of new enterprises, services, concepts, and other innovations in both the public and private sectors. If the intuitive is oriented more to people than tangible things, he or she may be exceptionally good at diagnosing the abilities and potential of other individuals. This diagnostic capacity may be combined with a talent for anything new. [20] The discussion of problem-solving styles to this point has focused on each of four pure and dominant psychological functions for differentiating individuals. As suggested earlier, each dominant type is likely to be supplemented and backed up by one of the other paired opposite types. Thus, the analysis for differentiating individual problem-solving styles needs to be carried one step further. This will be accomplished by considering the four major composite styles that might be derived when combing the two decision-making orientations with the two perceptual orientations.

COMPOSITE MODEL

Figure 5–4 presents a simplified composite model of individual problem-solving styles, which can be derived from the decision-making orientations of thinking and feeling and the perceptual orientations of sensation and intuition.

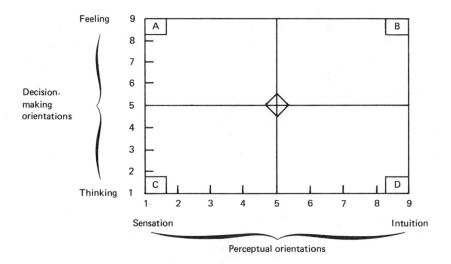

Figure 5–4   Composite Model of Individual Problem-Solving Styles

Since we have already presented the nature of the four psychological functions when each is dominant in an extroverted individual, the following will briefly review the four "pure" combined types as shown in Fig. 5–4. Following the explanation of each combined type, a profile of a specific individual that seems to approximate the attributes of the combined type is presented. Since the classification of these individuals is based on secondary data, the reader should be more concerned with the behaviors described than with whether the specific individuals are truly of a particular composite type.

Sensation–Feeling Type

Individuals in cell A of Fig. 5–4 rely primarily on sensing for purposes of perception, and on feeling for purposes of decision-making. These individuals are mainly interested in facts that can be collected and verified directly by the senses. They approach these facts with personal and human concern because they are more interested in facts about people than about things. When asked to write a paragraph or two as to what they perceive as the ideal organization, these individuals often describe an organization with a well-defined hierarchy and a set of rules that exist for the benefit of members and society. The organization should also satisfy member needs and enable them to openly communicate with one another. [21]

Steward Rowlings Mott, multimillionaire liberal and philanthropist, seems to manifest a number of the attributes of the sensation–feeling type. [22] Stewart Mott's fortune is derived from his father, who was one of the biggest stockholders of General Motors. Through 1974, Stewart Mott's annual income has ranged between $950,000 to $1.5 million. He greets individuals with a friendly and open smile and is quite willing to discuss any aspect of his life in an open and candid manner. His sixteenth story penthouse on New York's Park Avenue serves as his office and home. Mott's main office, his bedroom, is filled with piles of papers scattered around the room in an *organized* manner. He says "I don't know how to throw things out—people, old newspapers, or cigarette boxes." He is fascinated by details. The long hours he works are a consequence of his insistence on being informed on all the major and many of the minor activities of the organizations he helps support. Thus, he constantly reviews numerous reports and memoranda.

Since Mott contends that two major problems facing the world are population control and arms control, much of the approximate $6 million he has donated between 1964 and 1974 has gone to charitable and political groups concerned with these two causes. Insight into his "feeling" self was developed around 1960, when after psychoanalysis, he came to realize how supersensitive he was to possible rejection by his parents and girl friends.

While Mott is an activist for people causes, he is not interested in taking the time for abstract reflection or considering global philosophies. Mott says: "I'm no ideologue. I feel uncomfortable when asked to explain in some cogent, complete, lucid way a blueprint of my political perceptions. I believe in chipping away at the defects in the present system without attempting to change the way it fundamentally works."

Intuition–Feeling Type

Individuals in cell B of Fig. 5–4 rely primarily on intuition for purposes of perception, and feeling for purposes of decision-making. These individuals are predisposed to focus upon possibilities such as new projects, new approaches, new "truths," events which could happen, and the like. They approach these possibilities in terms of meeting or serving the personal and social needs of people in general. Intuitive–feeling types tend to avoid specifics and focus on broad themes that revolve around the human purposes of organizations, such as serving mankind or the organization's clientele. The ideal organization for these individuals tends to be described as one which is decentralized, has flexible and loosely defined lines of authority, no strong or central leaders, and few required rules and standard operating procedures. Intuitive–feeling types emphasize long-term goals and prefer organizations that are flexible and adaptive. [23]

Our profile of the intuitive–feeling type is Steve Carmichael, a pseudonym for a project manager with nine subordinates who worked for a city Neighborhood Youth Corps that was federally funded by the Office of Economic Opportunity. The following description is from Studs Terkel's book, entitled *Working.* [24] At the time of the interview, he was twenty-five years old, married, and had one child. The following are excerpts in Steve's own words.

> They say I'm unrealistic. One of the fellas that works with me said, "It's a dream to believe this program will take sixteen-, seventeen-year-old dropouts and make something of their lives." This may well be true, but if I'm going to think that I can't believe my job has any worth . . . We've got five or six young people who are burning to get into an automotive training program. Everybody says, "It takes signatures, it takes time." I follow up on these things because everybody else seems to forget there are people waiting. So I'll get that phone call, do some digging, find out nothing's happened, report that to my boss, and call back and make my apologies . . . The most frustrating thing for me is to know that what I'm doing does not have a positive impact on others. I don't see this work as meaning anything. I now treat my job disdainfully . . .

Sensation–Thinking Type

In cell C of Fig. 5–4, there is the sensation-plus-thinking type. These individuals emphasize and focus on external factual details and specifics of a problem. The facts of a problem are often analyzed through a step-by-step logical process of reasoning from cause to effect. Their problem-solving styles tends to be practical and matter-of-fact. When asked to describe their ideal organization, these individuals often describe an extreme form of bureaucracy. This organization is characterized by such attributes as: extensive use of rules and regulations; well-defined or prescribed positions, (i.e., the do's and dont's of each position are specific, and written down); technical ability is regarded as the primary if not the only basis for judging individuals; a well-defined organizational hierarchy; emphasis on high control, specificity, and certainty; and concern with realistic, limited, and short-term goals. [25]

While apparently not an extreme sensation–thinking type, John deButts, the chairman of the board of the American Telephone and Telegraph Company, seemed to reveal attributes of this type in an interview published in the *Harvard Business Review*. [26] To judge by this interview, he appears to focus on short-term problems, using standard operating procedures to solve problems, and keeping the system in control. To paraphrase deButts,

> the quality of your decisions depends on the quality of your input, on how unvarnished your information is after it has passed up the chain of command. And I do get information of that quality—the constant contacts I have with the key people at AT & T and the top people of our subsidiaries give me that quality. The organizational structure we have here helps provide quality information, too . . . Every other week, I meet with all the officers of AT & T; and practically every month I meet with all the presidents of our subsidiaries. In between, I have many conversations with individuals in these groups. These contacts give me a lot of my input.

In response to the question of whether he ever finds himself unprepared or surprised by something, deButts stated

> Seldom is there a significant surprise. Naturally, details come up with which I am not familiar. That's why we have discussions . . . The key, for me, has been to set up my broad objectives and then deal with the tasks within that framework . . .

In response to the question of how he spends his day, deButts replied:

> Usually, before I arrive at the office, I try to get into my mind the things I want to accomplish that day. I also jot down notes to myself. Today, for example, I've got several things I need to talk to people about. Then I'll try to take care of the mail. Incidentally, I read every letter that's addressed to me, either by name or by title . . . Nobody signs my name but me. I personally sign the reply on every letter that's addressed to me. Many answers are prepared for me, of course. I usually check the reply, and I frequently change it . . .

Intuition–Thinking Type

The last pure composite type is shown in cell D of Fig. 5–4. Intuitive–thinking individuals tend to focus on possibilities but approach them through impersonal analysis. Rather than dealing with the human element, they consider possibilities that are more often theoretical or technical. They are likely to enjoy positions that are ill-defined and require abstract skills (e.g., long-range planning, marketing research, and searching for new goals). The ideal organization for these individuals is one that is impersonal and conceptual. The goals of the organization should be consistent with environmental needs (such as pure air, clear water, and equal opportunity) and the needs of organizational members. However, these issues are considered in an abstract and impersonal frame of reference. In sum, intuitive–thinker people mention fuzzy, ill-defined, macro or global issues and problems. [27]

Our profile of the intuitive–thinking type is Irving Shapiro who, at the age of fifty-seven, became the chairman of the board and chief executive officer of E. I. duPont de Nemours and Company in 1974. The description of Shapiro is extracted from an article in *Fortune* magazine. [28] Shapiro is regarded by others in duPont as well suited to dealing with the wide-ranging changes affecting duPont and all other multinational corporations. It is said that no one else in duPont's top management has his ability to analyze risks, comprehend complex issues of law and politics, negotiate, and devise solutions that the company—and those watching it—can accept. He holds strong opinions but listens carefully to others. He is cautious but willing, if the odds are right, to take big risks. Bill McCoy, who chose Shapiro as his successor, says that he learns quickly how to make decisions.

Prior to joining duPont, Shapiro went to work at the Office of Price Administration (OPA) at the start of World War II. While there, he helped set up rationing systems for sugar, automobiles, and bicycles. After a while, he became bored with OPA and took a job in the Criminal Division of the Justice Department. Shapiro soon had a reputation as an outstanding writer of briefs, with an ability to grasp the critical issues in a case, clarify them, and argue in support of the government's position. The Justice Department at that time was divided into two factions and both considered him a member—he was smart enough to debate the intellectuals and practical enough to satisfy the activists. After joining duPont in 1951, Shapiro soon became known as the "can-do" lawyer. Instead of putting up legal roadblocks, he suggested how duPont management could accomplish their objectives legally. Shapiro's associates say that one of his greatest gifts is his ability to put complex and often emotional issues into simple, practical terms. One executive tells about a personal problem he was unable to resolve. He phoned Shapiro at home one afternoon and was immediately invited over for a drink. The executive said he laid out three alternatives and after talking for only fifteen minutes the best alternative became obvious.

OVERVIEW OF MODEL

The four pure, composite problem-solving styles of individuals represent only one of a number of useful models and sets of concepts that have been developed in this area. While the validity and long-term utility of this model for considering differences in individual problem-solving styles within organizations has not been firmly established, the research previously cited and our own applied research with about 1,000 college students and about 200 managers in various executive-development programs suggests it is worthy of recognition, discussion, and further research. In addition, the model presented is consistent with a number of key assumptions and findings of other models of individual decision-making. Among these assumptions and findings are:

1. Individual differences in judgments (decisions) reflect the characteristic styles in which individuals perceive, construe, and organize their environment;

2. These individual differences are reflected in differences in the weighting and combining of stimuli in the situation;

3. Judgmental differences are themselves mediated (intervened) by, and functionally related to, a wide variety of characteristics of individuals (which were not investigated in our model of problem-solving styles), such as intelligence and values; and

4. The dimensions of the stimuli in the environment, as well as the individual, need to be assessed. [29, p. 137]

SUMMARY

While we have discussed four pure, composite problem-solving styles, there is no intent to suggest that every individual can be characterized as one of the four pure types. An individual could exist any place within the grid shown in Fig. 5–4. According to Jung, the developing individual tends to move toward a balance and integration of the four psychological functions. This balance would exist in the center of Fig. 5–4. Since the individual is so rich in variety and complex in nature, we need to be especially cautious in pigeon-holing individuals and inferring that they cannot adapt to or learn from situations that do not "fit" their style. We hope this chapter has served to foster an empathy and understanding of the differences between individuals; facilitate self-insight as to your characteristic style and how it might influence your actions and reactions to certain problems, particularly in group problem-solving situations; and provide a framework for possible forms of desired individual growth and development. While there is no assumption that one composite style is inherently better than another, the requirements of certain positions or roles in an organization may be more natural to one style than another.

Discussion Questions

1. How would you characterize yourself in terms of the various problem-solving styles presented? What is the basis for your conclusions?

2. How would you characterize the problem-solving style of an individual who has served as your supervisor or manager? What is the basis for your conclusions?

3. How important do you think it is that a manager be extroverted? Are some management positions more likely to require extroversion than others?

4. Do you think an individual with a high feeling orientation can be effective and successful in an organization? Explain.

5. Should there be an attempt to select people for positions on the basis of their problem-solving styles? What virtues and problems might there be in such an attempt?

CRITICAL INCIDENT

John Jones had been made supervisor of a production line at Hercules Manufacturing, Inc. He was responsible for keeping the production line operating effectively and efficiently. Jones supervised five foremen who, in turn, had fifty assembly-line workers reporting to them. He felt his job was to maintain the assembly line at 80 units of output per hour.

Prior to Jones' being appointed supervisor (three months earlier), the production line was losing 100 minutes of production per day. There were a variety of causes that seemed to be contributing to this production loss—which amounted to over 20 percent of the daily production schedule. Jones tried to correct this problem through a number of steps, such as discharging several workers and keeping the main production line going even when some feeder lines broke down.

The production-line workers became increasingly disgruntled over these and other steps that had been taken. The workers claimed that Jones was using "speed up" tactics, and four of the workers filed a formal grievance one week ago against Jones. Many workers are also increasingly making verbal protests to their foremen. The plant manager, Bob Smith, became aware of the situation when the grievance was filed. After some checking, Smith is convinced that the situation is potentially explosive.

Questions:

1. How would Smith likely proceed if he has a strong sensation–thinking problem-solving style?

2. How would Smith likely proceed if he has a strong intuitive–feeling problem-solving style?

3. How would Smith likely proceed if he has a strong sensation–feeling problem-solving style?

4. How would Smith likely proceed if he has a strong intuitive–thinking style?

REFERENCES

1. Hoffman, G., "The Baker Scholar at Westinghouse," *MBA,* 1975, **9,** pp. 34–40.

2. Hall, C. S., and G. Lindzey, *Theories of Personality.* 2nd ed. New York: John Wiley & Sons, 1970, pp. 78–116.

3. Jung, C. G., *Collected Works* (esp. Vols. 7, 8, 9, Part I). H. Read, M. Fordham, and G. Adler (eds.). Princeton, Princeton University Press, 1953.

4. Campbell, J. (ed.), *The Portable Jung.* New York: Viking Press, 1971, pp. 70–74.

5. Hall, C. S., and G. Lindzey, *op. cit.,* pp. 90–91.

6. Wehr, G., *Portrait of Jung: An Illustrated Biography.* New York: Herder & Herder, 1971, pp. 64–65.

7. Myers, I. B., and K. C. Briggs, *Myers-Briggs Type Indicator.* Princeton: Educational Testing Service.

8. Campbell, J. (ed.), *op. cit.,* p. 179.

9. Harrel, T. W., *Managers' Performance and Personality.* Cincinnati: South-Western, 1961.

10. Campbell, J., *op. cit.,* p. 130.

11. Briggs, D. C., and I. B. Myers, *op. cit.*

12. Boyatzis, R. E., "The Need for Close Relationships and the Manager's Job" in *Organizational Psychology: A Book of Readings.* 2nd ed. Kolb, D. A., I. M. Rubin, and J. C. McIntyre, (eds.). Englewood Cliffs, N.J.: Prentice-Hall, 1974, pp. 183–187.

13. Myers, I. B., and K. C. Briggs, *op. cit.*

14. McKenney, J. L., and G. W. Keen, "How Managers' Minds Work," *Harvard Business Review.* 1974, **52,** pp. 79–90.

15. Mason, R. O., and I. I. Mitroff, "A Program of Research on Management Information Systems," *Management Science,* 1973, **19,** pp. 475–487.

16. Myers, I. B., and K. C. Briggs, *op. cit.*

17. Jacques, E., *Equitable Payment.* London: Heineman Educational Books, 1961.

18. Myers, I. B., and K. C. Briggs, *op. cit.*

19. McKinney, J. C., and G. W. Ken, *op. cit.*

20. Campbell, J. C. *op. cit.,* p. 224.

21. Kilmann, R. H., and W. W. McKelvey, "Organization Design: A Participative Multivariate Approach," *Administrative Science Quarterly,* March, 1975. *Also see:* Mitroff, I., and R. H. Kilmann, "On the Importance of Qualitative Analysis in Management Science: The Influence of Personality Variables on Organizational Decision-Making," working paper, Graduate School of Business, University of Pittsburgh, 1974. Mitroff, I. I., and R. H. Kilmann, "On Evaluating Scientific Research: The Contribution of the Psychology of Science," working paper, Graduate School of Business, University of Pittsburgh, 1975.

22. Ross, I., "The View From Stewart Mott's Penthouse," *Fortune,* 1974, **89,** pp. 134–133.

23. Kilmann, R. H., and W. W. McKelvey, *op. cit.*

24. Terkel, S., *Working.* New York: Pantheon Books, 1974, pp. 341–343.

25. Kilmann, R. H., and W. W. McKelvey, *op. cit.*

26. "An Interview: The Management Style of John deButts," *Harvard Business Review,* 1974, **52,** pp. 34–42+.

27. Kilmann, R. H., and W. W. McKelvey, *op. cit.*

28. Vanderwicken, P., "Irving Shapiro Takes Charge at duPont," *Fortune,* 1974, **89,** pp. 79–81+.

29. Wiggins, N., "Individual Differences in Human Judgments: A Multivariate Approach," in *Human Judgment and Social Interaction.* Rapport, L., and D. A. Summer. New York: Holt, Rinehart & Winston, 1973. *Also see:* Taylor, R. N., and M. A. Dunnette, "Influence of Dogmatism, Risk-Taking Propensity, and Intelligence on Decision-Making Strategies for a Sample of Industrial Managers," *Journal of Applied Psychology,* 1974, **59,** pp. 420–423.

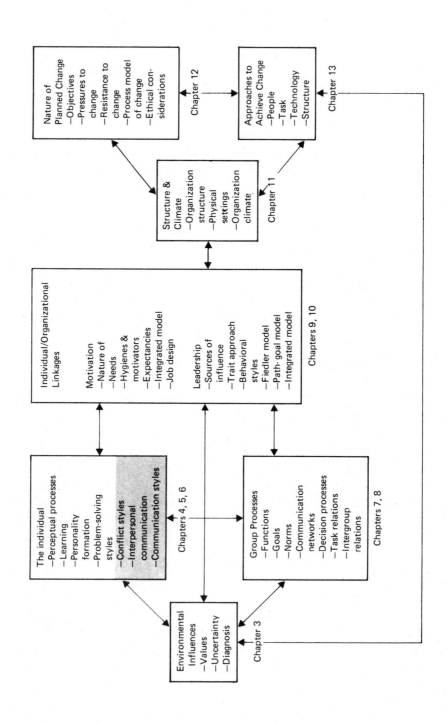

6
INDIVIDUAL STYLES: CONFLICT AND COMMUNICATION

This chapter further develops our discussion of individual styles into two additional domains—conflict and communication. The general objectives for this chapter are similar to those of the previous chapter. The key difference is that the areas of application are to conflict and communication styles of individuals. Accordingly, the major objectives of this chapter are:

1. To present and explain models for differentiating conflict and communication styles of individuals;

2. To develop an understanding of some contingencies under which certain conflict and communication styles are likely to be more effective for individual and organizational performance;

3. To further develop the ability to diagnose and recognize one's own and others' conflict and communication styles; and

4. To increase empathy and understanding of individual difference.

Relative to problem-solving styles, the conflict and communication styles to be discussed can be more readily developed through training as personal skills, which can be applied according to the contingencies in the situation. But even with these two sets of styles, individuals are often predisposed to approach interpersonal conflicts and communication with particular orientations and in predictable ways.

CONFLICT

In many chapters of this book, we discuss concepts, models, and research findings that are directly or indirectly related to conflict. Thus, our concern here is with the following limited objectives:

1. To explain the nature of and perspectives for discussing conflict;

2. To identify and explain five interpersonal conflict-handling styles;

3. To assess the implications for individual effectiveness of these conflict-handling styles; and

4. To suggest some contingencies that might influence the relative effectiveness of the alternative conflict-handling styles.

Nature

Conflict has been defined as referring ". . . to all kinds of opposition or antagonistic interaction." [1, p. 23] This definition of conflict is different from both competition and cooperation.[2] Competition denotes a striving for the same object, position, prize, etc., usually in accordance with certain fixed rules. Thus, there can be conflict that does not involve competition, competition that does not involve conflict, and overlap between the two such that they can't be distinguished from one another. Let's consider a couple of examples. Two departments can compete for the company's annual safety award without being opposed to each other or engaging in antagonistic interaction. Two individuals may argue and intensely dislike each other simply because of attitudinal differences, without necessarily competing for the same object, position, or prize.

The relationship between conflict and cooperation also needs clarification because sometimes these two concepts are viewed as opposite ends of the same continuum. Cooperation can be defined as acting or working together with another or others for a common goal. Thus, two individuals can simultaneously cooperate and engage in conflict. They may both have a goal of solving a common problem and be committed to working together on the problem but be in opposition to one another over the means of solving it. Or two individuals may be uncooperative and engaged in conflict.

There is no single definition that captures the essence of how we want to discuss the nature of conflict. However, Filley has nicely summarized the characteristics of a conflict situation, which is consistent with our perspective. Accordingly, we paraphrase his identification of the characteristics of a conflict situation as follows:

1. At least two individuals or groups are engaged in some kind of interaction (e.g., verbal, nonverbal, written, etc.).

2. Mutually exclusive goals or means actually exist, or are perceived to exist, between the involved individuals or groups.

3. Interaction often involves behavior designed to change, reduce, suppress, or defeat the other individual(s) or group(s) to attain one's own interests. This can involve a wide range of tactics and behaviors.

4. The individuals or groups face each other with at least some forms of mutually opposing actions and counteractions.[3]

Perspectives

With this explanation of the characteristics of conflict, competition, and cooperation, we might consider some perspectives taken toward social conflict. These perspectives can be identified in posing four questions.[4] Who or what is in conflict? What is the basis of the conflict? What are the effects of the conflict? What are the reactions to the conflict?

The question of who or what is in conflict is often considered in three groupings—intrapersonal conflict, interpersonal conflict, and intergroup conflict. Of course, any particular situation could involve all three of these groupings. *Intrapersonal conflict* involves psychological conflict that occurs within a single individual's mind and focuses on opposing feelings and/or thoughts. The identification of the characteristics of a conflict situation presented previously excluded intrapersonal conflict by suggesting that at least two individuals or groups must be present. However, intrapersonal conflict, while not explored in any degree here, can have a powerful impact on certain conflict situations. An extreme example is the occasional bizarre behavior of an employee who shows up in the workplace and shoots or attempts to shoot his superiors and peers. *Interpersonal conflict* focuses on interaction patterns and behaviors between two or more individuals. *Intergroup conflict*, on the other hand, involves conflict between opposing social systems such as labor-management groups, two or more departments within a firm, or two or more nations.

The question of what the basis of the conflict situation is focuses on whether the conflicting issues are affective, substantive, or both, in nature. Affective conflict focuses on emotional clashes between individuals, whereas substantive conflict involves clashes and opposition based on cognitive differences in ideas, goals, or means to be employed pertinent to some task.

Our third question concerns the effects of conflict in terms of whether it is destructive or constructive. One view is to consider conflict as inherently undesirable because it ultimately leads to disruption of an individual or social system. The contrary position is to regard conflict as essential to the effective functioning of a social system. Since the ugly and horrifying consequences of conflict are pressed upon us every day in newspapers and on television, it is easy to identify with the destructive aspects of conflict. However, conflict can have constructive functions, too:

> We do not believe that the elimination of conflict is invariable or even typically the desirable goal in wise management of conflict, as many who identify consensus with agreement tend to do. Conflicts stem basically from differences among per-

sons and groups. Elimination of conflict would mean the elimination of such differences. The goal of conflict management is, for us, better conceived as the acceptance and enhancement of differences among persons and groups . . . [5, p. 152]

In evaluating the constructive or destructive effects of conflict, we must add the caveat of "from whose point of view" are you evaluating it? Management may openly oppose and engage in conflict over the formation of a union because it threatens to limit their discretion over employees, whereas the union members may view this conflict process as functional and an inevitable part of attaining their goals. Our last question, which asks "What are the reactions to the conflicts?" focuses on the modes for resolving, reducing, or coping with the conflict. We will develop one set of modes, which we identify as styles for coping with conflict. Of course, there is no cure-all formula for conflict resolution or any of the other myriad human problems occurring in organizations. Two of the less meaningful prescriptions for conflict resolution are the simplistic recommendation of the need for "more communication" or "more cooperation."

Conflict-Handling Styles

This discussion of five conflict-handling styles is adapted and synthesized from the work of Thomas.[6] The conflict-handling styles are plotted within a two-dimensional model, as shown in Fig. 6–1. The first dimension, shown as the vertical axis, refers to the degree to which the individual desires to satisfy his or her own concern or interests. While this dimension should be viewed as a continuum, we simply dichotomize it as "low" (unassertive concern for self) and "high" (assertive concern for self). The second dimension, shown as the horizontal axis, refers to the degree to which the individual desires to satisfy the concern or interests of other individuals. This dimension is also dichotomized as "low" (uncooperative concern for others) and "high" (cooperative concern for others).

The choice and use of the five conflict-handling styles is likely to depend upon both the nature of the individual and situational factors. Figure 6–1 does not tell us *why* an individual has a low or high desire to satisfy his own concerns, or *why* an individual has a low or high desire to satisfy others' concerns. As each of these conflict-handling styles is explained, we need to recognize possible contingencies in the person and situation that could influence their utilization. One important contingency in the situation is the quality of the interpersonal relationship between the individuals prior to the conflict issue; the quality may be described as open, friendly, and positive, versus closed, hostile, and negative. There may be a greater tendency to cope with the conflict issue in a competitive style when relations are closed or hostile, and a tendency to use the collaborative style when relations are open and friendly.

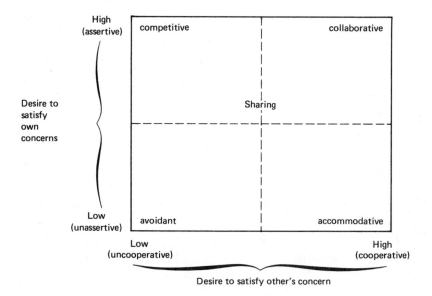

Figure 6–1 Model of Conflict-Handling Styles

Adapted from: Thomas, K. V., "Conflict and Conflict Management," Working Paper #74–3, Graduate School of Management, University of California at Los Angeles, February, 1974, p. 24(a). Used with permission.

A second important contingency in the situation is how the individual perceives the "size" of the conflict issue. "Large" conflict issues tend to be approached in a competitive style with the assumption of engaging in a win–lose (i.e., my gain is your loss, and vice versa) power struggle. Thus, the perceived "size" of a conflict may influence the tendency to utilize a particular style. From a conflict-management perspective, one author comments:

> The danger inherent in big disputes and the difficulty of settling them suggests that, rather than spend all of our time looking for peaceful ways of resolving big issues, we might better explore the possibility of turning big issues . . . into little ones.[7, p. 92]

Accordingly, the parties may be able to reduce large issues into a series of smaller ones. The assumptions in this approach are that conflicts may be more easily resolved when they are:

1. Considered as occurring between the people directly involved (such as a superior and subordinate);

2. Limited to a single specific issue at a time (such as inadequate performance on a specific task, versus performance over the previous three years);

3. Not treated as issues of principle or philosophy (such as management versus union "rights"); and

4. Considered as an issue to be assessed on its own merits without becoming excessively concerned with "What will others think?" or "How does this fit with past practice?" and the like.

A third contingency in the situation worthy of recognizing is the nature of the reward–punishment system within the organization. There might be more use of the competitive versus collaborative conflict-handling style if the reward–punishment system emphasizes:

1. Ranking employees against each other rather than in relation to achievement of goals and tasks;

2. Always trying to place "blame" on individuals for errors, rather than jointly seeking to understand causes of the errors and prevent them in the future; and

3. Always trying to differentially reward individuals, rather than rewarding a group when the individuals are highly interdependent and must cooperate for effective task accomplishment.[8]

Competitive Style.   The competitive style, in the upper lefthand cell of Fig. 6–1, represents a desire to attain one's own concerns, probably at the cost of one or more other individuals. A likely consequence of this relationship is the attempt by one individual to *dominate* or coerce one or more other individuals. A high desire to satisfy only one's own concerns can manifest itself in two strikingly different forms. In the raw form, the individual employs power in the dominance–submission mode. This form of power is associated with direct physical aggression and a heavy reliance on punishment, to gain control over others.[9] In the other form, the individual may use the competitive style because of factors in the situation, rather than within himself. An individual strongly desirous of a particular promotion may have been told that the decision is between two individuals—that person and another peer. Because the reward system is viewed as providing only one promotion opportunity, it may be extremely difficult and trying for each individual to be highly desirous about satisfying the other's concern.

Collaborative Style.   The collaborative style, which is shown in the upper right-hand corner of Fig. 6–1, represents a desire to satisfy the concerns of both oneself and others. The collaborative style has also been labeled as the problem-solving style or the confrontation style. Regardless of label, this approach has the common aim of attempting to *integrate* the interests of the individuals who are engaged in a conflict.[10] While the individual is still concerned with "self," the power orientation in satisfying one's own concerns is likely to be quite different than with the competitive style. Here, the power profile of the individual is:

> . . . characterized by a concern for group goals, for finding what goals will move them, for helping the group to formulate them, for taking some initiative in providing members of the group with the means of achieving such goals, and for giving group members the feeling of competence they need to work hard for such goals.[11]

Other common elements of the collaborative style include: openly sharing information and attitudes; sincerely attempting to listen and develop empathy, but not necessarily agreement, with the other individuals; engaging in intense discussions but not allowing them to degenerate into clashes between personalities; recognizing and separating conflicts over "facts" from conflicts over differences in attitudes and values; and a willingness to spend considerable energies on reevaluating the definition of the problem and generating additional alternatives.

The competitive style is often characterized by the reverse of these elements. While the competitive style focuses on the differences between the individuals, the collaborative style attempts to emphasize and search for positions and recommendations which are attractive to all involved. The collaborative style is quite effective where the conflict is related to semantic issues or the desired means for dealing with some problem. However, this approach is quite limited in dealing with conflicts over goals (such as a union's goal of a 10% wage increase and management's goal of a 5% wage increase to maintain profit levels) and differing value systems (such as a belief and desire to spread the free enterprise system versus the socialist system).

Sharing Style.   The sharing style, in the center of Fig. 6–1, represents a style for moderately, but incompletely, satisfying all individuals. The emphasis is on the processes of compromise, bargaining, or negotiation; i.e., all individuals give up something and keep or gain something. In other words, at some point in the conflict, there is some process of "splitting the difference." This does not necessarily mean an equal split. In union–management negotiations, it is common for the union to agree to a much lower wage settlement than their starting demands. This occurs because of the common and accepted practice of the union to start with demands far in excess of what they expect to attain during the current round of negotiations. Management's initial offers of a contract are also usually lower than they expect to receive.

The sharing style is particularly useful and common where the conflict involves differences in goals, attitudes, or values. The sharing style is also useful in conflicts where the individuals are interdependent and have power relative to each other; i.e., the individuals have the ability to impede as well as facilitate each other's goal attainment. The extent to which the sharing style needs to be utilized is somewhat dependent on the amount of agreement that exists on basic values and goals.[12] In sum, the sharing style is commonly used, widely accepted, and is often essential when conflicts are over goals and values.

The problem with this style is that it may be employed too soon with a conflict issue and it may be utilized for parts of the conflict that might be more effectively resolved through the collaborative style. The early use of the sharing style might result in a tendency for the individuals to accept the initial definition of their problem or assume that the alternatives are limited to those initially identified, and thus proceed to a process of sharing. An alternative approach is to reexamine the nature of the conflict issue, generate additional alternatives, and then begin to employ the process of sharing, if necessary.

Avoidant Style.   The avoidant style, in the lower lefthand corner of Fig. 6–1, refers to a process of withdrawing from situations that might create unpleasantness for oneself and postponing or suppressing issues.[13] This orientation has been described by behaviors and predispositions, such as withdrawal, indifference, evasion, apathy, flight, reliance upon fate, and isolation.[14] The prevalence of the avoidant style may be less evident than the other styles because it is not as readily observable. It may be subtly expressed in the decision not to decide.[15] A cartoon in the *Wall Street Journal* vividly portrayed the avoidant style with a group of managers sitting around a table and the secretary reading from the minutes: "The motion to take immediate and decisive action was tabled until next meeting." The frustration created for an individual who must work for a manager that overuses the avoidant style is nicely illustrated by Uris. Dan Fahey (pseudonym) states he is seeking another job "because my boss frustrates the hell out of me. He literally makes me sick. In the last few months I've been losing sleep, my digestion is shot."[16, p. 100] He goes on to say:

> The heart of the problem is my inability to get him to make a decision. Let me give you one example. A problem comes up, I wrestle with it and work out a plan of action. It needs my boss's approval, so I see him and explain what I have in mind. But he refuses to give me a go-ahead. And no explanation, either. I found it an impossible situation to live with.[17, p. 100]

Another subtle form of the avoidant style is for the individual to make decisions that are "acceptable" to others and thus serve to avoid conflict even if they are second-best solutions.[18] Let's assume a group of eight faculty members has interviewd three candidates for a new faculty position. The Department Head polls each of the eight faculty members regarding his preference among the three candidates. The results show that four faculty members rank candidate A as highest and candidate C as lowest, whereas four other faculty members rank candidate C as highest and candidate A as lowest. Candidate B appears to be ranked in the middle and has been evaluated as "so-so." With an avoidant style, the Department Head may decide to extend an offer to candidate B, rather than calling a meeting to openly explore the reasons for and the nature of the differences in rankings the other two candidates, because of the belief that faculty harmony might be disturbed.

Accommodative Style. The accommodative style, in the lower righthand corner of Fig. 6–1, focuses on appeasement, i.e., a desire to satisfy the concerns of others without attending to one's own concerns in the present conflict. The individual exercising this style may actually be generous or self-sacrificing in the present conflict issue because of a desire to preserve and maintain a relationship with the other individuals.[19] Implicit in this approach is the belief by the individual that others will cut off their relationship if he or she expresses self-oriented concerns.

The accommodative style seems to represent a conflict style that is likely to be employed by the "organization man" stereotype.[20] The organization man stereotype is based on three major assumptions: ". . . a belief in the group as the source of creativity, a belief in 'belongingness' as the ultimate need of the individual, and a belief in the application of science to achieve the belongingness."[21, p. 185] We are not suggesting that managers or other individuals working in today's large-scale organizations are primarily organization men. There is evidence suggesting just the opposite.[22] The accommodative style is likely to be overused by individuals with a docile, dependent, and submissive personality.[23] As one author notes, the "extreme of this form of behavior is a clinging, ingratiating dependency that may become very sticky indeed for the person toward whom it is directed."[24, p. 109]

In a conflict issue that is associated with the expression of intense and aggressive feelings, the accommodative style may be very beneficial as a starting point. If the desire to fully understand and empathize with the other individuals is sincere, it may serve to reestablish a relationship that can eventually employ the collaborative and/or sharing styles. A manager, when first confronted by a highly emotional subordinate who is shouting and pounding the desk, may well find the accommodative style beneficial as a starting point.

Overview

There have been several themes implicit in this discussion of conflict styles. First, in this discussion we have tried to provide a background for your thinking about the style or styles that are most characteristic of you, and the functional or dysfunctional consequences they may have had for you. Secondly, we have developed the theme that there is no single style that can be utilized successfully in all situations. Thus, the contingencies that may more appropriately call for one style over another were presented. We do, however, agree with the general prescription and value orientation that individuals should at least sincerely try to employ the collaborative style wherever possible.[25] Finally, we assume that individuals can learn to be more conscious and skillful in their choice of styles. To a considerable extent, the same themes, but applied to communication styles, will be of interest in the second major part to this chapter. The section on communication also has a broader focus than the conflict presentation and provides further insight into the process of conflict management—particularly the discussions on listening, feedback, and personal contingencies.

COMMUNICATION

The general objective in discussing communication is to identify patterns and characteristics of communication by individuals, rather than considering the content (what individuals might communicate). The more specific objectives of this discussion include:

1. To explain the forms of interpersonal communication—verbal and nonverbal;

2. To present selected personal contingencies that are likely to influence interpersonal communication styles;

3. To develop a general model of communication styles; and

4. To identify some recommendations for improving interpersonal communication.

There is an old cliché that goes "there are a lot of ways to skin a cat." The area of human communications seems to have a greater number of perspectives and points of view than any other field. As a consequence, there is no single adequate definition of communication encompassing all of the useful approaches human communication. One book, which attempts to capture the diversity in this area, identifies twenty-four approaches to human communication, including such points of reference as: art, general semantics, mass media, nonverbal behavior, linguistics, symbolic interaction, and the like.[26] While recognizing the inadequacy of any one definition, communication refers to the ". . . transmission and reception of ideas, feelings, and attitudes—verbally and/or nonverbally—which produce a response."[27, p. 10] The processes of reception, transmission, and response could occur at the levels of consciousness or unconsciousness. Our present interest is in face-to-face communications between two to about ten individuals.

FORMS OF INTERPERSONAL COMMUNICATION

Verbal Communication

From the perspective of interpersonal communication, verbal communication can actually take direct and indirect forms. As developed by Pfeffer and Jones, the two common types of indirect verbal communication involve the use of pseudo questions and clichés.[28]

Pseudo questions refers to questions that are not really designed to obtain information or answers. The individual uses questions to present opinions or statements. This reduces the risk of having one's ideas rejected and possibly increases the ability to force the other person(s) to agree with the speaker. Let's consider some types and examples of pseudo questions we are prone to use.

The *co-optive* question attempts to get the sender's desired answer by working in restrictions and limitations to the responses possible by the other person(s). Co-optive questions are likely to begin with phrases such as "Don't you think that . . .?", "Wouldn't you rather . . .?", and "Isn't it true that . . .?" The *imperative* question attempts to make a demand or request of another person(s). Imperative questions often start with phrases like "Have you done anything about . . .?" or "When are you going to . . .?" The *screened* question occurs when the individual asks the other person(s) what she or he likes or wants to do, while really hoping the responses will be what the questioner secretly desires. The screened question may be employed when the questioner is fearful of simply stating his or her own preferences. An example of a screened question is a manager asking a subordinate "Would you like to work overtime tonight on the Jones order?" when the real statement should be "I need you to work overtime tonight to get the Jones order out first thing in the morning, will you?" Even in the rephrased question there could be the possibility of its being intended or perceived as an imperative question. The last type of pseudo question we will cover might be called the *"got-cha"* or set-up question. The "got-cha" question is employed by the questioner to trap, intimidate, or embarrass the individual(s) rather than obtain a meaningful response.[29] "Got-cha" questions might start with phrases such as "Weren't you the one who . . .?", "Didn't you say that . . .?", or "Didn't I see you . . .?"

Clichés represent a second common type of indirect verbal communication. Clichés are standard, routine, habitual ways of responding to each other. They may be used when individuals don't really want to spend much effort in communicating anything of significance. All of us are likely to use clichés occasionally. It is the overuse of phrases such as the following that diminish communication effectiveness: "If you've seen one, you've seen them all"; "You hit the nail on the head"; "It's an open-and-shut case"; "Better late than never"; "Better safe than sorry"; "Let's get it over and done with"; etc . . .

Nonverbal Communication

Since about 1969, the interest in nonverbal communications has increased considerably. Nonverbal communication is defined as all behavior expressed consciously or unconsciously, done in the presence of another (or others) and perceived either consciously or unconsciously. Within this definition, ". . . it follows that no matter how one may try, one cannot *not* communicate. Activity or inactivity, words or silence all have message value; they influence others and these others, in turn, cannot *not* respond to these communications and are thus themselves communicating."[30, p. 49] Even if you are silent or inactive in the presence of others, you may send a message, which may or may not be your intended message, that you're bored, fearful, angry, or possibly even depressed. Let's consider a hypothetical example of this process. A manager calls the usual monthly review and planning meeting with his or her five subordinates. These meetings typically last four hours and are concerned with reviewing the previous month's accomplishments and problems and developing working plans for the coming month. Unknown to the subordinates, the manager attended a two-day communication-skills seminar three days before their meeting, and learned about such things as: the tendency for superiors to dominate communication flow when interacting with subordinates; the need for greater active listening by superiors; the impact of nonverbal communications, such as frowns or smiles as indicators of disapproval or approval; and many other things about interpersonal communications. Based on exercises in the seminar and personal introspection, the superior concludes that there is a need for major changes in how he or she communicates. For the up-coming meeting, the superior decides to vary past practice by being almost exclusively a listener, and to watch the nonverbals by using a "poker face." This is being done so the subordinates won't feel there is any attempt to pass judgment on what they are saying during the exploratory and problem-analysis phases of their meeting. What happens? The meeting is likely to be a complete disaster. One subordinate perceives the superior's "new" behavior as an obvious sign that the boss is terribly upset about "something," and thus becomes quite anxious. Another subordinate interprets the boss's behavior as a sure indicator of complete boredom and becomes quite frustrated because of the inability to draw the superior out. A third subordinate suspects the boss is fearful of something, such as getting fired or demoted, because the unit has been having more than its share of problems over the past three months. While the specifics of this incident are hypothetical, the issues and concepts within the incident are quite real. The overriding implication of this incident is the failure of the superior to communicate about how he or she would like to communicate in this meeting and how it might be different from past approaches. Any radical changes from the behavior that others have learned to anticipate, and hopefully interpret with reasonable accuracy, may result in different messages being interpreted by the different receivers and the sender's intended message never being received by anyone. Over the longer run, we could expect relearning to take place so that the intended verbal and nonverbal messages might more closely match the received or interpreted messages.

To develop a more specific understanding of the rich scope and depth of nonverbal communication, Fig. 6–2 provides a classification system and explanation of four major sets of nonverbal codes, including performance codes, artifactual codes, mediational codes, and contextual codes. The artifactual and contextual codes will be explored in greater depth in Chapter 11 in the discussion of the impact of physical settings on organizational behavior. The classifi-

Figure 6–2   Classification System of Nonverbal Communication Codes

Major Codes	Explanation and Examples
Performance Codes	Nonverbal signs originating through differences and changes in bodily action, such as facial expression, eye movement, gestures, body posture, tactile (touch) contact
Artifactual Codes	Nonverbal signs originating through differences and changes in cosmetics, dress, furnishings, art objects, status symbols (such as make of car), architecture, and the like.
Mediational Codes	Nonverbal signs originating through differences and changes in an intervening or intermediary communication medium such as television, radio, magazines, and newspapers. Through decisions by the intervening media, the sent nonverbal or verbal message can be influenced. For example, the message from nonverbal behavior can be influenced somewhat by use of color or black-and-white, photography or cartoon, and close-up or long-shot.
Contextual Codes	Nonverbal signs originating through differences and changes in the use of time and space. Time might be divided up very precisely and used efficiently, such as within work organizations or viewed and used casually in between. Space between individuals might vary for different types of interaction, such as a small zone for intimate interaction and a large zone for interaction with strangers.

Adapted from: Harrison, R. P., "Nonverbal Behavior: An Approach to Human Communication" in Budd, R. W. and B. D. Ruben (eds.) *Approaches to Human Communication.* Rochelle Park: Spartan Books, 1972, pp. 253–268.

cation scheme in Fig. 6–2 serves to dramatically illustrate the numerous ways by which we can and do communicate without saying a word. This figure also suggests the subtle, unrecognized, and often unconscious role of nonverbal communications. These subtle aspects have been expressed in recent book titles such as: *Body Language*[31], *The Hidden Dimension*[32], *The Presentation of Self in Everyday Life*[33], and *Personal Space*[34].

Contrary to some earlier thinking in the area of human communication, nonverbal communication appears to precede verbal communication in the development of individual humans. It may also strongly influence the content of verbal communication and the likelihood of its even taking place. The three major functions of nonverbal communication cues and examples of each have been nicely summarized by Harrison[35, p. 258], as follows:

First, they *define, condition,* and *constrain* the communication system [between individuals]. For instance, the time of day, or allotted time, the setting, and the arrangement of props may cue the participants on who is in the system, what the pattern of interaction will be, and what is appropriate or inappropriate conversational fare.

Secondly, nonverbal cues help to *regulate* the communication system. They signal status hierarchies, indicate who is to speak next, provide feedback about evaluations and intentions.

Finally, nonverbal signs (cues) communicate *content.* Sometimes, the nonverbal code is more efficient; for example, relationships are more easily preserved in an anologic code, such as a map, a blueprint, a picture, a model. Sometimes, the nonverbal code is more effective, perhaps because it uses an additional modality such as touch, or odor, or even taste. And sometimes, the nonverbal code increases the efficiency and effectiveness because it provides redundancy, another way of saying the same thing [italics added].

In sum, nonverbal communications are a crucial component of all interpersonal communications. In the following section, we consider some of the personal contingencies that might explain why the nature and quality of verbal and nonverbal communications are "what they are."

PERSONAL CONTINGENCIES IN COMMUNICATIONS

The objective of this section is to briefly consider several major contingencies that can be utilized to differentiate individuals and serve to influence their use of a predominant communication style. We will not be directly considering differences in the level of positions that individuals might occupy in a hierarchy, or differences in job-related abilities between individuals. The personal contingencies to be discussed are self-concept, self-disclosure, listening ability, and clarity of expression abilities.[36]

Self-Concept

Self-concept refers to how individuals see themselves and how they feel about what they see. It is a *personal* judgment of the degree of worthiness the individual holds towards herself or himself.[37] A person's self-concept is usually thought of as multidimensional, with some dimensions contributing more than others to the individual's overall self-concept.[38] Self-concept may include a wide range of dimensions such as height, weight, honesty, physical attractiveness, intelligence, and athletic ability. Evaluations of each dimension are determined by how the individual judges his own worth on that dimension and the degree of importance assigned to it. If a person evaluates his or her athletic ability very low, but does not regard it as an important issue, it is not likely to greatly affect his or her overall self-concept.

There are several crucial relationships between self-concept and communication styles. First, an individual whose self-concept involves inferiority, weakness, or inadequacy may have difficulty in conversing with others, expressing personal feelings, admitting when she or he has been wrong or in error, accepting constructive criticism from other individuals, or taking a position contrary to others. The individual with a weak self-concept is likely to be guarded and seclusive in interpersonal communication. Secondly, the relationship between self-concept and communication style seems to be circular. An important influence on the formation of and changes in our self-concept is the verbal and nonverbal communications we receive from individuals who are significant to us. Communications from others influence our learning about ourselves as to whether we are liked or disliked, loved or hated, acceptable or unacceptable, and the like. Individuals with strong self-concepts have usually had their needs for security, love, respect, and acceptance met from individuals who were significant, particularly in the childhood years.[39] As a result, their communication may be somewhat less inhibited and evaluative.

Self-Disclosure

Self-disclosure is defined as any information an individual consciously communicates verbally or nonverbally about himself to one or more other individuals. We often disclose much about ourselves unconsciously through what we do, how we act and react, mannerisms, and how we say what we say.[40] However, our discussion of self-disclosure is limited to verbal and nonverbal communication about ourselves that we consciously choose to transmit.

While self-concept may influence self-disclosure, the concepts are not the same and do not necessarily vary with one another. Individuals with positive self-concepts may vary from high to very little disclosure about themselves. One crucial intervening variable between self-concept and self-disclosure in interpersonal communications are the social norms (standards as to acceptable and unacceptable actions) that have been formed in the particular group. Norms are important in determining what, when, where, and with whom it is regarded as appropriate to be relatively open or closed about ourselves in interpersonal communications.

The ability to expose or express one's real self to one or a few significant other individuals is often a prerequisite for the development and maintenance of a healthy personality. The specific relationship between self-disclosure and mental health may be curvilinear. The nondisclosing individual may be repressing his "self" because to reveal it is seen as threatening. The total-disclosure individual who continuously exposes a great deal about himself or herself to anyone he meets may be unable to relate and communicate with others because of a preoccupation with the personal self. A medium level of disclosure may represent an individual who is quite open with a select number of very close individuals and moderately open with others consistent with the specific requirements of their social relationships. A healthy openness in a work setting might facilitate discussion and sharing of work-related problems you are having with your superior. Of course, we are assuming that the superior is approachable and receptive. A form of self-disclosure in the work setting that may not be consistent with a healthy personality would be a constant preoccupation with describing to your superior and peers your sexual experiences in great detail.

The possible ties between personality, self-disclosure, and communication style has been dramatically expressed by Jourard [41, pp. 46–47]:

> Healthy personality is manifested by a mode of what we call *authenticity*, or more simply, honesty. Less healthy personalities, people who function less than fully, who suffer recurrent breakdowns or chronic impasses, may usually be found to be *liars*. They say things they do not mean. Their disclosures have been chosen more for cosmetic value than for truth. The consequence of a lifetime of lying about oneself to others, of saying and doing things for their sound and appearance, is that ultimately the person loses contact with his real self.
>
> The authentic being manifested by healthier personalities takes the form of un-self-conscious disclosure of self in words, decisions, and actions.

The issue of authenticity and self-disclosure in interpersonal communications within organizations is often compounded between hierarchical levels. Individuals at one level have formal power (i.e., ability to influence the allocation of rewards such as pay raises and promotions, and punishments such as demotion or dismissal) relative to individuals at another level. Even if individuals are able and willing to engage in "appropriate" forms of self-disclosure at work, the degree to which superiors are perceived as trustworthy in not using the revealed information to punish, intimidate, or suppress is likely to influence the amount and form of self-disclosure. While this discussion has focused on self-disclosure as a function of the individual, the organization's climate and the leadership style of the superior will also influence levels of self-disclosure.

In recognition of hierarchical power relationships, the New England Telephone Company introduced an upward communications program that had the goal of increasing self-disclosure. To have a system that could be trusted rather than feared to increase self-disclosure, the communication program started with "private lines." This technique enables all employees to anonymously discuss or question any issue of concern by mailing in a form or calling the full-time coordinating staff that administers the upward communications program. This staff then transmits the issue, without identifying the employee, to the individuals who are responsible and/or have the necessary expertise to answer the problem. The coordinators receive the reply which is, in turn, fed back to the employee. Questions and answers of general interest are often published in the company newspaper. As of 1974, there had been 2,500 questions or comments processed, principally within the following categories: working conditions, benefits, promotions, transfers, assignments, and compensation. A survey of employees (75% nonmanagement and 25% management), using the private-line program, indicates that 79% were satisfied with the response to their questions and 93% indicated they would use it again.[42] While we personally find it unfortunate that a program such as this should even be necessary to get issues expressed, it does represent an attempt to constructively increase self-disclosure and thus communications within the context and realities of organizational power.

Listening Ability

Listening is defined as "... an intellectual and emotional process that integrates physical, emotional, and intellectual inputs in a search for meaning and understanding."[43, p. 126] Listening is effective when the sender's intended message is received and understood by the listener.

It has been estimated that as much as 40% of the work day of many white-collar workers is devoted to listening. However, tests of listening comprehension suggest that these employees listen at 25% efficiency.[44] While these figures might be quibbled over, the key point is that listening requires a meaningful portion of most employees' work day, particularly those in white-collar and managerial jobs. The quality and effectiveness of peer and superior–subordinate relationships is likely to be somewhat influenced by the listening ability of the interacting parties.

A potential basic barrier to listening ability may exist in the fundamental nature of the listener in terms of such dimensions as self-concept, attitudes and values, level of knowledge, and problem-solving styles. If an employee has developed an attitude of dislike for his or her superior, it may be extremely difficult to truly listen to the comments being made by the superior during a performance review season. If a trainer is trying to explain something that so exceeds the trainee's basic level of knowledge, frustration may develop to such a high level that the individual simply "turns off" the trainer.

There are a number of other barriers to listening, some of which are suggested in the following concepts and techniques that can aid in increasing one's listening skill.[45]

1. The individual should have a *reason* or *purpose* for listening. Good listeners are predisposed to search for value and meaning in what is being said, even if they are not predisposed to be interested in the particular issue or topic. On the other hand, poor listeners are predisposed to quickly rationalize any or all inattention, on the basis of initial interest or noninterest.

2. The listener should *suspend judgment,* at least initially. Good listening requires concentrating on the whole message of the sender, rather than forming evaluations of good or bad on the basis of the first few ideas presented.

3. The listener should *resist distraction;* such as noises, views, and other people; and focus on the sender.

4. The listener should *wait before responding* to the sender.

5. When the message is heavily emotion-laden or there is doubt as to what was intended, the listener should *rephrase* in his or her own words the content and feeling of what the sender appeared to be saying.

6. The listener should *seek the important themes* of the sender by listening for the overall content-and-feeling message.

7. The listener should use the time differential between rate of thought (400–500 words per minute) and rate of speech (100–150 words per minute) to *reflect* upon content and to *search* for meaning.

Most of these techniques and concepts for improving listening ability are interrelated; i.e., you can't practice one without improving the other. Unfortunately, it is much easier to understand or even be able to recall these techniques and concepts than to develop them as a skill to be employed in day-to-day interpersonal communications. A variety of experiential exercises are available for assisting the individual in diagnosing and improving his or her listening ability.[46]

We would like to capstone this section with a short, hypothetical incident between a college president and a student activist, which serves to capture the essence of the discussion of listening abilities or lack thereof. This incident is drawn from James and Jongeward.[47, pp. 227–230]

> *President:* What can I do for you, son?
>
> *Student:* Don't call me son! I'm not your son! I've talked to you before and you obviously didn't listen to a word I said. The demands I have represent a majority of the students here. You can't ignore them.
>
> *President:* I know those demands: I've read them before.
>
> *Student:* Do you understand them?
>
> *President:* Yes, I understand them, and for your own good, I can't accept any of these demands.
>
> *Student:* You and your pompous friends had better start listening to us, because we're going to sit in your office forever!
>
> *President:* O.K., I will listen to you, but I'll tell you right now, before you begin, that for your own good these demands are not being met.

One interpretation of the president's behavior is that he or she assumed the students must be controlled by authority, direction, and responsibility. The president was unwilling to discuss a new approach or listen to new ideas. Even when the president asserted, "O.K., I will listen to you. . . . ," there was no active listening involved. For the most part, the president's "listening" was used to form challenging questions, create diversions, and plan counterattacks. Given this analysis of the president's listening and communication approach, how would you charactrize and assess the student's listening skill? How would this script be rewritten if either party was trying to practice the concepts and techniques of listening previously outlined?

Expression Abilities

The fourth and last contingency to be considered in this section is one's facility of expression. Expression ability simply refers to the skill to say what one means or to express what one feels. The lack of expression is due to such things as carelessness in speech, assuming other individuals understand what one means, placing the burden of communication on the listener (i.e., "If it is clear to me, it must be clear to you"), and lack of knowledge or vocabulary in communicating one's thoughts so that they are interpretable by the listener. The process of feedback, which is crucial to our discussion of the communication model, is one means for improving expression abilities.

MODEL OF COMMUNICATION STYLES [48]

The model of communication styles, as shown in Fig. 6–3, is built upon a number of concepts and perspectives just presented. This model also serves to explicitly develop the concept and role of feedback in interpersonal communication styles.

Figure 6–3 is based upon two dimensions of interpersonal communications. One dimension, which is shown on the vertical axis as varying from "low" to "high," is labeled as openness to and from others. This dimension attempts to capture both the idea of self-disclosure (opening or revealing oneself to others) and being receptive to feedback from others, particularly about how they perceive you and your actions. The second dimension, which is shown on the horizontal axis as varying from "low" to "high," is labeled as giving feedback. This dimension refers to the degree to which the individual communicates his thoughts and feelings toward one or more individuals. The giving-feedback dimension could focus on very personal aspects of others, or on more abstract aspects such as feeding back your reactions to their ideas or proposals. Thus, the emotional impact of one's feedback is also likely to vary as to how "personally" it is focused.

By dichotomizing and cross-classifying the dimensions of openness to and from others and giving feedback, five styles of interpersonal communications are identified in Fig. 6–3.

The *self-denying* style refers to the individual who is isolated from others and very withdrawn. Introverted individuals are likely to be more prone to this communication style than would extroverted individuals. The *self-protecting*

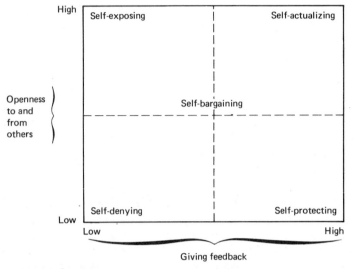

Figure 6–3   Model of Communication Styles

Adapted from: Polsky, H. W., "Notes on Personal Feedback in Sensitivity Training," *Sociological Inquiry,* 1971, **41**, p. 179. Used with permission.

style refers to the individual who probes others or makes comments to others. However, the motivation in giving feedback may be a defensive measure to prevent the possibility of self-exposure and comments from others about oneself.

With the *self-exposing style,* the individual attempts to get others to focus on himself by constantly asking for reactions to his behavior. Moreover, there is likely to be little internalization of the feedback by the individual. It's like "water off a duck's back." The *self-bargaining* style refers to the individual who is willing to give feedback and open up in direct relation to the same process taking place with the others in the interaction. Thus, the individual uses himself or herself as a point of bargaining or negotiation.

The *self-actualizing* style refers to the individual who spontaneously provides the appropriate amount of information about himself, asks for feedback, and provides feedback in a constructive and nondefensive manner. Under ideal conditions, the self-actualizing communication style might be one we would like to approximate. Even if predisposed and desirous of manifesting the self-actualizing style, an individual may experience situational factors that motivate him or her to employ some of the other styles. One key situational factor is the approach that others take in communicating with an individual. If a superior is not receptive to receiving feedback, the subordinate may be reluctant to give feedback. It is too simplistic and unrealistic to suggest that there should be only one communication style for all situations. But our biases, which are based on some research and personal values, lead us to conclude that the self-actualizing style is a desirable one to develop and employ when feasible.

Since giving feedback is a crucial dimension in the model of communication styles shown in Fig. 6–3, it is useful to consider some concepts and techniques for giving effective interpersonal feedback. These concepts and techniques are derived from a document utilized by Proctor and Gamble Company as part of its organizational development program to build more effective working relationships on the job.[49] Of course, researchers in other settings have found them helpful as well.[50] To be maximally *useful to the receiver,* giving feedback should be offered with the following concepts and techniques in mind.

1. Feedback should be *intended* to help the receiver. One question for testing this is to ask yourself: "Do I really feel that what I am about to say is *likely to be helpful to the receiver?*" While there may be circumstances in an organization where this is not possible, you are at least more likely to be aware of potential negative reactions by the receiver and possibly be prepared to cope with these reactions constructively rather than defensively.

2. Feedback should ideally be based upon a foundation of *trust* between the givers and receivers. If the organizational environment is characterized by extreme personal competitiveness, emphasis on the use of power to punish and control, rigid boss–subordinate relationships, and the like, we are surely not likely to find a level of trust necessary for effective helping feedback.

3. Feedback should be primarily *descriptive* rather than evaluative. If you describe a specific situation (in time and place) and tell the receiver(s) of the effect it had on you, the feedback is more likely to lead to further dialogue. This is in contrast to evaluating a situation or, more seriously, the receivers, in terms of good or bad and right or wrong.

4. Feedback should be *specific* rather than general, with clear and preferably recent examples.

5. Feedback should be given at a time when the receiver appears to be in a condition of *readiness to accept it.* Thus, if a person is angry, upset, or defensive, it is probably not the time to bring up other and new issues.

6. Feedback should be checked with the receiver, and/or others if it is a group situation, to determine it seems as *valid* to the receiver or others.

7. Feedback should include only those things that the receiver might be *capable* of doing something about.

8. Feedback should not include more than the receiver can *accommodate* at any particular time. Thus, the receiver may become threatened and defensive if you unload "everything that bothers you" about the receiver.

As with the techniques and concepts for improving listening ability, these guidelines for providing helpful feedback are easier to state and recall from our minds than to translate into communication skills that are practiced daily. Moreover, the guidelines for improving listening and feedback skills need to be linked up in the overall process of enhancing interpersonal communications.

This section concludes with some research findings, based on data collected from approximately 1,000 managers, as to how they perceive their interpersonal communications at work. The findings reported focus on the managers' perceptions of their use of self-disclosure and feedback with other employees, such as subordinates, peers, and colleagues. As noted in the following summary of findings, there are frequent deviations from the self-actualizing style (see Fig. 6–3) discussed previously. Some of Hall's findings of interest to us in this section include[51]:

1. The power differences among organizational members appeared to influence their willingness to communicate openly. More specifically, there seemed to be an implicit mistrust in relationships with peers and quasi-subservient withdrawal tendencies in relationships with superiors.

2. The strong correlations between personality traits and communication styles (for a subsample of Masters in Business Administration students) served to emphasize the importance of individual attributes in effective or ineffective communication. Thus, a portion of communication problems in organizations appears to be traceable to factors within individual members.

The model of communication styles in Fig. 6–3 should not be interpreted narrowly and mechanistically. It should serve as a diagnostic tool for considering one's own and other styles, a broad framework for considering the paths for improving interpersonal communications, and as a framework for consciously considering alternative styles that might be necessary and appropriate for the individual's "survival" under varying situations.

SUMMARY

This chapter and the previous chapter have explored the individual in terms of alternative styles that might be employed within three "semi-independent" domains of thought and behavior—problem-solving styles, conflict-management styles, and communication styles. Our overt strategy in these two chapters has excluded a "theory building" approach, which would involve systematically linking these domains to one another. This choice was made to avoid a discussion that might become excessively complex and irrelevant relative to our primary objectives. Moreover, the empirical literature is mixed and spotty in tying these domains together. While we have suggested certain connections in an *ad hoc* manner, we could well have gone further. If you are so inclined, a useful exercise in linking up the presentations of problem-solving styles, conflict-management styles, and communication styles would be to analyze each set of styles to determine whether there are any logical connections between specific styles that could be hypothetically derived from one another.

This and the previous chapter have focused on questions such as: How do you go about making important decisions? What are your typical ways of responding when you disagree with others? and How willing are you to communicate openly with others? If you now have ways for better understanding yourself and others in terms of questions such as these, the objectives of these two chapters have been met.

Discussion Questions

1. What similarities and differences are there in the recommendations for improving listening and feedback skills?

2. How would you compare the self-actualizing communication style with the collaborative conflict-handling style?

3. Describe a situation in which you have used one or more of the conflict-handling styles presented. Do you think the style was effective or ineffective? Why do you feel as you do?

4. Describe a situation in which you have used one or more of the communication styles presented. Do you think the style was effective or ineffective? Why do you feel as you do?

5. Describe the various nonverbal forms of communication utilized by someone you have worked for. Were the nonverbal communications consistent or inconsistent with her or his verbal communications? Explain.

6. What problems and limitations do you see in obtaining meaningful self-disclosure between superiors and subordinates?

CRITICAL INCIDENTS

A clerk with five years' experience tells the supervisor: "I've done a good job for years and nobody ever complained . . . and now you send my work back and tell me to do it over. It doesn't make sense and isn't fair. Maybe I do make mistakes now and then, but nobody is perfect. I don't think I should get all the blame for what goes on around here."

Question:

How would the supervisor likely respond and handle this situation if his or her communication style emphasized: self-exposing?; self-denying?; self-actualizing?; self-protecting?; or self-bargaining?

CRITICAL INCIDENT

George Heller, as manager of the Long-Range Planning Department of the McDonald's Manufacturing Company, thought that it would be desirable to reevaluate the firm's research and development activities. Heller noted that quite a bit of money had been invested in research and development over the past three years, with little payoff in the form of new products or major improvements in present products. Thus, Heller concluded, a total review of the research and development program was needed.

To start the review process, Heller thought it would be useful to conduct a survey of all research and development activities in the company. To this end, a lengthy questionnaire and evaluation form was sent to each of the company's three research and development units. Each of these units had about ten engineers, scientists, and other professionals. The questionnaires were placed in the company mail with a request from Heller that they be returned within 15 days.

When the three research and development group leaders received the questionnaires, they were furious. Some comments were: "Who does Heller and that long-range planning group think they are?" "Why are they asking all of these stupid questions?" "How can we answer these questions—doesn't he know our activities are too uncertain to answer such questions?" "I've been here ten years and all of a sudden Heller and his planners want to do my job."

The three research and development group leaders got together and wrote Heller a memo demanding that they meet to straighten him out on his "ridiculous questionnaire and request."

Questions:

1. How would Heller likely handle this situation if his conflict-management style emphasized: competition?; collaboration?; sharing?; avoidance?; or accommodation?

2. Why do you think the three group leaders responded this way?

REFERENCES

1. Robbins, S. P., *Managing Organizational Conflict: A Nontraditional Approach.* Englewood Cliffs, N.J.: Prentice-Hall, 1974.

2. Filley, A. C., *Interpersonal Conflict and Resolution.* Glenview, Ill.: Scott, Foresman & Co. 1975, p. 4.

3. Filley, A. C., *op. cit.,* pp. 25–28.

4. Fisher, B. A., *Small-Group Decision-Making: Communication and the Group Process.* New York: McGraw-Hill Book Co., 1974, pp. 103–110.

5. Bennis, W. G., K. A. Benne, and R. Chin (eds.), *The Planning of Change.* 2nd ed. New York: Holt, Rinehart, and Winston, Inc. 1969.

6. Thomas, K. W., "Conflict and Conflict Management," in *The Handbook of Industrial and Organizational Psychology.* Vol. II, Chapter 21. Dunnette, M. D. (ed.). Chicago: Rand McNally & Co. in press. Thomas' model is, in turn, derived from: Blake, R. R., and J. S. Mouton *The Managerial Grid.* Houston: Gulf Publishing, Co. 1964.

7. Fisher, R., "Fractionating Conflict," in *International Conflict and Behavioral Science: The Craigville Papers.* Fisher, R. (ed.). New York: Basic Books, 1964.

8. Cvetkovich, F., "Small-Group Dynamics in Extended Judgment Situations," in Rappaport, L., and D. A. Summers, *op. cit.*. Miller, L. K., and H. L. Hamlin, "Interdependence, Differential Rewarding and Productivity," *American Sociological Review,* 1963, **28,** pp. 768–778. Rappaport, L. H., and F. Cvetkovich, "Effects of Reward Structure and Cognitive Differences in a Mixed-Motive Two-Person Conflict Situation," *American Journal of Psychology,* 1970, **83** (1), pp. 119–125.

9. McClelland, D. C., "The Two Faces of Power," *Journal of International Affairs,* 1970, **24,** pp. 29–47.

10. McClelland, D. C., S. Rhinesmith, and R. Kristensen. "The Effects of Power Training on Community Action Agencies," *The Journal of Applied Behavioral Science,* **11,** 1975, pp. 92–115.

11. McClelland, D. C., *op. cit.*

12. Davies, M. R., and V. A. Lewis, *Models of Political Systems.* New York: Praeger Publishers, 1971, p. 146.

13. Kilmann, R. C., and K. W. Thomas, "A Forced-Choice Measure of Conflict-Handling Behavior: The 'Mode' Instrument," unpublished manuscript, 1974.

14. Stagner, R., and H. Rosen, *Psychology of Union-Management Relations.* Belmont, Calif.: Brooks/Cole Publishing Co., 1965.

15. Barnard, C. I., *The Functions of the Executive.* Cambridge, Mass.: Harvard University Press, 1938, p. 189.

16. Uris, A., *The Frustrated Titan: Emasculation of the Executive.* New York: Van Nostrand Reinhold Co., 1972.

17. Uris, A., *op. cit.*

18. Johnson, R. V., "Conflict Avoidance Through Acceptable Decisions," *Human Relations,* 1974, **27,** pp. 71–82.

19. Donnelly, L. I., "Toward an Alliance between Research and Practice in Collective Bargaining," *Personnel Journal,* 1971, **50,** pp. 372–397+.

20. Whyte, W. H., Jr., *The Organization Man.* New York: Simon & Schuster, 1956.

21. Jennings, E. E., *An Antomy of Leadership: Princes, Heroes, and Supermen.* New York: McGraw-Hill Book Co. 1960.

22. Porter, L. W., and E. E. Lawler, III, *Managerial Attitudes and Performance.* Homewood, Ill.: Richard D. Irwin, 1968.

23. Leary, T., *Interpersonal Diagnosis of Personality: A Functional Theory and Methodology for Personality Evaluation.* New York: Ronald Press Co., 1957.

24. Carson, R. C., *Interaction Concepts of Personality.* Chicago: Aldine Publishing Co. 1969.

25. Blake, R. R., and J. S. Mouton, "The Fifth Achievement," *Personnel Administration,* 1971, pp. 49–57.

26. Budd, R. W., and B. D. Rubin, (eds.), *Approaches to Human Communication.* Rochelle Park, N.J.: Spartan Books, 1972.

27. Sigband, H., *Communication for Management.* Glenview: Scott, Foresman & Co., 1969.

28. Adapted from: Pfeffer, J. W., and J. E. Jones, "Don't you Think That . . .? An Experiential Lecture on Indirect and Direct Communication," in Pfeffer, J. W., and J. E. Jones, *1974 Annual Handbook for Group Facilitators.* LaJolla, Calif.: University Associates, 1974, pp. 203–208.

29. Berne, E., *Games People Play.* New York: Grove Press, 1964.

30. Watzlawick, D., J. H. Beavin, and D. D. Jackson, *Pragmatics of Human Communication: A Study of Interactional Patterns, Pathologies, and Paradoxes.* New York: W. W. Norton & Co., 1967.

31. Fast, J., *Body Language.* New York: M. Evans & Co., 1970.

32. Hall, E. T., *The Hidden Dimension.* Garden City, N.Y.: Doubleday & Co., 1966.

33. Goffman, E., *The Presentation of Self in Everyday Life.* Garden City, N.Y.: Doubleday & Co., 1959.

34. Sommer, R., *Personal Space.* Englewood Cliffs, N.J.: Prentice-Hall, 1969.

35. Harrison, R. P., "Nonverbal Behavior: An Approach to Human Communication," in *Approaches to Human Communication.* Budd, R. W., and B. A. Ruben, (eds.). Rochelle Park, N.J.: Spartan Books, 1972.

36. Adapted from: Bienvenu, M. J., Jr., "An Interpersonal Communication Inventory," *The Journal of Communication,* 1971, **21,** pp. 381–388. Chartier, M. R., "Five Components Contributing to Effective Interpersonal Communications," in Pfeffer and Jones (eds.), *op. cit.,* pp. 125–128.

37. Coppersmith, S., *The Antecedents of Self-Esteem*. San Francisco: W. H. Freeman, 1967, p. 95.

38. Sherwood, J. J., "Self-Identity and Referent Others," *Sociometry*, 1965, **28,** pp. 66–81.

39. Arieti, S., *The Intrapsychic Self: Feeling, Cognition, and Creativity*. New York: Basic Books, 1967.

40. Cozby, P. C., "Self-Disclosure: A Literature Review," *Psychological Bulletin*, 1973, **79,** (2), pp. 73–91.

41. Jourard, S. M., *Disclosing Man to Himself*. New York: Van Nostrand Reinhold Co., 1968.

42. Harriman, B., "Up and Down the Communications Ladder," *Harvard Business Review*. 1974, **52,** pp. 143–151. *Aslo see:* Greenbaum, H. H., "The Audit of Organizational Communication," *Academy of Management Journal*, 1974, **17,** pp. 739–754.

43. Chartier, M. R., *op. cit.*

44. "Listening is a 10-Part Skill" in Nicholas, R. G., *Successful Management*. New York: Doubleday and Co., 1957.

45. Reik, T., *Listening With the Third Ear*. New York: Pyramid Publications, 1972.

46. Ruben, B. A., and R. W. Budd, *Human Communication Handbook: Simulations and Exercises*. Rochelle Park, N.J.: Hayden Book Co., 1975.

47. James, M., and A. Jongeward, *Born to Win: Transactional Analysis With Gestalt Experiments*. Reading, Mass.: Addison-Wesley Publishing Co., 1971.

48. Adapted from: Polsky, H., "Notes on Personal Feedback in Sensitivity Training," *Sociological Inquiry*, 1971, **41,** pp. 175–182.

49. Anderson, J., "Giving and Receiving Feedback," in *Managers and Their Careers: Cases and Readings*. Lorsch, J. W., and L. B. Barnes (eds.). Homewood, Ill.: Richard D. Irwin, 1972, pp. 260–267.

50. Golembiewski, R. T., "Planned Organizational Change: A Major Emphasis on a Behavioral Approach to Administration," in *Sensitivity Training and the Laboratory Approach: Readings, Concepts, and Applications*. Golembiewski, R. T., and A. Blumberg (eds.). Itasca, Ill.: F. E. Peacock Publishers, 1970, pp. 361–390.

51. Hall, J., "Interpersonal Style and the Communication Dilemma: Managerial Implications of the Johari Awareness Model," *Human Relations*, 1974, **27,** pp. 381–399.

*

PART III

GROUP PROCESSES

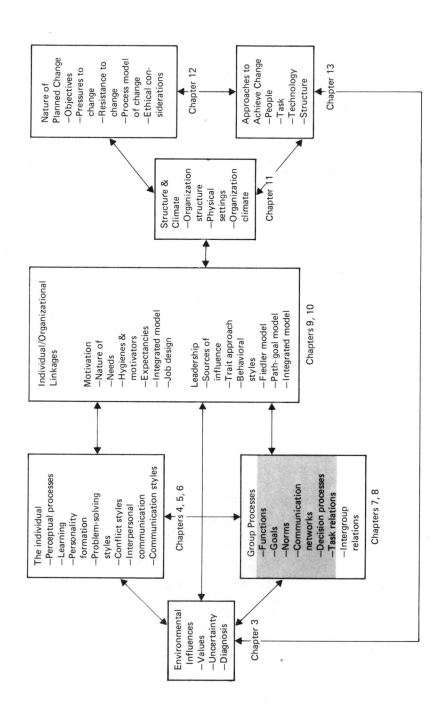

Nature of
Planned Change
—Objectives
—Pressures to
  change
—Resistance to
  change
—Process model
  of change
—Ethical con-
  siderations

Chapter 12

Approaches to
Achieve Change
—People
—Task
—Technology
—Structure

Chapter 13

Structure &
Climate
—Organization
  structure
—Physical
  settings
—Organization
  climate

Chapter 11

Individual/Organizational
Linkages

Motivation
—Nature of
—Needs
—Hygienes &
  motivators
—Expectancies
—Integrated model
—Job design

Leadership
—Sources of
  influence
—Trait approach
—Behavioral
  styles
—Fiedler model
—Path-goal model
—Integrated model

Chapters 9, 10

The individual
—Perceptual processes
—Learning
—Personality
  formation
—Problem-solving
  styles
—Conflict styles
—Interpersonal
  communication
—Communication styles

Chapters 4, 5, 6

Group Processes
—Functions
—Goals
—Norms
—Communication
  networks
—Decision processes
—Task relations
—Intergroup
  relations

Chapters 7, 8

Environmental
Influences
—Values
—Uncertainty
—Diagnosis

Chapter 3

7
INTRAGROUP
RELATIONS

Chapters 4, 5, and 6 focused on the individual, particularly in terms of the styles, personality, learning, and perception of individuals within organizational settings. In these chapters, we made some reference to external forces, such as other individuals, which might influence the very nature of individuals, their behavior, and attitudes. These external dimensions were presented with the primary intent of suggesting their possible relationship and influence on specific individuals within organizations. Thus, the preceding three chapters had an individual orientation. In the next two chapters, the discussion focuses on groups and relations between groups within formal organizations.

The perspectives, variables, and findings associated with groups and intragroup relations seem almost infinite. One researcher recently developed a bibliography of more than three thousand articles on groups. To avoid hopeless confusion on the part of ourselves and the reader, this body of literature will be dealt with selectively. We discuss only concepts and findings that are potentially useful in assisting individuals within organizations to better understand, diagnose, and possibly improve the groups within which they function. However, the specific "technologies" for improving the effectiveness of groups and intragroup relations will be considered more directly in the last part of the book, which is concerned with organizational change and intervention.

The strategy of this chapter is to discuss four major components for considering groups, while explicitly recognizing the interdependencies between them. The major components discussed in this chapter include: (1) the relation between individuals and groups; (2) the nature, types, and functions of groups; (3) major contingencies that have been identified as influencing group members and the ways groups operate; and (4) methods for studying, diagnosing, and assessing the nature and effectiveness of work groups. Of course, the issue of group effectiveness is also considered throughout the chapter. In sum, the primary objectives of this chapter are to assist you:

1. To better understand why you and others do what you do in work groups;

2. To perceive trouble spots and possible reasons why your work group is operating at a less than optimal level;

3. To consider alternative ways of behaving to increase the personal rewards available to you and fellow members of your work group;

4. To appreciate the complexity of contingencies that influence groups, and thereby understand how group members can play a positive role in determining their ultimate achievement level;

5. To recognize that the managerial role requires dealing with both individuals and groups; and

6. To present some ways for diagnosing and assessing your own work group.

INDIVIDUAL–GROUP RELATIONS

Within the United States, there is a strong belief in the importance and centrality of the individual. Our educational, governmental, religious and business institutions frequently proclaim their reason for existence is intimately related to enhancing the welfare of the individual. While the merits of this claim may be argued, our primary interest here concerns whether this view of the individual leads to a dysfunctional restriction in our understanding of organizational behavior. It is our opinion that viewing the individual as the major and/or only unit of analysis worthy of consideration limits our potential understanding of organizational behavior. We are in substantial agreement with the assertion that "individuals are the loci of human value, dignity, and worth; individuals are the source of new ideas; the growth of society depends on the creativity of individuals; and new values originate in the minds of individuals."[1, p. 85] At the same time, we are disturbed by the lingering of nineteenth century notions that idealized, in the extreme, thoughts of self-reliance, self-determination, and self-made men.

Nineteenth-century individualism seemed to ignore the social component of the individual. The social component, however, began to be acknowledged with the disappearance of the land frontier of the United States in the early 1900's. The abstractions of pure rugged individualism and self-sufficiency then began to lose their validity in the world. Thus, the complexity of relations between individuals has increasingly become apparent. We view the individual as playing a substantial role in choosing the kind of person he or she wants to become. At the same time, many skills, values, and modes of behavior must be acquired—usually from numerous group relations over one's lifetime. The importance of groups and their relation to the social component of individuals, who are often lauded as being "self-made," is expressed by Miss Marian Anderson (one of the great artists of this century, who, because of her race and sex, had less support than did many other Americans) this way:

> Dr. Stein asked Miss Anderson why she used "one does" and "we do" instead of using "I." "Possibly because the longer one lives," Miss Anderson replied, "one realizes that there is no particular thing that you can do alone. With the execution of the work that we do there are many people—those who write the music, those who made the piano on which the accompanist is playing, the accompanist who actually lends support to the performance. To go out without any of these things, to stand on your own, even the voice, even the breath, the notion that you have, to go to the platform, is not your own doing. So the "I" in it is very small after all.[2]

While neither society nor organizations can be adequately envisioned as a set of isolated individuals, the 1950's ushered in a new series of worries. Some social critics began to suggest that the pendulum had swung to excessive subordination of the individual to groups.[3] Similarily, in the late 1960's, more and more younger people began to worry that organizational life required conformity and "group-think" for success. This type of conformity and suppression of individual qualities was increasingly perceived as being antagonistic to one's personal self and immediate role as a unique being.

Although there is certainly the potential for individuals and groups to have incompatible interests, it is just as important to recognize that these interests and relations need not be conflicting and are often compatible. The position we will be developing is summed up by the five assertions presented by Cartwright and Lippitt about individuals and groups:

1. Groups do exist; they must be dealt with by any man of practical affairs, or indeed by any child, and they must enter into any adequate account of human behavior . . .

2. Groups are inevitable and ubiquitous . . .

3. Groups mobilize powerful forces that produce effects of the utmost importance to individuals . . .

4. Groups may produce both good and bad consequences . . .

5. A correct understanding of group dynamics permits the possibility that desirable consequences from groups can be deliberately enhanced.[4, pp. 423–425]

Accordingly, our position is a highly contingent one. Some processes and problems may appropriately use the individual as the unit of analysis, others the group, and still others may require consideration of both. For example, the previous discussions of individual styles naturally focused on the individual as the unit of analysis. However, this chapter needs to consider both the individual and the group as appropriate units of analysis.

NATURE, TYPES, AND FUNCTIONS OF GROUPS

Nature

A basic definition of a group is "... a number of persons who communicate with one another often over a span of time, and who are few enough so that each person is able to communicate with all the others, not at secondhand, through other people, but face to face."[5, p. 1] We are concerned with a group when the focus is on the interactions of group members and/or the outputs of the group as a whole, rather than on several individuals who just happen to be close to each other over some period of time. Groups differ from larger systems, such as a division of an organization or an entire organization, in several fundamental ways. First, for a group to exist, the members must usually be able to see and hear each other. Secondly, each group member must usually engage in two-way personal communication with every other member. Thirdly, there are usually minimal hierarchical distinctions in the sense of a chain of command such as one might find in the military or other formal organizations. However, this is not to suggest that there are no status distinctions or differences between members in their relative influence in the group.

Types

With this conception of groups clearly in mind, we might make further refinements by considering different types of groups. There is no ultimately right or wrong way of classifying groups. If you are concerned with the degree of difficulty in gaining membership or becoming accepted as a group member, you might develop a classification scheme that differentiates groups according to whether they are open or closed to new individuals. If you are evaluating groups in an organization setting according to the primary purpose they seem to be serving, the classifications of work (task) groups and friendship groups might be useful. Work groups refer to individuals who interact for the primary purpose of accomplishing organizationally defined goals. Friendship groups serve the primary purpose of meeting the members' personal needs of security, esteem, and the like. Of course, a single group in an organization can serve both work and friendship purposes.

Another way of classifying groups focuses on the nature of the interdependencies between group members in accomplishing some task or objective. Fiedler has identified three types of groups in terms of the nature of member interdependency: interacting, co-acting, and counteracting.[6]

An interacting group exists when one group member cannot perform a task until another member has completed a certain task. This is illustrated by a production group, such as the assembly teams utilized at Samsonite Luggage. Each team consists of about ten people who perform the tasks required to assemble a complete piece of luggage.

A co-acting group exists when the group members perform their jobs relatively independently, in the short run, of other members. We added the qualifying clause of "short run" because if there was *no* interdependency, we would not have a work group. For example, faculty members may be quite independent in the day-to-day teaching of their courses but highly interdependent in considering changes in courses or new course offerings.

A counteracting group exists when the members are interacting to resolve some type of conflict, usually through negotiation and compromise. Labor–management negotiating teams illustrate counteracting groups. The discussion in this chapter heavily emphasizes interacting and co-acting work groups, with some consideration of friendship groups.

Functions for Individuals

In the opening pages of this chapter, several desirable and undesirable impacts of groups on individuals were suggested. Now, we want to consider the sources of attraction of groups for individuals. Depending upon how the individual perceives them, each of the sources of attraction could also represent sources of rejection. This presentation draws heavily from the scheme presented by Shaw.[7] The types of personal needs satisfied from membership within a group might include interpersonal factors, group activities, and group goals. In addition, some personal needs could be satisfied outside the group, but only through group membership. In this instance, the group becomes a means and the ultimate attraction may be to others or goals outside the group. These sources of attraction to a group are summarized in Fig. 7–1.

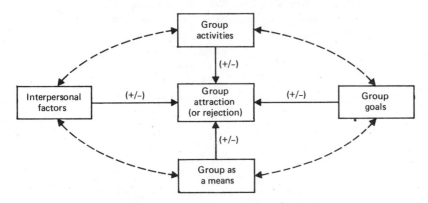

Figure 7–1   Possible Sources of Attraction to or Rejection by a Group

Although all these sources of attraction are discussed as if they were independent of each other, there are several complicating factors worthy of noting. First, each factor can vary in intensity or strength of attraction. For example, interpersonal factors could weigh heavily in the attraction a group holds for an individual, but the group activities may have little significance. Secondly, the presence and intensity of all four factors is likely to increase the strength of attraction relative to fewer factors and/or lower intensities. Third, these four types of factors are also potentially sources of rejection of the group, depending upon the individual's perception of them (as suggested by the minus signs in Fig. 7–1). Finally, some factors may be sources of attraction and others sources of rejection, raising the possibility of internal conflict for the individual.

Interpersonal Factors

An individual may obtain personal satisfaction in a group because of the perceived attractiveness in attitudes, values, physical appearance, and abilities of other members. In some cases, such as a work group where the members have little or no influence in the choice of individuals who join them, interpersonal attraction is not likely to have a major influence on an individual's decision to join the work group. Interpersonal attraction may well play a role between the job applicant and prospective superior and/or peers when they participate in the selection process.

One of the more obvious sources of attraction of an individual to a group or between two persons is the presence of physical attractiveness. Within work groups, the importance of this dimension can vary widely. The difficulties extensively reported by some women and minority members in gaining full acceptance into work groups composed of white males is a notable case. Apparently, color and/or sex are unfortunately sometimes defined as undesirable physical characteristics in the work group.

The similarity of an individual to the group, particularly in terms of attitudes and values, may well play a significant role in organizational settings. You can well imagine the potential for mutual rejection between an individual and group who may not share compatible values—for example, being competitive versus collaborative, distrusting versus trusting, closed to feelings versus open to feelings, and the like (see Fig. 3–1). In a 1973 CBS television special on Phillips Petroleum Co., several Phillips' executives indicated they do investigate and evaluate the attitudes and values of college recruits to determine whether they are compatible with the "company." While Phillips was explicit about the issue of attitude similarity, we suspect it plays some role, possibly at a subconscious level, in many work-group situations. Of course, the excessive demand and pressure for maintaining and creating attitude similarity raises the oftentimes expressed concerns about conformity, group-think, "sheeplike" behavior, and lack of individual freedom. While there is often considerable diversity evidenced in organizations and society, it is useful to note that much of this apparent diversity is *between* groups or organizations. Diversity within small groups is likely to be considerably less. This point will be developed later in the chapter.

The perceived ability or similarity in the ability of others may be a particularly strong form of attraction. If the individual needs to accomplish certain tasks that are interdependent with the tasks being performed by others (such as in interacting or co-acting groups), it is apparent that there might be a motivation to avoid affiliating with an incompetent and ineffective group.

Finally, the individual may simply be attracted to the group because it provides a setting in which one's needs for affiliation, survival, and security may be met. Membership in a group may serve to reduce a real or imagined threat, such as a new superior that threatens members of the work group with dismissal if they don't shape up. Of course, this may also be true for large-scale organizations such as labor unions or trade organizations. Regardless of group size, the underlying rationale is the same: "in unity there is strength." Even if a real threat does not exist, a group may serve to reduce the debilitating condition of excessive anxiety by meeting the individual's need for affiliation.

Group Activities

Attraction to a group may simply occur because the individual likes the activities or things done by the group. This has probably increased in relevance as individuals with higher educational levels seek out opportunities to apply their skills and talents within organizations. These individuals may seek out work groups in which the other members have complementary and supporting skills. For example, a student who has developed accounting skills and enjoys these activities is likely to seek out those work groups that need the application of these skills.

Group Goals

The goals of a group and its activities may be, but are not inherently, interrelated. Similar activities may be used to accomplish different goals. Moreover, we find ourselves immediately considering the goals and values of the individual and whether they are compatible, neutral, or incompatible with the group goals. An engineering graduate might be highly attracted to the general types of activities performed by a work group in a chemical firm, until he or she learns that the ultimate purpose of this group is to provide fundamental knowledge that can be used to increase the kill power of napalm manufactured by the firm. If the individual happens to be a pacifist, the group goals and personal goals are likely to be in sharp conflict with each other. Or a new employee might be attracted to the types of activities of a work group, but decide to leave when it is determined that their real purpose is to fight management, "goof off," and minimize output. The assumption here is that the individual's goals involve high achievement and performance.

The Group as a Means

A group is a means when the individual is attracted to it in order to attain one or more goals external to the group. This can occur in both small and larger groups like fraternities, sororities, country clubs, political groups, and the like. For example, one study found that belonging to certain business firms increased the recognition and status of the members in the community.[8] It is common to find some work groups receiving recognition and status from others outside the group because of such things as having more autonomy or more interesting work. Thus, the attraction to the group may be based on several factors, including the nature of the group activities and the ability of the group to serve as a means for obtaining external recognition and status.

In sum, a group can have a powerful attraction to an individual for a variety of reasons. At the same time, groups often hold an inherent dilemma for the individual. One author suggests that the individual ". . . wishes to be part of the group and at the same time to remain a separate, unique individual. He wants to participate, yet observe; to relate to, yet not *become* the other; to join, but to preserve his skills as an individual."[9, p. 368]

MAJOR CONTINGENCIES AFFECTING GROUPS

This section presents some of the major contingencies that can influence groups, particularly work groups, in terms of their behavior and outputs. By behavior, we mean the activities and interactions within the group. Activities of a group can be defined as ". . . things that people do: work on the physical environment, with implements, and with other persons."[10, p. 34] Activities is a very broad concept and can include a variety of behaviors, such as writing, walking, drinking, typing, sawing, giving instructions, etc. . . . Interactions in a group refers to the ". . . fact that some unit of activity of one man follows, or, if we like the word better, is stimulated by some unit of activity of another, aside from any question of what the units [of activity] may be."[11, p. 36] Again, interaction is a very broad concept and most often takes place through verbal and nonverbal communications. The outputs of a group might refer to such things as member sentiments and the achievement of certain tasks and goals. Sentiments refer ". . . to internal states of the human body . . . and range . . . all the way from fear, hunger, and thirst, to such probably far more complicated psychological states as liking or disliking for individuals, approval or disapproval of their actions."[12, p. 38] The achievement of tasks and goals could vary from the making of decisions to the creation of physical objects. Typically, a staff or managerial group primarily has decisions as their outputs, whereas a work group in a manufacturing plant might primarily have physical objects as their outputs, such as assembled luggage.

Figure 7–2 identifies a number of contingencies that can influence the behavior and outputs of a group, from the standpoint both of the group as a whole and of the individual members. Of course, these variables are quite interrelated, as suggested by the dashed line between each of them in Fig. 7–2. For example, the size of a group is likely to have an impact on the network of communication, which, in turn, is likely to influence the processes for making decisions. To keep the discussion from becoming excessively complex, we will explicitly mention only some of the more important interrelationships between these variables. In reading the following discussion, you should keep in mind three fundamental points. First, the nature of each of these contingencies can vary between groups and within a group over time. Secondly, these variables can be consciously influenced by the members, unconsciously influenced by the members, and/or influenced by factors external to the group. Thus, the variables affecting groups, particularly work groups, can be dynamic and changing over time. Thirdly, the behavior and outputs of groups can also be viewed as variables that can ultimately influence a group. This is suggested by the lines with double arrowheads between a contingency and the box labeled "Group Behavior and Outputs."

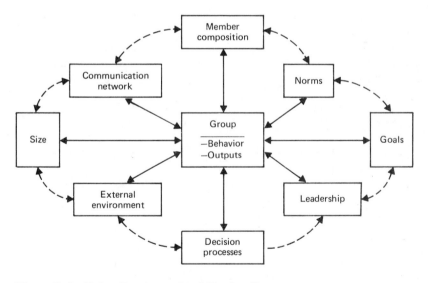

Figure 7–2   Major Contingencies Affecting Groups

Size

The size of a group is likely to range from two members to a normal upper limit of twelve members and rarely more than sixteen members. In the way we have defined a group, twelve members is probably near the upper limit of each member's capacity to react and interact with every other member simultaneously.[13] Some of the possible effects of size on groups are shown in Fig. 7–3. This figure shows nine dimensions of groups within the three categories of leadership, members, and group process. The likely effects of group size for each of these dimensions is shown as varying from "low," to "moderate," to "high." The tendencies identified indicate changes that are likely to occur with increases in the number of group members. As suggested in Fig. 7–3, groups of eight or more members are often quite different than groups with two to seven members. A sixteen-member board of directors is likely to operate quite differently than an executive group of seven members. Of course, boards of directors often form subgroups of five to seven members to consider specific decisions in greater depth than is possible with the whole board meeting at the same time.

Figure 7–3   Some Possible Effects of Size on Groups [15]

	Group Size		
Dimensions	2-7 Members	8-12 Members	13-16 Members
LEADERSHIP			
1. Demands on leader	Low	Moderate	High
2. Differences between leaders and members	Low	Low to moderate	Moderate to high
3. Direction by leader	Low	Low to moderate	Moderate to high
MEMBERS			
4. Tolerance of direction from leader	Low to high	Moderate to high	High
5. Domination of group interaction by a few members	Low	Moderate to high	High
6. Inhibition in participation by ordinary members	Low	Moderate	High
GROUP PROCESS			
7. Formalization of rules and procedures	Low	Low to moderate	Moderate to high
8. Time required for reaching judgmental decisions	Low to moderate	Moderate	Moderate to high
9. Tendency for subgroups to form within group	Low	Moderate to high	High

As with each contingency that can affect groups, a number of qualifications can be introduced to the tendencies identified in Fig. 7–3[14]. For example, if there is considerable time available to the group and the members are sufficiently committed to the group activities and goals, we might not expect the tendencies identified to become nearly so pronounced beyond seven members. If the group's primary activity and goal is to bring together the expertise of each respective member to arrive at decisions primarily based on expertise rather than judgment, a larger-sized group would not necessarily experience the tendencies identified. As will be emphasized in Chapter 10, leadership styles and practices can play a crucial role in influencing group processes to offset the direct effects of group size.

Communication Networks

From the previous discussion, it may be apparent that group size places limits on the possible communication networks within a group. In principle, as the size of a group increases arithmetically, the number of possible interrelationships increases *geometrically.*[16] Accordingly, there is a potential for disproportionately more variety and complexity in communication networks in a twelve-person group than in a three-person group. To obtain a better understanding of the possible direct effects of different communication networks, we will consider only a group of a single size. This will minimize the complicating effects of different numbers of members in a group.

A communication network is defined as the flow of verbal, nonverbal (gestures, facial expressions, and postural changes), written, or other forms of signals (data) between two or more group members. Further, the emphasis is on the pattern of signal flow, such as between member A and member B, or member A and all other members simultaneously, rather than on whether the signal sent was received as intended by the sender. Of course, communication networks can influence the likelihood of increased congruency between the intended sent signals and the signals received.

While every member may theoretically be able to communicate with all other members in real-life groups, the direction and number of communication channels is often somewhat limited.[17] Thus, groups may not always function in terms of the all-channel network illustrated in Fig. 7–4. For example, in committee meetings, there may be varying levels of formality in the rules and procedures influencing who may speak, what may be discussed, and in what order. The relative status or ranking of group members also may differ, with the likely consequence of higher-status members dominating the theoretically all-channel communication network. Finally, even where the all-channel (open) network is encouraged, the members may actually use a more constrained or limited network arrangement.[18]

Types of Network

As shown in Fig. 7–4, we are only concerned with five basic communication networks for a five-person group. There are actually about sixty possible communication networks for a five-person group. As a practical matter, the five networks presented illustrate the major differences that may be found in a five-person group. The five basic communication networks shown in Fig. 7–4 are labeled as the *star* (sometimes called the "wheel"), the Y, the *chain,* the *circle,* and the *all-channel* network. Each line between every pair of names represents a two-way communication channel. The networks are presented in terms of the degree of restriction on members in the use of communication channels. An inspection of the networks reveals the star configuration as the most restricted, since all communications must flow between Jane and each of the other members. At the other extreme, the all-channel network is the least restricted or most open, since each member may communicate with all other members simultaneously.

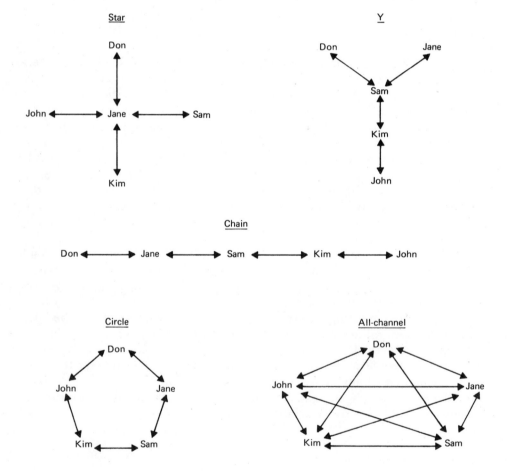

Figure 7–4   Some Communication Networks for Five-Person Groups

Effects of Different Networks

The importance of communication networks lies in the potential effects of different networks on such things as predicting group leaders, effectiveness, efficiency, member satisfaction, and the like.[19] Figure 7–5 attempts to provide a rough synthesis and comparison of the communication networks in terms of five assessment criteria. The first criterion, degree of centralization, refers to the degree to which some individuals have access to more communication channels than other individuals. The star network (see Fig. 7–5) is regarded as the most centralized, because all communications flow from and to only one individual. On the other hand, the all-channel network is the least centralized because any individual can communicate with any other individual or all other individuals at the same time. The second criterion, number of possible communication channels, is closely related (but in the opposite direction) to the degree-of-centralization criterion. The number of possible communication channels refers to the extent to which an increased number of individuals have access to channels of communication. The number of possible communication channels for the members as a whole is at a minimum in the star network and at a maximum in the all-channel network. The criterion of leadership predictability refers to the ability to anticipate which individual is likely to emerge as the group leader. In Fig. 7–4, the following individuals are likely to emerge as leaders: Jane in the star network; Sam in the Y network; and possibly Sam in the chain network. In each of these three networks, the anticipated leader should have greater amounts of information and greater control

Assessment Criteria	Types of Communication Networks				
	Star	"Y"	Chain	Circle	All-channel
Degree of centralization	Very high	High	Moderate	Low	Very low
Number of possible communication channels	Very low	Low	Moderate	Moderate	Very high
Leadership predictability	Very high	High	Moderate	Low	Very low
Average group satisfaction	Low	Low	Moderate	Moderate	High
Range in individual member satisfaction	High	High	Moderate	Low	Very low

Figure 7–5   Some Comparisons of Five Communication Networks for Five-Person Groups

over the dissemination of information, suggestions, and the like, than the other group members.

The fourth and fifth assessment criteria in Fig. 7–5 refer to overall (average) satisfaction of the group members as a whole within each network and the *range* in satisfaction between group members. There are a number of interesting relationships between these two criteria.

In the star network, the average member satisfaction in the group is likely to be the lowest compared to the other networks. But the *range* in individual member satisfaction is likely to be high relative to the other networks. Why might this be the case? First, Jane, in the star network, is the center of attention and has considerable influence over the group. Thus, she may find this network highly satisfying. On the other hand, the other members are highly dependent on Jane and may well play a peripheral role to her in the decision process. Accordingly, the average satisfaction of the group as a whole is likely to be relatively low.

In contrast, the all-channel network creates the potential for greater participation by all members in terms of their interest and ability to contribute to the group. Thus, while the average group satisfaction may be relatively high, there is likely to be a lower range between the satisfaction scores of individual members.

Complicating Factors

As usual, there are complicating factors in these and other findings regarding communication networks, particularly in terms of the relative effectiveness of different networks. At a basic level, we may differentiate between problems as being simple versus complex. With simple problems, there are few demands on the members in terms of:

1. Collecting, categorizing, and evaluating information;

2. Generating goals or objectives to be achieved;

3. Developing and evaluating alternatives; and

4. Coping with human problems associated with the task at hand.

Of course, complex problems are characterized by a high degree of one or more of these types of demands. As you might anticipate, the all-channel network is often most effective for complex problems and the star network may well be quite effective for simple problems. Another qualifying factor is the degree of member interdependence required to accomplish the group's task. Complex problems, in which there is little member interdependence, may be effectively handled through one of the more centralized communication networks. Since complex problems usually require member interdependence, we don't expect this to occur very often. For complex problems requiring a high degree of member interdependence, the all-channel network is much more likely to be effective. Additional contingencies, such as the degree of problem complexity and the degree of member interdependence, are likely to influence the effectiveness of different communication networks and our findings with respect to the assessment criteria presented in Fig. 7–5.

We need to be cautious about simplistic claims as to the "best" network. Nonetheless, our discussion of communication networks leads to several managerial implications. First, there is probably no single optimal network that is likely to prove effective for a work group with a variety of tasks and objectives. The seemingly efficient and low-cost star network, if used exclusively by a work group, may actually be dysfunctional. Member satisfaction may become so low that individuals will leave the group or lose motivation to contribute. Second, complex problems requiring high member interdependence may be dealt with ineffectively because of inadequate sharing of information, inadequate consideration of alternatives, and the like. Third, there are always trade-offs or opportunity costs to be considered. A work group committed to the exclusive use of the all-channel network could experience inefficiency in dealing with simple problems requiring little member interdependence. In such cases, members may also become bored and dissatisfied with group processes because they feel their time is being wasted. Another trade-off with the all-channel network is its implied labor costs. In sum, we contend that different networks should be used that most appropriately serve the group tasks or problems at hand with the simultaneous recognition of the impact on member satisfaction.

Member Composition

Another contingency or variable that may potentially influence the processes and outcomes of a group is simply the innate and acquired characteristics of the individual members. Let's consider a couple of ways by which group members can differ and how the types and levels of member skills can influence the outputs of a group.

Recall the discussion in Chapter 5 about possible differences in individual problem-solving styles. Individuals were differentiated by their preference for taking in information from the outside world, i.e., either by sensation or by intuition, and by the two basic ways of reaching a decision, either by thinking or by feeling. By combining the two information-input approaches and the two decision-making approaches, we arrived at a model of problem-solving styles, which included four basic types: sensation–thinking; sensation–feeling; intuition–thinking; and intuition–feeling. As discussed in Chapter 5, problem-solving groups can have their processes and decisions affected by the particular combination of member decision styles in the group.

Member composition could also differ in terms of the presence or absence of creative personalities in one or more members. Creative personalities are characterized by such attributes as: (1) unique and varied ideas; (2) openness to new and different information from a variety of areas; (3) ability to deal with uncertainty (but also trying to make some order out of it); and (4) the ability to think in terms of long decision-making chains (i.e., ability to see the problem as a whole), while simultaneously evaluating the consequences of each decision step for other parts of the problem.[20] Creativity is usually thought of as more than originality—it must also serve some useful purpose. A group faced with simple tasks may find the presence of creative personalities of little consequence for effectiveness. There is even the possibility that creative personalities in such a situation may side-track the group into other unrelated areas and tend to make its members apathetic. On the other hand, the potential utility of creative personalities in groups faced with complex and novel problems should be apparent. A manager in a work group needs to be sensitive to the members' abilities, and should attempt to draw upon and match them with types of problems faced by the group. Several approaches managers may use for increasing group creativity, regardless of the level of individual creativity in the group, will be discussed in Chapter 13.

In attempting to draw conclusions about the effects of member composition on effectiveness or performance, we should recognize that either too much or too little of certain attributes of members could adversely influence group effectiveness.[21]

Norms

In the most limited sense, group norms refer to the generally agreed upon standards of member and group behavior that have emerged as a consequence of member interaction over time. In the broader sense, a norm is the "behavior that is anticipated and expected by the group of its members."[22, p. 3] Thus, individuals may join or form groups in which many of the norms actually exist prior to group interaction. For example, bricklayers who have never worked together before may begin work at a construction site with a common norm as to about how many bricks should be laid on an average workday. Norms differ from organizational rules in that they are unwritten and must have some degree of acceptance and implementation by members before they can be said to exist. On the other hand, rules may be written and distributed to all members in the form of manuals and memorandums, but may be widely ignored and not accepted by members. A final possible difference between a norm and a rule is that the former must be backed up by some type of power or influence system. If a member consistently and excessively violates the group's norm(s), there is usually some type of negative and/or positive sanction of the individual by other members. This can range from physical abuse or threats, to the withdrawal of rewards such as praise, recognition, and acceptance. While we talk of norms in this section, it should be emphasized that groups need to be viewed in terms of normative systems, i.e., specific norms are often interdependent and mutually reinforcing to one another.

Group members often have only a vague conscious awareness of the norms by which they live, even though norms may be a powerful influence on group and member behavior. It is imperative we bring these subconscious group forces to the level of conscious awareness. This is important for two reasons. First, awareness increases the potential for individual and group freedom. This is based on the assumption that self-awareness and awareness of our environment is a necessary (even though insufficient) condition for freedom. Second, norms and normative systems can have positive and/or negative influences on the effectiveness of individuals, groups, and organizations.

Categories of Norms

Let's consider some of the categories of norms in terms of their possible positive or negative impact on the effectiveness of work groups, departments, or even entire organizations. Figure 7–6 identifies nine categories, which are obviously somewhat interrelated, around which work groups or entire organizations may hold positive and/or negative norms. A norm is labeled as positive or negative on the basis of whether it is likely to contribute or hinder the accomplishment of task objectives. For each category, an illustration of a possible positive and negative norm is given. There are also a number of popular criticisms of large-scale organizations for maintaining and encouraging norms like "It is best to keep opinions to yourself and play it safe" and "The most important thing is to appear to work hard, regardless of the results." Unfortunately, there is little good research-based data to demonstrate the extent to which such norms actually exist in organizations.

Conformity

An important issue for work groups is that the norms and the pressures to adhere to them may result in conformity. There are actually two types of conformity: *compliance* and *private acceptance.* [23] Compliance refers to the behavior of an individual which becomes or remains similar to the group's wishes because of real or imagined group pressure. The compliance type of conformity does not mean that the individual personally believes in the desirability or appropriateness of these actions. In our opinion, a considerable amount of the conformity found in organizations and/or work groups may be of this type. There may be a variety of reasons for compliance, without personal acceptance. The members might feel that the appearance of a "united front" is necessary for them to succeed in accomplishing their goals. The president of General Motors is not likely to announce "After considerable argument and debate, the majority of my executive committee finally agreed to increase car prices by an average of 6 percent this year." Rather, the G.M. president might say: "After considerable study, the Executive Committee of G.M. unanimously agrees that it is essential to raise the price of our cars by an average of 6

Figure 7–6   Categories of Organizational Norms with Possible Positive and Negative Examples

Categories	Examples	
	Positive Norms	Negative Norms
Organizational and personal pride	Members speak up for the company when it is criticized unfairly	Members don't care about company problems
Performance/ Excellence	Members try to improve, even if they are doing well	Members are satisfied with the minimum level of performance necessary
Teamwork/ Communication	Members listen and are receptive to the ideas and opinions of others	Members gossip behind the backs of others rather than deal with issues openly and constructively
Leadership/ Supervision	Members ask for help when they need it	Members hide their problems and avoid their superiors
Colleague/Associate relations	Members refuse to take advantage of fellow workers	Members don't care about the well-being of fellow workers
Customer/Consumer relations	Members show concern about serving the customers	Members are indifferent and, when possible, hostile to customers
Honesty and security	Members are concerned about dishonesty and pilferage	Members are expected to steal a little and be honest only when necessary
Training and development	Members really show they care about training and development	There is much talk about training and development but no one takes it seriously
Innovation and change	Members are usually looking for better ways of doing their job	Members stick to the old ways of doing their jobs

Adapted and modified by permission of the publisher from: Allen, R. F. and S. Pilnick, "Confronting the Shadow Organization: How to Detect and Defeat Negative Norms," *Organizational Dynamics,* 1973, 1, pp. 3–18.

percent, even though the costs of producing a car exceed this percentage." On a more personal level, individuals may conform because it is instrumental in meeting their needs to be liked and accepted by others. This may be especially true for lower-status members in relation to higher-status members, such as a subordinate and a superior. Finally, we might comply simply because the costs of conformity are much less than the costs of nonconformity, which could serve to threaten the maintenance of the existing relationship in the group. Another way of stating this is that the individual makes some trade-offs and attempts to maximize rewards and minimize costs.

The second type of conformity refers to compliance based on the personal acceptance of the group's wishes by the individual. In this type of conformity, the person's behavior and attitudes or beliefs are consistent with the group's wishes. The strength of this type of conformity is, by definition, much stronger than the compliance type of conformity.

Let's consider a hypothetical example of these two types of conformity for two employees in a work group. Let's assume that the work group has norms as to the appropriate output for a day's work, such as between 90 and 100 units. There is high conformity within this allowable range of output. Management feels the workers could produce substantially more units without sacrificing quality. After much study, management decides to implement an incentive system on an experimental basis, subject to modification or elimination by either party (workers or managers) after a six-month trial period. To minimize problems of possible distrust and meet the security needs of workers, the incentive plan is designed as a supplement to the present hourly pay system. What happens? Bob, who has been conforming to the output norms on the basis of compliance, is quite enthusiastic toward management's proposal. However, Sam, who has been conforming to the output norms on the basis of personal acceptance, might receive management's proposal with considerable distrust, anxiety, and opposition. These two types of conformity provide major insight into why some members of highly conforming groups may easily change behavior, while others may oppose and/or find the process of change quite stressful.

There is no simple answer to the issue of conformity in work groups.[24] Without norms and some conformity to them, work groups would be chaotic and random environments in which few tasks could be accomplished. At the other extreme, excessive and mechanistic conformity threatens the important place we claim to hold for the individual in our society, as well as the ability of groups to deal with change, uncertainty, and complex problems. One possible recommendation, in coping with the dilemmas of conformity, is that work groups can learn to become more self-aware of the conformity, and its possible positive and negative consequences, and reassess or change the norms and the sanction system which serves as the underlying base of conformity. From the standpoint of group members, it appears that the functional or dysfunctional nature of conformity may depend on the norms of the group itself.

Effects on Productivity

We need to be careful of assuming that work groups always have well defined norms regarding standards of productivity and/or strongly enforced conformity with them. This conclusion is brought into clear focus in an interview and questionnaire study of workers in the engineering divisions and power plants of the Tennessee Valley Authority. The subjects were asked "If a person on your job were known as a fast, energetic worker, how would this affect his chances of being close friends with people on his own level on the job?"[25, p. 108] The findings were somewhat surprising: 56 percent indicated it wouldn't matter one way or the other in terms of acceptance; 27 percent thought hard work would make it easier to gain acceptance in the work group; and 16 percent thought an energetic worker would find it harder to make friends. A possible criticism of these findings is that they are based on the conscious response of members and may not reflect what actually happens in the work group.

Goals

There is generally a natural correspondece between group goals and group norms. It is logical, but not always true, that groups would adopt norms to facilitate the attainment of their goals. One of the purposes of some organizational development efforts is to assist group members in assessing whether the norms they follow are consistent, neutral, or actually conflicting with the group and/or organizational goals. For example, a work group may claim and believe that one of its goals is to improve its efficiency, which is likely to be compatible with productivity goals "assigned" to the work group by higher management. Close inspection of the members' behavior might actually reveal norms counterproductive to this expressed goal. There may be norms of "Don't produce too much" and "Don't make too many changes." Norms such as these, even if the members are consciously aware of them, could be rationalized as being instrumental to their efficiency goal. Members could claim producing more than the norm will "burn them out," resulting in lower long-term efficiency. On the other hand, always looking for and introducing changes takes members away from their primary tasks and is too disruptive to their operation. However, if the work group goals are concerned with such things as minimizing managerial influence and increasing the opportunity for social interaction among members, norms placing some restrictions on worker output could be perceived by the members as functional.

Relation to Individuals

Group goals cannot exist outside the minds of the members in some metaphysical collective mind. Group goals, however, cannot be directly determined from the goals of individual members nor can they be summed up by simply adding together the individual member goals. Group goals are concerned with the objectives or states desired for the group as a whole, not just the objectives desired by each individual member. The concept implicit in our assertions is that the whole is greater than and different from the simple sum of the individual parts. For example, the positive and negative norms illustrated in Fig. 7–6 have primary meaning in relation to group goals and groups as a whole (where we focus on structure, size, norms, and the like). In sum, group goals refer to the group as a unit or system; i.e., they refer to desired states of the unit, not just individual members.[26]

Pervasiveness of Goals

Throughout this book, we keep returning to the concept of goals as important to understanding, predicting, and changing systems such as individuals, groups, and organizations. Each of these systems is partially defined as possessing the characteristic of being goal-oriented or purposive systems. Accordingly, if we are concerned about variables affecting group behavior and sentiments, we must always try to make some assessment of group goals. Of course, individual member goals and the organizational goals within which the group functions are likely to influence both the types of group goals and the actual behavior and outputs of the group. There are a number of possibilities for compatible and conflicting goals with each system (i.e., individual, group, and organization), as well as between systems. For example, work groups typically have socio-emotional goals and task goals. In effective groups, there appears to be concern with both of these goals, with about two-thirds of the time spent on task issues and one-third on socio-emotional issues.[27] The exclusive pursuit of only one or the other of these goals over the long run would reduce effectiveness, increase conflicts, and possibly result in dissolution of the group. The role of goals in influencing work-group behavior and outputs becomes even more complex when we consider the possible compatibilities and conflicts between group goals, individual member goals, and organizational goals. Since several other chapters have pursued these relationships, we won't do so here in depth.

Cohesiveness

One group attribute, cohesiveness, is substantially influenced by the degree of compatibility between group goals and individual member goals. Cohesiveness generally refers to the strength of the member's desires to remain in the group and his or her commitment to the group. Groups whose members have a strong desire to remain in the group and personally accept its goals would be considered a highly cohesive group relative to one where the opposite was found.

Relation to Conformity

There is no one-to-one relationship between cohesiveness and conformity. It may be reasonable to find low cohesiveness associated with low conformity.

While high cohesiveness probably exists along with at least a moderate level of conformity, there is no inherent requirement that high cohesiveness can exist only with the presence of high conformity. Mature groups may have high member commitment and stick-togetherness, while simultaneously respecting individual differences in terms of behavior and thought. This might occur more frequently when the cohesion is substantially based on a common commitment to group task goals. Moreover, if the group confronts complex problems, low or moderate conformity may not only be tolerated, but actually be encouraged and supported by members.

Impact on Productivity

The degree of group cohesion is especially important because of its potential impact on group productivity. Actually, it might be more appropriate to think of cohesion and productivity as potentially interdependent. This is particularly true for groups who have highly task-related goals. If the group is successful in reaching its goals, the positive feedback of its attainments may serve to enhance member commitment.[28] A winning football team, everything else equal, is likely to be more cohesive than one with a mediocre record. Of course, the cause-and-effect relation can work in both directions. Thus, a cohesive football team may also be more likely to win games.

On the other hand, low cohesiveness may interfere with the ability to obtain task goals because group resources are not as likely to be shared and interactions are not as likely to take place as frequently as necessary. High cohesiveness in work groups may actually be associated with low productivity *if* the group goals are contrary to organizational and/or managerial goals. Thus, the relation between cohesion and productivity cannot be anticipated or understood unless we also know the group's goals and norms.

The potential complexity between cohesion, productivity, and other variables was suggested in a study of 228 small work groups in a plant manufacturing heavy machinery.[29] Cohesiveness was evaluated in terms of the degree to which: members perceived themselves to be part of the group; members preferred to remain in the group rather than leave; and members perceived their group to be superior to other groups with respect to the way the members stuck together, helped each other out, and got along together. The productivity measure was obtained from a single productivity average for each respondent for a three-month period prior to completing the questionnaires. The following major findings were obtained:

1. Productivity between workers was more uniform in high-cohesiveness groups than low-cohesive ones, suggesting that cohesiveness had a conformity effect;

2. Productivity differences between work groups were greater in high-cohesive groups than low-cohesive ones; and

3. High cohesiveness was associated with high or low productivity, depending upon the degree to which members felt management was supportive or threatening to them.

Leadership

In our opinion, studies of small groups within organizations have placed excessive emphasis on the importance of emergent or informal leadership, especially as related to the accomplishment of task goals. An informal leader is usually thought of as the individual who emerges over time with relatively high influence in the group.

Multiple Leaders

Leadership in a group has popularly been regarded as the province of a single individual. As mentioned earlier, work groups often have at least two major classes of goals—socio-emotional goals and task goals. It is quite possible for a group to have two leaders, one who provides leadership with respect to socio-emotional issues and the other who provides leadership with respect to task issues. These two goals may require different personal skills for attainment and they may be somewhat conflicting at times—a combination of demands often difficult to fulfill in one person.[30]

Some research indicates that informal task leaders do emerge in groups with formal (designated) leaders. For example, in a study of seventy-two decision-making groups with between five and seventeen members, the informal emergent task leaders were generally characterized as follows: (1) very high on total participation; (2) members of conference groups in which the formal leaders did not engage in certain behaviors that would have facilitated discussion and problem-solving; (3) exhibited much more facilitating discussion and problem-solving behavior than did the formal leader or other high participators who were not identified as informal leaders; and (4) were called "more needed" significantly often by the chairman and other members.[31] This and other studies leads us to suggest that informal task leaders of work groups, where a formal leader already exists, are most likely to emerge only if the formal leader abdicates the task-related responsibilities and/or lacks the necessary abilities to carry them out. In contrast, there is some basis for suggesting that the socio-emotional leader of a work group is more likely to emerge informally.

Effective Group Leaders

Effective leaders of work groups generally exhibit more of the following types of behavior than other members:

Creating and maintaining a clear conception of the primary group task or goal;

2. Maintaining a unique position in the group by both participating in it and yet remaining sufficiently detached so as to observe the group as a whole;

3. Assuming primary responsibility for the regulation or control of interactions (i.e., exchanges and interrelationships) between the group and other groups or individuals; and

4. Permitting and encouraging some shifting of leadership tasks among group members who are more qualified to meet the changing demands on the group.[32]

These behaviors certainly provide only an outline of strategic qualities needed for effective work-group leaders. The extent to which activities and processes are accommodated by formal or informal leaders can have substantial impact on group behavior and outcomes, including productivity, member satisfaction, and the like.

The importance of group leadership may be especially profound in its indirect and subtle effects. Virtually all of the variables affecting groups previously discussed (i.e., size, communication network, member composition, norms, and goals will be disproportionately influenced by the person or persons in the group leadership position(s). For example, the effective group leader often assumes a key role in the relations between the group and its external environment. This person is likely to have substantial influence over the selection of new group members—a process that is virtually universal in work groups. Even when the work-group members participate in the selection of new members, it is common for the group leader to provide some screening of potential members, thereby limiting the alternative choices available to the members.

As will be seen, decision processes within groups are also directly and indirectly influenced by group leadership.

DECISION PROCESSES

This discussion of decision processes in groups will be limited to four areas of group decision making: (1) individual versus group decision-making; (2) levels of group decision-making; (3) types of group decisions; (4) some potential effects of group participation in decision making; and (5) interacting versus nominal groups.[33]

Individual Versus Group

Which is better—individual decision-making or group decision-making? While this is the way the issue of individual versus group decision-making is popularly formulated, it is probably an inappropriate and meaningless question. It accomplishes little more than locking people into "either–or" positions. It appears much more useful to ask: Under what conditions does individual or group decision-making, or some combination of the two, appear to be relatively more effective? Some research suggests that one of the key situational factors that indicate a superiority of one over the other is the nature of the problem. In making decisions, groups often appear to be superior to an individual (or the same number of individuals working independently) when the tasks involve: generating many ideas or very unique ideas; recalling information accurately; and estimating and evaluating ambiguous or uncertain situations. Individuals seem to have the edge for "thinking out" problems that require long chains of decisions to be made for solution.[34] The last type of task is concerned with the implementation of predesigned plans, rules, or instructions. If we have a group in which members can perform their jobs relatively independent of others, individual decision-making is likely to be the more appropriate mode. However, if work group members are interdependent and must cooperate with one another, we probably need greater group decision-making for effective performance.[35]

As suggested earlier in the chapter, work groups over time often confront different types of tasks and experience varying degrees of member interdependency for different problems. Thus, we would fully expect both individual and group decision-making in effective groups. Our intent here has been to suggest several underlying criteria that a work group or its leadership should consider in deciding when to use individual decision-making and when to use group decision-making. There are costs associated with inappropriate use of either individual or group decision modes. The inappropriate use of group decision-making may have dual costs: organizational resources have been wasted because members' time could have been used in other pursuits; and member motivation might be reduced because of boredom and a feeling that their time has been wasted. The inappropriate use of individual decision-making could result in poor coordination, lower quality and creativity in decision-making, greater errors, and the like.

The complexities of individual versus group decision-making are furthered when we realize there are a number of levels of group decision-making.

Levels of Group Decision-Making

In speaking of levels of group decision-making, we refer to whether the members are involved in none or all of the elements or steps in the decision-making process. Of course, a work group may use or experience various levels of group decision-making for different types of decisions (problems). The types of decisions that may be made by a group will be discussed in the next section.

The vertical axis in Fig. 7–7 outlines various levels to group decision-making. The horizontal axis indicates a qualitative range in group participation, from none to high. As suggested by the rising line in the figure, the amount of participation by members increases as the level of group decision-

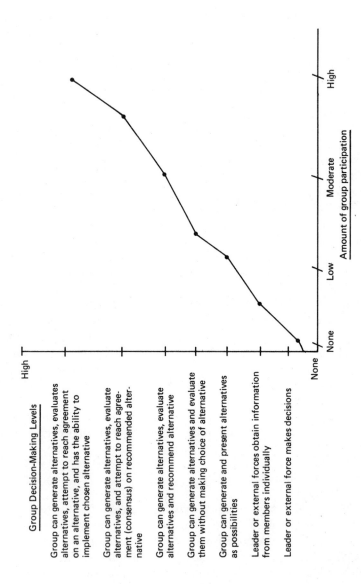

Figure 7–7   Relation Between Group Decision-Making Levels and Participation

making increases. At the lowest level in Fig. 7–7, we don't really have group decision-making because the leader (or some external force) simply makes the decision and announces it. An example of an "external force" might be an announcement by management about a new pay-incentive system being implemented within two months. It is conceivable that the work-group leadership, formal or informal, had no part in making decisions about the pay-incentive system. Another external force might be a federal inspector who orders a number of changes in the practices and procedures of the work group to bring them into compliance with the Federal Occupational Safety and Health Act. At the other extreme of group decision-making levels, we find the group engaged in virtually all phases of problem-solving. The group can generate alternatives, evaluate alternatives, and attempt to reach agreement on an alternative, and has the ability to implement its chosen alternative.

Increased group decision-making and autonomy implies certain responsibilities and the accountability for them will be shared by the group as a whole. Under conditions of high task interdependence and a need for cooperation, it may be appropriate to encourage group enlargement and accountability for certain tasks and goals, rather than job enlargement for the individual. A common mechanism for doing this might be an incentive scheme heavily weighted on the performance or outputs of the work group as a whole, rather than on each individual member.

Types of Group Decisions

The degree of work-group autonomy is concerned with the *types* of decisions made by the group. This is suggested by Fig. 7–8, which shows a variety of decisions that might be made by a work group. The autonomy of a work group increases as you read *up* the list of decisions in Fig. 7–8. Moreover, it is generally assumed that these types of decisions are cumulative. A group that can decide on questions of recruitment will also have an influence on questions of internal leadership and production methods.

The relationships between levels of group decision-making (as shown in Fig. 7–7) and degrees of work-group autonomy (as shown in Fig. 7–8) might be summed up this way: First, Fig. 7–7 is primarily concerned with the process or level of group decision-making, whereas Fig. 7–8 is concerned with the types (i.e., content or substance) of decisions made by and within the group. Secondly, a group may make extensive use of a high level of group decision-making without necessarily being highly autonomous. However, a highly autonomous group must use a high level of group decision-making. For example, a group may have a high level of group decision-making (e.g., generate alternatives, evaluate alternatives, implement alternative chosen, etc.) with respect to determining its internal distribution of tasks, but have little or no influence over the qualitative and quantitative goals "assigned" to it by higher management or others.

Types of Decisions	Level of Group Autonomy
	High
Group has influence on its qualitative goals.	
Group has influence on its quantitative goals.	
Group decides on questions of external leadership.	
Group decides on what additional tasks to take on.	
Group decides when it will work.	
Group decides on questions of production.	
Group determines internal distribution of tasks.	
Group decides on questions of recruitment.	
Group decides on questions of internal leadership.	
Group members determine their individual production methods.	
	Low

Figure 7–8   Continuum of Work Group Autonomy

Adapted from: Gulowsen, J., "A Measure of Work—Group Autonomy," in *Design of Jobs*. Davis, L. and J. Taylor (eds.). Middlesex: Penguin Books, 1972, pp. 374–390.

Group Participation

Work group participation is often closely linked to the distribution of power[36] and the control structure[37] of organizations. These issues will be taken up in the next chapter. For now, we would like to describe one organizational study indicating the possible benefits of group decision-making. This will be balanced by a presentation of several limitations to participation.

Possible Benefits.   This section reviews a field and experimental study conducted by Bragg and Andrews.[38] Participative decision-making (hereafter PDM) refers to a form of involvement in which decisions as to the work group's activities are heavily influenced, if not arrived at, by the work group that has to implement those decisions.[39] PDM was introduced into the laundry department of one hospital. Two other hospital laundries were used as comparison groups; i.e., there were no formal changes made in their level of PDM. Before PDM was implemented, the laundry foreman accepted the idea and fundamental changes involved in the experiment. When PDM was introduced to the 32 laundry workers, the foreman honestly stated the basic purpose of this change was to create more interesting jobs. Higher-level management was already quite happy with the productivity of the laundry. The laundry workers were assured they (the laundry workers) could discontinue PDM if they didn't like it. The union leadership gave their approval, but not active support, to the program. The major transfer in decision-making power was from the laundry foreman to the work group, consisting of all the laundry employees. The work group could consider any and all aspects of managing the laundry. It was agreed the meetings of the work group would be limited in length to 30 or 40 minutes and would only be called if there were specific problems or proposals to discuss. Much of PDM was also achieved outside of formal meetings. Typically, the work group's decisions could be implemented within one or two weeks, since prior approval from higher management was usually not necessary before taking action.

Measurements were taken in the areas of employee attitudes, absenteeism, and productivity. At the end of fourteen months, 90 percent of the employees had positive attitudes toward PDM. This is an increase from 62 percent with positive attitudes at the end of the first two months of the program. A superior absenteeism record (compared to the rest of the hospital) became significantly better after the introduction of PDM. The laundry group had an overall absence rate of 2.95 percent before PDM and only 1.77 percent after the introduction of PDM. Productivity averaged 50 pounds of laundry processed per paid employee hour in the year prior to the introduction of PDM. During the third six-month period after PDM, productivity had increased to 73 pounds per paid employee hour. The productivity in the two comparison hospitals had declined slightly over the eighteen-month study period.

Possible Limitations.   While this study seems to be building the case for PDM, we need to keep in mind some of the possible limitations with participatory groups. Participatory groups are generally faced with the potential limitations of time, emotion, and inequality.[40] First, a greater length of time is usually required with group decision-making. This could have the further consequences of making quick decisions in emergencies almost impossible, causing frustration and boredom among members, and creating conflicts among members who see their time as more or less valuable in relation to the group. Secondly, group decision-making may increase the possibility of issues becoming personalized. Members' ideas can become interrelated with their own emotional psychological selves. Members who present ideas may take criticism of these ideas as criticism of themselves. The members who are not subtle and possess little interpersonal skill may also have their ideas ignored or rejected, even though they are of high quality. Thirdly, group decision-making may not adequately consider inequalities of abilities between members in making decisions. We are the first to admit that problems of time, emotion, and inequality are not always inevitable and may be more than offset by other benefits. Yet they need to be recognized!

Interacting Versus Nominal Decision Groups

Much of our discussion in this section on decision-making has assumed the presence of an interacting work group. In this subsection, we would like to further narrow the definition of an interacting decision group as referring to:

"(1) an unstructured group discussion for obtaining and pooling ideas of participants; and (2) majority voting on priorities by hand count."[41, p. 1] Interacting groups may be most effective for the evaluative phase of a group decision process which involves: synthesis of information and development of alternative solutions; evaluation of information and assessment of alternative solutions; and development of group consensus and agreement on a particular solution.[42] While this and previous chapters have provided many suggestions for improving the effectiveness of interacting groups, the creative or fact-finding phase of group decision-making could benefit by a different group process.

One such process is the utilization of the *nominal group* technique in the creative and fact-finding phase of group decision-making. As outlined by Debecq, Van de Ven, and Gustafson, the process of group decision-making with the nominal group technique is as follows[43]:

1. A group size of about seven to ten individuals.

2. The members silently express their ideas in writing as to the nature of the problem or alternative solutions to the problem, if it has already been identified. The members may work alone in separate rooms [44] or around a table in full view of each other.

3. At the end of some time period (10 to 15 minutes), the members share their ideas with each other. This sharing is very structured in that each member presents, in round-robin fashion, only one idea in each round from her or his list.

4. In full view of all members, a recorder writes a short and paraphrased version of each idea on a flip chart or board. This continues until all ideas, possibly eighteen to twenty-five, have been expressed. There is no recorded identification of ideas with members.

5. Each idea is then openly discussed by asking for clarification or stating support or nonsupport of it.

6. Each member privately and in writing rank-orders the ideas in order of preference. The group decision or recommendation would be the mathematically pooled outcomes of the member rankings of each idea.

The potential advantages of the nominal group technique over the usual interacting group are greater emphasis and attention to idea generation, increased attention to each idea, and a greater likelihood of balanced participation and representation of each member in the group. However, some research suggests that nominal groups may not be superior to interacting groups ". . . when the task of problem identification is performed by persons who are both (a) pervasively aware of the existing problems and (b) willing to communicate them."[45, p. 72] It appears that the nominal group technique may be most effective when there are certain blocks or problems in a group, such as a few dominating members.

Review

There have been several themes running through this entire discussion of group decision processes. These themes might be summed up in the form of the questions we have addressed. How can we differentiate the levels or process of group decision-making? What is the relation between group decision processes and the relative autonomy of groups? What role do the process of group decision-making and the content of decisions made by a work group have in evaluating the concept of participation? What are the possible effects, both positive and negative, of group decision-making? What are some of the situational factors to be considered in group decision processes?

EXTERNAL ENVIRONMENT

In the most basic sense, external environment refers to the conditions and factors that are not substantially controlled by the work group and represent "givens" for the members.[46] Some dimensions that might be considered as part of the external environemnt for a work group include the technology, physical conditions, management practices, rules, leadership of the designated supervisors and managers, rewards and punishments from the organization, and the like. Since these external environmental factors are likely to play such a crucial role in the day-to-day behavior and output of a work group, it is likely that they will become blurred with the variables within the group, which can also influence group behavior and output.

The discussion of contingencies affecting groups has focused on the internal character and dynamics of the group. The external environment can affect each of the variables presented, such as member composition and leadership, as well as directly affect the behavior and outputs of a group. For example, management may want to introduce a technological change, such as automatically controlled machines, to a work group. From the perspective of the work group, this might be considered as an external force. By acting in a united manner, the work group might also be able to influence the conditions under which the machines are introduced. Thus, the influences between the external environment and work group can be two-way, rather than just from the external environment to the group.

Much of the discussion in Chapter 3, "Environmental Influences and Assessment," and the next chapter, "Intergroup Relations" addresses issues and concepts related to the external environment of work groups. Thus, we will not explore the "external environment" contingency any further here. But, there is one point we want to make explicit: Work groups can be and often are dramatically changed in response to higher management-initiated changes in the areas of technology, job design, structure, rules, formal supervision, and the like.[47]

DIAGNOSING YOUR WORK GROUP

The last part of this chapter presents several illustrative diagnostic and assessment approaches for evaluating work groups. This part of the chapter serves two objectives. First, it provides you with some knowledge and awareness of the limitations we face in learning about, diagnosing, and assessing groups. Secondly, it explains several of the available means for better understanding and possibly improving the groups in which we participate here and now and in the future. The two most common ways for diagnosing and assessing intragroup relations are the observational approach and the self-report approach.

Self-Report Approach

The self-report approach for collecting data and learning about intragroup relations requires the individuals to describe and/or evaluate their own group. There are numerous issues involved in accomplishing this (see Chapter 2). We will only briefly describe and present sample items and dimensions from two research instruments designed to assess group attributes or characteristics as perceived by group members. These instruments serve to illustrate how we can perceive a group as a distinct unit of analysis, how we can perceive different attributes of a single group, and how groups can differ from each other.

Group Dimensions Descriptions Questionnaire.   The Group Dimensions Descriptions Questionnaire, developed by John K. Hemphill and his colleagues at Ohio State University, represents a comprehensive measure of the attributes of groups.[48] The questionnaire consists of thirteen relatively independent group dimensions, which are measured by 150 questionnaire items. The individual responds to each questionnaire item on the following five-point scale: definitely true, mostly true, equally true and false, mostly false, and definitely false. For purposes of analysis, the five alternative choices are assigned a numerical weight from five points to one point. This questionnaire is particularly useful for obtaining insights in terms of the attitudes, perceptions, impressions, and knowledge possessed by individual members about their group. In previous sections of this chapter, findings and implications that are directly related to a number of the group dimensions and questions outlined in Fig. 7–9 were discussed.

As you read Fig. 7–9, it is useful to think about a group in which you are presently a member. You might find it useful to respond to each item in terms of this group. After responding to these items, you should look over these sample items to see if there is any patterns to your responses. If so, does your pattern of responses suggest any possible reasons for your overall feeling of satisfaction, indifference, or dissatisfaction with this group?

Figure 7–9   Selected Dimensions and Sample Items from the Group Dimensions Descriptions Questionnaire

Dimension	Sample Questions	Responses				
Control	Members fear to express their real opinions	DT	MT	TF	MF	DF
Stability	There is a large turnover of members within the group.	DT	MT	TF	MF	DF
Intimacy	All members know each other very well.	DT	MT	TF	MF	DF
Stratification	Every member of the group enjoys the same group privileges.	DT	MT	TF	MF	DF
	Certain members have much more influence on the group than others.	DT	MT	TF	MF	DF
Autonomy	The group works independently of other groups.	DT	MT	TF	MF	DF
Cohesiveness	Members of the group work together as a team.	DT	MT	TF	MF	DF
Participation	There is a high degree of participation on the part of members.	DT	MT	TF	MF	DF
	The work of the group is well divided among members.	DT	MT	TF	MF	DF
Polarization	The group operates with sets of conflicting plans.	DT	MT	TF	MF	DF
	The group knows exactly what it has to get done.	DT	MT	TF	MF	DF
Flexibility	The group is very informal.	DT	MT	TF	MF	DF
	The group has rules to guide its activities.	DT	MT	TF	MF	DF
Homogeneity	Some members are interested in altogether different things than other members.	DT	MT	TF	MF	DF
	The group contains members with widely varying backgrounds.	DT	MT	TF	MF	DF

Key: DT = Definitely True; MT = Mostly True: TF = Equally True and False;
MF = Mostly False; and DF = Definitely False

Adapted from: Hemphill, J. *Group Dimensions: A Manual for Their Measurement.* Columbus, Ohio: Bureau of Business Research, Ohio State University, 1956. Used with permission.

Semantic Differential Technique.   The semantic differential technique can be used to assess and diagnose feelings about intragroup relations, intergroup relations, specific individuals, organizations, and any other object or unit which can be conceived of by individuals. It is certainly not limited in application to only intragroup relations.

This technique can be used to assess and diagnose an individual's perceptions of two relatively independent dimensions—an evaluative dimension and a potency dimension.[49] The *evaluative dimension* assesses the individual's feelings along a continuum ranging from good to bad. The individual is asked to evaluate such things as whether the unit of analysis (such as the work group) is believed to be valuable and satisfying or worthless and dissatisfying. On the other hand, the *potency dimension* assesses the individual's feelings along a continuum ranging from strong to weak. The individual might evaluate the group in terms of how powerful or influential it is in affecting the respondent and/or group. The evaluative and potency dimensions for a particular concept are typically evaluated using a number of bipolar adjectives. For example, we might take the concept of group cohesion. Figure 7–10 shows one semantic differential measure that has been used to evaluate group cohesion in terms of the evaluative and potency dimensions. The individual is asked to check a box on the seven-point scale which best represents his or her feeling toward the member's group. You might want to respond to the bipolar adjectives shown in Fig. 7–10 in terms of a group in which you are a member. In looking over your pattern of responses, what do you see? How do you evaluate your group? Is it relatively potent or impotent? What does this mean to you?

Evaluative dimension

Fair ___:___:___:___:___:___:___:	Unfair
Good ___:___:___:___:___:___:___:	Bad
Valuable ___:___:___:___:___:___:___:	Worthless
Pleasant ___:___:___:___:___:___:___:	Unpleasant
Clear ___:___:___:___:___:___:___:	Lazy

Potency dimension

Strong ___:___:___:___:___:___:___:	Weak
Hard ___:___:___:___:___:___:___:	Soft
Large ___:___:___:___:___:___:___:	Small

Figure 7–10   Semantic Differential Measurement of Group Cohesion

Adapted from: Reif, W., R. Mongka, and J. Newstrom, "Perceptions of the Formal and Informal Organization: Objective Measurement through the Semantic Differential Technique," *Academy of Management Journal*, 1973, **16**, pp. 389–403.

Review.   The two self-report approaches presented to facilitate the diagnosis and assessment of one's group are intended as brief illustrations of many possibilities. Our purpose was to provide a concrete demonstration of how you might assess your group through self-report measures, and the types of group dimensions that might be evaluated. This should enhance your ability to better understand groups in which you are (or will become) a member. The rationale for illustrating self-report approaches can be extended to the following brief discussion of the observational approach.

Observational Approach

For our purposes, the observational approach is limited to well-developed techniques designed to record or collect information on the behavior of the group as a whole and/or the behavior of the group members. Observations are typically made by someone or some mechanical device (television or tape recorder) "external" to the group. By external, we mean the observing individual or machine is not intended to be an active participant or influence on the processes and behavior of the group. An analysis of the possible unintended effects of observation on group processes and behavior is beyond our purpose here. We will simply acknowledge that external observation may well influence the group's behavior. The observational approach is occasionally used where observations are recorded by someone who is both an active participant and observer of the group.

Observer Role.   The observer(s) is usually assigned one of two tasks, or both. One task may be to assign the behavior being observed into predetermined categories. This often involves counting how frequently certain kinds of behavior occur. For example, the observer may record the frequency of laughter or disagreement in the group. A second task may be to assign some numerical index to the observed behavior by rating it on some type of scale. For example, the observer might evaluate the amount of member participation on the scale ranging from high participation to low participation. A technique emphasizing the recording of the frequency of occurrence of specific kinds of behavior is Bales' Interaction Process Analysis.

Bales' Interaction Process Analysis.   Bales' Interaction Process Analysis (hereafter IPA) consists of twelve observational categories. It is called IPA because "it attempts to abstract from the raw material of observation . . . the . . . problem-solving relevance of each act for the total on-going process."[50, p. 258] IPA is particularly useful for gaining a specific understanding of the decision-making process within one's group and identifying areas for improvement. Bales suggests that group processes may be broken down into the broad areas of socio-emotional orientation and task orientation. The socio-emotional orientation may be further broken down into the two major categories of showing positive reactions and negative reactions. The task orientation is also further broken down into the categories of asking questions and giving answers. These categories are further subdivided as shown in Fig. 7–11. The various categories of behavior are related to six basic problems that must be solved if the group is to accomplish its objectives or task. Three of these problems are in the task area and three are in the socio-emotional area.

In the task area, the first problem is one of orientation. Orientation involves arriving at a common definition of the situation. The subcategories of behavior concerned with the problem of orientation are giving information and asking for information. The second problem is one of evaluation, which is primarily concerned with developing a common way of evaluating alternative solutions. This is indicated by the giving-opinion and asking-for-opinion categories. The third problem is one of control, and deals with efforts by the group members to influence one another. This is indicated by the behavior of giving suggestions and asking for suggestions.

In the socio-emotional area, the three major problems are those of decision, tension-management, and integration. The problem of decision is concerned with the resolution of the problem or problems before the group, and is indicated by the behavioral categories of showing agreement and showing disagreement. The problem of tension-management concerns the expression and reduction of tension. This is recorded in the categories of showing tension and tension release. Lastly, the problem of integration concerns the binding together and breakdown in the group. Integration is primarily evaluated through the behavioral categories of solidarity and antagonism.

Choosing a Diagnostic Approach

The choice involved in deciding to use some sort of self-report and/or an observational approach is certainly not a simple one. The self-report approach has the advantage of eliciting from the members what they see happening in their group and how they feel about it. Measurement of the members' attitudes is at times a relatively accurate and at other times a relatively inaccurate indicator of the group's behavior.[51] On the other hand, the observational approach may be somewhat more accurate in reporting actual group behavior. This is true only if the process of observing does not radically change the way the group would have behaved if it had not been under observation. However, the observation approach may not tell you as much about the significance and meaning of the group to the members (as would the self-report approach).

This part of the chapter has briefly reviewed the Group Dimensions Descriptions Questionnaire, the Semantic Differential Technique, and Bales' Interaction Process Analysis, to provide you with some tools for learning how your group processes might be diagnosed and assessed. A secondary purpose was to suggest ways and dimensions by which a group may be differentiated.

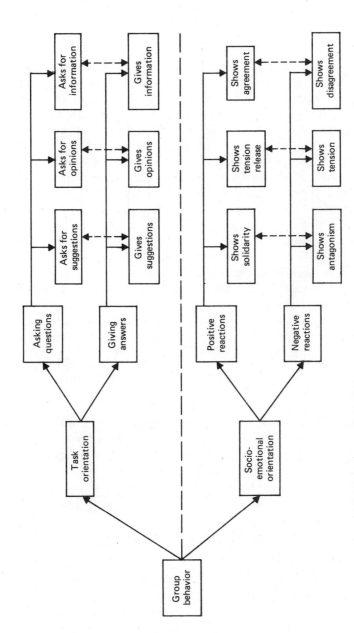

Figure 7–11   Simplified Bales IPA Scheme

There are also many other approaches for diagnosing a group and issues that could be considered; these are described in the literature.[52]

SUMMARY

There have been four major components to this chapter. First, some of the dilemmas associated between individuals and groups were discussed. Secondly, the nature, types, and functions of groups were reviewed. Thirdly, the chapter emphasized major contingencies which, independently and more likely in combination, can influence the behavior and outputs of work groups. Without becoming overly complex, some of the interrelationships between these contingencies were also noted. Fourth, the Group Dimensions Descriptions Questionnaire and the Semantic Differential Technique were presented as illustrations of self-report measures for assessing and diagnosing one's work group, whereas Bales' Interaction Process was an illustration of an observational approach.

The focus of attention, as mentioned, was on the major contingencies or variables that can play a role in influencing group behavior and outputs. These contingencies were identified as follows: size, communication networks, member composition, norms, goals, leadership, decision processes, and external environment. Although the following chapter focuses on intergroup relations, much of it naturally has implications for intragroup relations. Thus, this chapter has certainly not presented all issues or suggestions associated with intragroup relations, particularly work groups.

Discussion Questions

1. Identify a group in which are presently a member. By utilizing the framework presented in Fig. 7–1, analyze the specific sources of attraction and/or rejection of this group for *you* in terms of: interpersonal factors, group activities, group goals, the group as a means.

2. How would you characterize and assess the communication network(s) utilized by the group you identified in Question 1? Does the type of communication network tend to change with different types of problems and issues in your group? Can you give examples? By utilizing the dimensions presented in Fig. 7–5, how would you assess your group?

3. Identify three prevalent norms of a work group in which you have been a member. Figure 7–6 might be helpful in stimulating your thinking. Do you think that you or other group members conformed to these norms on the basis of compliance or personal acceptance? Explain.

4. Describe the leadership process of a work group in which you have been a member. Did there seem to be a task leader and a socio-emotional

leader, or did one person perform both of these tasks? Evaluate the group leader or leaders in terms of the types of behavior identified for effective group leaders in the chapter.

5. Describe and evaluate the level of group decision-making and types of group decisions which were (or are) made by your work group. Figures 7–7 and 7–8 should be helpful in performing this task. Should the level and types of group decisions be changed for improved effectiveness? Explain.

CRITICAL INCIDENT

Alvin Brown, a plant manager of the Parma Plant of Wiley Corporation attended a management seminar conducted at a large university. The two-week seminar primarily emphasized managerial decision-making.

Professor Scholar of the university staff especially impressed Alvin Brown with the lectures on group processes and decision-making. On the basis of research and experience, Professor Scholar told the managers that employees, if given the opportunity, could diagnose and evaluate many problems and arrive at quality decisions that would be enthusiastically accepted.

Upon returning to his plant, Mr. Brown decided to practice some of the principles presented. He called together the fifteen employees of Department A and told them that production standards established several years previously were now too low, in view of the recent installation of automated equipment. He was giving them the opportunity to discuss these circumstances and to decide among themselves, as a group, what their production standards should be. On leaving the room, Mr. Brown believed the workers would establish much higher standards than he would ever dare propose.

After three hours of discussion over a three-day period, the workers summoned Mr. Brown and notified him that, contrary to his opinion, their group decision was that the standards were already too high, and since they had been given the authority to establish their own standards, they were making a reduction of 5 percent. Mr. Brown knew these standards were far too low to provide an adequate profit on the owners' investment. Yet, as Professor Scholar emphasized in the seminar, the refusal to accept a work group's decision could be disastrous. Before doing anything, Mr. Brown called Professor Scholar at the university for his opinion.

Questions

1. Assuming you are Professor Scholar, what "errors" do you think were made by Mr. Brown?

2. What advice might you give to Mr. Brown?

REFERENCES

1. Miller, D., *Individualism: Personal Achievement and the Open Society.* Austin: University of Texas Press, 1967.

2. An account by Edward R. Murrow, in *S. Hurok Presents Marian Anderson;* quoted from David L. Miller, *op. cit.*

3. Riesman, D., *Individualism Reconsidered.* New York: Free Press, 1954.

4. Cartwright, D., and R. Lippitt, "Group Dynamics and the Individual," *International Journal of Group Psychotherapy,* 1957, **7,** pp. 86–102.

5. Homans, G. C., *The Human Group.* New York: Harcourt, Brace & World, 1950. *Also see:* Miller, J., "Living Systems: The Group," *Behavioral Science,* 1971, **16,** pp. 302–398.

6. Fiedler, F., *A Theory of Leadership Effectiveness.* New York: McGraw-Hill Book Co., 1967.

7. Shaw, M., *Group Dynamics: The Psychology of Small Group Behavior.* New York: McGraw-Hill Book Co., 1971. *Also see:* Hill, R. A. "Interpersonal Compatibility and Work-Group Performance," *Journal of Applied Behavioral Science,* 1975, **11,** pp. 210–240.

8. Ross, I., and A. Zander, "Need Satisfaction and Employee Turnover," *Personnel Psychology,* 1957, **10,** pp. 327–338.

9. Turquet, P., "Leadership: The Individual and the Group," in *Analysis of Groups.* Gibbard, G., J. Hartman, and R. Mann (eds.). San Francisco: Jossey-Bass Publishers, 1974, pp. 349–386.

10. Homans, G. C., *op. cit.*

11. *Ibid.*

12. *Ibid.*

13. Turquet, P., *op. cit.,* p. 350.

14. Bouckard, T., J. Baraloux, and G. Drauden, "Brainstorming Procedure, Group Size, and Sex as Determinants of the Problem-Solving Effectiveness of Groups and Individuals." *Journal of Applied Psychology,* 1974, **59,** pp. 135–138.

15. Berelson, B., and G. Steiner, *Human Behavior: An Inventory of Scientific Findings.* New York: Harcourt, Brace & World, 1964, esp. pp. 356–360.

16. Graicunas, A., "Relationships in Organizations" in *Papers on the Science of Administration.* Gulick, L., and L. Urwick (eds.). New York: Institute of Public Administration, 1937, pp. 181–188.

17. Glazer, M., and R. Glaser, *Techniques for the Study of Team Structure and Behavior.* Part II: "Empirical Studies of the Effects Structure." Pittsburgh: American Institute for Research, 1957.

18. Guetzkow, H., and H. Simon, "The Impact of Certain Communication Nets upon Organization and Performance in Task-Oriented Groups," *Management Science,* **1,** 1955, pp. 233–250.

19. Miller, J., "Living Systems: The Group." *Behavioral Science,* 1971, **16,** pp. 302–398.

20. Barron, F., "Some Studies of Creativity at the Institute of Personality Assessment and Research." Rokeach, M. "In Pursuit of the Creative Process," in *The Creative Organization.* Steiner, G. (ed.). Chicago: University of Chicago Press, 1965.

21. McGrath, J. E., and J. E. Altman, *Small Group Research.* New York: Holt, Rinehart & Winston, 1966, p. 65.

22. Allen, P. F., and S. Pilnick, "Confronting the Shadow Organizations: How to Detect and Defeat Negative Norms," *Organizational Dynamics,* 1973, **1,** pp. 3–18.

23. Kiesler, C., and S. Kiesler, *Conformity.* Reading, Mass.: Addison-Wesley Publishing Co., 1969.

24. Rothlisberger, F. J., and W. J. Dickson, *Management and the Worker: Technical Versus Social Organization in an Industrial Plant.* Cambridge, Mass.: Harvard University Press, 1939.

25. Patchen, M., *Participation, Achievement, and Involvement on the Job.* Englewood Cliffs, N.J.: Prentice-Hall, 1970.

26. Mills, T. M., *The Sociology of Small Groups.* Englewood Cliffs, N.J.: Prentice-Hall, 1967.

27. Philip, H., and D. Dunphy, "Developmental Trends in Small Groups." *Sociometry,* 1954, **22,** pp. 162–174.

28. Sherif, M., and C. Sherif, *Groups in Harmony and Tension.* New York: Harper & Row Publishers, 1953.

29. Seashore, S., *Group Cohesiveness in the Industrial Work Group.* Ann Arbor, Mich.: Survey Research Center, University of Michigan, 1954.

30. Bales, R., *Interaction Process Analysis.* Cambridge, Mass.: Addison-Wesley Publishing Co., 1950.

31. Crockett, W., "Emergent Leadership in Small, Decision-Making Groups, *Journal of Abnormal and Social Psychology,*" 1955, **51,** pp. 378–383.

32. Cohen, G., *The Task-Tuned Organization of Groups*. Amsterdam: Swets and Zeitlinger, 1969.

33. *See:* "A Symposium: Workers' Participation in Management: An International Comparison." *Industrial Relations,* 1970, **9,** pp. 117–214.

34. Geer, J., *A Psychological Study of Problem-Solving.* Haarlem: de Toarts, 1957. Schoner, B., and G. Rose, "Quality of Decisions: Individual versus Real and Synthetic Groups," *Journal of Applied Psychology,* 1974, **59,** pp. 424–432.

35. Wood, M. T., "Effects of Decision Processes and Task Situations on Influence Perceptions," *Organizational Behavior and Human Performance,* 1972, pp. 417–427.

36. Wood, M., "Power Relationships and Group Decision-Making in Organizations," *Psychological Bulletin,* 1973, **74,** pp. 280–293.

37. Levine, E., "Problems of Organizational Control in Microcosm: Group Performance and Group Member Satisfaction as a Function of Differences in Control Structure." *Journal of Applied Psychology,* 1973, **58,** pp. 186–196.

38. Bragg, J., and I. Andrews, "Participative Decision-Making: An Experimental Study in a Hospital," *Journal of Applied Behavioral Science,* 1973, **9,** pp. 727–735.

39. Lowin, A., "Participative Decision-Making: A Model, Literature Critique, and Prescriptions for Research," *Organizational Behavior and Human Performance,* 1968, **3,** pp. 68–106.

40. Mansbridge, J., "Time, Emotion, and Inequality: Three Problems of Participatory Groups," *Journal of Applied Behavioral Science,* 1973, **9,** pp. 351–368.

41. Van de Ven, A. H., "Group Decision-Making and Effectiveness: An Experimental Study," *Organization and Administrative Sciences,* 1974, **5,** pp. 1–110.

42. Van de Ven, A. H. "Nominal Versus Interacting Group Processes for Committee Decision-Making Effectiveness," *Academy of Management Journal,* 1971, **14,** pp. 203–212.

43. Delbecq, A. L., A. H. van de Ven, and D. H. Gustafson, *Group Techniques for Program Planning: A Guide to Nominal and Delphi Processes.* Glenview, Ill.: Scott, Foresman & Co., 1975, pp. 7–10, 17–18.

44. Taylor, D. W., P. C. Berry, and C. H. Block, "Does Group Participation When Using Brainstorming Facilitate or Inhibit Creative Thinking?" *Administrative Science Quarterly,* 1958, **3,** pp. 23–47.

45. Green, T. B., "An Empirical Analysis of Nominal and Interacting Groups," *Academy of Management Journal,* 1975, **18,** pp. 63–73.

46. Scott, W. G., and T. R. Mitchell, *Organizational Theory: A Structural and Behavioral Analysis.* Homewood, Ill.: Richard D. Irwin and Dorsey Press, 1972, pp. 117–122.

47. Johnson, D. P., "Social Organization of an Industrial Work Group: Emergence and Adaptation to Environmental Change," *The Sociological Quarterly,* 1974, **15,** pp. 110–125.

48. Hemphill, J. K., *Group Dimensions: A Manual for Their Measurement.* Columbus, Ohio: Bureau of Business Research, Ohio State University, 1956.

49. Osgood, C. E., G. I. Suci, and P. H. Tannenbaum, *The Measurement of Meaning,* Urbana, Ill.: University of Illinois Press, 1957.

50. Bales, R., "A Set of Categories for the Analysis of Small Group Interaction," *American Sociological Review,* 1950, **15,** pp. 257–263.

51. Liska, A., "Emergent Issues in the Attitude–Behavior Consistency Controversy," *American Sociological Review,* 1974, **39,** pp. 261–272.

52. Madron, T., *Small-Group Methods and the Study of Politics.* Evanston, Ill.: Northwestern University Press, 1969.

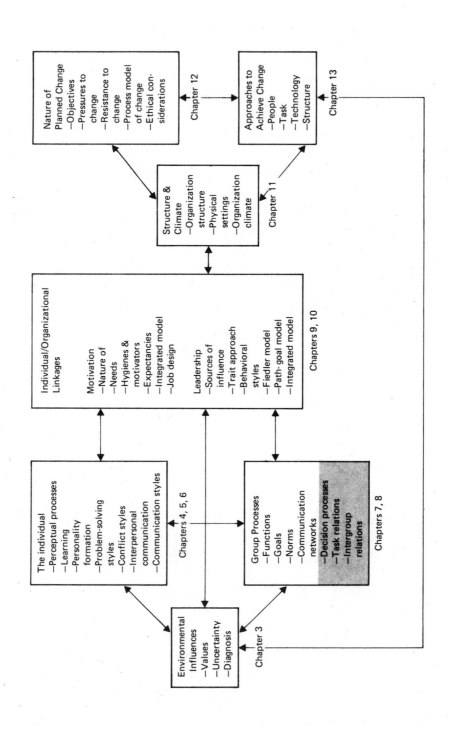

Nature of Planned Change
—Objectives
—Pressures to change
—Resistance to change
—Process model of change
—Ethical considerations

Chapter 12

Approaches to Achieve Change
—People
—Task
—Technology
—Structure

Chapter 13

Structure & Climate
—Organization structure
—Physical settings
—Organization climate

Chapter 11

Individual/Organizational Linkages

Motivation
—Nature of
—Needs
—Hygienes & motivators
—Expectancies
—Integrated model
—Job design

Leadership
—Sources of influence
—Trait approach
—Behavioral styles
—Fiedler model
—Path-goal model
—Integrated model

Chapters 9, 10

The individual
—Perceptual processes
—Learning
—Personality formation
—Problem-solving styles
—Conflict styles
—Interpersonal communication
—Communication styles

Chapters 4, 5, 6

Group Processes
—Functions
—Goals
—Norms
—Communication networks
—Decision processes
—Task relations
—Intergroup relations

Chapters 7, 8

Environmental Influences
—Values
—Uncertainty
—Diagnosis

Chapter 3

8
INTERGROUP
RELATIONS

The previous chapter focused on concepts, issues, and processes of particular importance within an interacting group of sixteen or fewer individuals. In this chapter, the primary focus is on relations between groups of various sizes. Most of the following discussions could be relevant for: two groups within a single functional area, such as marketing research and sales; two different functional departments, such as personnel and production; a product unit, such as a car division, and corporate headquarters; a staff unit, such as a planning group, and top management; or other formal or informal groupings that can be identified as being interdependent. Thus, our use of the word "group" in this chapter goes beyond the definition of group (i.e., face-to-face relations) utilized in the previous chapter.

An understanding of intergroup relations is important to all of us since we often have to work with and through other groups to accomplish our objectives; and other groups often create problems and demands on the various work groups in organizations. In brief, the primary objectives of this chapter are to assist you:

1. To develop an understanding of the major contingencies that can influence intergroup relations, including the level and types of conflicts that often occur between groups;

2. To create an awareness of the major mechanisms and processes for managing intergroup relations;

3. To improve one's skills in diagnosing and assessing intergroup relations;

4. To develop skills and techniques that can be useful in managing intergroup relations, including intergroup conflict and conflict resolution; and

5. To introduce some concepts and techniques that serve as the basis for forming the structure of complex organizations.

MAJOR CONTINGENCIES AFFECTING INTERGROUP RELATIONS

Consistent with the discussion of intragroup relations, there is no single contingency or cause that can serve as a simple explanation of the relations between two groups. Our primary strategy in this section is to discuss each contingency as to how and why it can influence relations between two groups. The secondary strategy is to selectively explain how two or more of these contingencies can interact to affect intergroup relations. There will be no attempt to relate how all of these contingencies could simultaneously interact to influence intergroup relations. This would result in a degree of complexity and involvement with intergroup relations well beyond the scope of this book. Moreover, not all of the contingencies identified are equally important or of even minor importance in every intergroup situation.

Figure 8–1 identifies six major contingencies that may have an impact on the relations between two or more groups. The dashed lines between the forces are intended to reflect their potential interconnectedness. The contingencies, in order of their discussion, are goal orientation, uncertainty absorption, substitutability, nature of task relations, degree of resource sharing, and attitudinal sets. The order of discussion is not intended to imply the relative importance of each contingency. Throughout the following discussion, we will use the words department, unit, and group as synonymous and general terms.

Goals

The goals of two groups can have a powerful impact on their relationships with one another. Goals may be thought of as desired states. Decision-makers often use goals to indicate their relative preferences. In the short run, one goal of a business firm might be a 10 percent increase in profits. To reach this goal, the firm's production department might have a goal of a 5 percent increase in efficiency; the marketing department might have a goal to introduce the three new products or services; the research department might have a goal to develop less expensive materials of equal quality for one of the firm's product lines; the personnel department might have a goal to reduce turnover of blue-collar workers by 10 percent; and the finance department might have a goal to reduce the average time period for accounts receivable from 40 days to 37 days. Three ideas are important in these examples. First, they represent examples of only one of the many goals each of these departments are likely to have. Second, the goals for each of the groups (i.e., production, personnel, marketing, etc.) are intended as subgoals to help the organization obtain the stated broader goal of a 10 percent increase in profits. Third, the accomplishment of the stated goal of each group may require interaction with one or more

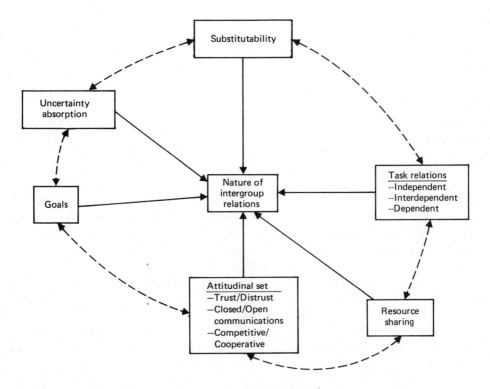

Figure 8–1 Some Contingencies Affecting Intergroup Relations

of the other groups. For example, the personnel department might need the cooperation of production supervisors in reducing turnover, or the finance department might need more information from the marketing department regarding the financial status of customers. The ideal state might exist when each group perceives its goals, the goals of the organization as a whole, and the goals of other groups as compatible with one another and mutually reinforcing. This is frequently referred to as a "win–win" situation. Each group can gain or attain its goal if the other groups attain their goals. In this case, we are more likely to find open and free-flowing communications between groups, cooperation, mutual concern, and respect for each other's problems, rapid problem-solving, and the like. However, goals are not always perceived or designed in such a way as to be quite so compatible and mutually reinforcing.

Goal Incompatibility

The perception of goal incompatibility implies that goal attainment by one group may prevent or reduce the level of goal attainment by one or more other groups.[1] We are unlikely to find widespread goal incompatibility of the win–lose variety within an organization. A win–lose situation exists when one group's goal attainment is at the direct expense or cost of another group. In keeping with our earlier discussion, this might occur when the production department perceives that the introduction of three new products by the marketing group might decrease the former's reported efficiency by 5 percent rather than enable it to realize its goal of a 5 percent increase in efficiency.

Goal incompatibility between departments is more often a mixed, rather than a total win–lose, variety. This may mean that up to a certain level of goal attainment for each group, there is no perceived or real incompatibility. To continue our example, the production department might believe that it can attain its 5 percent efficiency goal if marketing introduces only *one* new product, a 2 percent improvement in efficiency with the introduction of two products, and a 5 percent *drop* in efficiency with the introduction of three products. This example assumes that three new products are likely to have an impact on the production department's efficiency because of the new learning and start-up costs incurred by production personnel. It also assumes that certain thresholds exist for the production department—one new product can be accommodated and still allow the department to meet its goals; some impact occurs with two new products; and chaos starts to set in for the production unit with the introduction of three new products.

Under these assumptions, it is clear why the production department might perceive its goals, at some point, as being potentially incompatible with those of marketing. Production may claim the lost efficiencies are not offset by the possible gains of introducing three new products within a one-year time period. Moreover, the introduction of these products over three years, rather than one year, could enable production to meet its efficiency goal and marketing to meet its long term goal of being responsive to changing customer needs. We can well imagine the types of counterarguments from marketing.

One of the ways for reducing this goal incompatibility in our example is for higher management to simply relax the requirement of a 5 percent improvement in efficiency for the production department. However, if the members of the production department had personally accepted (internalized) the efficiency goal, the willingness of higher management to relax or modify it may not reduce resistance to or questioning of the desirability of introducing three new products. In the first place, it is extremely difficult to establish meaningful production goals for the new products when they are first manufactured because each production worker has to be trained to perform the new task, new machine standards have to be set, and the like. Thus, the production members could experience some short-run felt losses in the reduced sense of accomplishment or achievement, unless new standards and goals are reached. New products may also require changing comfortable habits and work patterns, necessitate new habits and work patterns, and require new skills. If the production unit had not been accustomed to change, these new requirements could create considerable frustration and anxieties for workers.

Assessment

The degree to which two groups perceive their goals as compatible or incompatible with each other may have considerable impact on the nature of their relations. We do not want to leave this section by giving the impression that complete compatibility in goals between units is possible or necessarily even desirable. The specialization of labor that is inherent in organization creates the inevitable condition of some degree of "tunnel-visionedness" or narrowness in goal orientation by the members comprising a group. The question of goal incompatibility is not whether or not it occurs. The important questions are to what degree goal incompatibility occurs, what its effects are, and what mechanisms are available to manage it creatively.

Absorption of Uncertainty

As noted in previous chapters, organizations, groups, and individuals have been viewed as open systems, somewhat unpredictable and faced with uncertainty. As we discussed in Chapter 3, uncertainty is the complement of knowledge.[2] "It is the gap between what is known and what needs to be known to make correct decisions."[3, p. 1] One way of managing uncertainty is to create certain groups and/or assign certain individuals to deal with it. The focus here is on uncertainty absorption by a group rather than individual. Thus, we might say that some groups absorb particular types of uncertainty for other groups in the organization.[4] This occurs when one group makes certain decisions for another group and/or sets the decision premises for another group. For example, the accounting department might develop uniform procedures and guidelines for handling travel expenses. Thus, a sales manager would have many ready-made answers provided by accounting regarding how to process travel expenses and how to determine what is allowable. We could say accounting has absorbed the uncertainty the sales manager might have experienced in handling travel-expense matters with salesmen.

Consequences

An important consequence of uncertainty absorption is the impact it can have on the relative power of groups. The power of one group (or individual, organization, etc.) may serve as the basis for affecting the behavior of another group (or individual, organization, etc.). There are three major dimensions of power: weight, domain, and scope.[5] The *weight* of power refers to the degree to which one group can affect the behavior of another group. The *domain* of power for a group refers to the number of other groups it affects. The *scope* of power refers to the range of behaviors or decision issues that are determined by one group for another group. In relation to our earlier example, we are likely to find that accounting carries a heavy weight with respect to expense-account procedures; that the scope of behaviors affected in marketing by these procedures is probably inconsequential relative to marketing's important behaviors and goals; and that the domain of accounting in expense-account matters is relatively encompassing, affecting virtually all members in marketing as well as in other groups.

The actual power of accounting relative to marketing in expense-account procedures (or any two groups on any issues) cannot be assumed. For example, we could find marketing requiring accounting to change its expense-account procedures because they are too cumbersome or time-consuming; or accounting might have to discuss and obtain prior approval from the top management in marketing before making any changes in expense-account matters. In this case, it would be very deceiving to see the statement of procedures and rules from accounting regarding expense-account matters and to conclude that they have high power even in this single area. The real power of accounting relative to expense accounts may be more to enforce the procedures and rules. Of course, even this could become a major source of power.

Since uncertainty absorption is such a pervasive and crucial process in understanding intergroup relations, an abridged version of an actual case study that dramatically demonstrates this concept is provided below. This case study, by Fred Goldner, focuses on the relationship between an industrial relations department and a production department.[6]

Case Study of Uncertainty Absorption

This case focuses on the industrial relations department and the production department of one of the companies of a multicompany corporation. Most of the data was obtained from the main plant of the company. This plant used a continuous-process technology which converted a raw material into a product used in construction. About 750 of the 1,100 workers were employed at the main plant.

The most important tasks of the industrial relations department were those related to the unions; including negotiating union–management agreements, processing worker grievances, interpretation of issues covered in the agreement, etc. The mechanisms and practices by which the industrial relations department absorbed uncertainty for the production department stemmed heavily from the union's existence. A significant source of the industrial relations power relative to other departments within the scope of plant-level issues stemmed from their (I.R.'s) use of the union as an "outside" threat that could adversely permeate the whole organization.

One of the industrial relations managers recognized that their supposed antagonists, the unions, were a major source of their internal power in these words: "As I told one of the (other I.R.) guys who was damning the unions, 'Don't bite the hand that feeds you.' "[7, p. 105] The union increased the need to maintain uniformity and coordination in industrial relations policies, practices, procedures, and rules. Without coordination, one plant might yield on union demands unimportant to them but of relevance to other companies or plants.

To maintain and increase its autonomy and power, the industrial relations department always claimed to possess the "bigger picture," which must be considered for decision-making related to the organization's human resources. There was considerable uncertainty and some conflict created by the inconsistent pressures of maintaining uniform labor relations policies, rules, procedures, and the like, while also trying to give a reasonable amount of autonomy to managers within the companies and plants. Because of these conflicting pressures both within management and between management and the union, the industrial relations department played a key role in absorbing many of the uncertainties created.

The industrial relations department had superior knowledge of the bargaining agreements. They also had a greater ability to apply the knowledge. The industrial relations people often asserted: "You never go by the wording in contracts. You go by the interpretation."[8, p. 127] Thus, the uncertainties as to the meaning and interpretation of agreements were primarily absorbed by the industrial relations department. Since the industrial relations department was not part of the production department's chain of authority, it could obtain information unavailable to others and bypass the plant's hierarchy. For example, industrial relations personnel regularly obtained information in their tours of all plant facilities. Employees also came to industrial relations personnel when they were fearful of going to their supervisors. Through such means, they could legitimately pick up bits and pieces of information and feelings about the true state of the organization that didn't get into the production unit's communication channels. As a consequence, the industrial relations department absorbed considerable uncertainty as to emerging human problems.

Substitutability

The nature of relations between groups can be affected by the degree to which one group can obtain the services, inputs, or activities provided by another group from alternative sources. If alternative services, inputs, or activities are readily available, the power of the "service" group is likely to be weaker than if no alternatives existed.[9] For example, in the previous case, there was no ready substitute for the industrial relations department. However, if the organization had been willing to spend the additional resources, they could have hired external industrial relations consultants. The external agents could evaluate the same issues as the industrial relations department and provide independent diagnoses and assessments to management. While the external consultants would also be absorbing uncertainty, it might enable top management to more effectively question and evaluate the activities of the industrial relations department.

Limits on Substitutability

To increase the probability of full utilization of resources, top management frequently issues rules requiring that departments use the services provided by other units within the organization. For example, a marketing department that wants a new sales brochure run off might have to go through the printing department, rather than contracting with an outside printing firm. This rule might well be enforced even if the marketing department could get the job done quicker and at a lower price from the outside firm. From an organizational standpoint, the increased costs to marketing might be much less than the lower utilization of manpower and equipment in the printing department.

The impact of limitations on substitutability was experienced by one of your authors when he served as coordinator of a committee that was responsible for the development and planning of a Behavioral Learning Center in the College of Business at Penn State. The University had a rule that all electronic design work had to be done by a special internal department, rather than an external consultant. Once the design work was completed, it was given to the purchasing department, who sought the approval of this facility from a government agency in the state capital. When the approval was forthcoming, it was possible to request bids from private firms for the equipment and the installation. Since the internal department had so many demands for its services, it took approximately nine months to obtain the specifications statement from the time the desired capabilities were indicated for the Behavioral Learning Center. Because the rules prevented the use of any substitute for this department, the full use of the Behavioral Learning Center was delayed by over one year.

In sum, we might conclude that, everything else equal, the lower the substitutability of the services or activities of a department, the greater its power within the organization.[10]

Task Relations

The issues of task relations is somewhat related to the concept of substitutability. In essence, the question of substitutability would not exist if there were no task relations between two groups. There are three basic types of possible task relations between any two groups within an organization—independent, interdependent, and dependent. It is useful to think of relations between groups as varying along a continuum from relative independence, through varying degrees of interdependence, to relative dependence.

Types of Task Relations

An *independent* task relation between two groups is almost a contradiction in terms. If the groups are independent of each other, how can it be said that they have task relations? We use the term to denote infrequent task relations between two groups that occur at the discretion of both groups.[11] For example, some large organizations maintain internal consulting groups that will contract, on mutually agreeable terms, to work with other units. Corning Glass Company has an Organizational Development Group that operates principally along these lines. If a unit at Corning would like to improve its problem-solving effectiveness in committee meetings, it might call in a representative from the Organizational Department Group to diagnose the problems and assist in changing the processes. Once the groups start working together, it is probably more reasonable to identify their relations as interdependent for the duration of the project. However, if both groups have the discretion to withdraw from the relationship at will, they are likely to perceive a relatively independent task relationship.

Interdependent task relations often exist when the two groups coordinate or collaborate with one another. *Collaboration* occurs when the two groups share joint responsibility for certain tasks. *Coordination* exists when the subtasks allocated to different units need to be sequenced and agreed upon by the two groups. For instance, there often needs to be considerable coordination and sometimes collaboration between production and marketing. Marketing needs to be careful not to promise customers orders that would create chaos for the production unit. On the other hand, production must be responsive to customer wants. For an effective interdependent task relation to exist, neither group can have the power to dictate or unilaterally determine the outcome of the interaction.[12] As illustrated in this and other chapters, there are numerous issues and problems in organizations that create interdependent task relations between groups.

A *dependent* task relation probably exists between two groups if one group absorbs uncertainty for the other group, the activities of the latter group are readily substitutable, or the latter group is dependent upon the former for resources. A dependent rask relation may result in one group having the ability to dictate or unilaterally determine the outcome of their interaction. One of the most dramatic examples of a dependent task relation may occur between the top-management planning or budget committee and lower-level organizational units. The budget levels and possibly survival of these lower-level units may be dependent upon the stroke of a pen by the top-management planning committee of an organization.

To develop a firmer understanding of task relations, the following study is provided as an illustration. This series of case studies by George Strauss also serves to bring out several of the previously mentioned contingencies affecting intergroup relations,[13] such as uncertainty absorption and substitutability.

Task Relations Between Purchasing and Other Groups. This study concerns the tactics used by purchasing departments in their interactions with other units such as engineering, manufacturing, sales, and production scheduling. We will focus on the tactics used by purchasing in dealing with task interdependencies with other units and the conflicts that frequently result. The majority of contacts between purchasing and other units were handled routinely, according to standard operating procedures, and without conflict, but there were still many difficult task interdependencies that couldn't be handled in a standardized or routine way.

On the surface, purchasing had two major functions in the firms studied: (1) to negotiate and place orders at the best terms possible, according to specifications laid down by other units; and (2) to expedite orders by making sure deliveries are made according to schedule. However, the purchasing unit and/or many of its member agents often viewed their responsibilities more broadly. While purchasing recognized that its job was to serve the needs of departments, it also considered its job to be *proactive* with other departments. Purchasing often was proactive in making suggestions to other units regarding such issues as: (1) the use of alternative parts or raw materials; (2) modifications in specifications or parts that might increase quality, speed up delivery, save money, and the like; (3) the most economical size of orders; and (4) the determination of decisions to purchase or make various parts. Thus, purchasing sought to be consulted during the planning and decision-making process of other units before requests for purchase orders were drawn up.

Interdependencies and Conflicts with Engineering.   Purchasing was often expected to buy products based on specifications from the engineering department. If engineering specifies a particular brand or writes up its specifications too tight, the purchasing department had little discretion in choosing among suppliers. This could reduce the status of purchasing internally and reduce its bargaining power with suppliers. Within organizations, the degree to which a unit can exercise discretion or make significant decisions is often a key factor in determining its relative status. Purchasing sometimes contended that engineering put undue emphasis on quality and reliability and were somewhat indifferent to speedy delivery and low cost. These issues may be further aggravated if purchasing attempts to change specifications and the like after engineering considers these tasks to be completed.

Interdependencies and Conflicts with Production Scheduling.   Production scheduling usually takes the initiative in determining the size of orders and the dates on which they are to be delivered. A variety of interdependencies and conflicts between purchasing and production scheduling ensue: (1) purchasing may claim too short a notice is given, and try to get production scheduling to revise their date of needed delivery; (2) purchasing may claim that production scheduling engages in sloppy planning with the result that purchasing has to choose from a limited number of suppliers, pay higher prices, and ask special favors of salesmen for quick delivery (thus creating future obligations); and (3) production scheduling may claim the short delivery times are due to such factors as delays by engineering in the preparation of blueprints (plans) or the sales unit's acceptance of rush orders. Another source of interdependence and potential conflict becomes evident when purchasing disagrees with requested order sizes from production scheduling because of their failure to adequately consider inventory costs and/or savings from quantity discounts.

We have described some issues around which purchasing and engineering or production scheduling can experience task interdependencies and conflicts. In the following section, we briefly describe the range of techniques purchasing used for relating to other units.

Tactics Used by Purchasing.   A variety of tactics were used by purchasing units in dealing with other departments on problems or decisions that could not be easily routinized, programmed, or standardized. The tactics used by purchasing can be grouped into five general categories: rule-oriented tactics; rule-evading tactics; personal-political tactics; educational tactics; and organizational-interactional tactics. Brief explanations and examples of these tactics are presented in Fig. 8–2. We are not suggesting that all of these tactics were necessarily "right," "good," or "best." They were simply the ones found to be followed in various circumstances. It may well be that some tactics would be effective in the short run for purchasing, but would increase interunit conflicts and difficulties over the long term and/or not be in the interests of the organization as a whole.

There are several major conclusions worthy of noting that probably have implications well beyond purchasing. First, the major types of tactics used by purchasing may be used by other departments in organizations. Secondly, departments that are often formally defined as staff (such as purchasing, personnel, and quality control) may exercise influence in the decision-making process well in excess of the advisory role implied in being formally identified as a staff unit. Thirdly, to understand intergroup relations, it is necessary to assess the work flow or task interdependencies between the departments.

Resource Sharing

The relations between two groups can be affected by the degree to which the two groups must draw from a common pool of resources, and the degree to which this common pool of resources is adequate to meet the needs of each group.[14] Let's assume that two groups must make use of the same typing pool for the preparation of most letters, memoranda, reports, and the like. There are few skills and resources within each group to perform this type of work. If the typing pool has adequate resources (typist, typewriters, paper, reproduction equipment, and the like) to meet the demands of both groups, we are likely to expect few, if any, problems between the two groups that share the same typing pool.

Let's now assume that each group expands its workload and the number of employees, but the typing pool's resources remain constant. This might even be a deliberate strategy by higher management if they felt the typing pool

Figure 8–2   Tactics Used by Purchasing in Relations with Other Units

Classification of Tactics	Explanation and Example
Rule-oriented	a) Appeal to some common authority to direct that the requisition be revised or withdrawn. b) Refer to some rule (assuming one exists) which provides for longer lead times. c) Require the scheduling department to state in writing why quick delivery is required. d) Require the requisitioning department to consent to having its budget charged with the extra cost (such as air freight) required to get quick delivery.
Rule-evading	a) Go through the motions of complying with the the request, but with no expectation of getting delivery on time. b) Exceed formal authority and ignore the requisitions altogether.
Personal-Political	a) Rely on friendships to induce the scheduling department to modify the requisition. b) Rely on favors, past and future, to accomplish the same result. c) Work through political allies in other departments.
Educational	a) Use direct persuasion, that is, try to persuade scheduling that its requisition is unreasonable. b) Use what might be called indirect persuasion to help scheduling see the problem from the purchasing department's point of view (in this case it might ask the scheduler to sit in and observe the agent's difficulty in trying to get the vendor to agree to quick delivery).
Organizational-Interactional	a) Seek to change the interaction pattern, for example, have the scheduling department check with the purchasing department as to the possibility of getting quick delivery before it makes a requisition. b) Seek to take over other departments, for example, to subordinate scheduling to purchasing in an integrated materials department.

Adapted and modified from: Strauss, G., "Tactics of Lateral Relationship: The Purchasing Agent," *Administrative Science Quarterly*, 1962, **7**, pp. 161–186.

is staffed to meet the peak demands from the other two groups with the consequences of underutilization much of the time. Higher management might feel that better planning and/or more realistic deadlines to the typing pool could enable it to produce much more with little added costs. Their belief might be reinforced by previous complaints from several workers in the typing pool of having to work frantically one day and being bored by inactivity the next day. Initially, the two units may simply respond by pressuring the typing pool to the point that everything is urgent. The next step might be for each department to establish priorities on its own materials to be typed. If this does not solve the problem, we would hope representatives of the two groups and the typing pool might try to work out a set of priorities and understandings through group problem-solving. One of these understandings could be that if one group encounters a true emergency requiring the typing pool to set aside another group's work, there would be direct contact between the two groups to work out some accommodation. The representative from the typing pool is likely to claim they have been "put in the middle too often for too long and what's been going on is upsetting the staff and lowering output."

The need to share resources between groups can result in competition or cooperation between the groups. The hypothetical example just presented assumed that the groups were initially competitive and became more cooperative when they confronted the problems.

Attitudinal Sets

The sets of attitudes[15] that members of groups hold toward each other can be both a cause and a consequence of the nature of their relationship. The relations might begin with the groups being trusting, cooperative, and open with each other. In this situation, we are likely to find the ways by which the other contingencies in group relations (i.e., goals, uncertainty absorption, substitutability, task relations, and resource sharing) are met to be somewhat influenced as well. For example, if the groups trust each other, there is likely to be greater acceptance of joint responsibility for mutual problems, greater consideration of the other group's point of view, greater willingness to avoid blaming the other group when problems occur, and a greater tendency to check with each other before making decisions that might have a mutual impact. If the group relations begin with attitudes of distrust, competitiveness, secrecy, and/or closedness in communications, we might expect just the opposite.

The attitudinal sets of groups toward one another can also be a consequence of the previous contingencies discussed as affecting intergroup relations. If an auditing group in an organization is evaluated solely on the basis of finding and reporting errors in other groups and reporting them to higher management, the other groups may have attitudes of distrust, competitiveness, and closed communications toward the auditing group. Of course, these attitudes are more likely to prevail if higher management uses the reports from auditing primarily as a means of punishing the other groups, rather than as an aid to improvement. These other groups are quite likely to give the auditing group the appearance that they are being cooperative and open in their communications,[16] though in fact they are not.

Consequences of Cooperative versus Competitive Attitudinal Sets

The sets of attitudes that groups come to hold toward one another often form into stereotypes. Since the nature of stereotypes is explained in greater depth in Chapter 4, we will simply state that "Stereotypes are standardized short-cut evaluations that reflect present or past relations between groups or a picture of these relations presented to the group." [17, p. 231] A number of possible attitudinal and behavioral consequences have been identified if the groups basically stereotype their relationships as competitive or cooperative.

Figure 8–3 summarizes some of these attitudinal and behavioral consequences.[18] Each dimension is presented as varying along a continuum. In extremely competitive relationships, the groups are likely to be distrusting and unresponsive, to emphasize self-interests, to interact only when required, to resist influence or control from each other, and so on. On the other hand, a highly cooperative relationship is more likely to be characterized by trust, responsiveness, emphasis on mutual interests, easy and frequent interaction, acceptance of mutual influence or control, and the like. We have personal doubts that intergroup relations are as often at one or the other ends of the continuum as one might be led to believe. The reader should not assume that intergroup relations in organizations usually fit either the extreme cases of full cooperation or competition.

Intergroup problem-solving and effectiveness is likely to be greater when relations are more indicative of the attributes along the lefthand side of Fig. 8–3 than along the righthand side. This may be especially true for intergroup relations within organizations and when the effectiveness criteria are based on what's desirable for the organization as a whole. However, within the broader United States political and economic arena, there is some evidence suggesting that groups (such as business firms, industry groups, occupational groups, reform groups, political groups, and the like) that are characterized by some of the attributes toward the righthand column of Fig. 8–3 may be more likely to attain their goals.[19]

In sum, we need to be careful not to assume that there is only one set of desirable intergroup relations. Desirability and the definition of effectiveness can be somewhat influenced by the goals and particular perspectives of the involved groups. The following case study is summarized to illustrate attitudinal sets as both a cause and consequence of intergroup relations. Rolf Rogers, the author of this study, provides a more complete description and analysis of it elsewhere.[20]

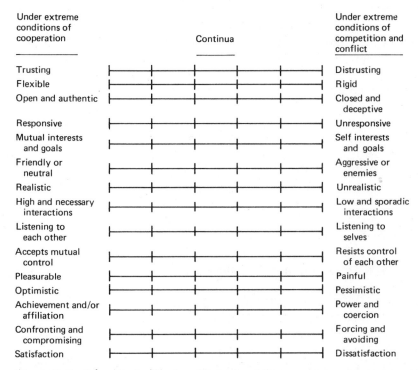

Under extreme conditions of cooperation	Continua	Under extreme conditions of competition and conflict
Trusting		Distrusting
Flexible		Rigid
Open and authentic		Closed and deceptive
Responsive		Unresponsive
Mutual interests and goals		Self interests and goals
Friendly or neutral		Aggressive or enemies
Realistic		Unrealistic
High and necessary interactions		Low and sporadic interactions
Listening to each other		Listening to selves
Accepts mutual control		Resists control of each other
Pleasurable		Painful
Optimistic		Pessimistic
Achievement and/or affiliation		Power and coercion
Confronting and compromising		Forcing and avoiding
Satisfaction		Dissatisfaction

Figure 8–3 Some Attitudinal and Behavioral Consequences of Intergroup Relations

Interdepartmental Relations: A Case of Failure

This study is concerned with the Management Analysis Department and Data Processing Department within the Weapon Systems Division of a multidivisional aerospace firm located in a large West Coast city. Both departments had responsibility for operating and developing a management system within the division. Management systems refer to activities designed to increase control of the operations in the division. The Management Analysis Department reported to the Vice President for Administration and the Data Processing Department reported to the Controller, who was the chief financial officer. These two executives, in turn, reported to the President of the division.

Formally, the Management Analysis Department would be presented operating and management problems for analysis. A report was usually issued to the "client" describing the problem, assessing alternatives, and recommending a solution. If part of the solution required a data-processing computer system and this recommendation was accepted by the "client," the report would be turned over to the Data Processing Department for more detailed computer systems design.

The conditions leading to the problems and dysfunctional stereotyping between the two departments began in June, 1967. There had been a steady decline in profitability of the weapons division, which had been underbid by competitors a number of times and was consequently not obtaining new contracts. The President asked Dr. Robert Benson, Manager of the Management Analysis Department, to have his unit develop a system for working up cost estimates. One of the major recommendations of the study was to develop a computer-based estimating system. It was intended that this system would take the accounting and production data already in the computer and integrate them for purposes of preparing cost estimates.

At the September 1967 staff meeting, the President directed Dr. Benson to submit the report to the Data Processing Department for design, programming, and implementation. The President also instructed Mr. Bowen, the Controller, to direct Don Ludden, the Director of Data Processing, to give his project high priority and to provide monthly progress reports.

Incidents

To develop a personal feel for the attitudinal sets which were forming, we will quote directly from samples of conversations that took place during the next month. At the next staff meeting (October 15), the following discussion took place [21, pp. 93–94]:

President:	Mr. Bowen, I have not received a progress report from your organization on the status of the new estimating system. Why not?
Mr. Bowen:	I don't know, Sir, but I'll check on it immediately.
President:	Please do. (Mr. Bowen leaves the room to call Don Ludden, the Director of Data Processing.)
Mr. Bowen:	(on the phone) Don, where is the progress report to the President on the new estimating system? I told you that this report is due every month in my office on the 10th and in the President's office on the 12th.
Don Ludden:	We are having problems making sense out of the system proposed by Management Analysis (department). I tried to reach Carl Abel (project leader in Management Analysis Department), but he is out of town.
Mr. Bowen:	O.K., but I want action on this project immediately. I'll talk to Dr. Benson about Abel. (Mr. Bowen returns to the staff meeting.)
President:	Well, Mr. Bowen?
Mr. Bowen:	My data processing people tell me that they can't make sense out of the Management Analysis report and they have not been able to reach the Project Chief, Carl Abel.

President:	Dr. Benson?
Dr. Benson:	Well, I don't know why there should be any problem in understanding the proposal. Mr. Abel is out of town on another assignment but they could have talked to Dr. Dolan or any one of the team members.
President:	I suggest that you two gentlemen get together on this and "get the show on the road." I should have been informed immediately of any problems, Mr. Bowen, instead of my having to bring the subject to *your* attention. I suggest that you personally keep track of this project from now on.
Mr. Bowen:	Yes, Sir.

On October 18, a meeting was held with the following individuals: Benson, Dolan, and Abel from the Management Analysis Department; and Bowen, Ludden, Warick, and Sorensen from the Data Processing Department. The following conversation ensued [22, pp. 94–95]:

Dr. Benson:	Well, what's the problem in your shop with getting this new system "off the ground"?
Mr. Bowen:	I'll let Sam (Warick) describe some of the initial problems.
Sam Warick:	Well, to begin with, your proposal is too vague for us to do any detail design work. None of my systems people can make sense out of the "interface" model in the system. Secondly, your proposal calls for the use of the XL–2 programming language; we have never used that language here and I don't have anyone who can program in it.
Phillip Sorensen:	Yes, that's right. The XL–2 is so new that nobody has had any experience with it. I called several computer manufacturers and none of them have used it; they are still testing whether the language can be used at all.
John Dolan:	To answer your first point, it is not our responsibility to do detail design work; that is your job and you are supposed to have the people to do it. If you don't, that's your problem not ours. Secondly, on the XL–2 language, I'll ask Carl to answer that.
Carl Abel:	I don't know who you have been talking to, Phil, but that language is used by the Computer Center at the State University and they tell me it's the best approach to the type of computation required in our proposed system.

Phillip Sorensen:	That's just great. Who do you think we have for programmers here? Ph.D.'s in computer science? We are lucky if we can get people with Bachelor's degrees. If you people would check your "high-level" solutions with us practical people instead of writing all this theoretical ____, we wouldn't have half of the problems we have now.
Don Ludden:	That's right. We are handed the dirty work without being consulted and then told it's our problem.
Dr. Benson:	Now let's not get personal. It seems to me that we have two problems. First, there is some problem in understanding the proposed system; second, there is a problem with the programming language. Now I suggest that Carl, Sam, and Phil sit down together and work these problems out. We will meet again, as a group, one week from today at the same time to discuss what solutions you three have come up with. Is that O.K. with you Sam (Bowen)?
Mr. Bowen:	O.K.

During the next week, Carl, Sam, and Phil attempted to work out the design and programming language problems with no success. The relationships between the two departments were hostile and rigid, and involved accusations of incompetency. Further meetings between the two groups were cancelled. On October 26, a meeting with the division president was called.[23] After little progress in this meeting, the President indicated he would think over this problem and let them know of his decision.

"Solutions."   At the November 15 meeting, the President announced he had retained an outside consulting firm to assess the current problems between the two departments. There was little interaction between the two departments during the period of the consultant's study. At a special staff meeting on January 14, 1968, the president announced the formation of the Management Systems Department, which would report directly to him. Basically, the new department consisted of the present Management Analysis Department and Data Processing Department. Mr. O'Connel from the Corporate Management Audit Staff, was made the new director. He, along with the Directors of Personnel from the division and headquarters, were given the responsibility for the staffing and appointment of managers. Abel, Benson, and Dolan resigned; Bowen and Sorensen requested transfers; and there was no unusual turnover reaction in the lower levels of the two units. A follow-up in June, 1968 indicated that the new departmental arrangement was working quite effectively. The consultant's

recommendation that "study teams" be established (so that all affected units would be represented right from the start of a project) was implemented.

In this case, changes in organization structure, task relations, and personnel were used to solve the conflict situation, negative attitudinal sets, and problems in task relations. We have no way of second-guessing whether the changes represented the "best" solutions to the problems. As will be seen in Chapter 13, the decisions actually made do not represent the only change approaches that might have been pursued.

Implications. The importance of this case is not in how this organization "solved" the problems. Rather, the case serves to dramatically demonstrate the possible role of attitudinal sets, task relations, goals, power, and the like as contingencies that can influence the nature of intergroup relations. Moreover, the case suggests that a number of the contingencies discussed are likely to be in effect simultaneously or at least interconnected in having an influence on intergroup relations. Finally, the relative importance of the six contingencies discussed (i.e., goals, uncertainty absorption, substitutability, task relations, resource sharing, and attitudinal sets) cannot be generalized and may even be quite difficult to discern in assessing relations between the two actual groups. In the next major part of this chapter, we present some of the mechanisms used for managing intergroup relations.

MECHANISMS FOR MANAGING INTERGROUP RELATIONS

This part of the chapter is presented in two major sections. The first section discusses formal mechanisms for managing lateral intergroup relations. Lateral relations refer to groups that are interdependent and have the ability to influence each other. Six major mechanisms are presented. The second section focuses on the relations between "management" and "workers" as separate classes or groups. The formal mechanisms in management–worker relations presented are the hierarchical approach, collective-bargaining approach, joint-consultation approach, and workers' control approach. Of course, many of the behavior processes, issues, and mechanisms discussed in other chapters, like those on individual styles, motivation, and leadership, can have major impacts on intergroup relations as well.

Formal Lateral Relations

Impact of Differentiation, Integration, and Uncertainty

There are three major factors that are likely to influence the extensiveness and sophistication of formal mechanisms or devices in managing intergroup relations. The three factors are the degree of differentiation between the groups, the degree of integration required between the groups, and the degree of uncertainty confronting the groups. As suggested in Fig. 8–4, each of the factors can vary in degree or amount. For our purposes, each of these factors is identified in the figure as varying from low to high within a three-dimensional framework.

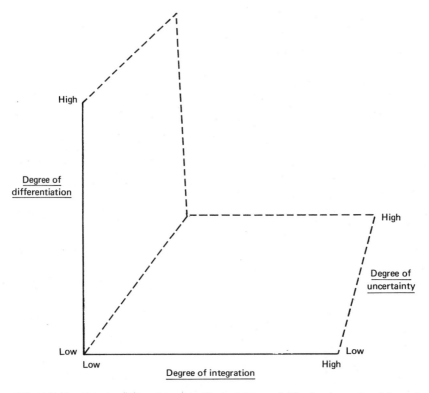

Figure 8–4   Forces Affecting the Use of Formal Mechanisms for Managing Lateral Intergroup Relations

The *differentiation* factor is defined as the degree to which organizational units differ from one another in terms of the extent of departmental structure (high to low), members' orientation toward time (short to long), members' orientation toward others (permissive to authoritarian), and members' orientation toward environmental sector (certain to uncertain, see Chapter 3).[24] Each of these components of differentiation has been discussed previously in this and prior chapters. Thus, an example or two should be sufficient here. Production units often have a high degree of departmental structure, including many rules and procedures, tight supervisory control, and frequent and specific reviews of individual and departmental performance. The opposite situation is often found in research departments. With respect to members' orientation toward others, research and sales personnel tend to prefer open, interpersonal relationships while those in production units tend to prefer more directive and structured relationships with co-workers. In terms of time orientation, sales and production have shorter time horizons and accordingly think more about immediate problems and profits, whereas research units tend to think several years into the future.

The *integration* factor is defined as "the degree of collaboration (cooperation) and mutual understanding actually achieved among the various organization units."[25, p. 21] The emphasis in this section is on the formal mechanisms that can be used to achieve the desired level of integration between groups. Since Chapter 3 featured an extensive discussion of *uncertainty*, it is simply defined here as "the difference between the amount of information required to perform the task(s) and the amount of information already possessed by the organization (or its units)."[26, p. 5]

Logic and research have suggested several general conclusions regarding the combinations of the differentiation, integration, and uncertainty factors. First, the easiest intergroup situation to manage occurs under conditions of low uncertainty, low differentiation, and low integration requirements. In this situation, the departments are practically autonomous or independent of each other, such as custodial groups in different buildings on a college campus. Second, increases in the degrees of uncertainty, differentiation, and required or desired integration need to be accompanied by increases in the expenditure of resources to obtain integration, increases in the variety of formal mechanisms to obtain integration, and increases in the use of certain behavioral processes or mechanisms to obtain integration. Third, the most difficult interunit relation to manage is likely to occur under conditions of high uncertainty, high differentiation, and high required integration. For example, the initial production of the first Boeing 747 airplanes was accompanied by all of these conditions. Moreover, we are likely to find the greatest expenditure of resources and greatest variety of formal and behavioral mechanisms being utilized to manage interunit relations under this set of conditions.

Organizations can err in trying to establish too much or too little integration between units. With too little integration, there is likely to be a lower quality of decisions and consequent underutilization or misutilization of resources. In the other case, the costs associated with integration are likely to far exceed any possible benefits. Moreover, the two units are likely to prove more obstructionist than facilitating task accomplishment for each other.

Types of Formal Mechanisms

There are at least six formal managerial mechanisms that might be utilized to establish integration between two or more organizational units that are in an approximate lateral relationship with each other. Figure 8–5 identifies these mechanisms. It is important to keep in mind that increases in, or higher levels of, uncertainty and differentiation are primarily important in the choice of formal mechanisms only if it is desirable or required that the units be integrated. While somewhat of an oversimplification, these mechanisms are placed along a single continuum to indicate the varying levels of sophistication and resource requirements associated with each mechanism. The continuum in Fig. 8–5 represents a combination of the three factors presented in Fig. 8–4. Thus, the continuum ranges from low to high for uncertainty, differentiation, and desired integration. The types of mechanism(s) that may be most appropriate for varying levels of uncertainty, differentiation, and desired integration are shown to the right of the continuum. The plus sign (+) between each mechanism suggests there is likely to be a use of the prior identified mechanisms along with the new mechanism, as one moves to higher intergroup relations on the continuum. For example, if linking roles are appropriate to help integrate two or more units, we are likely to find some use of hierarchy and plans to be appropriate as well. Let's briefly consider each of the mechanisms.

Hierarchy

The use of hierarchy as a mechanism for obtaining integration is based on the process of resolving differences and problems between two units primarily through a common superior. You will recall the case involving the Management Analysis Department and Data Processing Department, which was discussed in relation to the role of attitudinal sets in intergroup relations. The manager of the Management Analysis Department reported to the Vice President for Administration and the Manager of the Data Processing Department reported to the Controller. In turn, the Vice President for Administration and

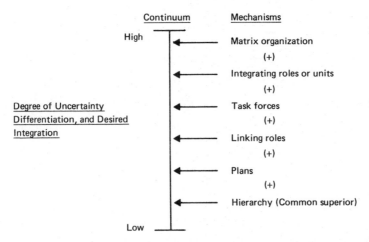

Figure 8–5   Mechanisms for Managing Intergroup Relations Under Varying Conditions

the Controller reported to the President of the Division. In this case, the problems and differences between the two units involved the active participation of the President. He represented the common superior between the two units. After consultation, he also made several structural and personnel changes to resolve the interunit differences.

The use of hierarchy (common superior) to help integrate units is based on the assumption that individuals at upper levels have more power and/or expertise than those at lower levels. However, the *exclusive* use of hierarchy to cope with integration between units, as well as a number of other issues, is being questioned on several grounds. While many of these have been presented previously, we might briefly review some of the major concerns with undue emphasis on the use of hierarchy:

1. It might create or increase personal alienation, conflict, and frustration;

2. It might interfere with trained specialists, who may have more expertise in the problem area, preventing them from interacting as needed;

3. It might interfere with the flexibility needed to respond to uncertain and changing environments and technologies;

4. It might be inconsistent with the values of openness, participation, and self-control; and

5. It might overload higher-level managers, with the result that they spend too much time on less important issues.

As suggested in Fig. 8–5, the primary use of hierarchy to resolve interunit problems and possible coordination issues may be especially appropriate under conditions of low uncertainty, few integration requirements, and minor differences between the units.[27] Of course, the use of hierarchy does not necessarily prevent representatives from the involved units from sitting down with the common superior and working through the issues together, or at least having an opportunity to influence and discuss the problem.

Plans

A second mechanism for managing intergroup relations is through the use of plans and planning processes. In the broadest sense, planning has been defined as:

> . . . the continuous process of making present entrepreneurial (risk-taking) decisions systematically and with the greatest knowledge of their futurity; organizing systematically the *efforts* needed to carry out these decisions; and measuring the results of these decisions against the expectations through organized systematic feedback.[28, p. 125]

Planning need not always be as well defined a process as this.[29] Nonetheless, through accepted or agreed upon plans, it is possible for two or more groups to act and make decisions on a day-to-day basis without constantly interacting with one another. Yet they could be quite integrated and interdependent in terms of their objectives. For example, two construction firms might start working on a section of highway many miles apart from one another. As long as both groups make their decisions in relation to the requirements or constraints of the plan (and the plan is accurate), we can be fairly sure the road surfaces being laid by each group will meet. Of course, this example involves virtually no uncertainty regarding the ability to accurately measure and plot the path of the roadway. A less restricted view of plans and planning as mechanisms for integrating two or more groups is suggested in the following example of the planning at Babcock and Wilcox. This example also demonstrates the role of hierarchy in achieving integration.

Planning at Babcock and Wilcox. [30]   Babcock and Wilcox is a multidivisional firm operating in such areas as electrical power-generation equipment, tubular products, and nuclear materials. The firm has grown from $500 million in 1965 to over one billion dollars in 1975. There are a number of ways in which integration is established or increased through their plans and planning processes. While each division in the company has considerable planning autonomy, all plans must be coordinated and related to overall corporate objectives. This is a first step in obtaining integration between the corporation as a whole and its divisions. The basis and forms of integration between the corporation and divisions are explicitly presented in a Comprehensive Business Plan (CBP) prepared annually by each division. Through this process, top management may conclude that certain activities or programs in one division offer greater advantages to the organization's future than those in another, and change priorities accordingly. The Comprehensive Business Plan also calls for "systematic feedback" of results within subunits of the divisions and between divisions and headquarters. This monthly reporting of the relation between planned performance and actual performance provides tangible feedback as to developing problems.

Babcock and Wilcox claim they do not view their plans as "straightjackets" on the divisions and their subunits. Their business plans are said to be dynamic, may continuously change as conditions change, and make reasonable allowance for contingencies. If all factors could be controlled and predicted, there would be virtually no uncertainty. The plans could be specified in great detail for extended time periods and provide the mechanism for tight integration. This is rarely the case for organizations.

In sum, Babcock and Wilcox's case has been used as a brief example of how plans and hierarchy can be used as a mechanism for achieving some degree of integration between units that are in a hierarchical and/or lateral relationship with each other. It is also apparent that as uncertainty, differentiation, and desired integration increase, the ability to rely only on plans and/or hierarchy becomes more difficult, requiring the use of additional mechanisms.

Linking Roles

A linking role refers to a specialized position in which the individual attempts to facilitate communications and problem-solving between two or more interdependent units. This type of role might be thought of as an incremental mechanism to facilitate integration when the exclusive use of hierarchy and/or plans becomes too slow or time-consuming. For example, if minor issues are continuously referred up the hierarchy, the common superior might become overloaded and the response time increased. In the earlier part of this chapter, a case study of the industrial relations and production units in terms of uncertainty absorption was described. You might recall that there was a key industrial relations representative physically located in each manufacturing facility. This representative was also regarded as a member of the industrial relations department located at company headquarters. While the industrial relations representative helped serve the manufacturing department, this individual also was the primary link between the two functional departments.

At the simplest level, the linking role may be little more than a convenient mechanism for systematically handling the flow of paperwork and following up on issues as required. In a more complex linking role, such as the industrial relations representative mentioned previously, the linking individual may have expertise in such areas as:

1. Helping the linked departments develop a better understanding of each other's functions and responsibilities;

2. Assisting in interpreting to one department the terminology and semantics unique to the other;

3. Serving to reduce the tendency for differences in the average educational levels in two departments to create such status differences that they become barriers to problem-solving; and

4. Providing a continuous way of keeping each department aware of its interdependencies with other units in the day-to-day decision-making.

Although our focus is on linking roles between units within the organization, there may also be specialized roles created to link the organization to external groups or other organizations. These roles are often called "boundary-spanning" roles. They provide an essential mechanism for facilitating the flow of information and decision-making between the organization and its environment.[31] For example, a safety manager might be in a boundary-spanning role between the organization and the Occupational Safety and Health Administration of the Federal government, with respect to safety and health issues.

Task Forces

When *ad hoc* issues or problems arise involving a number of departments, it may be desirable to establish a task force consisting of one or more representatives from each of the affected departments. The task force normally exists until decisions are made to resolve the current issues or problems. Some members could be engaged in the task force on a full-time basis and others part time. Each representative may also be thought of as providing a linking role between one's department and the task force. It is usually assumed that each representative can provide information and ideas regarding the common problems, serve as a transmitter of ideas and information between the task force and his or her department, and help assess the impact of decisions by the task force on his own department.

Task forces may emerge on a formal or informal basis. An informal task force may simply involve several individuals getting together to consider a mutual problem. A formal task force is one which higher management specifically recognizes and creates, usually in writing, through such means as stating the problem area to be of concern to the members. Once the objectives of the task force are attained, it is disbanded. Task forces, as well as the other integrating mechanisms being discussed, are used in business and nonbusiness organizations. The following is an example of a task force in a nonbusiness setting.

External Affairs Task Force. In January 1974, the Dean of the College of Business Administration (CBA) of a major university created a "CBA External Affairs Task Force." Six faculty members from various departments and disciplines within the College were appointed by the Dean after consultation. The purpose of the task force was to develop "a recommended plan of action for CBA external affairs activities that would encompass a three-to five-year time horizon with special emphasis on year one." During the first six months, the task force engaged in such activities as: holding brainstorming sessions; interviewing managers and executives; meeting with administrators in the University concerned with various aspects of external affairs, such as alumni and government relations; personally visiting and interviewing representatives from schools of business around the country; and seeking faculty ideas and attitudes through hearings and a questionnaire. Finally, a five-year strategic plan was approved at a faculty meeting in September 1974. This document represents a series of recommendations regarding priorities, programs, and activities related to external affairs. Upon completion and acceptance of this plan, the task force was disbanded. For the most part, further consideration and implementation of the recommendations will occur through the established organizational channels.

There should be no assumption that task forces are always successful. You will recall, in the earlier case involving the Management Analysis Department and the Data Processing Department, that the President created a task force consisting of Carl, Sam, and Phil to work out the design and programming-language problems. This task force obviously failed.

Integrating Roles or Departments

As the need for integration and the amount of differentiation and uncertainty continue to increase, interunit and intergroup difficulties and problems may occur with such frequency and/or be of such magnitude that more permanent, complex and powerful integrating mechanisms need to be utilized. Since integrating roles and specialized integrating departments can vary together in so many basic ways, we have decided to discuss them together. An integrating role implies that it is being filled by one individual, whereas an integrating department or group implies that several individuals have been formally assigned the task of facilitating integration between two or more other departments. The degree of formal authority for integrating roles or groups can vary widely, as can the types of roles or groups that have integration as one of their functions. Some examples of roles and groups that serve the integrating function (in addition to those previously discussed) are product or brand manager, program coordinator,[32] project manager,[33] group vice president, group management committees, annual meetings between corporate and division general managers,[34] and boards of directors.[35]

The role of the integrating position or department usually involves facilitating the resolution of nonroutine, unanticipated problems that develop among other departments, particularly between functional areas such as marketing, production, and research. Integration may revolve around interunit conflicts, major capital-investment decisions, numerous tactical decisions regarding service or product features, production levels or mix, schedules, cost estimates, standards of quality, and the like.[36]

The decision to use a position or a specialized department to achieve integration is likely to depend upon the contingencies in the situation. Obviously, a specialized department is likely to be a more costly integrating mechanism than a single role. There should probably be a tendency to move toward integrating units of increasing sophistication under the following types of circumstances: as the degree of differentiation between the units needing integration increases; as the degree of needed integration increases; as the degree of uncertainty increases. In addition, a variable that has been found to influence the use of integrating mechanisms, particularly between headquarters and divisions in large-scale organizations, is top management's philosophy.[37] If top management has a philosophy of tight control and authoritarianism, there is more likely to be a greater number of integrating mechanisms, greater formal authority assigned to them; and greater emphasis on domination and uniformity than on shared decision-making.

Degrees of Formal Authority.   Figure 8–6 provides a general continuum of the varying degrees of formal authority that might be assigned to an integrating role or department by higher management. At the lowest level of formal

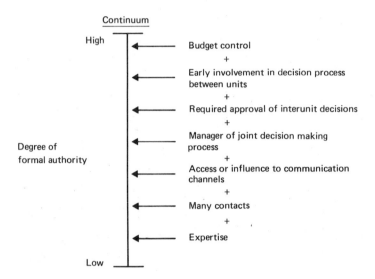

Figure 8–6   Degrees of Formal Authority for Integrating Roles or Units

Adapted and modified from: Galbraith, J., *Designing Complex Organizations*. Reading, Mass.: Addison-Wesley Publishing Co., 1973, pp. 93–102. Used with permission.

authority, higher management simply recognizes a particular individual with expertise (specialized knowledge or interpersonal skills) that is relevant to the relations between two or more departments. This individual is assigned to assist in helping the departments with their relationships, but the departments can decide when and whether it is used. However, it should not be concluded that expertise is a weak form of power. If the units are receptive and recognize that they need the expertise being made available the expert may have a considerable impact. As we move up the continuum in Fig. 8–6, there are examples representing increasing levels of formal authority with respect to obtaining integration between departments. The highest level of formal authority shown suggests that the integrating role or unit would have a budget (i.e., financial control over certain resources in its decision-making area). We could have the integrating manager or department essentially purchasing resources from other departments. The integrating role or department obviously becomes more active and influencial in the decision-making process, particularly in terms of planning and resource allocation. The next level of integration would likely lead to a matrix organization.

Matrix Organization

The matrix form of organization represents a balance between organizing resources around products, programs, or projects, and functional classifications, such as marketing, production, finance, personnel, and research. An organization may decide not to organize solely around products, programs, or projects because it might reduce desired functional specialization, or create the need to duplicate too many resources. For example, Dow Corning Corporation uses a matrix form of organization, in conjunction with product units such as rubber and sealants, resins and chemicals, fluids and compounds, specialty lubricants, and consumer products.[38]

The distinguishing feature of a matrix organization is the existence of at least dual authority, information, and reporting relationships and systems. In essence, the integrating role or department has a dual authority, information, and authority relationship with at least one functional (specialist) and one project or product group. In terms of authority relations, the integraging role or department is evaluated by both a project (or product unit) and a functional department. The project and functional units (usually their managers) affect the chances for promotion and salary increases for those involved with integration and their performance goals. Ideally, this results in a power balance between the influence of the project (or product) department and the functional unit on the integrating department (or individuals).

To assist in visualizing a matrix organization, a simple hypothetical example is shown in Fig. 8–7. We paraphrase the explanation of the figure offered by Delbecq and Filley, as follows.[39] First, a review of the overall figure does indicate the presence of hierarchy in the matrix organization. Hierarchy in the matrix approach is often overlooked because of the attention given to lateral or diagonal relations, shared and dual authority, flexible decision-making based upon expertise, and the like. The tendency to play down hierarchy probably occurs because it is not the distinguishing feature of the matrix design. Near the top of Fig. 8–7, there is a *program unit,* which consists of program coordinators who represent project (or product) groups. The program unit focuses on coordination of the functional units and trying to maintain a balance between the needs of project units and the needs of the functional units. The *staff service unit(s)* in Fig. 8–7 are primarily concerned with planning, budgeting, scheduling, and other support issues. As implied in the word "staff," the involvement in these issues would primarily be of an advisory nature. The *executive committee* consists of the top executive and at least one top manager from the program unit, staff service unit(s), the project director, and each functional unit. Among other functions, this committee also serves as a top-level integrating mechanism. The *functional departments* provide for groupings of specialists and the development of expertise and knowledge in each specialty area. On the other hand, the *project departments* usually have relatively well-defined goals that can be obtained within the foreseeable future. Upon goal attainment, it is assumed that a project department is disbanded or reorganized around some new project. However, if a *product* department is interfacing the functional department, it is likely to remain in existence as long as it is beneficial for the continued manufacture of the product.

Individuals from functional departments are typically assigned to project departments. The assignment patterns might vary as follows: (1) full-time for

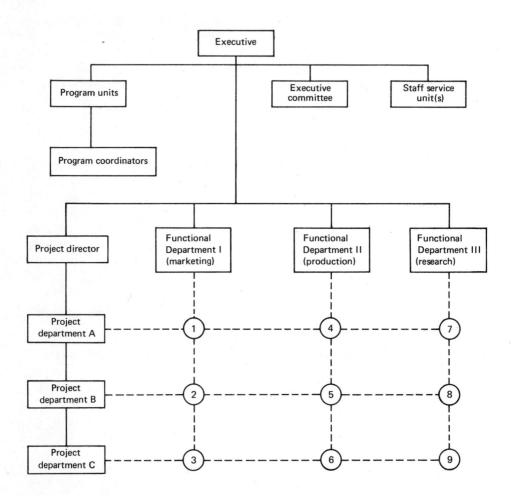

Figure 8–7   Simplified Matrix Structure

Adapted and modified from: Delbecq, A. and A. Filley, *Program and Project Management In A Matrix Organization: A Case Study.* Madison, Wisconsin: Graduate School of Business, University of Wisconsin, Madison, 1974, p. 16. Used with permission.

the duration of the project; (2) full-time assignments for one phase of the project; (3) part-time assignment; and (4) contract for services from the functional specialty. In this last assignment pattern, the functional specialist never becomes a part of the project department. The project manager simply arranges for certain services from the functional department.

As mentioned earlier, the key distinguishing feature of the matrix organization is the presence of at least dual authority, reporting, and information relationships. In terms of Fig. 8–7, dual relationships would exist within and/or for the subunits numbered 1 through 9. For example, some of the dual relationships would be as follows: group #1 to project department A and functional department I (marketing); group #2 to project department B and functional department I (marketing); and group #8 to project department B and functional Department III (research).

While a matrix structure is a costly form of organization and the power balances are subtle and difficult to maintain, it may be superior to other organizational forms under conditions of high uncertainty, high differentiation, and high need for integration. Some of the specific advantages claimed for the matrix form include:

1. It identifies a specific individual as the central point for all activities associated with a particular project;

2. It facilitates flexible use of individuals, because functional specialists can be obtained from the functional departments and shifted among projects, as needed;

3. It provides a home base to which functional specialists, who assist in the development of expertise and knowledge, can "return" between projects; and

4. It provides for built-in checks and balances between cost considerations, project considerations, and functional specialist (technical) considerations.[40]

Summary

This section has summarized and briefly evaluated the contingencies under which six different formal mechanisms would be utilized to assist in managing intergroup (or department) relations. As indicated in Fig. 8–5, these mechanisms were identified as hierarchy, plans, linking roles, task forces, integrating roles or units, and matrix organization. It was emphasized that one mechanism does not necessarily substitute for or preclude the use of other mechanisms.

Management–Worker Relations

The second major section in this part of the chapter focuses on formal mechanisms involving workers and management. These mechanisms are the hierarchical approach, joint-consultation approach, collective-bargaining approach, and workers' control approach. Since the hierarchical approach was presented previously in this and other chapters, we will not discuss it here. While our discussion will be somewhat of an oversimplification, we can differentiate these approaches in the formal sense on the basis of the amount of influence, participation, and/or control by workers in various decision-making areas (it might be useful to refer to Fig. 7–7, entitled "Relation between Group Decision-Making Levels and Participation"). Figure 8–8 differentiates these approaches along a continuum of the amount of worker influence or control in the decision-making process. As always, we need to keep clearly in mind that these formal approaches and how they are supposed to operate may differ substantially in practice. The above classification and the following discussion draw from the work of Strauss and Rosenstern.[41]

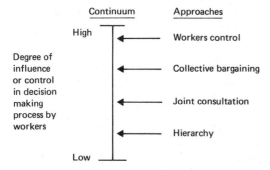

Figure 8–8 Continuum of Workers' Influence with Various Formal Worker-Management Approaches

Joint–Consultation Approach

The joint-consultation approach permits workers and/or their representatives to be heard on various decision issues, but management usually retains the ability to make the final decisions. The Tennessee Valley Authority (TVA) is one of the major examples of the joint-consultation approach. TVA is a semiautonomous agency of the United States government. Its 18,000 employees are primarily concerned with flood control, electric power generation, agricultural and forest improvement, and the like, in the Tennessee Valley area.

Their program, called the cooperative program, provides for a formal system of consultation and joint decision-making between employees and management representatives.[42] An underlying assumption of the cooperative program, and all joint-consultation approaches, is that there is a substantial commonality of interests or goals between management and the workers. The basic purpose of the formal cooperative program is to provide an additional outlet through which the mutual goals can be realized. Since the TVA workers are also represented by a union, the regularly held meetings by employee and management representatives focus on the discussion of mutual problems outside the scope of collective bargaining. The size of each cooperative unit or committee is typically quite large, such as an engineering division or a power plant. The representatives of management normally include the top managers of each unit, while the workers are represented by eight to ten elected individuals chosen by employees in various subparts of the unit. The employee representatives are usually union members, but not union officers. The meetings, normally several hours long, are held once per month. The areas of discussion include issues of mutual concerns such as improvements in working methods, safety, hospitalization plans, training, park facilities, community fund drives, and the like. While decisions are often made by consensus rather than by voting, management retains the ultimate authority for accepting, rejecting, and implementing decisions.

The activities of the cooperative committee are supposed to be communicated to workers through their representatives and printed summaries. Between major monthly meetings, various subcommittees work on issues and report back to the committee as a whole.

The enthusiasm, strength, and perceived significance of the cooperative program varies widely among major units of the TVA. A key variable seems to be the degree of support and enthusiasm for it from the management group in each unit. A lower-level supervisor indicated that the management of his engineering division assigned little importance to the program in these words:

> Now these cooperative conferences don't impress us much here at _____ division. The things they do don't seem to get to us as much as in other parts of TVA. We don't seem to appreciate the benefits. We do get information, suggestions, and the committees are good, but there is no real enthusiasm for them here.[43, p. 183]

On the other hand, an assistant unit operator in one steam plant commented:

> Yes, we have a cooperative committee here and if you have an idea you draw it up and submit it to the job steward, who goes to the monthly meeting. Then they take it and have a committee survey it. And if they think it will work, they'll OK it. I could show you numerous changes around here suggested by employees. I've got three or four changes out there myself.[44, p. 184]

In sum, the joint-consultation approach, as illustrated through the TVA cooperative program, is a formal mechanism for bringing management and workers together. It provides a systematic basis to consider issues of mutual concern and to resolve these issues, whenever possible, in a mutually beneficial manner.

Collective-Bargaining Approach

All bargaining relationships, whether they are between two or more individuals, departments, or organizations, have certain basic features in common.

Features of Bargaining Relationships.   The prominent characteristics or features of all bargaining relationships have been synthesized by Rubin and Brown as including the following:

1. At least two parties are involved.

2. The parties have a conflict of interest with respect to one or more different issues.

3. . . . the parties are at least temporarily joined together in a special kind of voluntary relationship (for bargaining to exist, the parties must believe they are participants by choice rather than compulsion).

4. [The primary activity in the bargaining relationship] . . . concerns: the division or exchange of one or more specific resources and/or (b) the resolution of one or more intangible issues among the parties or among those whom they represent.

5. The activity usually involves the presentation of demands or proposals by one party, evaluation of these by the other, followed by concessions and counterproposals. The activity is thus sequential rather than simultaneous.[45, p. 18]

There have been literally thousands of volumes of material written on bargaining, including collective bargaining. We can mention only a few of the basic elements and assumptions of collective bargaining as a formal mechanism for coping with worker–management relations. Somewhat in contrast to the joint-consultation approach, the collective-bargaining approach assumes that workers and management have some conflicting interests and some power struggles. Up to a point, these differences may be inevitable, necessary, and legitimate. Collective bargaining provides the formal structure and mechanisms through which various differences can be resolved. At a fundamental level, collective bargaining as a negotiating process has been regarded as relatively unchanging. It has been suggested that if a five-thousand-year-old Babylonian were to sit opposite present-day management or worker representatives, his methods would be almost the same as those currently used.[46] Some individuals have called for the introduction of new processes for utilizing collective bargaining, and have identified various social and mechanical technologies for doing so.[47] In many parts of this book, concepts and approaches that are relevant to intergroup decision-making and conflict are discussed. Thus, we do not deal with these issues here. While we are focusing on the collective-bargaining approach, it is useful to recognize that it really represents only one of the numerous areas in which the process of negotiation takes place.[48] For example, negotiations go on in interpersonal relations as well as in international relations.[49]

Framework.   A useful framework for considering the collective-bargaining approach has been developed by Walton and McKersie.[50] They identify four major subprocesses for collective bargaining, including distributive bargaining, integrative bargaining, intraorganizational bargaining, and attitudinal structuring.

Distributive bargaining refers to situations in which the goals of management and workers are considered to be in conflict. In the extreme, it is assumed that a "zero sum" situation exists in which management's gain is a loss to the workers, or vice versa.

Integrative bargaining refers to situations in which the goals of each group are perceived as mutually reinforcing, or at least not in conflict with one another. Integrative bargaining requires attitudes and behaviors such as joint problem-solving, joint fact-gathering, joint exploration of problems, and mutual concern and interest in each other's welfare. In contrast, distributive bargaining implies a continuous process of offensive and defensive positions being taken by each group. Distributive bargaining is probably more prevalent than integrative bargaining within the area of union–management relations today.

Intraorganizational bargaining refers to the activities and bargaining that take place within the worker group (union) and within the management group, about the positions to be taken by the representatives of each group in the actual collective-bargaining sessions.

Attitudinal structuring refers to the types of attitudes and the activities that serve to change attitudes and relationships. (See Fig. 8–3 for contrasting types of attitudes under conditions of cooperation and competition.) As you might expect, the attitudes the two groups hold toward each other are likely to be relatively positive where there is an emphasis upon integrative bargaining and somewhat negative where the emphasis is on distributive bargaining. Attitudes and other noneconomic factors can influence the relationships between the two groups, in addition to the more traditional economic issues.[51] Of course, any given collective-bargaining relationship may consider some issue areas primarily in an integrative style, such as day-to-day administration of a collective-bargaining agreement, and other issue areas primarily in a distributive style, such as negotiating over a wage increase in a new contract.

The conduct of collective bargaining can accentuate forces and factors such as goals, power, and conflict in management's attempts to change organizations.[52] If outside consultants or behavioral scientists are to operate successfully in change efforts, they must accept and respect the appropriateness of the differences in goals between management, workers, and union organizations. Accordingly, change agents should seek to use change processes that recognize the needs and goals of each of these groups.[53] We will directly consider change processes and issues in Part Five of this book.

Workers' Control Approach

In contrast to the joint-consultation approach, where management has final decision-making authority, the workers' control approach calls for final decision-making authority resting in elected representatives of the workers. In theory, these worker representatives determine policy and employ management to implement it. The workers' control approach is most common in Yugoslavia, although other socialist countries have some versions of it. Some of the formally stated characteristics of the workers' control approach will be described by using the Yugoslavian system as a case illustration. However, as of this writing (1975), some important constitutional changes were being considered for the workers' self-management system in Yugoslavia. It cannot be emphasized too strongly that some research suggests that this approach does not always operate or function in reality as claimed on paper.[54] For example, management may have so much information, expertise, and education that in some areas the workers' representatives can do little more than go through the motions of approving management's recommendations.

Yugoslav System.   Yugoslav enterprises are socially owned.[55] This means that ownership of the enterprise is by society as a whole. The management of a firm is delegated (by the state) to a workers' collective consisting of those individuals who work within the firm. The only limitation on the workers' collective is that it is responsible for enhancing and maintaining the value of the firm. This system provides for direct and indirect participation by all workers. Direct participation can occur through meetings of the whole workers' collective (usually once or twice per year), meetings of the immediate work unit (once or more per month), and referenda (voting on issues, such as whether to merge with another enterprise). Indirect participation occurs through elected representatives. Each enterprise has an elected Workers' Council consisting of ten to fifty individuals, depending upon the size of the enterprise. The Council is the ultimate operating authority and is accountable to the collective as a whole. The Council and/or subgroups of the Council, created to handle particular decision areas, makes decisions concerning issues such as approval of production plans, prices of products and services, investments, use of profit, distribution of salaries and wages, and hiring and firing of employees, particularly management and staff personnel. The Workers' Council also selects the top managers, normally for a four-year period. The top managers may be reelected after each term of office. However, public announcements are made regarding the expiring terms of managers, and candidates would be invited to apply.

The stated rationale of the Workers' Council approach in Yugoslavia claims to provide a mechanism for: (1) resolving class conflict by abolishing classes, through the elimination of private property, and (2) humanizing work and creating conditions to assist in the development of the individual.

Overview

This section has served to briefly explain three rather contrasting formal mechanisms for coping with management–worker relations. The hierarchy approach (which was not discussed here), joint-consultation approach, collective-bargaining approach, and workers' control approach are all based on different starting assumptions, and involve different processes for coping with worker–management relations.

SUMMARY

This chapter was presented in two major parts to discuss various aspects of intergroup relations. The first part presented six major contingencies which can, independently or in combination, affect intergroup relations. These contingencies include goals, uncertainty absorption, substitutability, task relations, resource sharing, and attitudinal sets. The second part outlined various mechanisms for managing lateral relations between groups or units, and formal mechanisms for managing relations between management and workers as distinct groups. In general, the nature of these mechanisms and concrete examples of each were developed. Moreover, we wove into the discussion key contingencies which can influence the use of these formal mechanisms.

Discussion Questions

1. How serious a problem do you think goal incompatibility is between units within organizations? Explain. Can you think of any personal examples where goal incompatibility occurred between a group in which you were a member and some other group? Describe this situation.

2. In what ways might a marketing research department absorb uncertainty for a sales department?

3. Are there any conditions under which a department should be able to substitute services provided by a firm outside of the organization for those provided by another unit within the organization? Explain.

4. Can there be interdependent task relations between two or more groups that are also characterized as being "autonomous" groups? (See Chapter 7, especially Fig. 7–8.) Explain.

5. By utilizing the continua in Fig. 8–3, how would you describe the intergroup relations between any two groups with which you have a personal familiarity? Does your diagnosis have any implications for the relative effectiveness or ineffectiveness of these groups? Explain. You should try to develop your example from some setting such as a business firm, educational institution, religious organization, government, or social groups.

6. Discuss and evaluate the following statement: "Hierarchy in organizations and society in general is nothing more than a mechanism to enable a few individuals at the top to control and suppress the many individuals at the bottom."

7. Discuss and evaluate the following statement: "The matrix form of organization is one of those mechanisms advocated by the eggheads in the university. Its use within an organization would surely lead to confusion, with everyone being responsible for everything but no one accountable for anything."

8. Should there be a widespread utilization of formal joint-consultation programs between "workers" and "management" in business and nonbusiness organizations? Explain.

9. Do you think the utilization of the workers' control approach is likely to increase in the future within the United States and other countries? Explain.

CRITICAL INCIDENT

Doug Stone, Project Leader for the Ajax Company, had fifteen computer programmers reporting to him. These programmers were working on the development of three major information systems, and each of his programmers was assigned to one of three teams. Each team was responsible for one of the information systems.

Mr. Stone decided that he could better control the development of the projects, and free more time for his administrative responsibilities, by assigning team leaders to each project area. The team leaders, he decided, would be called "lead programmers." Before announcing his decision to all of his programmers, Mr. Stone decided to discuss it privately with each of his three prospective lead programmers. He wanted to be sure that they understood the project and were willing to accept this new responsibility.

Mr. Stone called Dave Fleet into his office and told him that he would like him to be the lead programmer on projects related to the billing and pricing systems. Mr. Stone carefully explained to Dave that this position carried the authority to direct the project-related activities of the people assigned to the project area. These people were Bob Strawser, Dave Crumley, Clint Phillips, and Jo Ann Thomas. Mr. Stone clearly explained what was meant by project-related activities vs. areas of administrative authority, which he would retain. Dave Fleet accepted the new position, and as he was leaving the office, asked Mr. Stone to announce and explain the new position to the other programmers. Mr. Stone assured Dave that he would on the next day. The following week Mr. Stone began his annual vacation.

One morning, while Mr. Stone was still on vacation, Dave Fleet asked Howard Chamberlain to prepare the computer operator procedure for a system test which had to be run that night. Later that day, Dave asked Howard if the test procedure was ready. Howard replied that it was not.

Dave asked, "Why not, didn't you have enough time?"

"No," Howard replied, "I had enough time, but where I worked before, that task was the responsibility of the project's systems analyst."

Dave was getting upset. "Fortunately or unfortunately, it is a programming responsibility here; I've explained that to you earlier. I'm the lead programmer on this project; now why didn't you do as I asked?"

"You're the lead programmer?" Howard seemed surprised. "To my knowledge, we don't have a lead programmer on this project."

Dave pondered what his next step should be. He knew that the test procedure had to be done within three hours, and Howard was the only one who had the knowledge to prepare it.

Question:

Analyze the issues and problems in this incident in terms of the following contingencies affecting intergroup relations: goals, uncertainty absorption, substitutability, task relations, resource sharing, and attitudinal sets. Which contingencies seem to be important and unimportant? What are the bases for your conclusions?

REFERENCES

1. Schmidt, S., and T. Kochran, "Conflict: Toward Conceptual Clarity," *Administrative Science Quarterly,* 1972, **17,** pp. 359–370.

2. Arrow, K., "Control in Large Corporations," *Management Science,* 1964, **10,** p. 404.

3. Mack, R. P., *Planning on Uncertainty: Decision-Making in Business and Government Administration.* New York: Wiley-Interscience, 1971.

4. Thompson, J. D., *Organizations in Action.* New York: McGraw-Hill Book Co., 1967.

5. Kaplan, D., "Power in Perspective," in *Power and Conflict in Organizations.* Kahn, R. L., and E. Boulding (eds.). London: Tavistock, 1964, pp. 11–32.

6. Goldner, F. H., "The Division of Labor: Process and Power," in Zald, M. N., *Power in Organizations.* Nashville, Tenn.: Vanderbilt University Press, 1970, pp. 97–143.

7. *Ibid.*

8. *Ibid.*

9. Dubin, R., "Power, Function, and Organization," *Pacific Sociological Review,* 1963, **6,** pp. 16–24.

10. Hickson, D. J., C. R. Hinnings, C. A. Lee, R. E. Schneck, and J. M. Pennings, "A Strategic Contingencies Theory of Intraorganizational Power," *Administrative Science Quarterly,* 1971, **16,** pp. 216–229.

11. O'Brien, G. E., "The Measurement of Cooperation," *Organizational Behavior and Human Performance,* 1968, **3,** pp. 427–439.

12. Emerson, R. M., "Power-Dependence Relations," *American Sociological Review,* 1962, **27,** pp. 31–40.

13. Strauss, G., "Tactics of Lateral Relationship: The Purchasing Agent," *Administrative Science Quarterly,* 1962, **7,** pp. 161–186.

14. Mack, R., and S. Synder, "The Analysis of Social Conflict: Toward an Overview and Synthesis," *Journal of Conflict Resolution,* 1957, **1,** pp. 212–248.

15. Browne, P. J., and R. Golembiewski, "The Line–Staff Concept Revisited: An Empirical Study of Organizational Images," *Academy of Management Journal,* 1974, **17,** pp. 406–417.

16. Sayles, L., *Managerial Behavior.* New York: McGraw-Hill Book Co., 1964.

17. Sherif, M., and C. W. Sherif, *Groups in Harmony and Tension: An Integration of Studies on Intergroup Relations.* New York: Octagon Books, 1966.

18. Blake, R. R., and J. S. Mouton, "Comprehension of Own and of Outgroup Positions Under Intergroup Competition," *Journal of Conflict Resolution,* 1961, **5,** pp. 304–310. Cafferty, T. P., and S. Streugert, "Conflict and Attitudes Toward the Opponent: An Application of the Collins and Hoyt Attitude-Change Theory to Groups in Interorganizational Conflict," *Journal of Applied Psychology,* 1975, **59,** pp. 48–53. Dutton, J. M., and R. E. Walton, "Interdepartmental Conflict and Cooperation: Two Contrasting Studies," *Human Organizations,* 1966, **25,** pp. 207–220. Stern, L. W., B. Sternthal, and C. S. Craig, "A Parasimulation of Interorganizational Conflict," *International Journal of Group Tensions,* 1973, **3,** pp. 68–90.

19. Gamson, W. A., "Violence and Power: The Meek Don't Make It," *Psychology Today,* 1974, **8,** pp. 35–41. Gamson, W. A., *The Strategy of Social Protest.* Homewood, Ill.: Dorsey Press, 1975.

20. Rogers, R. E., *The Political Process in Modern Organizations.* Jericho: Exposition Press, 1971, pp. 84–117. Used with author permission.

21. *Ibid.*

22. *Ibid.*

23. *Ibid.*

24. Lorsch, J. W., and P. R. Lawrence, "Organizing For Product Innovation," *Harvard Business Review,* 1965, **42,** pp. 109–122.

25. Lorsch, J. W., and S. A. Allen, III, *Managing Diversity and Interdependence: An Organizational Study of Multidivisional Firms.* Boston: Harvard University, Graduate School of Business Administration, 1973. *Also see:* Lawrence, P. R., and J. W. Lorsch, *Organization and Environment: Managing Differentiation and Integration.* Homewood, Ill.: Richard D. Irwin, 1969.

26. Galbraith, J., *Designing Complex Organizations.* Reading, Mass.: Addison-Wesley Publishing Co., 1973.

27. Tannenbaum, A. S., B. Kavcic, M. Rosner, M. Vianello, and G. Wieser, *Hierarchy in Organizations: An International Comparison.* San Francisco: Jossey-Bass Publishers, 1974.

28. Drucker, P. F., *Management: Tasks, Responsibilities, Practices.* New York: Harper & Row Publishers, 1973.

29. McCaskey, M. B., "A Contingency Approach to Planning: Planning with Goals and Planning without Goals," *Academy of Management Journal,* 1974, **17,** pp. 281–291.

30. Allio, R. J., "The Corporate Road-Map Planning at Babcock and Wilcox," *Long-Range Planning,* 1972, **5,** pp. 9–15.

31. Keller, R. T., and W. E. Holland, "Boundary-Spanning Roles in a Research and Development Organization: An Empirical Examination," *Academy of Management Journal,* 1975, **18,** pp. 388–393.

32. Lawrence, P. R., and J. W. Lorsch, "New Management Job: The Integrator," *Harvard Business Review,* 1967, **45,** pp. 142–151.

33. Butler, A. G., "Project Management: A Study in Organizational Conflict," *Academy of Management Journal,* 1973, **16,** pp. 84–101.

34. Lorsch, J. W., and S. A. Allen, *op. cit.*

35. Pfeffer, J., "Size and Composition of Corporate Boards of Directors: The Organization and its Environment," *Administrative Science Quarterly,* 1972, **17,** pp. 218–228. Pfeffer, J., "Size, Composition, and Function of Hospital Boards of Directors: A Study of Organization–Environment Linkage," *Administrative Science Quarterly,* 1973, **18,** pp. 349–364.

36. Lawrence, P. R., and J. W. Lorsch, *op. cit.,* pp. 142–144.

37. Vance, S. C., *Managers in the Conglomerate Era.* New York: Wiley-Inter-Science, 1971, esp. pp. 255–269. Lorsch, J. W., and S. A. Allen, *op. cit.,* pp. 1–30.

38. Goggin, W. C., "How the Multidimensional Structure Works at Dow Corning," *Harvard Business Review,* 1974, **52,** pp. 54–56.

39. Delbecq, A., and A. Filley, *Program and Project Management in a Matrix Organization: A Case Study.* Madison, Wis.: Graduate School of Business,

University of Wisconsin—Madison, 1974. *Also see:* Evans, P. B., "Multiple Hierarchies and Organizational Control," *Administrative Science Quarterly,* 1975, **20,** pp. 250–259.

40. Cleland, D. I., and W. R. King, *Systems Analysis and Project Management.* New York: McGraw-Hill Book Co., 1968.

41. Strauss, G., and E. Rosenstein, "Workers' Participation: A Critical View," *Industrial Relations,* 1970, **9,** pp. 197–214. *Also see:* Flanagan, R. J., G. Strauss, and L. Ulman, "Worker Discontent and Workplace Behavior," *Industrial Relations,* 1974, **13,** pp. 101–123.

42. Patchen, M., *Participation, Achievement and Involvement on the Job.* Englewood Cliffs, N.J.: Prentice Hall, 1970. *Also see:* Ruh, R. A., R. L. Wallace, and C. F. Frost, "Management Attitudes and the Scanlon Plan," *Industrial Relations,* 1973, **12,** pp. 282–288. Ruh, T. A., R. G. Johnson, and M. P. Scontrino, "The Scanlon Plan: Participation in Decision-Making, and Job Attitudes," *Journal of Industrial and Organizational Psychology,* 1973, **1,** pp. 36–45.

43. Patchen, M., *op. cit.*

44. *Ibid.*

45. Rubin, J. Z., and B. R. Brown, *The Social Psychology of Bargaining and Negotiation.* New York: Academic Press, 1975.

46. Karrass, C. L., *The Negotiating Game.* New York: World, 1970.

47. Balke, W. M., K. D. Hammond, and G. D. Meyer, "An Alternative Approach to Labor-Management Relations," *Administrative Science Quarterly,* 1973, **18,** pp. 311–327.

48. Nierenberg, G. I., *Fundamentals of Negotiating.* New York: Hawthorn Books, 1973.

49. Editorial, *Journal of Conflict Resolution,* 1957, **1,** pp. 1–3.

50. Walton, R. E., and R. B. McKersie, *A Behavioral Theory of Labor Negotiations: An Analysis of a Social Interaction System.* New York: McGraw-Hill Book Co., 1965. *Also see:* Benson, J. K., "The Interorganizational Network as a Political Economy," *Administration Science Quarterly,* 1975, **20,** pp. 229–244.

51. Tracy, L., "The Influence of Noneconomic Factors on Negotiators," *Industrial and Labor Relations Review,* 1974, **27,** pp. 204–215.

52. Dyer, L., and T. A. Kochan, "Labor Unions and Organizational Change: A New Frontier for OD." Paper presented at the Annual Meeting of the Academy of Management, Seattle, Washington, 1974.

53. Fisher, R. J., "Third-Party Consultation: A Method for the Study and Resolution of Conflict," *Journal of Conflict Resolution,* 1972, **16,** pp. 67–94.

Lewiski, R. J., and C. P. Alderfer, "The Tensions between Research and Intervention in Intergroup Conflict," *The Journal of Applied Behavior Science,* 1973, **9,** pp. 424–449.

54. Obradovic, J., "Workers' Participation: Who Participates?" *Industrial Relations,* 1975, **14,** pp. 132–144. Adizes, I., *Industrial Democracy: Yugoslav Style.* New York: Free Press, 1971. Garson, G. D., and J. Case (eds.), *Workers' Control.* New York: Randon House, 1973.

55. Tannenbaum, A. S., *et al., Hierarchy in Organization.* San Francisco: Jossey-Bass Publishers, 1974, pp. 27–32.

*

PART IV

INDIVIDUAL ORGANIZATIONAL LINKAGES

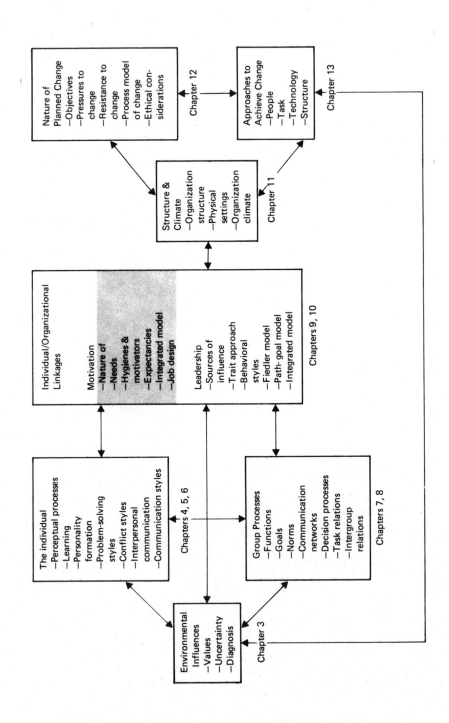

Nature of Planned Change
—Objectives
—Pressures to change
—Resistance to change
—Process model of change
—Ethical considerations

Chapter 12

Approaches to Achieve Change
—People
—Task
—Technology
—Structure

Chapter 13

Structure & Climate
—Organization structure
—Physical settings
—Organization climate

Chapter 11

Individual/Organizational Linkages

Motivation
—Nature of
—Needs
—Hygienes & motivators
—Expectancies
—Integrated model
—Job design

Leadership
—Sources of influence
—Trait approach
—Behavioral styles
—Fiedler model
—Path-goal model
—Integrated model

Chapters 9, 10

The individual
—Perceptual processes
—Learning
—Personality formation
—Problem-solving styles
—Conflict styles
—Interpersonal communication
—Communication styles

Chapters 4, 5, 6

Group Processes
—Functions
—Goals
—Norms
—Communication networks
—Decision processes
—Task relations
—Intergroup relations

Chapters 7, 8

Environmental Influences
—Values
—Uncertainty
—Diagnosis

Chapter 3

9
MOTIVATION IN ORGANIZATIONS

Suppose, as a foreman, you notice two carpenters building packing crates for several large generators, which your organization manufactures and ships to customers. They work the same shift and build the crates to the same specifications. When a crate is completed, the carpenter then places it on a conveyor belt and proceeds to gather materials to begin the construction of another crate.

After watching these two carpenters working for a week or so, you notice that one carpenter has completed about twice as many crates as his fellow worker. This chapter is about one of the major reasons why workers produce at different rates: motivation. Motivation is certainly not the only reason that causes people to produce at different rates, since the performance level of an individual is influenced by many factors, such as ability, manual dexterity, intellectual capacity, and the like. In addition to these factors, mechanical breakdowns, low-quality materials, an inadequate supply of materials, inequitable reward structures, or unpopular supervisory behavior can influence the productivity rate of a worker. Still, particularly in most managerial jobs, motivation seems to be a major determinant of performance. If we want to have effective organizations, we must understand how to encourage effective individual performance. We must understand why one employee works at 50 percent of standard and another works at 100 percent of standard. To understand the motivational process, this chapter will:

1. Define motivation and illustrate some methods used to measure it;

2. Discuss the relationship between motivation and satisfaction;

3. Review Maslow's, Herzberg's, McClelland's and the Expectancy theories of motivation;

4. Propose an integrated model of motivation;

5. Discuss how job design can affect an individual's motivational process; and,

6. Study the effects of job-enrichment programs on workers' satisfactions and performance.

CONCEPT OF MOTIVATION

Motivation has been defined as a predisposition to act in a specific goal-directed manner.[1] This definition of motivation is restricted to purposive or goal-directed behavior, but we must note that some behavior, such as reflexes, is not considered goal-directed. Reflexes are strictly determined by the reaction of various nerves to external stimuli, such as heat, cold, and the like, and will not be dealt with in this chapter. We are concerned with why a person does what he does, and to what degree he or she does it.

The motivational process can best be understood by examining the employee's goals and how he or she feels these goals can be attained. For example, suppose the two carpenters previously mentioned both had an equal desire for high salaries, which could only be attained through performance. One of these carpenters believes that it is probable that he can achieve this goal by working hard. The other carpenter does not believe that he can achieve a high salary by working hard. In this case, we expect the first carpenter to be more motivated to work hard than the second. The problem in studying the motivational process of individuals, therefore, is to explain the voluntary choices made by the workers to reach the same goal.

Just as organizations differ in the products they manufacture or services they render, people differ in what motivates them to work. Some people work primarily for money, others for companionship, others for the challenge their work offers them, and still others for a combination of reasons. Organizations have tried numerous methods to motivate employees on the job; giving employees interesting jobs, using participative management, use of pay-incentive systems, exercising close supervision, and the like. The variety of approaches is not surprising. Among other factors, the type of technology influences the way in which the organization can design its jobs, and the environment influences the organization's products and/or services.

It is important to distinguish between motivation and job satisfaction, for too often these terms are confused one with the other. Most workers' responses toward various aspects of the work itself, the pay, supervision, promotional opportunities, and the like can be classified as attitudes. Attitudes have been defined as affective responses (feelings), cognitive responses (beliefs and thoughts), and behavioral acts.[2] Attitudes are most commonly used in reference to the affective component. A worker's attitudinal response to a questionnaire or some other research instrument that is designed to measure factors affecting a worker's job are often called "facets of job satisfaction." *Satisfaction* is an end-state resulting from the attainment of some goal. It is the worker's feelings about, or affective responses to, aspects of the work situation. Motivation is primarily concerned with the individual's desires, and how they can be fulfilled in the work situation. The differences between motivation and satisfaction might be highlighted by reviewing the measurement of each concept.

Assessment of Motivation

One way to answer the questions "What does a person do?" and "To what degree does he or she do it?" is to assess the *meaning* of work and what it can provide to the individual. Behavioral scientists have identified many worker desires: security, esteem, self-actualization, autonomy, prestige, and so on. There are two methods frequently used to assess the strength of these desires. First, we can construct questions pertaining to the specific desires and simply ask employees to indicate the presence or absence of these desires for them. The list of desires each of us could generate might be substantial. The problem with following this approach is that it does not enable the worker to respond according to the strength of each desire, nor does it take into account the influence of one desire on another.

A second procedure is to assume that each worker has a hierarchy of needs, some stronger than others, and that an individual will seek fulfillment of his strongest desires first.[3] If we measure the relative strength of desires, we can compare groups and individuals with respect to differential fulfillment of desires.[4] This approach would provide us with information with respect to the absolute level of desire strength for a single employee, and/or it could provide a comparison of desire strengths among employees.

Porter and Lawler have designed an instrument to assess the fulfillment of needs.[5] The first question asks "How much of the desired characteristic is now in the workplace?" The second asks "How much of the desired characteristic *should* there be in the workplace?" Fulfillment of needs can be assessed by subtracting the response to the first question from the response to the second. The smaller the difference, the more the fulfillment of that need in the work situation. For example, suppose that the following question was used to measure degree of fulfillment of the self-actualization need, and the responses are as circled:

The opportunity, in my management position, for participating in setting goals:

How much is there now?

Minimum   1   2   3   ④   5   6   7   Maximum

How much should there be?

Minimum   1   2   3   4   5   ⑥   7   Maximum

The difference (2) indicates some lack of fulfillment in this need. We would expect that the worker would take some action to try to decrease the discrepancy between what there is and what there should be. Discrepancy scores should be interpreted with some caution.[6] One problem is that a deficiency score can be derived in many ways (e.g., $5 - 7 = 2$; $4 - 6 = 2$; $3 - 5 = 2$, and so on), and yet will mean quite different things for the employees. Nonetheless, it is a widely used method to tap the motivational desires of individuals.

Assessment of Job Satisfaction

Job satisfaction has been defined as the feelings about various aspects of the worker's work setting. Various formats have been developed to measure job satisfaction. One such format asks the respondent to indicate a choice of "yes," "no," or "uncertain" in response to whether or not the statement or adjective is descriptive of the job. This approach is illustrated in Fig. 9–1. For example, consider a job that you have performed, and answer the following questions either "yes," "no," or "uncertain." This technique does not ask you directly about your satisfaction with the five related job factors, but infers the level of satisfaction from the adjectives that you consider descriptive of the job. For example, it is unlikely that you would be satisfied with your co-workers if you responded "yes" to the adjectives of lazy, slow, and stupid. On the surface, this technique simply asks you to describe the various aspects of your work. In describing your work, you do, however, provide information that is used to infer a state of satisfaction or dissatisfaction. Most of the adjectives are evaluative (e.g., satisfying, good, bad). There is a clear attempt to avoid the use of needs, wants, or desires since these are aspects of *motivation*.

THEORIES OF MOTIVATION

At this point, we would like to turn our attention from the assessment of motivation and job satisfaction to a discussion of how outcomes become goals for people. We will consider two general types of theories: first, those theories that attempt to specify why certain outcomes are valued by people, and what factors influence the values people assign to their goals; second, a theory of motivation that tries to explain how behavior is directed, and why people choose a particular way of behaving in order to reach a particular goal. As previously indicated, to understand motivated behavior, we need to know both what the goals of people are and how people decide which way to try to achieve them.

An adequate explanation of why certain goals are desirable must deal with three separate but interrelated questions:

1. What is it about the nature of individuals that causes goals to become desirable to them?

2. What general classes or groups of goals do people find desirable or undesirable?

Work
fascinating	____
routine	____
satisfying	____
boring	____
good	____
creative	____
respected	____

Pay
income adequate for normal expenses	____
barely live on income	____
bad	____
insecure	____
underpaid	____

Promotions
good opportunity for advancement	____
dead-end job	____
regular promotions	____
unfair promotion policy	____

Supervision
asks my advice	____
hard to please	____
impolite	____
tactful	____
up-to-date	____

Co-workers
stimulating	____
lazy	____
slow	____
ambitious	____
stupid	____
fast	____

Figure 9–1 A Measure of Job Satisfaction

Adapted from: Smith, P., L. Kendall, and C. Hulin, *The Measurement of Satisfaction in Work and Retirement.* Chicago: Rand McNally & Co., 1969, p. 83.

3. What factors influence the desirability of these goals?

Unless the second and third questions are answered, it is impossible to predict the kind of behavior choices a person will make. In order to predict behavior, several theorists—A. Maslow, D. McClelland, and F. Herzberg—have found it necessary to make assumptions about what causes goals to be important in the first place. These three theorists are among the best known and most widely accepted authorities in the management field. However, as we shall point out, there are controversies and concerns regarding each of the theories.

Need Hierarchy

Maslow's hierarchical classification of needs has been the most widely used theory for the study of motivation in organizations.[7] Maslow proposed that individuals have a complex set of needs, which are arranged in a hierarchy of prepotency. There are four basic assumptions in this hierarchy:

1. A *satisfied* need is not a motivator. When a need is satisfied, another need emerges to take its place, so that man is always striving to satisfy a need.

2. The need network for most people is very complex, with a number of needs affecting the behavior of an individual at any one time.

3. Lower-level needs must be satisfied, in general, before higher-level needs are activated sufficiently to drive behavior.

4. There are many more ways to satisfy higher-level needs than for lower-level needs.

Maslow's theory postulates that there are five need categories: Physiological, safety, social, esteem (or ego development) and self-actualization. These five need categories are arranged somewhat in the hierarchical order indicated in Fig. 9–2.

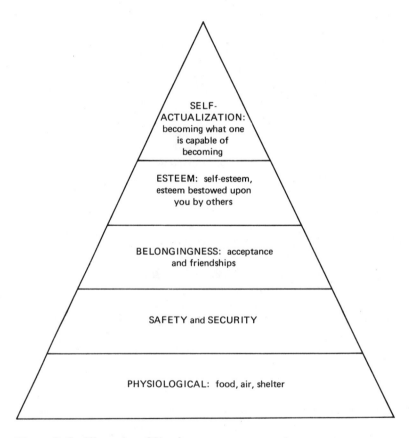

Figure 9–2 Hierarchy of Needs

Physiological Needs

These needs include the need for food, water, air, and so on. These needs are at the lowest level in the hierarchy, and we generally concentrate on satisfying these needs before we concentrate on the higher-order needs. If an individual is extremely hungry, no other interests exist and he or she is primarily motivated to obtain food. Sadly enough, in today's society, there are large segments of people that are dangerously deprived of the basic physiological essentials. Most of us, however, experience an *appetite* for something, rather than being dangerously hungry. Within organizational settings, managers usually express little concern with needs at this level, and have turned their attention to the security need, as the lowest-level need, in their analysis of worker behavior.

Once the physiological needs have been satisfied, their strength or importance decreases, and the next higher-level need becomes the strongest motivator of behavior. This process of "increased fulfillment/decreased importance/increased importance of the next higher need" repeats itself until the highest level of the hierarchy is reached. This is what Maslow means by saying that there is a hierarchy of needs that serve to motivate individuals.[8]

Safety Needs

These needs include the need for security, stability and absence from pain, threat or illness. As in the case with the physiological needs, when the safety needs are not satisfied, the individual becomes preoccupied with satisfying this need. The safety needs for many workers are expressed in the desire for a job with security, medical, pension, unemployment, and old age insurance benefits. In the mid-sixties, many of the contractual agreements between labor and management focused on job retention for workers. Several industries, most notably the airlines, newspapers, railroads, and shipping, have negotiated extensive provisions for workers whose jobs have been eliminated by a change in technology. The Occupational Safety and Health Act of 1970 and the Pension Act of 1974 are indicators that the U. S. government is trying to reduce the number of safety and health hazards in industry, and to assure workers that the monies they have invested in pension plans will be there upon retirement. Another evidence of the need for safety is the preference for individuals to undertake tasks or live in environments that are familiar rather than unfamiliar.

Belongingness and Love Needs

These needs include the need for affection, belongingness, love, and so on. When the physiological needs and the safety needs are satisfied, the belongingness and love needs emerge and serve to motivate the individuals. This level in the hierarchy represents a clearcut step above the first two (physical) needs;

nonfulfillment of this need may affect the mental health of the employee. Examples of nonfulfillment of this need may be evidenced in high absenteeism rates, poor productivity, low job satisfaction, and emotional breakdowns. As indicated in Chapter 7, membership in groups may serve many of the belongingness and love needs that employees bring with them to the work situation.

Esteem Needs

These needs include both a need for personal feelings of achievement or self-worth, and recognition or respect from others. The desire for excellence, a mastery of some problem or skills, independence, and the like, are internal or personal feelings that may be indicators of self-esteem. The desire for respect, prestige, recognition, and appreciation by others are external indicators of one's self-esteem that can also fulfill the individual's need for esteeem. The fulfillment of the esteem need leads to feelings of worth, adequacy, and self-confidence. The inability of the individual to fulfill these needs may lead to a feeling of discouragement. There is a real danger to the individual's mental health when esteem is bestowed upon the individual by others if it is based upon external celebrity or fame, rather than upon actual competence or capacity to perform the task.

This need differs from the needs at the social level, in which the person wants people to accept him for what he is. At the esteem level, he wants to be perceived as competent and able. He is concerned about the achievement, prestige, status, and promotional opportunities that others will provide as recognition of competence and capabilities.

Need for Self-Actualization

These needs include self-fulfillment, or the realization of one's potential. The actualizing person may be described as one who has increased acceptance of self and others, increased problem-solving ability, increased spontaneity, increased detachment and a desire for privacy, and the like.[9] To fulfill this need of becoming everything that one is capable of becoming requires that the individual has at some time partially fulfilled the other needs. However, self-actualizers may focus on the fulfillment of this highest need to such an extent that they, consciously or unconsciously, make sacrifices in the fulfillment of lower-level needs. Figure 9–3 identifies some behaviors that might be thought of as suggesting the self-actualization need.

In short, Maslow's theory of needs assumes that each individual is motivated by an attempt to satisfy the need(s) that is (are) most important at that point in his or her life. Further, the strength of any particular need is determined by its position in the need hierarchy and by the degree to which it and all lower-level needs have been satisfied. The theory predicts a dynamic, step-

Some indicators of self-actualization

1. Self-actualization means experiencing fully, vividly, selflessly, with full concentration and total absorption.
2. Life can be thought of as a process of choices, one after another.
3. Talk of self-actualization implies that there is a self to be actualized.
4. When in doubt, be honest rather than not. Looking within oneself for many of the answers implies taking responsibility.
5. One cannot choose wisely for a life unless he dares to listen to himself—his own self—at each moment in life, and to say calmly, "No, I don't like such and such."
6. Self-actualization is not only an end-state but also the process of actualizing one's potentialities at any time, in any moment.
7. Peak experiences are transient moments of self-actualization. They are moments of ecstasy which cannot be bought, cannot be guaranteed, cannot even be sought.
8. Finding out who one is, what one is, what one likes, or doesn't like, what is good for him and what bad, where one is going and what one's mission is—opening up one's inner self—means the exposure of psychopathology. It means identifying defenses, and after defenses have been identified, it means finding the courage to give them up.

Figure 9–3   Some Indicators of Self-Actualization

Source: Maslow, A. H., *The Farther Reaches of Human Nature.* New York: Viking Press, 1971, pp. 45–49.

by-step, causal process of motivation, in which behavior is governed by a continuously changing set of "important" needs. As indicated, Maslow did not propose that the hierarchy be rigidly fixed in only one set for all individuals. This is specially true for the middle-level needs (esteem and belongingness), where the order would probably vary from person to person. However, Maslow clearly indicates that the physiological needs are the most prepotent and the self-actualization needs are the least fulfilled.

From the point of view of the three questions asked on page 250, the hierarchical concept provides fairly complete answers to the last two questions. That is, Maslow's theory makes specific statements about what goals people will value and also suggests what type of behavior will influence the fulfillment of various needs. It provides less complete information as to *why* the needs originate. It does, however, imply that lower-level needs are innate and that higher-level needs are potentially present in most people. Moreover, these higher-level needs will motivate most people if the demands of the situation do not block them from appearing.

Controversies Regarding the Need Concept

The hierarchical concept has received a great deal of attention among those interested in the study of behavior in organizations,[10] undoubtedly because the concept, if valid, would provide managers with a powerful tool for predicting behavior in their organizational settings. For example, the hierarchy suggests that, when an individual is permitted to exercise more discretion in the job and his lower-level needs have been satisfied, he or she will become more concerned with middle-level and upper-level need fulfillment. Unfortunately, the research evidence does not provide a clear indication that the hierarchy is a valid predictor of an individual's motivational desires. While it is beyond the scope of this book to examine all the criticisms of the theory, several relevant questions can be asked.

Is There a Need Hierarchy?

There is strong evidence to support the notion that unless basic needs are satisfied, none of the higher-level needs can affect behavior. However, there is very little evidence to support the view that there are five levels of needs. If anything, research seems to indicate that most people are simultaneously motivated by needs at the same level, but not motivated by needs at two different levels.[11] One person, for example, might be motivated by hunger and thirst needs, while another may be motivated by social and autonomy needs. However, it is less likely that a person would be motivated by a physiological and esteem need at the same time. The lower-level need would assume greater importance until it has been fulfilled and the individual would engage in behavior (e.g., searching for food, water, shelter) that would be directed at fulfilling this prepotent need.

Can Outcomes Fulfill More Than One Need?

There is a considerable amount of research evidence that some outcomes are relevant to the fulfillment of more than one need.[12] For example, adequate pay appears to satisfy not only the physiological and safety needs, but also the esteem need. The more a manager is paid, the higher his security and esteem-need fulfillment. It is not difficult to see how pay can fulfill the need for food and other necessities by giving the employee money to buy articles that satisfy the lower-level needs, and also afford him or her a certain amount of esteem and respect in our society. Another example is the midmorning coffee break. In most organizations, workers take a morning coffee break, which serves to fulfill the workers' physiological hunger need and their social needs for affiliation and belongingness.

How Important Are Different Needs?

Many researchers have tried to measure the importance of different employee needs. The data in Fig. 9–4 are taken from a sample of over 1900 managers. The lines in the figure clearly indicate that the higher-level needs are the most important. Other studies show that the managers' lower-level needs are easily fulfilled by the organization, but that most of the higher-level needs are not fulfilled in the work setting.[13]

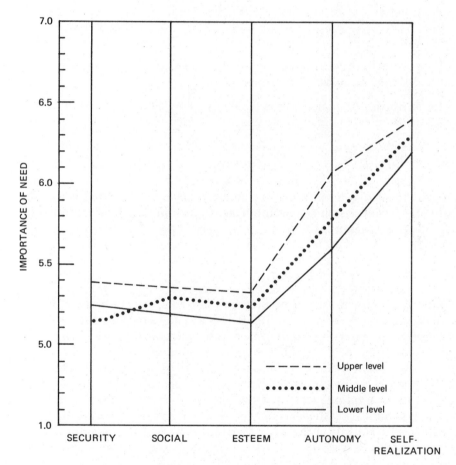

Figure 9–4   Importance Attached to Five Needs by Managers from Three Organization Levels

Source: Porter, L., *Organizational Patterns of Managerial Job Attitudes.* New York: American Foundation for Management Research, 1964.

Studies have also shown that the fulfillment of needs differs according to such factors as the job a person performs in the organization, his or her age or race, the size of the company, and the cultural background of the employee.[14] Briefly, these studies have found:

1. Line managers perceived greater fulfillment than staff managers did in the areas of security, socialization, esteem, and self-actualization needs. The largest differences between line and staff managers occurred in the esteem and self-actualization needs.

2. Young workers (25 years old or less) have greater need deficiencies than older workers (36 years old or more) in esteem and self-actualization categories.

3. Black managers report a greater lack of need fulfillment in every need than do their nonblack counterparts.

4. At lower levels of management, small-company managers were less deficient in their needs than managers who worked for larger companies.

5. Workers in different cultures have different hierarchies from those workers employed in North American firms.

Perhaps the most significant thing to remember from these studies is that the employee rates different things as important depending on the work situation and his own personality.

Individual Differences in Need Strength

As implied in the previous section, there are large differences in the needs of individuals, and these differences are attributable to numerous factors. If we relate differences in need strength to personal characteristics, we might begin to understand some of these differences. For example, urban workers have different values from those of rural workers.[15] Urban workers seem to be more alienated (e.g., estranged or separated) from their work and are less concerned about fulfillment of their higher-level needs on the job than are rural workers. Similarly, Mexican workers place a greater importance on the fulfillment of their needs in the work situation than do North Americans. An interesting profile of a worker for whom money is the only important work related factor is:

> The employee is a male, probably in the twenties; his personality is characterized by low self-assurance and high neuroticism; he comes from a small town or farm background; he belongs to few clubs, and he owns his own home and is probably a Republican.[16]

The list of individual differences affecting the fulfillment of needs could go on and on. The important thing to note is that there are individual differences among employees, and that these differences affect the importance of different needs and outcomes. This point has some interesting implications for managers. For example, it means that it is possible to identify those employees for whom a particular need is likely to be important. Moreover, it may suggest the desirability of tailoring the organization's environment and management systems to make them flexible enough to recognize need differences among people in the organization.

How Changeable is the Importance of Needs?

There is some evidence that organizational and personal events can and do change the importance of needs. For example, the importance of needs can be shaped in early childhood experiences by the parents. Similarly, organizational practices strongly influence the arousal and fulfillment of many higher-level needs. The esteem need can be aroused by a promotion based on past competence in a position. One study has found that as managers advanced in the organization, their safety needs tended to decrease, with a corresponding increase in their needs for affiliation, achievement, esteem, and self-actualization.[17]

The following statements summarize the major points regarding the hierarchy of needs.

1. Needs can be thought of as desires that individuals strive to fulfill.

2. The higher-level needs will motivate the individual only when the lower-level needs have been fulfilled.

3. All needs except self-actualization can be fulfilled and as they become fulfilled, they decrease in importance for the individual.

4. An individual can be motivated by more than one need at any given point in time; individual differences can affect the hierarchy of needs for any one individual, and the hierarchy of needs is changeable over a period of time.

Achievement Motivation

The achievement motive has been extensively studied by McClelland,[18] especially with regard to entrepreneurship. The achievement motive has been defined as a desire to perform in terms of a standard of excellence or a desire to be successful in competitive situations. While McClelland indicates that nearly everyone feels that he has an "achievement motive," probably only 10 percent of the U.S. population is strongly motivated for achievement. The amount of achievement motivation people have is dependent upon childhood, occupational and personal experiences, as well as upon the type of organization the individual is working for.

Motives are located mentally just below the level of full awareness in the preconscious mind—the borderland between the conscious and unconscious. This is the area of reverie, of daydreams, where people talk to themselves without quite being aware of it. But the pattern of these reveries can be tested, and a person can be taught to change his or her motivation by changing these reveries.

Assessment of Achievement Motive

McClelland measures the strength of people's achievement motive by scoring their responses to a number of projective pictures (see Chapter 2 for a detailed description). These pictures permit the individual to verbalize his other reveries. The stories are analyzed on the basis of the subject's desire to be successful or to show a desire for excellence in performance. We would like you to stop reading for a few minutes and take a brief look at Fig. 9–5; then write a short story about the picture by answering these questions:

1. What is going on in the picture?

2. What is the man thinking?

3. What has led up to the situation?

After writing your story, you may wish to compare your story with the story given by one manager, which is an example of a story showing a strong achievement motive. (It was written in response to the picture in Fig. 9–5).

> This individual is an engineer who wants to win a competition in which the man with the most practical drawing will be awarded the contract to build the bridge. He is taking a moment to think how happy he will be if he wins. He has been baffled by how to make such a long span strong, but remembers to specify a new steel alloy of great strength, and submits the entry, but does not win and is very unhappy.[19]

Does your story sound like that? If so, then you might fit McClelland's description of a high achiever.

Characteristics of High Achievers

The major characteristics of the self-motivated achiever have been identified. First, achievers like to set their own goals. They are nearly always trying to accomplish something. They are seldom content just to drift aimlessly and let life "happen to them." They are quite selective about the goals to which they

Figure 9-5   Just look at the picture briefly (10–15 seconds), and write the story it suggests.

Source: David A. Kolb, Irwin M. Rubin, and James M. McIntyre, *Organizational Psychology: An Experiential Approach,* © 1971, p. 57. Reproduced by permission of Prentice-Hall, Inc., Englewood Cliffs, New Jersey.

become committed. For this reason, they are unlikely to automatically accept goals that other people—including their supervisors—select for them. They do not tend to seek advice or help, except from experts who can provide needed skills. The achiever prefers to be as fully responsible for the attainment of his goal as possible. If they win, they want the credit, and if they lose, they accept the blame. For example, let's assume that you are given a choice between rolling dice with one chance in three of winning, and working on a problem with one chance in three of solving the problem in the time allotted. What would you do? A high achiever would choose to work on the problem, even though rolling the dice is obviously less work and the odds of winning are the same. High achievers prefer to work at a problem rather than leave the outcome to chance or to others.

Second, high achievers tend to avoid the extremes of difficulty in selecting goals. They prefer moderate goals that are neither so easy that winning them would provide no satisfaction, nor so difficult that winning or attaining them would be more a matter of luck than ability. They gauge what is possible, and then select a goal that is as tough as they think they can make—the hardest practical challenge. An ordinary example of ring-tossing might illustrate this point. In most carnivals, there are ring-tossing games that require the participant to throw rings over a peg from some minimal distance, but no maximal distance. Most people throw more or less randomly, standing now close, now far away, but those with a high achievement motive seem to calculate carefully where they should stand to be most likely to have a chance of winning a prize. These individuals seem to stand at a distance that is not so close as to make the task ridiculously easy, and not so far away as to make it impossible. They set a distance that is moderately far away, but where ringing a peg is potentially achievable. In other words, they set challenges for themselves and tasks that will make them stretch themselves a little.

Third, achievers prefer tasks that provide them with more or less immediate feedback, that is, measurements of how well they are progressing toward their goal. Because of the importance of the goal to them, they like to know how well they are doing. This is one reason why achievers often decide upon a professional career or a career in sales and/or engage in entrepreneurial activities.[20] A golfer, for example, knows his or her score and can compare how he or she is doing (compared to "par") or with his or her own performance yesterday or last week. Performance is related to both feedback (golf score) and goal specificity (handicap) for high achievers.

McClelland points out that the effect of monetary incentive on achievers is actually rather complex. On the one hand, achievers usually have a fairly high opinion of the value of their services, and prefer to place a high price tag on themselves. They are unlikely to remain for long in an organization that does not pay them well if they are performing well. On the other hand, it is questionable whether an incentive plan actually increases their performance, since they are normally working at peak efficiency anyway. Thus, money is a strong symbol of their achievement and adequacy, but may create dissatisfaction because of feelings of inadequacy relative to their contribution.

When the achievement motivation is operating, good job performance becomes very attractive to people. However, achievement motivation does not operate when achievers are performing tasks that are routine or boring, or where no competition is involved.

Developing Achievement Motivation

How can you improve your achievement motivation? McClelland has suggested four ways. First, arrange for some *accomplishment feedback.* This is the art of designing tasks so that you succeed bit by bit, gaining a reward each time, and thus strengthening your desire to achieve more. (This has worked for your authors. When we got bogged down in writing this book, we decided to publish articles and participate in executive development programs. The sense of accomplishment in these tasks kept us going.) Second, seek *models of achievement.* If people around you succeed, it will stimulate your desire to succeed. (For example, Harry Truman came from a modest home, but he attributed the prominence he attained to the heroes he modeled himself after—the famous statesmen he had read about in books). Third, modify your *self-image.* People with high achievement motivation seek personal challenges and responsibilities and require continual feedback of success. These are experiences that they desire so much that they may be said to *need* them. McClelland believes that it is possible to develop such wants by reconceptualizing oneself as someone who *requires* these things. (As a first step, imagine yourself as a person who must have success, responsibility, challenge, and variety.) Fourth, *control* your reveries. Just beyond the borderline of awareness, most of us are constantly talking to ourselves. Athletes, such as Billie Jean King, for one, talk to themselves during matches, repeating words of encouragement. Conversely, negative ideas should be discouraged.

Overall, research on the achievement motivation suggests that the theory provides answers to our second and third questions (see page 250), but again falls short of explaining *why* the achievement motivation is learned. That is, McClelland's theory clearly indicates what types of job-related experiences achievers desire from their work and some of the factors (feedback, pay, moderate goal-setting) that influence the desirability of their work experiences. It is hard to see, however, that achievement could be classified as a primary drive, in the sense of Maslow's lower-level needs. Situational factors, such as child-rearing practices of parents, culture, organizational practices, and the like, affect the development of the achievement motive.

Two-Factor Theory

This is the last theory that we shall consider that has, as its primary focus, an attempt to specify why certain job related outcomes are valued by employees. Currently, this theory is one of the most controversial theories of motivation developed. Two aspects of the theory are unique and probably account for most of the attention it has received. First, it stresses that some job factors lead to satisfaction while others can only *prevent* dissatisfaction. Second, the theory states that job satisfaction and dissatisfaction do not exist on a single continuum. In order to understand these major points, let's briefly look at the development of the theory.

Herzberg and his associates conducted a study of accountants and engineers, in examining the relationship between job satisfaction and productivity.[21] Through the use of semistructured interviews, they accumulated data on various factors which these workers indicated affected their feelings toward their jobs. The result was the emergence of two different factors.

Motivator and Hygiene Factors

The first factor, called "motivators," included items such as recognition, the work itself, advancement, and responsibility. These factors were associated with positive feelings about the job and related to the content of the job itself. These positive feelings were associated with the individual's having experienced achievement, recognition, and responsibility in the past. These positive feelings were predicated on a lasting rather than temporary achievement in the work setting.

The second factor, called "hygienes," included items such as company policy and administration, technical supervision, salary, working conditions, and interpersonal relations. These factors were associated with negative feelings about one's work, and related to the context or environment in which the job was performed. That is, these factors were *extrinsic* or external to the job or the work itself. In contrast, the motivators are related to the *intrinsic* factors associated with the job.

Viewed somewhat differently, extrinsic outcomes can be largely determined by the formal organization (e.g., salary, company policies and rules, and the like). These types of outcomes can serve as a reward for high performance only if the organization recognizes high performance. On the other hand, intrinsic outcomes, such as feelings of accomplishment after successful task performance, are largely administered internally by the individual, and the organization's policies can have only an indirect impact on them. For example, by stating what defines exceptional performance, the organization may be able to influence individuals to feel that they have performed their tasks exceptionally well.

Although motivators or intrinsic factors were usually associated with positive feelings toward one's job, they were sometimes associated with negative feelings. However, the hygiene or extrinsic factors were almost never associated with positive feelings, but were associated with states of mental depression, quitting the organization, absenteeism, and the like.

Figure 9–6 illustrates the two-factor theory. The figure shows the frequency with which each factor was mentioned by the accountants and engineers in connection with high (satisfying) and low (dissatisfying) work experiences. As can be seen, achievement was present in over 40 percent of

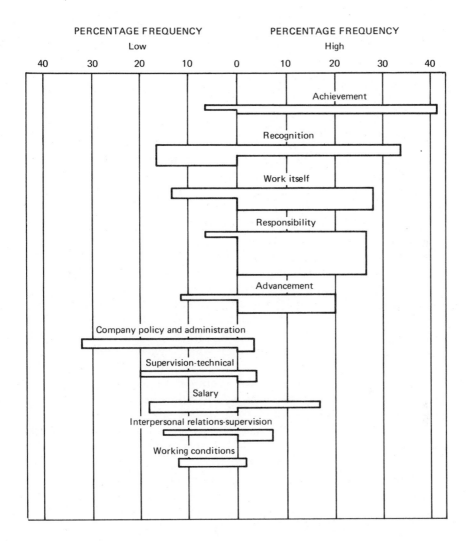

PERCENTAGE FREQUENCY   PERCENTAGE FREQUENCY
Low   High
40   30   20   10   0   10   20   30   40

Achievement

Recognition

Work itself

Responsibility

Advancement

Company policy and administration

Supervision-technical

Salary

Interpersonal relations-supervision

Working conditions

Figure 9–6   Comparison of Motivators and Hygiene Factors

Adapted from: Herzberg *et al., The Motivation to Work.* 2nd ed. New York: John Wiley & Sons, 1959.

the satisfying experiences and in less than 10 percent of the dissatisfying experiences.

The second major point of the theory is the concept that satisfaction and dissatisfaction are not on a single continuum, but are *separate and distinct,* as indicated in Fig. 9–7. One of the most interesting things about these dual continua is that the person can be satisfied and dissatisfied at the same time. The dual continua also imply that hygiene factors, such as working conditions, salary, etc., cannot increase or decrease job satisfaction; they can only affect the amount of job dissatisfaction.

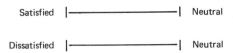

Figure 9–7   Satisfaction Continua

Controversies Surrounding the Dual-Factor Theory

The research designed to test Herzberg's theory has not provided clearcut evidence either supporting or rejecting the theory.[22] It is beyond the scope of this chapter to review these numerous studies. However, we can consider some of the major criticisms levied against the theory.

One of the major criticisms is that the use of the semistructured interviews made the results "methodologically bound"; that is, the *method* used to measure the factors determined the results. People have a tendency to attribute good results from their job to their own efforts and to thrust reasons for their poor performance onto others. A review of the studies indicates considerable support for this position: The more the methodology deviates from that used by Herzberg, the more variable the results. Two key questions were asked: "Can you describe, in detail, when you felt exceptionally good about your job?" and "Can you describe, in detail, when you felt exceptionally *bad* about your job?" To the extent that the respondents tend to give what have been termed "socially desirable" answers, the theory is method-bound. Socially desirable answers are those that the respondents think the researcher wants to hear and/or that sound "reasonable."

A second major criticism is whether satisfaction and dissatisfaction really are two dimensions, as indicated in Fig. 9–7. Research results are mixed. It has been found that some factors can contribute to *both* satisfaction and dissatisfaction, while other researchers have found that motivators contribute to *dissatisfaction* and hygiene factors contribute to *satisfaction.* Although these findings raise serious questions about the theory, the concept that satisfaction and dissatisfaction are two different continua has not been destroyed.

While a considerable amount of effort has been directed at resolving these two criticisms, few efforts have been directed toward answering the three questions posed on page 250. The evidence, although not strong, suggests the kinds of experiences that might lead to a strong motivation to perform well. For example, increasing job responsibility, challenge, advancement opportunities have been linked to high performance. Unfortunately, Herzberg provides little theoretical basis for these findings. Little attention has been paid to constructing a theory that explains why certain job factors should affect performance positively or negatively. Similarly, few attempts have been made to explain why certain outcomes are attractive to employees, and why a person chooses a certain type of behavior versus another, in order to obtain a desired outcome. Thus, in terms of our three questions, the dual-factor theory is not a theory of motivation because it does not: (1) specify how outcomes become desirable for people, and (2) specify the factors that influence the desirability of the goals. It does, however, explain the determinants of job satisfaction and dissatisfaction, and has pointed out important concepts for those individuals concerned with job enrichment programs in industry. These concepts will be dealt with later in this chapter.

Expectancy Theory

In its general form, expectancy theory attempts to understand how behavior is directed and why individuals choose a particular way of behaving in order to reach a goal(s). While a number of developments have taken place since Vroom originally stated his expectancy theory in 1964,[23] the model appears to still be based on four assumptions:[24]

1. Individuals have *preferences* for various *outcomes* (goals) that are potentially available to them. The higher the preference, the greater the desirability of that outcome for the individual. On the other hand, if the outcome is not desirable and/or dissatisfying, the individual will actively seek to avoid it.

2. Individuals have *expectancies* about the likelihood that an action on their part will lead to intended behavior. If the amount of effort is too great and the probability of this effort leading to intended behavior is low, the individual will usually not perform the act.

3. People have certain *instrumentalities* (probabilities) about the likelihood that certain behaviors will lead to the attainment of desirable outcomes. In other words, we mentally calculate the various actions available to us, such as high performance, absenteeism, leaving the organization, asking for a higher pay raise, and a promotion, and the likelihood that each of these actions will lead to the satisfaction of our desirable goals.

4. In any situation, the action a person chooses to take is determined by the expectancies and the preferences that person has at the time.

Basic Expectancy Model

Figure 9–8 shows, in diagrammatic form, the basic expectancy model, including some of the major factors that might influence motivation of a particular person at a particular time. The various boxes have examples of behaviors and outcomes. We would expect these examples to change depending on the situation.

Valence.   As can be seen by the Figure, there are three important concepts. First, various outcome goals are attractive to the individual. The amount of attractiveness or desirability is referred to as *valence.* Generally, there are two

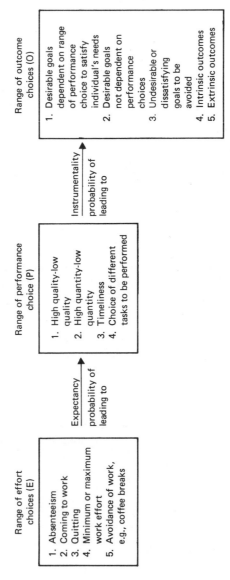

Range of effort choices (E)

1. Absenteeism
2. Coming to work
3. Quitting
4. Minimum or maximum work effort
5. Avoidance of work, e.g., coffee breaks

Expectancy probability of leading to

Range of performance choice (P)

1. High quality-low quality
2. High quantity-low quantity
3. Timeliness
4. Choice of different tasks to be performed

Instrumentality probability of leading to

Range of outcome choices (O)

1. Desirable goals dependent on range of performance choice to satisfy individual's needs
2. Desirable goals not dependent on performance choices
3. Undesirable or dissatisfying goals to be avoided
4. Intrinsic outcomes
5. Extrinsic outcomes

Figure 9–8   A General Expectancy Theory Model

major classes of outcomes available to individuals in organizations: intrinsic and extrinsic. Extrinsic outcomes are largely determined by the formal organization, and typically include salary, working hours, company policies and rules, and fringe benefit. Intrinsic outcomes are derived from the individual's feelings of accomplishment, such as recognition, achievement, and a sense of fulfillment. It is important to bear in mind that only those outcomes, intrinsic or extrinsic, that the individual finds desirable will motivate him. The fact that the organization offers certain rewards for high performance, for example, does not necessarily mean that the individual will expend effort to achieve high performance.

The attractiveness of any outcome can be thought of as varying from very desirable (+) to very undesirable (−). Valence is usually measured by asking the worker to select the desirability of a number of outcomes. The identification of outcomes would be generated by the employees themselves. For example, the list of outcomes may include salary, leisure time, friendly co-workers, technical supervision, and the like. Each employee would then rate the desirability of the outcomes for himself or herself. There are two reasons why outcomes associated with the various performance choices may be valent: (1) they directly satisfy an individual's needs, or (2) they lead to an outcome or set of outcomes that satisfy a particular need or set of needs.

Besides knowing about the individual's preferences, we must know something about two contingencies: expectancy and instrumentality.

Expectancy. *Expectancy* is the subjective probability that the individual assigns to the likelihood that his or her efforts can influence the range of performance choices. An individual might feel that his or her effort-performance probability is low because he or she lacks the ability to perform well, or because the mechanical pacing of the assembly line dictates the amount of work that can possibly be accomplished, or for a variety of other reasons. The expectancy variable has been measured by asking each employee to react to statements such as "I feel that the amount of effort that I put into my job will affect my production rate." Responses range from 1.0, certainty, to 0.0, no relationship at all.

Instrumentality. The second contingency refers to the individual's expectations that his performance will result in the satisfaction of various extrinsic and/or intrinsic outcomes. This contingency is often referred to as *instrumentality*. Instrumentality is the probability that high performance, for example, will lead to the satisfaction of current desires. The instrumentality variable can be measured by Likert-type scales. The worker indicates the extent to which he or she believes that high performance, for example, would lead to the attainment of each outcome.

For both of these contingencies, it is the individual's perception that is most important, and not the "real" contingency. For example, if the individual believes that he or she cannot affect the rate of production either by varying his level of effort or by expanding his abilities, the relationship does not exist for that worker. Similarly, if an incentive system is used in the organization but the employee sees little relationship between his or her salary and the number of units he produces, the relationship does not exist as far as that worker's motivation to produce is concerned.

Application of Expectancy Theory.   A specific example might be helpful here. A particular foreman may think that he has a 50 percent chance of producing 30 axles per shift with a concentrated effort. If we consider this kind of expectancy as varying from 0 to 1, the foreman's expectancy could be represented as 0.5. This same foreman may be sure that if he produces 30 axles per shift, a pay increase will be forthcoming. This expectation (instrumentality) of a pay increase would equal 1. The expectation of performance leading to the satisfaction of a particular outcome is certain in the mind of our foreman. Expectancy and instrumentality concepts are both expressed in terms of probabilities that can range from 0 to 1.0. Returning to our example, let's assume that the foreman believes that if he or she does produce 30 axles per shift, there is a 50 percent probability that he or she will receive a promotion. Moreover, the foreman has a strong preference to be promoted. In addition, there may be a number of other extrinsic and intrinsic outcomes associated with producing 30 axles. Also, the foreman may see still other outcomes associated with trying but *failing* to produce 30 axles.

Overall, then, the expectancy model suggests that a person's motivation to choose a particular performance goal will be influenced by one's expectancies about trying to reach this goal (E $\longrightarrow$ P), one's instrumentalities about the outcomes associated with performing at that level (P $\longrightarrow$ O), and the attractiveness of the outcomes involved. These factors combine to produce a motivational force to perform in a specific manner. Returning to our specific example, this means that the foreman's E $\longrightarrow$ P expectancy for producing 30 axles, his P $\longrightarrow$ O instrumentality for producing 30 axles, and the perceived attractiveness of a salary and promotion increase combine to determine the motivation to produce 30 axles per shift. Expectancy theory predicts that an individual will be a high performer when he or she (1) sees a high probability that personal efforts will lead to high performance, (2) sees a high probability that high performance will lead to outcomes, and (3) views these outcomes to be positively attractive.[25]

If the worker's perception of the situation is that both good and poor performers receive the same outcomes, this will affect his or her decision to produce. For example, the Vega plant at Lordstown, Ohio, has experienced numerous labor troubles since it began production several years ago. Some of these problems may be understood if we look at the situation from the assembly-line worker's perspective. Pay is typically not affected by performance. Rather, performance is substantially determined by the mechanical pacing of the line, which the worker does not control, and pay is determined through union-management labor negotiations. Most of the jobs are so simple that there is probably little opportunity to derive intrinsic satisfaction from performing them. Being highly productive may be perceived as leading to nothing more than tiring oneself out. So why produce?

In most organizations, people are often forced to choose among a limited number of performance range choices (see Fig. 9–8). The theory predicts that the individual will choose that performance option that has the highest motivational force. That is, the individual will choose that alternative which maximizes his or her expectancy, instrumentality, and valence. For example, our foreman will be motivated to produce 30 axles per shift if he feels that he can be highly productive and if he sees that being highly productive is positively related with a number of highly valent outcomes. If the foreman sees relatively few benefits to be derived from being a high performer, then he will probably not choose to do so.

Controversies Surrounding Expectancy Theory.   A number of studies have found that expectancy theory can predict some of the variance in an employee's performance. For incentive workers, it was found that workers with high expectancy perceptions were significantly higher producers than those with low expectancy perceptions.[26] Similarly, researchers found that job candidates who perceive a future job to be very desirable will select that job over other jobs months before they actually join the organization.[27] The importance of a variety of outcomes has been investigated. Pay has generally shown up as an important outcome. However, no other outcomes have consistently emerged.

While these results are encouraging, there are problems. First, it is important to understand all the factors affecting the employee's expectancy perception. Several factors influencing this $E \longrightarrow P$ relationship are: (1) self-esteem, (2) past experience in similar situations, (3) ability, (4) style of supervision and (5) a host of other factors. Secondly, what are the factors influencing the $P \longrightarrow O$ relationship? Again, while several factors have been identified (e.g., attractiveness of outcomes, belief in internal versus external control, communications, and the like), more need to be identified. Third, individuals can *misperceive* the situation. Because of their needs, emotions, values, and beliefs, people do sometimes misperceive the situation in which they find themselves. These misperceptions can lead them to consider only inappropriate behavior and/or not to consider all the relevant factors. Fourth, there has been relatively little research to reach some important conclusions on how these expectancies and instrumentalities develop and what influences them.

In summary, the expectancy model answers two questions that were raised on page 250. First, it argues that both the attractiveness of the outcomes and the person's expectancies and instrumentalities influence the range of performance alternatives a person will try to obtain. The model also details how these alternatives will be sought. The choice of a behavior also implies that the individual *has* a choice of what behavior will be attempted. However, it still does not address the question of how an individual develops expectancies and instrumentalities and what influences them.

INTEGRATED MODEL OF MOTIVATION

As indicated at the beginning of this chapter, there are no complete theories of motivation and there is no one theory of motivation on which all managers agree. As a result, we will attempt to pull together the parts of the four theories previously discussed to provide an overall framework for considering motivations in organizations.

Figure 9–9 indicates that job-related motivation is a function of the particular individual, the perceived job situation, the range of behavioral choices confronting the individual, and the range of goals available to the person. While it is not our intention to make an in-depth analysis of each major component, we will briefly discuss them. For simplicity's sake, it is assumed that the individual's behavioral choice is to be a high producer. However, the individual usually has a wide range of behavioral choices available, such as absenteeism, low productivity, lateness, quitting work, and shoddy work.

Individual performance is seen as most directly a consequence of the individual's ability, motivation, and organizational variables. These three variables interact to determine the individual's intention to be a high performer. For example, someone with no ability to complete the task cannot successfully complete the task no matter how highly motivated he may be to do so. Likewise, in most jobs, the individual has a range of different effort choices available to him. Except for extremely restricted jobs, such as those on an assembly-line, the individual can vary the effort and energy expenditure depending on what he or she wants to do. Therefore, we would conclude that effort and abilities are multiplicative in determining job performance. High effort and the correct abilities to perform the task will usually lead to a high job performance.

The model also states that there is a relationship between abilities, efforts, and organizational variables. For example, equipment malfunctions often place limits on the amount of output obtainable from a production worker. Then, too, particular sales territories may give certain salesmen advantages resulting in extra output unrelated to extra effort and/or ability.

Perhaps the most important organizational variable is how the organization goes about designing the task(s) to be performed by the individual. In the next section of this chapter, we will explore how the task's design can influence the individual's relative ability and also the amount of intrinsic outcomes that may be derived from a task. The organization, by the way it designs the tasks, assigns rewards to employees, and so on, influences the individual's expectancies about performance. For example, the assembly line is designed in such a way that the individual has little to say about scheduling work and selecting the procedures to be used in doing the task. The individual's abilities will probably not affect his or her performance. Individuals who work on a job that restricts the use of their abilities tend to show less personal ambition and a lesser desire for satisfaction of higher-level needs than do individuals who perform less routine tasks. It seems that challenging tasks increase the individual's desires

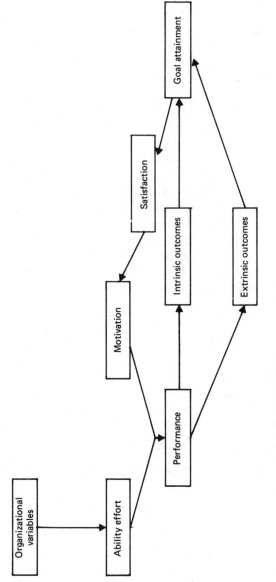

Figure 9–9 An Integrated Model of Motivation

From *Performance in Organizations: Determinants and Appraisal* by L. L. Cummings and Donald P. Schwab. Copyright © 1973 by Scott Foresman and Company. Reproduced by permission of the publisher.

for personal growth, self-esteem, and self-actualization. Thus, over the long term, the design of the job can affect the worker's personal characteristics.

The individual has preferences about various levels of performance—above average, average, below average. The higher the preference, the more likely the individual is to engage in behavior required to reach this goal. Thus, performance is the net effect of a person's effort as modified by his abilities and the organization's task constraints. Performance is valued because it leads to the satisfaction of the individual's goals. Broadly viewed, performance can be tied to intrinsic and/or extrinsic outcomes. Intrinsic outcomes include recognition, self-esteem, advancement, the work itself, and other "motivator" factors mentioned by Herzberg. Extrinsic outcomes include salary, interpersonal relations, status, salary, working conditions, and other "hygiene" factors. The attainment of these factors is influenced by the individual's subjective probability that performance will lead to these valued outcomes. The degree of connection that an individual sees between his job performance and his personal work-related goal(s) is an integral key of our model. The greater this relationship, the more likely a person is to exert effort to obtain a high level of job performance. In other words, the individual mentally calculates the various performance levels available, the probability that a certain performance level will bring about the outcome, and the attractiveness of the outcome. If the individual's job performance can satisfy a goal(s), the individual should be motivated to high productivity. In short, job motivation is present when the individual perceives the opportunity to fulfill a need through behavior on the job.

JOB DESIGN AND JOB PERFORMANCE

Motivation can be affected by the design of an employee's job. In determining the relationship between performance and goal outcomes, the job influences the individual's beliefs concerning the nature of intrinsic rewards, such as self-esteem, achievement, and responsibility.

It also affects the valence for certain performance levels and the expectancy-performance beliefs about good performance. In this section of the chapter, we examine job enrichment in relation to the various motivational concepts.

Job Enrichment

Since the 1950's, many managers have argued against the scientific management approach to the design of jobs. This approach, in brief, suggests that jobs are to be machine paced, standardized, specialized, and simplified. In theory, this enables a supervisor to know exactly what each worker is doing, making it easy to determine whether the work is being done properly. Training is simple and the company has little investment in the worker. Because of the short training cycle, workers can easily be replaced if they don't perform correctly.

The problems with jobs designed according to the principles of scientific management are several.[28] Some companies report turnover in excess of 100 percent per year for their assembly-line jobs. If too many workers leave, even minimal training costs per person become significant. Further, recruitment, selection, payroll, accounting, and other costs can become significant. Absenteeism also tends to be high on standardized, specialized, and simplified jobs. Employees are likely to use all of their sick leave and vacation time. As a result, many organizations report that they get fewer hours per employee per dollar spent. Another problem is that it is very difficult to obtain a balanced line. Every time consumer demand fluctuates and the number of people on the line changes, the line must be balanced again. Industrial engineers must be hired for this time-consuming task, and this means an additional expense for the organization.

It is because of these problems and many others that some organizations have turned to job-enrichment programs, where applicable. Job enrichment refers to adding activities and some power of discretion to a job, in order to provide the person with a "whole" job. The rationale behind job enrichment is that individuals experience higher-level need satisfaction when they learn that they have accomplished something they believe is personally worthwhile. That is, higher-level need satisfaction should occur when an individual has a job that: (1) allows the individual to feel personally responsible for a portion of the job, or for the entire job; (2) provides outcomes that are intrinsically meaningful for the individual; and (3) provides feedback about what is accomplished. The more the individual's job embraces these three things, the greater his potential for higher-level need satisfaction. Further, as the individual gains job-related experience, he will be more motivated to perform effectively because he will learn that good performance does lead to the desirable job-related outcomes.[29]

Integrated Framework

Figure 9–10 provides an integrated framework for considering changes in individual responses to work and several job characteristics.[30] At the most general level, five "core" dimensions are seen as leading to three psychological states which, in turn, lead to a number of positive personal and work-related outcomes. The three psychological states (experienced meaningfulness of the work, experienced responsibility for the outcomes of the work, and knowledge of the results of work activities) are the central part of the framework. This framework is closely linked to the materials presented in Chapter 4 on learning theory. That is, an individual experiences positive feelings toward the job to the extent that he or she learns (knowledge of results) that he or she personally has performed well (experienced responsibility) on a task that he or she cares

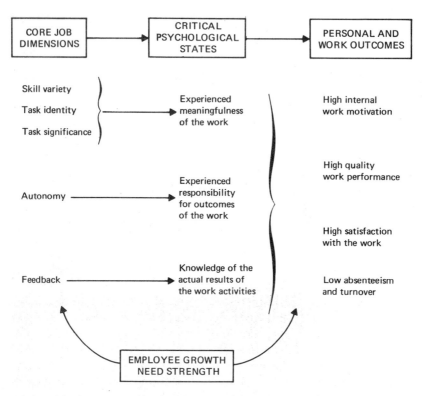

Figure 9-10   The Relationships Among the Core Job Dimensions, The Critical Psychological States, and On-the-Job Outcomes

Adapted from: Hackman, J. and G. Oldham, "Development of the Job Diagnostic Survey," *Journal of Applied Psychology,* 1975, **60**, p. 161. Copyright 1975 by the American Psychological Association. Reprinted by permission.

about (experienced meaningfulness). This positive feeling is reinforced to the individual and serves as an incentive for the individual to continue to try to perform well in the future. When the individual does not perform well, there is no internal reinforcement of the task and the individual may elect to try harder in the future so as to regain the internal rewards that good performance brings to the individual. The result of this process is a self-perpetuating cycle of positive work motivation based on self-generated rewards. This cycle will continue until the individual either no longer values the rewards derived from the three psychological states, or the task has been redesigned and no longer provides the individual with the opportunity to satisfy these psychological states.

It should be noted that self-generated motivation should be highest when all three psychological states are present. If the individual feels fully responsible for work outcomes on a meaningful task, but never receives feedback on his or her performance, it is doubtful that the worker will experience the internal rewards that can lead to self-generated motivation. Similarly, if the individual has full knowledge of the results of the work, but experiences the task as routine (or feels no personal responsibility for the results of the work), internal motivation will not be high. The three psychological states may be defined as:

Experienced meaningfulness of the work. The degree to which the individual views the job as one that is generally meaningful, valuable, and worthwhile.

Experienced responsibility for work outcomes. The degree to which the individual feels personally accountable and responsible for the results of the work he or she does.

Knowledge of results. The degree to which the individual knows and understands, on a continuous basis, how effectively he or she is performing the job.

Of the five job characteristics shown in Fig. 9–10, three contribute to the experienced meaningfulness of the work, and one each contributes to experienced responsibility and to knowledge of results. *Toward experienced meaningfulness* has three components. First, *skill variety,* which refers to a job that requires a variety of different activities in carrying out the work and the use of a number of personal skills of the worker. For example, many recreational sports and activities achieve much of their popularity because they tap and test the intellectual and/or motor skills of the people who do them. When a job draws upon several skills of the employee, that individual may consider the job to have a lot of personal meaning. Second, *task identity* refers to the degree to which the job requires completion of a whole and identifiable piece of work. For example, if an individual assembles a complete product, he or she should find the work more meaningful than would be the case if he or she was responsible for only a small part of the whole job. Third, *task significance* refers to the degree to which the task has an impact on the lives or work of other people. For example, employees who tighten nuts on aircraft assemblies are more likely to perceive their work as meaningful than are workers who fill boxes with rubber bands.

The second major job characteristic is *experienced responsibility.* The extent to which the individual can use his or her own efforts, initiatives, and decisions to control the quality and quantity of work, rather than "follow the book," is a measure of responsibility. Where the individual has freedom to make decisions, the individual should feel a sense of autonomy. In the AT&T example that follows on pages 278–281, the autonomy job dimension was critical to the program's overall success.

Knowledge of results is the last critical psychological state. If the task permits the individual to receive feedback on a task, it should increase the individual's motivation to go on performing that task. One important aspect of feedback is that, regardless of how much feedback management gives to the workers regarding their task performance, an employee's reactions to this feedback will be filtered through the individual's perceptual processes. That is, a pro golfer who scores an 80 and a fifteen handicapper who also scores an 80 will perceive their scores (feedback) quite differently. The pro will regard this knowledge of results as an indication that he or she played a poor round, while the fifteen handicapper will regard this round as highly indicative of an improvement in his or her game.

Effects of Job Enrichment

In a survey of 276 selected firms from *Fortune's* list of the 500 largest firms, 20 percent of the firms said that they were using a job-enrichment program. Among these are IBM, AT&T, Gaines Pet-Food Manufacturing, Travelers Insurance Company, Texas Instruments, Corning Glass Works, Imperial Chemical, Polaroid, United Airlines, and Donnelly Mirrors. The major advantages that the companies found in using these programs were increased job satisfaction of employees and reduced operating costs. The most common criteria for the measurement of the program's success, in decreasing order of importance, were improved profit, improved employee job satisfaction, product quality, and output. To acquaint you with the process of enriching a job, let's examine how AT&T implemented its job-enrichment program.

Applications at AT&T.   Early in the 1960's, the Bell system was experiencing high turnover rates among typists and service-order clerks and correspondingly high employment and training costs.[31] Robert Ford was hired to remedy the situation. His strategy was to break work down into three aspects: the Work Module; the Control Module; and Feedback.

The Work Module.   Changing the work module in Indiana's Bell system involved job redesign for thirty-three clerical workers compiling telephone directories. The traditional work process included twenty-one steps and a lengthy verification routine, with one clerk checking another clerk's work. This process was instrumental in having workers develop apathetic attitudes toward their jobs and the company, and a high turnover rate. In 1968 turnover was so high that twenty-eight new clerks had to be hired to maintain an employment level of thirty-three clerks.

To remedy this situation, Ford cut the twenty-one production steps to fourteen, eliminating some of the verification. Observing improvement in the turnover rate and job attitudes, Ford encouraged each clerk to perform all fourteen steps in compiling thinner telephone books, while splitting thicker larger-city books alphabetically. This important change increased two of the core dimensions, autonomy and task identification in Fig. 9–10.

The Control Module.   Ford encouraged the supervisors to give the clerks some responsibility for handling the procedures used in compiling the telephone directories. For example, allowing the worker to help determine when to discontinue the ad sales for the Yellow Pages in South Central Bell's book, in order to reach the printer on time, saved Indiana Bell more than $100,000 in costs per year. Several other decisions delegated to the clerks included setting credit ratings, cutting off service for nonpayment, and rejecting material because of poor quality. These procedures increased the worker's skill variety and task significance, other core dimensions in Fig. 9–10.

Feedback. The success of the work and control modules depended on the employees' internalizing these procedures. The elimination of the verification procedure by another clerk permitted each worker to have a knowledge of the quality of his or her own performance and to monitor his or her own performance. This is the fifth core dimension in Fig. 9–10.

Decision Centers. From these experiments, AT&T concluded that job enrichment could be successfully implemented. Ford then began working on a technique that involved the grouping of several jobs to create *decision centers,* to upgrade performance and improve job satisfaction. It also involved rearrangements of the physical work setting.

Prior to job enrichment, the office arrangement appeared as indicated in Fig. 9–11. Notice that the supervisors are in front of the employees and facing them. This permits the supervisors to exercise close control. After the job-enrichment program was instituted, each service representative was given a separate geographic location. Each location defined a set of customers to be taken care of. The service representatives and their supervisors were then moved into a circular "wagon train" arrangement, as indicated in Fig. 9–12. In this new office design, the clerks were no longer facing their supervisors. The next step was to move the typists and service order reviewers (SOR) into a corner of the service representatives' room. This caused unforeseen problems. Within the next few months, six of the eight typists quit their jobs and the efficiency of the service representatives began to decline. The problem was that any typist could be called on to type any order for any service representative. This work-flow arrangement, combined with the physical isolation of the typists from other typists in the room, were diagnosed as the causes of the problem(s). To offset this problem, Ford placed the typists and service order reviewers in the center of the circular layout as members of a specific unit. This revised arrangement is indicated in Fig. 9–13. With this new spatial arrangement, the distinction between the typists and reviewers was abolished and the typists were upgraded in pay.

The success of the nesting procedure has been clearly demonstrated. Before nesting began, the processing of a service order took ten steps. With the changeover in layout, the procedure was reduced to only three steps. Besides removing seven steps in the process, most of which involved repetitious transmittals and reviews, the effectiveness of the unit markedly improved. Before the typists were moved into a circular configuration, the group was

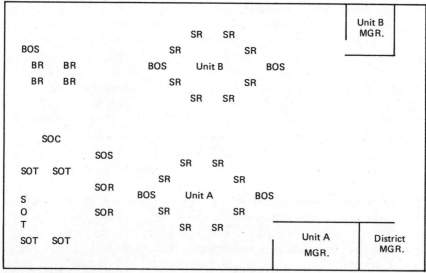

```
┌─────────────┬────────────────────┬──────────────┐
│  Unit B     │       Unit A       │   District   │
│  MGR.       │       MGR.         │   MGR.       │
├──────────┐  └──┐              ┌──┘  ┌───────────┘
│                                              │
│        BOS                   BOS             │
│  SR          SR        SR         SR      SR │
│  SR   Unit   SR        SR   Unit  SR Unit SR │
│  SR    B     SR        SR    A    SR   A  SR │
│  SR          SR        SR         SR      SR │
│                                              │
└──────────────────────────────────────────────┘
```

SR: Service Representative
BOS: Business Office Supervisor

Figure 9–11   Office Layout Before Nesting

Adapted from: Ford, Robert N., "Job Enrichment Lessons from AT&T," *Harvard Business Review,* January–February, 1973, **51**, p. 102. Reproduced with permission, *Harvard Business Review.*

```
┌──────────────────────────────────────────┬─────────┐
│                   SR   SR                 │ Unit B  │
│  BOS           SR        SR               │ MGR.    │
│    BR   BR   BOS  Unit B    BOS          ─┴───┐     │
│    BR   BR      SR        SR                   │     │
│                   SR   SR                      │     │
│                                                │     │
│       SOC                                      │     │
│           SOS         SR   SR                  │     │
│  SOT  SOT       SR         SR                  │     │
│           SOR  BOS  Unit A   BOS               │     │
│  S        SOR   SR         SR                  │     │
│  O                SR   SR              ┌───────┴─────┤
│  T                                     │ Unit A │District│
│  SOT  SOT                              │ MGR.   │ MGR.  │
└────────────────────────────────────────┴────────┴──────┘
```

SR: Service Representative
BR: Business Representative
SOC: Service Order Control
SOS: Service Order Supervisor
SOR: Service Order Reviewer
SOT: Service Order Typist
BOS: Business Office Supervisor

Figure 9–12   Initial Nesting Arrangement

Adapted from: Ford, Robert N., "Job Enrichment Lessons from AT&T," *Harvard Business Review,* January–February, 1973, **51**, p. 103. Reproduced with permission, *Harvard Business Review.*

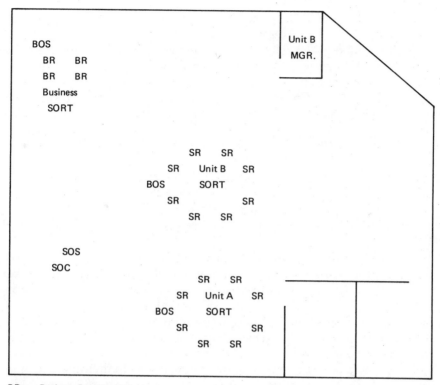

BR: Business Representative
SR: Service Representative
BOS: Business Office Supervisor
SOC: Service Order Control
SOS: Service Order Supervisor
SORT: Service Order Review and Typing

Figure 9–13   Final Nesting Arrangement

Adapted from: Ford, Robert N., "Job Enrichment Lessons from AT&T," *Harvard Business Review,* January–February, 1973, **51**, p. 104. Reproduced with permission, *Harvard Business Review.*

operating at 27 percent of efficiency; thirty days after moving into the circle, the rate was 90 percent. The elimination of the seven steps meant that 88 man-weeks per year of unnecessary work was saved. Finally, the turnover among typists for job-related reasons had virtually ceased.

Obstacles to Job Enrichment

The approach outlined is one that Ford has found successful in the Bell system and has been used by other firms (e.g., Corning Glass Works, Emerson Electric, Travelers Insurance) as well. However, there are several obstacles to job-enrichment programs that should be considered. Not all job-enrichment programs have had the success that Ford has been able to generate at Bell.[32]

Not all jobs lend themselves to enrichment. The technology of the task may represent the greatest obstacle to the implementation of a successful job-enrichment program. Firms that are heavy users of assembly-line technology, such as G.M., Ford, Chrysler, and Maytag, are faced with high costs if the technology must be changed to enrich employees' jobs. The capital investment per worker in these plants is extremely high when compared to the types of jobs enriched in the Bell system. Most assembly-line jobs are of a physical nature. Increased efficiency comes through increasing the pace of the line, minimizing physical motion, and/or increased mechanization. Another problem in these types of industries is that the worker has a difficult time identifying with the product. This occurs because the assembly-line worker's contribution to the final product is often very small, and in some cases, not even externally visible.

Another obstacle to job enrichment is that not all workers want to satisfy their needs in the work environment. Some unskilled or semiskilled workers may be so involved in attempts to satisfy lower-level needs that they are not interested in self-actualization or intrinsic rewards from their jobs. It is not uncommon to find that workers who are continuously trying to satisfy their lower-level needs tend to exclude higher-level needs from motivating them.[33] Workers with a few years to retirement and many years of service probably have adjusted their expectations to the reality of their job situations. Similarly, workers on the assembly line or those who are performing routine and repetitive tasks often report that their tasks are not dissatisfying. Some workers prefer these types of jobs because it permits them to daydream and socialize with their fellow workers.[34] These workers, who *prefer* to perform the repetitious, unenlarged, familiar job, might resist a change. For example, in one case the jobs were redesigned to increase two of the five core dimensions in Fig. 9–10. The result was a decrease in the quality of interpersonal relationships in the work group. Apparently, this job change disrupted traditional interpersonal relationships in the group and the employees had difficulty establishing new, equally satisfying relationships. The supervisors were also unhappy with the changes because they had to redefine their jobs, and it put pressure on them to manage in a different way.[35]

Union opposition may represent another obstacle to job-enrichment programs. Negotiated job classifications, job seniority, and work rules may place practical limitations on the extent to which a job's-core dimensions can be changed. However, companies with good labor-management relations, such as AT&T and Maytag, have experienced little union opposition to job enrichment.[36]

Overall Assessment

While the list of obstacles is longer than the aforementioned items, job-enrichment programs have had favorable results for both management and the employee.[37] In most instances, job-enrichment programs have had a positive effect on the quality of production and on workers' job attitudes. However, job-enrichment programs should not be regarded as a panacea for all problems affecting the worker's performance and job satisfaction and motivation. Rather, job-enrichment programs have been designed to deal with problems where job content has been identified as the cause.

SUMMARY

This chapter has emphasized that individuals engage in job-related activities to reach certain goals and/or satisfy certain needs. We asked three questions. First, what is it about individuals that cause outcomes to become desirable to them? Second, what general classes or groups of outcomes do people find desirable? Third, what factors influence the desirability of these outcomes? The theories of Maslow, McClelland, and Vroom all provide plausible answers to the second and third questions, while Herzberg provides answers primarily to the second question. None of the theories could adequately answer the first question.

Also, in this chapter, we have pointed out that an individual's perception of the job is directly related to his or her job behavior. The more directly the worker perceives that a given performance level is directly related to a given goal or reward he or she desires, the more highly motivated he is. Motivation is related to both organizational and individual goals.

Finally, we discussed job enrichment as one approach to increasing a worker's performance, motivation, and job satisfaction. Job enrichment can have a profound influence on these factors, but not all individuals or organizations are ready for enrichment programs.

Discussion Questions

1. Explain the sequence by which needs are translated into action in a work situation.

2. Explain how the same need or motive can cause different behavior (a) among different people, and (b) by the same person at different times.

3. Discuss how the following jobs might be enriched: cashier in a McDonald's restaurant; salesclerk in a department store; and a secretary.

4. Explain the differences between expectancy theory and McClelland's achievement-motivation theory.

5. How might variations in job designs affect employee motivation? Explain using (a) Maslow's need hierarchy and (b) expectancy theory.

6. What is the basic difference between "motivators" and "hygiene" factors? Which are more important in work motivation? Why?

7. Of what practical value is the expectancy model for managers? What can managers learn from the model that would improve their effectiveness on the job?

8. If high need-achievement people tend to be superior performers, why could a manager not increase organizational performance simply by hiring only high need-achievement employees?

9. Why do you think Maslow's theory of motivation has been so popular among managers and organizational researchers?

10. Exactly how might rewards, such as pay, promotion, and positive feedback affect the determination of job satisfaction? How might they affect performance?

CRITICAL INCIDENT

Paul Archibald, 43 years old, began working at Standard Steel Corporation in the Metallurgical Department as a Quality Control Inspector eighteen years ago. After spending five years in this position, Paul progressed to be Head of the Quality Control program. After he had spent six years as head of this program, Paul advanced to Head of the Melting Control Program. He has been working on that job for the last seven years.

Paul was able to move upward in the Metallurgical Department much faster than most men his age, bypassing several managerial positions and individuals. Paul possesses above average intelligence and potential, and had been identified in high school and college as very talented. Of the four heads of program in the Metallurgy Department, he is the youngest and lowest in seniority. Paul's next possible advancement would be Chief of the Metallurgical Department.

Each major shop in the steel mill has one metallurgist assigned to it. For example, the melting department, rolling department, ring department, and the like, each have a senior metallurgist assigned to them. Each metallurgist is given supervisory responsibilities for quality control, the training of observers, and the conduct of safety meetings in the various departments. Weekly and monthly quality-control reports and other observations are given to the Chief Metallurgist.

Each metallurgist has one or more observers reporting to him. These individuals are responsible for making routine quality-control checks. Their job description has a very detailed set of instructions outlining the procedures to follow. For example, the observer in the rolling ring mill has a job description that includes activities such as checking the weights of the rings, the interior and exterior diameters, hardness results, surface defects, and the like.

Paul apparently did an outstanding job during his first several years at Standard, as evidenced by his rapid movement upward in the department. However, during the past five years, Paul's performance has deteriorated, according to the Chief Metallurgist and some of the subordinates reporting to Paul. Some of the complaints are: (1) lack of technical detail in the melting process reports; (2) lack of job interest; (3) absence at safety meetings; (4) late reports; and (5) loss of confidence in subordinates.

During the past five years, business has been increasing at Standard. However, with the shortage of natural resources in mid-1974 and the loss of three major government contracts, the company was forced to make some production cutbacks. As a result of these economic conditions, Paul was asked to return to his previous job as Head of the Quality Control Program. Although Paul had not worked on this job the last seven years, the Chief Metallurgist thought that he should have no problem. However, during the first month on the job, Paul was absent for three safety meetings and made some errors in a report concerning the hardness of a finished ring for the government. Whether it was a deliberate attempt to falsify the report or a slip-up, the Chief Metullurgist laid Paul off for one week.

In late 1975, as business improved to its pre-1974 condition, Paul was advised by the Chief Metallurgist that his previous behavior would no longer be tolerated. Just before Christmas of 1975, Paul was called in by the Chief Metallurgist and was again disciplined for these continued behaviors. This time, Paul was laid off for two weeks and was advised that he was subject to discharge for his performance if it did not come up to that of other program heads immediately.

In his spare time and on weekends, Paul was a housing contractor. While he subcontracted most of the work to others, this activity took a lot of his time. Business was profitable for the past six years and these profits were invested in a restaurant with another partner. However, during 1974, the interest rate on mortgages was high and most contractors in the area found that they could not sell homes that they had erected.

Questions:

1. Explain Paul's actions at work.

2. What is Paul looking for in his job?

3. Predict what Paul will do.

CRITICAL INCIDENT

James Davis is an accountant in a large insurance company. Jim comes from a small rural farming community in which his family had low income and followed strict rules for behavior. In order to achieve his college degree, he worked on numerous odd jobs.

Jim is an intelligent and capable worker. His main fault is that he does not want to take any risks. He hesitates to make decisions for himself, often referring small or routine decisions to his supervisor or to other accountants for a decision. Whenever he does a major audit, he brings it in rough draft to his supervisor for approval before he finalizes it.

Since Jim is a capable person, his supervisor wants to motivate him to be more independent in his work. The supervisor believes that this approach will improve Jim's performance, relieve the supervisor from extra routine, and give Jim more self-confidence. However, the supervisor is not sure how to go about motivating Jim to improve his performance.

Question

In the role of the supervisor, plan how to motivate him. Give reasons.

REFERENCES

1. Zedeck, S., and M. Blood, *Foundations of Behavioral Science Research in Organizations.* Belmont, Calif.: Wadsworth Publishing Co., 1974, p. 174.

2. Shaw, M., and J. Wright, *Scales for the Measurement of Attitudes.* New York: McGraw-Hill Book Co., 1967, pp. 1–14.

3. Maslow, A., *Motivation and Personality.* Rev. ed. Harper & Row Publishers, 1971.

4. For a complete description of this procedure, see Porter, L. A., "Study of Perceived Need Satisfactions in Bottom and Middle Management Jobs," *Journal of Applied Psychology,* 1961, **45,** pp. 1–11. Sheridan, J., and J. Slocum, "The Direction of the Causal Relationship Between Job Satisfaction and Work Performance," *Organizational Behavior and Human Performance,* 1975, **14,** pp. 159–172.

5. Porter, L., and E. Lawler, *Managerial Attitudes and Performance.* Homewood, Ill.: Richard D. Irwin and Dorsey Press, 1968.

6. Wall, T., and R. Payne, "Are Deficiency Scores Deficient?" *Journal of Applied Psychology,* 1973, **58,** pp. 322–326.

7. Maslow, A., "A Theory of Human Motivation," *Psychological Review,* 1943, **50,** pp. 370–396. *Motivation and Personality.* Rev. ed. New York: Harper & Row Publishers, 1970.

8. Maslow, A., *Toward a Psychology of Being.* 2nd ed. Princeton, N.J.: Van Nostrand Reinhold Co., 1968, p. 30.

9. Smith, B., "On Self-actualization: A Transambivalent Examination of a Focal Theme in Maslow's Psychology," *Journal of Humanistic Psychology,* 1973, **13,** pp. 17–33.

10. For those desiring a more critical review of the literature, see Wahba, M., and L. Bridwell, "Maslow Reconsidered: A Review of the Research on the Need Hierarchy Theory," *Organizational Behavior and Human Performance,* 1976, in press. Miner, J., and P. Dachler, "Personal Attitudes and Motivation," *Annual Review of Psychology.* 1973, **21,** pp. 379–402.

11. Lawler, E., and L. Suttle, "A Causal Correlational Test of the Need Hierarchy Concept," *Organizational Behavior and Human Performance,* 1972, **7,** pp. 265–286.

12. Lawler, E., and L. Porter, "Perceptions Regarding Management Compensation," *Industrial Relations,* 1963, **3,** pp. 41–49. Lawler, E., *Pay and Organizational Effectiveness: A Psychological View.* New York: McGraw-Hill Book Co., 1971.

13. Berger, C., and L. Cummings," "Organizational Structure, Attitudes, and Behavior," paper presented at 35th Academy of Management Meeting, New Orleans, August, 1975.

14. For references in this section, see (1) Porter, L., "Job Attitudes in Management: II. Perceived Importance of Needs as a Function of Job Level," *Journal of Applied Psychology,* 1963, **47,** pp. 141–148. (2) Altimus, C., and R. Tersine, "Chronological Age and Job Satisfaction: The Young Blue-Collar Worker," *Academy of Management Journal,* 1973, **11,** pp. 53–66. (3) Slocum, J., and R. Strawser, "Racial Differences in Job Attitudes," *Journal of Applied Psychology,* 1972, **56,** pp. 28–33. (4) Porter, L., "Job Attitudes in Management: IV. Perceived Deficiencies in Need Fulfillment as a Function of Size of the Company," *Journal of Applied Psychology,* 1963, **47,** pp. 386–397. (5) Slocum, J., P. Topichak, and D. Kuhn, "A Cross-cultural Study of Need Satisfaction and Need Importance for Operative Employees," *Personnel Psychology,* 1971, **24,** pp. 435–445.

15. Robey, D., "Task Design, Work Values and Worker Response: An Experimental Test," *Organizational Behavior and Human Performance,* 1974, **12,** pp. 264–273.

16. Lawler, E., *op. cit.* p. 51.

17. Hall, D., and K. Nougaim, "An Examination of Maslow's Need Hierarchy in an Organizational Setting," *Organizational Behavior and Human Performance,* 1968, **3,** pp. 12–35.

18. McClelland, D., *The Achieving Society.* Princeton, N.J.: Van Nostrand Reinhold Co., 1961.

19. Adapted from McClelland, D., *Assessing Human Motivation.* Morristown, N.J.: General Learning Press, 1971, p. 12.

20. Steers, R., "Task–Goal Attributes in Achievement and Supervisory Performance," *Organizational Behavior and Human Performance,* 1975, **13,** pp. 392–403. Durand, D., "Effects of Achievement Motivation and Skill Training on the Entrepreneurial Behavior of Black Businessmen," *Organizational Behavior and Human Performance,* 1975, **14,** pp. 76–90.

21. Herzberg, F., B. Mausner, and B. Snyderman, *The Motivation to Work.* New York: John Wiley & Sons, 1959.

22. For those individuals interested in some excellent reviews, see Kerr, S., A. Harlan, and R. Stogdill, "Preference for Motivator and Hygiene Factors in a Hypothetical Interview Situation," *Personnel Psychology,* 1974, **25,** pp. 109–124. House, R., and L. Widgor, "Herzberg's Dual-factor Theory of Job Satisfaction and Motivation: A Review of the Evidence and Criticism," *Personnel Psychology,* 1968, **20,** pp. 369–389. Dunnette, M., D. Campbell, and M. Hakel, "Factors Contributing to Job Satisfaction and Dissatisfaction in Six Occupational Groups," *Organizational Behavior and Human Performance,* 1967, **2,** pp. 143–174.

23. Vroom, V., *Work and Motivation.* New York: John Wiley & Sons, 1964.

24. Lawler, E., *Motivation in Work Organizations.* Belmont, Calif.: Brooks/Cole, 1974, p. 49. Much of this section is based on materials discussed by Lawler.

25. For those interested in a more complete description of the model, see Mitchell, T., "Expectancy Models of Job Satisfaction, Occupational Preference, and Effort: A Theoretical, Methodological, and Empirical Appraisal," *Psychological Bulletin,* 1974, **81,** pp. 1053–1077. House, R., J. Shapiro, and M. Wahba, "Expectancy Theory in Managerial Performance and Motivation: An Integrative Model and Empirical Evidence," *Decision Sciences,* 1974, **5,** pp. 481–506.

26. Sheridan, J., J. Slocum, Jr., and B. Min, "Motivational Determinants of Job Performance," *Journal of Applied Psychology,* 1975, **60,** pp. 119–121.

27. Sheridan, J., J. Slocum, Jr., and M. Richards, "A Longitudinal Test of Expectancy Theory and Heuristic Models of Job Selection," *Journal of Applied Psychology,* 1975, **60,** pp. 361–368.

28. For many examples of these behaviors, see *Work in America.* Cambridge, Mass.: Report of a Special Task Force to the Secretary of Health, Education, and Welfare, MIT Press, 1972. Davis, L., and J. Taylor, *Design of Jobs.* Baltimore, Md.: Penguin Books, 1972. Flanagan, R., G. Strauss, and L. Ulman, "Work Discontent and Workplace Behavior," *Industrial Relations,* 1974, **13,** pp. 101–124.

29. Hackman, J., and E. Lawler, "Employee Reactions to Job Characteristics," *Journal of Applied Psychology,* 1971, **55,** pp. 259–286. Greller, M., and D. Herald, "Sources of Feedback: A Preliminary Investigation," *Organizational Behavior and Human Performance,* 1975, **13,** pp. 244–256.

30. Hackman, J., and G. Oldham, "Development of the Job Diagnostic Survey," *Journal of Applied Psychology,* 1975, **60,** pp. 159–170.

31. Most of the section was drawn from Ford, R., "Job-Enrichment Lessons from AT&T," *Harvard Business Review,* 1973, **51,** pp. 96–106.

32. Sirota, D., and A. Wolfson, "Job Enrichment: What are the Obstacles?" *Personnel,* 1972, **49,** pp. 12–17. Hackman, J., G. Oldham, R. Janson, and K. Purdy, "A New Strategy for Job Enrichment," *California Management Review,* 1975, **17,** No. 4, pp. 57–71. Malone, E., "The Nonlinear Systems Experiment in Participative Management," *Journal of Business,* 1975, **48,** pp. 52–64.

33. Fein, M., "Job Enrichment: A Reevaluation." *Sloan Management Review,* 1974, **15,** pp. 69–88. Schrank, R., "Work in America: What Do Workers Really Want?" *Industrial Relations,* 1974, **13,** pp. 124–130.

34. Collins, D., and R. Raubolt, "A Study of Employee Resistance to Job Enrichment," *Personnel Journal,* 1975, **54,** pp. 232–235, 248.

35. Lawler, E., J. Hackman, and S. Kaufman, "Effects of Job Redesign: A Field Experiment," *Journal of Experimental Social Psychology,* 1973, **3,** pp. 49–62.

36. Myers, S., "Overcoming Union Resistance to Job Enrichment," *Harvard Business Review,* 1971, **49,** pp. 37–49.

37. Sandler, G., "Eclecticism at Work: Approaches to Job Designs," *American Psychologist,* 1974, **29,** pp. 767–773.

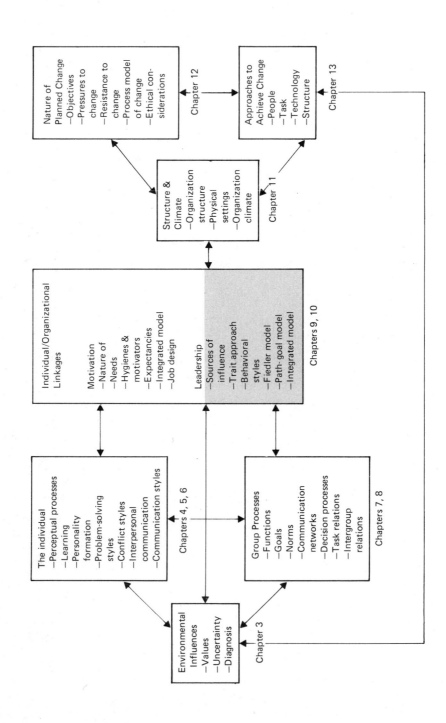

The individual
—Perceptual processes
—Learning
—Personality
 formation
—Problem-solving
 styles
—Conflict styles
—Interpersonal
 communication
—Communication styles

Chapters 4, 5, 6

Individual/Organizational
Linkages

Motivation
—Nature of
—Needs
—Hygienes &
 motivators
—Expectancies
—Integrated model
—Job design

Leadership
—Sources of
 influence
—Trait approach
—Behavioral
 styles
—Fiedler model
—Path-goal model
—Integrated model

Chapters 9, 10

Structure &
Climate
—Organization
 structure
—Physical
 settings
—Organization
 climate

Chapter 11

Nature of
Planned Change
—Objectives
—Pressures to
 change
—Resistance to
 change
—Process model
 of change
—Ethical con-
 siderations

Chapter 12

Approaches to
Achieve Change
—People
—Task
—Technology
—Structure

Chapter 13

Group Processes
—Functions
—Goals
—Norms
—Communication
 networks
—Decision processes
—Task relations
—Intergroup
 relations

Chapters 7, 8

Environmental
Influences
—Values
—Uncertainty
—Diagnosis

Chapter 3

10
LEADERSHIP

The previous chapters on motivation, groups, and individual's styles have described and illustrated many of the factors that influence the behavior and attitudes of people in organizational settings. While many different sets of factors are potentially important, it is clear that leaders are in a position to exercise great influence over these factors. The effectiveness of the manager is probably the single most important factor affecting the performance of subordinates. In spite of this, very little is known about the effectiveness of leader behavior. While managers confidently discuss the characteristics of successful managers, and while many managers think that they can select good leaders on the basis of their personal experience, the need to develop effective leaders is still a problem. Peter Drucker points out that leaders are the basic and the scarcest resource of any business enterprise.[1] In most organizations there is a continuous search for persons who have the necessary ability to lead effectively. This search is not confined to the business organizations, but also includes educational, military, governmental, and religious institutions.

One point of departure for the understanding of leadership is to study the behavior of individual leaders in different institutional settings, i.e., business, governmental, military, civil rights, and religious. This strategy might focus on the study of celebrated leaders such as Winston Churchill, Mahatma Gandhi, Golda Meir, George Patton, Martin Luther King, and others. Much can be learned about leadership through the biographies of such people, but most of the evidence bearing on the leadership process stems from numerous studies conducted in factories, offices, college laboratories, military units, and voluntary organizations. While a thorough understanding of all the leadership studies is beyond the scope of this (and most) book(s), we shall attempt to bring you an understanding of the dynamics involved in the leadership process that cannot be developed from what is known of a few outstanding, charismatic individuals.

In this chapter we will examine the dynamic nature of the leadership process and various models of leadership, and propose an integrated leadership model. To accomplish these purposes, the chapter has six objectives:

1. To define the nature of the leadership process;

2. To indicate sources and the nature of a leader's influence;

3. To assess the trait approach to the study of leadership;

4. To examine various leadership styles as they affect subordinates' job satisfactions and performance;

5. To assess two contingency models; and

6. To identify the critical factors affecting the leadership process in complex organizations.

NATURE OF THE LEADERSHIP PROCESS

Let us begin by considering a potentially dangerous phenomenon that is frequently overlooked by both experienced and inexperienced managers. Specifically, what is the difference between "leadership" and the "leader"? A popular definition of a leader is a person who draws people to himself. This is the person others want to follow, the one who commands their trust, as well as their loyalty. These are the folk heroes others want to emulate. Unfortunately, most of the work in an organization is accomplished by individuals who are not so inspiring. These are managers of insurance offices, chairmen of PTA committees, foremen at the local mills, bank vice-presidents, and the like. These managers (leaders) are the people who plan, organize, control, communicate, delegate, and accept the responsibility to reach the organization's goals. In other words, the leader is appointed to a job with authority, responsibility and accountability to accomplish the goals and objectives of the organization. The manager of a local insurance company, for example, has the responsibility and authority to write insurance policies, train secretaries and other agents, handle client insurance claims, process changes in insurance policies, and investigate claims. The manager usually accomplishes these tasks through the exercise of leadership.

Leadership is the process of influencing group activities toward the achievement of goals.[2] This statement is relatively simple, but it seems to capture the essence of what we mean by leadership. There are two important threads in this definition. First, leadership is a relationship between two or more individuals in which influence and power are unevenly distributed. For example, the formal charter of an organization may give the director of industrial relations legitimate power to negotiate a salary settlement with a union, and this agreement will specify certain wages, hours, fringe benefits, and the like. It also binds the worker to perform certain tasks in return for payments.

Second, there can be no leaders in isolation. If you want to know whether or not you are exercising leadership, look behind you. Is anyone following you? In most instances, you cannot really coerce people into behaving in certain ways. Therefore, leadership implies that followers must *give their consent* to be influenced. In accepting an individual as a leader, the followers voluntarily give up some of their freedom to make decisions, in order to achieve a goal. The individual who finds it difficult to give up some decision-making freedom will not be a satisfied group member, just as the individual who finds it hard to make decisions for others will not find leadership very rewarding. In effect, the followers suspend their judgment, allowing another individual to make certain decisions in specific situations. This leader–member relationship involves some kind of psychological or economic exchange.[3]

Thus, a leader is considered valuable by subordinates and to be an integral part of the group or team only after proving his or her value as a leader, to his or her subordinates. For example, Dick Williams, baseball coach of the California Angels, has demonstrated his leadership abilities on the baseball diamond because he has led Oakland, his former ball team, to two successive World-Series championships. The ballplayers followed his advice on the baseball diamond and suspended their decision-making judgments because of Williams' ability to bring extra economic and psychic rewards to them. Psychic rewards include a sense of achievement when the group reaches desired goals, as when a ball team wins the World Series.

The emotional relationship is by no means one-sided. The leader also becomes involved with subordinates, and their feelings toward him are important. Whether he or she is perceived as fair or unfair, liked or disliked, friendly or unfriendly, all are integral parts in determining whether the leader has the support of the group.

There is little doubt that the leadership position provides economic and psychic rewards for the holder. In many organizations, the persons at the top of the organization may be paid ten to twenty times as much as the lowest paid employees. Notwithstanding the possibility that people may not be worth that much, it is clear that somebody thinks so. However, leadership is sought even when economic rewards are absent. The captain of a collegiate football team, union steward, chairman of a civic or church committee, and PTO chairmen are not paid positions, but individuals occupying these positions usually exercise leadership. Why? Leadership gives one influence or power over others, and with this power comes satisfaction in the knowledge that one can influence, to some extent, the well-being of others, and can affect one's own destiny.[4] Therefore, the leader receives his or her authority from the group because the group has accepted that individual as a leader. For an individual to maintain a leadership position, the person must enable the members to gain satisfactions that are otherwise outside their reach. In return, the group satisfies the leader's need for power and prominence, as well as giving the leader the power necessary to reach the organization's goals.

Sources and Nature of Leader Influence

What, then is required to influence others? Since not all leaders derive their sources of influence from their role in the organization, the leader must somehow be able to rely more on the formal organization to influence others. One of the ways to answer this question is to consider the sources of power available to a leader. These have been identified as: legitimate, reward, coercion, referent, and expert.[5]

Legitimacy. This type of power is vested in a manager's position in the organization hierarchy. Each manager has authority to make decisions in a specific area. For example, the rank-and-file worker who has been promoted to a foreman's position now has legitimate power over other rank-and-file workers in his efforts to achieve the company's goals. If the new foreman has been accepted by the co-workers, his or her influence is likely to be great.

Reward. This type of influence stems from the capability of the leader to specify rewards that are valued by subordinates. A subordinate who complies with the leader's requests does so with the expectation that this behavior will lead to positive rewards, either psychological or economic. Therefore, this type of influence derives from the ability of the leader to provide desired outcomes for others, in exchange for compliance.

Coercion. This type of power is based on fear. A subordinate perceives that failure to comply with the orders from a superior could lead to punishment or some other outcomes that are undesired (for example, an official reprimand for not following orders, poor work assignments, and/or stricter enforcement of all work rules). Unfortunately, the effect of this type of power on the worker's behavior is uncertain. As indicated in Chapter 4, negative reinforcement does not necessarily encourage desired behavior. The worker who receives an official reprimand for shoddy work, for example, may find other ways to avoid the punishment, such as not performing the task at all, falsification of performance reports, and absenteeism.

Referent. Referent power is based on the follower's identification with the leader. This identification may be based upon a personal liking of the leader. Usually, this identification includes a desire on the part of the follower to "be like" the person with referent power. Referent power is usually associated with individuals who possess admired personality characteristics, charisma, or a "good" reputation.

Expert.   Expert power stems from the perceived and demonstrated competence of the leader to implement, analyze, evaluate, and control the task that the group has been assigned to complete. Street gangs usually assess and ascribe expert power to those who can fight the best; academicians to those colleagues who write journal articles and books, and advance new theories. Expert power is narrow in scope; i.e., we tend to be influenced by another person only within the individual's area of expertise.

It is worth noting that a leader can possess varying amounts of these sources of power. The area of rewards, punishment, and legitimate power are largely specified by the hierarchical structure of the organization. For example, the first-line foreman is at a lower level in the organization's hierarchy than the vice-president for manufacturing. Consequently, the foreman's bases of legitimate, reward, and punishment power are less than the vice-president's. On the other hand, some supervisors may possess personal characteristics that increase their referent or expert power, regardless of their position in the organization's hierarchy.

MODELS OF LEADER BEHAVIOR

Many individuals believe that they possess the intuitive ability to identify outstanding leaders. The personnel director may believe that people with pleasing personalities will be highly successful managers. Imbued with this belief, the personnel director will recommend as foremen individuals who have a great deal of personal charm, rather than basing his choices on merit or effort. Why does this happen? One answer is that it is very difficult to determine, in most managerial situations, how well a leader has performed. Getting a manager to evaluate a subordinate's leadership style is almost impossible. The manager will tell you what the individual does, how much time is spent doing various tasks, and the like. However, because a manager performs many tasks, trying to single out good performance criteria has been extremely difficult. A second answer is that the personnel manager would not have been in that position unless somebody else spotted certain personal qualities in him. Therefore, the personnel manager thinks "If these qualities enabled me to get this position and carry out my responsibilities successfully, I will pick others who have qualities similar to my own, so they can also be successful." This statement means that an individual's leadership ability and success depend on a manager's personality. If a subordinate has a manager whose personal qualities are similar to his, the chances of the subordinate's getting a high recommendation are greater than if the subordinate has a manager with dissimilar personal qualities. While it may be true that some managers have the ability to select individuals who become good leaders, it is equally true that some managers do not possess this ability.

In an attempt to analyze the leadership process, we shall discuss four models. As indicated in Fig. 10–1, the models vary along numerous dimen-

Figure 10–1　Comparison of Selected Leadership Models on Critical Dimensions

Dimensions	Leadership Models			
	Trait	Behavioral	Fiedler	Path-Goal
Data collection methods	Questionnaire and observation	Questionnaire	Questionnaire	Questionnaire
Emphasis on individual leader behavior	High	Moderate	High	Moderate
Characteristics of subordinates	Low	Moderate	Moderate	High
Situational factors	Low	Low	High	High
Task structure or technology	Low	Low	Moderate	High
Complexity of model	Low	Moderate	High	High
Validity of model in predicting leadership success	Low	Low/ moderate	Moderate	Moderate
Reliability of model	Low	Low/ moderate	Moderate	Moderate

sions, which, however, are only illustrative of the differences between the models, and should not be taken as exhaustive. The essence of each of these dimensions will be analyzed in our discussion of each of the models.

Trait Model

The study of traits of both successful and unsuccessful leaders is hardly new to the field of management. The trait model has attempted to isolate the attributes of successful and unsuccessful leaders, and implies that the reason why one individual was successful was because he or she possessed traits differing from those of leaders who were less successful. While there is considerable support for the notion that effective leaders have different interest patterns, different abilities, and perhaps also some different personality traits, than do less effective managers, most researchers have come to regard the trait approach as not very effective in predicting successful leadership.[6] Why?

First, although over a hundred essential personality attributes of successful leaders have been identified, no consistent relationship has been found between these attributes and leader behavior. Effective leader traits include intelligence, fairness, understanding, self-confidence, and dominance. The list of unsuccessful leader traits include indecisiveness, lack of communication, lack of aggressiveness, insensitivity, unsureness, and arbitrariness.[7]

The general implications of these findings is that successful leaders rate higher than less successful leaders on self-assurance, dominance, and the like. These findings make it abundantly clear that individual personality cannot be left out of the leadership picture. Individual differences clearly affect the social perceptions of some individuals, and consequently play an important part in determining individuals' behavior. It is clear that these relationships are contingent upon a situation, but leadership cannot be exclusively a function of the situation.[8]

Second, physical and constitutional factors have also been related to effective leadership. Individuals' height, weight, appearance, physique, energy, health, and intelligence have all been related to successful leadership. However, it seems that most of these factors are also correlated with many other situational factors which, in some cases, significantly affect a leader's effectiveness. For example, in the military or in the police force, members must have a certain minimal height and weight in order to perform their tasks effectively. While these attributes may assist an individual to rise to a leadership position, the number of inches of height or the number of pounds of weight do not relate highly to performance. In other organizations (e.g., educational or business), height and weight requirements are not requisites for rising to a leadership position.

Third, situational factors may, and sometimes do, override personality factors. For example, intelligence has been found to be moderately related to performance of first-line managers, but becomes increasingly important at higher managerial levels.[9] In this case, the level of the individual in the organization is important. Other studies have found that different managerial traits are associated with different functional roles in the organization. For example, successful sales managers are optimistic, enthusiastic, masculine, and dominant, whereas successful production managers are progressive, have a genuine respect for people, are introverts, and are cooperative.[10] Therefore, what is an important personality attribute for one role may not be important for a different role in the same organization.

Fourth, personality description and measurement themselves may be inadequate. It may be that leadership researchers have not investigated the really significant aspects of a leader's personality. That is, most of the traits are measured by pencil-and-paper questionnaires, which were designed to be valid indicators of other behaviors, such as stability, neuroses, achievement, and the like. Trait theorists assumed that these questionnaires would also be valid indicators of leadership ability.

Fifth, leadership itself is known to be a complex and probably not a consistent pattern of individual roles. There could be a relation between personality and taking of particular roles, which is not reflected in a study relating personality to a measure of effectiveness. For example, one study found that high earners (a measure of success) in small firms were more ascendant, they tended to have interests similar to those of personnel managers, they were more open-minded, and described themselves as more considerate, than low earners. In these firms, each individual is required to perform numerous roles and those individuals who are predisposed to performing a multiplicity of roles will seek out small firms that permit them to do so.[11]

Behavioral Models

Following the failure of the trait model to predict successful leader behavior, researchers turned to an examination of the structure and functions of groups. The emphasis turned from identifying what traits are important in the leadership process to the study of what leaders actually do and how they do it. Effective leaders performed the tasks of assisting the group in achieving certain task-goals by being task-centered in their relations with subordinates. To assist the members to achieve certain personal goals, such as work satisfaction, promotions, and the like, leaders are also viewed as being considerate or supportive. Examples of task behavior would be to focus attention on production, reviewing the quality and quantity of work accomplished, and the like. Examples of considerate leader behavior would include settling disputes, keeping the group happy, providing encouragement, giving positive reinforcements, and the like.

Continuum of Leader Behaviors

There are, of course, a variety of styles of leader behavior between being task-oriented and considerate. One way to look at these styles is depicted as a continuum (illustrated in Fig. 10–2). Leaders whose behavior is observed to be task-directed and who use their formal authority to influence their subordinates, appear on the lefthand side of the figure. Leaders whose behavior appears to be considerate of the needs of their subordinates, thus giving them more freedom in their work, are located on the right side. The continuum illustrates that a manager has a large number of styles from which to choose and can shift his or her style. The manager who has capable and talented subordinates might prefer a more democratic or relations-oriented approach, as opposed to the manager who perceives subordinates as incapable of self-judgment and control. If a manager has more confidence in his own capabilities than in those of his subordinates, he will not delegate many decision-making functions to the subordinates. A manager's own value system will also determine his or her particular style of leadership. How strongly does the manager

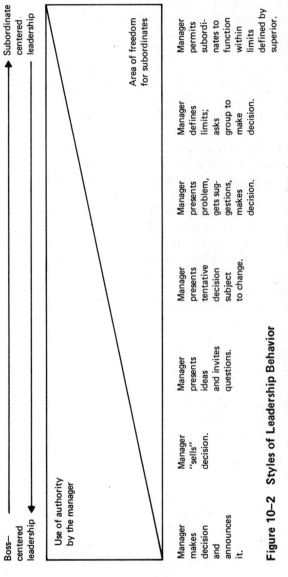

Figure 10–2 Styles of Leadership Behavior

Source: Tannenbaum, R. and W. Schmidt, "How to Choose A Leadership Pattern," *Harvard Business Review*, 1973, 51, p. 164. Reproduced with permission, *Harvard Business Review*.

feel that individuals should have a share in the decisions that affect them? The strength of convictions on questions such as this will tend to move the manager from one end of the continuum to the other. The last factor facing a manager is the situation. The manager who delegates decision-making functions to subordinates reduces the predictability of the decision to some extent. Some managers have a greater need than others to know the outcome of the decision, and have a lower tolerance for ambiguity than others.

Before deciding how to lead, the manager will also want to consider a number of factors affecting subordinates' behavior. For example, do the subordinates have a need for independence? Are they ready to assume the responsibility for decisions? Do they understand the goals and objectives of the company? Generally speaking, if the manager can answer yes to these questions, the manager can permit his or her subordinates greater freedom.

In addition to forces in both manager and subordinates, certain general characteristics of the situation will also affect the manager's behavior. Among the more critical situational circumstances are those that stem from the organization, the work group, the nature and scope of the problem, and the pressures of time.

These, then, are the critical forces that affect a manager's leadership style at any one instance and tend to determine his or her behavior in relation to his subordinates. As the manager works on problems that arise day by day, the most effective leadership will change. Thus, a leader has a continuum of styles to choose from, as indicated in Fig. 10–2.

Sometimes, this leadership continuum is extended to include a laissez-faire style. This behavioral style permits the subordinates to do whatever they want to do. No policies or procedures are established by the leader. As indicated by the absence of this style on the continuum, it is felt that a laissez-faire leadership style represents an *absence* of leadership. The leadership role has been abdicated, and therefore no leadership is being exhibited.

In recent years, leadership styles have been found to vary considerably from leader to leader. Some leaders tend to emphasize the task, while others stress the more interpersonal relationships. There are even some leaders whose style seems to be both task- and relations-oriented.

Ohio State Leadership Studies

The leadership studies initiated in the late 1940's by the Bureau of Business Research at Ohio State University attempted to identify dimensions of leader behavior. This effort resulted in the specification of two dimensions of leader behavior: consideration and initiating structure. *Consideration* reflects the extent to which a leader is likely to have job relationships characterized by mutual trust, two-way communication, respect for subordinates' ideas, and consideration of their feelings. This style emphasizes the needs of the individual. Some statements posed to subordinates to measure the considerate behavior of the immediate supervisor are:

"He (she) looks out for the personal welfare of group members."

"He (she) is friendly and approachable."

"He (she) treats all of his (her) co-workers as equals."

Initiating structure refers to the extent to which a leader is likely to define and structure his or her role, and those of subordinates, toward goal accomplishment. This style emphasizes directing group activities through planning, communicating information, scheduling, trying out new ideas, and the like. Some typical guidelines used to measure a leader's initiating structure are: "He (she) schedules work to be done," "He (she) assigns group members to particular tasks," and "He (she) maintains definite standards of performance."

The overall results from the Ohio State leadership studies can be summarized by an examination of Fig. 10–3. This leadership grid depicts considerate leader behavior on a continuum ranging from low to high on the horizontal axis. Initiating structure may also vary from low to high, as indicated on the vertical axis. Leaders who were rated highly on initiating structure by their immediate subordinates were generally rated highly by their immediate supervisors and had subordinates who were high producers. Perhaps it is not surprising to note that this style of leader behavior was related to high absenteeism, employee grievances, turnover, and low job satisfaction for workers performing routine tasks. On the other hand, highly considerate leaders were found to be in charge of satisfied workers, who displayed high degrees of group harmony and cohesiveness.[12] Leaders with low consideration and high initiating structure experience higher grievance rates and turnover than leaders high in consideration but low in initiating structure.

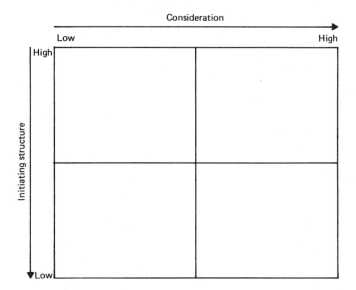

Figure 10–3 Ohio State Leadership Grid

The underlying assumption made by the researchers at Ohio State was that leader behavior was related not only to indirect measures of performance, such as absenteeism, grievances, and turnover, but also to direct measures of performance, such as the number of units produced. In one review, the author concludes that we know very little about how these styles affect work group performance. While this comment may appear harsh, many studies have failed to find a significant relationship between these dimensions of leader behavior and performance.[13]

Some of the reasons for these findings are that an individual's productivity is influenced by other factors such as (1) the individual's social status within the group; (2) the type of technological process employed; (3) the individual's expectation of a certain style of supervision; and (4) the individual's psychological rewards from working with a particular type of leader. Some of the reasons derived from these findings can be noted in Fig. 10–1. The early Ohio State studies tended not to emphasize situational factors, such as the expectations of subordinates, task design, and the role of the leader's personal characteristics. Recently, the researchers have altered their position, and now place a great emphasis on situational factors; the validity of the model has improved, as indicated in Fig. 10–1.

University of Michigan Leadership Studies

Occurring almost simultaneously with the Ohio State leadership studies were those of the Survey Research Center at the University of Michigan. The focus of this group of researchers was on locating characteristics of leaders that seemed to be related to measures of performance effectiveness. Through these studies, two styles of behavior were identified: employee-centered and production-centered.

A leader who was described by his or her subordinates as employee-centered stressed the interpersonal aspects of the job. That is, the leader took a personal interest in the needs of the employees, accepted their individuality, and felt that every employee was important as an individual. Production-centered leaders were described as emphasizing the technical aspects of the job, viewing employees as tools to accomplish the organization's tasks, and concerned with extablishing well-defined patterns of task relationships. These two leadership styles are similar to the two styles developed by the Ohio State researchers.[14] That is, "production-centered" and "initiating structure" measure similar leader behaviors, while "employee-centered" and "consideration" are similar. In a wide variety of industrial situations (including railway maintenance crews, insurance office staffs, heavy industry production lines, trucking companies), the Michigan researchers found that employee-centered leadership was associated with high productivity, whereas production-centered leadership was associated with low productivity. These researchers also found that employee-centered attitudes in supervisors were associated with higher job satisfaction and morale, whereas production-centered attitudes were associated with poor morale and less job satisfaction.

While there is a great temptation to conclude that considerate leader behavior increases group effectiveness and morale while task-directed leader behavior has the opposite effect, there are several questions that need to be answered. First, it was not possible to show whether the leader's behavior caused the group to be effective and satisfied, or whether the effective group caused the leader to be employee-centered. Second, there is considerable evidence that the behavior of leaders changes from situation to situation.[15] The leader who is quite employee-centered and considerate in one situation can become production-centered and initiate structure in another situation. Third, groups that are highly cohesive and satisfied and that are attracted to the leader are more apt to describe the leader as considerate than are groups that are torn by conflict and that actively demonstrate their dislike for the leader.

As indicated in Fig. 10–1, the Michigan researchers used questionnaires to measure leader behavior, and did not emphasize the nature of the subordinate's task or personal characteristics, or other situational variables. More recently, these researchers, just like the Ohio State researchers, have started to consider many more situational variables (i.e., organizational climate, group processes, technology) and the complexity of the model has increased. Along with this shift in emphasis, the validity of the model has increased.

While considerate or employee-centered leader behavior should not be viewed as the "one best way to lead," there is good evidence that when subordinate attitudes and the work environment are appropriate, it can have a substantial impact on both satisfaction and performance. Some of the conditions that contribute to greater effectiveness of considerate leader behavior are:

1. The extent to which subordinates have relevant skills and information to perform the tasks;

2. The extent to which subordinates perceive that their decision-making involvement is legitimate and will affect their job performance;

3. The extent to which subordinates are motivated to participate in the decision-making process;

4. The less the status difference between the leader and followers; and

5. The greater the degree of trust and support exhibited by the leader.[16]

Contingency Models

As pointed out in earlier parts of this chapter, no single personality trait, trait pattern, or particular style of leader behavior has been consistently related to effective organizational performance. A person may be an effective leader in one situation but very ineffective in another. Two recent theories of leadership —those of Fiedler and House—have suggested the conditions under which one or another type of leader behavior is most effective in terms of leading the group to accomplish its task goals and attaining the satisfaction of its members' needs.

Fiedler's Contingency Model

The first contingency model of leadership effectiveness was developed by Fiedler and his associates.[17] This model represents a departure from the trait and behavioral models of leadership in that it specifies that performance of a group is contingent upon both the motivational system of the leader and the degree to which the leader has control and influence in a particular situation. The effectiveness of a leadership style depends on the interaction of the leader's behavior with three situational variables: task structure, group atmosphere, and leader's position power. Let's briefly look at these variables.

Assessing Leadership Style.   The leadership style of a person is measured by using an instrument called "esteem for least preferred co-worker" (LPC). The instrument asks the respondent to think of all co-workers one has ever had and to describe the person with whom he or she could work least well, the "least preferred co-worker." The description is made by rating that person on a simple bipolar scale. Examples of these bipolar adjectives are indicated in Fig. 10–4. Each bipolar scale is scored from one to eight, with eight indicating the most favorable perception of one's least preferred co-worker. The LPC score is obtained by totaling up point values for all the items. A low score indicates the degree to which an individual is ready to reject those with whom he or she cannot work. This attitude is reflected by describing in negative terms co-workers' attributes that are not directly related to their work. The lower the LPC score, the greater the task orientation of the leader. A more positive score indicates a willingness to perceive even the worst co-worker as having some reasonably positive attributes. A high LCP person sees both good and bad points in his least preferred co-worker and is more motivated to use a "relations-oriented" leadership style.

Fiedler interprets a leader LPC score to be an index of a motivational hierarchy, or of behavioral preferences. The high LPC person, who perceives his or her least preferred co-worker in a more favorable light, has as his basic goal the desire to be related with others. That is, the leader seeks to have strong emotional ties with the co-workers. If the leader reaches this goal, he or she will want to reach the secondary goals of status and esteem. In return, the leader wants the subordinates to show admiration and recognition.

The low LPC person has a different motivational system. This person's basic goal is task accomplishment. Self-esteem is gained through achievement of task related goals. However, as long as accomplishing the task presents no problems, this person also tends to be friendly and pleasant in relations with subordinates. It is only when task accomplishment is threatened that good interpersonal relations assume secondary importance to accomplishing the task.

Task Structure.   Task structure represents the extent to which the task is simple (or routine), can only be done one (or numerous) ways, and is highly specific (or vague). If the task is routine, it is likely to have clearly defined goals, only a few steps or work procedures, be verifiable, and have a correct solution. An axle assembler in an auto plant who secures front and rear assemblies to chassis springs is performing a highly structured task because the goals are clearly spelled out, the method to accomplish the task is detailed and specific, and whether the task was correctly performed is verifiable. Under these conditions, the leader's ability to influence the group is restricted because the task dilutes the leader's potential influence.

Think of the person with whom you can work least well. He may be someone you work with now, he may be someone you knew in the past. He does not have to be the person you like least well, but should be the person with whom you have the most difficulty in getting a job done. Describe this person as he appears to you. The farther you go from the middle of each scale toward the end to place your check mark, the stronger the person has the quality described.

Friendly	: 8 : 7 : 6 : 5	4 : 3 : 2 : 1 :	Unfriendly
Rejecting	: 1 : 2 : 3 : 4	5 : 6 : 7 : 8 :	Accepting
Helpful	: 8 : 7 : 6 : 5	4 : 3 : 2 : 1 :	Frustrating
Unenthusiastic	: 1 : 2 : 3 : 4	5 : 6 : 7 : 8 :	Enthusiastic
Tense	: 1 : 2 : 3 : 4	5 : 6 : 7 : 8 :	Relaxed
Distant	: 1 : 2 : 3 : 4	5 : 6 : 7 : 8 :	Close
Cold	: 1 : 2 : 3 : 4	5 : 6 : 7 : 8 :	Warm
Cooperative	: 8 : 7 : 6 : 5	4 : 3 : 2 : 1 :	Uncooperative
Supportive	: 8 : 7 : 6 : 5	4 : 3 : 2 : 1 :	Hostile
Boring	: 1 : 2 : 3 : 4	5 : 6 : 7 : 8 :	Interesting

Figure 10–4   Leadership Style: LPC

Adapted from: Fiedler, F. and M. Chemers, *Leadership and Effective Management.* Glenview, Ill.: Scott, Foresman & Co., 1974, p. 75.

At the other extreme is the task that is completely nonroutine. In this condition, the leader may possess no more knowledge than the subordinates. The goals are unclear, the path to achieve the goals are multiple, and the task cannot be done by the "numbers." Tasks performed by social workers, detectives, policy-makers, executives, marketing researchers, and the like would be examples of individuals performing tasks.

Group Atmosphere.   This variable measures the leader's feelings of being accepted by the group. The leader's authority partly depends on his or her acceptance by the group. If others are going to follow him because of his referent power, for example, they are following the leader because of the leader's personality, trustworthiness, and the like. Also, they are likely to accept the person as their leader. Many of the factors influencing this factor have been discussed at length in Chapter 7.

Position Power.   Position power is the extent to which the leader possesses reward punishment and legitimate power bases. These bases of power were mentioned earlier in this chapter. Some typical questions asked to determine the leader's position power are: Does the leader have the right to promote or demote a subordinate? Can the leader instruct the subordinates concerning task goals? In most business organizations, foremen, supervisors and managers have high position power. In most voluntary organizations, committees, and other social organizations, leaders tend to have low position power.

Determinants of Favorable Situation.   The three aspects of the situation that appear to be the most important in determining the leader's influence and control are (1) whether the leader has been accepted or rejected by his work group (group atmosphere); (2) whether the task is relatively routine or non-routine (task structure); and (3) whether the leader has high or low position power (power position). A particular group may be classified first by its leader-member relations, then by its task structure, and finally by its leaders' position power. The higher each of these is (i.e., the more pleasant the relations, the more structured the task, and the greater the power), the more favorable the situation for the leader.

Figure 10–5 shows the basic contingency model. The three basic variables are shown on the horizontal axis. The eight octants represent combinations of the three variables and are arranged in order of leader favorableness from most favorable to least favorable. The model assumes that a leader will have the most control and influence in groups that fall into octant 1; that is, in which he is accepted, has high position power, and has subordinates performing relatively structured tasks. The leader will have somewhat less control and influence in octant 2, where he is accepted and has a structured task, but little position power. As we proceed along the continuum to groups in octant 8, the leader's control and influence will be very small. In this situation, the leader

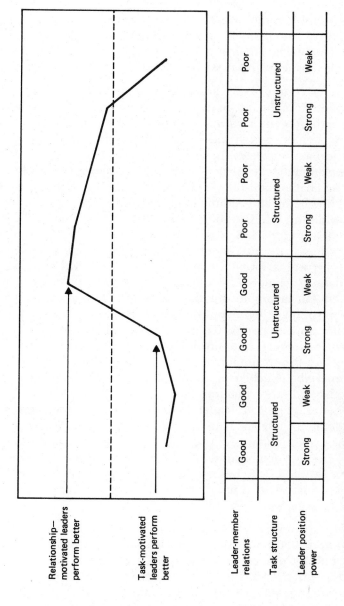

Figure 10–5 Basic Contingency Model

Source: Fiedler, F., ("Engineer the Job to Fit the Manager," *Harvard Business Review*, 1965, 45, p. 118. Reproduced with permission, *Harvard Business Review.*

is not accepted by the group, the group is performing vague and unstructured tasks, and the leader has little position power.

Some typical groups that might be placed in these various octants are: octants 1 and 5, telephone offices, craft shops, meat departments, grocery departments; octants 2 and 6, basketball and football teams, surveying parties; octants 3 and 7, general foremen, ROTC groups, research chemists, military planning groups; and octants 4 and 8, racially divided groups, disaster groups, church groups, and mental health groups. The critical question is "What kind of leadership style is most effective in each of the different group situations?"

Findings. The average results of the various studies conducted by Fiedler and his associates are plotted in Fig. 10–5. As indicated previously, the horizontal axis of this figure indicates the favorableness of the situation, with the most favorable octant (#1) on the far left and the least favorable octant (#8) on the far right. The vertical axis indicates the leader's LPC score. The solid line on the graph above the midline indicates a positive relationship between LPC and group performance. That is, high-LPC leaders performed better than low-LPC leaders. The solid line below the midline indicated that low-LPC leaders performed better than did high-LPC leaders. The solid line represents the best predictions between a leader's LPC score and work group effectiveness.

As Fig. 10–5 shows, the task-motivated (low-LPC) leaders performed most effectively in the very favorable situations, octants 1, 2, and 3, and in the least favorable situation, octant 8. Low-LPC leaders are basically motivated by task accomplishment. In favorable situations in which their group supports them, their power position is high, and the task is structured, they will strive to develop pleasant work relations. Their behavior will seem friendly and considerate toward co-workers. In unfavorable situations, in which the task is unstructured, they lack group support, and their position power is low, they will devote their energies to achieving the primary goal of the group.

Figure 10–5 also indicates situations in which a high-LPC leader is most likely to perform better. High-LPC leaders obtain best group efficiency under conditions of moderate or intermediate favorableness, octants 4, 5, 6, and 7. Octants 4 and 5 describe situations in which (a) the task is structured but the leader is disliked and must demonstrate that he or she cares for the emotions of subordinates, or (b) the leader is liked, but the group has an unstructured task and the leader must depend upon the willingness and creativity of the group's members to accomplish the goals.

Implications. There are several important implications of this model. First, both relationship-motivated and task-motivated leaders perform well under certain situations but not others. An outstanding manager at one level who gets promoted to another level may fail at higher levels because his or her motivational base does not match the demands of the situation.[18] For example, the practice of a company taking its most successful foreman and promoting the individual to production manager is such a case. The contingency model suggests that the foreman's failure in the new position may not indicate a lack of intellectual ability, but rather a change in leadership situation to one in which the individual is no longer able to function at his or her best. The structure of the task has probably changed from a relatively structured one to a less structured task situation. Assuming that this person's position power and ability to get along with the group didn't change, the contingency model would predict two different leadership styles as being effective. That is, the foremen may move from a situation requiring a task-motivated style to a situation requiring a more human-relations style. Second, it is not totally accurate to speak of a good or poor leader. Rather, one must think of a leader who performs well in one situation but not in another. The preceding example of the foremen promoted to general foremen illustrates this point. Third, the performance of a leader depends upon both the leader's motivational bases and the situation. Therefore, the organization can change leadership effectiveness by attempting to change the motivational states of the leader, or by modifying the favorableness of the leader's situation.

Validity of Model. A number of fairly detailed reviews to validate the model have been published.[19] Studies to determine the validity of this model have been conducted in a wide variety of groups, teams, and organizations (e.g., research teams, department stores, military units, basketball teams, hospital wards, and the like). While it is beyond the scope of this book to evaluate critically all of the studies, there have been several important issues raised.

First, what does LPC mean? Early in his research, Fiedler assumed it was a measure of the leader's personality, while his most recent interpretation is that it reflects an individual's motivation structure with respect to need gratification from groups. Despite the fact that the interpretation of a leader's LPC score is cloudy, it does seem to reflect a leader's underlying motivational bases and not a leader's cognitive ability or a basic personality.[20] While the debate continues to specify what LPC means, it has been highly related to group productivity.

Second, we must question the reliability of a leader's LPC score over a period of time. The lack of reliability of the LPC score seriously limits the validity of the research supporting the model. It seems hardly worthwhile to change a work situation on the basis of a leader's LPC score if there is a probability that the leader's LPC score will change within a short period of time, and will vary according to group performance. That is, high performance of a group can increase a leader's LPC score, while low performance can cause a decrease.[21] While it is true that changes in the LPC score occur as a result of changes in a individual's life and the leader's success or nonsuccess, we cannot engineer the job to fit the manager if the manager's motivational bases are constantly changing.

Third, the model does not take into account that the leader can influence the task structure because of his knowledge of the situation. That is, a leader can take a nonroutine task and provide some structure to it before assigning it to subordinates. They, in turn, perceive the task to be more structured than unstructured. The leader can also affect the group's atmosphere through a particular style of behavior.[22] A leader who has been described as approachable, friendly, and supportive may facilitate the development of group harmony and high group cohesiveness. On the other hand, a leader who is aloof, unapproachable, and unfriendly may create hostility and resentment in the work group.

Fourth, since LPC is a unidimensional concept, it implies that if an individual is highly motivated toward task accomplishment, he or she must be completely unconcerned with relations among group members, or oriented away from social concerns, and vice versa. As discussed in the previous section on behavioral models of leadership, it is possible for an individual to be both task- and relations-motivated. Thus, a leader's orientation with respect to one dimension should not completely determine the orientation on the other. The leader may well be one who is motivated by both task and relational concerns.

In summary, Fiedler's contingency model stresses that both relations-oriented and task-oriented leaders can perform well, but under different conditions. The task-motivated leaders perform best in situations in which their power and influence are either very high or low, as well as in situations in which their task is highly structured and there are good leader–member relations. Relations-motivated leaders perform best under conditions of moderate favorableness, in which the power and influence they have are mixed, leader–member relations are low, and the structure is either high or low.

House's Path—Goal Model

Puzzled by the contradictory findings in the leadership area, House developed a model that is based on Vroom's theory of motivation (see Chapter 9). House's model of leadership effectiveness does not indicate the "one best way" to lead, but suggests that a leader must select a style most appropriate to the particular situation.[23]

The basic idea of the model is that one of the functions of a leader is to enhance the psychological states of subordinates that result in motivation to perform a task or in satisfaction with the job. The leader's function consists of increasing the personal satisfactions to subordinates for work-goal attainment, and making the path to these satisfactions easier to obtain. This is accomplished by clarifying the nature of the task, reducing the road blocks from successful task completion, and by increasing the opportunities for the subordinates to obtain personal satisfactions. The model states that, to the extent the leader accomplishes these functions, the motivation of the subordinates will increase. A subordinate is satisfied with his or her job to the extent that performance will lead to things that the individual highly values. The function of the leader is to help the subordinate reach these highly valued job-related goals. The specific style of leader behavior is determined by two situational variables—characteristics of the subordinates and task structure.

Characteristics of Subordinates.   With respect to subordinates' characteristics, the theory states that leader behavior will be viewed acceptable to subordinates to the extent that the subordinates see such behavior as either an immediate source of satisfaction, or as needed for future satisfaction. For example, if subordinates have a high need for esteem and affiliation, supportive leader behavior may serve as an immediate source of need satisfaction. On the other hand, subordinates with high needs for autonomy, responsibility, and self-actualization are more likely to be motivated by leaders who are directive than by leaders who are supportive. Similarly, individuals who are internally oriented (believe they can control their own behavior) as opposed to externally oriented (believe that the behavior is controlled by fate) prefer leaders who demonstrate more supportive behavior than those low on this dimension.

Supportive leadership is demonstrated by a friendly and approachable leader who shows concern for the status, well-being, and needs of subordinates. This leadership style is similar to the employee-centered or the considerate styles discussed earlier in this chapter. Such a leader does little things to make the work more pleasant, treats members as equals, and is friendly and approachable. Similarly, where subordinates perceived themselves to have the ability to perform the task, a leader who demonstrates constant coaching and directiveness is likely to be perceived unfavorably. Directive leadership is characterized by a leader who lets subordinates know what is expected of them, gives specific guidance as to what should be done and how it should be done, makes his part in the group understood, schedules work to be done, maintains definite standards of performance, and asks that group members follow standard rules and regulations.

Task Structure.   The second major variable is the task's structure. Where path–goal relationships are apparent because of the routine nature of the task, attempts by the leader to further clarify path–goal relationships will be perceived by subordinates as unnecessarily close control. While such close control may increase performance by preventing "goofing off," it will also result in decreased job satisfaction. For example, the axle assembler in an auto plant who secures front and rear assemblies to chassis springs is performing a highly structured and repetitive task. Under these conditions, many workers cannot derive any intrinsic satisfactions (i.e., esteem, self-actualization) from the performance of the task. If a leader is directive, this leadership style is likely to be perceived by the workers as redundant and excessive, and directed at keeping them working on unsatisfying tasks. Within this task structure, a leader who is supportive is likely to have more satisfied employees than one who is directive. A supportive leadership style is likely to increase the worker's extrinsic satisfaction (e.g., satisfaction within supervising company, and the like) on a job that provides little intrinsic satisfaction. On the other hand, when the tasks are highly unstructured, i.e., more complex and varied, a more directive leadership style is appropriate to the extent that it helps subordinates cope with task uncertainty, and clarifies the paths leading to highly valued goals. For example, a manager of an industrial relations team who gives subordinates guidance and direction on how to process a grievance for arbitration is attempting to clarify the direction of his subordinates for the attainment of an organizational goal. This style of leadership is not perceived as excessive and/or redundant since it helps the subordinates reach their goals, a source of intrinsic job satisfaction.

Figure 10–6 illustrates the effect of task structure on leader behavior and subordinates' job satisfaction. On the vertical axis is a continuum of job satisfaction, ranging from low to high. On the horizontal axis is a leader's directive behavior, ranging from high to low. Task structure moderates the relationship between leader behavior and subordinate job satisfaction. When the task is highly structured, the leader who does not give direction and excessive coaching is likely to have highly satisfied subordinates. On the other hand, when the task is unstructured, a directive leadership style is likely to increase subordinates' job satisfaction. There are several other variables (e.g., performance, supervisor satisfaction, promotion satisfaction) that could replace job satisfaction, and the relationships in the figure would not change.

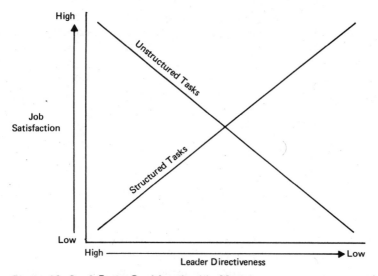

Figure 10–6   A Path–Goal Leadership Model

Findings. It is too early to make anything but a preliminary assessment of House's path–goal theory of leadership, because there is so little research data to go on. However, the early research findings have been encouraging. Workers performing highly structured tasks have reported high job satisfaction when their immediate supervisor uses a supportive (as opposed to directive) leadership style. On the other hand, managers performing in unstructured task environments are more productive when their immediate supervisor uses a more directive leadership style. However, this style does not always lead to high job satisfactions.[24]

Implications. The implications of these findings for managers indicate that the kind of leadership style needed varies according to the situation. The findings support the notion that while shop-floor personnel prefer a supportive leader, to gain some extrinsic satisfaction from performing routine and often boring tasks, middle and professional employees work better with a more directive leadership style. At these levels, job descriptions are usually written without much specification and a directive leader can clarify the task(s) and the goal(s) for the subordinates. It does not seem unreasonable that different leadership styles will be required for different occupational groupings and levels of the organization's hierarchy.

The Leader in Complex Situations

The primary need of a supervisor is to assist subordinates in task–goal achievement and provide personal satisfactions. The degree to which a leader accomplishes these functions will determine his or her effectiveness. The approach that we have taken throughout this chapter tells us that no single factor, such as the personality of the leader, the characteristics of the subordinates, or the nature of the task, explains a group's performance. Our aim in this section of the chapter is not to write the final work on leadership, but rather to point out a number of variables affecting the leadership process in complex organizations.

The eight factors that we consider as affecting the leaderships process are indicated in Fig. 10–7. Because of the interactive and multiplicative relationships between these variables, it is not possible to discuss all the interrelationships. However, we will discuss each factor separately. It is important to note that a leader's behavior can also affect some of the factors, as indicated by the dotted lines between leader behavior and these factors.

Nature of the Work Task. As discussed by House and his associates, in simple, highly routine and structured tasks, a considerate or supportive leadership style may be more closely related to high job satisfaction and performance than a more directive leader style. In many instances, workers find highly routine jobs unrewarding and boring. Where a supervisor is in frequent contact with the workers, this contact is likely to be perceived as a source of harassment. Under these conditions, workers do not need much supervision and therefore prefer a leader who is not continually looking over their shoulders.

On the other hand, in less structured tasks, subordinates appreciate more direction by their immediate supervisor. In these tasks, it seems that the supervisor who can contribute to the subordinates' effective and satisfying work experience by giving them direction and guidance is perceived as the most effective leadership style.[25] Also note that a leader's behavior can affect his subordinates' perceptions of the structuredness of the task.

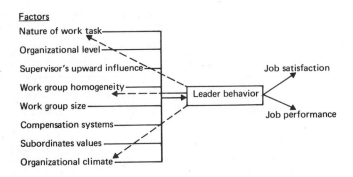

Figure 10–7 Factors Affecting the Leadership Process

Adapted from: Ritchie, J., "Supervision," in *Organization Behavior: Research and Issues,* Strauss, G., C. Snow, and A. Tannenbaum (eds.). Madison, Wis.: Industrial Relations Research Association, 1974. pp. 51–76.

Organizational Level. [26]   Different leadership styles are often needed at different levels in the organization. Most high-level executives are implicitly asked to operate at two organizational levels. That is, an executive may be in charge of other executives, peers, or subordinates or both. For example, in a nursing unit, the head nurse is in charge of other nurses, licensed practical nurses, orderlies, nurses' aides, and the like. The head nurse's leadership style may be directly related to the performance or satisfaction of nurses' aides, and orderlies, and also other nurses. Higher-level supervisors may also compensate for lower-level supervisor behavior. The head nurse's considerate style of leader behavior may compensate for the ward nurse's directive style with aides and orderlies.

Supervisor's Upward Influence.   The degree to which subordinates perceive their supervisor as a means of securing valued work-related goals from higher management may also determine the effectiveness of the leader. Those supervisors who are advocates of their subordinates' positions to higher management may be able to bring to their subordinates payoffs that they perceive as desirable.[27] Thus, the considerate, upwardly influential supervisor can act as a facilitator to higher management for subordinates and, by doing so, satisfy his employees' needs.

Work-Group Homogeneity.   As pointed out by Fiedler and his associates, the homogeneous nature of the work group, the similarity of the members and the leader, is a variable that can affect the performance and satisfaction of the work group.[28] This is especially true for groups whose members are dependent upon each other for successful accomplishment. In a football team, the team's score depends on the coordination of each of the individual's efforts on offense and defense. If the team is highly cohesive, a considerate style of leader behavior may be appropriate to motivate team members for task accomplishment. If the team is torn by strife, the leader may choose to use a more directive style. Similarly, in the waning seconds of a close football game, the coach may become more directive in his leadership style. This increase in leader directiveness will be tolerated by the members so that they may win the game. Group cohesiveness will not decline under these conditions because the players need additional direction to win.

Work-Group Size. As pointed out in Chapter 7, group size affects member satisfaction, locus of decision-making, communication channels, and leadership style. In small work groups, leaders tend to perform more like social specialists, emphasizing interpersonal functions. In larger groups, where individual members are relatively autonomous, leaders tend to emphasize task–goal accomplishment and resolution of conflict between the individual members of the group.

Compensation Systems. Lawler stresses the point that one of the easiest ways to motivate many employees toward task accomplishment is to demonstrate to them that there is a direct relationship between performance and monetary rewards.[29] Where organizational pay policies make this relationship specific, the leader's behavior can play an important role in determining the individual's pay. Where policies make this impossible, such as for the assembly-line worker, supervisor efforts to increase performance may be to no avail.

Subordinate Values. As indicated in Chapter 9, there are movements to increase the humanization of work. The subordinate's attainment of challenging and responsible jobs is a task for supervisors at all levels where workers are seeking advancement. Supportive leader behavior provides a means for employees to satisfy their ego and social needs. That is, this style of leader behavior gives the employees greater opportunities for regulating and controlling their own activities and has been found to increase the degree to which individuals can express their various and diverse needs. Directive or task-centered leader behavior will reduce the degree to which social needs can be satisfied through the accomplishment of a task. Therefore, subordinates seeking to satisfy social needs on the job will find greater opportunity to satisfy these needs with supportive leadership styles, and less opportunity with directive leadership styles.[30]

Organizational Climate. Organizational climate refers to a set of attributes that workers perceive about their organization.[31] Organizations having a large number of rules and regulations, use of the formal organization hierarchy to make all decisions, and the like, would elicit expression of one set of attributes about the organization, whereas organizations that use few of these mechanisms will be perceived differently by employees. The significant fact to note is that the organization's climate can be partially created by the leader's behavior. If employees perceive both the organization and their leaders as autocratic, the employees are likely to have low job satisfaction, negative attitudes toward the company, low innovation and productivity. On the other hand, if the organization is perceived as achievement-oriented and the leaders are considerate, the employees are likely to respond by exhibiting high levels of achievement, high job satisfaction, positive attitudes toward the company and high performance.

SUMMARY

We have tried to point out some of the problems relevant to leadership in modern complex organizations. The material presented in this chapter is not meant to be a comprehensive analysis of leadership, but only to show how certain styles of leader behavior affect subordinates under various stiuations. Leadership does have an important impact on organizational effectiveness and the satisfactions that employees can derive from their jobs. It was pointed out that an effective leadership pattern varies as a function of the conditions facing the leader, subordinate, group, and organization.

Discussion Questions:

1. Why has the trait approach to leadership failed? Why, then, do managers still believe in the trait approach?

2. What is the difference between a leader and the process of leadership?

3. What are the functions that a leader has to exercise in most work groups?

4. Describe Fiedler's contingency model.

5. Explain why initiating structure, as a leadership strategy, produces effectiveness in a managerial task situation but ineffectiveness and dissatisfaction for shop-floor employees.

6. Develop a contingency model of leadership that incorporates Fiedler's and House's works.

7. Define "influence." Why does the leader whom subordinates can influence have considerable influence himself?

8. Is it feasible to alter the job to fit the particular style of a leader, in order that the leader be more effective?

9. What are some of the concepts in motivation that a leader should be aware of?

CRITICAL INCIDENT

John Pawl, a new foreman in the rolling ring mill at ABS Steel Corporation, was introduced to his new job duties on the Friday afternoon shift. He was to be in charge of an assembly and packing crew. Since he was a former assembler and packer in another firm, he approached his new job with energy and self-confidence.

Most of the first afternoon on the job he spent circulating among the men, trying to get to know them and letting them meet him. The manager of the ring mill decided to let John introduce himself around since he was an experienced mill hand. During the conversation with some of the mill workers, John asked "Is that all you do, pack rings for shipment?" or "Haven't you thought of another way to pack that ring after all these years on the job?" At one point, he even packed a ring himself to demonstrate how things should be done. He left at the end of the shift thinking that he had done an excellent job.

When he arrived on the job Monday afternoon, he was called into the manager's office and the following conversation took place:

Bill Olson:	(manager) Well, John how did it go Friday afternoon?
John:	Just great, Bill. I even showed the men a few new tricks.
Bill:	Oh, what were the men's reactions?
John:	Very positive. They probably learned a lot from watching a "pro" in action.
Bill:	I think that the men had a different reaction than you stated. See this list of grievances. They have been filed against you by the men in the ring mill.
John:	I don't understand.

Questions:

1. Explain John's behavior.
2. If you were Bill, what would you do?

CRITICAL INCIDENT

Kirk Downey is a typist in a university academic department. He is one of the few male typists employed in the college, and he has been there for two months. He was in the Army before attending a business school to become a secretary, and has had no other industrial experience.

Kirk's work has been borderline since entering the department. Carl Anderson, his supervisor, decided to chat with Kirk about his work. After a routine discussion of football and other non-work-related matters, Carl asked Kirk how he felt about his quality and quantity of output during the first two months on the job. Kirk replied, "It's different than in the Army, and I know that my quality and quantity are not up to par with the rest of the secretaries in the department. However, my reason is you! The problem is that you are always shouting and yelling out orders which I cannot understand. When I misinterpret your orders, you shout at me and make me upset for the rest of the day. Therefore, I cannot keep my mind on the job long enough to maintain a high level of secretarial proficiency."

Question:

You are the supervisor, so prepare your reply. You know that you are rather loud and curt with all employees, but this is a part of your personality, and this is your behavioral style.

REFERENCES

1. Drucker, P., *Management: Tasks, Responsibilities, and Practices.* New York: Harper & Row Publishers, 1974.

2. Stogdill, R., "Definitions of Leadership," *Handbook of Leadership.* New York: Free Press, 1974, pp. 7–16.

3. Organ, D., "Social Exchange and Psychological Reactance in a Simulated Superior–Subordinate Relationship," *Organizational Behavior and Human Performance,* 1974, **12**, pp. 132–142.

4. Bavelas, A., A. Hastorf, E. Gross, and W. Kite, "Experiments on the Alteration of Group Structure," *Journal of Experimental Social Psychology,* 1965, **1**, pp. 55–70.

5. French, J., and B. Raven, "The Bases of Social Power," in *Studies in Social Power.* Cartwright, D. (ed.); Ann Arbor, Mich.: Institute for Social Research, 1959, pp. 150–167.

6. Nash, A., "Vocational Interests of Effective Managers: A Review of the Literature," *Personnel Psychology,* 1965, **18,** pp. 21–38. Ghiselli, E., *Explorations in Managerial Talent.* Pacific Palisades, Calif.: Goodyear Rubber Co., 1971.

7. Sank, L., "Effective and Ineffective Managerial Traits Obtained as Naturalistic Descriptions from Executive Members of a Supercorporation," *Personnel Psychology,* 1974, **27,** pp. 423–434.

8. Gibb, C., "Leadership," in *The Handbook of Social Psychology.* 2nd ed. Lindzey, G., and E. Aronson, (eds.). Reading, Mass.: Addison-Wesley Publishing Co., 1969, pp. 205–283.

9. Korman, A., "The Prediction of Managerial Performance: A Review," *Personnel Psychology,* 1968, **21,** pp. 259–322.

10. Harrell, T., *Manager's Performance and Personality.* Cincinnati, Ohio: Southwestern Publishing Co., 1961.

11. Harrell, T., "The Personality of High Earning MBA's in Small Business," *Personnel Psychology,* 1970, **23,** pp. 369–375.

12. Kerr, S., C. Schriesheim, C. Murphy, and R. Stogdill, "Toward a Contingency Theory of Leadership Based upon the Consideration and Initiating Structure Literature," *Organizational Behavior and Human Performance,* 1974, **12,** pp. 62–82.

13. Korman, A., "Consideration, Initiating Structure, and Organizational Criteria: A Review," *Personnel Psychology,* 1966, **19,** pp. 349–362. Fleishman, E., "Twenty Years of Consideration and Structure," in *Current Developments in the Study of Leadership.* Fleishman, E., and J. Hunt (eds.). Carbondale, Ill.: Southern Illinois University Press, 1973, pp. 1–38.

14. Likert, R., *New Patterns of Management.* New York: McGraw-Hill Book Co., 1961.

15. Hill, W., "Leadership Style: Rigid or Flexible," *Organizational Behavior and Human Performance,* 1973, **9,** pp. 35–47. Hill, W., and D. Hughes, "Variations in Leader Behavior as a Function of Task Type," *Organizational Behavior and Human Performance,* 1974, **11,** pp. 83–97.

16. Ritchie, J., "Supervision," in *Organizational Behavior: Research and Issues.* Strauss, G., R. Miles, C. Snow, and A. Tannenbaum, (eds.). Madison, Wisconsin: Industrial Relations Research Association, 1974, p. 65.

17. Fiedler, F., *A Theory of Leadership Effectiveness.* New York: McGraw-Hill Book Co., 1967. "Personality, Motivational Systems and Behavior of High and Low LPC Persons," *Human Relations,* 1972, **25,** pp. 391–412.

18. Hunt, J., "Leadership-style Effects at Two Managerial Levels in a Simulated Organization," *Administrative Science Quarterly,* 1971, **16,** pp. 476–485.

19. Fiedler, F., and M. Chemers, *Leadership and Effective Management.* Glenview, Ill., 1974. Chemers, M. and R. Rice, "A Theoretical and Empirical Examination of Fiedler's Contingency Model of Leadership Effectiveness," in *Contingency Approaches to Leadership.* Hunt, J., and L. Larson (eds.), Carbondale, Ill.: Southern Illinois University Press, 1974, pp. 91–123.

20. Larson, L., and K. Rowland, "Leadership Style and Cognitive Complexity," *Academy of Management Journal,* 1974, **17,** pp. 37–45.

21. Stinson, J., and L. Tracy, "Some Disturbing Characteristics of the LPC Score," *Personnel Psychology,* 1974, **27,** pp. 477–485. Katz, R., and G. Farris, "Does Performance Affect LPC?", unpublished manuscript, Massachusetts Institute of Technology, Cambridge, Mass., 1976.

22. Korman, A., *Industrial and Organizational Psychology.* Englewood Cliffs, N.J.: Prentice-Hall, 1971, p. 129.

23. House, R., "A Path–Goal Theory of Leader Effectiveness," *Administrative Science Quarterly,* 1971, **16,** pp. 321–338. House, R., and T. Mitchell, "Path–Goal Theory of Leadership," *Contemporary Business,* 1974, **3,** pp. 81–98.

24. Downey, H. K., J. Sheridan, and J. Slocum, "The Path–Goal Theory of Leadership: A Longitudinal Analysis," *Organizational Behavior and Human Performance,* 1976, in press. Schriesheim, C., and M. VonGlinow, "Tests of the Path–Goal Theory of Leadership: A Theoretical and Empirical Analysis," unpublished manuscript, Faculty of Administrative Sciences, Ohio State University, 1976.

25. Vroom, V., and A. Jago, "Decision-Making as a Social Process: Normative and Descriptive Models of Leader Behavior," *Decision Sciences,* 1974, **5,** pp. 743–770.

26. Hunt, J., R. Osborn, and L. Larson, *Leadership Effectiveness in Mental Institutions.* Carbondale, Ill.: Technical Report, Department of Administrative Sciences, University of Southern Illinois, 1973, pp. 20–23.

27. Herold, D., "Interaction of Subordinates and Leader Characteristics in Moderating the Consideration–Satisfaction Relationship," *Journal of Applied Psychology,* 1974, **59,** pp. 649–651.

28. Stogdill, R., "Critical Dimensions of Leader–Group Interaction," paper presented at 34th Annual Meeting, Academy of Management, Seattle, Washington, August, 1974. *Handbook of Leadership.* Glencoe, Ill.: The Free Press, 1974.

29. Lawler, E., *Pay and Organizational Effectiveness: A Psychological View.* New York: McGraw-Hill Book Co., 1971.

30. Kerr, S., C. Schriesheim, C. Murphy, and R. Stogdill, "Toward a Theory of Leadership Based upon the Consideration and Initiating Structure Literature," *Organizational Behavior and Human Performance,* 1974, **12,** pp. 62–82.

31. Hellriegel, D., and J. Slocum, "Organizational Climate: Measures, Research, and Contingencies," *Academy of Management Journal,* 1974, **17,** pp. 255–280.

*

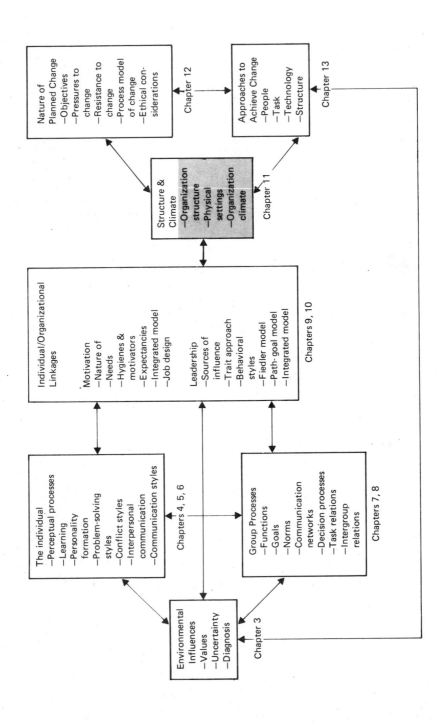

Nature of Planned Change
- Objectives
- Pressures to change
- Resistance to change
- Process model of change
- Ethical considerations

Chapter 12

Approaches to Achieve Change
- People
- Task
- Technology
- Structure

Chapter 13

Structure & Climate
- Organization structure
- Physical settings
- Organization climate

Chapter 11

Individual/Organizational Linkages

Motivation
- Nature of
- Needs
- Hygienes & motivators
- Expectancies
- Integrated model
- Job design

Leadership
- Sources of influence
- Trait approach
- Behavioral styles
- Fiedler model
- Path-goal model
- Integrated model

Chapters 9, 10

The individual
- Perceptual processes
- Learning
- Personality formation
- Problem-solving styles
- Conflict styles
- Interpersonal communication
- Communication styles

Chapters 4, 5, 6

Group Processes
- Functions
- Goals
- Norms
- Communication networks
- Decision processes
- Task relations
- Intergroup relations

Chapters 7, 8

Environmental Influences
- Values
- Uncertainty
- Diagnosis

Chapter 3

11
ORGANIZATION STRUCTURE AND CLIMATE

This chapter focuses on the nature and effects of organizational structure, physical settings, and organizational climates. Thus, the chapter zeroes in on the internal environments of organizations. We need to be concerned with the patterns and design of internal environments because they influence, directly and indirectly, organizational goal attainment, successful relations with the external environment, and member satisfaction and growth.

Several of the topics discussed in this chapter have been introduced in various preceding chapters. Let's review a few of these. In Chapter 3, the change-complexity model of organizational environments was used to demonstrate the need to employ various organizational structures in different environments. For example, when environmental change and complexity are high, complicated structural mechanisms are needed, such as project management and task forces. The alternative profiles of individual and managerial values presented in Chapter 3 also have implications for the types of structures, physical settings, and climates found in organizations. For example, if top management's values are primarily characterized by the profit-maximizing value system, there may be a tendency toward rigid, top-down, and centralized structures. Chapter 8 presented several formal mechanisms for managing intergroup relations, including hierarchy, plans, linking roles, task forces, integrating roles or units, and matrix organizational structure; and climate was implicit in the discussion of job enrichment. Lastly, the Fiedler and path–goal leadership models, that were developed in Chapter 10, considered variations in structure and work-group climates and how these might influence leadership styles and practices.

As this chapter unfolds, we will build on some of the materials presented in earlier chapters. To a certain extent, this chapter emphasizes the impersonal and global aspects of the organization. However, the personal significance of these impersonal dimensions will be addressed, especially in the "case" studies reviewed to illustrate various concepts and approaches, as well as in the discussion of perceived organizational climates. Accordingly, the specific objectives of this chapter are to assist you:

1. To understand the dimensions and differences in organizational structures;

2. To know some of the strategies for designing organizations;

3. To increase your ability to diagnose several key contingencies that influence and should be considered in designing organization structures;

4. To develop insight into impacts that structures can have on organization members;

5. To enhance your awareness of how physical settings in organizations can directly and indirectly influence task accomplishment and member behavior; and

6. To appreciate how organization structures, physical settings, leadership, motivation, and the like can interact together to create different organizational climates.

DESIGNING STRUCTURES

Organization structure refers to the formal systems of communication, authority, and responsibility. This general definition will be made explicit by presenting four strategies for structuring an organization. It needs to be emphasized that these strategies are not mutually exclusive. An organization or one of its units, such as an automobile plant, may utilize all of the strategies for dealing with its different types of problems.

These structural strategies include the bureaucratic model, "autonomous" or self-contained units, vertical information systems, and lateral relations.

BUREAUCRATIC MODEL

To a certain degree, the bureaucratic model is universally employed as a structural strategy by organizations. In everyday usage, the words bureaucracy (or bureaucratic) often conjure up thoughts and feeling of rigidity, incompetence, red tape, inefficiency, and ridiculous rules. Even Webster's dictionary views bureaucracy negatively, by defining it as a system of departments which are managed by officials who follow an inflexible routine. Max Weber, a German scholar who wrote in the early 1900's, used "bureaucratic model" as a scientific tool and frame of reference for evaluating, characterizing, and comparing all types of organizations. It is primarily in this sense that we want to utilize the term bureaucratic model. Most individuals are likely to find a number of the aspects of the formal bureaucratic model reasonable and desirable. Thus, we need to be careful, in discussing the bureaucratic model, to distinguish between the way it should "ideally" function and popular conceptions of the way some large-scale organizations actually operate.

Dimensions

As suggested in Fig. 11–1, there are six major dimensions in the bureaucratic model, including hierarchy of authority, division of labor, rules, procedural specifications, impersonality, and technical competence.[1] The continua are intended to convey the idea that the relative and absolute degree to which the structure of an organization emphasizes each dimension can vary substantially. A single organization or its subsystems (such as an assembly plant, or research and development facility) can also vary in these dimensions. Organization A in Fig. 11–1 would represent a relatively high level of bureaucracy across all dimensions, whereas organization B is much less of a bureaucracy and is more varied in its emphasis on each dimension. For example, organization B is characterized as having a relatively low emphasis on hierarchy of authority but a very high emphasis on technical competence.

It would not be surprising to find an automobile assembly plant illustrative of organization A and a research and development facility illustrative of organization B. This same pattern could also be found if the automobile assembly plant and the research and development facility were part of the same organization, such as General Motors, Ford, or Chrysler.

Let's briefly consider each of these dimensions.

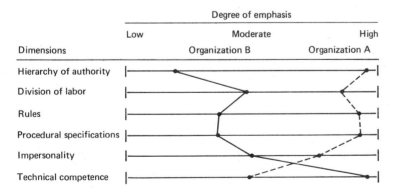

Figure 11–1   Dimensions in the Bureaucratic Model

Hierarchy of Authority.   This refers to the extent to which decision-making is prestructured by the organization and the degree to which participation in decision-making varies in direct relation to one's position level in the hierarchy. Virtually all organizations utilize a hierarchy of authority. Higher-level units or individuals often assign or approve of goals and budgets for lower-level units or individuals. An advertising department may have considerable decision-making discretion over the form and content of the organization's advertising program, but it probably is carried out within certain budget guidelines previously approved from top management.

The hierarchy of authority dimension is sometimes confused with centralization. Centralization, a relative concept, is said to prevail when all major, and possibly many minor, decisions are made only at the very top levels of the organization. In contrast, hierarchy of authority primarily means that there has been a rather complete specification of the decisions that can be made by the individuals occupying the various positions in the organizations. If our advertising department had to have virtually all decisions relating to its advertising program approved by higher management, we might conclude that the organization is highly centralized relative to the advertising function. If the organization simply specifies in detail the types of decisions which can and can't be made by the advertising manager, there exists a hierarchy of authority that could permit considerable discretion. For example, higher management might specify that 40 percent of the advertising dollars should be expended in TV media, 40 percent in magazine media, and 20 percent in newspaper media. The timing and the specific choice of TV stations, magazines, and newspapers are left to be worked out by the advertising department and the firm's advertising agency. In this instance, a number of crucial advertising decisions have been *decentralized* to the advertising department. A final implication of the hierarchy-of-authority dimension is the idea that each higher level has the authority to withdraw any authority that has been delegated to a lower level.

Division of Labor.   This refers to the extent to which the tasks to be performed are subdivided and carried out by different individuals and units. The degree of division of labor is one of the key factors influencing differentiation (see Chapter 8) in organizations. As suggested in the discussion of job enrichment in Chapter 9, there has been recent concern over the high degree of division of labor in organizations, particularly for individuals at lower organizational levels, where many employees perform simple, routine tasks that require virtually no skills. This may have the personal consequences of boredom, indifference, low productivity, and dissatisfaction. While the division of labor may be carried to the point where it becomes dysfunctional for both task accomplishment and employee needs, it remains as a fundamental dimension in all organizations.

A simple example would be a firm with three major functions: marketing, production, and finance. A greater or lesser degree of division of labor might be illustrated by examining some possibilities in the marketing function.

Figure 11–2 shows two hypothetical structures for performing similar marketing functions, each with eight individuals. In the marketing function that shows "low" division of labor, each sales representative may call on three types of customers of the firm (i.e., retailers, wholesalers, and manufacturers), handle all service requests and complaints for their accounts, and be responsible for performing marketing-research tasks. In a case where the marketing function has a "high" division of labor, there has been some attempt to divide certain tasks among several positions. Without going into a discussion of the possible pros and cons of each approach, it should be emphasized that the case showing "high" division of labor could provide challenging and meaningful positions for all of the individuals.

Rules. This dimension refers to the degree to which there are formal written statements specifying acceptable and unacceptable behaviors and decisions by organization members. One of the ironies in the proliferation of rules that attempt to reduce individual discretion is that someone must still exercise discretion as to which rules apply to specific situations. Rules are often associated with negative feelings, and for good reason. In July 1975, New York City was engaged in making substantial layoffs of policemen, firemen, and other city employees. One fireman, who was scheduled to be laid off at 9:00 A.M., had been called to fight a fire at about 8:45 A.M. At approximately 9:05 A.M., the fireman climbed a ladder several times and carried three people out of the fire. As a result, the fireman suffered burns, smoke inhalation, and other personal harm. When it was determined that this rescue took place after 9:00 A.M., the "bureaucracy" concluded he was not, at that time, employed by the city. Thus, he had acted as a "civilian" and was therefore ineligible for medical and other benefits normally available to firemen injured on the job. It is the narrow and ridiculous application of rules, such as in this case, that often results in much resentment among workers. After the news media made the fireman's plight public, the decision to deny benefits was reversed.

Good rules often go unrecognized. The rule that everyone must wear a hard hat on construction sites of high-rise buildings is likely to be universally accepted as a good and necessary rule. Rules designed to prevent or stop favoritism, or nepotism (hiring one's own relatives), and discriminating on irrelevant grounds may often be viewed favorably.

The dual character of rules has been succinctly summarized this way:

> Rules do a lot of things in organizations; they protect as well as restrict; coordinate as well as block; channel effort as well as limit it; permit universalism as well as provide sanctuary for the inept; maintain stability as well as retard change; permit diversity as well as restrict it.[2, p. 32]

Universalism refers to the idea of treating people on the basis of merit or achievement in performing their jobs.

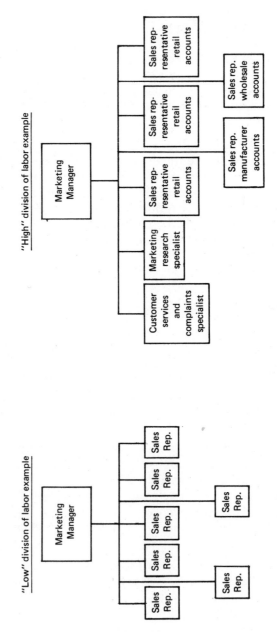

Figure 11-2 "High" versus "Low" Division of Labor for a Marketing Function

There are three final points with respect to organizational rules. First, rules viewed as "bad" today may have been desirable when first formulated. This suggests that rules often need modification to accommodate changing values, tasks, employee abilities, and other circumstances. Second, rules are a means to assist the organization in reaching its goals. When a rule hinders rather than helps goal achievement, it should be eliminated or changed. Third, we need to distinguish whether our common frustration is over the need for rules covering certain behavior and decisions, or over the substance of the rules. It is one thing to argue that there should be no rules covering the layoff of employees. It is quite another to argue whether the rules should emphasize seniority or degree of merit as a basis for layoffs.

Procedural Specifications.   This dimension refers to the degree to which members are expected to follow a predetermined sequence of steps in performing tasks and dealing with problems. Procedural specifications often consist of a number of rules that are to be implemented in a particular sequence. To obtain reimbursement for expenses, the employee must often adhere to a well-defined set of procedures, such as (1) obtaining prior approval for the travel from one's superior; (2) providing hotel and transportation receipts; (3) limiting food expenditures to $12 per day; (4) stating the purpose of the trip and listing the individuals contacted on a travel voucher form; (5) obtaining signatures on the form from the higher levels of management plus the budget officer. Since procedures are substantially made up of rules, they can have many of the same positive or negative features.

In Fig. 11–1, we suggested that an entire organization or its various departments can be generally portrayed as having a low-to-high emphasis on rules and procedures. Within a single organization or department, the utilization of rules and procedures can also vary substantially among task and problem areas. For example, the workers on the assembly line of an automobile plant are required to adhere to well-defined rules and procedures regarding how their work is to be performed and the accompanying safety requirements. In contrast, the professionals in a research and development facility working with radioactive materials may have to adhere to safety rules and procedures that are much more elaborate than those required of the assembly-line workers. But there are likely to be fewer rules and procedures specifying the tasks they are to perform.

Impersonality.   This dimension refers to the extent to which organizational members, as well as outsiders, are treated without regard to certain individual qualities. Of course, individual qualities are considered if they are related to predetermined and specified standards. The ability to pass a physical examination when applying for a position is usually viewed as an appropriate individual quality for assessment. On the other hand, individual qualities such as sex, race, color, creed, or national origin have been formally stated as attributes that are *not* to be used as bases for rejecting an applicant. Organizations, particularly government agencies, are often expected to treat "outsiders" the same, regardless of their personal wealth or position in other organizations. The public, and critics such as Ralph Nader, often decry the favoritism and cronyism found in and between the top officials of some bureaucracies. Max Weber (the seminal writer on bureaucracy) in the early 1900's was also calling for the same thing in the impersonality dimension. He was very concerned over the tendency of some individuals, especially those at high levels, to utilize their positions and organizations for excessive personal gain.

A simple example of a breakdown in the impersonality dimension occurred when a U.S. Senator and his family appeared at the loading gate of a major airline demanding a seat on the plane which was being loaded and was soon to depart for Washington D.C. The ticket agents discovered the U.S. Senator and his family had no tickets; and the flight was already booked to capacity. Nonetheless, the airline agents gave the Senator and his family the needed seats. The airlines officials also knew that the Senator was a powerful member of a congressional committee responsible for legislation affecting the airline industry. Because of the ticket agents' actions, several angry passengers with confirmed tickets were left behind. Many passengers who did board the plane and observed these actions openly criticized the Senator during the flight. The news media also widely reported the incident. The Senator made a public apology, and high airline executives publicly claimed it was not their policy to show such favored treatment. Presumably, the impersonality dimension, for this type of issue, would be widely supported by the public.

Technical Competence.   This dimension refers to the extent to which standards of individual skill and performance are utilized in the selection, retention, demotion, dismissal, or advancement of employees. To the extent that technical competence and achievement, rather than family lineage, friendships, personal loyalties, social class of the individual, and the like, are the primary determinants of one's position, the organization is regarded as "high" on that dimension.

The technical competence and achievement among a limited number of individuals may be difficult to evaluate. To reduce competitive pressures among individuals and to maintain a sense of "impersonality," seniority is often used as a substitute criterion for technical competence, on either a formal or informal basis.[3] Of course, unions are quite explicit (and often adamant) in placing a high emphasis on seniority. The best we can conclude is that seniority may be compatible with technical competence in some cases, and in other cases it may not.

Seven–Eleven as a Bureaucratic Organization

This section provides a personalized account of how the Seven–Eleven organization was perceived as fitting the bureaucratic model to a very high degree. It is based on a discussion by a student, written under the direction of one of the authors, reporting on his experiences as a clerk in one of the Seven–Eleven grocery stores in Florida.[4]

We are aware of the limitations of anecdotal accounts such as this one. In reading this account, try to apply a personalized and concrete sensitivity to the nature of the bureaucratic model in its more extreme form. You should think about how some of the structural arrangements could be functional for the organization in achieving its goals of profit, control, and growth, but dysfunctional for a skilled individual at a low organizational level because of the simplicity and routinization of these jobs.

Becoming an Employee

Technical competence was one of the key elements of the hiring procedure at Seven–Eleven. A battery of standardized tests was administered, and each employee was expected to fulfill a set number of company qualifications. These varied from previous work experience to avowals of never having used "hard drugs" and not having shoplifted more than twenty-five dollars' worth of merchandise during one's life. To illustrate the degree to which the management ensured "organizationally defined" competence, part of the hiring procedure included a polygraph test to verify the factuality of portions of the personal information submitted. Of course, there is research suggesting polygraphs are not nearly as accurate as believed by some individuals.

Impersonality was tied to technical competence in the hiring procedure. While one's personality was a partial consideration in obtaining a clerical position, it was evaluated as impersonally as possible through standardized tests and successful fulfillment of standard requirements. The requirement of sound personal health was assessed by a physical examination that finally determined one's fitness for a position in the Seven–Eleven organization.

In line with procedural specifications, each employee was then introduced to his or her district supervisor. This wasted little time in acquainting an employee with who the main boss would be during the period of employment and what the written rules of the organization were. The supervisor explained how rules would guide a clerk's job performance (" . . . *a clerk shall wear . . . a clerk shall always report on time* . . . "), and how obedience to the rules is required in order to perform a good job. The entire organization was heavily rule-oriented and the rules were used to control the employees' behavior.

A clear chain of command existed throughout the hiring and orientation process of clerks. The most important questions to be considered, such as my fitness for membership in the organization, were left to be answered by higher management. The final referral was to the store manager who had been entrusted to guide and train clerks, a task not requiring the expertise or time of someone located in top management.

Working in the Organization

In fulfilling the duties of clerk, I encountered many applications of the bureaucratic model. Rules existed for washing the floor (including the cleaning agents to be employed) and the frequency of waxing. Rules existed limiting the amount of money allowed in the register at any one time, the denominations of this cash, and the denominations of bills employees were allowed to accept from customers. The effective operation of the store seemed to be determined by properly tabulating how closely the rules were being met, which were believed to lead to high profits.

There was one particularly revealing example of the organization's reliance on rules for meeting its end goals. Once a month the store would receive a promotional packet from its district headquarters, alerting the store manager to the company marketing plans and promotions for the coming month. This packet came complete with promotional banners, window displays, and other needed materials. Rather than giving the store manager the discretion to use the materials as he or she saw fit, the packet came complete with a store diagram of the front windows, presenting the predetermined positioning of banners upon particular glass sections. In-store banners came with similar diagrams, commanding where they were to be displayed.

While tying into the bureaucratic model's concept of rules for limiting the behavior of the employees, this one example also touches on the model's concept of hierarchy. Greater discretion was exercised by those in power above, with the decisions being implemented by employees located in the hierarchy below.

This great use of rules in organizing the workplace helped contribute to another concept of the bureaucratic model—the division of labor. Because the clerk position was so controlled by rules, the amount of decision-making required of an individual in that position was quite low. Anyone capable of learning and following the rules would be able to perform an adequate job in the workplace. The job was reduced to a form that required no great skills, nor any great level of training. The following incident dramatically illustrates the high division of labor.

Once a week the store would receive its grocery order from the warehouse. Groceries came into the store prepriced, ready to be placed directly on the shelves. While this may have been done because many items were ordered in less than case quantities for each store, it also served to simplify the running of the store, thus dividing the otherwise required labor among more individuals. Night-shift clerks were given responsibility for leaving the store clean, making a final sales reading for the day, depositing the day's receipts, and ensuring that shelves were well stocked for the following day's business. The day-shift clerks, on the other hand, were responsible for compiling the weekly orders, checking and storing the orders as they arrived, and making price changes on items as the need arose. While these particular responsibilities were assigned according to time availability and need, they still display the clear markings of a division of labor.

One of the reasons the rules led to the desired employee behavior appeared to be the threat of a polygraph test. Store inventories took place every four to seven weeks. Inventory day was the "day of reckoning." It revealed where shortages existed; and if shortages were above a predetermined level, all employees would be required to take a polygraph test. Even when they were not guilty of stealing, there seemed to be a high level of anxiety among store employees who feared the finger of guilt might erroneously point toward them. This singular threat had the employees highly aware of their individual behavior in any area that could affect inventory or shed some light on the misapplication of the organization's rules. Bad produce and damaged items were almost religiously recorded on the store write-off list, as were inventory items used within the store.

As each employee had already encountered one polygraph test in the hiring procedure, the likelihood of a second test for a large cash shortage or inventory shortage was accepted as the likely procedure for the organization to follow. Not only did the polygraph act to ensure the proper enforcement of rules; it also reinforced the impersonality of the entire organization. When shortages occurred above a given level, all members of the store who could have played some part in the shortage were required to answer questions while on the polygraph. In fact, there was much talk about several managers who had lost their jobs because of their personal involvement in inventory shortages, showing the rule's universal application to all involved.

It was startling to witness the degree to which the hierarchy of authority of the bureaucratic model would be followed as long as the rules of the organization were being met. A case in point involves the rules and procedures employees were required to follow after an armed robbery. Having learned the "proper procedure" in the training period for dealing with a robbery ("... *Give them the money; do not resist ... Lock the front door behind them ... Call the police ... Call your manager ...*"), I began to wonder how far up in the hierarchy it would be necessary to be to personally report the details of this occurrence. Having given the police the information they required, the manager instructed me to immediately write out a report of what happened, how much I thought was stolen, date the paper, and sign my name. As a result of following this procedure correctly, I was never required to issue an oral report or answer directly to any member of higher authority in the Seven–Eleven organization. Even the supervisor never questioned me directly about the robbery, making notice of its occurrence only in his remarks that he was glad to hear I was not hurt.

Leaving the Organization

The procedures for leaving the organization were explained prior to the first day of work. The organization required a written, two weeks' notice prior to departure. There would also be a hold on the final paycheck to make sure there were no outstanding debts (store grocery bills unpaid, possible involvement in register or inventory shortages, or unreturned uniforms).

According to procedures, I very carefully filed the letter of resignation with the supervisor two weeks prior to the last day on which I expected to work.

The final week of work coincided with part of the supervisor's vacation. If there had been well-defined rules for dealing with this situation, there should not have been any difficulties. However, as clearly defined rules could not be found by the substituting supervisor, a lack of complete utilization of the bureaucratic model did allow a problem to occur.

The pay period fell every two weeks at the Seven–Eleven Stores, on a one-week delayed basis. Thus, one would work three weeks before receiving the first two weeks' pay. My last week of work coincided with a two-week pay period and, according to the rules, I expected to receive this next-to-last paycheck. When pay day arrived, however, my check was not forwarded to the store and, to my mind, the rules of the organization had been broken. I contacted the substitute supervisor to explain my problem and reported the immediate need of the check to cover expenses in preparing to return to school. He apologetically informed me that the check had been purposely withheld to fulfill the requirement of holding the last check while the company reviewed my accounts for any unpaid debts. As my next check would have been only one week's pay, he said the "company" likes to hold onto the larger of the two checks. Personally, I believe this was merely his personal interpretation of the existing rule; he did not desire to make use of his personal discretion as a supervisor while substituting in someone else's district. I state this rather assuredly because, within a single day of my contact, the two-week paycheck was made available. Since the organization was very rule-oriented, I do not believe the check would have been provided so quickly if it was the stated policy to withhold "two weeks'" pay, rather than the *final* check, as I was originally told. Bureaucratic rules were involved in this area of conflict. Yet a full application of the bureaucratic concept of clearly defined rules would have removed the conflict surrounding the interpretation of the "final paycheck."

As I "retired," a new worker was hired, according to the rules and procedural specifications of the organization, with an absolute minimum of conflict and uncertainty.

Conditions for Effectiveness

Apparently, the Seven–Eleven organization has successfully applied, with a relatively high degree of emphasis, the dimensions of the bureaucratic model to its lower organizational levels. Cases such as this, and other more systematic research studies, have suggested that a relative high degree of application of the bureaucratic model may be associated with organizational effectiveness under certain conditions.[5] A consideration of the more detailed aspects of different versions of the bureaucratic model is beyond our scope.[6] Some of the contingencies that seem to be compatible with a high emphasis on the bureaucratic model for an organization or one or more of its subsystems include: (1) routine tasks that are not highly difficult or changing; (2) a relatively simple and unchanging external environment; (3) an employee and management group whose values and attitudes are compatible or neutral toward the "requirements" of the bureaucratic model; and (4) a well-defined technology that can be simple (as in the Seven–Eleven stores) or somewhat more complex (as on the assembly line of an automobile plant).

Research has suggested that certain patterns of structure are associated with organizational effectiveness under specific conditions. However, this research also implies that there is considerable discretion available to the people in organizations in designing, shaping, and modifying their structures.[7] In addition to designing the structure of an organization by applying the dimensions of the bureaucratic model in varying degrees, there are several additional strategies (that can be utilized along with the bureaucratic model) for structuring an organization. These strategies include "autonomous" or self-contained units, creation of lateral relations, and vertical information systems.[8]

"AUTONOMOUS" OR SELF-CONTAINED UNITS

This strategy for structuring an organization or its subunits involves designing units so that they consist of virtually all of the resources and skills needed to produce a specific output and/or serve a particular geographic area or clientèle. Several aspects of "autonomous" or self-contained units were presented in Chapter 7, in our discussion of work-group autonomy (see Fig. 7–8). The consequences of this structural strategy include: fewer decision problems are referred up the hierarchy and less information is transferred up in the hierarchy; less integration is needed between different units, because almost all of the resources required to create a given output are located within one unit; and the members of the units usually have clearly defined goals, can readily perceive these goals, and are probably subject to less division of labor. The concepts within the strategy of "autonomous" or self-contained units are quite similar to the concepts within job enrichment—only now tasks and goals are being allocated to a group of people rather than to a single individual.

Volvo's Use of "Autonomous" or Self-Contained Units

Volvo is one of the more dramatic examples of a firm that has made some substitution of the autonomous or self-contained unit strategy for the bureaucratic strategy.[9] In one of its plants, 600 employees have been divided into teams of 15 to 25 members each. This is in contrast to situations where the 600 employees would be performing a few simple tasks repeatedly along a conveyor belt. Each team ("autonomous" or self-contained unit) is responsible for assembling a complete part of the car, such as the electrical system, steering and controls, instrumentation, brakes and wheels. These teams work in areas that are self-contained, with their own entrances, changing rooms, and relaxation areas.

336 Organization Structure and Climate

Within the limits of being able to complete their assigned parts of the assembled car, the teams can decide for themselves how the work will be done, including who will do which jobs. To increase familiarity with each operation in a team, members are encouraged to rotate jobs. While the teams are responsible for attaining output goals (such as 20 electrical systems assembled, of acceptable quality, per day), they have some control over the pace at which they work. This is possible because the area between each team is used for storing inventory. As long as a team has at least three completed units in inventory ready for the next team, the team can vary its work rate as it pleases. One of the motivating forces for trying the self-contained unit strategy was the high rate of turnover and absenteeism being experienced by Volvo, especially in 1969 when it reached 52 percent. Since these changes, there has been a substantial decline in turnover and absenteeism.

The self-contained unit strategy was also implemented in the higher managerial levels of the firm in 1972. In stages, Volvo has gone from a functional to a divisional structure while also pushing decentralization. Headquarters personnel consist of ten staff units reporting directly to a five-person executive committee, for a total of about 100 individuals. This contrasts with the 1,700 individuals at headquarters before the changes, most of whom were reassigned within the divisions. Volvo has established profit centers within its four divisions, with a high degree of independence for attaining specific objectives.

Conditions for Effectiveness

Several of the potential *limitations* with the self-contained unit strategy include:

1. A possibility of reduced expertise, because members of each unit must have skills in more areas (e.g., engineers do their own computer programming rather than go to a programmer for assistance);

2. A possibility that some economies of scale and efficiencies in utilizing equipment will be lost (e.g., a small Xerox machine in each department rather than one more economical and faster Xerox machine to be used by all departments);

3. A possibility of increased costs due to higher levels of inventory between units (in the previous Volvo example, inventories were maintained between each team);

4. A possibility that a high level of integration and day-to-day problem-solving between units is necessary for the accomplishment of objectives.

If these limitations or problems are not severe or can be offset by other advantages, the self-contained unit strategy might be quite effective. From a more positive point of view, self-contained units often serve to (1) reduce the amount of interaction and communication flowing between departments and thereby reduce manpower and other costs; and (2) enhance employees' desire to achieve and other forms of motivation by providing somewhat greater discretion and identifiable goals.

CREATION OF LATERAL RELATIONS

As a design strategy, the various formal mechanisms for facilitating lateral relations serve to reduce the amount of information and problems that need to be referred up the hierarchy. This simultaneously increases the probability that those individuals with the relevant expertise will be involved in decision-making. As with self-contained units, lateral relations may increase the capability of a larger number of individuals to make decisions, particularly those of an unstructured nature.[10]

In Chapter 8, the main types of formal lateral relations were addressed in the discussion of mechanisms for managing intergroup relations (see especially Fig. 8–5). The structural mechanisms included hierarchy, plans, linking roles, task forces, integrating roles or units, and matrix organization. Thus, a rereading of this section in Chapter 8 may be appropriate. The following case serves to illustrate the informal lateral relation of direct contact and the formal lateral mechanisms of integrator role, task force, and integrating unit.

Hershey Foods Use of Lateral Relations

In previous chapters, a number of examples and concepts associated with formal lateral relations have been presented. This section will serve to provide a specific example of how a variety of lateral mechanisms can be utilized by a single department. It is based on a paper prepared under the direction of one of your authors.[11]

The setting is the Environmental Affairs Department of the Hershey Foods Corporation, located in Hershey, Pennsylvania. This department was formed in 1969 to deal with in-plant and community pollution detection and abatement. Let's identify some of the forms of lateral relations for the unit.

The most basic and common form of lateral relation employed was probably one of direct contact. The manager of the Environmental Affairs Department had direct contact with the managers of quality assurance, project engineering and construction, product and process development, and drafting and planning.

A second lateral mechanism was task forces. An example of their use occurred when a problem developed with the internal plant water-pipe system. There were no existing complete and updated drawings of the entire system, so that maintenance personnel were not sure what the system looked like, or what effects it was having on internal and the external environments. A task force was set up that included employees from several departments and an external consultant. This task force drafted a complete, revised and updated map of the plant's water-pipe system. Upon completion of this task, the group was disbanded and members returned to their previous departments.

A third type of lateral mechanism was that of an integrator role. This role was occupied by a Senior Section Leader. He was a founding member of the Environmental Affairs Department and had a close and trusting relationship with all of its members. His role involved the coordination of the subdepartments of Noise and Solid Waste, Water Management, Air Management, and Fish Studies. Although he didn't make the decisions for the subdepartments, he did try to see that the best overall decisions were made. This was accomplished by sharing and translating the nature and significance of the findings from one unit to another and by conducting joint meetings in a manner so that the "big picture" was always kept before the subdepartments.

A fourth lateral mechanism employed was a managerial integrating committee called the Environmental Control Committee. It was comprised of the following members; Director of Personnel (Chairman); Manager, Environmental Affairs; Safety Administrator; and Corporate Medical Director. The committee operated directly under the President of the Hershey Foods Corporation. It recommended specific actions to appropriate department heads and prepared programs of capital improvement to ensure safe, healthful, working conditions for all employees. This committee was involved early in the decision-making process and influenced the budgets of other corporate departments.

Conditions for Effectiveness

As suggested in Chapter 8, it may be desirable to utilize lateral mechanisms to a greater extent as the degrees of uncertainty, differentiation between departments, and desired integration (coordination) between departments increase. From this perspective, lateral relations are considered desirable because they facilitate the accomplishment of organizational goals. Even if short-term organizational goal accomplishment would not improve through lateral relations, they are sometimes recommended as a partial substitute for the bureaucratic model because of their ability to enhance certain human needs and values such as self-actualization and participation. From this perspective, lateral relations can also be effective because they should: (1) enable wider participation by organizational members in decision-making and thereby reduce the use of centralized hierarchies; (2) give some emphasis to mutual confidence, trust, and interaction as integrating forces in the organization, rather than position-based authority; and (3) enhance the growth of members toward greater shared and individual responsibility and self-control, rather than external and imposed controls.[12]

VERTICAL INFORMATION SYSTEMS

The last strategy for structuring an organization that we will consider is vertical information systems. For the most part, this strategy is concerned with the application of computers and related information technology to perform tasks that might also be carried out through the other structural strategies, including bureaucracy, self-contained units, and lateral relations. Of course, vertical information systems are often used in conjunction with these other strategies. As with the other structural strategies, vertical information systems can serve the basic functions of communication, problem-solving (particularly for well-structured and routine problems), and control.

Since the late 1950's, there has been considerable controversy over the organizational implications of the new vertical information systems, particularly computer-based information systems. On the one hand, predictions and research have suggested that the organizational impacts of computer-based information systems include: (1) greater centralization; (2) fewer departments and levels in the organization; (3) worker displacement; (4) downgrading and reduction of middle managers; and (5) the rapid and early takeover of the solving and control of well-structured problems.[13]

On the other hand, predictions and research have also suggested that the effects of computer-based information systems on organizations include: (1) greater opportunity to decentralize the decision-making process by providing lower organizational levels with the information necessary to make decisions; (2) relief from the boredom of performing dull and repetitive tasks; (3) greater opportunity to engage in creative thinking; and (4) the enlargement and upgrading of jobs.[14]

British Petroleum Use of Vertical Information Systems

Since computer-based information systems are most often associated with centralization in the organization and we will give a research example of this in Chapter 13, we thought a case to the contrary would be appropriate here. The case study focuses on British Petroleum, a large international oil firm that has made extensive use of computer-based information systems. The specific incident focuses on the investment planning model utilized by British Petroleum. This model provides information that aids in making decisions about capital investments. Before computerized systems were installed, the information needed to make effective capital decisions could only be brought together in corporate headquarters. When the model was computerized, regional coordinators were allowed to exercise greater discretion over investments than before. Moreover, subsidiaries and associate companies were given greater responsibility for planning, since they now had access to the accurate and timely information provided by the computerized models. Since the many environments of the units in British Petroleum are apparently complex and changing, this seems to have been a creative design configuration.[15]

Conditions for Effectiveness

Modern information systems have been effectively utilized in virtually all levels and types of organizations for a variety of tasks. The most extensive use of computer-based information systems is probably with organizations that have massive volumes of data to process in a repetitive fashion. These would be illustrated by financial institutions, like banks and insurance companies, and government agencies, such as the Internal Revenue Service and the Social Security Administration.[16] It has been claimed that if the information technology employed by the Bell Telephone System in 1900 were utilized today it would require over 100 million telephone operators alone. One can only imagine what the organizational structure of the Bell System would look like.

In a review of the literature on computers and organization structure, Robey concludes: " ... (1) computers do not cause changes in the degree of delegation; (2) computerized systems are sufficiently flexible to facilitate either centralized or decentralized structures; and (3) the degree of delegation in these studies is related to task environmental conditions of the organizations studied."[17, p. 1] He found a consistent pattern. Under stable environmental conditions, the introduction of computer-based information systems seemed to be followed by centralization of decision-making. Under dynamic environmental conditions, the computer systems reinforced or increased decentralization in decision-making.

INTEGRATION AND ENVIRONMENTAL IMPACT

We have presented four strategies for structuring an organization, bureaucracy, "autonomous" or self-contained units, lateral relations, and vertical information systems. These strategies are often used in combination with one another in a single organization. Brief applications of each strategy were presented and some of the conditions under which they might be effectively utilized were noted. While our treatment has been brief, it has tried to be consistent with the following theme expressed by Drucker:

> ... in designing organizations, we have to choose among different structures, each stressing a different dimension and each, therefore, with distinct costs, specific and fairly stringent requirements, and real limitations. There is no risk-free organization structure. And a design that is the best solution for one task may be only one of a number of equally poor alternatives for another task, and just plain wrong for yet a third kind of work.[18, pp. 50–51]

Figure 11–3 provides a general framework for providing an integrated overview of a number of our previous comments, as well as reemphasizing possible relationships between the external (and/or internal) environment of an organization and/or its various units. In the lefthand column, four general types of external (and/or internal) environments are identified. These environ-

| External (and/or internal) environments | Design strategies | | | |
	Bureaucratic model	"Autonomous" or self-contained unit	Vertical information systems	Lateral relations
Static, simple	Moderate to high	Low	Low processing emphasis; low control emphasis	Low
Static, complex	High	Moderate to high	High processing emphasis; high control emphasis	Low
Dynamic, simple	Moderate	Moderate	Moderate processing emphasis; moderate control emphasis	Moderate
Dynamic, complex	Low to moderate	Moderate	High processing emphasis; low control emphasis	High

Figure 11–3 Relative Emphasis on Four Design Strategies Within Four Environments for Organizational Effectiveness

ments are based on the change–complexity model presented in Chapter 3 (see Fig. 3–2). You will recall that this model consisted of two dimensions—the degree-of-change dimension (ranging from static to dynamic) and the degree-of-complexity dimension (ranging from simple to complex). The lefthand column of Fig. 11–3 consists of the four extreme combinations derived from these two dimensions. Across the top of the figure, the four design strategies discussed are identified. To develop a more integrated view of each of these strategies and their possible combined pattern of usage within a single organization (and/or unit), we have presented the degree of utilization or emphasis on each strategy that should probably exist in the four extreme "environments." The degree of emphasis is simply identified as varying from low to moderate to high. It is also suggested that the pattern of emphasis on the four structural strategies in organizations (or units) with the different environments could represent effective combinations in the ways of structuring an organization. Of course, conflicting research in the area of organization structure permits modifications in these conclusions and interpretations.

A word or so is in order about the degree of emphasis on vertical information systems, particularly in terms of the role and the impact of computer-based information systems. The emphasis on vertical information systems is considered in terms of two dimensions. The first refers to the degree of emphasis on processing information and data, and the second dimension refers to the extent to which it is used for purposes of organizational control. In the first instance, computer information systems are little more than a tool of the users, while in the other instance they serve in the capacity of "managing" organizational members. For example, the programs in the computer systems may provide signals to individuals indicating when certain tasks should be performed, or provide feedback signals indicating whether certain tasks have been properly performed.

PHYSICAL SETTINGS

In recent years, there has been increasing recognition of the often "hidden," but significant, impacts that physical settings can have on organizational behavior. As suggested in Chapter 6, physical settings can serve as a powerful form of nonverbal communications. The physical environment may be supportive, neutral, or a hindrance in relation to various functions. As illustrated by the assembly line, "efficiency" experts have long been involved with creating physical layouts that were intended to optimize the flow of materials, arrangement of machines, and sequencing of tasks. While the goal of these efficiency experts has been noble, they have been prone to assume that (1) a physical setting has a limited function, such as moving paper or goods from one spot to another; (2) the higher-level needs of people working in these settings are not an important design consideration; (3) physical settings should control people rather than enhance (or at least not dampen) opportunities for the realization of intrinsic motivations; or (4) only a narrow range of physical factors like temperature and lighting affect organization members.

It is often concluded, as in Herzberg's dual-factor theory of motivation discussed in Chapter 9, that physical settings do not motivate. Moreover, individuals in organizations often do not think of their physical settings as influencing their work motivation. However, physical settings may influence a variety of functions and may often be a necessary condition, even if an insufficient condition, for optimal work motivation and achievement. This position will become clearer in a consideration of the possible functions of physical settings.

Functions of Physical Settings

Steele has developed a relatively simple, but insightful system for categorizing the functions of physical settings.[19] Physical settings in one's immediate environment may be diagnosed in terms of six functions, including security, social contact, symbolic identification, task instrumentality, pleasure, and growth. As suggested in Fig. 11–4, a particular physical setting and its constituent parts may vary from highly positive, to neutral, to highly negative, in serving each of these functions. A complete diagnosis of one's immediate physical setting requires breaking it down into subparts and assessing each subpart in terms of the six functions. For an office worker, this could include walls, floor, furniture, machines, other people in the immediate area, arrangements of chairs and desks, relative location of offices, and social factors such as norms as to who may use a physical setting and how it is to be used.

A "positive" response to the questions in Fig. 11–4 cannot necessarily be interpreted as "good" or desirable. A setting may promote so much social contact that it is difficult for members to obtain privacy when needed or focus on tasks requiring periods of quiet and concentration. While the components of the setting may have a positive influence on certain functions, they may also be regarded as relatively unimportant. For example, an individual whose job is to perform routine tasks may find that working in a quiet setting by himself or herself (which could be desirable for purposes of concentration) is quite irritating and boring.

Security Function.   The security function corresponds directly with the physiological and safety needs in Maslow's need hierarchy (see Chapter 9). This function refers to the degree of unwanted physical and psychological stimuli in the physical surroundings.

Since passage of the Occupational Safety and Health Act in 1970 and the Coal Mine Health and Safety Act in 1969, many organizations have been required by the federal government to increase the amount of attention they give to the security function. The reaction to this legislation and its enforcement has ranged from regarding it as inadequate and poorly implemented, to

Functions	Assessment		
	Positive	Neutral	Negative
Security			
1. Does the setting provide protection from physical and psychological stresses?	+3 +2 +1	0	−1 −2 −3
2. Can you "withdraw" and secure privacy when necessary?	+3 +2 +1	0	−1 −2 −3
Social Contact			
3. Does the setting permit or encourage interaction between individuals?	+3 +2 +1	0	−1 −2 −3
4. Does the setting permit or promote the mobility of individuals?	+3 +2 +1	0	−1 −2 −3
Symbolic Identification			
5. Does the setting suggest images about the degree of emphasis on formal positional power?	+3 +2 +1	0	−1 −2 −3
6. Does the setting convey whether people can modify or "tailor" some- what the settings to their own desires?	+3 +2 +1	0	−1 −2 −3
Task Instrumentality			
7. Does the setting help in performing physical tasks (like typing or machine operation)?	+3 +2 +1	0	−1 −2 −3
8. Does the setting help in performing interactional tasks (like group prob- lem solving)?	+3 +2 +1	0	−1 −2 −3
9. Does the setting help in performing internal tasks (like thinking or con- centrating)?	+3 +2 +1	0	−1 −2 −3
Pleasure			
10. Does the setting provide a sense of gratification (rather than only serving as a means to some end)?	+3 +2 +1	0	−1 −2 −3
11. Does the setting provide stimuli that influence a sense of enjoyment?	+3 +2 +1	0	−1 −2 −3
Growth			
12. Does the setting promote learning new skills?	+3 +2 +1	0	−1 −2 −3
13. Does the setting promote feedback and understanding about the results of members' actions?	+3 +2 +1	0	−1 −2 −3

Figure 11–4   Simplified Framework for Diagnosing One's Physical Setting

Adapted and modified from: Steele, F. I., *Physical Settings and Organization Development,* Reading, Mass.: Addison-Wesley Publishing Co., 1973, pp. 96–99. Used with permission.

considering it excessive and too rigidly enforced. Regardless of personal feelings about the need for this legislation, there has been a greater emphasis since 1970 on the security function in organizations.[20]

Social Contact Function.   This dimension refers to the extent to which the setting promotes or hinders interaction of a social or interpersonal nature. Social contact is often influenced by the way facilities are arranged (chairs bolted to the floor, versus movable ones, in the classroom), the relative locations of facilities and people (social and friendship groups often thrive in direct relation to their physical proximity to one another), and the extent to which individuals are allowed (or required) to move around. Mobility of workers and social contact can also be affected by the technology employed. Workers on the automobile assembly line may not develop meaningful social groups because they are tied to the steady movement of the belt in one location. The noise on the line also may not permit interaction with other nearby workers. On the other hand, in some automated chemical process plants, the workers are freer to move about and interact with others because they are primarily engaged in monitoring of equipment and maintenance tasks.[21]

Symbolic Identification Function.   This function refers to the extent to which the setting allows employees to perceive certain things about the organization's structure, its interpersonal processes, and other individuals. Physical settings are often used to symbolize the relative status of individuals in the formal structure.[22] There are numerous physical elements utilized as status indicators. Figure 11–5 vividly illustrates these status indicators in operation by comparing the president's and vice presidential offices at the headquarters of the Ohio Bell Telephone Company in Cleveland, Ohio.[23] In this example, status differences in the offices occurred in quality, amount, and variety. There was little question about the "seat" with the greatest formal organization status. These and other status differences had been carefully designed and considered throughout the building when it was first occupied.

A number of organizations, including parts of the Bell Telephone system (as indicated by the example in Chapter 9; see Fig. 9–13), have recently tried to reduce the tendency of narrowly lock-stepping hierarchical levels with differences in physical environments. These extreme differentiations might serve to hinder task accomplishment by directing an employee's motivation more toward reaching for physical symbols than for the attainment of organizational goals.

Task Instrumentality.   This dimension refers to the extent to which the setting promotes or hinders the performance of physical, interactional, or mental (internal to people) activities necessary to achieve organizational goals. Some of the obvious elements in a setting that are likely to affect physical activities are the size of the workplace, the quality of materials, temperature, humidity, noise, and air quality. Interaction activities are likely to be somewhat in-

Figure 11–5   Some Status Indicators in the Executive Offices of Ohio Bell

Indicators	President's office	Vice presidential offices
Room size	Huge	About ½ size of President's office
Floor	Parquet wood and oriental rug	Wall-to-wall carpeting
Windows	Two window walls with direct view of Lake Erie	One window wall with angled view of Lake Erie
Chair	High back to rest neck; padded	Padded and comfortable
Desk	Huge and decorative and luxurious	Smaller, but nice
Fixtures	Button to open and close drapes, plus rheostat to control lighting level	Pull rope to open and close drapes, plus switch to turn lights off and on
Furniture	Luxurious; many pieces plus liquor cabinet	Nice, fewer pieces; no liquor cabinet
Bathroom	Shower; sink with cabinet, large mirror, toilet; decorative wall covering	Sink, toilet; painted walls
Entrance	Huge and decorative entry; door at end of hall	Smaller and plainer; doors along side of hall

fluenced by the distance between individuals or work areas, size of the area (too small or too large), noise conditions, and the opportunity to flexibly alter or move locations or work areas. Finally, physical settings can help or hinder the performance of tasks taking place *within* individuals (thinking, reflecting, associating, reading, etc.).

Pleasure Function.   The pleasure function refers to the extent to which individuals receive a sense of gratification or aesthetic satisfaction from the space itself. While the pleasure function appears to be infrequently considered in the design of manufacturing facilities, a number of large companies, when designing new corporate headquarters, have explicitly recognized it. The following description of the world headquarters for E. R. Squibb (near Princeton, New Jersey) which opened in 1972, provides a sense of this.

A hill-hugging complex comprised of seven buildings, incorporating 11 modules in a campus-like setting, complete with manmade lake, extensive exterior and interior landscaping, parking lots that are convenient while almost hidden from view, and abundant design and systems innovations for working effectiveness . . . Environmentally the offices make liberal use of live plants, bright colors, natural sunlight ... Expanses of glass in walkways and the spectacular lobby and the vertical sweep of the stairways here linking floor to floor, give each worker a greater sense of his relationship to the whole. He is not "filed away" as in some anonymous urban high-rise; he is part of an organization—and he sees it.[24, p. 21]

Growth Function.   This function refers to the extent to which the setting promotes (or retards) individual development in the form of new skills, greater self-insight, improved understanding, and the like. Forces in a setting facilitating growth include: encouraging contact with others; enabling individuals to see how things work; providing feedback on the consequences of their actions (knowledge of results); changeability to meet different purposes; and the like. While individuals are likely to vary in their tendency to grow in different settings, there tends to be a curvilinear relationship between physical settings and growth. Growth may be optimal when the stimulation from the setting is neither too low nor so high that the individual feels overwhelmed.[25] One generalized conclusion about the growth and other functions is the realization that individual differences (such as values, problem-solving styles, motivation orientations, attitudes) can result in differences being perceived about a given setting.[26]

Relationships Between Functions.   Most of the preceding discussion has considered each function of the physical setting separately. In practice, these functions are all operating simultaneously. In some situations they may be complementary to one another, while in other cases they may be competing. In the design of physical settings, trade-offs between functions are often necessary. There may also be high economic costs associated with satisfying one or more functions. For those expressing opposition to the Occupational Safety and Health Act and its enforcement, a common theme is that the economic costs of compliance are felt to exceed the possible benefits.

The following example is intended to provide a more personal and "holistic" sensitivity for the functions of physical settings in operation. After you read this section, it may be beneficial to refer again to Fig. 11–4 and undertake a diagnosis of a setting in which you have been employed. This should serve to increase your awareness and provide possible insight as to why certain events occurred and how the physical setting might be improved.

A Frito-Lay Plant's Physical Setting

This analytical case study of the functions of physical settings is adapted from a paper written under the direction of one of the authors.[27] It is based on a student's perceptions (as a summer employee, over two years) at a Frito-Lay snack-food processing plant. This plant manufactured Cheetos, Munchos, and three varieties of Doritos Corn Chips. During the first summer of employment, the firm started a major plant expansion that was completed by the time the student returned the second summer. There will be a number of comparisons made with respect to the changes in the physical setting.

Security

With respect to stressfulness in physical settings, part of the Frito-Lay plant had substantial noise and heat. Without a major change in technology, it is doubtful that much could be done about the noise created by the packaging machines closing and sealing the product into plastic bags. Besides, one unconsciously tended to tune it out and not really be aware of the noise. As for the heat problem, which was especially bad in the summer, the firm constructed a wall during the plant expansion to divide the kitchen area from the packaging area. Holes were cut in this new wall for the conveyor belts that carried the cooked product to the packaging machines.

This dividing wall brought about a variety of changes in the physical setting. First, it separated the production department into distinct areas. Workers in the packaging area were no longer distracted by what was happening in the kitchen, and vice versa. Each section was enclosed in its own unique setting, instead of being scattered over one large production floor. The wall not only helped to control the excess heat given off by the gas jets in the kitchen, but made it possible for the packaging area to be air-conditioned. The people in the kitchen apparently accepted and were accustomed to working in the heat. Workers in the packaging side, who were predominantly women, seemed quite happy with the changes.

Social Contact

Social contact was illustrated by the location of the bulletin board on the wall in the packaging area. Job openings (up for bid) and the daily production schedules for each product line were always posted on it. It was a natural gathering place for workers and managers alike. Unfortunately, it was located along an aisle and people who stopped to read would block forklift traffic into the shipping warehouse.

The only really good setting for informal contact was the self-service cafeteria, which was moved from the front office area to make room for more office space. It was reconstructed exactly as it had been and was relocated in a corner of the receiving department's warehouse. This new place brought it into a more central part of the plant. The cafeteria had many small movable tables and chairs that allowed people to sit together in any groupings they chose. It was here that informal groups really seemed to operate. Employees picked up a lot of information about plant operations, especially from listening to maintenance men who were able to move freely about the plant.

Mobility is a crucial aspect of social contact. Frito-Lay's technology produced a whole range of physical mobility. Just within the packaging area, the packers were virtually tied to their tables trying to keep pace with the packaging machines. The operators, who ran the machines, were able to move about and talk with each other. As long as operators could see their machines or were in shouting distance of another operator who could operate them, they were free to wander about while their machines ran smoothly unattended. In the kitchen, physical mobility was even greater. Each product line was automated. Thus, the operators primarily made routine checks on temperature and seasoning from time to time. This allowed them free movement within their own area as well as the mobility to talk with the machine operators in the packaging area.

Symbolic Identification

Symbolically, the most impressive change in the physical setting was external. When driving into the parking lot the second summer looking for a job, one was overwhelmed by the massive new storage facilities which had been constructed. There were three brightly painted storage tanks for cooking oil, a large corn silo with an automatic system that fed corn directly into the plant, and a fenced-off area enclosing natural gas tanks. A new railroad track also led right up to the warehouse receiving door. All these exterior physical changes very vividly symbolized that this plant was growing to meet the demand for its products.

Inside the plant were additional changes that provided more information about the expanding operations. A new conference room was built, comfortably furnished, and even equipped with a televisionlike monitor for viewing video tapes. Managers now had a definite place for meeting as a group, instead of just in someone's office. The quality-control laboratory had been moved from its old cramped quarters near the front office to spacious new facilities right next to the kitchen. This change was important for two reasons. First, it enhanced the importance of the quality-control function. Secondly, it brought the quality-control lab physically closer to its intended area of concern. A new warehouse was constructed that became the shipping department's place of operation. Receiving took over the old location that both departments had previously shared. With shipping in its new location, they both had their own separate identity that could be easily recognized.

Task Instrumentality

The shipping department not only got a new warehouse but also new machinery for accomplishing its task. The old method involved loading tractor trailers by pushing individual cartons down a line of roller tracks. New equipment was purchased that would take a whole skid from the warehouse and place it right into the back of the truck. These battery-powered devices were innovations (and naturally expensive). The warehouse was two stories high, and the loaders were capable of extending right to the top, with the driver going along. This enabled the driver to see exactly what he was doing, as opposed to a forklift, where the operator is left on the ground.

An additional corn cooker was installed, with a system of vats that rotated into position for dumping cooked corn automatically instead of requiring it to be pushed by hand. This technological improvement in the kitchen made it easier and more efficient to feed the additional line of Dorito ovens. With these innovations, tasks progressed faster and smoother.

Pleasure

Pleasure is subjective. A setting will be pleasurable to a particular person depending on the qualities of the physical setting itself and some combination of that person's past history and his or her present mood. Some workers managed to put in overtime just about every night, while others struggled through eight hours.

It has been claimed that people can psychologically block out their dis-pleasure and dissatisfaction with a setting, thus reducing their awareness of how they feel. In the packaging area, the constant noise of the machinery was apparently unconsciously tuned out by many.

Packing boxes were really just an extension of the packaging machine, forcing people to do mechanical labor. One job in particular left workers really numb. In the kitchen, after the potato chips came out of the cooking oil on the Muncho line, they were vibrated down the line and salted. While they were moving past, the chips were still very hot but had to be inspected immediately (and any burnt or undercooked product picked out by hand). Imagine a noisy, vibrating table constantly filled with product flowing past, and it is your job to sort through it, sometimes burning your hand. You couldn't even look around because your attention must remain focused on that table. In a setting like this, it's no wonder a worker tends to lose touch with reality.

Growth

A setting's physical qualities affect perception and hence growth. At the end of the shift, one night, a line manager conducted a tour around the plant for a group of packers. It may have seemed odd to pay overtime to show them around the same place they worked at every day, but the manager real-ized that these packers probably had never seen the entire operation. The manager was giving them a visual picture of just where they fit in the total scheme. Unlike some classes of workers, packers were virtually fixed in their setting.

Summary

There were many interconnections among the functions in the examples given above. The massive change in the exterior physical setting was undoubtedly task-oriented, but it also provided symbolic information about the organiza-tion. By following the functions of physical settings, it may be possible to perceive past, present, and future experience in new ways.

Overview

Physical settings can be supportive, a hindrance, or neutral, in realizing the six functions discussed. There may be trade-offs between functions, as well as between the benefits realized in serving the particular functions and the economic costs required in doing so. It is hoped that this part of the chapter has served to: (1) highlight some of the linkages between physical settings, organization structure, and behavioral processes; (2) increase your awareness and competence for managing physical settings; and (3) develop your understanding of the often subtle and hidden role of physical settings.

ORGANIZATIONAL CLIMATE

In the final part of this chapter, we bring together a wide variety of processes and components of organization discussed in this and previous chapters. This is being done to develop a more integrated understanding of the patterned ways by which an organization, or one or more of its subsystems, may differ. The phrase "organization climate" could be misleading. In large and differentiated organizations, there may well be a *number* of organizational climates. Consistent with the contingency view, we may find one type of climate effective when a department or larger organizational unit faces high task uncertainty, nonroutine problems, and a changing environment (possibly a research and development unit); and another type of climate effective when a department or unit faces low task uncertainty, routine problems, and a static environment (such as an assembly-line unit). Of course, the values and expectations of employees and other members of the environment within which the firm operates must be considered. Thus, even if a particular output (such as an assembled automobile) has been produced in one type of climate, it may be desirable to create another type of climate because of changing values and expectations of employees. In the earlier discussion of Volvo, a key motivation for creating a new organization climate was the skyrocketing turnover and absenteeism of employees—with its attendant adverse consequences on organizational effectiveness and productivity. Before considering some possible patterns of organization climates, let's consider a little more closely what is meant by the term and why it is significant.

Nature

Organizational climate refers to a set of attributes that can be perceived about an organization and/or its units and may be described by the practices, processes, and ways of dealing with members of the unit and its environment.[28] Let's discuss this definition in greater detail.

First, the perceptions being sought from individuals are primarily descriptive rather than evaluative. For example, one common dimension of organization climate is concerned with determining the perceptions of members over the degree to which they participate in decision-making, rather than how they feel (such as satisfied or dissatisfied) about their participation. As discussed in previous chapters (especially Chapter 4), some differences in the perceived climate may be attributable to the differences among individuals. Thus, an organization climate could vary somewhat by virtue of the particular individual doing the perceiving. Secondly, the perceptions being sought are primarily macro rather than micro. The emphasis is often on a department or organization as a whole. In relation to participation in decision-making, there would be an attempt to determine the general types and degrees of participation in decision-making over a period of time, rather than the amount of participation in decision A at time B. That is, the assessment of an organization's climate might be concerned with the perceived degree of participation by a subordinate that generally exists in setting one's job objectives, rather than how much a subordinate participated in setting the job objective of getting a particular market survey report out by 4:00 P.M. on Friday. Thirdly, the perceived attributes being sought are primarily those of the organization or department rather than of specific individuals. Of course, individuals, particularly those in managerial positions, may create or impose organizational processes and practices that are strongly influenced by their own unique styles and personalities. The discussion in Chapter 5 suggested some possible links between individual problem-solving styles and differences in organizational practices. For an ongoing organization, there could be a tendency to employ and promote managers whose problem-solving styles are congruent with the prevailing climate. Thus, ST (sensation–thinking) individuals may be quite compatible with certain managerial positions in an assembly-line operation whereas NT (intuitive–thinking) individuals may be quite compatible with certain managerial positions in planning or research and development. Fourth, differences in perceived organization climates could have varying consequences for individual motivation, productivity, organizational innovation or change, and the like.

In sum, assessing the climate of an organization is an attempt to capture the essence, order, and pattern of an organization, department, or other unit as a "system." The assessment or measurement of climate usually involves soliciting perceptions about the various attributes and elements of the organization or unit. Where there are extreme differences in the members' perceptions of organizational climate, there is often an interest in assessing whether these differences in perception adversely affect the functioning of the organization and its members.

Diagnosis

The diagnosis of organizational climate is most often undertaken through the use of structured survey instruments. A sample of the items in such an organizational-climate instrument and how they might be assessed was presented earlier, in Chapter 2 (See Fig. 2–3). The following examples outline a method for tapping the overall perceived pattern of two key dimensions of climate for a unit or organization—*structure* and *autonomy*. Some of the other dimensions of organizational climate might include decision centralization, flexibility and innovation, motivation to achieve, and social relations. The following items were developed for administration to managers.[29]

> *Structure*—Degree to which the organization specifies the methods and procedures used to accomplish tasks. This factor does *not* involve the presence or absence of supervision or evaluation. It is really the degree to which the organization likes to specify and codify, set up organizational structures, and write things down in a very explicit form.

> -1 Practically no attempt is made to specify procedures and structure.

> -2

> -3

> -4 If something is important, the procedures and methods are outlined fairly specifically, written records are kept, etc.

> -5

> -6

> -7 No matter how small a project or task is, all aspects of it are specified and recorded, and a work group structure is specified.

> *Autonomy*—Degree of freedom that managers have in day-to-day operating decisions such as when to work, when not to work, and how to solve job problems. Includes freedom from constant evaluation and close supervision. Once the job has been defined and the objectives and methods set, the individual has complete freedom to do as he pleases within those broad constraints; the freedom to be your own boss.

> -1 Virtually a complete lack of autonomy; no freedom for a manager to be his own boss.

> -2

> -3

> -4 The individual manager makes the majority of the everyday operating decisions, but his boss usually exercises fairly close supervision whenever anything really important comes up.

> -5

> -6

> -7 Virtually complete autonomy; a manager can do almost anything he wants in any way he pleases.

There is considerable unresolved controversy as to whether it is possible to meaningfully diagnose climate by obtaining perceptions that are primarily descriptive rather than evaluative and aren't excessively colored by the personal attributes of the individual respondent.[30] In the above structure and autonomy items, the statements clearly seek to obtain descriptive assessments. There is some concern that one's personal feelings of satisfaction or dissatisfaction about items, as well as the personal attributes of respondents, make it virtually impossible to obtain descriptive statements. At the present, the authors feel the construct of organizational climate is valuable and the problems of measurement can be adequately controlled through various techniques.

Patterns of Climates

The purpose of this section is to suggest possible profiles or patterns of different organizational climates. Various patterns of climates are important because they can serve as a constellation of powerful forces to influence individuals, groups, and organizations. Figure 11–6 presents the possible characteristics of climate patterns at two ends of a five-point continuum. These continua suggest that organization climates are not necessarily *either/or* types. Some dimensions or elements that may be a part of an organization climate are shown in the lefthand column of Fig. 11–6. To the extent possible, we have taken dimensions discussed in previous chapters and have identified ways by which they might vary along certain continua. We have also suggested dimensions that are *not* as likely to vary in any particular pattern. For example, organizations along the lefthand side of the continuum may place just as much emphasis on the security function in physical settings as those along the righthand side. A particular organization or department need not be described at the same point in the continua for each dimension. However, these dimensions and their characteristics are part of a system. A system perspective implies interdependent parts and processes. Thus, we may expect to find that the dimensions are within a similar range on each continuum, resulting in a fairly consistent pattern in climate.

As mentioned, Fig. 11–6 is essentially limited to some of the dimensions that have been discussed in previous chapters. Thus, we have not exhausted the various dimensions and ways by which they can be differentiated, in identifying patterns of organizational climates.[31]

General Implications

From a review of Fig. 11–6 and a reading of previous chapters, it is clear there are several overall implications of different climates, particularly the two extreme patterns presented. First, the climate pattern toward the right column in Fig. 11–6 tends to be necessary if the organization or department is faced with high rates of change and must be innovative for survival and growth.[32]

Secondly, the climate pattern toward the left in Fig. 11–6 may be adequate, but not necessarily required, for effectiveness if the organization or department is faced with little change and high certainty. While combining the *tasks, technology, structure,* and *people* parts of organization places some bounda-

Figure 11–6 Continuum of Patterns in Organizational Climates

Dimensions	Continuum of Patterns		
	Characteristics 1	2 3 4	Characteristics 5
Inter-Group Relations			
Goal relations	Independent and/or competitive		Interdependent and/or collaborative
Relative differences in power	High emphasis		Low emphasis
Task relations	Emphasis on independent or dependent relations		Emphasis on interdependent relations
Rule usage	High emphasis		Low emphasis
Attitudinal sets	Tendency toward distrust and rigidity with each other		Tendency toward trust and flexibility with each other
Motivation			
Levels of needs	Emphasis on physiological security and belongingness		Recognition of lower needs plus emphasis on esteem and self-actualization
Achievement	Low to moderate emphasis on tapping achievement motive		High emphasis on tapping achievement motive
Performance → reward probabilities	Low to moderate		Moderate to high
"Complete" and "enriched" jobs	Low to moderate emphasis		High emphasis
Leadership			
Sources of power			
Legitimate	High		Low
Reward	Moderate to high		Moderate high
Coercion	Low to moderate		Low
Referent	Low		Low to moderate
Expert	Low to moderate		High
Role orientation	Emphasis on day-to-day direction and control		Emphasis on planning, facilitating, and guiding
Technology	Stable		Dynamic

Figure 11-6 (Continued)

Dimensions	Continuum of Patterns		
	Characteristics 1	2 3 4	Characteristics 5
Problem Solving			
Structured problems	High emphasis		Low emphasis
Unstructured problems	Low to moderate		High emphasis
Uncertainty	Low		High
Styles	Few and fixed		Multiple and flexible
Goals	Few and simple		Multiple and complex
Conflict			
Resolution by higher authority	High emphasis		Low emphasis
Dominant mechanisms	Compromise, forcing, or smoothing		Multiple and complex
Dominant attitudes under conflict	Win-lose or mixed		Mixed or win-win
Communication			
Openness to others	Low and guarded		High and authentic
Feedback	Top → down emphasis for corrective feedback		All-directional emphasis for corrective feedback
Flow	Emphasis on formal channels		Emphasis on using the channel which gets to source of information
Intra-Group Relations			
Individual–group	High conformity emphasis		Low to moderate conformity emphasis
Functions for individuals	Social and security emphasis		Social and growth emphasis
Communication network	Well defined and stable		Varied and changing
Member composition	Uniform		Diverse
Norms	Well defined and stable		Varied and changing
Leadership	Single individual		Some variation according to who has the needed expertise
Participation in decision making	Low and prescribed		High and flexible

Figure 11–6   (Continued)

Dimensions	Continuum of Patterns		
	Characteristics 1	2 3 4	Characteristics 5
Structure			
Bureaucratic			
Hierarchy of authority	High emphasis		Low emphasis
Rules	Many, and high emphasis		Few, and low emphasis
Procedural specifications	Many, and high emphasis		Few, and low emphasis
Impersonality	High emphasis		Low impersonality (high consideration to situational factors)
Technical competence	Low to high		High
"Autonomous" or self-contained units	Low emphasis		Moderate to high emphasis
Vertical information systems			
Processing	High emphasis		High emphasis
Control	High emphasis		Low emphasis
Lateral relations	Low emphasis		High emphasis
Physical Settings			
Security	High		High
Social contact	Low emphasis		Moderate to high emphasis
Symbolic identification	High formal emphasis		Low formal emphasis
Task instrumentality	High		High
Pleasure	Low		High
Growth	Low to moderate		High
Environmental Relations			
Reactive orientation	Moderate and low		High and fast
Proactive orientation	Low and weak		High and strong
Other organizations	Few with well defined relations		Many and diverse organizations with changing relations

ries around the types of climate that are likely to be effective, we need to realize that the boundaries may be sufficiently wide to leave considerable discretion in the evolution or design of organizational climates.

Finally, we remain concerned about the problems of trying to prescribe the conditions under which one climate may be more effective than another. In part, this is because definition of effectiveness always depends on the values or goals that various groups "assign" to organizations. Accordingly, effectiveness can be somewhat of a relative matter, depending on the value set of the particular individual or group. For example, a group with the profit-maximizing management value orientation could define an organization as highly effective because of its growth in profits; another group with a quality-of-life management value orientation might see the same organization as relatively ineffective because (while profit is defined as important) it has ignored or traded off other goals in the pursuit of reporting higher and higher profits.

SUMMARY

This chapter has dealt with three aspects of organizations—structure, physical settings, and climates. Four strategies for structuring an organization were discussed, including the bureaucratic model, "autonomous" or self-contained units, vertical information systems, and lateral relations. The conditions under which each strategy, separately or in combination, might be applied were developed.

Related to the structure of an organization is its physical setting. Thus, part two of the chapter addressed the subtle and often "hidden" functions of physical settings. The functions presented were security, task instrumentality, social contact, symbolic identification, pleasure, and growth.

Part three of the chapter focused on the nature of organization climate, a common means for diagnosing climates, different patterns of climates, and the implications of different climates for organizational effectiveness. The latter section also served as a means of reintroducing and showing some possible relationships among a variety of the materials presented in earlier chapters. In the next two chapters on organizational change, we will relate and draw upon this and earlier chapters to further develop an integrated sense of organizational behavior.

Discussion Questions

1. Describe an organization in which you are presently a member in terms of the dimensions of the bureaucratic model. By utilizing Fig. 11-1, how would you characterize the degree of emphasis placed on each of the bureaucratic dimensions?

2. Give some examples of organizational rules you have encountered that seemed to be functional and dysfunctional from the standpoint of enhancing organizational effectiveness.

3. Do you think there should be greater use made of "autonomous" or self-contained units? Explain.

4. What are some factors that might serve to increase and decrease the commitment of individuals to task forces? Some of the materials presented in the motivation chapter may be especially useful in developing your response.

5. By utilizing the framework presented in Fig. 11-4, how would you diagnose a place you have worked or are now working?

6. If you are or have been enrolled in a university, describe some of the status indicators in the physical setting of this institution. Which of these seemed to be functional and which dysfunctional?

7. Do you think organizations should take measurements of their "climates" on a systematic basis, such as once per year?

8. How could data on the perceived organizational climate be effectively utilized?

CRITICAL INCIDENT

Dale Myers is an accounting supervisor in a national insurance company. His group handles many detailed transactions every day, and handles them smoothly, on the whole. Dale prides himself on his department's efficiency and also on its high morale. But lately the morale has been threatened—and, oddly enough, by the most conscientious, most dependable worker in the group.

Lois Heller is Dale's key accounting clerk. A widow, she has spent most of her life working for the company and is now nearing retirement age. She has been in the accounting group for the past three years and knows all phases of its work thoroughly.

It's this very thoroughness that seems to be causing trouble. Lois automatically sees all charges that go out of the division, because she needs the figures for Dale's weekly reports. She is in no way responsible for checking the accuracy of these charges, but in balancing her figures she has, on occasion, found errors made by others. She has gradually slipped into the habit of checking all the work going through her hands so that she can feel, as she puts it, that "everything that goes out of here is *right.*" This extra checking takes extra time, but she puts in the overtime voluntarily without being paid and without complaining. When she finds an error, she points it out—sometimes rather sharply—to the person concerned.

Lois' approach is, of course, highly conscientious, but the others in the group actively resent it. They say it's not Lois' job to correct them, and they contend further that many of her corrections are "picky" and unnecessary.

Dale once heard Stella Maculin, another clerk, tell Lois, "You must be off your rocker to spend so much time checking into other people's business." And Bonnie Theis, whose telephone Lois often uses to check the accuracy of other departments' figures, has, on occasion, invented excuses to deny Lois the use of the phone. When Dale asked Bonnie about this, she replied, "Lois leans over my desk and breathes down my neck, using the phone all day long to check up on information we are not even supposed to question. Most of us are getting fed up with her constant picking."

Another clerk asked Dale, "Why should I bother to check my work when I know Lois will check it anyway?"

Dale called Lois in to discuss the situation. He suggested that she show him any errors she found, rather than take them up with the people concerned.

"That would be fine . . . I guess," Lois said. "But you're away from your desk so much that it might delay things. Besides, most of this is small stuff that I can handle without bothering you."

"But the way you handle it seems to bother other people," said Dale.

Lois flared up: "If they would do their own jobs right, there wouldn't be so many errors, and they wouldn't all be picking on me."

Questions:

1. By generalizing from this limited information, what is the apparent climate of this work group? You should feel free to make any necessary assumptions that are consistent with the information given.

2. What recommendations, if any, would you make for changing the work climate? Explain.

REFERENCES

1. Hall, D., "Some Organizational Considerations in the Professional-Organizational Relationship," *Administrative Science Quarterly,* 1967, **12,** pp. 461–478.

2. Perrow, C., *Complex Organizations: A Critical Essay.* Glenview, Ill.: Scott, Foresman & Co., 1972. *Also see:* Anderson, J. G., "Bureaucratic Rules: Bearers of Organizational Authority," *Educational Administration Quarterly,* 1966, **11,** pp. 7–34.

3. Maniha, J. K., "Universalism and Particularism in Bureaucratizing Organizations," *Administrative Science Quarterly,* 1975, **2,** pp. 177–190.

4. (*Name withheld*). "The Seven-Eleven Organization in Relation to the Bureaucratic Model," unpublished paper, November, 1974.

5. Burns, T., and G. M. Stalker. *The Management of Innovation.* London: Tavistock Publications, 1961. Duncan, R. B., "Multiple Decision-Making Structures in Adapting to Environmental Uncertainty: The Impact on Organizational Effectiveness," *Human Relations,* 1973, **26,** pp. 273–291. Khandwalla, P. N., "Mass Output Orientation of Operations Technology

and Organizational Structure," *Administrative Science Quarterly,* 1974, **1,** pp. 75–97. Lawrence, P. R. and J. W. Lorsch, *Organization and Environment.* Boston: Graduate School of Business Administration, Harvard University, 1967. Van de Ven, H. H., A. L. Delbecq, D. C. Emmett, and J. S. Mendenhall, "A Structural Examination of the Model of Unit Design," *Proceedings of the National Academy of Management,* 1974. Woodward, J., *Industrial Organization: Theory and Practice.* London: Oxford University Press, 1965.

6. Pugh, D. S., *et al.,* "An Empirical Taxonomy of Structures of Work Organizations," *Administrative Science Quarterly,* 1969, **14,** pp. 115–126. Reimann, B. C., "Dimensions of Structure in Effective Organizations: Some Empirical Evidence," *Academy of Management Journal,* 1974, **17,** pp. 693–708.

7. McCaskey, M. B., "An Introduction to Organizational Design," *California Management Review,* 1974, **17,** pp. 13–20; Pugh, D. S., "The Measurement of Organization Structures: Does Context Determine Form?" *Organizational Dynamics,* 1973, **1,** pp. 19–34.

8. Conceptualization of these as other design strategies was adapted from: Galbraith, J., *Designing Complex Organizations.* Reading, Mass.: Addison-Wesley Publishing Co., 1973.

9. Willatt, N., "Volvo Versus Ford," *Management Today,* January, 1973, pp. 44–48. Gyllenhammer, P. G., "Participation at Volvo," *Journal of General Management,* 1974, **1,** pp. 34–47.

10. Galbraith, J., *Designing Complex Organizations,* Reading, Mass.: Addison-Wesley Publishing Co., 1973, p. 46.

11. Mariskovic, S., "The Implementation of Five Design Strategies into the Hershey Foods Corporation—Environmental Affairs Department," unpublished paper, November, 1974.

12. Argyris, C., *Integrating the Individual and the Organization.* New York: John Wiley & Sons, 1964. Bennis, W., *Changing Organizations.* New York: McGraw-Hill Book Co., 1966. Kelmann, R. H., and B. McKelvey, "The Maps Route to Better Organization Design," *California Management Review,* 1975, **17,** pp. 23–31. McGregor, D., *The Human Side of Enterprise.* New York: McGraw-Hill Book Co., 1960. Kingdon, D. R., *Matrix Organization: Managing Information Technologies.* London: Tavistock, 1973.

13. Leavitt, H. J., and T. L. Whisler, "Management in the 1980's," *Harvard Business Review,* 1958, **36,** pp. 41–48. Whisler, T. L., *Information Technology and Organizational Change.* Belmont, Calif.: Wadsworth Publishing Co., 1970.

14. Burlingame, J. F., "Information Technology and Decentralization," *Harvard Business Review,* 1961, **39,** pp. 121–126. Klatsky, S. R., "Automation, Size, and the Locus of Decision-Making: The Cascade Effect," *Journal of*

Business, 1970, **43,** pp. 141–151. Stewart, M., *How Computers Affect Management.* London: Macmillan Press, 1971.

15. *Ibid.*

16. Sanders, D. H., *Computers and Management in a Changing Society.* 2nd ed. New York: McGraw-Hill Book Co., 1974, pp. 483–494.

17. Robey, D., "Computers and Organization Structure: A Review and Appraisal of Empirical Studies," *Proceedings of the National Academy of Management,* August, 1974.

18. Drucker, P. F., "New Templates for Today's Organizations," *Harvard Business Review,* 1974, **52,** pp. 45–53.

19. Steele, F. I., *Physical Settings and Organization Development,* Reading, Mass.: Addison-Wesley Publishing Co., 1973.

20. Foulkes, F., "Learning to Live with OSHA," *Harvard Business Review,* 1973, **51,** pp. 57–67. Nicholas, J., "OSHA, Big Government and Small Business," *MSU Business Topics,* 1973, **23,** pp. 57–64.

21. Blauner, R., *Alienation and Freedom.* Chicago: University of Chicago Press, 1964.

22. Korda, M., "Office Power—You are Where You Sit," *New York,* 1975, , pp. 36–44.

23. Personal observations made by one of your authors.

24. "Multi-Modular Office Wins First Award," *Administrative Management* 1972, **34,** pp. 20–27. *Also see:* "Montgomery Ward's New Headquarters Wins First Award," *Administrative Management,* 1975, **36,** pp. 20–25.

25. Schroder, H., M. Drever, and S. Steufert, *Human Information Processing.* New York: Holt, Rinehart & Winston, 1967.

26. Brookes, M. J., and A. Kaplan, "The office Environment: Space Planning and Affective Behavior," *Human Factors,* 1972, **14,** pp. 373–391. Nemecek, J., and E. Grandjian, "Results of an Ergonomic Investigation of Large-Space Offices," *Human Factors,* 1973, **15,** pp. 111–124.

27. Ulmer, G., "Applications Paper: Functions of Physical Settings at Frito-Lay," unpublished paper, Pennsylvania State University, May, 1975.

28. Hellriegel, D., and J. Slocum, "Organizational Climates: Measures, Research, and Contingencies," *Academy of Management Journal,* 1974, **17,** pp. 255–280. *Also see:* James, L. R., and A. P. Jones, "Organizational Climate: A Review of Theory and Research," *Psychological Bulletin,* 1974, **81,** pp. 1046–1112. Pritchard, R. D., and B. W. Karasick, "The Effects of Organizational Climate on Managerial Job Performance and Job Satisfaction," *Organizational Behavior and Human Performance,* 1973, **9,** pp. 126–146.

Schneider, B., and R. A. Snyder, "Some Relationships between Job Satisfaction and Organizational Climate," *Journal of Applied Psychology*, 1975, **60,** pp. 318–328; Sims, H. P., and W. LaFollette, "An Assessment of the Litwin and Stringer Organization-Climate Questionnaire," *Personnel Psychology*, 1975, **28,** pp. 19–38.

29. "Organizational-Climate Questionnaire," developed by Institute of Industrial Relations, University of Minnesota, 1969.

30. Johannesson, R. E., "Some Problems in the Measurement of Organizational Climate," *Organizational Behavior and Human Performance*, 1973, **10,** pp. 118–144. LaFollette, W. R., and H. P. Sims, "Is Satisfaction Redundant with Organizational Climate?" *Organizational Behavior and Human Performance*, 1975, in press. Lirtzman, S., R. House, and J. Rizzo, "An Alternative to Organization Climate: The Measurement of Organization Practices," paper presented at National Academy of Management meetings, 1973.

31. Kast, F. E., and J. W. Rosenzweig (eds.), *Contingency Views of Organization and Management.* Chicago: Science Research Associates, 1973, pp. 315–318.

32. Zaltman, G., R. Duncan, and J. Holbeck, *Innovations and Organizations.* New York: John Wiley & Sons, 1973.

*

PART V

CHANGE PROCESSES

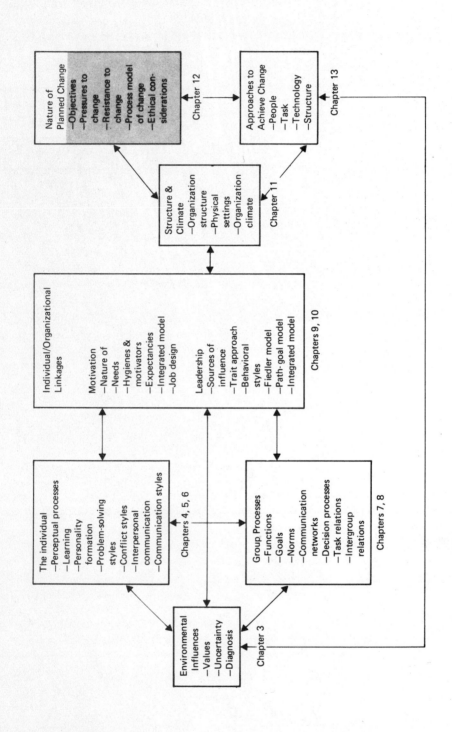

Nature of
Planned Change
—Objectives
—Pressures to
change
—Resistance to
change
—Process model
of change
—Ethical con-
siderations

Chapter 12

Approaches to
Achieve Change
—People
—Task
—Technology
—Structure

Chapter 13

Structure &
Climate
—Organization
structure
—Physical
settings
—Organization
climate

Chapter 11

Individual/Organizational
Linkages

Motivation
—Nature of
—Needs
—Hygienes &
motivators
—Expectancies
—Integrated model
—Job design

Leadership
—Sources of
influence
—Trait approach
—Behavioral
styles
—Fiedler model
—Path- goal model
—Integrated model

Chapters 9, 10

The individual
—Perceptual processes
—Learning
—Personality
formation
—Problem-solving
styles
—Conflict styles
—Interpersonal
communication
—Communication styles

Chapters 4, 5, 6

Group Processes
—Functions
—Goals
—Norms
—Communication
networks
—Decision processes
—Task relations
—Intergroup
relations

Chapters 7, 8

Environmental
Influences
—Values
—Uncertainty
—Diagnosis

Chapter 3

12
NATURE
OF PLANNED
ORGANIZATIONAL
CHANGE

Managers are increasingly concerned today with the dilemma of how to fully utilize the human resources of organizations and, at the same time, to design work roles, work environments, and the relationships of organizational members so that basic and higher-level needs (such as achievement and self-actualization) can be met more fully in the work environments. To resolve this dilemma, new organizational forms and work roles need to be developed, more effective goal-setting and planning processes need to be learned, and teams of employees, which can consist of managers and subordinates alike, should spend time improving their methods of working, decision-making, and communicating.

To design modified or new organizations, employee roles, and interpersonal processes and to bring them into reality is the domain of organizational change and development. Even if it were possible for a single individual or small group to develop a master blueprint for introducing organizational change, it is doubtful whether the organizational members who are affected would readily accept the change or have the required skills for implementing the change. For these reasons, it is critical that change agents, whether they be managers, change specialists, or employees with ideas, be as competent in deciding *how to introduce change* as they are in diagnosing *what needs to be changed.*

In examining the nature of planned organizational change, this chapter has the following objectives:

1. To explain the objectives of planned organizational change;

2. To identify several key pressures encouraging changes in today's organization;

3. To identify individual and organizational resistances that often impede the introduction of change;

4. To propose a general model of processes that are likely to take place and the organizational variables that are likely to be affected in introducing any type of change;

5. To examine the types of change agents that may be utilized to facilitate the introduction of change; and finally

6. To discuss some key ethical considerations inherent in any planned change process.

OBJECTIVES OF PLANNED CHANGE

Planned changes in an organization are undertaken to attain or maintain goals. These goals may include higher productivity, acceptance of new engineering techniques, greater motivation, and more innovative behavior. These goals, and a host of others, have two underlying objectives: (1) modification of the organization's mode of adaptation to changes in its environment, and (2) modification of attitudes, interpersonal communication, and conflict styles of individuals within the organization.[1]

Organizational Adaptation

Effective organizations are continually trying to adjust their internal organization environment to allow them to cope more effectively with their changing external environments. The *external* environment consists of those important physical and social factors outside the boundaries of the organization, such as suppliers, customers, regulatory groups, societal values, and so forth. The *internal* environment consists of those relevant physical and social factors within the boundaries of the organization, such as departments, consisting of marketing, operations, accounting, finance, personnel, and so forth.[2] Most innovative organizational changes are introduced in anticipation of, or in reaction to, new pressures from the firm's external environment. Therefore, it is essential that the organization obtain information from its environment to maintain or increase its effectiveness. Companies such as DuPont, Scott Paper, Lever Brothers, Monsanto, and Honeywell Corporation have established permanent staffs at corporate headquarters charged with the responsibility for monitoring the multiple environments of the corporation and alerting management to developing environmental trends.[3] These staffs maintain contacts with a wide variety of organizations, including governmental agencies, future research centers, planning staffs of other corporations, professional societies, advisory services, and universities. While it is beyond the scope of this chapter to discuss how an organization's structure facilitates the gathering and processing of information from its relevant external environment, it is important for the organization to get feedback from its external environment in order to make appropriate changes in its internal structure.[4] In Chapter

13, we examine several strategies that focus on how internal changes in the organization can assist an organization in acquiring information from its environment.

Individual Adaptation

The second goal of organization change is to achieve modifications in the attitudes, styles, and behavioral patterns of individuals within the organization. An organization may not be able to change its adaptation strategy for reacting to its relevant environment unless the members in the organization behave differently in their relationships to one another and to their jobs. Organizations survive, grow, decline, or fail because people make decisions. Every organization has its unique decision-making process. Thus, any organization change, whether it is introduced through a new structural design or a company training program, is basically trying to get employees to change their behavior. In a highly turbulent environment, such as parts of the aerospace, electronics, and pharmaceutical industries, a rigid authority hierarchy may restrict the channels of communication and reduce the amount of information available to the organization's top managers to make effective decisions. Even if the structure of the organization changes to a more decentralized one, there is a high probability that unless the employees' behavioral patterns are changed, the new structure will have little impact on the effectiveness of the organization. In order for organization-wide effects to be felt, new employee behavior must emerge, to be consistent with the demands of the organization's environment. In Chapter 13, several change strategies that focus on changing the attitudes, styles, and/or behavior of employees will be examined.

PRESSURES TO CHANGE

One of the demands for managers operating in turbulent environments is to diagnose these important changing factors in the environment that affect the organization. It is the purpose of this section to discuss the major pressures facing organizations to change their adaptation patterns.

Changing Environments

The rate of social and technological change is greater today than it has been at any time in the past. This much repeated statement has been made by managers, philosophers, statesmen, scholars, and the like. Sir Charles P. Snow, in his lecture on the *Two Cultures,* comments that during all human history until this century, the *rate* of social change has been very slow[5]—so slow that it could pass unnoticed in one person's lifetime. That is no longer so. The rate of change has increased so much that our imagination can't keep up. For example, in the area of individual freedoms, we are far from the days of slavery and serfdom in many domains (e.g., civil rights, equal employment opportunity, quality of working life, and the like).

Accelerating technological change is also widely recognized. It is the principal theme of Alvin Toffler's book *Future Shock.* [6] Toffler's central thesis is that our society's inability to adapt to the increasing rate of change—not to its content or direction—is the most critical problem of our times. During the last hundred years, the speed of communications has increased by a factor of 10^7, speed of handling data 10^6, and the speed of travel 10^2.[7] Thus, the technological environment in which private and public organizations operate is becoming increasingly turbulent. This turbulence increases the relative uncertainty for individuals and organizations alike. The problem for organizations is that the forms of adaptation developed to meet a simpler and more stable environment are no longer sufficient to meet the higher levels of complexity and turbulence now confronting them. The dimensions of this highly turbulent environment can be grouped into three major categories, including knowledge explosion, rapid product obsolescence, and the changing nature of the work force.[8]

Knowledge Explosion.   The rate at which society has been storing useful information about itself has been spiraling upward at an increasing rate. Today, for example, the number of scientific journals and articles is doubling about every fifteen years, and the number of different book titles produced each day has been estimated at 1,000. As a result, knowledge in a particular field quickly becomes obsolete. In addition, organizations that depend on highly sophisticated knowledge bases can easily become obsolete unless planned change efforts are continuous. For example, Bowmar, the manufacturer of the first pocket calculator in 1971, lost its dominance in the market in 1975. This occurred because, as the technology to make calculations became simpler and cheaper, competitors moved into the market, prices fell, and Bowmar couldn't adapt. Industry sales of pocket calculators made quantum jumps—from an estimated four million sold in 1972 to 28 million in 1975—but Bowmar mismanaged the knowledge explosion in terms of consumer wants and needs. Left with outdated equipment and large overhead expenses, Bowmar's management could not adapt its technology to compete with other firms in the industry.[9] Another example of inadequate adaptation to the knowledge explosion has occurred with Volkswagen.[10] By 1972, VW had sold over 15 million Beetles, but success blinded VW to the change signals of rising affluence and changing consumer taste, of new Japanese competition (Toyota, Datsun, and Mazda), of U.S. companies producing economy cars, as well as from the imbalance of payments resulting in major currency revaluations and devaluations. In an attempt to close these strategic gaps that resulted in reducing its share of the market, VW has increased its capital investment from a total of $177 million in 1968 to a projected $600 million in 1975. VW has followed a crisis-change approach by developing new models without the simplicity of its unbelievably successful Beetle. By mid-1975, VW had the capability of manufacturing fourteen different models, including the Rabbitt and Dasher, with variations of air-cooled motors in the rear, water-cooled motors in the front, one with a motor in the middle, and with both front- and rear-wheel drive. Unfortunately, as of 1975, not one of these new models has been an unqualified success in terms of sales and return on investment for VW. VW reported a $347 million loss in 1974, and will probably lose an equal amount in 1975. Of course, VW's problems just mirror the automobile industry' problems in 1975.

Rapid Product Obsolescence. Fast-shifting consumer preferences, interacting with frequent technological changes, have shortened the life cycle of many products and services. Every consumer has had the experience of trying to buy certain items in the supermarket only to find that the product is impossible to locate or that the brand no longer exists. Approximately 55 percent of the items sold today did not exist ten years ago, and of the products sold then, about 40 percent have been taken off the shelf. In the volatile pharmaceutical and electronics fields, a product is often obsolete in as short a period as six months. As the pace accelerates, managers may well create products with the knowledge that they will remain on the market for only a matter of months. When Bowmar introduced the first pocket calculator in 1971, it sold for $247. In 1975, it appeared that almost every month a new, less expensive, but more complex instrument was introduced to the market, rendering older ones obsolete, to some extent. When product life cycles are shortened, organizations must be able to shorten their "lead times" to get into production. Thus, flexible organizations, or at least flexible subsystems, are likely to be required for continued viability in the future. These temporary or flexible organizations will permit managements to assemble small groups of personnel for the purposes of developing strategies and analyzing decisions. Aside from its value in permitting flexibility and adaptation for the corporation, this type of structure enables the corporation to react quickly to information gathered by an early-warning system, facilitates transitions to new forms of operations, encourages broadly based and participative decision-making, and provides a multitude of situations in which potential future leadership can be observed and developed.

Changing Nature of the Work Force. One major change in the work force is the decrease in the average age of the worker. Organizations are confronting younger, better educated individuals who do not readily accept certain management styles. In 1969, 15 percent of a national survey of employees were less than 24 years old, compared to 21 percent in 1973. Similarly, the percentage of workers over 55 years old has steadily decreased over the past decade. Besides having younger workers in the labor force, these workers have a higher average level of education. For example, in 1969, a U.S. Department of Labor survey indicated that less than 30 percent of the labor force held a college degree, compared to 36 percent of the labor force in 1973.[11]

Quality of Working Life.   In addition to the younger and more educated work force, there has been increased emphasis on the quality of working life. Several studies issued by the U.S. Department of Health, Education, and Welfare[12] indicate that the North American work force is becoming dissatisfied with dull, unchallenging, and repetitive jobs. A worker's attitude toward his employer is not solely a product of the salary, but also depends on the nature of the work, the environment in which it is accomplished, the opportunity for participation in the design of the work, and the prospects for advancement. Those most satisfied with their working conditions, according to one report, were middle-aged workers, workers who had college degrees or education in excess of a college degree, whites, and workers who were in professional, technical, or managerial occupations. Those least satisfied are those workers less than 21 years old, workers with grade-school education or less, blacks, operatives, and nonfarm laborers.[13] While the women's movement may have helped make women more conscious of sex discrimination, wage inequities and other qualities of working life between men and women still remain great. Managements have attempted to improve the quality of working life with experiments involving working hours, job enlargement, and the like.

Life Styles.   Life style has been described as an individual's values, beliefs, and perspectives about organizationally related issues. There are three dimensions of a person's life style that are important for managers: formalistic, interpersonal, and personalistic. An individual's life style can be viewed as containing a certain proportion of each of these three dimensions, as indicated in Table 12–1.

The table depicts nine basic values or behaviors and how these interrelate with a person's three major life styles. The *formalistic* life-style dimension reflects the value that an individual places on having his or her actions guided by directives from formal authorities. Control over the individual's behavior should come from rules, regulations, policies, and standard operating procedures. Direction should come from the top positions in the organization. The individual grows and develops by following an established order set forth by the organization. The traditional bureaucratic organization, characterized by a detailed list of rules, policies, and regulations, closely follows this life style. Communications are mostly downward; decisions are made at the top, and implemented by individuals down the organization's hierarchy.

The major value dimensions in the *interpersonal* life style are those developed through interaction with others. The values are derived from accepted group norms and serve as a basis of control of the individual's behavior. The individual grows and develops through interaction with others. The informal work group is the organization's parallel to this life style. In a work group, authority is vested in the standards and norms developed by the group. Decisions are made by group consensus. Communication is, for the most part, carried on between members of the group, and conflict is resolved through group consensus.

Table 12-1 The Values and Behaviors of Three Major Life Styles

Value/Behavior	Formalistic	Interpersonal	Personalistic
Direction from	Authorities and those responsible	Discussion, agreement with others who are close	Within individual
Guidance from	Precedent and policy	Close relationships with others	Self-knowledge of what one wants to do
Desired condition	Clear pathways for advancement and reward	Friends and colleagues who are committed	Freedom to choose how one lives
Basis for growth and progress	Learning from and following the established order	Learning from and sharing with others	Learning from one's own experience, acting on one's own awareness
Faith in	Rules, laws, policies, orders	Group norms, what close friends say and advise	One's own sense of justice
Strives for desired state	Advancement and prestige, compliance, respect	Intimacy and acceptance collaboration, agreement, consensus	Freedom and independence self-determination and realization
Incentive	Security and comfort	Intimate relationships and shared values	Experimentation and self-discovery
Responsible to	Those in positions of higher responsibility	Those with whom one has close personal relationships	Self
Feelings and emotions	To be channeled and made rational	To be shared with others who are close	To be totally experienced

Source: Friedlander, F., "Emergent and Contemporary Life Styles: An Intergenerational Issue," Human Relations, 1975, **28**, 329–347.

The last major value dimension is the *personalistic* style. This style emphasizes that an individual's actions are guided by his or her own personal experience and feelings. Growth and awareness development should result from increased self-awareness. The individual strives for freedom, independence, and the development of a sense of values. In many organizations, this dimension can be seen in the use of temporary systems, such as project management, committees, and task forces. In these systems, two or more people come together because they share some common concern, and stay together because of it. Each individual decides what he or she wants to do and directs himself or herself toward achieving that goal. Communication is mostly within each individual in terms of ideas, reactions, and feelings, and progress toward goal achievement. Conflict between members is dealt with openly and resolved by the persons involved.

An individual who is low in formalistic life style, and is forced to work in a job characterized by a high degree of rules, regulations, and directives from top management, is likely to be dissatisfied with his or her job.[14] The bureaucratic organization places control and responsibility in formally appointed leaders. These leaders assign goals and objectives for their department and direct subordinates toward those goals. The activities to be performed are decided by the leader. Thus, there is little opportunity for the individual to experience values in his or her interpersonal or personalistic life styles. It is important for the manager to match the individual's life styles with the task and climate of the organization, in order to achieve maximum performance and high job satisfaction for the individual.

Most individuals today are deeply concerned with the problem of developing managerial strategies appropriate to the changing conditions of their environment. The changes through which our organizations and society are going are not independent of one another. They reflect some of the basic changes noted in the previous pages. Successful managers and/or organizations are continually seeking to develop flexible organizations that can change with the requirements of the environment, and can also anticipate and be proactive in influencing the environment. It is not enough to carry out piecemeal efforts to patch up a problem here, redesign a job there, or rewrite a rule. There is an increasing need for systematic planned-change efforts that coordinate the ways of work, relationships, and communication systems with the predictable and unpredictable requirements of the future.

RESISTANCES TO CHANGE

This section examines some of the reasons why individuals and organizations resist change. Resistance to change is one of the most baffling problems that managers face because it can take so many forms. Overt resistance may take the form of strikes, reduction in productivity, and shoddy workmanship. Implicit resistance may be manifested in the form of increased absenteeism, requests for transfer, resignations, loss of motivation to work, "mental errors," and lateness in arriving at work. The effects of resistance, either overt or implicit, may be subtle and cumulative. That is, minimal reactions to small changes (for example, a change in location of an office machine or a change in office routine) can take place without a superior being aware of employee resistance. In contrast, a major overt indicator of resistance may be some type of wildcat strike or work slowdown.

Resistance by the Individual

For the purposes of this section, we shall focus on resistances as they operate within the individual. This list of resistances is somewhat arbitrary and many of the individual and organizational resistances interact.[15]

Habit. As discussed in Chapter 4, most learning theory includes the assumption that, unless the situation changes noticeably, individuals will continue to respond to stimuli in their accustomed way. Once a habit is established, it may become a source of satisfaction for the individual. If an organization were suddenly to announce that every employee was to immediately receive a 20 percent pay raise, few would object. However, if the company were suddenly to announce that every employee was to immediately receive a 20 percent reduction, many would object. In the latter case, many habits—taking vacations, buying new cars every three years, shopping for convenience foods—would have to be changed because of the individual's inability to finance these activities. In the recession of 1974–1975, it appeared that individuals' buying habits changed slowly and only under severe economic conditions (after unemployment benefits were exhausted).

Selective Perception and Retention. Once an attitude has been established, a person responds to others' suggestions within the framework that has been established. Situations may be perceived as reinforcing the original attitude when they actually do not. Individuals successfully resist the possible impact of change on their lives by reading or listening to what agrees with their present views, by conveniently forgetting any learning that could lead to opposite viewpoints, and by misunderstanding communications that, if correctly perceived, would not be congruent with pre-established attitudes. For example, many managers who enroll in training programs and are exposed to different managerial philosophies may do very well at discussing and answering questions about these philosophies. But they may carefully segregate in their minds the new approaches which "of course, would not work in my job" and those which they are already practicing.

A change will usually be opposed by an employee unless he or she has specifically requested the change. Since the employee's status, prestige, or job may be at stake with the coming change, the employee must be convinced of the need for the change. The employee must see some personal benefit to be gained before he or she is willing to participate in the change process.

Dependence.   All human beings begin life dependent upon adults. Parents sustain life in the helpless infant and provide major satisfactions. The inevitable outcome is that children tend to incorporate the values, attitudes, and beliefs of their parents. The dependency of individuals on others can be a resistance to change if the individual has not developed a sense of self-esteem. Individuals who are highly dependent on others and lack self-esteem are likely to resist changes until significant others endorse the changes and incorporate them into their behavioral activities. The individual who is highly dependent on his or her boss for feedback on performance will probably not incorporate any new techniques or methods unless the boss personally okays the decision and indicates to the employee how these changes will improve performance.

Security and Regression.   Another obstacle to change is the tendency of some individuals to seek security in the past. When life becomes frustrating, individuals think with nostalgia about the happy days of the past. The irony is that this frustration–regression sequence occurs just when old ways no longer produce the desired outcome, and experimentation with new approaches is most needed. Even under these conditions, individuals with a high degree of insecurity are apt to cling even more desperately to the old, unproductive behavior patterns. The manager who does not recognize the effects of equal-opportunity legislation on his policy of hiring only white males, or the changing composition of the labor force, seeks somehow to find a road back to the old days when he ran the shop according to his personal likes. The accountant who was trained in the 40's to hand-post accounts may resist new electronic data-processing equipment because he or she feels threatened by the possible loss of a job or loss of prestige through lessened authority and responsibility.

Resistance to Change by Organizations

Most organizations have been designed to be innovation-resisting. That is, like fully automated factories, organizations have customarily been designed to do a narrowly prescribed assortment of things and to do them reliably. To ensure reliability of prescribed operations, the organization may create strong defenses against change. Moreover, change often runs counter to vested interests, and probably violates certain territorial rights or decision-making prerogatives that have been established and accepted over time.

Stability of Systems.   The first resistance to change by organizations are the benefits derived from their collective stability. To assure predictability, the typical bureaucratic organization narrowly defines jobs, delimits lines of authority and responsibility, and stresses the hierarchical flow of information from the top to the bottom. It stresses discipline through the use of rewards and punishments. Novel ideas and/or the use of resources in a new way may be perceived as threats to the internal distribution of power and status. For example, the conservative financial policy of Montgomery Ward immediately after World War II assured Ward of great organizational stability. But since the retail environment was changing, this drive for economic stability was instrumental in Ward's decline in the merchandising field. On the other hand, Sears assumed that risk-taking, in terms of opening new stores in suburban areas, and adding new lines of merchandise, was needed to gain prominence in the market. As a result of these different strategies, Sears' sales, in 1974, were 240 percent of Ward's.[16] Under periods of crisis, such as earthquakes, floods, bankruptcy, and other disasters, organizations start searching for new solutions to the basic problem of survival. A state of crisis does not in itself generate innovative ideas, but the uncertainty and anxiety generated by the crisis make organization members more eager to adopt new structures that promise to relieve the anxiety of instability.[17]

Resource Limitations.   While some organizations desire to emphasize stability, others would change their structure and behavior if they had available the resources necessary to implement a change. Bethlehem Steel Corporation made a decision to close down its Johnstown, Pa., operation because it couldn't comply, without expending huge sums of money, with the environmental standards proposed by state and federal governmental agencies. Only after the agencies modified their environmental regulations was Bethlehem able to continue its Johnstown operations. Another example is the decline in central business districts. Many firms watch their customers desert them for the greater convenience of suburban shopping centers. Yet the companies find themselves unable to raise the funds needed to provide the public parking facilities and rapid transit systems required to counter this trend.

Sunk Costs.   Resource limitations obviously are not confined to organizations lacking assets. Rich organizations may find themselves as hard put because they have invested much of their capital in fixed assets (e.g., equipment, building, land, etc.). They may be locked into the present by their assets, for those represent sunk costs. Again, the plight of many central business districts may serve to illustrate this resistance. Most of our larger cities were planned in the era before automobiles, and they can hardly begin to handle today's motor traffic. Therefore, these cities have had an increasingly difficult time meeting the competition of suburban shopping centers. Sunk costs are not always limited to physical things. They can also be expressed in terms of people. What happens to an employee who is no longer making a significant contribution to the organization but has enough seniority to maintain his or her job? Unless the employee can be motivated to higher task performance, he or she will likely stay with the company until retirement. Fringe benefits, salary, and the like are payments to the individual for past services and represent sunk costs for the company.

Interorganizational Agreements.   Agreements between organizations usually impose obligations on people that can act as restraints on their behavior.[18] Labor contracts are the most pertinent examples because some things that were once considered major prerogatives of management (right to hire and fire, assignment of personnel to tasks, promotions, etc.) now have become subjects of negotiation. Labor contracts are not the only kinds of contracts that restrain management. Exponents of change in an organization's structure may also find their plan delayed by arrangements with competitors, commitments to suppliers, pledges to public officials in return for licenses or permits, promises to contractors, and the like. While agreements can be ignored or violated, potential legal costs may be expensive, lost customers might be hesitant to buy the product again, and credit rating declines can be disastrous.

Does it follow, therefore, that managers must be forever saddled with the task of trying to achieve change in organizations or individuals that resist change? Our answer is *no.* Resistance to change will probably never cease completely, but managers can learn to succeed and to minimize the resistance by planning the change. In the next section of this chapter, we shall identify a model that managers can use to understand the process of change.

GENERAL PROCESS MODEL OF CHANGE

One of the difficulties that a manager often encounters in situations involving change is that he or she finds it difficult to get a handle on the situation. The problems sometimes become quite complex because of the variety of interrelationships.[19] The expectations of people within the organization, or of customers buying its products or services, the demands of the technology used to manufacture the product, and the organization's structure utilized to make decisions, all must be examined.

Several years ago Kurt Lewin, a pioneering social psychologist, developed a way of looking at change that has proved to be highly useful to action-oriented managers.[20] Lewin saw change not as an event, but as a dynamic balance of forces working in opposite directions in any given situation. Any situation can be considered in a state of equilibrium resulting from a balance of forces constantly pushing against each other. For example, a manager may wish to delegate decision-making authority to subordinates more effectively.[21] There are certain forces in the situation that tend to maintain the *status quo*—to resist more delegation. These forces are called "resistances to change" and were described in the previous section of this chapter. At the same time, acting opposite to these forces, pushing for change, are certain pressures to change. The combined effect of these two sets of forces results in the current situation, as illustrated in Fig. 12–1. Resistances to change and

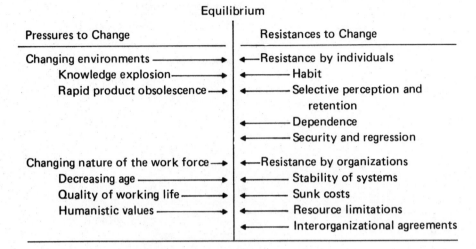

Figure 12-1   A Basic Process Model of Change

pressures to change are categorized as discussed in the text. Note that you don't have to have an equal number of resistances and pressures to change. If you identify five pressures to change, there is no reason why you must also identify eight resistances to change. Often one resistance may offset the effects of several pressures to change.

Strategy for Change

To initiate a change, the manager will have to take some action to modify the current equilibrium of forces. In other words, the current equilibrium must be "unfrozen." The manager can do this by:

1. Increasing the strength of the pressures for change;

2. Reducing the strength of the resisting forces or removing them completely;

3. Changing the direction of a force; i.e., make a resistance into a pressure for change.

Going back to the example of a manager who would like to delegate more effectively, we might find that the current situation is characterized by the resistances and pressures shown in Fig. 12-2.

After a diagnosis of the resistances and pressures to change, the manager is then faced with the task of determining what action to take to affect the situation. For example, although we identified only six resistances, two or three may have relatively greater impact on the organization than the others. These

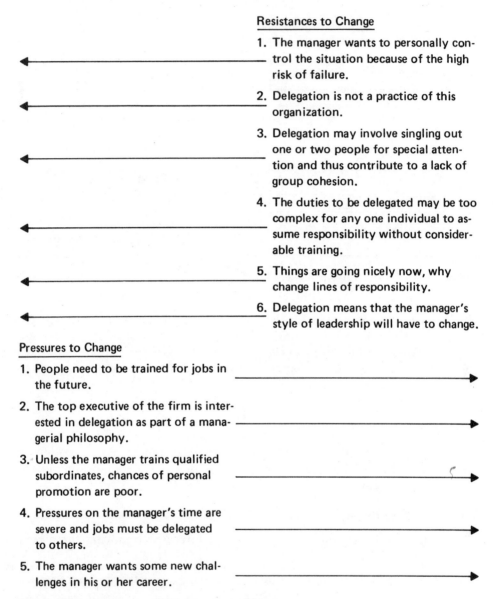

Resistances to Change

1. The manager wants to personally control the situation because of the high risk of failure.

2. Delegation is not a practice of this organization.

3. Delegation may involve singling out one or two people for special attention and thus contribute to a lack of group cohesion.

4. The duties to be delegated may be too complex for any one individual to assume responsibility without considerable training.

5. Things are going nicely now, why change lines of responsibility.

6. Delegation means that the manager's style of leadership will have to change.

Pressures to Change

1. People need to be trained for jobs in the future.

2. The top executive of the firm is interested in delegation as part of a managerial philosophy.

3. Unless the manager trains qualified subordinates, chances of personal promotion are poor.

4. Pressures on the manager's time are severe and jobs must be delegated to others.

5. The manager wants some new challenges in his or her career.

Figure 12–2   Pressures and Resistances to Change

resistances, if modified, will have a greater impact on the proposed change than will the less powerful resistances. Of course, the same situation may exist with regard to the pressures for change. Some are stronger than others and are more important in the current situation. Thus, the process of planned change is one of altering the forces that support a particular level of equilibrium so that one set of forces replaces another.

There are several benefits from this model for understanding the processes of change. First, it requires that the individual change agent get a specific picture of the current situation. By examining the forces pressing for change and the resistances to change, the individual should have an idea of the relevant forces under consideration. In addition, the concept of equilibrium provides the individual with some kind of useful framework to analyze a complex situation. Finally, the model serves to highlight those factors that can be changed and those that cannot. Too many managers spend a great deal of time considering actions related to forces over which they have little control. When the manager directs attention to those forces over which he or she has some control, the likelihood is increased that the options chosen will be likely to have the most impact.

To carry through on the aforementioned example, let's assume that the manager has decided to delegate more decision-making responsibility and authority to qualified subordinates. The manager's first task is to *unfreeze* the attitudes, beliefs, and personal styles of subordinates. As indicated in Fig. 12–3, when this occurs, the subordinates' performance is likely to decrease, in the short run. In this example, the subordinates' performance of 100 units per day is assumed to decrease fairly quickly to 60 units per day. During this period of time, indicated on the horizontal axis, subordinates must develop new attitudes, skills, and techniques to handle their enlarged decision-making responsibilities. This transition period is the *moving* stage, when attitudes or beliefs are changing. The equilibrium of the situation has been disturbed and the forces resisting the change are greater than the pressures supporting the change. During the moving period, days 7 through 16, the manager should attempt to reduce some of the resistances. For example, the manager's own

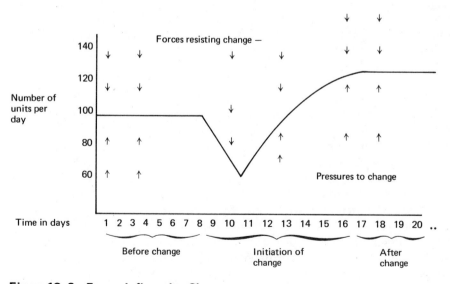

Figure 12–3   Forces Influencing Change

leadership style might be changed to be more compatible with the philosophy of delegation of decision-making. Similarly, the manager's superiors must provide him or her with the necessary psychological and financial support, in case a subordinate fails to complete the task as desired. As the manager and subordinates gradually overcome these resistances to change, the forces pressing for the change increase. When the change process has been completed, the performance may be 20 units higher than before the change was initiated (i.e., 120 versus 100 units per day). At that point in time, the manager and subordinates must *refreeze* this newly established equilibrium—that is, rearrange the forces in the situation to maintain the higher level of productivity.

While this example illustrates the benefits of a change in decision-making, many managers are unsuccessful in creating meaningful change. One reason is that some managers have a strong tendency to increase the pressures to change in order to produce the desired change. This will, of course, disrupt the balance and result in short-run changes. Unfortunately, an increase in the pressures to change also has negative effects on the stability of the system. This was illustrated in our previous example when production dropped from 100 to 60 units per day. This process is much like inflating a balloon. As you increase the air on the inside, you also decrease the strength of the balloon and at some point, the balloon explodes because it cannot absorb any more pressure. What is needed is an understanding of resistances to change and how these resistances and pressures to change interact, so that the system will be able to remain stable and not reach the breaking point over the long run.

Major System Variables in the Change Process

Before leaving the general model of planned change, it is important to review some of the major variables that can be changed. There are at least four interacting variables in an organization—task, structure, people and technology.[22] The *task* refers to whether the job is simple or complex, novel or repetitive, or standardized or unique. Some tasks, such as the placement of a bumper on an automobile, are highly standardized, repetitive, and simple, whereas the design of a new jet liner is often unique, novel, and complex. The task's nature can also create independent, interdependent, or dependent relations among departments in an organization (see Chapter 8 for a complete description of these processes). The *structure* means the systems of communication, authority, and responsibility. Each organization has its own structure that specifies power relations among individuals in it. The *people* variable are those individuals working within the organization. This includes their attitudes, personal styles, and motivations to work in the organization. Finally, the *technological* variable refers to problem-solving methods or techniques, such as computers, typewriters, drill presses, and so forth. These four variables are highly independent as indicated in Fig. 12–4. A change in any one usually results in a change in one or more of the others. A structural change, for example, toward decentralization of decision-making, should result in assign-

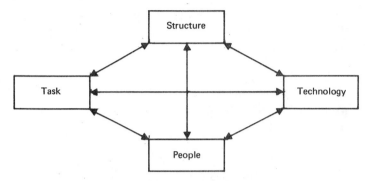

Figure 12–4   Factors in Organization Change

Source: Leavitt, H., Applied Organizational Change in Industry: Structural Technological and Humanistic Approaches. In *Handbook of Organizations,* March, J., ed. Chicago: Rand McNally & Co., 1965, p. 1145.

ment of different people to certain organizational tasks. But decentralization of decision-making will also probably change the technology for performing the tasks, as well as the attitudes and values of the employees performing the task. The introduction of computers (technology change) in insurance companies in the mid-50's caused changes in the structure (i.e., communication channels, number of hierarchical levels, locus of decision-making), change in people (their numbers, skills, motivations), and changes in the performance of tasks (the ability to use complex operation-research models to solve unique and novel problems).

Organizational change can be introduced through alteration of any one of these variables, singly or in combination. Obviously, organizational members need to decide "what is to be changed" before undertaking a planned change effort. Leavitt's framework provides us with an opportunity to examine some change approaches. While specific approaches to change will be spelled out in great detail in Chapter 13, an overview is presented in the following section.

People.   The *people* approach attempts to change organizations by modifying the attitudes, values, styles, behavior, and interpersonal processes of organizational members. It is assumed that people are the major force pressing for and/or resisting the change. One common thread in this approach is the redistribution of power among organizational members. This redistribution of power can be accomplished by encouraging independent decision-making by subordinates, and by opening communication channels.

One example of this approach is the Scanlon Plan, a union–management plan used by many companies, that focuses on (1) money bonuses to all members of the organization in proportion to their base rates, for all improvements in the firm's efficiency; and (2) a system of work-improvement committees that cross organizational levels. The plan has had a great impact on the nature of the interpersonal relations between managers and workers and among the workers themselves. In general, the plan has fostered a greater acceptance of responsibility by lower-level personnel, and a sharing of responsibility for decision-making by higher managerial personnel with lower-level groups in the hierarchy.[23] This approach, along with others, such as T-group training, Grid training, and transactional analysis, focuses on the forces affecting an individual's behavior in the organization.

Structure.   The structural approach involves changing the internal structure of the organization, i.e., the role responsibilities and relationships of organizational members and their centers, coordinative mechanisms within the organization, span of control, number of hierarchical levels, and the like. An example of a structural change is decentralization of decision-making authority and responsibility. One reason for decentralization is that it reduces the need for coordination between departments and also increases a manager's control over the departments. That is, each department is given more decision-making discretion and autonomy.[24]

Technology.   The technological approach focuses mainly on problem-solving mechanisms and the processes by which new problem-solving methods are generated and adopted by the organization. Historically, this approach has its bases in the pioneering work of Frederick Taylor and the scientific-management movement. Out of Taylorism there emerged a group of individuals (industrial engineers) who were primarily trained in planning and measuring units of production. Since Taylor, the technological approach has been expanded to include not only measurement of specific jobs, but work flow among departments, information systems, and the like. For example, Volvo's redesign of the car manufacturing process is an example of a technological change. For half a century, it has been argued that the economics and technology of making cars left no alternative but the assembly line. However, Volvo has redesigned this process to emphasize team work and job enrichment.

Task.   The task approach focuses on the job performed by the individual. Examples of task approaches would include job enrichment, job rotation, and behavioral modification. The case study of Emery Air Freight (see Chapter 4), demonstrates the practical and economic benefits of dealing with specific task behavior and its consequences. This company put a few behavioral modification techniques (such as providing feedback, reinforcements, and the like) to the practical test of modifying on-the-job behavior and succeeded. Under the general direction of Edward Feeney, Emery was able to save a reported $2 million over a three-year period by identifying performance-related behaviors and strengthening them with positive reinforcement.

It should be pointed out that all of these variables are usually present in a change process. A systems approach to change requires that all these variables be understood before one variable is disturbed.[25] For example, a redesign of jobs to permit more decision-making authority by employees should probably be accompanied by more participative supervision, by a pay system that recognizes and rewards performance, and by a communication system that encourages open channels of communication.

TYPES OF CHANGE AGENTS

Behavioral scientists have frequently taken somewhat divergent positions on the question of who should initiate an organizational change, what type of person would this be, and what methods should be followed. The particular approach to change is, to some extent, a function of the *change agent*. This section will be devoted to understanding how certain qualities, characteristics, and behavior patterns affect the functioning of a change agent.

Many authors have addressed these questions, and alternative answers are readily available in most textbooks.[26] However, few models are available that portray the actual behavior of change agents. Figure 12–5 provides a model for describing various types of change agents. The model, proposed by Tichy, was derived from a study of 91 well-known social-change agents.[27]

There are five basic components to the model, all of which interact with each other. First are the *background* characteristics of the change agent. These typically would include the agent's educational training, income, religion, age, sex, relationships to clients, and so forth. The second part of the model is the *value* component. The value component represents the agent's evaluative orientation toward change, such as his or her attitudes toward important social

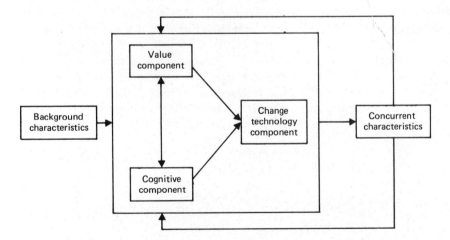

Figure 12–5 Framework for Change Agent's Role

Source: Tichy, N. Agents of Planned Social Change: Congruence of Values, Cognitions and Actions. *Administrative Science Quarterly,* 1974, **19**, p. 165. Reprinted by permission.

changes, political orientation (left, liberal, moderate, conservative), his or her own social-change goals (increased range of individual freedom and choice, improved satisfaction of members, equalization of power between organizational members, and so forth), and the goals he or she feels change agents should have. This component represents behavior expected of a change agent. The third basic component is the agent's *cognitive* component—the change agent's concepts about means of affecting change. Tactics such as shifting organizational power and authority, changing the selection system, management training, job redesign, and so forth, represent different means for affecting change. The relative emphasis placed on the four variables—task, structure, people, technology—discussed earlier in this chapter would be still other examples of cognitive components. The fourth basic component is the agent's *technology.* This refers to the tools and skills the change agent uses to effect social change. To make use of his other knowledge (cognitive component) and to act on his other values (value component), each change agent has a set of techniques, such as sensitivity training, operations research, survey feedback, team development, and so forth, that can be applied to a situation. Finally, the *concurrent* characteristic refers to the actual behavior of the change agent. The relationship among the five components of the model assumes that stress or tension exists in the change agent when the value component and concurrent characteristics or the cognitive component and actions are not in agreement with each other. For example, an agent whose values are openness, trust, etc., will most likely use tactics such as transactional analysis or T-group training, which reflect these values, and not operations-research techniques, to understand an organizational problem and bring about a planned change.

Based on consistent differences in the patterns of these five components of the model in Fig. 12–5, four different types of change agents have been identified. These are (1) People-Change-Technology (PCT); (2) Analysis-from-the-Top (AFT); (3) Organizational Development (OD); and (4) Outside Pressure (OP). Since the "Outside Pressure Type" (e.g., Ralph Nader, John Gardner, Eldridge Cleaver) is rarely used by managers to bring about changes, we shall discuss only the three other types of change agents. Table 12–2 outlines the change tactics likely to be used by each type of change agent and the frequency with which they are used. Many of the change tactics listed in this figure will be discussed in Chapter 13.

People-Change Technology (PCT)

This type of change agent often works to achieve change in the way members behave. These agents are usually concerned with improving motivation, job satisfaction, and productivity. One PCT person described his role as:

> To help individuals and organizations focus on goals, obstacles which stand in the way of goal attainment, individual motivation patterns and requirements of the task, organizational goal attainment, emphasis on individual and organizational self-development.[28]

Table 12-2 Percentage of Different Change Tactics Used by Change Agents

Change tactic	People-change technology type (PCT)	Organization development type (OD)	Analysis-from-the top type (AFT)
Confrontation meetings	47	95	39
Survey feedback	46	50	38
Job training	65	22	75
Sensitivity training	41	79	21
Team development	65	100	31
Technological innovations	71	63	89
Change in reward structure	82	58	71
Change in decision-making structure	76	94	96
Role clarification	100	100	95

Adapted from: Tichy, N, "Agents of Planned Social Change: Congruence of Values, Cognitions and Actions," Administrative Science Quarterly, 1974, 19, p. 177.

Methods used by the PCT change agent, as listed in Table 12–2, include job enrichment, behavioral modification, need-achievement training, management by objectives, and the like. The basic assumption of these change agents is that if individuals change their behavior, the organization, too, will change, especially if enough (or the right) individuals in the organization change.

The data gathered by Tichy indicate that PCT change agents usually hold academic positions with doctorates, range in age between 35–40, and have median incomes ranging between $20–30 thousand. Their political orientation is liberal, and they express a moderate degree of societal criticism. The linkages between political orientation and values indicates that their primary value is to improve system efficiency, increase output, and to equalize the power and responsibility within the organization.

Analysis-From-the-Top (AFT) Type

This type of change agent relies primarily on the operations research model. These agents work on creating, improving decision-making, and maintaining and controlling employee performance. One AFT describes his role as:

> ... to work with groups concerned with problems of design and operation of system, in order to aid in resolving their problems. Normally the work involves technological remodeling and analysis.[29]

Methods used by the AFT change agent, listed in Table 12–2, include changing the decision-making structure of the organization, technological innovations, and job training in areas such as computerized information-processing systems, development of new tasks, and so forth. These change agents assume that if the organization's impersonal technical and structural processes are changed, the organization's efficiency will increase.

The AFT change agents are likely to be older than either the PCT or organizational development (OD) change agents (ranging in age from 40–50), have a median income over $40,000, and are not necessarily associated with an academic institution or holders of doctorates. They are moderates with respect to their political orientation and are not critical of society.

Organization Development (OD) Type

This type of change agent works to improve the organization's problem-solving capabilities by helping people learn to help themselves. This involves assisting members of the organization to work out their interpersonal problems and communications, conflicts of interest, career plans, and the like. As indicated in Table 12–2, OD change agents rely on tactics such as team building, role clarification, confrontation meetings, and sensitivity training to achieve their goals. One of the basic goals of the OD change agent is to increase democratic participation in decision-making by all members. In this way, the organization can develop problem-solving mechanisms so key executives can work with each other.

The background characteristics of the OD change agent include a median age of 40–50, primarily Protestant religious beliefs, a high proportion holding degrees, and a median income of $30–40 thousand. Their political affiliation tends to be liberal or toward the moderate side. They do not advocate radical changes in organizations to achieve their objectives.

Summary

This typology of change agents suggests that each type of change agent appears to have somewhat different goals and tactics for facilitating organizational change. The PCT change agent's goals, however, seem to be closely aligned with the goals of the OD agent, which are the improvement of organizational problem-solving, while the AFT change agent's primary goal is to increase organizational output and the organization's efficiency. In addition to these different goals, the tactics used by each change agent are different. OD change agents emphasize team development, confrontation meetings, and the like. The PCT's focus more on individually oriented tactics, such as role clarification and job training, whereas the AFT's rely more on impersonal technical and structural tactics to achieve their goals.

The data in Table 12–2 illustrate the relative emphasis on tactics used by these three types of change agents. However, you should notice that all three types of change agents, depending on the situation and their individual values and philosophy, can rely on similar tactics to bring about planned change. For example, all three types of change agents report they use tactics such as confrontation meetings, survey feedback, job training, and role clarification. In other words, although the values and cognitions may differ among the three types of change agents, the change tactics may be quite similar, with major differences being those of relative emphasis and focus.

The establishment of the three types of change agents can be linked to Leavitt's model. The OD change agent is more likely to examine people as forces either supporting or resisting change; the PCT agent is more likely to examine both people and structure, and the AFT change agent is more likely to examine the technological forces. The change agent's selection of forces is influenced by his own goals, and sometimes by those of the organization.

Internal and External Change Agents

Change agents can be members of the organization as well as outsiders. Many large organizations, such as General Electric, Corning Glass Works, TRW Systems, Imperial Chemical Industries Limited, and Shell Oil Corporation, among others, employ full-time change agents. These organizations often set up a department in the corporate headquarters, usually reporting either to the vice-president of industrial relations or of human resources, called an organization-development or organization-improvement department. This department frequently functions as an internal consulting organization available to various departments of the organization to help them with diagnosis, planning of changes, and conducting various types of training programs. Most smaller firms cannot sufficiently utilize such personnel to warrant the cost associated with a full-time staff. These firms usually rely on external change agents for assistance.

There are several differences between internal and external change agents. In general, the roles of internal and external change agents cannot be interchanged.[30] The role of the external change agent is much more clearcut than that of the internal consultant, who may have more difficulty in explaining his or her role to organizational members. Further, internal change agents are more likely to accept the system as given and try to accommodate their change tactics to the needs of the organization. Thus, internal change agents are more likely to focus on activities such as team building, improving the quality of meetings, and other tactics. By accepting the norms of the organization, these change agents spend little time in helping the organization move toward self-renewal, growth, and change. In contrast, the external change agents appear to be freer to examine the organization from a total systems viewpoint, and are much less affected by organizational norms. Similarly, external change agents are likely to have easier access to top managers since they are usually the people who initiate contact with the external agents.

ETHICAL CONSIDERATIONS

The change agent is often in a situation analogous to that of a nuclear physicist.[31] The knowledge about the control and manipulation of human behavior that the change agent is capable of applying is beset with enormous ethical ambiguities, and he or she must accept the responsibility for the social consequences. The change agent must be concerned with the question of how his or her knowledge is likely to be used by the organization and at the same time be concerned with choosing an approach that will facilitate the organization's reaching its goal(s). For those individuals who are concerned with the individual's fundamental freedom of choice, any manipulation of the behavior of others constitutes a violation of this basic "right." This would be true regardless of the tactics used by the change agent. However, some degree of manipulation and control of individual behavior is an inherent part of every planned change. An implicit imposition of the change agent's values, cognitions, and technology on the organization he or she is trying to influence is accepted by the organization that hires the change agent. In attempting to provide answers to these questions, many of the ethical dilemmas can be grouped into two major categories: power and freedom.[32] Although these categories are tightly interwoven, we shall treat each of these separately.

Power

Two important questions are raised in this area. The first is one of justice. Is it fair for those who already possess power and control over others to exert influence over the change process? This question is especially important because many of the tactics used by change agents will likely change or reinforce the balance of power, influence, and authority in the organization. For example, an OD tactic of team development depends on the willingness of members to look at the way in which they interact with each other, the activities formed by members of the team, and the like. Behavioral patterns are often modified which may strengthen the influence of some members relative to others.

The second question centers on the degree of openness regarding the power implications of a change effort. Important issues are:

What is to be defined as a problem?

Where can the change realistically be brought about with maximum benefit and minimum damage?

Who will evaluate the effectiveness of the change?

How will the information be gathered?

Typically, information is collected in an atmosphere of trust, where no one will be harmed by his or her honesty, but trust and openness have their limits in organizations where power and status differences exist.

Freedom

Some of the most critical issues in a planned change effort lie in the area of personal freedom and the related value of individual welfare. The essential points of freedom are: (1) an awareness by the individual of options for choice, knowledge of the consequences for each option, and the ability to act upon a decision; (2) manipulation; and (3) misuse of information.

Informed Consent.   From our observation, many employees have only the vaguest notion of what the change will mean to them personally at the time they agree to participate or are persuaded to participate. "The boss thinks this is a good idea" is too often used as the rationale for enlisting employees in a change effort. While there is no easy solution for this problem, several guidelines have been suggested by practicing change agents. First, the change agent should clearly articulate the tactics likely to be used in the change effort. Second, the results of the change effort are likely to be more effective when participation is voluntary and the participants have had a voice in whether or not the change should be undertaken.

A study conducted by Coch and French in a clothing factory illustrates the possible benefits of participation and informed consent.[33] The change agents (PCT type) introduced changes in work methods by varying the amount of participation in the change process. This set up a "field experiment" research design (see Chapter 2 for a detailed description of this). The first group, "no-participation," was told that there was a need for a minor methods change in their work procedures and were given instructions on how to perform their work in accordance with the new method. In the second group, "participation-through-representation," the workers were given the problem facing the company. After they had reached agreement about the need for change, the group was asked to name workers who would be given the needed specialized training. In the third and fourth groups, "total-participation," all workers were introduced to the work change on a total participation basis and were asked to discuss how existing work methods could be improved and unnecessary operations eliminated. The results clearly indicate the effects of varying amounts of participation. The output of Group 1 dropped immediately to about two-thirds of its previous output. There were marked expressions of hostility—deliberate restrictions of output, conflict with the methods engineers—and a 17 percent quit rate. In contrast, the productivity rate of the total participation group exceeded the previous rate and there were no signs of hostility and conflict. The results of the second group were intermediate between Group 1 and Groups 3 and 4.

Manipulation.   This refers to deliberate attempts to change the structure of the individual's personal, social and/or physical environments without their knowledge. Some change agents encourage participants to "open up" and reveal their true feelings and thoughts. That is, they place the individual in situations that may involve an invasion of privacy, and through group pressure force the individual to respond.

Misuse of Information.   A basic component in many change tactics is an honest expression of problems and the expression of negative feelings. Unfortunately, these revelations by employees can sometimes be used against them by their superiors. For example, in the U.S. Foreign Service, where status differences are accentuated, promotions depend heavily on the favorable impressions of superiors, and transfer to other organizations in the same career line is difficult. Thus, the effects of honesty could be devastating on the career development for certain organizational members. Differences in power and authority could give some members of the organization the opportunity to retaliate for unpleasant revelations. However, change agents are usually in a "doctor–patient" relationship were norms of confidentiality have been formed and are usually adhered to.

SUMMARY

This chapter has focused on several global change-related issues. The first theme developed was the various forces encouraging organizational change. The increasing rate of technological innovation and knowledge, coupled with the changing nature of the workforce and its values, poses serious problems for many organizations in terms of profitability and stability. The second theme was to address various sources of individual and organizational resistances to change. To adapt to their changing environment(s), organizations need to systematically plan their changes.

To understand the change process, we proposed a systems model of planned change. Major changes involve a multitude of factors that affect the entire organization. Four factors—technology, task, structure, and people— were identified as the major factors that are likely to be altered in a change effort. The selection of a factor to be changed depends on the type of change agent. Three different types were discussed: organization development (OD); people-change technology (PCT); and analysis-from-the top (AFT). A number of the tactics employed by the three types of change agents are similar, but the relative emphasis placed on the tactics and the change agent's personal philosophy often differ.

The last section of the chapter examined some of the ethical dilemmas in the change area, with particular emphasis on power and freedom. Awareness by the individual, knowledge about the tactics used, and the misuse of information were discussed as major ethical issues.

Discussion Questions

1. What internal and external forces have stimulated the necessity for changes in many of today's organizations? What has been the response of these organizations to such changes?

2. How may an individual's resistance to change have desirable consequences in an organization?

3. Why are organizations referred to as "innovation-resisting" by many change agents?

4. What is meant when one refers to equilibrium in an organization?

5. What are the four major system variables affecting an organization's ability to change? How are these interrelated?

6. What are the principal differences between PCT, OD, and AFT change agents?

7. What are the implicit value differences between an internal and external change agent?

8. What are some of the ethical considerations facing change agents?

CRITICAL INCIDENT

The manufacturing operations at the Phelps plant of the Macungie Corporation consist of fabricating and assembling trucks—over-the-road, fire engines, and panel trucks. Traditionally, the manufacturing systems have been designed and built around an assembly-line operation.

As general production manager of the Phelps plant, Mr. Schaadt, who has developed through the management ranks largely by following the basic principles of management, must give final approval to all system changes that will affect the operations of this plant. A new design for an engine of the over-the-road truck has been completed by product engineering. In turn, it has been released to manufacturing engineering for implementation into the assembly-line system.

The manufacturing engineering group recently studied the available research relative to the advantages of job enrichment and how it compares to the traditional method of an assembly line, in terms of providing the workers with more challenging tasks, relief from boredom, and greater responsibility for the product. Management realized that job satisfaction and motivation continued to be an apparent problem on assembly-line work, and a system that included job enrichment was developed to assemble the new components of the engine along with the traditional conveyor-paced system. After the systems had been in operation for six months, the results of each system were presented to Mr. Schaadt for his approval. The manufacturing engineering group recommended that he adopt the job enrichment system because it relieved workers from performing dull, meaningless, and repetitive tasks. Mr. Schaadt, being aware of the perceived monotony and boredom of the assembly line, decided to accept the recommendation from the manufacturing engineering group.

As the production date arrived, the facilities were completed and a number of operators moved from the assembly line process to a new job. They, in turn, were told to completely assemble the engine and stamp their work with a personalized identification stamp that Macungie had provided.

Output and quality during the first week were 10 percent below that expected and during the next few weeks very little improvement was shown. In fact, the output was significantly below that of similar engine work at an adjacent conveyor-paced system.

Mr. Schaadt's boss was upset, since efficiency was low and excessive overtime was necessary to meet the heavy demands for trucks. Mr. Schaadt, realizing that he is responsible for the production at the Phelps plant, is trying to determine what happened and what course of action to take.

Questions:

1. What should Mr. Schaadt do?

2. What factors should Mr. Schaadt consider changing?

CRITICAL INCIDENT: CHANGE

In 1974, the management of Weis Market, located in Sunbury, Pa., realized that demand for grocery products was increasing in the central Pennsylvania region. Expansion of existing facilities and a wider diversity of products carrying the Weis label was necessary if this demand were to be met and the market position of the firm maintained. As a result, Weis began to expand its retail stores, constructed warehouses, and purchased several food-processing plants in central Pennsylvania.

One of the retail outlets affected by this expansion plan was located in a university town of State College, Pa. Having served the university community for more than fifteen years, it was still the kind of store where clerks waited on each individual customer. According to the central headquarters in Sunbury, the location was above average in sales potential because the university's enrollment was increasing, light industry was locating in the town, and customers were on friendly terms with the employees of the store.

In addition to the store manager, there were five clerks working in the grocery department, one clerk in the produce department, and five butchers. All of the employees were friendly with one another because most had gone to the same high school, and often stopped to chat or joke with each other about the "good old days." Mr. Cannon, the store manager, was a very efficient and cordial person. He insisted on certain work standards, but seldom interfered with the work of his subordinates. All the employees, including Mr. Cannon, had been working for Weis Markets for at least ten years. Consequently, it was understood and evident that each individual knew his particular job.

The congenial relations that existed among the employees may be exemplified further. Certain informal customs existed. Mathews, Wilson, Bither,

Dolich, and Olson—the five grocery clerks—were equally capable workers. When they had nothing to do, they often loaded the grocery bags of customers for the checkers, unloaded deliveries, or helped the produce clerk. Mitchell, the produce clerk, generally had enough work to keep himself busy, and when he couldn't handle all the work, Olson gave him a hand. Besides helping each other with their jobs, vacations were mutually scheduled so that more than one clerk could be absent at a time. All belonged to the Elks Country Club, and played on the store's softball team.

This was the situation in 1975 when the division manager came to the State College store to acquaint Mr. Cannon with the plan for Weis expansion. He stated that the company directors had decided to open a new supermarket in State College to replace the old store because of the increase in sales in the area and the opening of a new shopping center with a large K-Mart. Mr. Cannon was told that the new store would be ready within ten months and that all employees, except himself, would become part of the staff of the new store. Mr. Cannon was to report to the main office in Sunbury as part of the staff there. The employees received the news enthusiastically, realizing the advantages of the new store and feeling that their experience and seniority would provide them with opportunity for better jobs.

Ten months later, the new Weis store was completed, and the eleven employees of the old store reported to the supermarket for their assignments. All the grocery clerks were assigned to their usual job with no pay increases; Homan, the meat manager in the old store, was made assistant meat manager in the new store at $20 per week more; the other four butchers from the old store were given meat-cutting jobs with no raise; Mitchell, the produce clerk, was transferred to the dairy department with no salary adjustment.

During the next several months the old employees found that routines in the new supermarket were quite different from the old. Within a short time they found that work assignments were received from the various department heads at the beginning of each day, and there was little time for fraternizing. In addition, they found that the new store manager, Mr. Kelley, had little to do with the employees directly. Once when Olson asked for a day off, he was told by Mr. Kelley to go through proper channels.

The butchers from the old store had even greater problems. Homan, the assistant meat manager, had fifteen years of experience with the company but reported to a meat manager who had just recently graduated from the local university. The latter, a Ms. Straka, placed most of the work load on Homan and gave him great freedom in running the department. When other managers were around, Straka took most of the credit for running the department, something that Homan resented.

Even worse, the other four butchers found that they now had to cater to a group of women packers. These women packaged the meat when cut, and distributed it to the self-serve boxes in the store. Often the girls blamed the butcher for any shortage in supply, even if he had nothing to do with the situation.

As time passed, tremendous pressure was put on all employees because the ratio of sales to labor was declining. Contact between employees was almost nonexistent. When Mathews, Wilson, Bither, and Dolich learned that two better jobs in the store had been filled by new employees, they all quit Weis and found employment at Dean's Market in State College. Within two months after this, Homan asked for a transfer to another store in the Weis chain, and Olson quit.

Questions:

1. What type of change strategy was used by Weis management?

2. Assuming you are Mr. Cannon, what would you recommend to remedy the situation?

REFERENCES

1. Greiner, L., and L. Barnes, "Organization Change and Development," in *Organizational Change and Development,* G. Dalton, P. Lawrence, and L. Greiner (eds.). Homewood, Ill.: Richard D. Irwin and the Dorsey Press, Inc., 1970, p. 2.

2. Zaltman, G., R. Duncan., and J. Holbek, *Innovations and Organizations.* New York: John Wiley & Sons, Interscience Publication, 1973, pp. 110–121.

3. Nanus, B., "The Future-Oriented Corporation," *Business Horizons,* 1975, **18,** pp. 5–12.

4. For those who wish to pursue this line of reasoning more closely, see Galbraith, J., *Designing Complex Organizations.* Reading, Mass.: Addison-Wesley, 1973. Weick, K., *The Social Psychology of Organizing.* Reading, Mass.: Addison-Wesley Publishing Co., 1969.

5. Snow, C., *The Two Cultures: A Second Look.* New York: Mentor Books, 1964.

6. Toffler, A., *Future Shock.* Random House, 1970. *Also see:* Toffler, A., *Learning for Tomorrow.* New York: Random House, 1974.

7. Schmidt, W., *Organizational Frontiers and Human Values.* Belmont, Calif.: Wadsworth Publishing Co., 1970, p. 28.

8. Adapted from Huse, E., *Organization Development and Change.* St. Paul, Minn.: West Publishing Co., 1975, pp. 9–12.

9. Langway, L., "Corporations: Brain Drain," *Newsweek,* March 24, 1975, pp. 76 ff.

10. Mayer, A., "Sick Bug," *Newsweek,* May 26, 1975, p. 67.

11. Quinn, R., and L. Shephard, *The 1972–1973 Quality of Employment Survey.* Ann Arbor, Mich.: Survey Research Center, Institute for Social Research, The University of Michigan, 1974, pp. 19–20.

12. *Work in America: Report of a Special Task Force to the Secretary of Health, Education, and Welfare.* Cambridge, Mass.: The MIT Press, 1973. Quinn, R., and T. Mangione, *The 1969–1970 Survey of Working Conditions: Chronicles of an Unfinished Enterprise.* Ann Arbor, Mich.: Survey Research Center, 1973.

13. Quinn, R., and L. Shephard, *op. cit.*

14. DiMarco, N., and S. Norton, "Life Style, Organization Structure, Congruity, and Job Satisfaction," *Personnel Psychology,* 1974, **27,** pp. 581–591.

15. Watson, G., "Resistance to Change," in *Planning to Change,* 2nd ed., Bennis, W., K. Benne, and R. Chin (eds.). New York: Holt, Rinehart & Winston, 1969, pp. 488–498.

16. Brown, K., and J. Slocum, "An Application of Systems Concepts in Diagnosing Organizational Strategies," in *Management and the World Today.* D. Hellriegel and J. Slocum (eds.). Reading, Mass.: Addison-Wesley Publishing Co., 1975, pp. 54–70.

17. Thompson, V., *Bureaucracy and Innovation.* University, Ala.: University of Alabama Press, 1969.

18. Kaufman, H., *The Limits of Organizational Change.* University, Ala.: The University of Alabama Press, 1971. Shepard, H., "Innovation-Resisting and Innovation-Producing Organizations," *Journal of Business,* 1967, **40,** pp. 470–477.

19. For a description of these interrelationships, see Huse, E., *op. cit.* Sashkin, M., W. Morris, and L. Herst, "A Comparison of Social and Organizational Change Models," *Psychological Review,* 1973, **80,** pp. 510–526.

20. Lewin, K., "Frontiers of Group Dynamics," *Human Relations,* 1947, **1,** pp. 5–41.

21. The example used draws upon the work of H. Knudson, R. Woodworth, and C. Bell. *Management: An Experiential Approach.* New York: McGraw-Hill Book Co., 1973, pp. 341–356.

22. Leavitt, H., "Applied Organizational Change in Industry: Structural, Technological and Humanistic Approaches," in *Handbook of Organizations,* J. March (ed.). Chicago, Ill.: Rand McNally & Co., 1965, pp. 1144–1170.

23. Frost, C., J. Wakeley, and R. Ruh, *The Scanlon Plan for Organization Development: Identity, Participation, and Equity.* East Lansing, Mich.: Michigan State University Press, 1974.

24. Luke, R., *et al.* "A Structural Approach to Organizational Change," *Journal of Applied Behavioral Science,* 1973, **5,** pp. 611–636.

25. Beer, M., and E. Huse, "A Systems Approach to Organization Development," *Journal of Applied Behavioral Science,* 1972, **8,** pp. 79–101.

26. Havelock, R., and M. Havelock, *Training for Change Agents.* Ann Arbor Mich.: Institute for Social Research, The University of Michigan, 1973.

27. Tichy, N., "Agents of Planned Social Change: Congruence of Values, Cognitions, and Actions," *Administrative Science Quarterly,* 1974, **19,** pp. 164–182.

28. *Ibid.,* p. 170.

29. *Ibid.,* p. 169.

30. Huse, E., *op. cit.*

31. Steele, F., *Consulting for Organization Change.* Amherst, Mass.: University of Massachusetts Press, 1974. Kelman, H., "Manipulation of Human Behavior: An Ethical Dilemma for the Social Scientists," *Journal of Social Issues,* 1965, **21,** pp. 31–46.

32. This section draws heavily on the work of Walton, R., and D. Warwick, "The Ethics of Organization Development," *Journal of Applied Behavioral Science,* 1973, **9,** pp. 681–689. Warwick, D., and H. Kelman, "Ethical Issues on Social Intervention," in *Process and Phenomena of Social Change.* G. Zaltman (ed.). New York: John Wiley, 1973, pp. 377–417. Walter, A. "Some Criteria for Ethical Considerations in Organizational Development." Paper presented at 35th Annual Meeting, Academy of Management, New Orleans, August, 1975.

33. Coch, L., and J. French, "Overcoming Resistance to Change," *Human Relations,* 1948, **1,** pp. 512–532.

*

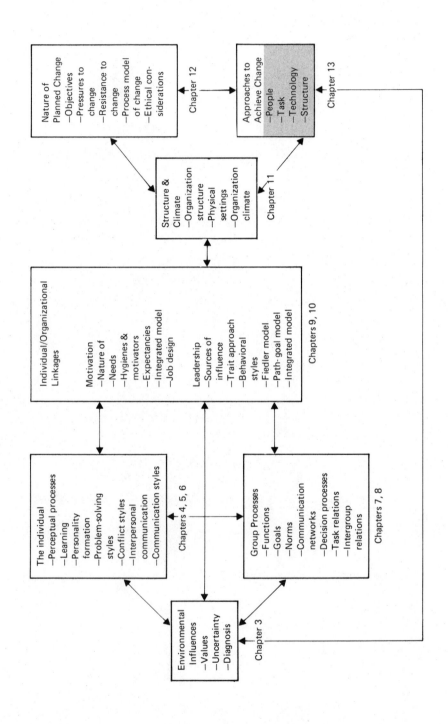

Nature of
Planned Change
—Objectives
—Pressures to
 change
—Resistance to
 change
—Process model
 of change
—Ethical con-
 siderations

Chapter 12

Approaches to
Achieve Change
—People
—Task
—Technology
—Structure

Chapter 13

Structure &
Climate
—Organization
 structure
—Physical
 settings
—Organization
 climate

Chapter 11

Individual/Organizational
Linkages

Motivation
—Nature of
—Needs
—Hygienes &
 motivators
—Expectancies
—Integrated model
—Job design

Leadership
—Sources of
 influence
—Trait approach
—Behavioral
 styles
—Fiedler model
—Path-goal model
—Integrated model

Chapters 9, 10

The individual
—Perceptual processes
—Learning
—Personality
 formation
—Problem-solving
 styles
—Conflict styles
—Interpersonal
 communication
—Communication styles

Chapters 4, 5, 6

Group Processes
—Functions
—Goals
—Norms
—Communication
 networks
—Decision processes
—Task relations
—Intergroup
 relations

Chapters 7, 8

Environmental
Influences
—Values
—Uncertainty
—Diagnosis

Chapter 3

13
APPROACHES TO ORGANIZATIONAL CHANGE

There is considerable controversy over the "best" approach for changing an organization, one of its units, and its members. We certainly make no claim of resolving such controversy within this chapter. From the pragmatic perspective of "Does it work?" a number of different approaches have been successfully utilized in organizational change efforts. But an approach to organizational change that was considered a success in one organization may also be a dismal failure in another organization. While there are numerous potential explanations for such conflicting outcomes, we want to re-emphasize the contingency perspective. In terms of organizational change, the contingency perspective suggests that there is not a single best approach to change, but that any approach is not likely to be equally effective under all circumstances. Accordingly, the major objectives of this chapter are:

1. To explain and illustrate a limited, but representative, number of specific approaches for changing an organization, one of its units, and its members;

2. To identify some of the key contingencies that should influence the choice of a particular approach and may influence the likelihood of its being effective;

3. To emphasize the close relationship between the concepts, models, and techniques presented in previous chapters with the treatment in this chapter;

4. To increase your knowledge and skills in using a representative range of change approaches in organizational settings; and

5. To develop your ability to anticipate the consequences and constructively respond to various types of change efforts initiated by others, but of which you are a part.

OVERVIEW OF APPROACHES

The chapter is, to some extent, organized as though each approach discussed is independent and mutually exclusive of the others. There is nothing that could be farther from the truth. The decision to present each approach somewhat independently is based on these considerations. First, an understanding of the various approaches that are commonly utilized and referred to within organizations is enhanced. Secondly, the desire to avoid becoming excessively complex and esoteric impels us not to focus on detailed similarities and differences in the approaches.

Interdependence in Approaches

The approaches to organizational change we shall be discussing are often quite interdependent and can be utilized in conjunction with each other. Thus, there is not a zero-sum or win–lose relationship between the approaches. This idea can be demonstrated by sharing some aspects of the Corning Glass Works Corporation's orientation to organization development and change.[1] Corning is a good example of a firm that applies the contingency perspective because it ". . . doesn't believe that it's possible to label any one intervention strategy [approach] as the most effective strategy, equally appropriate to all circumstances and adequate for all problems."[2, p. 22] A key contingency, which influences the choice of approach or combination of approaches, is the nature of the problem Corning is trying to resolve. For example, an approach that emphasizes the development of group problem-solving for production workers who are basically dissatisfied and frustrated with highly controlled, boring, and routine jobs could easily increase the problem. The opportunity for the production workers to discuss openly and explicitly the nature of their work, without the opportunity to make any changes in the ways by which the tasks are performed, may well increase the feelings of deprivation and misery. In this example, the key approach to change should probably focus on the nature of the production workers' jobs and opportunities to enrich the tasks performed. A supplementary approach may involve group problem-solving sessions with the production workers, to gain their assistance and embrace their ideas, in redesigning the tasks to be included in the jobs.

Medfield Operation of Corning

The Medfield operation of Corning, which produces various types of electrodes, provides a concrete example of a change program involving the combined use of several approaches. At the time of intervention in 1968, Medfield was new and small, with about 120 employees. The operation was nonunion and had a technology that permitted major changes in the task factor. The redesign of tasks was supplemented with approaches emphasizing people and structure factors. As suggested by Fig. 12–5 and discussed in the previous chapter, a major change program is likely to have an impact on task, structure, technology, and people, and may require a combination of approaches that facilitate change in each of these factors. At the Medfield operation of Corning, the variety of interventions and changes included:

1. Widespread introduction of job enlargement, particularly at the level of production workers, that enabled them to be responsible, individually or as an autonomous group, for the production of substantial components;

2. Monthly group meetings at every organizational level;

3. Weekly meetings between the plant manager and representatives of production and clerical employees;

4. Special meetings to consider technical and productivity issues or problems;

5. Creation of autonomous groups in some departments with responsibility for scheduling, assembly, training, and some quality issues;

6. Involving hourly workers in influencing their own productivity goals in relation to overall plant goals;

7. Redesigning pay systems to make them consistent, and as a means of reinforcing these other changes, such as more use of group versus individual pay incentives.

The many positive effects of these changes were shown within six months of introduction and have been retained during the following years. The qualitative and quantitative indicators improved substantially. Michael Beer, the director of organization development at Corning Glass when this change program was completed, summarizes the results this way.

> Voluntary turnover among hourly employees has consistently been below that for the area; productivity and quality have improved as changes have been made in department after department. The plant handles more volume with less supervision and indirect labor; management is able to introduce new and highly complex products without drops in productivity.[3, p. 31]

Implications

One of the generalizations from the experience at Corning and other organizations is that successful major change programs are likely to require the use of a variety of approaches that need to be employed simultaneously or sequentially. Of course, there are also many minor change efforts frequently underway in organizations that can be successfully implemented through a limited number and intensity of approaches.

When the tasks to be performed are routine, structured, and involve little uncertainty, some suggest it may be best to start with one or more approaches that emphasize the structural factor and are followed by one or more approaches that emphasize the people factor. Structural changes in this situation may be more readily utilized to "unfreeze" the organization, especially since decision-making, power, and information are more likely to exist at the highest management levels. In contrast, where the tasks are nonroutine, unstructured, and involve considerable uncertainty, it may be best to start with one or more approaches that emphasize the people factor and are followed by one or more approaches that emphasize the structural factor. In this set of circumstances, it is assumed that relevant information and knowledge are spread throughout the organization. Moreover, crucial technical competencies may be greatest at the lowest organizational levels.[4, pp. 75–77] While the logic and empirical evidence for these guidelines are appealing, the area of organizational change is too new and has been inadequately investigated to date to warrant a hard conclusion on this question.

Diagnosing Choice of Approaches

There is no ready-made or agreed-upon formula for determining the approach or combination of approaches to utilize in changing an organization. As mentioned previously, one key factor should be the nature of the problem the organizational members are attempting to resolve. However, as implied in the discussion of types of change agents in Chapter 12 and problem-solving styles in Chapter 6, individuals may be predisposed to perceive problems in particular ways and to choose particular change approaches.

Although this phenomenon cannot be fully eliminated, Beckard has suggested some guidelines for choosing an approach or combination of approaches. It is assumed that the approach chosen is believed to provide the greatest and most effective leverage to begin the change process. Beckard identifies four issues that should be diagnosed: (1) definition of the change problem; (2) determination of the readiness and capability for change; (3) identification of the change agents' own resources and motivations for the change; and (4) determination of the intermediate change strategy and goals.[5]

While widespread agreement may exist among organizational members as to the need for change, there may be very different perceptions among organizational members as to the change approaches that should be utilized and/or where they should be implemented. To increase accuracy in defining the change problem, there should be a systematic attempt to determine whether the primary initial focus requires a change (1) of attitudes? If so, whose? (2) Of behavior? If so, by whom and to what? (3) Of knowledge and understanding? If so, where? (4) Of organization procedures? If so, where and to what? (5) Of practices and ways of work? If so, whose? The initial approaches or interventions that are most likely appropriate can be partially determined by rank-ordering the relative importance of these questions.

The second issue focuses on assessing the attitude and motivational levels concerning the change, as well as the physical, financial, and organizational capacity to make the change. This issue was explicitly addressed in the previous chapter. Approaches that require a massive commitment of personal energies and organizational capacity are likely to be doomed if there is not a corresponding level of readiness and capacity. In such circumstances, it may be more effective to start with more moderate and less demanding approaches and increase the depth and breadth of the change approaches as the organization develops the necessary capacity and commitment. If the organization is in a state of crisis, the luxury of staged interventions over a long time span may not be a viable option. Given this contingency, there may be a tendency to do whatever is felt to be necessary. A prevailing attitude may be "after all, if you're at the bottom, there is no way to go but up."

The third issue consists of two components: self-awareness by the change agent, if one is used; and openness with the client system. First, the change agent should know himself before dealing with others. Secondly, the change agent should be open with the client about the knowledge and skills he or she brings to the organization, and what knowledge and skills he or she doesn't possess. The various types of change agents and their predispositions were discussed in Chapter 12.

Finally, the fourth issue concerns the determination of intermediate approaches and goals to enable movement toward the ultimate goals and approaches. This is illustrated by the earlier discussion of possibly starting with some structural approach and then moving to a people approach, or vice versa. While these four issues are quite interdependent, a conscientious consideration of each of them should increase the probability of appropriate judgments in the development of a change program.

Comparison of Approaches

The approaches to change considered in this chapter are intended to be a representative, rather than an exhaustive inventory. Some of the approaches to change that have been woven into previous chapters, such as job enrichment and behavioral modification, will not be discussed here. Obviously, job enrichment, behavioral modification, and other possibilities should not be viewed as irrelevant or unimportant simply because they are not extensively discussed in this chapter.

Relative Emphasis on Major System Variables.   Table 13–1 provides an overview of the change approaches to be discussed, the focus of each approach, and the relative direct impact of each approach on four major system variables (people, task, technology, and structure).

Table 13–1 Comparisons in Relative Direct Impact of Selected Change Approaches

Change approaches	Relative direct impact on major system variables			
	People	Task	Technology	Structure
People focus:				
Survey feedback	High	Low to moderate	Low	Low to moderate
Management by objectives	Moderate to high	Low to high	Low	Low to moderate
Grid organization development	High	Low to high	Low	Low to high
Transactional analysis	High	Low	Low	Low
Sensitivity training	High	Low	Low	Low
Task focus:				
Autonomous groups	High	High	Low to high	Low to high
Technology focus:				
Computer systems	Low to moderate	Moderate to high	High	Low to high
Structure focus:				
Role relations	Moderate to high	Low to high	Low	High

In Table 13–1, we characterize each approach in terms of whether it usually has a high, moderate, or low *direct* impact on each of the four systems variables. For those approaches that can often vary in their degree of direct impact on a particular system variable, we indicate such a range. For example, the management-by-objectives change approach may vary between a low and a high direct impact on the task variable. In reviewing the matrix in Table 13–1, a word of caution as to interpretation is in order. Any one of the change approaches could ultimately have a substantial impact on all four of the major system variables. Our interpretation of *direct* impact is based on the typical nature, focus, and orientation of each change approach, rather than its unanticipated, indirect, or ultimate consequences. It will also become evident that the nature of some of these approaches has certain common and overlapping attributes. For example, the management-by-objectives approach and the managerial-grid approach have several elements in common.

Since the objective of this book is to give special emphasis to the human element in organizations, we have a corresponding concentration on change approaches with a people focus. Thus, the fact that we consider only one approach under those that have a task, technology, or structure focus should not be interpreted as meaning that these are of minor importance in organizational change programs. It is our judgment, based on the literature on organizational change, that approaches with a people focus are more likely to be effective if preceded, accompanied, or followed by one or more approaches with a task, technology, and/or structural focus.

Relative Emphasis on Other Dimensions

A second set of comparisons for assessing the change approaches is shown in Table 13–2. This figure suggests the typical relative emphasis of each approach in terms of four dimensions: types of change agents most likely to utilize each approach (see Chapter 12); degree of cognitive emphasis; degree of affective/emotional emphasis; and the degree of need for trusting behaviors.[6] Again, each approach is characterized as high, moderate, or low in relation to three of the four dimensions. If an approach can often vary in terms of these dimensions as a result of different forms of application, we shall indicate our judgments as to the *typical* range.

In Table 13–2, you will note that several types of change agents may be likely to utilize the same change approach. However, the styles employed by the different change agents for implementing a particular approach could vary substantially. For example, the organizational development (OD) change agent tends to consider changes in role relations by involving the individuals who are likely to be affected by the changes, whenever possible. The analysis-from-the-top (AFT) type of change agent is also likely to utilize the role relations approach, but to involve members at lower organizational levels who might be affected by the changes to a very limited extent. Another example is

Table 13–2 Comparisons Along Four Dimensions of Selected Change Approaches

Change approaches	Types change agents	Dimensions		
		Cognitive emphasis	Affective/ emotional emphasis	Need for trusting behaviors
People focus:				
Survey feedback	OD	Moderate	Low to moderate	Moderate
Management by objectives	PCT, OD	Moderate to high	Low to moderate	Low to high
Grid organization development	OD	High	Moderate to high	Moderate to high
Transactional analysis	OD	Moderate to high	Moderate to high	Moderate to high
Sensitivity training	OD	Low to moderate	High	High
Task focus:				
Autonomous groups	PCT, OD	High	Moderate	High
Technology focus:				
Computer systems	AFT, PCT	High	Low	Low
Structural focus:				
Role relations	AFT, PCT, OD	High	Low to moderate	Low to moderate

OD = Organizational development type

PCT = People-change technology type

AFT = Analysis-from-the-top type

between the people-change technology (PCT) type and the organizational-development (OD) type in their use of the management-by-objectives approach. The PCT type is more likely to focus on individual objectives and overt behavior. On the other hand, the OD type is more likely to employ a management-by-objectives approach by first considering group attitudes, norms, and objectives.

The cognitive emphasis in a change approach refers to the extent to which it focuses on observable and overt aspects of the organization, as well as task-related knowledge and skills of individuals. The affective/emotional emphasis in a change approach refers to the extent to which it focuses on hidden or covert aspects of the organization, as well as attitudes or sentiments and personal styles of members. The trusting behavior dimension refers to the extent to which the change approach requires actions that increase one's vulnerability: . . . (a) to another whose behavior is not under one's control, (b) in a situation in which the penalty (disutility) one suffers if the other abuses that vulnerability is greater than the benefit (utility) one gains if the other does not abuse that vulnerability.[7, p. 230] The ranking of an approach as requiring low trusting behavior by those directly affected by the change should not be interpreted as distrust. It simply means the change approach is not heavily dependent on a high-trust relationship. We may expect any of the change approaches to be met with hesitation, skepticism, and resistance if there exists a high degree of distrust.

PEOPLE-FOCUSED APPROACHES

This part of the chapter explains and assesses five change approaches that are roughly classified as "people-focused." These approaches include survey feedback, management by objectives, grid organization development, transactional analysis, and sensitivity training. The key contingencies that are likely to be associated with the successful utilization of each approach are also reviewed.

Survey Feedback Approach

Nature.   Although this discussion draws from a number of sources, it appears that Floyd Mann and other members of the Institute for Social Research at the University of Michigan have been most heavily involved in the development of the survey feedback approach and research on it.[8] The primary objective of this approach ". . . is not to introduce a systematic change [such as a new computer system] but to improve the relationships among the members of each organizational family and between organizational families, through their discussion of their common problems."[9, p. 424] An organizational family refers to the supervisor or manager at any hierarchical level plus the employees reporting directly to her or to him.

The survey feedback approach involves a number of interrelated elements. Typically, the process starts with obtaining commitment and endorsement by top management. A standardized questionnaire is usually completed anonymously by members of the whole organization, or by members of a particular subsystem, such as a plant or department. It is generally preferred to include members of the whole organization or at least all the members in a particular chain of command, such as from the Vice-President of Marketing on down through all members in the marketing unit. The questionnaire usually asks for members' perceptions and attitudes on a wide range of areas, including: communication processes; motivational conditions, decision-making practices; coordination between departments; and satisfaction with company, supervisor, job, and work group. A sample of items included in one questionnaire that provided the data for the survey feedback program is shown in Fig. 13–1. A survey-feedback questionnaire may be a combination of standardized items that can be completed by all employees in many organizations; it may also include specially developed items for a particular organization or department. The questionnaire normally contains items which focus on the respondents' department as well as processes that may characterize the organization as a whole. In one reported case, top management retained only questionnaire items that related to practices and processes they were willing and able to change.[10] Since this approach requires the feedback of data from these completed questionnaires to all respondents, there was apparently concern about raising expectations of lower-level members toward possible areas of change that top management had no intention or ability to modify. Moreover, in this case, the relations between the union, which represented the production employees, and management were strained and tense.

The data from the questionnaire are usually prepared in a format that breaks out a summary of the responses for each organization, department, or unit. At a minimum, each member of an organization unit obtains a report that tabulates his or her group's responses, as well as those obtained from all other parts of the organization.

Group discussion and problem-solving meetings are then held by organizational units to discuss the data being fed back. Under ideal conditions, these group sessions would move from a discussion of the tabulated perceptions and attitudes, to identifying possible implications, and concluding with commitments to various action steps. Of course, a single group session may deal only with particular parts of the data fed back, and the organization unit may have several meetings over a period of time to process these data fully. In any event, these meetings are conducted in a very task-oriented and problem-solving manner that consciously tries to avoid focusing on "personalities."

Prior to conducting these meetings, an external agent often counsels the immediate superior in each organizational unit as to: nature of the responses; the basis and meaning of the questionnaire measures; suggestions regarding the interpretation and use of the data; and possibly guidelines for conducting the group problem-solving sessions. There are two basic ways of timing the

Instructions: To indicate how descriptive each statement is (or should be) of your situation, write a number in the blank beside each statement, based on the following scale.

1	2	3	4	5
To a very little extent	To a little extent	To some extent	To a great extent	To a very great extent

_____ 1. To what extent is this organization generally quick to use improved work methods?

_____ 2. To what extent does this organization have a real interest in the welfare and happiness of those who work here?

_____ 3. How much does this organization try to improve working conditions?

_____ 4. To what extent does this organization have clear-cut, reasonable goals and objectives?

_____ 5. To what extent are work activities sensibly organized in this organization?

_____ 6. In this organization to what extent are decisions made at those levels where the most adequate and accurate information is available?

_____ 7. When decisions are being made, to what extent are the persons affected asked for their ideas?

_____ 8. People at all levels of an organization usually have know-how that could be of use to decision-makers. To what extent is information widely shared in this organization so that those who make decisions have access to all available know-how?

_____ 9. To what extent do different units or departments plan together and coordinate their efforts?

How friendly and easy to approach are the persons in your work group?

_____ 10. This is how it is now.

_____ 11. This is how I'd like it to be.

When you talk with persons in your work group, to what extent do they pay attention to what you're saying?

_____ 12. This is how it is now.

_____ 13. This is how I'd like it to be.

To what extent are persons in your work group willing to listen to your problems?

_____ 14. This is how it is now.

_____ 15. This is how I'd like it to be.

To what extent does your supervisor offer new ideas for solving job-related problems?

_____ 16. This is how it is now.

_____ 17. This is how I'd like it to be.

To what extent does your supervisor encourage the persons who work for him to work as a team?

_____ 18. This is how it is now.

_____ 19. This is how I'd like it to be.

Figure 13–1   Sample Questions in Feedback Program [11]

feedback of the data: Everyone gets the data almost simultaneously, or a "waterfall" pattern is used, in which group meetings are held at the highest organizational levels first and followed by group meetings at each succeeding lower level.

Conditions for Effectiveness.   There are several conditions that probably should exist if the survey feedback approach is to have a maximum impact. The first condition has already been mentioned: the sessions need to be conducted in a factual, task-oriented environment. Secondly, each organizational unit must have sufficient discretion to consider and take positive action, or at least recommend changes, based on its findings and analysis for its own unit. A pattern of usage involving only the measurement of perceptions and discussion of them, without the opportunity to determine or strongly influence corrective actions, may actually be counterproductive. With this pattern, the members are likely to sense that they were deceived, manipulated, and misrepresented. The third condition serving to enhance the effectiveness of the survey-feedback approach is the practice of reporting up the line the results of the group problem-solving meetings from the immediate lower organization unit. This serves several purposes. Higher management is more likely to rapidly become involved in recommendations requiring some action on its part. There is more likely to be a recognition at all levels that this process is important and not mere window dressing. Thus, the commitment by all parties may be greater if there is a belief that their efforts could make a difference.

Assessment.   It has been suggested the effectiveness of the survey feedback approach ". . . in comparison to traditional training courses, is that it deals with the system of human relationships as a whole (superior and subordinate can change together) and that it deals with each manager, supervisor, and employee in the context of his own job, his own problems, and his own work relationships."[12, p. 5]

A strength and a limitation of this approach is that it relies upon, and might actually reinforce, the prevailing organization structure. This might occur because there is a major emphasis on improving working relationships and two-way communications between the various organizational levels within the existing structure. Another impact of the survey feedback approach may be to increase the influence of lower-level units with respect to higher organizational levels. But higher levels may also have greater influence with lower levels because their policies are better understood and the competencies and knowledge throughout the organization are being brought to bear on organizationally related issues. Fundamental structural changes, such as the movement from a functional to a matrix form of organization, are not usually a direct part of the survey feedback approach. But the survey feedback approach may be quite useful in surfacing problems and clarifying issues that serve to indicate the need for a major structural change.

One of the major studies of the relative long-term effectiveness of the survey feedback approach involved a five-year time span and was launched in 1966.[13] The survey feedback approach was used in five organizations and involved about 5,700 respondents. The respondents and organizations ranged widely, including blue-collar and white-collar workers in varying technologies and functions. The assessment of the effectiveness of the survey feedback was limited to repeated administrations, usually one year apart, of a standardized questionnaire, which focused on 18 scales or indices including decision-making practices, leadership, work-group support, job satisfaction, and the like.

The results of this assessment process indicated that the survey-feedback approach was associated with a significant frequency of improvement. The effectiveness of this approach was substantially attributed to: (1) the broad coverage of the process to include virtually all members; (2) the amount of unfreezing (see Chapter 12) that the approach stimulated; and (3) the members' tendency to perceive the data generated and the process as being directly relevant to the problems and goals of the organization and their units.

In sum, the survey-feedback approach can be effective in meeting both organizational goals and individual needs.[14] However, it is not a "radical" approach in the sense of bringing about fundamental changes in the structure, task design, or technology of the organization.

Management by Objectives

Management by objectives (MBO) is a widely employed and recognized approach to change and management. While it has been generally recognized in the business world since about 1965, MBO is gaining considerable attention and enthusiasm in the public sector as well. Although MBO goes under a single label, there are major differences between the ways by which it is prescribed in its ideal form and the ways by which it is practiced. One model of MBO tends to have a very strong emphasis on the individual while the other, less frequently discussed model places the emphasis on work teams and interdependent groups.

Impact of Managerial Values.   Several different managerial or value systems seem to underlie the different forms of application in the management-by-objective approach. In Chapter 3, three models of managerial values were presented: traditional profit-maximizing management, trusteeship management, and quality-of-life management. One of the key issues and elements in the management-by-objectives approach is the degree to which subordinates are involved in the process of setting objectives or goals. The prevailing managerial value system may play a crucial role in determining whether objectives are set by higher management and handed down to each lower level, or an interaction process takes place between superiors and subordinates in the

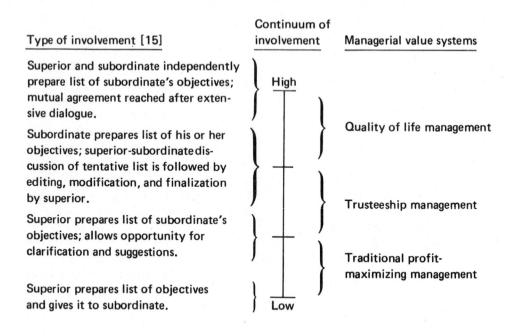

Type of involvement [15]	Continuum of involvement	Managerial value systems

Superior and subordinate independently prepare list of subordinate's objectives; mutual agreement reached after extensive dialogue.

Subordinate prepares list of his or her objectives; superior-subordinate discussion of tentative list is followed by editing, modification, and finalization by superior.

Superior prepares list of subordinate's objectives; allows opportunity for clarification and suggestions.

Superior prepares list of objectives and gives it to subordinate.

High

Quality of life management

Trusteeship management

Traditional profit-maximizing management

Low

Figure 13–2 Subordinate Involvement in Objective-Setting Process and Managerial Value Systems

goal-setting process. Figure 13–2 suggests the general relationship likely to be found between the level of subordinate involvement in goal setting and the three managerial value systems.

With profit maximizing management, we expect objectives to be established and tightly controlled by each higher level of management for the immediate lower level. The important value of the organization is to maximize profits, and all other decisions and actions should be directed toward this singular end. A recent study of the largest firms in the United States found a number of cases where MBO was used in an authoritarian manner with minimal subordinate involvement in objective setting.[16] This represents one of the key differences often found between the prescribed approach to MBO and the way it may actually be practiced. While there are some notable exceptions, MBO is usually prescribed as an approach that should have a moderate to high level of subordinate involvement in the objective-setting process.

In the trusteeship-management value system, there is a strong sense of organizational self-interest and the need to earn certain targeted profit levels. There is also likely to be a recognition of the value of some group and individual participation in decisions. Organizational members are viewed as both a means and an end and should have certain rights that must be recognized. Consistent with this value system, employees will probably be involved in the objective-setting process. While subordinates may be able to actually negotiate and formulate certain objectives with one's superior, there are likely to be other job-related objectives over which the subordinate has little influence. For example, a production supervisor may have little influence over the number of units to be produced by his or her unit, but may be able to negotiate with the superior so that the quantity objectives be established on a weekly rather than daily basis. This could serve to give the supervisor more flexibility in planning and coping with unanticipated contingencies, such as machine breakdowns, absenteeism, and set-ups for new runs.

The quality-of-life management value system is totally consistent with a high level of subordinate involvement in establishing both levels and types of objectives he or she is to pursue. You will recall that this value system maintains individual and group participation in the organizing, planning, and controlling of work relevant to one's job domain is necessary and desirable.

In sum, as an organizational change approach and process of management, MBO may well be found and practiced in substantially different forms as a consequence of different prevailing managerial value systems. With this recognition clearly in mind, the next section primarily focuses on one prescriptive model of the MBO approach that has an individual orientation.

Individual MBO Model

The individual-oriented MBO model includes four basic elements, each of which consists of a number of dimensions. As suggested in Fig. 13–3, these include an objectives-setting element, a subordinate participation element, an implementation element, and a review and feedback element. The arrows in Fig. 13–3 are intended to imply that all of the elements should be simultaneously operating to make the MBO process effective and there is a high degree of linkage between each of the elements.

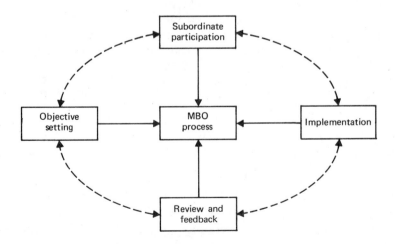

Figure 13–3   Individual MBO Model

Objective-Setting Element.   MBO is a system that tries to get subordinates and superiors to define and focus on the objectives of jobs, rather than placing so much emphasis on means, activities, procedures, or specific tasks. Our use of the word objectives is synonomous with terms such as goals, outputs, results, ends, or standards of performance. The objective-setting process includes identifying specific areas of responsibility for the job, the objectives or standards of performance in each area, and possibly a work plan for achieving the desired results. Figure 13–4 provides a hypothetical example for a salesman of selected task-related responsibility areas and possible specific objectives.

Over a period of time, the responsibility areas in a particular job are likely to change less dramatically and frequently than the specific objectives associated for each responsibility area. Thus, in Fig. 13–4, the salesman is surely going to have sales volume as a responsibility area on a continuing basis, but the specific level and changes in sales volume could vary dramatically. These changes might be due to general economic conditions, changed market acceptance, greater or less opportunities in one's sales territory, and the like.

There are two obvious recommendations in the process of setting objectives. First, objectives should not be stated in such global and general terms that they have little personal significance to the individual, such as stating that your job objective is to maximize the welfare of the firm and society. Secondly, objectives should not be stated in such narrow and detailed terms that the individual is expected to concentrate on dozens of different objectives.

One author did an analysis of what the various writers in the area of MBO regard as criteria or indicators of a "good" formulation of objectives.[18] He identified nine criteria often prescribed as indicators of a "good" set of objectives. Figure 13–5 outlines these criteria. In the righthand column, the percentage of MBO writers who agree on the inclusion of each criterion is indicated. These criteria might serve as useful guidelines for both developing statements of objectives and assessing an established MBO process. Many additional guidelines and criteria have also been prescribed for formulating objectives.

However, consistent with the contingency view, we need to keep in mind throughout this discussion several limitations with the seemingly clearcut na-

Figure 13–4   Hypothetical Responsibility Areas and Objectives for a Salesman [17]

Selected responsibility areas	Specific objectives
Sales volume	Increase sales volume by 10 percent
Gross margin of goods sold	Keep average gross margin on goods sold at 40 percent
Number of calls per day	Increase the average number of calls per day to 8
Order-call ratio	Increase order-call ratio to 25 percent
Average order size	Increase average order size to 200 dollars
New accounts	Generate 20 new accounts

Figure 13-5   Criteria Prescribed for Developing Statements of Objectives

Criteria	Percentage of agreement by MBO writers
Statements of objectives for a job should:	
be defined in terms of measurable results	100%
include the indicators or methods of measuring the attainment of the objectives	94%
specify the time period for accomplishing the objectives	88%
be in writing	82%
be reviewed two to four times a year	73%
include both routine and new developmental objectives	73%
have priorities or weights assigned to each objective	67%
include personal developmental objectives	55%
include a plan of action for accomplishing the objectives	55%

Source: Adapted and modified from: Kirchoff, B. A., "MBO: Understanding What the Experts are Saying," *MSU Business Topics,* 1974, 22, 53-59.

ture of the management by objectives process. As Steers and Porter conclude in their analysis of numerous studies on management by objectives and the process of objective setting, ". . . performance under goal [objective]-setting conditions appears to be a function of at least three important variables: the nature of task goals, additional situational–environmental factors, and individual differences."[19, p. 448]

For example, one researcher found that the performance of individuals with a high need for achievement significantly increased when objectives were made more specific and there was clearcut feedback on their efforts. On the other hand, the performance of individuals low in need for achievement significantly increased with greater opportunities to participate in the objective-setting process.[20]

With these limitations in mind, there may be a number of potential advantages in developing objectives for certain jobs, some of which might include: (1) increased knowledge of expectations; (2) reduction in goal displacement; and (3) systematic linking of jobs to departmental and organizational objectives.[21] MBO should increase each individual's knowledge of what is expected of him or her. This is often a precondition for improved work performance because the individual has better information about priorities, methods by which results will be assessed, resources available, and the outputs expected. Moreover, there should be greater clarification and understanding of inevitable types of role conflict and ambiguity between superior and subordinate. MBO may reduce the tendency for goals or objectives to be displaced because of an undue emphasis on rules, conformist behavior, and rigid behavior in light of changed or special job circumstances. This may be exaggerated to the point where primary concern with conformity to rules interferes with the purpose of the organization (or job).[22] Since the underpinning of MBO requires a conscious and systematic consideration and modification in job-related objectives, there should be less possibility for serious cases of goal displacement. Finally, MBO may have the potential merit of attempting to link the objectives of jobs to those of the individual's department which are, in turn, linked to a higher organizational unit such as a whole function or division.

Subordinate Participation Element. Some aspects of the amount of subordinate participation in the MBO process were previously discussed and summarized in Fig. 13–2. While there is not uniformity of agreement on the issue, it is frequently contended there should be a moderate to high level of participation by the subordinate in the objective-setting process. Before there can be any significant participation by the subordinate, there must already exist (or an increase be planned) a discretionary content to the job. This discretionary content should enable the individual to perform planning and controlling tasks in addition to "doing" tasks.

MBO, in and of itself, requires increasing or stimulating planning and control tasks on the part of the subordinate. Jobs that are highly routinized and programmed are likely to require enrichment and redesign through the task approach to change before considering the utilization of the MBO approach.

Black and Decker, a firm with an MBO program, has the following stated objectives for their program, which includes a high level of subordinate participation:

1. To help the individual to improve his (her) knowledge and skill;

2. To assure continuing two-way communications between the individual and his immediate supervisor;

3. To convert Black and Decker's goals into targets for the individual;

4. To realistically appraise the individual's performance.[23, p. 195]

The ways by which subordinate involvement has been systematized is expressed in their overall performance worksheet. The general instructions for the procedures to be followed in establishing objectives at Black and Decker are as follows:

1. The manager of each division, department, or section should meet with his or her subordinates in a briefing session to discuss how the group's targets can be converted to targets for each individual.

2. After the briefing session, each individual should review the group's targets and determine what his or her own targets should be to help the group achieve its overall targets. Then the individual should prepare the first three elements of the Work Sheet concerning personal development, principal job responsibilities, and specific objectives. Each manager should do the same for each individual reporting to him or her.

3. Finally, the individual should again meet with the manager and mutually agree on the personal and job targets and principal job responsibilities for the next year.

4. Both the manager and the individual will have a copy of the Work Sheet. The individual's copy is the working copy to be used throughout the year. The manager's copy is his or her working copy and becomes the permanent file copy at the end of the year.[24, p. 195] [Slightly edited from original.]

The Black and Decker example departs from the individual MBO model because there is some degree of group problem-solving and consideration of the objectives for the unit as a whole. There could also be more than one meeting between the superior and subordinate in developing the statement of objectives and working through of differences. A number of the group problem-solving skills, communication skills, conflict management skills, and the like discussed in previous chapters could be instrumental in making these sessions a constructive experience for both the superior and subordinates. Of course, if the parties have a low level of interpersonal competence or if there are unresolved political issues, we can anticipate numerous difficulties in these objective-setting sessions. In this regard, Odiorne has noted:

One of the major reasons for the failure of MBO in many organizations is that those in charge fail to recognize the political character of the implementation process. MBO is indeed logical and systematic, but it must also deal with a number of factors, including power and authority, the organization form, and the values and expectations of people.[25, p. 13]

After the objective-setting session(s) are completed, the subordinate should also engage in behaviors such as: personally reviewing progress toward objectives on a regular basis; renegotiating objectives when major changes occur; taking the initiative in letting the superior know when progress is lagging, and informing the superior when she or he feels there is lack of coordination with others or lack of resources that require action.[26]

In previous chapters, we have addressed the potential advantages and limitations of subordinate participation in decision-making. For the most part, we might expect these findings to hold with respect to participation in the objective-setting process. While recognizing the potential limitations to participation, some of the advantages might include: higher and better performance levels, greater job satisfaction, greater acceptance of objectives, lower turnover and absenteeism, improved understanding and communication between superior and subordinate.

Implementation Element.   This element refers to the idea of translating the outcomes from the objective-setting process into new day-to-day behaviors that will ultimately lead to the attainment of the desired objectives. For the superior, it often means he or she must give greater latitude and choice to subordinates. Accordingly, the superior might need to discontinue managing the hour-by-hour and day-to-day activities of subordinates. A key behavior and attitude of the superior is to be available to coach and counsel the subordinate as needed. Thus, the superior assumes somewhat less of a judgmental role and more of a helping or facilitating role. At Black and Decker, the superior is expected during the year to hold periodic meetings with the individual to review progress, discuss any assistance or help needed, and to make any changes in objectives if they are necessary. This last point needs special emphasis. It is generally considered desirable to change or modify objectives as warranted. This serves to keep MBO from being perceived as a rigid system and encourages major new problems or changes to be addressed as they occur.

   In sum, to increase the probability that MBO will be a successful change approach, the implementation element requires a conscientious consideration of the types of behaviors the superior and subordinate need to engage in on a day-to-day basis. A few of these behaviors have been suggested above.

Review and Feedback Element.   This element focuses on the subordinate developing a clear understanding of one's progress through feedback and review. As applied to MBO, feedback is a key element because it provides knowledge as to the correspondence between one's objectives and their degree of attainment. As discussed in Chapter 9, knowledge of results of one's behavior is often essential to changes in job performance and personal development in the form of new skills, attitudes, and/or knowledge.

   Unlike some other approaches, MBO places heavy emphasis on the subordinate engaging in self-control to review and participate in evaluating one's own performance.[27] By knowing one's objectives, the measures or indicators of achievement of these objectives, and having information available regarding these areas, the subordinate should be able to gain substantial insight into his or her performance and the possible need for modified behaviors. For example, two of the objectives for the salesman illustrated in Fig. 13–4 called for an increased sales volume of 10 percent and the maintenance of average gross margin on goods sold at 40 percent. So long as the salesman has information fed back regarding these areas, it is possible to have a very concrete self-understanding of his or her results in relation to the objectives. Unfortunately, the review process is often not so simple. In the case of the salesman, there may be factors, other than the salesman's own behavior, influencing possible gaps between the stated objectives and actual results. Secondly, significant parts of many jobs may not lend themselves to the development of indicators of performance that are based on "objective" measures.[28] As might be expected, an objective evaluated on the basis of judgment can result in a variety of different perceptions. Thus, the problem of determining whether or not the objective was achieved exists even before getting to questions of why it was or was not attained.

While MBO does not recommend a passive role by the superior in the review and feedback element, it does require the superior to shift from a judgmental and critical posture to more of a helping and mutual problem-solving role. At times, we have found individuals interpreting this element and the whole MBO process as "soft." Quite to the contrary! Individuals can be demoted and dismissed under this system. This is because the rationale and basis for such actions should be more apparent and it should be easier for the superior to confront the necessity of making such decisions. On the other hand, the MBO process is intended to reduce and prevent the need for such decisions.

Under ideal conditions, what might the feedback and review sessions between superior and subordinate look like? Carroll and Tosi have summarized the relevant literature for the common guidelines often suggested for reviewing performance. They are quick to recognize the day-to-day relations between the superior and subordinate are most likely to be the major influences in setting the tone and quality of the interview.[29]

Since a number of these guidelines have been discussed previously as general recommendations for improved managerial feedback, we only briefly mention them below (see especially Chapters 6, 10, and 11).

1. Meet on "neutral grounds" such as a conference room rather than the superior's office. This is to reduce the possibility of the superior being perceived as sitting in the "judge's" chair or actually behaving in such a manner.

2. Before the meeting, the superior and subordinate should review progress during the designated time period (such as 3 months, 6 months, a year), bring data they regard as relevant, and prepare a list of items they want to discuss.

3. The superior should create an atmosphere of a mutual problem-solving session.

4. The superior should listen attentively.

5. The superior should use reflective summaries to make sure there is an understanding of the subordinate's perceptions and feelings about a particular situation.

6. The superior should remain quiet if it appears that the subordinate is resisting discussion of a certain issue.

7. The superior should encourage and accept self-insight and criticism by the subordinate, especially through nonverbal communications like smiling and nodding.

8. The superior should give direct, rather than evasive, answers to the subordinate's questions.

9. The superior should minimize, but not necessarily eliminate, criticism of the subordinate. If there is criticism, it should be oriented toward the problem rather than the person. Whenever possible, descriptive and nonevaluative feedback is preferred.

10. The superior should allow the subordinate to release frustration through an open expression of feelings without being criticized or attacked for doing so.

11. The superior should use probing questions to encourage the subordinate to consider causes of problems and possible solutions.

12. The superior should encourage the confrontation and resolution of disagreements before the review session is ended. If not, the disagreements should be openly acknowledged.

These guidelines are not intended to be exhaustive nor a mechanistic, cookbook approach. As emphasized in previous chapters, guidelines such as these are easy to state, but difficult to put into practice. These guidelines are primarily valid under conditions of a high level of subordinate involvement and participation in the MBO process.

Overview.   The purpose of this section has been to outline a model of the MBO approach which has a strong focus on the individual. While the previous discussion has assumed a positive posture supportive of the MBO process, there have been a number of concerns expressed about it, particularly in terms of how it is actually applied in organizations. The criticisms of the MBO process seem to be in terms of how individuals actually use it, rather than in terms of how it is supposed to be utilized. A sampling of the criticisms of MBO include: (1) too much emphasis develops on a reward–punishment psychology (i.e., you are rewarded for accomplishing objectives and punished for not doing so); (2) MBO develops an excessive amount of paperwork and red tape —the very thing it is intended to reduce; (3) the process is really controlled and imposed from the top, allowing little opportunity for real participation; (4) it turns into a zero-sum (win–lose) game between superior and subordinate; (5) those aspects of the job that can be assessed quantitatively receive undue emphasis, relative to the more qualitative aspects of the job; and (6) there is too much emphasis on individual objectives and performance, which drives out recognition of the need for collaborative teamwork and group objectives.[30] This last criticism is considered in the following discussion of the team MBO model.

Team MBO Model

The team MBO model is fundamentally consistent with the key elements of the individual MBO model. One of the key differences is that the process encompasses entire work units or teams, as well as individual jobs. This model attempts to overcome two major deficiencies in the individual MBO model. First, the team model explicitly recognizes the interdependencies between jobs, especially those at the supervisory and managerial levels. Second, it encourages coordination of objectives between the individuals occupying the interdependent jobs, rather than placing the entire responsibility for integration upon the common superior.

Nature.   As with the individual MBO model, the degree of participation and influence in setting objectives by work groups can vary widely in the team model. French and Hollman have developed a nine-phase approach to the team MBO model, which incorporates a number of aspects of the Managerial Grid. Since the Grid is discussed as our third approach to organizational change, we will merely highlight here the distinguishing aspects of the team MBO model developed by these authors.[31]

1. Overall organization objectives to be achieved within a certain time period are developed in team meetings of the top executives, primarily on the basis of consensus. Of course, prior to this, it is assumed that there would have been inputs and interaction from lower levels.

2. Departmental or unit objectives to facilitate the attainment of overall organizational objectives are again developed in team or group sessions, primarily through a consensus process.

3. Individual objectives are developed within this framework. However, a major difference with the individual MBO model in this phase is that team members may discuss each other's objectives, make suggestions for change, and openly discuss the interdependent nature of their responsibilities.

4. While performance reviews still take place between superior and subordinate, matters of concern to the work unit are discussed in regularly scheduled meetings.

The team MBO model is likely to have the greatest potential for success only if certain contingencies exist: (1) The top management group desires to cooperate and offer mutual assistance, rather than engage in political power struggles. (2) The participants have some degree of skill in group processes and interpersonal relations. (3) There is a real need for integration between individuals.

Assessment.   Throughout the previous discussion, we have made a number of comments involving an assessment of the MBO model based on personal observations, case studies, or one-time attitudinal measures. There are very few studies reporting objective performance measures before and after the implementation of an MBO program. Even worse, it is difficult to determine from these studies how fully the MBO model was actually implemented.

One of the more recent and complete studies of changes in performance due to the implementation of an MBO program has been presented by Ivancevich.[32] The following is an outline of his procedure.

1. His study involved 181 supervisors in the production and marketing departments of three of the six similar plants of a manufacturing firm that had about 5,000 employees.

2. Objective performance data were collected at five points in time over a 36-month period.

3. Two plants had MBO introduced (experimental plants) and one plant was used as a comparison unit (control).

4. One of the MBO plants had a reinforcement schedule introduced 30 months after the program was initiated. The reinforcement schedule consisted of letters, memos, meetings, and telephone discussions from higher management to (and between) lower levels of management. These reinforcements emphasized expression from higher management of appreciation for implementing the MBO program, support for the program, and encouragement to keep at it.

Although the results from this study were quite involved and there were some differences between marketing and production, it appeared that: (1) the MBO program generally had a positive impact on performance; (2) the introduction of the positive reinforcement schedule in the one plant was followed by significant improvements in performance; and (3) the MBO program didn't seem to have much, if any, impact on one of the two production departments.

This and other studies suggest that the MBO approach to planned change can be effective, but its introduction is no guarantee of instant success.

Grid Organization Development

Grid organization development includes a number of aspects of the MBO model, in both its individual and team versions. For those overlapping parts, we will make only brief mention. Grid organization development (hereafter grid) tends to be a more encompassing change approach and addresses cognitive as well as affective/emotional issues normally unexplored in the MBO model, particularly in its individualistic form. The grid approach covers a wide range of organizational and behavioral issues, concepts, and skill areas. Correlative discussions of many of these have been presented in earlier chapters: the individual level (Chapters 5 and 10); the group level (Chapter 7); the inter-group level (Chapter 8); and the total organization level (Chapters 3 and 11). Robert Blake and Jane Mouton advanced the grid approach in book form in 1964 and since that time have been enthusiastically involved in writing and consulting on the approach.[33] The following discussion is primarily drawn from their various writings.

The grid approach to change in a large organization is thought to require three to five years for complete implementation. It requires a very systematic approach, consisting of six phases that are designed to be logically connected and to build upon each other.

Underlying Model.   The model that underlies the concepts, attitudes, and skills of all six phases in this change approach is the *managerial grid,* which serves as a framework for describing different ways of managing, as well as prescribing how one *ought* to manage. As shown in Fig. 13–6, the managerial grid consists of two dimensions, each of which can vary along a nine-point continuum. The vertical axis refers to the manager's degree of *concern for people,* particularly her or his subordinates. This is shown as ranging from "1," low concern for people, to "9," suggesting a high concern for people. The horizontal axis refers to the manager's degree of *concern for production,* especially by one's subordinates. Again, this is shown as ranging from "1," low concern for production, to "9," which indicates a high concern for production. Concern for production is used in the broadest sense to include number and quality of outputs, ideas developed, quality of decisions, activities performed, and the like.

Since Fig. 13–6 is a 9 by 9 grid, there are 81 possible combinations between concern for people and concern for production. As a practical matter, the focus is on the five critical combinations (four extreme and one central). Blake and Mouton utilize questionnaires to assess various aspects of a manager's style and behavior. The scoring process for these questionnaires usually enables the manager to plot where he or she fits on the 81-cell grid. There is nothing sacred about this 9 by 9 grid. It could just as easily have been developed as a 7 by 7 grid, an 11 by 11 grid, or on some other numerical scaling.

Let's briefly consider the five critical managerial styles noted in Fig. 13–6. Blake and Mouton suggest that each manager is likely to have a dominant style, such as 9,9, and a backup or secondary style, such as 5,5. There is alleged to be no natural link between a particular dominant style and the concomitant backup style. The combination will depend on the situation and individual.

The *1,1 managerial style* has been called impoverished management. The manager tends to put people on jobs and then avoid them, to follow the rules, and to serve as little more than a conduit of messages and orders from his or

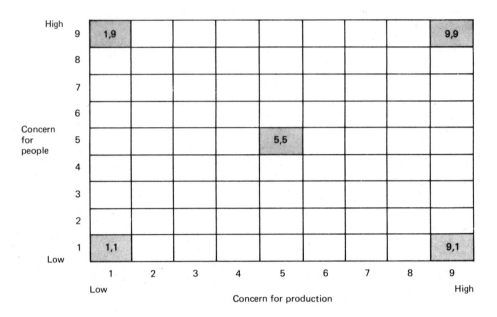

Figure 13–6   The Basic Managerial Grid

Source: Adapted and modified from: Blake, R. and J. Mouton, "An Overview of the Grid," *Training and Development Journal,* 1975, 5, p. 31.

her superiors. The *1,9 managerial style* has been called country-club management because of the exclusive emphasis on the feelings, comfort, and needs of subordinates. The concern is with obtaining loyalty from subordinates that will motivate them to produce without pressure. The *9,1 managerial style* has been called task management. The manager does the planning and pushes to get the work out, since subordinates are assumed to be lazy and indifferent. The subordinates are expected to follow the manager's rules, instructions, procedures, and schedules. The *5,5 managerial style* has been called middle-of-the-road management. The manager assumes there is an inherent conflict between concerns for people and production. Accordingly, there is an attempt to compromise and balance these two dimensions. The *9,9 managerial style* has been labeled as team management. It is regarded as the ideal style and the one that managers and the organization are encouraged to adopt. This style focuses on people's higher-order needs, involves subordinates in decision-making, and assumes that the objectives of the organization and the subordinates are compatible. All six phases of the grid organization development approach rest on the assumption that there is a potential win–win relationship between the people side and production side of organizations.

Each of the phases of OD can become quite complex and efforts to implement them may be time-consuming. It should therefore be recognized that the following represents a skeleton description of each phase.

Phases

Phase I: The Managerial Grid.   Phase I is essentially a seminar for the involved supervisors and managers. It is normally conducted outside of the organization. The seminar lasts about a week and involves all-day sessions, including evening assignments. The participants study reading materials, listen to short lectures, and, most importantly, diagnose their personal styles and approaches to management. This is accomplished through completion of questionnaires and small-group discussion sessions. There are also sessions dealing with methods for improving group (team) processes and assessments of the organization's norms, past practices, and organizational climate.

Phase II: Work Team Development.   This phase focuses on assisting the members of all work teams in the organization, such as a manager and his or her subordinate supervisors, to apply directly what they learned in Phase I to their specific situation. This process may start with the chief executive and individuals reporting directly to her or him, and then move downward to work groups at succeedingly lower levels. The work-team development phase encourages: (1) the diagnosis and resolution of barriers interfering with the effectiveness of the work team; (2) development of agreement on how the members want to operate; (3) setting of objectives, with a timetable, for improving their team functioning; and (4) creation of skills and a climate for introspecting and critiquing their own patterns of operation.

Phase III: Intergroup Development.   The objective of the intergroup development phase is to improve working and problem-solving relationships between groups (work teams) requiring closer integration. Many of the concepts and contingencies presented in Chapter 8, entitled Intergroup Relations, would be of relevance in this phase.
 Interventions in the intergroup development phase focus principally on the representatives from each unit who are primarily responsible and are involved in actual and direct contact with each other. These individuals are often assigned the tasks of: (1) developing an *ideal* model of what their relationships should be like; (2) comparing and exchanging group images of each other; (3) identifying problems and blockages in moving toward this ideal; and (4) developing an action plan for progress. Of course, an internal or external change agent is normally quite influential in sequencing the flows of activities and preventing sessions from degenerating into name-calling, scapegoating, or placing blame.

Phase IV: Developing an Organization Blueprint.   This phase focuses on designing an *ideal* model of what the organization should become, with a decreased emphasis on "what it is." As may be expected, the organization blueprint phase requires a particularly heavy commitment of time and energy by the top executives. This phase is also intended to move down through the lower levels, at least through all management and professional classifications. The output of this phase should include statements and understandings of changes in and new organizational strategies, objectives, structures, policies, and the like. If the organization blueprint phase is seriously implemented, there could be fundamental changes in the people, task, and structural variables (see Fig. 12–4). However, this phase of grid organization development does not generally seem to directly consider the technological variable.

Phase V: Blueprint Implementation.   Phase V is designed to bridge the gap from "what is" to "what should be." This phase requires the greatest period of time, possibly two or three years. Although there is no simplistic formula for the blueprint-implementation phase, a common recommendation is to create planning teams for logical parts or subsystems of the organization. These teams often have the tasks of conducting conversion studies of how they are to change and what specific changes they need to make. Of course, it is recommended that an overall planning team of top executives be actively engaged in the tasks of taking initiatives that don't naturally fall within the scope of other planning teams, and facilitating and reviewing the progress and outputs of these other planning teams.

Phase VI: Stabilization.   This phase involves an overall critique and evaluation of the organization's progress and the development of insights about the need for new changes and replanning. There is concern for reinforcing the new patterns developed from Phase I through Phase V, and making them "standard practice."

The stabilization phase may require administering questionnaires, interviewing individuals, reviewing performance data, and the like, to assess the degree of change, identify weaknesses, and plan ways of eliminating them.

Assessment.   The grid approach is potentially the most comprehensive of the people-focused approaches to organization change that we shall discuss. It represents an example of our earlier point that specific change approaches may well call for alterations in two or more of the four basic variables we have focused on; namely, people, task, technology, and structure.

Like the MBO approach, it is difficult to draw hard conclusions about grid organization development. This is because the studies on the grid do not make clear that: (1) the processes were always implemented as prescribed; (2) there was even an attempt to implement the full range of phases[35]; and (3) the research designs permit limited opportunity for drawing inferences about change.

The grid appears to be based on the assumption that there is *one best way* to manage and change organizations. This is certainly not consistent with some of the other research we discuss in this and other chapters, nor with the overall theme of the book. It is our judgment that the grid approach can be effective particularly where: the managerial value system approaches quality-of-life management; the external environment (such as governmental regulations or customer demands) does not tightly mandate internal processes; and the technology can be modified or does not tightly control people. Unfortunately, the best we can conclude is that the research suggests that the grid approach has had successes, failures, and mixed results.[36] This may be due to some of the contingencies suggested above.

Transactional Analysis

As of this writing (1975), transactional analysis seems to be approaching the status of a "fad" in terms of its use within organizations and the current levels of public attention. Sensitivity training, discussed in the next section, appears to have gone through the same process of simplistic attention and reached its peak as a "fad" about 1971. Like many ideas or things that develop into fads, there is a tendency for individuals who are attempting to exploit the fad to make excessive and misleading claims about what can be accomplished, as well as presenting *desired* objectives as *guaranteed* promises. There are numerous qualified and competent change agents who are capable of effectively utilizing transactional analysis and sensitivity training. It is unfortunate that these practitioners are sometimes faced with a need to overcome the disillusionment or embitterment created by such misrepresentation by other sources.

Although the processes of transactional analysis and sensitivity training differ considerably, their objectives, particularly when utilized for organizational purposes, are quite similar. Both approaches are often intended in an organizational change program designed to help the organization members:

1. Improve interpersonal communications;

2. Develop improved ways and styles for managing interpersonal conflict;

3. Gain self-insight by becoming more aware of their own behavior and obtaining feedback from others;

4. Develop diagnostic skills, particularly as related to the individual and small groups;

5. Acquire an understanding of the factors that interfere with or facilitate group functioning; and

6. Reduce self-defeating attitudes and behaviors.

Although some difference in interpretation is possible, we feel that both approaches strongly focus on the people variable, especially in terms of individual and small-group processes. Compared to the other approaches already discussed, there tends to be: relatively (and absolutely) little direct emphasis on the task, technology, and structural variables (see Table 13–1); relatively high affective/emotional emphasis; and relatively high need for trusting behaviors (see Table 13–2). Thus, the careful utilization of transactional analysis or sensitivity training could be effective initial approaches to unfreeze the organization for a consideration of other changes.

Basic Transactional Analysis Model [37]

Transactional analysis was first formally developed by Eric Berne in 1961 and was elaborated upon by him in a number of succeeding books.[38] As suggested in Fig. 13–7, the basic model of transactional analysis consists of seven interdependent elements.

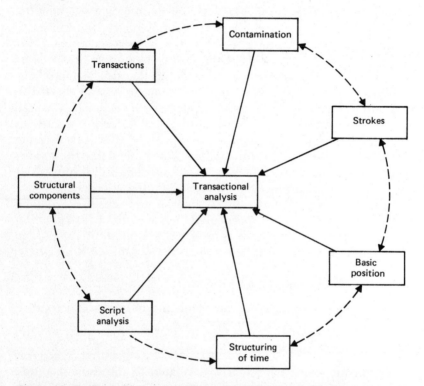

Figure 13–7   Basic Elements in Transactional Analysis Model

Structural Components.   The model contends that each of us is capable of displaying *three ego states:* Parent, Adult, and Child. An *ego state* refers to typical ways of feeling, thinking, and reacting.

The *Parent* ego state in each of us refers to the feelings, thoughts, and reactions that are similar to those perceived by us in our mothers, fathers, or other important individuals who might have reared us. The Parent in us assumes numerous functions, including: setting limits; giving advice; disciplining; guiding; protecting; making rules and regulations about how life should be (the musts, shoulds, always, nevers, goods, bads, etc.); teaching how to's; keeping traditions; nurturing; judging; criticizing; and the like. In themselves, the parental functions, like those of the other ego states, are not necessarily to be regarded as good or bad. One of the objectives of the transactional analysis change approach is to assist in becoming more aware of the Parent and then helping each of us determine for ourselves what forms and parts of it are relevant or irrelevant to our current lives. This is to help us live our own lives and not those of our parents. The ways by which parents or significant others use and communicate these functions strongly determines how children view parents, authority, and society.

The *Adult* ego state is the part that computes, stores experiences, and uses facts to make decisions. The Adult is the cognitive part of us and is unemotional. In the transactional analysis model, the Adult is not intended to mean or suggest maturity. The Adult functions include: data-gathering on the Adult, Parent, and Child; identifying and assessing alternatives; setting objectives and determining how to attain them; and all of the components of ordered planning and decision-making process. The manner of functioning of the Adult ego state varies between individuals, as well as in the extent to which it includes all of these functions.

The *Child* ego state refers to what we were in our younger years. There could be a number of "children" in us from the past. The Child in us could range from angry, rebellious, frightened, or conforming, to creative, carefree, funloving, adventurous, trusting, and so on.

All three of these ego states (Parent, Adult, and Child) exist within us, and all are important. It is desirable to have our Adult operating at all times so that it can keep us aware of the Parent, the Child, and the situation, as well as help us with our decisions. Thus, latitude of choice and freedom to be ourselves is increased.

Transactions.   Transactions refers to interactions we have with others and with our internal selves. It includes verbal and/or nonverbal communications that can vary from an exchange of compliments to a brawl. There are three basic forms of interpersonal transactions; parallel, crossed, and ulterior. These transactions occur between the three ego states of one person and the three ego states of another person. In the examples below, the following notation is used: P = Parent; A = Adult; and C = Child.

Transactions are *parallel* when the lines of communication between two individuals are complementary, such as Parent to and from Parent, Parent to and from Child, and Parent to and from Adult. The following are examples of parallel transactions which have been suggested by Luchsinger and Luchsinger.[39]

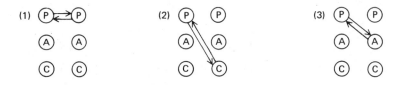

1. Parent–Parent Transaction.

> *Manager:*   An effective maintenance repair program always reduces costs.
>
> *Employee:*   I always say that a stitch in time saves nine.

2. Parent–Child Transaction.

> *Manager:*   An effective maintenance repair program always reduces costs.
>
> *Employee:*   Yes, sir.

3. Parent–Adult Transaction.

> *Manager:*   An effective maintenance repair program always reduces costs.
>
> *Employee:*   The problem is the new supplier. Maintenance and production records show that his parts don't last as do the parts from Acme Company.

In the above three examples, the employees are acting in the perceived expected ego states.

A *crossed* (noncomplementary) transaction occurs when the interactions do not have common origination and terminal ego states. Difficulties in communication and arguments often arise from crossed transactions, as illustrated below:

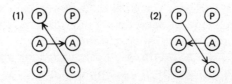

1. Crossed Transaction

> *Joe:*   Do you know how long it takes (the bus) to get to Philadelphia?
>
> *Jack:*   I wish we could stop for a milkshake.

2. Crossed Transaction

> *Doting Mother:*   You can never trust a man. They're just no good.
>
> *Sally:*   You can't judge a man you haven't met.

Ulterior transactions occur when one individual attempts to create the impression of relating to one ego state when, in fact, he or she is responding to another. These transactions represent attempts to be dishonest, manipulate, or engage in unconscious "game playing." Ulterior transactions involve the simultaneous activity of more than two ego states and are the basis for psychological games, as illustrated below.

1. Ulterior Transaction.

> *Joe Supersales:*   You'd get a better vacuum for another $30.00, but I don't think you can afford it.
>
> *Patsy:*   I'll take it.

Here, the salesman addresses Patsy Adult–Adult on the social level, but Adult–Child on the psychological level. This is done in the hope of hooking the Child into responding "Yes, I'll take it." A wary Adult would realize the financial irresponsibility and squash the offer.

Contamination.   This refers to the Child's acceptance in us of our parents' or significant others' prejudices, opinions, and feelings as our own. Thus, we may be prone not to use our Adult to check out the "facts" for ourselves. Contamination may be conveyed and illustrated as follows.

1. Contamination Transaction.

> *Father:*   Joe, let me warn you that you can never trust managers; they are no good and only try to exploit you.
>
> *Grandfather:*   That's right, Joe. This family is proud of its tradition of fighting management by sticking together.
>
> *Joe:*   O.K.

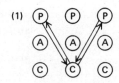

Strokes.   Strokes refer to the positive or negative ways we acknowledge the existence of others. This occurs through verbal and/or nonverbal means. Positive strokes would include expressions of love, respect, friendship, recognition, and the like. Negative strokes would be characterized by just the opposite.

Basic or Existential Position.   The Child in each of us has its own characteristic way of experiencing itself and perceiving others. The general intrapersonal and interpersonal view taken by the Child is called the *existential,* or basic, position. Individuals may differ by taking one of four different basic positions. These positions as described below are *pure types,* and individuals can fall along a continuum from one extreme to the other. The four pure positions include:

1. I'M OK: YOU'RE OK. This is obviously the healthy position and the ultimate change objective in transactional analysis.

2. I'M OK: YOU'RE NOT OK. This is a position of distrust. The child in us is very suspicious of other people.

3. I'M NOT OK: YOU'RE OK. The child in us has a negative self-concept and is likely to feel low or depressed.

4. I'M NOT OK: YOU'RE NOT OK. The Child in us feels that other people, itself, and life in general "just aren't any good." At the extremes of this position, the Child could sense total helplessness of rage, and possibly engage in suicide or homicide.

As might be expected, transactional analysis as a change approach aims at increasing the probability of realizing the I'M OK: YOU'RE OK position.

Structuring of Time.   Our particular basic (existential) position will strongly influence how we structure our time. There are six types of time structuring, which are expressed through transactions. These are withdrawal, rituals, activities, pastimes, games, and intimacy. *Withdrawal* involves psychologically removing ourselves from the people around us, as, for example, by daydreaming. *Rituals* include transactions that are socially agreed upon ways of behaving toward each other. *Activities* are established as spontaneous transactions between or among individuals, such as eating, playing tennis, and working. *Pastimes* are transactions that serve to fill time with others, such as "bull sessions," discussing Saturday's football game, and gossiping. Games are ". . . recurring set(s) of transactions, often repetitious, superficially plausible, with a concealed motivation, or . . . gimmick."[40, p. 48] Games always have an ulterior motive and are designed to obtain a payoff for one of the individuals, which was the real reason for playing the game. Over ninety games have been described, including such types as "Yes, But," "Ain't it Awful (about them),"

"See What You Made Me Do," and "Now I've Got You, You S.O.B." *Intimacy* involves transactions concerned with the mutuality of two people in a shared identity. Mutuality occurs through giving, sharing, taking risks, and trusting one another.

Script Analysis.   Our script refers to the life plan we feel compelled to act out. It is closely related to our life position and our ways of structuring time. A script is thought to be a subconscious life-plan formed within our Child by about the age of seven. Although decisions have been made about our script at one point in time, it can be redecided. Individuals with problems often have scripts with unfavorable outcomes (sickness, badness, stupidness, craziness, etc . . .). One of the aims of transactional analysis is to assist us in freeing ourselves from these scripts.

There are many other aspects of transactional analysis that could be considered, but to do so would take us well beyond our limited objectives.

Assessment.   Transactional analysis, as should be clear from the preceding dicussion, has a well-developed theoretical framework that is fairly easy for most individuals to learn. Transactional analysis differs from sensitivity training in several respects:

1. It is a relatively nonthreatening approach to self-evaluation.

2. It places more emphasis on examining oneself than others.

3. It requires less self-disclosure between individuals.

4. It requires less risk-taking by participants.

5. It places greater emphasis on each individual controlling and consciously deciding upon the types and the depth of personal change he or she would like to achieve.

Because these factors offer the potential for accomplishing many of the same objectives as does sensitivity training, we feel that the transactional-analysis approach is more readily usable with many types of organizations and individuals.

Because of the recency in applications of transactional analysis within organizational settings, most of the reports assessing its effectiveness are based on single-time attitude surveys and case-study reports from those utilizing it. Among the larger organizations making some use of transactional analysis are Bank of America, American Airlines, Mountain Bell Telephone Co., and the Data Processing Division of IBM.[41] The applications of transactional analysis by these firms seem to be in a training format, where individuals are expected to attend a certain number of indoctrination sessions. In a few cases, there have been attempts to apply the transactional approach to entire work teams. Our search of the literature has not uncovered any reports of efforts to apply the transactional-analysis change approach that incorporates an organization-wide reassessment of task, structural, and technology variables.

Sensitivity Training

Sensitivity training is sometimes referred to as T-group or laboratory training. It is an experience-based approach that focuses on individual and small-group development and change. Sensitivity training sessions are often conducted in group settings of about eight to fifteen individuals. The duration of the sessions can vary widely, with most groups meeting from a total of ten to forty hours. The sessions could be continuous, as in a marathon, weekend T-group; conducted over one to two weeks, as in a live-in program; or spread out over a year, as in a college program.

T-groups may be utilized as part of a larger change approach which is usually referred to as laboratory education. Laboratory education may involve the additional use of such things as: case studies; a wide variety of structured exercises, often involving role-playing; lecturettes on cognitive material relevant to interpersonal relations; and the utilization of instruments or questionnaires.

Basic Sensitivity Training Model

While the nature of T-groups can vary widely, they usually contain the following elements: here-and-now focus; unstructured to semi-structured group; self-disclosure; intense interpersonal feedback; creation of ambiguity, dilemmas, and anxiety; and generalizations from direct experience.[42] Sensitivity training should not be, although it commonly is, confused with some forms of the "let it all hang out" encounter groups.

The trainer of a T-group may start the process by defining her or his role and immediately form an environment to bring about "unfreezing" by creating ambiguity, dilemmas, and anxiety within the members. The following statement is an example of how a trainer might start.

> This group will meet for many hours and will serve as a kind of laboratory where each individual can increase his understanding of the forces that influence individual behavior and the performance of groups and organizations. The data for learning will be our own behavior, feelings, and reactions. We begin with no definite structure or organization, no agreed-upon procedures, and no specific agenda. It will be up to us to fill the vacuum created by the lack of these familiar elements and to study our group as we evolve. My role will be to help the group to learn from its own experience, but not to act as a traditional chairman or to suggest how we should organize, what our procedure should be, or exactly what our agenda will include. With these few comments, I think we are ready to begin in whatever way you feel will be most helpful.[43, p. 1]

In this ambiguous situation, members may try to organize the group by selecting a chairman, selecting a topic for discussion, withdrawing and waiting in silence, getting the trainer to take a more active role, etc . . .

Regardless of what takes place, the "here-and-now" focus means that the members should eventually start discussing why they responded as they did, how they personally felt, their feelings about the actions of others, etc . . . In other words, the basic focus for the interactions is on what is happening and being experienced in the group, and not on something that happened a year ago or in some other place. The emphasis on the "here-and-now" is contrary to most of our previous learning experiences and consequently may generate considerable frustration and anxiety.

Disclosure refers to the process of making more of oneself known to the other members. As discussed in Chapter 6, random and wide-open disclosure may suggest personal difficulties. T-groups usually encourage disclosure and operate on the position that we tend to conceal too much of our feelings and self-reactions for maximum psychological adjustment.

Feedback is the other face of disclosure in a T-group. Feedback enables us to know how we are perceived by others and what impact we are having on others. Through feedback, we can gain insight as to our tendency to be evaluative versus descriptive, and learn how to give helpful (instead of hurtful) feedback. This insight could occur through feedback from others on whether they perceive your communications as based on inferences or observations, and on how they experienced your communications. Throughout the T-group process, there are likely to be segments of time devoted to drawing inferences, generalizations, and conclusions from the group members' here-and-now experiences. Rather than imposing a concept or model on the group, the trainer may intervene by asking members to reflect and introspect on the meaning of what has just taken place.

Assessment.   Individuals may experience the same T-group quite differently, and they may vary in their experiences of different T-groups. Figure 13–8 summarizes some possible effects of T-groups and their consequences for individual members. One example of a possible positive or negative consequence for individual members is shown for each group effect.

Two of the contingencies appearing to influence the effects of a T-group are the trainer and each member's personality. There are some data suggesting that T-group trainers who provide excessive stimulation and give inordinate attention to the control function are associated with negative outcomes for the members.[44] Excessive stimulation is illustrated by behaviors that emphasize revealing feelings, challenging, confrontation, revelation of personal values, and frequent participation. The control function refers to behaviors emphasizing suggestion of rules, setting limits, managing time, and sequencing activities.

Possible group effects	Diverse consequences for individuals	
	Positive	Negative
1. Achieving and maintaining group cohesiveness	Feeling a part of the group, experiencing a sense of belonging	Giving up autonomy in order to belong, losing oneself in the group
2. Conforming to group norms	Awareness of participating in creating group norms	Feeling pressured to abide by group norms
3. Validating personal perceptions through group consensus	Reality testing and correcting personal distortions	Sharing illusions of the group
4. Expression of affective feelings	Free expression of feelings	Feeling inadequate unless expressing group approved emotions
5. Group perception of problems	Unblocked thinking	Forced to share problems with groups
6. Potency of group	Chance to feel influential	Feeling manipulated
7. Role differentiation	Achieving role flexibility	Type-cast in a role
8. Self-disclosure	Insight into personal blind spots	Becoming shaken in belief in self

Figure 13-8   Possible Effects of T-Groups on Individuals

Source: Adapted from: Likin, M., *Experiential Groups: The Uses of Interpersonal Encounter, Psychotherapy Groups, and Sensitivity Training.* Morristown: General Learning Press, 1972, p. 11.

Second, the personality of the individual is likely to determine whether the reactions to the T-group process are basically positive or negative. There are some tentative data suggesting that individuals strongly characterized by introversion, sensation, or thinking orientations (especially when two of these are combined in a single person) are more likely to reject and have unfavorable experiences from standard T-groups.[45] You will recall from Chapter 5 that:

1. Introvert types like quiet for concentration, have some problems communicating, work contentedly alone, etc . . .;

2. Thinking types are unemotional, are uninterested in people's feelings, like analysis and putting things into logical order; and

3. Sensation types dislike new problems unless there are standard ways to solve them, like an established routine, etc. . . .

Since the processes and requirements of T-groups are so contrary to the introvert, thinking, and sensation types, it also seems logical that individuals with these predispositions would be less receptive.

Sensitivity training is probably the most controversial of the various change approaches, particularly when utilized as part of an organizational change program. One issue area concerns possible harm to the individual and invasion of privacy, especially when the T-groups consist of members from the same organization [46]. A second issue area concerns its effectiveness as a change approach. While well-conducted T-group training can bring about change in the individual in the work situation (in terms of increased flexibility, more openness, better listening skills, etc.), the effect on individual role performance and overall organizational change remains a debatable question.[47]

Overview

One way to develop an overview of the various people-focused approaches we have discussed is to refer again to Table 13–1, entitled Comparisons in Relative Direct Impact of Various Change Approaches, and Fig. 13–2, entitled Comparisons along Three Dimensions of Selected Change Approaches. In our judgment, each of the people-focused approaches has the potential for creating positive outcomes. With the possible exception of Grid Organization Development, they do not strongly and directly address the task, technology, and structure variables in organizations. However, most versions of the management by objectives approach place at least moderate emphasis on the task variable. It may often be desirable to utilize one or more people-focused approaches even if a change program is oriented to approaches that focus on the task, technology, or structure variables.

TASK-FOCUSED APPROACHES

Depending upon the orientations of the authors, task-focused approaches are sometimes classified under structure or technology. While there are close relationships with these two variables and a degree of overlap, we consider the task approach as focusing on making changes in the activities each person or work group does, when, where, with whom, how long, and how often. The change process normally begins with an analysis of the nature and flow of tasks that are performed at the lowest organizational levels. We may say changes in tasks are developed from the "bottom up." This "bottom-up" style does not necessarily mean that the individuals at the lowest organizational levels are heavily involved in the redesign of the tasks performed and work flow employed.

Basic Task-Focused Model

From a change perspective, the task approach basically involves increasing or decreasing the task difficulty and/or task variability in a position or work unit. *Task difficulty* refers to the degree to which the work itself is easily understandable and there are well defined procedures or steps for performing the tasks.[48] A position or work unit low in difficulty is illustrated by assembly-line or record-keeping activities. High difficulty may be illustrated by an airline crew and an intensive-care nursing unit. *Task variability,* on the other hand, refers to the degree to which exceptional or nonroutine problems are experienced that also require different or new procedures and steps for doing the work.[49] Low task variability is illustrated by receptionists and watch guards, whereas high task variability is illustrated by lawyers, physicians, and many managers. Of course, all the positions and work units we have mentioned above need to be considered in terms of both task variability and difficulty,

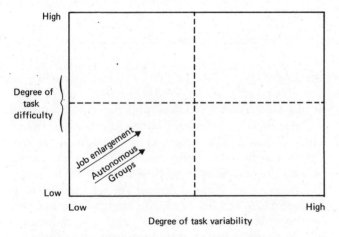

Figure 13–9   Simplified Model of Task Structure

which are independent dimensions varying along separate continua. This is suggested by Fig. 13–9, which shows a simplified model for assessing the task structure of a position or work unit. The vertical axis shows the degree-of-task-difficulty dimension ranging from low to high and the degree-of-task-variability ranging from low to high. As shown in Fig. 13–9, the change strategies of *job enlargement* [see Chapter 9] and the creation of *autonomous groups* [see Chapter 7] involve increasing the amount of task variability and/or task difficulty.

Assessment

As discussed in previous chapters (especially 7 and 9), job enlargement and the creation of autonomous groups have been two common change strategies for reducing boredom from repetitive, unchallenging jobs and/or work groups. These two strategies are often employed with the idea of increasing employee satisfaction, democratization, and humanization of work. From a broader perspective, the task approach can also involve increasing the specialization of labor. This can result in individuals performing tasks that are less variable and difficult.

While job enrichment and the creation of autonomous groups have been successfully employed, there are contingencies that might limit their applicability, such as technology, costs, and attitudes and norms.[50] One contingency is the technology employed in the production process. Even in the Volvo plant, where management was willing to make substantial changes in the technology utilized, the work teams have no choice in the selection of parts to be installed and they must be assembled in a given sequence. While the technologies employed to reach a common objective may vary substantially (such as from one small group assembling a whole car to the mass production line), the economic costs and benefits of alternative technologies may be the crucial deciding factor. Limits on job enrichment and utilization of autonomous groups may also be imposed by the skill and educational levels of certain classes of employees. Of course, there are different degrees of job enrichment and group autonomy, thereby enabling applications to vary according to the current ability and trainability of employees. Finally, while these two strategies are designed to improve workers' attitudes and norms toward work, it is sometimes the negative attitudes and norms of workers that serve as contingencies to resist the introduction of such changes. This has apparently been particularly true with some types of unionized craft groups, which frequently try to protect job security by maintaining jurisdiction and control over a well-defined set of tasks.

TECHNOLOGY-FOCUSED APPROACHES

The technological approach is probably the most pervasive and common contemporary perspective for explaining changes in organizations, changes in society and its institutions, changes in people (by wiping out certain types of jobs and creating new ones), creation of new organizations, elimination of established organizations, and growth in large-scale and multinational organizations.[51]. While recognizing that it is not the only source of change, Toffler characterizes technology as "... that great, growling engine of change."[52, p. 25] Of course, the organizational, cultural, or social setting into which technological changes are introduced can have much to do with whether these changes are experienced as benefits and/or problems.

NATURE

Definitions of technology have changed from a narrow perspective including only machines to the extremely broad definition that equates it with rationality. For our purposes, technology is defined as:

> ... tools in a general sense, including machines, but also including such intellectual tools as computer languages and contemporary analytical and mathematical techniques. That is, we define technology as the organization of knowledge for the achievement of practical purposes.[53, p. 25]

Although somewhat of a simple generalization, the "information" technological approach to change can be classified as falling within three distinct (and increasingly sophisticated) stages, all of which may be applied in today's organizations.

1. The first stage involved devices that mechanized communication, enabling the transmission of symbols. The telephone, telegraph, radio, and television are illustrative.

2. The second stage involved devices that can observe, record, generate, and remember symbols (data). The thermometer, speedometer, and radar are illustrative.

3. The third stage, which appeared in the 1940's, involved devices that can generate symbols, store, transmit, and manipulate them to make decisions. The computer and its various software is the best illustration of this phase. [54, p. 17]

Machines have long been used as a substitute for human labor in the performance of physical and routine tasks. The bulk of computer applications appear to be oriented toward tasks that are highly routine and must be performed repeatedly. However, computer information technology, especially since 1955, has made possible increasing numbers of applications where it automatically performs planning, control, and decision-making activities, in the place of individuals, including managers.

Assessment

There is little question that technology in general and computer information technology in particular has and will continue to have a major effect on society and organizations. Figure 13–10 outlines the major impacts of technology on society and organizations along seven dimensions: goal accomplishment, unintended effects, knowledge of effects, alternatives, new needs and goals, tools, and self-knowledge.[55]

Although technology is clearly a major approach to change, there can be considerable variations in the nature of its effects on an organization's members, structure, and task design. In one long-term study of nineteen insurance companies, the wide-scale introduction of computer information technology appeared to lead to changes in many other aspects of these organizations. Some of these effects included:

1. Increases in managerial productivity by improving the ability to control and coordinate complex activities;

2. Increases in employee productivity, by performing tasks previously undertaken by humans and accomplishing the same (or more) objectives (outputs) with fewer employees;

3. Reduction in the number of organizational levels, particularly at the lower levels where routine tasks were performed;

4. Changes in the pattern of departmentalization and size of some departments because certain previously separated information-handling tasks were moved into a computer center;

5. Some shift to a greater degree of centralization of control and decision-making;

6. Some shift in control of certain organizational activities from individuals to the computer information technology, so that these systems participate in the managerial control function;

7. Increased task interdependency between lower-level workers and less individual discretion; and

8. Change in job requirements and skill levels.[56]

Computer information technology is not always a source of such widespread changes in organizations. There are some studies suggesting that this technology can be consistent with "decentralization" and may actually make possible increased decentralization. It appears that the applications and the effects of computer information technology can vary somewhat as a function of the prevailing managerial philosophy and the degree of uncertainty in decision-making within the organization.[57]

Figure 13–10   Selected Impacts of Technology on Society and Organizations

Dimensions	Explanations
1. Goal accomplishment	It enhances our abilities to accomplish individual and collective goals (e.g., to produce an adequate supply of food);
2. Unintended effects	It often produces unintended and unwanted side effects, typically proportional in magnitude to its intended effects (e.g., the amount of sulfur oxides vented to the atmosphere grows proportionally with the production of energy);
3. Knowledge of effects	It provides knowledge about these same side effects, which might otherwise go undetected, so that we can take account of them in our decisions to use or eschew the use of particular technologies (e.g., chromatography, an example of advanced technology, enables us to detect trace quantities of possibly noxious substances in air or water or food);
4. Alternatives	It provides alternative routes among which we may choose in pursuing our goals (e.g., planes, trains, and cars as alternative modes of transportation);
5. New needs and goals	It makes us aware of new needs, and sets new goals (e.g., technology taught us that we need adequate quantities of vitamins in our diets);
6. Tools	It provides tools for analyzing and understanding complex systems (e.g., the standard tools of management science which may then be applied to the decision processes for selecting technologies);
7. Self-knowledge	It provides knowledge of ourselves, helping to define the terms of the human condition (e.g., it instructs us about how human aspiration levels are determined, and how human beings manage frequently to redefine the situations in which they find themselves as zero-sum games).

Source: Adapted and modified from: Simon, H. "Technology and Environment," *Management Science,* 1973, **19**, p. 111.

STRUCTURE-FOCUSED APPROACHES

The structure-focused approach can be most easily grasped by noting that it emphasizes changes in the dimensions discussed in Chapter 11 and in certain parts of other chapters, particularly our discussion in Chapter 8 on mechanisms for managing intergroup relations (hierarchy, plans, linking roles, task forces, integrating roles or units, and matrix organization), as well as the contingency models of leadership in Chapter 10.

NATURE

In the broadest sense, the structural approach focuses on changing organizations by changing position (roles) definitions, relationships between positions, and the expected behavior of people in positions, through modification of variables or forces "external" to them. The structural approach can be employed along collaborative–unilateral continua. At the collaborative end of the continuum, the people to be affected by the changes are heavily involved in defining what the changes should be and how they should be implemented. At the unilateral end of the continuum, top management or some other group (such as the federal government whose action may break up a company into several independent firms) defines the changes and implements them. The structural approach has probably most frequently been employed along the unilateral end of the continuum, especially when the structural changes focus on: (1) use of profit centers; (2) use of functional, product, or geographic departmentation (or some combination); (3) use of matrix structures and project groups; (4) more or fewer organization levels; (5) wider or narrower spans of control; (6) levels of formal authority in positions (such as changing the amount of money a manager can authorize, without prior higher-level approval, from $100 to $500); (7) formal reward systems (such as implementing an individual or group incentive system); and (8) changes in certain types of formal rules (e.g., requiring receipts to accompany all requests for reimbursement of travel expenses). Figure 13–11 summarizes some of the elements and dimensions often regarded as part of the structural approach.

Assessment

The structure-focused approach has long been utilized to change organizations. At times, structural changes may be made to accommodate changes brought on by new technologies. At other times, structural changes may be made to better serve or cope with environmental pressures (competitors, customers, government, and the like). At still other times, structural changes may be made to accommodate varying managerial, work force, or societal values. For example, increased decision-making discretion at lower levels, increased participation by those from lower levels in decisions normally made at the top

Figure 13–11   Elements Often Included in the Structural Approach to Change

Rules	Number of organization levels
Procedures	Committees
Formal economic reward systems	Staff-line
Reporting requirements	Performance criteria
Plans	Formal decision-making authority
Basis of departmentation	Promotion criteria
Span of control	Selection criteria
Matrix structure	Project groups
Schedules	Budgets
Communication systems	Formal training

of the organization, fewer organization levels, and the like, are often regarded as structural changes that may democratize and humanize the workplace.

An example of the structural approach is provided by the top-level changes made by R. H. Jones, when he became Chairman and Chief Executive Officer of General Electric in 1973.[58] Jones redefined the role of his job and those of several other top G.E. officers. Prior to Jones, G. E.'s chief executive had three vice-chairmen who served as a corporate executive staff, with responsibility for policy development, but no direct financial accountability for the operations they watched and reviewed. The three vice-chairmen are now financially accountable for the operating groups reporting to them and are more involved with line operations. Jones also gave up the direct review function he had over the power generation and power delivery groups. Jones stated: "I want to give myself a little more time to step back from the operating responsibility I had, to work on the general thrust of the corporation."

There is little question that the structural approach is potentially powerful as a change strategy. From the standpoint of enabling or enhancing the achievement of organizational goals, structural changes have ranged from smashing successes to dismal failures and have been attributed as a cause of organizational death.[59] While there may be many reasons for the failure of a structural intervention, one common theme seems to reoccur—lack of consideration-of-the-people variable. This raises the point we introduced earlier in the chapter. While a change program may have a particular emphasis and/or begin with a particular focus, it may ultimately have to include approaches with other foci to increase and enhance effectiveness.

SUMMARY

There is no single approach for changing an organization. There is no single point or variable (i.e., people, task, technology, or structure) for gaining leverage to begin the process of planned change. It is increasingly recognized that the people-focused approaches to change need to take account of the technology, task, and structure variables. More importantly, there is a growing awareness of an organization as a system, which means that there are interrelationships between the people, task, technology, and structure variables. Accordingly, major organizational change programs may need to incorporate a combination of approaches to maximize the positive and minimize adverse and dysfunctional unanticipated consequences.

Discussion Questions:

1. By utilizing the continuum of individual values in organizational settings that were presented in Fig. 3–1, how would you describe the values that seem to be implicit or explicit in each of the change approaches discussed in this chapter?

2. Evaluate this statement: "The survey feedback approach should be effective in any type of organization with virtually every class of employees."

3. What difficulties, if any, do differences in formal power between individuals create in the implementation of a management-by-objectives system? Explain.

4. Is it always possible for employees (including managers) to have a high level of involvement in the objective-setting process?

5. Can an organization simultaneously utilize the individual MBO model and the team MBO model? Explain.

6. What are the similarities and differences between grid organization development and management by objectives?

7. Do you think higher management should have the right to require an employee to engage in transactional analysis or sensitivity training? Explain.

8. What are some of the limitations that an organization's technology may place on task-focused approaches to change?

9. Philip M. Hauser has stated: "It may well be that our present chaos will engulf and drag us down as a nation which achieved the miraculous in technology but was unable to adapt itself to the new world man created. The United States may well collapse and bring down most, if not all, of humanity. We do have the means to destroy ourselves; it is naive to assume that the use of these means is beyond the realm of possibility. We also have within our grasp the means to deal with our problems in an effective manner." Discuss this quote in relation to the materials presented in this chapter.

CRITICAL INCIDENT

The Philippine Consulting Corporation*

In 1964, the Philippine Consulting Corp. (PCC) was organized to "accelerate the development of the economy by providing professionalized management services to industry and government." In spite of the entry of various firms into the industry, the PCC had consistently ranked second in terms of industry sales. In addition to its traditional business services, the firm was noted for having pioneered in the areas of management development and industrial research.

In December, 1969, Mr. Celestino Rivera was appointed Chief Executive Officer of the company. He announced that his management style would be "participatory," in contrast to what was viewed as a highly "authoritative" style of his predecessor. This was interpreted by many consultants to mean that they would be allowed to participate in important policy matters, particularly those related to performance evaluation and salary scales. As the former Chief Executive officer hardly consulted anyone in making a decision, the announcement made by Mr. Rivera was very well received and was considered by employees to facilitate their goal of becoming number one in industry sales.

Six months later, the organization was in a state of "crisis." Two vice-presidents and several top consultants had resigned. As a result of this unfavorable publicity, sales had started to decline and clients were reported to have sent out "feelers" for new consultants. Internally, the atmosphere was quite tense—in the words of one consultant, "things were run under conditions of martial law."

Part One: The PCC—Management and Organization

At the time of Mr. Rivera's appointment, the PCC was organized in three main departments: Management Consultancy, Management Training and Development, and Industrial Research. Each department was headed by a vice-president and was considered a profit center of the firm.

The departments were organized on a "project-management" basis. After the review of the project contracts by the vice-president, these were assigned to senior consultants who were responsible for organizing their project teams. At this point, all liaison with clients became the responsibility of the senior consultant and the project team. As a final "quality-control" measure, the senior consultant, the project team, and the vice-president reviewed the project report before it was submitted to the client.

---

*This case incident was prepared by Gerardo R. Ungson, Research Assistant, Pennsylvania State University, with the assistance of Professors John Slocum and Lawrence Hrebiniak. Used by permission.

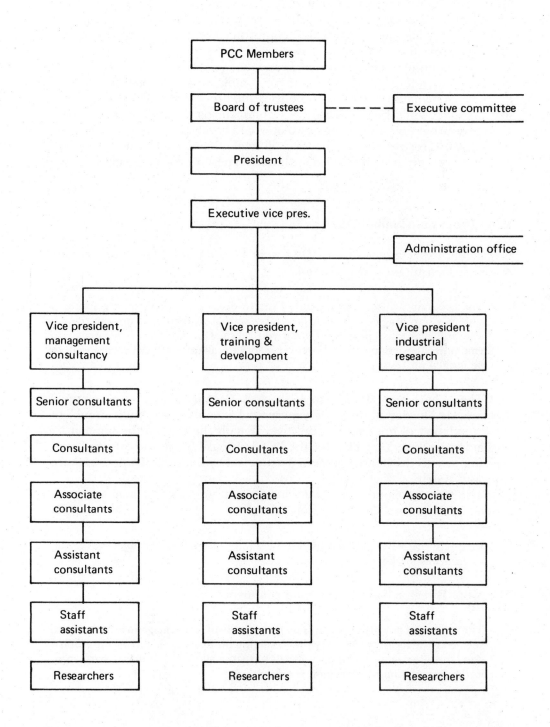

PCC—December, 1969

Mr. Celestino Rivera was appointed Chief Executive Officer to replace Mr. Jaime Casas. For a long time, the staff had resented the latter's "authoritative" style; he had made decisions without conferring with the staff and was highly secretive about the firm's salary structure.

As second-in-command (Vice President, Consulting), Mr. Rivera had been the "sounding board" for all these complaints. Following his appointment, he immediately initiated new policies and procedures: (1) He announced that his style would be "participative," commencing with a management-by-objectives program for the company that would be started by external consultants. (2) A directive was issued that all senior consultants should discuss performance ratings with their subordinates. These were well received by the staff.

MBO Program—January 1970

In general, expectations of the MBO were high. Prior to the program, one Associate Consultant had remarked:

> The program will serve as a good forum to discuss our performance-appraisal system. Consulting is quite difficult; it takes several years to build up your reputation and one lousy project to bring you down. Our present system seems to emphasize these drawbacks. Moreover, a lot of evaluation is subjective: I want to be judged on results . . .

The behavior of Mr. Rivera at the MBO seminar came as a complete surprise. He "lorded it" over the experiential exercises and "pulled rank" in the formulation of operational objectives. Finally, he capped the seminar by presenting his Five-Year Plan for the PCC. Ostensibly, he had attached very little importance to an area perceived as critical by the staff: the performance appraisal system.

The tenor of comments made during and after the seminar was quite disturbing. One associate consultant said:

> I thought the MBO was supposed to be a joint formulation of objectives . . . all I heard was his Five-Year Plan . . .

The MBO Director had the following comments:

> The success of any MBO depends on the attitude of top management. Mr. Rivera seemed to be more concerned with presenting his plans . . . in fact, he de-emphasized the other important aspect of MBO—that of allowing the staff to participate in the formulation of evaluation standards.

In defense of his position, Mr. Rivera said:

> You cannot redesign a program in days! I am working on the appraisal system now
> . . . To have discussed it during the seminar would have resulted in our getting
> bogged down on some details . . . I know the sentiments of the staff . . . I intend
> to incorporate all suggestions in the new system.

Post-MBO Policies

A few weeks after the seminar, PCC made the local headlines when one of its
major clients complained about what it considered "substandard quality services." Following this fiasco, Mr. Rivera announced that he would be sitting
in on all project meetings for "quality-control" reasons. The move was resented by many consultants:

> I agree that there should be quality control. But he (Rivera) is overdoing it . . .
> I meet with client and we agree on basic study premises . . . suddenly, he "sits in"
> and suggests sweeping changes which I feel are totally irrelevant to the project
> . . . let us have some control but let us not overdo it . . .

Mr. Rivera, however, had justified his actions as follows:

> Being new in my position, I cannot afford "early" mistakes . . . I have been a
> consultant for ten years and made no major mistakes . . . I know this is hard on
> the staff but after the XYZ project I cannot take another fiasco.

By March, 1970, he had presented the revised performance appraisal
system: each department was given corporate "target quotas" based on its
budget. Following the MBO method, they had full options of developing their
own programs to meet their objectives. Many consultants were quick to point
out some deficiencies but Mr. Rivera simply snapped:

> What are you complaining about? Under Cases, you did not even see your rating
> . . . now you can develop your own programs to meet your objectives and you will
> be evaluated on this basis . . . I repeat: every man will be evaluated on the basis
> of performance . . . is this not in keeping with MBO which all of you wanted?

In May, 1970, the two vice-presidents and three senior consultants announced their resignations. The papers extensively covered all these events
and PCC clientèle were alarmed. To curb off the "exodus," Mr. Rivera was
meeting every staff member individually. His response was a bit philosophical:

> I knew I was well liked when I became EVP . . . I have provided opportunities
> which Casas did not even want to discuss. How could this happen to me, when
> I was so sincere?

Question

Prepare a five-to-seven-page report covering a *diagnosis* and your *recommendations* for the Philippine Consulting Corporation. In your diagnosis, make sure to include a discussion of both *structural* changes and *motivational* factors, realizing, of course, that the two may be interrelated. Moreover, develop both short-range (e.g., immediate) and long-range (e.g., policy-orientations) recommendations for the corporation.

REFERENCES

1. Dowling, W. F., "To Move an Organization: The Corning Approach to Organization Development," *Organizational Dynamics*, 1975, **3**, pp. 16–34.

2. *Ibid.*

3. *Ibid.*

4. Tushman, M., *Organizational Change: An Exploratory Study and Case History*, ILR Paperback No. 15, Ithaca: New York State School of Industrial and Labor Relations, Cornell University, 1974. Guest, R., *Organizational Change: The Effects of Successful Leadership*, Homewood, Ill.: Richard D. Irwin and the Dorsey Press, 1962.

5. Beckhard, R. "Strategies for Large System Change," *Sloan Management Review*, 1975, **16**, pp. 43–55.

6. Harrison, R., "Choosing the Depth of Organizational Intervention," *Journal of Applied Behavioral Science*, 1970, **6**, pp. 181–202. Selfridge, R. J., and S. L. Sokolik, "A Comprehensive View of Organization Development," *MSU Business Topics*, 1975, **23**, pp. 46–61. Zand, D., "Trust and Managerial Problem Solving," *Administrative Science Quarterly*, 1972, **17**, pp. 229–239.

7. Zand, D., *op. cit.* Kegan, D. L., and A. H. Rubenstein, "Trust, Effectiveness and Organizational Development: A Field Study in R&D," *The Journal of Applied Behavioral Science*, 1973, **9**, pp. 498–513.

8. Aplin, V. C., and D. E. Thompson, "Successful Organizational Change," *Business Horizons*, 1974, **17**, pp. 61–66. Baumgartel, H., "Using Employee Questionnaire Results for Improving Organizations: The 'Survey' Feedback Experiment," *Kansas Business Review*, 1959, **12**, pp. 2–6; Bowers, D. G., *Development Techniques and Organizational Change: An Overview of Results from the Michigan Inter-Company Longitudinal Study*, Springfield: National Technical Information Service, U. S. Department of Commerce, 1971. Katz, D., R. L. Kahn, *The Social Psychology of Organizations*, New York: John Wiley, 1966, esp. pp. 416–425. Mann, F. C., "Studying and Creating

Change: A Means To Understanding Social Organization," *Research in Industrial Human Relations,* Madison, Wis.: Industrial Relations Research Association, no. 17, 1957, pp. 146–157. Taylor, J. C., and D. C. Bowers, *Survey of Organizations: A Machine-Scored Standardized Questionnaire Instrument,* Ann Arbor: University of Michigan, 1972.

9. Katz, D., and R. L. Kahn, *op cit.*

10. Aplin, J. C., and D. E. Thompson, *op cit.*

11. Taylor, J. C., and D. G. Bowers, *op cit.*

12. Baumgartel, H., *op cit.*

13. Bowers, D. G., *op cit.*

14. Huse, E. F., *Organizational Development and Change,* St. Paul, Minn.: West Publishing Co., 1975, pp. 163–174.

15. French, W. L., and R. W. Hollman, "Management by Objectives: The Team Approach," *California Management Review,* 1975, **16,** pp. 13–22.

16. Schuster, F. E., and A. F. Kendall, "Management by Objectives: Where We Stand—A Survey of the *Fortune* 500," *Human Resource Management,* 1974, **13,** pp. 8–11.

17. Adapted from: Jackson, D. W. and R. J. Aldag, "Managing the Sales Force by Objectives," *MSU Business Topics,* 1974, **22,** pp. 53–59.

18. Kirchoff, B. A., "MBO: Understanding What the Experts Are Saying," *MSU Business Topics,* 1974, **22,** pp. 17–22. *Also see:* Kleber, T. P., "Forty Common Goal-Setting Errors," *Human Resource Management,* 1972, **11,** pp. 10–13.

19. Steers, R. M., and L. W. Porter, "The Role of Task–Goal Attributes in Employee Performance," *Psychological Bulletin,* 1974, **81,** pp. 434–452.

20. Steers, R. M., "Task–Goal Attributes, N Achievement, and Supervisory Performance," *Organizational Behavior and Human Performance,* 1975, **13,** pp. 392–403.

21. Huse, E., "Putting in a Management Development Program that Works," *California Management Review,* 1966, **9,** pp. 73–80. Odiorne, G. S., "Management by Objectives and the Phenomenon of Goal Displacement," *Human Resource Management,* 1974, **13,** pp. 2–7.

22. Merton, R. K., "Bureaucratic Structures and Personality," *Social Forces,* 1940, **18,** pp. 560–568.

23. Carroll, S. J., and H. L. Tosi, *Management by Objectives: Applications and Research,* New York: MacMillan Co., 1973.

24. *Ibid.*

25. Odiorne, G. S., "The Politics of Implementing MBO," *Business Horizons,* 1974, **17,** pp. 13–21.

26. Slusher, E. A., and H. P. Sims, "Commitment through MBO Interviews," *Business Horizons,* 1975, **18,** pp. 5–12. *Also see:* Raia, A. P., *Managing by Objectives,* Glenview, Ill.: Scott, Foresman & Co., 1974.

27. Drucker, P. F., *The Practice of Management,* New York: Harper, 1954.

28. Jamieson, B. D., "Behavioral Problems with Management by Objectives," *Academy of Management Journal,* 1973, **16,** pp. 496–505.

29. Carroll, S. J., and H. L. Tosi, *op. cit.*

30. Jamieson, B. D., *op cit.* Levinson, H., "Management by Whose Objectives?" *Harvard Business Review,* 1970, **48,** pp. 125–134. Kerr, S., "Some Modifications in MBO as an OD Strategy," *Proceedings, 1972 Annual Meeting,* Academy of Management, 1973, pp. 39–42. Thompson, P., and G. Dalton, "Performance Appraisal: Managers Beware," *Harvard Business Review,* 1970, **48,** pp. 149–157. Wickens, J., "Management by Objectives: An Appraisal," *Journal of Management Studies,* 1968, **5,** pp. 365–379.

31. French, W. L., and R. W. Hollman, *op. cit.*

32. Ivancevich, J. M., "Changes in Performance in a Management-by-Objectives Program," *Administrative Science Quarterly,* 1974, **19,** pp. 563–574.

33. Blake, R., and J. Mouton, *The Managerial Grid,* Houston: Gulf Publishing Co., 1964. Blake, R., and J. Mouton, *Building A Dynamic Corporation through Grid Organization Development,* Reading, Mass.: Addison-Wesley Publishing Co., 1969. Blake, R., and J. Mouton, "An Overview of The Grid," *Training and Development Journal,* 1975, **29,** pp. 29–36.

34. Blake, R. R., H. A. Shepard, and J. S. Mouton, *Managing Intergroup Conflict in Industry,* Houston: Gulf Publishing Co., 1964.

35. Rush, H., *Behavioral Science: Concepts and Applications,* New York: National Industrial Conference Board, 1969.

36. Beer, M., and S. Kleisath, "The Effects of the Managerial Grid On Organizational and Leadership Dimensions," in *Research on the Impact of Using Different Laboratory Methods for Interpersonal and Organizational Change.* Zalkind, S. S. (ed.). Washington, D. C.: Symposium presented at the American Psychological Association, 1967. Blake, R., J. Mouton, L. Barnes, and L. Greiner, "Breakthrough in Organization Development," *Harvard Business Review,* 1964, **42,** pp. 133–155; Kreinick, P., and N. Colarelli, "Managerial Grid Human Relations Training for Mental Hospital Personnel," *Human Relations,* 1971, **24,** pp. 91–104. "Using the Managerial Grid to Ensure MBO," *Organization Dynamics,* 1974, **2,** pp. 54–65.

37. Adapted from: Anderson, J. P., "A Transactional Analysis Primer," in Pfeiffer, J., and J. Jones, *The 1973 Annual Handbook for Group Facilitators,* Iowa City: University Associates, 1973, pp. 145–157.

38. Berne, E., *Transactional Analysis in Psychotherapy,* New York: Grove Press, 1961. Berne, E., *The Structure And Dynamics of Organizations and Groups,* Philadelphia: Lippincott, 1963. Berne, E., *Games People Play,* New York: Grove Press, 1964. Berne, E., *Principles of Group Treatment,* New York: Oxford University Press, 1966. Berne, E., *What Do You Say After You Say Hello?,* New York: Grove Press, 1972.

39. Luchsinger, V. P., and L. L. Luchsinger, "Transactional Analysis for Managers, or How to be More OK with OK Organizations," *MSU Business Topics,* 1974, **22,** pp. 5–12.

40. Berne, E., *Games People Play,* New York: Grove Press, 1964.

41. Jongeward, D., and contributors, *Everybody Wins: Transactional Analysis Applied to Organizations,* Reading, Mass.: Addison-Wesley Publishing Co., 1973. *Also see:* James, M., and D. Jongeward, *Born To Win: Transactional Analysis With Gestalt Experiments,* Reading, Mass.: Addison-Wesley Publishing Co., 1971. Harris, T. A., *I'm OK—You're OK,* New York: Harper & Row Publishers, 1967. Meininger, J., *Success through Transactional Analysis,* New York: Grosset & Dunlap, 1973.

42. Buchanan, P. C., "Innovative Organizations—A Study In Organization Development," in *Applying Behavioral Science Research in Industry.* New York: Industrial Relations Counselors, 1964. Back, K., *Beyond Words: The Story of Sensitivity Training and the Encounter Movement.* New York: Russell Sage Foundation, 1972. Golembiewski, R., and A. Blumber (eds.), *Sensitivity Training and the Laboratory Approach: Readings about Concepts and Applications.* Itasca: F. E. Peacock, 1970. Schein, E., and W. Bennis, (eds.), *Personal and Organizational Change through Group Methods: The Laboratory Approach,* New York: John Wiley, 1965.

43. Seashore, C., "What Is Sensitivity Training?" *NTL Institute News and Reports,* 1968, **2,** pp. 1–2.

44. Lieberman, M. A., L. D. Yalom, and M. B. Miles, *Encounter Groups: First Facts,* New York: Basic Books, 1973. Lundgren, D. C., "Trainer–Member Influence In T-Groups: One-Way or Two-Way," *Human Relations,* 1974, **27,** pp. 755–766.

45. Kilmann, R. H., and Taylor, V., "A Contingency Approach to Laboratory Learning: Psychological Types Versus Experiential Norms," *Human Relations,* 1974, **27,** pp. 891–909. Steele, F., "Personality and Laboratory Style," *Journal of Applied Behavioral Science,* 1968, **4,** pp. 25–45; Ivancevich, J., "A Study of a Cognitive Training Program: Trainer Styles and Group Development," *Academy of Management Journal,* 1974, **17,** pp. 428–439.

46. Scott, W. G., "Schmidt is Alive and Enrolled in a Sensitivity Training Program," *Public Administration Review*, 1970, **30**, pp. 621–625.

47. Buchanan, P., "Laboratory Training and Organization Development," *Administrative Science Quarterly*, 1969, **14**, pp. 466–480. Dunnette, M., J. P. Campbell, C. Argyris, "A Symposium: Laboratory Training," *Industrial Relations*, 1968, **8**, pp. 1–45. House, R. J., "T-Group Education and Leadership Effectiveness: A Review of the Empiric Literature and A Critical Evaluation," *Personnel Psychology*, 1967, **20**, pp. 1–32.

48. Van de Ven, A., and A. Delbecq, "A Task Contingent Model of Work-Unit Structure," *Administrative Science Quarterly*, 1974, **19**, pp. 183–197. *Also see:* Perrow, C., *Organizational Analysis: A Sociological Approach.* Belmont: Wadsworth Publishing Co., 1970.

49. Van de Ven, A., and A. Delbecq, *op. cit.*

50. Fein, M., "Job Enrichment: A Reevaluation," *Sloan Management Review*, 1974. **15**, pp. 69–88. Lammers, C., "Self-Management and Participation: Two Concepts of Democratization in Organizations," *Organization and Administrative Sciences*, 1975, **5**, pp. 17–33. Lynch, P. O., "An Emprical Assessment of Perrow's Technology Construct," *Administrative Science Quarterly*, 1974, **19**, pp. 338–356. Meisner, M., *Technology and the Worker's Technical Demands and Social Processes in Industry*, San Francisco: Chandler Publishing, 1969. Miller, E., "Socio-Technical Systems in Weaving, 1953–1970: A Follow-Up Study," *Human Relations*, 1975, **28**, pp. 349–386. Sayles, L., *Behavior of Industrial Work Groups: Prediction and Control*, New York: John Wiley, 1958. Shepard, J., "Specialization, Autonomy, and Job Satisfaction," *Industrial Relations*, 1973, **12**, pp. 274–281. Walton, R., "How To Counter Alienation In The Plant," *Harvard Business Review*, 1972, **50**, pp. 70–81.

51. Ellul, J., *The Technological Society*, New York: Vintage Books, 1964. Jaffe, A., and J. Froomkin, *Technology and Jobs: Automation in Perspective*, New York: Frederick A. Praeger Publishers, 1968. Galbraith, J., *The New Industrial State*, Boston: Houghton Mifflin, 1967. Kheel, T., *Technological Change and Human Development: An International Conference*, Ithaca, N.Y.: Cornell University, 1970. Sanders, D. (ed.), *Computers and Management in A Changing Society*, 2nd ed., New York: McGraw-Hill Book Co., 1974. Whisler, T., *Information Technology and Organizational Change*, Belmont, Calif.: Wadsworth Publishing Co., 1970.

52. Toffler, A., *Future Shock*, New York: Bantam Books, 1970.

53. Mesthene, E., *Technological Change: Its Impact On Man and Society*, Cambridge, Mass.: Harvard University Press, 1970.

54. Ackoff, R., *Redesigning the Future: A Systems Approach to Societal Problems*, New York: Wiley-Interscience, 1974.

55. Simon, H., "Technology and Environment," *Management Science,* 1973, **19,** pp. 1110–1121.

56. Whisler, T., *op. cit.* Myers, C., (ed.), *The Impact of Computers on Management,* Cambridge, Mass.: M.I.T. Press, 1967.

57. Robey, D., "Computers and Organization Structure: A Review and Appraisal of Empirical Studies," paper presented at annual meeting of the National Academy of Management, 1974. Stewart, R., *How Computers Affect Management.* London: Macmillan Press, 1971.

58. "G.E.'s Jones Restructures His Top Team," *Business Week,* June 30, 1973, pp. 38–39.

59. O'Connell, J., *Managing Organizational Innovation,* Homewood, Ill.: Richard D. Irwin, 1968. Chandler, A. D., *Strategy and Structure,* Cambridge: M.I.T. Press, 1962. Duncan, R., "Modifications in Decision Structure in Adapting to the Environment: Some Implications for Organizational Learning," *Decision Sciences,* 1974, **5,** pp. 122–142. Golembiewski, R., R. Hilles, M. Kagno, "A Longitudinal Study of Flexi-Time Effects: Some Consequences of an OD Structural Intervention," *Journal of Applied Behavioral Science,* 1974, **10,** pp. 503–532. Kingdon, D., *Matrix Organization: Managing Information Technologies,* London: Tavistock Publications, 1973. Luke, R., P. Black, J. Davey, V. Averch, "A Structural Approach to Organizational Change," *Journal of Applied Behavioral Science,* 1973, **9,** pp. 611–635. Tushman, M., *op. cit.* Vosburgh, W. and D. Hyman, "Advocacy and Bureaucracy: The Life and Times of a Decentralized Citizen's Advocacy Program," *Administrative Science Quarterly,* 1973, **18,** pp. 433–448. Zaltman, G., R. Duncan, and J. Holbeck, *Innovations and Organizations.* New York: Wiley-Interscience, 1973.

Note: Page 458 is Blank

CASES

HOW HIGH THE DOC?*

Ms. Barret was Head Nurse of the operating room at Mountain View Hospital. She was experiencing some difficulties in scheduling scrub technicians and circulating R.N.s to certain surgery rooms. People who had been doing fine during one surgery had come to the nursing station during clearance of the operating room to ask to be relieved of their next surgery. They complained of feeling dizzy or just in need of a break. This often put the R.N. at the desk on the spot as she had difficulty in replacing personnel in the middle of the day. Requests were always granted and the employees would break for fifteen minutes to an hour, and then ask to be reassigned.

After about two weeks of this, the problem was brought to Ms. Barret's attention and she told the nurses to send all relief requests to her personally. Gary, a Certified O.R. Technician who had been with the hospital for two years, was the first to come to her with a request.

Barret: Gary, what seems to be the problem?

Gary: Well, Ms. Barret, I just don't feel very good and I'd just like to lie down for a while.

Barret: If you don't feel good you'd better take the rest of the day off.

Gary: I don't think I need to do that.

Barret: Gary, can you tell me what's going on around here?

*This case was prepared by Professor Richard B. Chase, for the University of Arizona, as a basis for class discussion.

459

Gary: Well, most people just don't like to work for Dr. Collins. He's pretty slow and seems to be out of it most of the time.

Barret: Have you talked to Ms. Johnston the circulating R.N. about this?

Gary: I've talked to her and Dr. Martin. Ms. Johnston gave me a hard time as usual. She says I am getting too big for my britches and if I don't like the situation I can ask for a transfer. Dr. Martin says that he's with Dr. Collins most of the time and he looks fine to him.

Barret: Thank you Gary, this will be kept confidential.

Ms. Barret went to ask Ms. Johnston to come into see her. After four days without seeing her, Ms. Barret went to find her.

Barret: Ms. Johnston I'd like to ask you some questions. I asked to see you four days ago.

Johnston: I have been trying to find time to see you.

Barret: I have some questions to ask you about Dr. Collins. Do you feel he's competent in surgery?

Johnston: As far as I know.

Barret: Have you ever seen him overly tired or not feeling well?

Johnston: Well, he did come in last week hung over but that was an emergency. He was on call and had just been to a cocktail party the night before. That's what those techs are complaining about isn't it?

Barret: How many times has this happened?

Johnston: Well, I don't know. But if Dr. Collins has any problems, Dr. Martin is always there to take over. I always circulate for him and I know my business. The techs are complaining because they don't like to be told what to do. They just can't take orders and Dr. Collins gives it to them when they don't. They think just because they have been through a few cholesectomies they can start questioning the doctors and R.N.'s orders.

Barret: Thank you Ms. Johnston that is all the questions I have.

Two days later Gary gave his notice and quit working three weeks later. Relief requests stopped coming in but two other O.R. techs gave their notice. Absenteeism rose.

Ms. Barret scheduled Ms. Johnston to work under another doctor and assigned Ms. McEvers to circulate for Dr. Collins. Later that day Ms. Barret went to visit the O.R. room where Dr. Collins was working. There she found

Dr. Collins, head anesthesiologist, Dr. Martin assisting, and Ms. Johnston circulating as usual. She inquired into where Ms. McEvers was as she was scheduled for this surgery. She was informed by Dr. Martin that this operation could involve complication and they needed an experienced circulator.

> *Barret:* Dr. Martin you have every right to request certain circulators. I would appreciate some notice before you tamper with room scheduling.

> *Martin:* I am giving you notice that I would like to have Ms. Johnston circulate for me and Dr. Collins.

> *Barret:* Due to some difficulties in scheduling Ms. McEvers will circulate for you for the rest of the week. After that if I have your request in writing I will have no choice but to assign Ms. Johnston to you scheduling problems or not.

Ms. McEvers worked out the week under the two doctors and at the end of the week Ms. Barret asked to see her in her office to inquire into Dr. Collins' competence.

> *McEvers:* I refuse to make waves here so I want this confidential. Dr. Collins often looks hung over in the morning when he does his patient's pre-op. I wouldn't stand up in court and swear he had been drinking but he sometimes smells of alcohol.

> *Barret:* Have you ever inquired into his behavior?

> *McEvers:* I asked Dr. Martin about it. He always has some story of Dr. Collins just being called in or not feeling up to par.

Later that week, Ms. Barret confronted Dr. Martin with this information.

> *Martin:* Those are pretty serious charges you're leveling at Dr. Collins.

> *Barret:* No one is accusing anybody of anything at this point.

> *Martin:* What you're saying could have serious repercussions around here. If anyone got wind of this it could look very bad, not only for us but for the profession and the hospital.

> *Barret:* I am concerned here with the patient's safety.

> *Martin:* No one is in danger. Ms. Johnston and I are always with him.

> *Barret:* That isn't the point.

> *Martin:* Take it to the Chief of Staff then but let me give you some advice. You need some hard facts to make anything stick. You need the testimony of at least four nurses and under the circumstances that might be hard to get. You might like to know Dr. Collins is retiring next year.

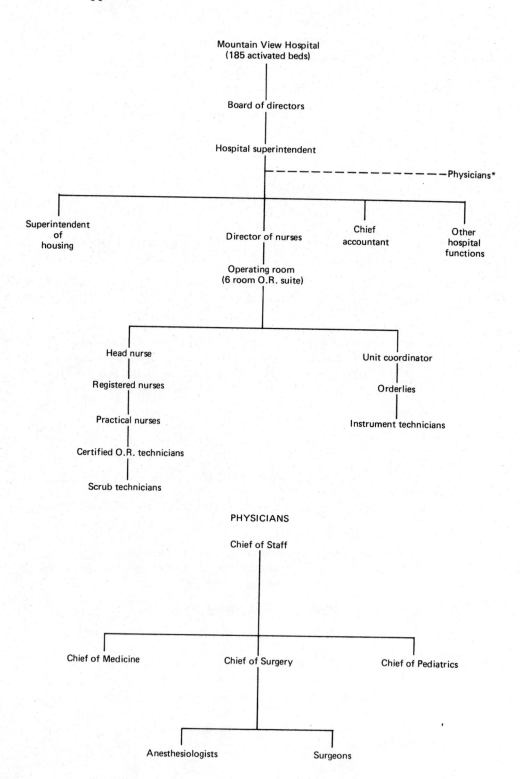

JACK DOBBIN'S PROBLEM*

Jack Dobbins left the vice president's office feeling elated as well as concerned about the new responsibilities he was about to assume. Ralph Barnes, State College's vice president and comptroller, had just told Jack of the Executive Committee's decision to appoint him Superintendent of Buildings. Jack was concerned because Mr. Barnes had gone into considerably more detail about the many management and morale problems among the College's custodial workers and their supervisors than in any previous interviews.

The Situation

State College was located in a suburban area just outside of a major southern metropolitan area. It was one of several universities run by the state and was less than 10 years old. In this short time it had grown rapidly to 9500 students, the majority of whom lived off campus and commuted to school each day.

The Superintendent's major function was to plan, organize, direct and control the activities of about 80 employees and supervisors involved in keeping all college buildings (except for dormitories) in clean and orderly condition. There were 10 major buildings, ranging in size from 24,000 square feet to 137,000 square feet. Total square footage under the jurisdiction of the Superintendent amounted to 1,025,000. This space included classrooms, faculty offices, administration and library buildings, student center, etc.

Of the 80 employees in the department, 16 were women, 64 were men, including the 4 supervisors who reported to the Superintendent. Starting wages for maids had just been raised to $2580 per year from $2300. By some quirk of the state's budgeting system, starting wages for male janitors had just been lowered to $2700 per year from $2900. Employees could receive only one raise per year, usually on July 1st at the beginning of the fiscal year. It was within the Superintendent's authority to grant raises up to a maximum of 10% the first year, 7½% the second year, and 5% the third year. In order to qualify for the maximum, however, employees had to receive a rating of "outstanding." The work week was 40 hours. Vacation leave of 10 working days was allowed while sick leave was accrued at the rate of one day per month to a maximum of thirty days. Group life and health insurance was available by payroll deduction at employee expense. State employees were not covered under Social Security but did participate in the state retirement system under which both the State and the employee contributed. The total budget for the department amounted to about $280,000, with $250,000 for wages and salaries and $30,000 for supplies and materials.

*This case was prepared by Assistant Professor David R. Kenerson, University of South Florida, as a basis for class discussion. Distributed by the Intercollegiate Case Clearing House, Soldiers Field, Boston, Mass., 02163. All rights reserved to the contributors. Printed in the U.S.A.

Turnover among employees was unusually high. In July and August of 1967, turnover amounted to 15% and 20%. Typically in this type of work in universities, turnover normally runs 100% per year. Most of the employees were Negroes, and the majority of them were holding down other full time jobs outside of the College.

Departmental Work Organization

There was no organization chart for the department, but Jack Dobbins felt it would look pretty much like the chart shown in Exhibit 1.

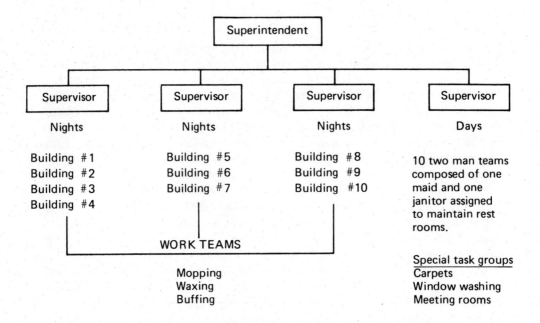

Work was organized on the basis of special tasks. Although supervisors were assigned responsibility for different buildings, work was specialized into floor mopping crews, followed up by waxing and buffing crews. Supervisors decided when particular floors were mopped, waxed, and buffed and coordinated and scheduled the different crews in proper sequence. The day crews worked largely on restroom detail in all buildings with special groups assigned for carpet cleaning, window washing, and straightening and cleaning up meeting rooms before and after meetings.

Jack Dobbins' Background

Jack Dobbins was a retired military man with 20 years service in various posts as management analyst and operations and training officer. On resigning from the military, he had enrolled as a student in the College of Business Administration in order to earn a degree in management and business administration. At 45 he was looking forward to a new career in a new environment in a field where he felt his experience, knowledge and training could be most effectively used.

During the last hour and one-half in his talk with Mr. Barnes, he had learned much about the current problems of the department. Harry Kraft, the man he was replacing, had come to State College when the first students were admitted. He was about 50 years old, of limited education, and with a varied background as foreman or supervisor in construction firms. When the College was small with only a few buildings and few employees, he was reasonably successful. However, four months previously, Harry had fired one of the supervisors with rather disastrous results. Rank and file employees were indignant and had sent a petition all the way to the state capital in an attempt to get Harry's decision reversed. Some were threatening not to come to work. Morale was low, turnover high, and top officials of the College, as well as the department itself, were being deluged with complaints about the lack of good housekeeping in all buildings. Toilets were not adequately serviced, classrooms and offices frequently went untouched for a week at a time.

Although Jack was concerned, he was not dismayed because he felt strongly that his recent exposure to a wide variety of management courses would make it relatively easy to show substantial improvements in this department, even despite the fact that no raises could be given to any employees before the next fiscal year 11 months away.

CENTER CITY ENGINEERING DEPARTMENT*

The Engineering Department of Center City employed approximately 1,000 people, all of whom worked under the provisions of the Civil Service System.

*Prepared by Professor H. R. Knudson, Jr., College of Business Administration, University of Washington, Seattle, Washington. Appeared in *Human Elements of Administration;* 1964. © Holt, Rinehart & Winston, New York. Reprinted by permission.

Of these employees, about 100 worked in the Design Division. Parker Nolton, an Associate Engineer, had been employed in the Design Division for 19 years and was known personally by virtually everyone in the division, if not in Center City itself. Nolton had held the position of Associate Engineer for seven years on a provisional basis only, for he had never been able to pass the required civil service examinations to gain permanent appointment to this grade, although he had taken them often. Many of his co-workers felt that his lack of formal engineering education prevented him from passing the examinations, but Nolton felt that his failures were the result of his tendency to "tighten up" when taking an examination. Off the job, Nolton was extremely active in civic affairs and city sponsored recreational programs. During the past year, for example, he had been president of the High School Parent Teacher's Association, captain of the bowling team sponsored by the Engineering Department in the Municipal Bowling League and a member of the Managing Committee of the Center City Little League.

As Center City grew and the activities of the Engineering Department expanded to keep pace with this growth, younger men were hired into the Department in relatively large numbers. Among those hired were Ralph Boyer and Doug Worth. Both of these young men were graduate engineers, and had accepted the positions with the Engineering Department after fulfilling their military obligations. Ralph Boyer had been an officer in the Army Corps of Engineers. In order to give the new men opportunities to achieve permanent status in the Civil Service System, examinations were scheduled with greater frequency than they had been in the past. Nolton's performance on the examinations continued to be unsatisfactory. The new men, however, passed the exams for successively higher positions with flying colors. Ralph Boyer in particular experienced marked success in these examinations and advanced rapidly. Three years after his initial employment he was in charge of a design group within the design division. Parker Nolton, in the meantime, had been shifted from the position of a project engineer to that of the purchase order coordinator. The position of purchase order coordinator was more limited in scope than that of a project engineer, although the responsibilities of the position were great. He continued to be classified as an Associate Engineer, however.

Ralph Boyer continued his successful career and soon qualified for the position of Senior Engineer. A new administrative group that had been created to meet the problems that arose in the Design Division because of the expanding activities of the Engineering Department was placed under his direction. Doug Worth, too, was successful in his examinations and was shortly promoted to the grade of Associate Engineer and transferred into the administrative group headed by Ralph Boyer.

One of the functions under the new administrative group was that of purchase order coordination. This relationship required that Parker Nolton report to Ralph Boyer. Nolton, however, chose to ignore the new organizational structure and dealt directly with the Chief Engineer, an arrangement which received the latter's tacit approval. Nolton was given a semiprivate office and the services of a Junior Engineer to assist him in his activities. His assistant, John Palmer, soon requested a transfer on the grounds that he had nothing to do and there was no need for anyone in this position. Nolton, on the other hand, always appeared to be extremely busy and was continually requesting additional manpower and assistance to help him with the coordination of purchase orders.

Some four months after the organizational changes noted above had taken place, the Chief Engineer left the Company and his replacement, Stan Matson, was appointed from within the division. Matson was the logical successor to the position; his appointment came as no surprise and was well received by all the employees. His appointment was shortly followed by the assignment of Ralph Boyer to a special position which took him completely out of the Design Division. Doug Worth was assigned to the position thus vacated, Supervisor of the Administrative Group and consequently inherited the supervision of Parker Nolton's activities. This assignment, initially made on a provisional basis, was soon made permanent when Worth passed the required examinations and was awarded the grade of Senior Engineer. Doug Worth had never worked closely with Parker Nolton but had been on cordial terms with him since his arrival in the Engineering Department. He had had contact with Nolton in several recreational activities in which they both had participated.

During the months which followed, Parker Nolton continued his direct reporting relationship with the Chief Engineer, now in the person of Stan Matson, and never consulted or advised Doug Worth regarding the progress of his activities as purchase order coordinator. His former assistant, John Palmer, has been transferred and had been replaced by an engineering aide. Both the aide and Nolton appeared to be busy most of the time, and Nolton was still requesting more manpower for his activity through formal channels. When occasions arose which required that Doug Worth check on Nolton's activities, he was always forced to go to Nolton's office for information. Nolton always claimed to be too busy to leave his own office. During the conversations which occurred when Worth visited Nolton, Nolton frequently gave the impression that he regarded Worth's activities and interest as superfluous. Several times he suggested that in future situations Worth just send the inquiring party directly to him if questions arose about his activities. He often made the comment that he knew everyone in the department and often it was better to handle many situations informally rather than through channels.

Doug Worth was concerned with Nolton's attitude, for he did not feel that he could effectively carry out his responsibilities as Supervisor of the Administrative Group if he did not know the current status of activities in all of the functions under his control. Consequently, he attempted to gain more cooperation from Nolton by approaching the subject at times when the two men were engaged in common off-hours recreational activities. These attempts were uniformly unsuccessful. Nolton always quickly brought the conversation around to the standing of the bowling team, the progress of the P.T.A., or any other unrelated subject close at hand.

After several attempts to talk with Nolton in a friendly way off the job, Worth concluded that the situation as it currently stood was intolerable. While he realized he must do something, Worth felt he understood Nolton's attitude and reactions and was sympathetic. After all, Nolton had been in the department for years and had been relatively successful. He knew all the "ropes" and had many friends. Worth reflected that it must be a blow to a man like Nolton to have to report to young, relatively inexperienced men. Worth had faced similar problems during his military career, when he had had more experienced men many years his senior under his command. After much thought, he decided his best approach would be to appeal to Nolton in a very direct manner for a greater degree of cooperation. Thus, Worth approached Nolton on the job and suggested that they have a talk in his private office where they would not be disturbed by all the activity in Nolton's office. Nolton protested that he could not take time away from his duties. Worth was firm, however, and Nolton reluctantly agreed to come to Worth's office, protesting all the way that he really could not spare the time.

During his opening remarks to what Worth had planned as a sympathetic discussion of the situation, Worth referred to "the normal relationship between a man and his superior." Nolton's reaction was violent. He stated that he didn't regard any young upstart as a "superior," especially his. He told Worth to run his own office and to let him, Nolton, run his. He concluded by stating "if you haven't anything more to say I would like to get back to my office where important work is being neglected." Worth, realizing that nothing more could be accomplished in the atmosphere which prevailed, watched in silence as Nolton left.

Doug Worth subsequently reported his latest conversation with Nolton to Stan Matson, the Chief Engineer. He also related the events which had led to this conversation. In concluding his remarks, he stated that he could no longer take responsibility for Nolton's actions because Nolton would neither accept his guidance, nor advise him of the state of his work. Matson's reply to this last statement was "yes, I know." This was the only comment Matson made during the interview, although he listened intently to Worth's analysis of the situation.

At the next meeting of the Supervisory Staff of which Worth was a member but Nolton was not, Worth proposed that Nolton be transferred to the position of Design Drafting Engineer, in effect a demotion. As Worth was explaining the reasons for his proposed action regarding Nolton, one of the other members of the Supervisory Staff interrupted to proclaim very heatedly that Nolton was "one of the pillars of the entire Engineering Department" and that he would be violently opposed to the demotion of "so fine a man." Following this interruption, a very heated, emotional discussion ensued concerning the desirability of demoting Nolton.

During this discussion Stan Matson remained silent; yet he reflected that he should probably take some action during the meeting regarding the Nolton situation.

PARTS DISTRIBUTION DEPARTMENT*

Corporate Personnel representative Bruce Pritchard has spent the afternoon observing operational characteristics of Parts Distribution Department and interviewing its manager, Bob Warren. Parts Distribution, together with Marketing and Warehousing, comprise the Operations section of Midwest Sales, a division of an electrical parts manufacturing corporation. A relatively small department of thirty people, Parts Distribution is responsible for coordinating the stock of primary parts/inventory for the corporation's warehouse and distributor operations throughout the United States.

Pritchard's visit from corporate headquarters was made at the request of Charlie Elsley, Operations Director. Elsley is perturbed with continuing signs of poor morale in Parts Distribution as well as with its failing reputation among the sister departments of Operations.

Before starting his afternoon of observations, Pritchard was made aware of Bob Warren's past history with Parts Distribution: Warren has been its manager for the past twelve years, having risen through the ranks of the department over a thirteen-year period. He now anticipates Charlie Elsley's retirement. With Charlie's retirement—certain within the next two years—Warren believes that he could become new Operations Director.

According to Warren, Parts Distribution has achieved an optimal organizational structure under his direction. The department's newest structure, he relates, allows him to make the most of the personnel who have "accumulated" over the years. "I've never been particularly happy with the supervisors; I've got to keep on their backs. But what do you do? They were the only ones available at the times we needed new supervisors." To compensate for individual weaknesses among the supervisors, he has reallocated certain tasks among them so that each might concentrate on those activities at which he is best.

Each supervisor typically oversees the work of two or three schedulers. The scheduler's job is core to the functioning of Parts Distribution. A scheduler (1) conducts a monthly survey on the inventory status of his assigned

*This case was prepared by Larry J. Bossman, Jr. of University of Detroit as a basis for class discussion rather than to illustrate either effective or ineffective handling of an administrative situation. Presented at the Northwestern University Case Workshop of the Intercollegiate Case Clearing House, October 28–30, 1973. Copyright © 1973 by Larry J. Bossman, Jr. Distributed by the Intercollegiate Case Clearing House, Soldiers Field, Boston, Mass. 02163. All rights reserved to the contributors. Printed in the U.S.A.

parts-line, (2) determines what should be purchased by part number, (3) executes purchase orders, (4) maintains warehouse contact by phone, message, or teletype, as well as supplier relations by telephone contact, expediting, and follow-up by phone. In addition, the scheduler maintains upgraded record sheets. This task accounts for over thirty percent of the scheduler's time. It is accomplished by hand-recording computer print-out data of end-of-month part stocks in the scheduler's book of monthly stock records.

Each scheduler receives from his supervisor a monthly-turnover estimate which represents the number of times a parts-line is expected to be restocked to full inventory in an average month's time.

The monthly-turnover estimate, also used by the supervisor in his yearly estimate of each part-line's projected annual volume, originates from Bob Warren's office. Warren and his assistant, Harold Frain, compute the monthly-turnover figures, using market forecasts received from Marketing and inventory open-order data received from Warehousing.

Employment turnover among schedulers is a growing problem. Some seek transfers to the "more glamorous" Marketing Department. Others quit. Of the sixteen schedulers, nine are the college graduates of the department. In-fighting has occurred among some scheduler groups.

Warren's former strategy for promoting interest and morale among the department's personnel was to upgrade the job classifications, and thus the salary ranges, of both schedulers and supervisors. However, corporate Personnel Activity has not approved Warren's last four requests for higher classifications. In turn, Warren has implemented several organizational changes in the department. He believes that he has arrived at an optimal structure because greater promotional opportunities are provided for his people. He has assigned one of the younger schedulers to "Systems," a one-man operation, to debug computer errors in end-of-month inventory print-outs; he has created two "general supervisor" positions for Dave Wilson and Sid Ladimere such that the six remaining supervisors report to them; he has appointed Harold Frain, his right-hand man, as "assistant manager" to whom Wilson and Ladimere report.

In addition to their direct line involvement, Wilson and Ladimere are responsible for all plant visitations. They visit the operations of seventy suppliers—both within and without the corporation—to improve plant shipment times and order clearances.

Warren is proud of his reorganization design. In addition to rewarding some of his key men with higher positions, he has focused plant visitation responsibilities on two men who can handle themselves well in the field. As Warren related to Bruce Pritchard, "Plant visitations used to be the responsibility of each supervisor for his part-lines. But some of them were so damned lousy at it, I just couldn't trust them anymore."

Over dinner cocktails that evening, Bruce listens to Charlie Elsley reiterate his concern for the Parts Distribution schedulers. He admits that his own prior attempts to persuade Warren to reshape the department's activities have led to little, if any, improvements. Parts Distribution continues to carry its "Operation Ostrich" reputation among other divisional departments.

At one point, Charlie turns his thoughts to the topic of a brochure which corporate Personnel Activity had recently issued to the Divisions. Charlie states that he was impressed with the concepts of job enrichment described in the brochure, and saw their direct application to the Parts Distribution situation. After admitting that an enrichment project could "gain much . . . but lose little for that department," Charlie asks for Bruce's opinion.

After a pause, Bruce questions whether Bob Warren would accept an enrichment project. He is immediately assured by Charlie: "I've already bounced the idea off Bob, and he'll be willing to give it a try. That's why I've called you in, Bruce."

THE CASE OF THE CHANGING CAGE*

Part I

The voucher-check filing unit was a work unit in the home office of the Atlantic Insurance Company. The assigned task of the unit was to file checks and vouchers written by the company as they were cashed and returned. This filing was the necessary foundation for the main function of the unit: locating any particular check for examination upon demand. There were usually eight to ten requests for specific checks from as many different departments during the day. One of the most frequent reasons checks were requested from the unit was to determine whether checks in payment of claims against the company had been cashed. Thus efficiency in the unit directly affected customer satisfaction with the company. Complaints or inquiries about payments could not be answered with the accuracy and speed conducive to client satisfaction unless the unit could supply the necessary document immediately.

Toward the end of 1952, nine workers manned this unit. There was an assistant (a position equivalent to a foreman in a factory) named Miss Dunn, five other full-time employees and three part-time workers.

The work area of the unit was well defined. Walls bounded the unit on three sides. The one exterior wall was pierced by light-admitting north windows. The west interior partition was blank. A door opening into a corridor pierced the south interior partition. The east side of the work area was enclosed by a steel mesh reaching from wall to wall and floor to ceiling. This open metal barrier gave rise to the customary name of the unit—"The Voucher Cage." A sliding door through this mesh gave access from the unit's territory

*The following case was taken from "Topography and Culture, The Case of the Changing Cage," *Human Organization*, 1957, **16**,(1), by C. B. Richards and H. F. Dobyns. Reproduced by permission of the Society for Applied Anthropology from *Human Organization*, 1957, **16**(1).

to the work area of the rest of the company's agency audit division, of which it was a part, located on the same floor.

The unit's territory was kept inviolate by locks on both doors, fastened at all times. No one not working within the cage was permitted inside unless his name appeared on a special list in the custody of Miss Dunn. The door through the steel mesh was used generally for departmental business. Messengers and runners from other departments usually came to the corridor door and pressed a buzzer for service.

The steel mesh front was reinforced by a rank of metal filing cases where the checks were filed. Lined up just inside the barrier, they hid the unit's workers from the view of workers outside their territory, including the section head responsible for over-all supervision of this unit according to the company's formal plan of operation.

Part 2

On top of the cabinets which were backed against the steel mesh, one of the male employees in the unit neatly stacked pasteboard boxes in which checks were transported to the cage. They were later reused to hold older checks sent into storage. His intention was less getting these boxes out of the way than increasing the effective height of the sight barrier so the section head could not see into the cage "even when he stood up."

The girls stood at the door of the cage which led into the corridor and talked to the messenger boys. Out this door also the workers slipped unnoticed to bring in their customary afternoon snack. Inside the cage, the workers sometimes engaged in a good-natured game of rubber band "sniping."

Workers in the cage possessed good capacity to work together consistently and workers outside the cage often expressed envy of those in it because of the "nice people" and friendly atmosphere there. The unit had no apparent difficulty keeping up with its work load.

Part 3

For some time prior to 1952 the controller's department of the company had not been able to meet its own standards of efficient service to clients. Company officials felt the primary cause to be spatial. Various divisions of the controller's department were scattered over the entire 22-story company building. Communication between them required phone calls, messengers, or personal visits, all costing time. The spatial separation had not seemed very important when the company's business volume was smaller prior to World War II. But business had grown tremendously since then and spatial separation appeared increasingly inefficient.

Finally in November of 1952 company officials began to consolidate the controller's department by relocating two divisions together on one floor. One was the agency audit division which included the voucher-check filing unit. As soon as the decision to move was made, lower level supervisors were called in to help with planning. Line workers were not consulted but were kept informed by the assistants of planning progress. Company officials were concerned about the problem of transporting many tons of equipment and some 200 workers from two locations to another single location without disrupting work flow. So the move was planned to occur over a single weekend, using the most efficient resources available. Assistants were kept busy planning positions for files and desks in the new location.

Desks, files, chairs, and even wastebaskets were numbered prior to the move, and relocated according to a master chart checked on the spot by the assistant. Employees were briefed as to where the new location was and which elevators they should take to reach it. The company successfully transported the paraphernalia of the voucher-check filing unit from one floor to another over one weekend. Workers in the cage quit Friday afternoon at the old stand, reported back Monday at the new.

The exterior boundaries of the new cage were still three building walls and the steel mesh, but the new cage possessed only one door—the sliding door through the steel mesh into the work area of the rest of the agency audit division. The territory of the cage had also been reduced in size. An entire bank of filing cabinets had to be left behind in the old location to be taken over by the unit moving there. The new cage was arranged so that there was no longer a row of metal filing cabinets lined up inside the steel mesh obstructing the view into the cage.

Part 4

When the workers in the cage inquired about the removal of the filing cabinets from along the steel mesh fencing, they found that Mr. Burke had insisted that these cabinets be rearranged so his view into the cage would not be obstructed by them. Miss Dunn had tried to retain the cabinets in their prior position, but her efforts had been overridden.

Mr. Burke disapproved of conversation. Since he could see workers conversing in the new cage, he "requested" Miss Dunn to put a stop to all unnecessary talk. Attempts by female clerks to talk to messenger boys brought the wrath of her superior down on Miss Dunn, who was then forced to reprimand the girls.

Mr. Burke also disapproved of a untidy working area, and any boxes or papers which were in sight were a source of annoyance to him. He did not exert supervision directly, but would "request" Miss Dunn to "do something about those boxes." In the new cage, desks had to be completely cleared at the end of the day, in contrast to the work-in-progress piles left out in the old cage. Boxes could not accumulate on top of filing cases.

The custom of afternoon snacking also ran into trouble. Lacking a corridor door, the food bringers had to venture forth and pack back their snack tray through the work area of the rest of their section, bringing this hitherto unique custom to the attention of workers outside the cage. The latter promptly recognized the desirability of afternoon snacks and began agitation for the same privilege. This annoyed the section head, who forbade workers in the cage from continuing this custom.

Part 5

Mr. Burke later made a rule which permitted one worker to leave the new cage at a set time every afternoon to bring up food for the rest. This rigidity irked cage personnel, accustomed to a snack when the mood struck, or none at all. Having made his concession to the cage force, Mr. Burke was unable to prevent workers outside the cage from doing the same thing. What had once been unique to the workers in the cage was now common practice in the section.

Although Miss Dunn never outwardly expressed anything but compliance and approval of her superior's directives, she exhibited definite signs of anxiety. All the cage workers reacted against Burke's increased domination. When he imposed his decisions upon the voucher-check filing unit, he became "Old Grandma" to its personnel. The cage workers sneered at him and ridiculed him behind his back. Workers who formerly had obeyed company policy as a matter of course began to find reasons for loafing and obstructing work in the new cage. One of the changes that took place in the behavior of the workers had to do with their game of rubber band sniping. All knew that Mr. Burke would disapprove of this game. It became highly clandestine and fraught with danger. Yet shooting the rubber bands *increased.*

Newly arrived checks were put out of sight as soon as possible, filed or not. Workers hid unfiled checks, generally stuffing them into desk drawers or unused file drawers. Since boxes were forbidden, there were fewer unused file drawers than there had been in the old cage. So the day's work was sometimes undone when several clerks hastily shoved vouchers and checks indiscriminately into the same file drawer at the end of the day.

Before a worker in the cage filed incoming checks, she measured with her ruler the thickness in inches of each bundle she filed. At the end of each day she totaled her input and reported it to Miss Dunn. All incoming checks were measured upon arrival. Thus Miss Dunn had a rough estimate of unit intake compared with file input. Theoretically she was able to tell at any time how much unfiled material she had on hand and how well the unit was keeping up with its task. Despite this running check, when the annual inventory of unfiled checks on hand in the cage was taken at the beginning of the calendar year 1953, a seriously large backlog of unfiled checks was found. To the surprise and dismay of Miss Dunn, the inventory showed the unit to be far behind schedule, filing much more slowly than before the relocation of the cage.

SUSSEX OIL COMPANY*

The Sussex Oil Company was a relatively small, rapidly growing regional distributor of gasoline, lubricating oils, and other petroleum products. Throughout several contiguous seaboard states the products distributed under the Sussex company's own brand names had enjoyed increasing consumer acceptance. The company had built or purchased a number of gasoline stations to distribute its products. Growth had also been achieved through what the company regarded as advantageous contracts with bulk-station operators and independently owned chains of gasoline stations. The success of the company was generally attributed in part to technically competent buying, but more especially to unusual skill in negotiations with refiners, customers, and bankers, and to a continuing, dynamic, "all-out" advertising program. The company had achieved some fame in local trade circles for its willingness to spend freely on promotional activities. Over the years, profits of the company had also grown, but by no means in proportion to the expanding scale of operations.

While the company paid salaries, wages, and commissions in line with those of competitors, it had attracted many of its employees, including even district managers, away from them. Employees of the company regarded a job with Sussex as very desirable and as carrying with it considerable prestige. Employee turnover at all levels was low, and few people left the company of their own accord. While the company was not ruthless in its handling of inept employees, "people took care to see to it that their work was satisfactory," as one executive phrased it.

The men who had founded the company still retained positions in its top management in the winter of 1940. The seven district managers who worked directly under this home-office group, as well as others throughout the entire organization, frequently commented on the founders' enthusiasm and energy. People in the organization sometimes said that this infectious aggressiveness had even permeated the managements of some of the company's customers.

The top-management group determined major policies, managed the company's finances, and negotiated contracts with suppliers and with some few of the more important customers. They delegated considerable authority in the actual operations of the company to the district managers, and gave some weight to their managers' views on broad policy matters.

During the year he had been with the company, Richard Hicks, manager of the company's Botany Bay district, attended many conferences and "pep meetings" at the home office, and scarcely a week went by that he did not receive a personal visit from some top official from the head office. These contacts generally amounted to pressure for increasing volume and injunctions—progressively urgent—to keep expenses down. Hicks responded in a negative way to this pressure to cut costs and expressed himself openly, both to his superiors and to his own office staff. Sussex, he asserted, was getting to be as bad as the large national refiner and distributor with which he had formerly been employed.

The Botany Bay district offices had been located in one of the newest office buildings in the center of the city, in the vicinity of the better hotels, shops, and theaters. The rental of this suite of offices amounted to about $25,000 a year, and renewal of the lease, which was about to expire, would raise the amount to at least $30,000. In addition to this cost the office paid monthly not inconsiderable sums for several direct telephone lines to the company's bulk-storage terminal. This plant, which consisted of large storage tanks and pumping facilities for unloading ocean-going tankers and for loading railroad tankcars and trucks, was located in a general area of docks and shipyards, warehouses, factories, and other oil terminals, all rather closely grouped together along the waterfront.

The top officials of the company had stated on a number of occasions that they thought Richard Hicks should move his district office from the central downtown location to a frame building located at the storage terminal in order to reduce costs. Hicks had been emphatic in his opposition to moving the offices, and the management, in accordance with its practice of giving authority to its district managers and respecting their judgment, had been reluctant to force the issue. On a recent visit, however, the president had indicated what Hicks thought were strong feelings on the subject. Hicks therefore had agreed to move.

The frame building at the plant had once housed the district office; but after the latter had been moved to the city location, it had remained largely vacant. It was, however, in a good state of repair; but in anticipation of the move it was painted, soundproofed, and otherwise renovated. In March of 1941 the 30-odd employees, including Richard Hicks, established themselves in their new quarters.

Within several weeks after the move to the plant, a noticeable unrest, which caused Hicks serious concern, developed among the office employees. This new atmosphere, in which strained relations, repressed spirits, and lack of enthusiasm about the work were outstanding characteristics, was totally different from that which he had known during the previous year. Even his immediate assistants stiffened in their relations with him; the banter and kidding in which almost the whole force used to engage disappeared; the performance of the whole group seemed somehow lethargic and lackluster. For example, the stock-records man frequently complained about being swamped

and seemed always behind in his records. The bookkeepers and credit department workers found it hard to keep up with their work and of their own volition
began to cut their lunch periods short to resume their duties before the period
was up. All in all, the work of the office was far behind the par of promptness
which had prevailed in the past. The attitude of the workers was apparently
reflected not only in the results of their work, but also members of the office
continually complained about the time they wasted driving to work, about the
noise and the dirt and the inconvenience of having to remain around the plant
during the lunch period to eat at nearby lunch counters. They were used to
eating at the better restaurants uptown, where they did not mingle with factory
laborers, truck drivers and other industrial workers. Although no one on the
force had actually quit, many had requested higher wages or talked about
finding better jobs.

Richard Hicks turned over in his mind these facts and others in the
situation at considerable length. He discounted many of the complaints. He
had made no changes in the organization's structure or its personnel. All
procedures and systems were as before. The jobs performed were all substantially the same as before. In fact, several had been simplified by the proximity
of office and plant. Members of the office force could now take up many
problems directly and personally with the plant personnel, whereas formerly
they had had to spend much time on lengthy and inconvenient telephone
conversations and on visits down to the plant.

Hicks was sure the new offices, because of the soundproofing, were in fact
not nearly so noisy as the old. He himself was glad to get away from the street
noise which used to well up from the busy intersection which his office had
overlooked. While there were, to be sure, some additional transportation
problems, all workers now had free parking space on the grounds of the plant;
before they had had to pay up to $10 a month for space several blocks from
the office. To avoid the congestion of transportation facilities at rush hours,
the office of the Sussex Oil Company opened and closed one-half hour earlier
than the main shift at the shipyards. Hicks estimated that with this early closing
time his people had at least an hour to shop and do errands in the city before
the stores closed. Along with the entire staff, Hicks had his lunch at "Mam-
my's" where the food was excellent and well served, although the clatter of
dishes, the babble of voices, and the music of a jukebox contrasted with some
of the mid-town restaurants.

Nevertheless the pressure for wage and salary increases continued. This
Hicks resisted for two or three months because the company not only paid
competitive scales but, indeed, paid better than many types of business. Further, he was much concerned lest the savings of the move be offset by increased
salary costs. On the other hand, he felt he could not possibly risk having to
replace efficient people of long experience with the company at a time when
the general demand for competent personnel far exceeded the supply, a condition which promised to become even more acute. As the pressure increased
and the morale of the organization continued to deteriorate, Hicks eventually

concluded there was no alternative to increasing wages and salaries of the office force. Because, it seemed to Hicks, the company could not raise the wages of the office force without raising those of the plant workers, he proposed to the home office that an increase be extended to the whole district organization. After some discussion and delay, the company accepted Hicks's proposal.

After the increase, there was much less talk about wages and salaries, but the office force seemed to devote an increasing portion of the working day to complaining about working conditions and about "the company." Several weeks later, after the morale of the organization had continued to degenerate, Hicks felt something positive and immediate had to be done. The breakdown was spreading to the plant workers, who had previously been a loyal and efficient group. The plant manager reported this development to Hicks and stated that while his men had made no specific complaints, they talked about the company "going to the dogs," and losing its spirit of competitive aggressiveness. Hicks was surprised to get this reaction from the plant workers. He was inclined to share their sentiment, even though he knew, as a matter of fact, that the company's sales and profits in the preceding year had reached the highest levels in its history. His own earnings were the largest of his career. The "penny-pinching" attitude of the home office, however, disturbed him more and more. One of his best salesmen had commented, "The company is on the down-grade; we are no longer pushing ahead; it's all 'retrenchment.'"

Hicks was thoroughly perplexed. It seemed clear to him that he could not move the office back to the city. The company, he thought, having just raised wages, would almost certainly not raise them again; in any event, he somehow thought that higher wages would not solve the problem. Yet, he felt, something had to be done if the situation were not to get completely out of hand.

JOSEPH LONGMAN*

Joseph Longman was hired in the spring 1938 as a tank operator on the night shift of the anodizing department at the Mallard Airplane Company. He was placed in this kind of work with a promise from the personnel department that he would be transferred to another job when the opportunity arose. Before working at the Mallard Airplane Company he had been employed as an arc welder. Almost all the welding in airplane production was done by acetylene torches and electric spot-welding machines. Longman was not qualified along these lines. He was, however, a good mechanic.

Longman was a red-haired Scotchman about 38 years of age. He was married and had a 13-year-old daughter of whom he was very proud. He had attended high school in California, and frequently referred to the fact that Robert Young was in the same school. Raising silver foxes was his hobby, and he hoped some day to have sufficient money and time to own a large fox farm. The small farm he owned, however, netted him an average income of $500 a year, an amount almost large enough to feed his family and keep up his house which was located in the country.

In the anodizing department where Longman worked, the duraluminum parts used in airplane construction were given a protective coating to increase their resistance to corrosion. The parts to be anodized were suspended by duraluminum clamps in tanks of chromic acid solution (dirty brown in color) and then charged with an electric current. There were two principal jobs in the department: tank operating and drying. Tank operators loaded and unloaded the tanks and washed the acid from the parts, once they had been removed from the tanks. During the 20-minute period when the electrolytic process was going on, they prepared the next tank load by tying parts together with aluminum wire. Dryers wiped and counted the parts and placed them on racks to be sent to the next department.

At first sight, working conditions in the anodizing department seemed both arduous and repulsive, especially for the tank operators. They wore rubber boots, rubber coveralls, and rubber gloves, and were required by law to wear masks to keep the acid from their lungs. The heat from the acid and their nonporous rubber clothing caused them to sweat profusely. The department was generally known as the "tank hole," and the men who worked there were referred to as "those dirty tank men." The tank men, however, were congenial and enjoyed working together. By speeding up the preparation of a load for the tanks, they could have a few minutes to loaf and gossip before it was time to pull out the parts already in the anodizing bath. The department supervisor made no objection to their practice of talking with one another between loads as long as they got the required amount of work done.

There were approximately 20 workers in the department. Since it was the company policy to hire young men for the department, most of the workers were from 19 to 23 years of age. The work did not require previous training and could be learned in four to six weeks. Wage rates in the department were about average for the company. Stephen Gifford was the supervisor of the department. He was attending college during the day at this time.

The morale of the night shift in the anodizing department was very high. A number of the men, as well as Gifford, attended college in the daytime. They planned many social functions together. In the winter months they attended the college ice hockey games and cheered for their supervisor, who played on one of the teams. During the summer, when college students were not in school, the group frequently took their lunches to the beach and played volley ball before coming to work. Once in a while they had a steak fry at a nearby lake to which they took girl friends or wives.

Longman did not participate in playing volley ball on the beach because his fair complexion could not stand the sunshine. He was, however, active in other group activities. He enjoyed helping to plan parties, and his wife was congenial and eager to purchase the hot dogs and rolls or to bake a cake. In fact, one night Mrs. Longman sent a cake which was passed around the department at midnight. This cake-eating at midnight became a habit thereafter, each man taking turns buying or having his mother, wife, or best girl bake a cake.

In addition to helping load and unload the tanks, Longman was in charge of running the electric current through the acid in one of the tanks. It was a position with some responsibility. He also instructed and oriented new men, a task which he enjoyed, and he always went out of his way to help people with a problem. He was well liked and respected by the rest of the men. However, there were no opportunities for advancement within the department.

An opportunity for Longman's transfer to another job did not arise until he had been in the anodizing department for two years. It would not have arisen then except that Gifford knew that it had been promised to him at the first opportunity. Gifford thought highly of Longman and wanted to see him promoted. Consequently, he was glad to arrange the transfer. A position was open in the sheet metal department, and Longman was assigned there to operate a punch press. There were over 200 men in this department, all of whom worked on individual machines. They had higher wages, cleaner working conditions, and more chance for advancement than the men in the anodizing department. They were not free to talk to each other, however, for each one had to be busy with his own machine. Moreover, the sheet metal supervisor seldom spoke to his men but stared at them with his hands on his hips when they were not working at their machines.

The quality of Longman's work was satisfactory from the start, and his weekly earnings would have increased as soon as his transfer had been made permanent, which would have taken two weeks. Nevertheless before this time had elapsed, Longman requested that he be transferred back to the anodizing department, and the request was granted.

After Stephen Gifford finished college in the spring of 1940, he transferred to the company's personnel department where he was concerned with employee relations. Late in 1941 he visited the plant and had the following conversation with Longman.

Gifford: Hello, Joe.

Longman: Well, it's a long time since I've seen you. How are you?

Gifford: Good. How are you?

Longman: Okay.

Gifford: How are those foxes coming along?

Longman: Better than ever. I've got some good pelts on foot this season —46 of them. With this war raising prices I ought to do okay. I'm going to make up a coat for Ruth. She's my daughter, you know.

Gifford: How's Ruth?

Longman: Mighty fine. She's a junior in high school now and doing mighty fine work. We got a letter from the principal telling us how fine Ruth was doing in her subjects. She wants to go to college, wants to be a school teacher some day. I guess college is pretty expensive, isn't it?

Gifford: A great deal depends upon which college she attends.

Longman: I've got to start putting some money away for Ruth's college education. After this war is over this airplane business isn't going to be so hot! In fact, it isn't so hot right now.

Gifford: What do you mean by that?

Longman: Oh, I don't mean we haven't got enough work. As far as a lot of the boys are concerned, we've got too damn much work. I guess the company has got a backlog of orders for the next two years, at least. What gripes me is all the changes that are being made around here.

Gifford: I can see there have been a number of changes.

Longman: You said it! A fellow just doesn't know where he stands these days. I used to help set up a load for the tanks, put the parts in the tank, and operate the generator. Now the generator is automatic. Since the two new tanks have been added and since the new conveyer system has been put in, the only thing I do is tie up the parts for each load. It keeps seven or eight of us busy just doing that. I don't like it around here the way I used to. No steak fries, no parties, no talking with the guys—just work and plenty of it. I don't get to know any of the other guys in the department. There's twice as many now as there used to be. We've got over 40 now, mostly all new kids.

Gifford: Do you still help to break them in?

Longman: Our new foreman has changed things a lot. With all the expansion we each do just one job. You might say we're specialists. I don't think my foreman likes me. When I would try to help a new fellow with his job, the foreman would say, "Mind your own business, Longman. You do too much talking for your own good. You just take care of your own job." All I was ever trying to do was to help the new guys get straightened out on their new assignments. It's not easy when you're new around here, and I think they appreciate your helping them. But the foreman, he's just jealous or afraid that I'll show him up in front of the other guys. He's not as smart as he thinks he is. See that new conveyor belt up there on the ceiling? It breaks down quite frequently and instead of fixing it ourselves, the

> foreman runs to the maintenance department. Once I offered to arc-weld a part of the track, and he told me to get back on my job and stay put. Personally, I don't think he knew what arc-welding was.

Gifford: Did the maintenance men fix it?

Longman: Sure they did. They arc-welded it! And it works fine now. You ought to see us turn out the orders with the new setup around here. With the two additional tanks and the new conveyor system we really pour out the work. You see each guy does just one thing, over and over again. Sort of a line production with each of us specializing. It's really okay. Our output has about tripled since you were here.

Gifford: That's good.

Longman: Of course we're working six days a week, and that makes quite a difference. Sure helps the old pay check with time and a half for Saturday work. That strike we had really helped out.

Gifford: What do you mean?

Longman: We got a raise in pay, and it also gave us seniority rights.

Gifford: What does that mean?

Longman: Well, any layoff within a department or section must be made according to seniority. It's a pretty good deal for us older fellows.

BETTY RANDALL*

On March 15, 1949, Betty Randall came in to talk over a problem with Mr. Robbins. Betty was a production worker doing hand assembly work in a modern branch plant, which employed approximately 600 people in a large eastern city. Mr. Robbins was the Personnel Director for the plant. After Betty had told Mr. Robbins her story, he asked Betty to write out her description of the situation. The resulting written statement is reproduced below.

> I consider this case not unusual nor typical, but as having happened to me and to a few others. As I am not equipped to do the work, it offers little or no solution to the problem at hand. I wouldn't be writing this report if I had not remembered

the advice given by Mr. Robbins of Personnel. He told a group that should we have a problem, to please consult him before walking out. However, I will mention here that I have seen a few very conscientious workers walk out without "fighting the case."

When I was first hired, Mr. Lipton, the foreman, introduced me to the young lady who taught me the process of soldering lead wires. I asked her how much production I would be expected to turn in daily, and she secured this information for me from the other girls. This seemed at the moment like a fantastic sum, but she assured me that after a few days I would become quite efficient, which I soon did. I'm not one to "bite the hand that feeds me," so I began working and finally developed the system into sort of a game. A few weeks later one of the girls asked me how I was doing, and I told her that I was doing fine. She looked at my production sheet and swore. She was astonished to see how much I was producing each hour. She bitterly reminded me that girls that had been here for several months or even years were not producing what I had accomplished in a few weeks. I laughed that off as somewhat of a compliment. That was my big mistake as far as cooperating with the company or satisfying my gregarious tendencies was concerned. I was immediately and severely ostracized.

During the weeks that ensued I noticed I was not completely alone, there were a few others who were also "friendless." However, it was soon apparent that ostracism was not satisfying the desires of their fiendish little plan. Threats were to follow, and follow they did. Having worked in the violent ward of a psychopathic hospital, I was not the least bit nervous because of these threats, but others were. I noticed a few things about the character, temperament, and education of those who were apparently "bossing." They were usually the "oldtimers" and loafers. Girls with a great deal of confidence and little reason for it. Sometimes their reasons for fighting the enormous business organization, which represents their security, were quite convincing. Your work is never appreciated. They'll always want more and more. You haven't got a chance to get a merit wage increase unless you go out with the boss and. . . . After this general talking to the poor girls began to wonder; some of them stayed a few days and then didn't turn up for work. The clique had scored again.

I sat and wondered as I worked. What to do? I was assured I had the bosses on my side, but then. . . . The long dead silence and the vulgar, stupid remarks of the other girls soon began to get under my skin. I worked quite a while at the psychopathic hospital and "they" never bothered me, but those stupid little people and their moronic remarks soon began to annoy me something terrible. Because my production was high I was asked to work Saturdays. This brought a violent counterthrust from the rebels.

Soon their campaign began to affect me exactly as they had planned. (Or am I giving them too much credit?) My production was dropping. The assistant foreman, Bert, asked me if I was ill. When I told him my troubles, he advised me to see Mr. Lipton, which I did. Mr. Lipton listened attentively, asked the names of the rebels, which I readily gave, not feeling at all like an informer. He then assured me, though stammering, that justice would prevail. I noticed little change.

The little minds had other desires than to keep their jobs secure; they wanted to jeopardize the position of their immediate superiors. Bert, who had advised me to talk to Mr. Lipton, commonly held the reputation of a communist, nailed on him by "my rebels." I have always maintained in my philosophy that if one cannot become great by one's own methods of accomplishment, then one will probably pull everyone else down below them, until by comparison they are above the mob, hence great. This is commonly known as scapegoatism. These girls carry this farther than I ever dreamed would be done. Scapegoating is a common activity of the uneducated. Education of the population, while not the solution, will greatly aid in the eventual solution of this problem.

However, back to the practical aspects of the problem at hand. I had convinced myself that most of the girls were not the kind I would care to associate with anyway, so my scope of activity was not ruptured too severely. As they ignored me, I ignored them. As they cursed me, I ignored them. However, something happened that I had not counted on. I became physically ill from the entire situation. Having had a few lectures on psychosomatic diseases, I knew I had not incorrectly diagnosed the case.

My relief came in the form of a temporary transfer to another department. I knew it would take some time before the girls would become acquainted with my case, and the rest was welcome. I was shocked to find that no one was interested in my "reputation." I was further shocked when I began to notice that harmony, tranquility, and cooperation prevailed in this department. It is my opinion that part of the cause for such cooperation in this department may be attributed to the fact of one boss, and a capable, understanding man at that.

Then I was told to return to my former department, where I was greeted by my boss with, "Enjoy your vacation?" This does not strike me as being very complimentary to one who has been conscientious from the beginning.

I had been taught to report all inferior grade materials, and this particular morning I found the wire defective. After reeling yards of red tape from a few of my bosses, I finally was sent to Mr. Lipton. Again Mr. Lipton was glad to see me. "I want you to get back to your machine, sit down, and mind your own business. Your production is failing. Why?" This I was told before I had a chance to speak. Here I explained about the strain I was under and about the inferior materials. He then told me to work as best I could with the inferior materials as he didn't want to send any of the girls home. I then told him I had thought of leaving. He sarcastically mentioned that perhaps it was for the best. This shock drove me to Mr. Robbins of Personnel and to standing here in my living room dictating this to my husband, the typist of the family.

ROLAND-OLIVER, S.A.*

"We've just a real fight in my group. I think I've got things straightened out now. But for a time I was worried."

*This case was made possible by a firm which chooses to remain anonymous. It is identical to the "Acting Out of Character" case with the exception of some minor alterations of names and places undertaken for pedagogical purposes. It was prepared as the basis for class discussion rather than to illustrate either effective or ineffective handling of an administrative situation. Copyright © 1973 by the President and Fellows of Harvard College. Reproduced by permission. Distributed by the Intercollegiate Case Clearing House, Soldiers Field, Boston, Mass., 02163. All rights reserved to the contributors. Printed in the U.S.A.

The speaker was Dr. Andre Dupas, a section head in the Sounds System Laboratory of Roland-Oliver, S.A., a medium-sized producer of electronic signalling systems. Dr. Dupas went on to explain to the casewriter how the conflict had arisen.

My group received this project. Potentially it had a large payoff—100 million francs or more. My boss, Dr. Menez, considered it top priority and it looked to both of us like an outstanding opportunity to make a breakthrough. We put three of our senior associates on the project, and right away they were fighting.

I won't confuse you with technical details but we were working with transducers which had to have very low breakdown voltages. I called together the three associates, Dr. Pierre Boyer, Dr. Jean Rault, and M. Kurt Kalcheck. Almost right away Dr. Boyer objected to the project on grounds that it was theoretically doubtful, if not impossible. Dr. Boyer is only about 26 years old. He received an advanced degree last year and demonstrated his first device three years ago. Frankly, I think he's brilliant. He's going to move up in this organization rapidly.

The rest of us were rather surprised by the speed and certainty with which Dr. Boyer responded. I'm not sure what Dr. Rault would have said if Dr. Boyer hadn't been so positive. At any rate Dr. Rault was lukewarm at best. However, I received immediate support from M. Kalcheck. He is much older than the other two, who are close friends. M. Kalcheck must be in his fifties. He has very little advanced mathematics and a background in engineering. He's one of the very few senior associates without an advanced degree. But M. Kalcheck is very loyal, diligent, practical and reliable and he'll work tremendously hard. We get along very well. M. Kalcheck said he would set up an experiment and see what happened.

It was agreed that the three of them should meet together and plan a preliminary investigation to decide whether the project should proceed. I remember thinking at the time that Dr. Boyer wasn't going to do any collaborating with anyone and I was right.

At 9:30 the next morning, Dr. Menez received an elaborate theoretical report, which demonstrated the mathematical impossibility of the project's objective. There was a forceful summary to the effect that we would be wasting our time proceeding any further. Dr. Boyer must have stayed up half the night to complete it. Both Dr. Menez and I were impressed by Dr. Boyer's speed and thoroughness. It was typical of him.

It was going to take time for us to evaluate the report and Dr. Menez was very busy that week. I was wondering whether to call M. Kalcheck off the project when some five days after Dr. Boyer's report had been submitted, M. Kalcheck came to see me. He had assembled the transducers and they worked. He'd done it! I was tremendously excited and so was Dr. Menez. Many people were congratulating M. Kalcheck. Dr. Boyer and Dr. Rault were called in and told the news. Dr. Boyer said nothing about having been wrong but began to examine M. Kalcheck's setup minutely.

A couple of hours later I received a call from Dr. Menez. Dr. Boyer was in his office complaining that M. Kalcheck refused to share information with him. I said I would handle it and I called Dr. Boyer, Dr. Rault and M. Kalcheck into my office. I said that this was M. Kalcheck's discovery and that no one must deprive him of the full credit for it. Probably Dr. Boyer could write a better article for the professional journals but M. Kalcheck must be permitted to exploit his work. I sympathized with M. Kalcheck's fear that his ideas would be taken over.

Dr. Boyer shrugged this off. He denied that he had the smallest intention of depriving M. Kalcheck of any credit. He merely wished to build on M. Kalcheck's work, for which he required information. Shared information was the basis of science.

That fight was two weeks ago and I think I resolved it. In a way M. Kalcheck was acting out of character. He isn't *expected* to discover new things. In fact Dr. Rault has announced that M. Kalcheck was only following my orders, which isn't true. M. Kalcheck is expected to be the practical one.

But you know something, I think M. Kalcheck has a lot of talent, if only he and others would start to believe it.

The casewriter asked to speak to Kurt Kalcheck. M. Kalcheck was a thin, balding man with glasses. He had a polite but earnest style of speaking and a distinct Polish accent. He was asked about his background and his life up to the present.

> *M. Kalcheck:*   I was born in Poland and educated in Munich, Germany. I studied engineering in France on a scholarship. After obtaining a degree, I accepted a job here at Roland-Oliver. At the time, it did not seem necessary to go on for an advanced degree. I had been here only a few months when the war broke out in 1939 and I was fired as a security risk. It was my Munich background and the fact that Poland was occupied.
>
> It was a pretty bad time to be a security risk or to speak with any sort of mid-European accent. During the war I could not afford to return to the university and had to take temporary jobs. After the war the company rehired me and I did some really important work on vacuum tubes. Thousands of systems used the miniature tubes I had developed. Then, quite suddenly the technology changed over to solid state devices and I was given only routine assignments on tubes. The creative work was no longer coming my way and hundreds of young men with advanced degrees just out of the university were way ahead of me.
>
> Have you ever stopped to think what happens to people in these technical upheavals? I often wonder what it must have been like to be an expert on propeller-driven airplanes and then suddenly find oneself at the bottom, nobody wanting all your knowledge. Industry makes these studies on how to use waste products and it never stops to think of the human beings it consigns to the scrap pile. Management says it's "up to the individual." There's all these orientation programs for newcomers but what about *reorientation* for some of us?
>
> Sometimes I think of all the brilliant people we have here and yet most of us are alone. Just a few yards away behind a wall there are probably a dozen men from whom we could learn so much. And yet there are high walls everywhere with many noncommunicating peo-

ple duplicating each other's efforts. We do *emphasize* "team work" but we work so much as individuals that we just don't notice each other. People here are strongly opinionated and individualistic. They like to work by themselves. Maybe they fear others will steal their ideas.

I'll give an example of the quite needless rivalry that goes on here. One of the production division's development groups has been sent over here—to the research laboratory. The idea is to "facilitate" the production of our ideas. They'll come in and take your idea and five days later they'll be developing it in an unfinished state before we've even evaluated it ourselves. And since this new pressure on us to do application work is intensifying—we are converging with this fiercely competitive marketing-oriented group, who seem intent on rushing everything through. This is duplication and it's hurting the company. Why doesn't management give us clearer assignments, which don't overlap? We're doing some work on defense systems as you may know. Now what happens when the government receives competitive bids from different parts of this company? Because that's going to happen any day now. I've complained several times about this. The other day the marketing manager of this manufacturing division which has invaded us was in here. He told me, "Don't cry about it. Get in quickly—that's life!" He wants all our information. I must confess I've always found it difficult to push in front of people. We spend hours laying down a list of priorities, than all of a sudden it turns into a game of how to get around them. It seems so destructive to me. Beyond a certain point competition becomes detrimental to the organization. While I'm waiting my turn—as I promised to do—someone else comes in and grabs the needed equipment. It gets so that my civilized behavior is just exploited. There has to be a better way!

It's bad enough when this fighting goes on between departments but when it's *inside* the very group you are working with, when you cannot even trust your closest associates, then things are really falling apart.

Casewriter: I understand that there has recently been a dispute between you and Dr. Boyer. Is that what you were referring to?

M. Kalcheck: Well, that was typical, although more unpleasant than usual because it was so close to us all. We were called into Dr. Menez's office to discuss the development of very low-frequency transducers. There was a definite application in mind. We all agreed to explore it but after the meeting Dr. Boyer walked off by himself and began writing a paper. He likes to show how quickly he can respond. He didn't consult us, of course, and the paper virtually told us "That's my conclusion, and that settles it."

Well, Dr. Boyer has a good brain—but it doesn't matter how brilliant you are, it's always dangerous to say that something can't be done and even more dangerous to put it into writing. I couldn't follow Dr. Boyer's theoretical arguments very closely and he didn't seem inclined to explain them to me. Dr. Dupas had told me to go ahead and so I did.

I went to the manufacturing division and succeeded in getting some low-frequency devices from them, which they had recently developed. It was difficult getting them and they made me promise not to let anyone else use them. That's the sort of suspicion we have around here! I set up some experiments and within eight days I'd achieved 20% efficiency, which Dr. Boyer had argued couldn't be done.

Well, you never saw a faster change of attitude from anyone than Dr. Boyer's. Instead of offering to work with me he began taking notes and a couple of hours after my first demonstration he was setting up a duplicate experiment on his own. Every few minutes he would come down from his laboratory and look at what I had done. It was quite clear that he was imitating my setup. I didn't protest until his lab technician came into the room, went over to my setup and without asking me picked up a couple of filters. I said, "I'm using those!" He said, "You're not. They were on the table." I explained that I borrowed the equipment from many different people. I'd waited my turn until it was ready and that I would need all the filters I had. "Why can't you wait your turn," I said, "and why duplicate this setup? Aren't we supposed to be working together?" "That's what *I* thought," he said. "All right, keep your filters!" and he threw them down hard onto the table and walked out. Why did he have to do that? We've been friends for ten years. We used to sit together at lunch—now he won't speak to me. And it's all so silly and unnecessary. I'm really ashamed to discuss it.

Well, a few moments later Dr. Boyer comes into the room. He says, "I understand you obtained some special devices from the product division. Can I have some of them or at least their specifications?" I said I was sorry but the information was confidential. If he went to the product division they might help him but I had been made to promise that I would keep the devices to myself. He didn't argue but went straight to Dr. Dupas, who followed him back into this room. He said, "Dr. Dupas, tell M. Kalcheck that he must share information or I'll go straight to Dr. Menez." I said, "The information is confidential." As Dr. Dupas hesitated for a moment, Dr. Boyer left the room, heading straight for Dr. Menez's office.

I repeated my story to Dr. Menez who said if the information was confidential that was that. A promise was a promise. I told Dr. Boyer he could have all my measurements but not the product division's specifications. I said, "Dr. Boyer, we can go on fighting but people do get hurt in these fights. No one really comes out ahead."

He said he could do nothing without the specifications and I knew it. Last I heard, he was trying to order a duplicate set of devices from the division. And I've got all we need already!

> People like Dr. Boyer don't realize that one *has* to work with other people. The equipment we use is expensive and we have to borrow back and forth all the time. No one can afford to be an island in this place. If you don't cooperate with other people, then they are not going to help you when you're in trouble and need equipment. There's no point appealing upstairs to Dr. Menez. He can't tell us how to cooperate. We have to learn.

The casewriter next tried to meet Dr. Boyer. After a series of delays he eventually managed to speak to him. Dr. Boyer was very cautious, would pause some time before answering, and chose his words carefully. Of the many persons interviewed in this company he expressed the most concern that his opinions could get him into trouble.

Dr. Boyer: Yes, I'd say I was satisfied with my job. Very satisfied on the whole, although there are always exceptions. I've sought employment elsewhere from time to time. Complaints? Well, it's a loose organization —too loose in my opinion. We don't always get cooperation from the other divisions and from each other. I feel we should be apprised of what other people are doing and have access to their work. People upstairs should take tighter control, insure better cooperation and that we get the equipment we need. It's a false economy being as short of equipment as we are. My technician takes a week to get equipment together. It shouldn't take that long. There isn't enough attention to doing what is best for the company. That has been my chief objective.

Casewriter: I've been talking with M. Kalcheck. That's his chief objective too.

Dr. Boyer: Well, of course you have to have some trust of people and he hasn't. It is in his make-up, his personality. He thinks someone is going to take something away from him. He's an extreme case as far as I'm concerned. I've never come across such distrust. . . . But I don't see how you're going to disguise all this I'm saying. It's bound to get out, isn't it? As far as I'm concerned this incident is closed. Who's going to read this case?

Casewriter: Well, I'm not sure how to reassure you. My experience has been that by the time these cases are typed up, disguised, and presented to the company for clearance, the incidents described have been forgotten. I've talked to about a dozen people. They have all expressed several opinions which were more negative than any expressed by you.

Dr. Boyer: Hm-m . . . all right. Well I assured M. Kalcheck that my motives were entirely honorable. I had no intention at all of depriving him of credit. All I wanted was to set up some more advanced experiments. There was a good opportunity for collaboration between us. He had made an interesting discovery. I could have come up with a model and proposed a further series of experiments.

Of course I do move a great deal faster than most other people. I realize, even if they don't, that a relatively small laboratory like this has some running to do. I attend professional conferences and I know what's going on. One of our competitors has ten people on a project similar to ours. I suspect that another competitor has thirty. We have the advantage of flexibility and concentration on one area provided we react fast. M. Kalcheck doesn't realize that I chose him to work with us. I'm all for cooperation. When you're working by yourself, just one small mistake can put you weeks behind. M. Kalcheck is thorough and he checks things. I've worked by myself here for five years and I felt the need for collaboration. That's the only way we're going to beat our competitors. Every time I work on a project I think will they beat me to it? We're up against tough competition make no mistake about it.

I've got a good record so far. A number of awards from the company and a couple from the industry. I'm seeking a reputation as an inventor and an original theorist. Most of my friends are professionals and the people I want to impress are fellow theoreticians and people at home. There was an article about me in the local newspaper last week.

Casewriter: Dr. Dupas feels that he helped to resolve the dispute between you and M. Kalcheck.

Dr. Boyer: Dr. Dupas didn't solve anything. I solved it. I solved it by keeping right away from M. Kalcheck. It's the only thing to do. I can work with Dr. Rault but not with M. Kalcheck. He wants to keep everything secret. Dr. Dupas gets very enthusiastic and so does M. Kalcheck, but we need to inject some realism into our work. But I'd rather not say anything more. . . .

SUBJECT INDEX

491

AUTHOR INDEX